Make the Connection

For trip planning and local activities, AAA guidebooks are just the beginning.

Open the door to a whole lot more on **AAA.com**. Get extra travel insight, more information and online booking.

Find this symbol for places to look, book and save on AAA.com.

iStockphoto.com_shapecharge

Kentucky, Ohio & West Virginia

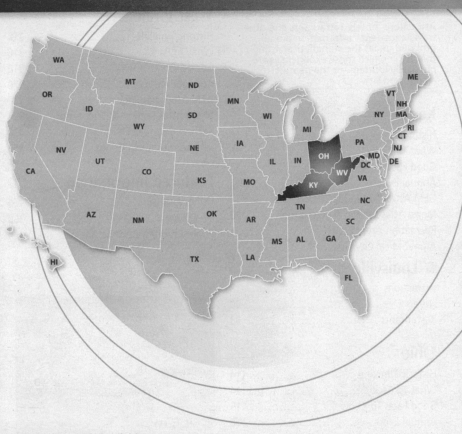

Published by AAA Publishing
1000 AAA Drive, Heathrow, FL 32746-5063
Copyright AAA 2020, All rights reserved

The publisher has made every effort to provide accurate, up-to-date information but accepts no responsibility for loss or injury sustained by any person using this book. TourBook® guides are published for the exclusive use of AAA members. Not for sale.

Advertising Rate and Circulation Information: (407) 444-8280

Printed in the USA by Quad/Graphics

This book is printed on paper certified by third-party standards for sustainably managed forestry and production.

Printed on recyclable paper.
Please recycle whenever possible.

Stock #4668

CONTENTS

Get more travel information
at AAA.com/travelguides
and AAA.com/traveltips

Attractions, hotels, restaurants and other travel experience information are all grouped under the alphabetical listing of the city in which those experiences are physically located—or the nearest recognized city.

free to
rock the boat

TripAssist travel insurance allows you to go with the flow. It can free you up to make the most of your vacation. Nothing will hold you back knowing that you and your travel plans are safe.

Talk to your AAA Travel Agent today for more information.

400003588_053018

ESCAPE

SHOP

ENJOY

FROM EVERYDAY TO EXTRAORDINARY

APPLY TODAY!

Visit your local AAA office or AAA.com/CreditCard

Using Your Guide

AAA TourBook guides are packed with travel insights, maps and listings of places to stay, play, eat and save. For more listings, more details and online booking, visit **AAA.com/travelguides**.

Helping You Make the Connection
Look for this symbol 🔗 throughout the guides for direct links to related content.

A to Z City Listings
Cities and places are listed alphabetically within each state or province. Attractions, hotels and restaurants are listed once — under the city in which they are physically located.

Cities that are considered part of a larger destination city or area have an expanded city header. The header identifies the larger region and cross-references pages that contain shared trip-planning resources:
- Destination map – outline map of the cities that comprise a destination city or area
- Attraction spotting map – regional street map marked with attraction locations
- Hotel/restaurant spotting map and index – regional street map numbered with hotel and restaurant locations identified in an accompanying index

Cities that are not considered part of a larger destination city or area but have a significant number of listings may have these resources within the individual city section:
- Attraction spotting map
- Hotel/restaurant spotting map and index

Location Abbreviations
Directions are from the center of town unless otherwise specified, using these highway abbreviations:

Bus. Rte.=business route
CR=county road
FM=farm to market
FR=forest road
Hwy.=Canadian highway
I=interstate highway
LR=legislative route
R.R.=rural route
SR/PR=state or provincial route
US=federal highway

About Listed Establishments
Hotels and restaurants are listed on the basis of merit alone after careful evaluation by full-time, professionally trained AAA inspectors. An establishment's decision to advertise in the TourBook guide has no bearing on its evaluation or designation; nor does inclusion of advertising imply AAA endorsement of products and services.

Information in this guide was believed accurate at the time of publication. However, since changes inevitably occur between annual editions, please contact your AAA travel professional, visit **AAA.com/travelguides** or download the free AAA Mobile app to confirm prices and schedules.

Attraction Listing Icons
SAVE AAA Discounts & Rewards® member discount

⊟ Electric vehicle charging station on premises. Domestic station information provided by the U.S. Department of Energy. Canadian station information provided by Plug'n Drive Ontario.

GT Guided Tours available

🅐 Camping facilities

🍴 Food on premises

❌ Recreational activities

🐾 Pet friendly (Call for restrictions/fees.)

🎏 Picnicking allowed

In select cities only:

🚇 Mass transit station within 1 mile. Icon is followed by station name and AAA/CAA designated station number within listing.

▼GEM AAA/CAA travel experts may designate an attraction of exceptional interest and quality as a AAA GEM — a *Great Experience for Members®*. See GEM Attraction Index (listed on CONTENTS page) for a complete list of locations.

Consult the online travel guides at **AAA.com/travelguides** or visit AAA Mobile for additional things to do if you have time.

Hotel Listing Icons
May be preceded by CALL and/or SOME UNITS.

Member Information:

SAVE Member rates: discounted standard room rate or lowest public rate available at time of booking for dates of stay.

ECO Eco-certified by government or private organization.

⊞ Electric vehicle charging station on premises. Domestic station information provided by the U.S. Department of Energy. Canadian station information provided by Plug'n Drive Ontario.

⊠ Smoke-free premises

In select cities only:

⊞ Mass transit station within 1 mile. Icon is followed by station name and AAA/CAA designated station number within listing.

Services:

⊕ Airport transportation

🐾 Pet friendly (Call for restrictions/fees.)

🍴 Restaurant on premises

🍴→ Restaurant off premises

🍽 Room service for 2 or more meals

🍸 Full bar

🚼 Child care

BIZ Business center

♿ Accessible features (Call property for available services and amenities.)

Activities:

♠ Full-service casino

🏊 Pool

🏋 Health club or exercise room on premises

In-Room Amenities:

HS High-speed Internet service

$HS High-speed Internet service (Call property for fees.)

📶 Wireless Internet service

$📶 Wireless Internet service (Call property for fees.)

📶 No wireless Internet service

📺 Pay movies

🧊 Refrigerator

📻 Microwave

☕ Coffeemaker

🅰 No air conditioning

📺 No TV

☎ No telephones

Restaurant Listing Icons

SAVE AAA Discounts & Rewards® member discount

ECO Eco-certified by government or private organization.

⊞ Electric vehicle charging station on premises. Domestic station information provided by the U.S. Department of Energy. Canadian station information provided by Plug'n Drive Ontario.

🅰 No air conditioning

♿ Accessible features (Call property for available services and amenities.)

⊠ Designated smoking section

B Breakfast

L Lunch

D Dinner

24 Open 24 hours

LATE Open after 11 p.m.

🐾 Pet friendly (Call for restrictions/fees.)

In select cities only:

⊞ Mass transit station within 1 mile. Icon is followed by station name and AAA/CAA designated station number within listing.

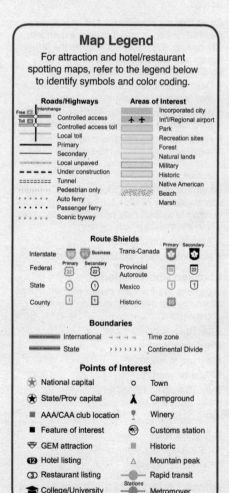

Map Legend

For attraction and hotel/restaurant spotting maps, refer to the legend below to identify symbols and color coding.

Roads/Highways

Free — Interchange
Toll —
Controlled access
Controlled access toll
Local toll
Primary
Secondary
Local unpaved
Under construction
Tunnel
Pedestrian only
Auto ferry
Passenger ferry
Scenic byway

Areas of Interest

Incorporated city
Int'l/Regional airport
Park
Recreation sites
Forest
Natural lands
Military
Historic
Native American
Beach
Marsh

Route Shields

				Primary	Secondary
Interstate	95	95 Business	Trans-Canada	♦	♦
Federal	Primary 22	Secondary 22	Provincial Autoroute	22	22
State	1	1	Mexico	1	1
County	1	1	Historic	66	

Boundaries

International
State
Time zone
Continental Divide

Points of Interest

National capital
State/Prov capital
AAA/CAA club location
Feature of interest
GEM attraction
Hotel listing
Restaurant listing
College/University

Town
Campground
Winery
Customs station
Historic
Mountain peak
Rapid transit
Stations
Metromover

Understanding the Diamond Designations

Hotel and restaurant inspections are unscheduled to ensure our trained professionals encounter the same unbiased experience members do.

- The first step for every hotel and restaurant is to demonstrate they meet expected standards of cleanliness, comfort and hospitality.

- Only hotels and restaurants that pass AAA's rigorous on-site inspection receive a AAA Diamond designation.

Learn more at **AAA.com/Diamonds**.

Hotels	**Restaurants**
 APPROVED	 APPROVED
Noteworthy by meeting the industry-leading standards of AAA inspections.	Noteworthy by meeting the industry-leading standards of AAA inspections.
THREE DIAMOND	**THREE DIAMOND**
Comprehensive amenities, style and comfort level.	Trendy food skillfully presented in a remarkable setting.
FOUR DIAMOND	**FOUR DIAMOND**
Upscale style and amenities enhanced with the right touch of service.	Distinctive fine dining, well-served amid upscale ambience.
FIVE DIAMOND	**FIVE DIAMOND**
World-class luxury, amenities and indulgence for a once-in-a-lifetime experience.	Leading-edge cuisine, ingredients and preparation with extraordinary service and surroundings.

Guest Safety

Inspectors view a sampling of rooms during hotel evaluations and, therefore, AAA/CAA cannot guarantee working locks and operational fire safety equipment in every guest unit.

Contacting AAA/CAA About the TourBook Guide

Tell us what you think about the TourBook guides or your experience at a listed hotel, restaurant or attraction. If your visit doesn't meet your expectations, please contact us **during your visit or within 30 days**. Be sure to save your receipts. We also welcome your recommendations on places to inspect.

Use the easy online form at **AAA.com/MemberFeedback**, email memberrelations@national.aaa.com or mail your feedback to: AAA Member Comments, 1000 AAA Dr., Box 61, Heathrow, FL 32746.

Kentucky

Shaker Village of Pleasant Hill, Harrodsburg

As strains of the state song drift across the track on the first Saturday in May, the sight of mint juleps conjures visions of stately manors and acres of blue-green grass. Imagine summer evenings on a porch, watching a canopy of trees swing gently in the breeze, golden fields of tobacco swaying in the distance.

Then they're off! You're brought back by the pounding hooves and the roar of the crowd. Jockeys battle for position and the first jewel of the Triple Crown. The climactic conclusion of 2 weeks of parties and festivals takes place in a scant 2 minutes, as the winner races across the finish line and collects a blanket of roses. The Kentucky Derby is over, but your adventure is just beginning . . .

Not far from Louisville's interstates are quiet country roads that take you to legendary horse farms and underground caverns known for their surreal beauty.

Daniel Boone National Forest

Slow down the pace as you take scenic drives past white-painted fences surrounding paddocks and pastures. Small but historic towns along the way offer tours of distilleries, Civil War landmarks and the grand mansions that were Stephen Foster's inspiration.

But modern Kentucky is more than just plantations and Thoroughbred farms. Louisville and Lexington have become thriving metropolitan areas without losing a drop of their Southern charm. Their urban skylines have grown up through the bluegrass, shadowing the historic homes of the past.

Scenic Wonders

The Appalachian mountain pass of Cumberland Gap was the first entryway settlers used to reach the nation's vast interior. During its 1775-1796 heyday, more than 200,000 men, women and children passed through, leaving behind everything familiar for a new life in a virtually unknown land. Today you can hike a 3-mile trail to the top of White Rocks, a limestone outcropping heralding the approach to the gap, and on a clear day you may even see as far as the Great Smoky Mountains.

Within Daniel Boone National Forest, the terrain takes an unusual turn. Here the steep-sided, narrow valleys are dotted with ancient, erosion-carved rock arches. The forest's Red River Gorge Geological Area boasts 80 such landmarks, including much-photographed Sky Bridge, which airily stretches 75 feet atop a lofty ridge overlooking the gorge.

Sporting whimsical names like River Styx and Grand Central Station, the unusual formations at Mammoth Cave National Park range from 192-foot-high Mammoth Dome to 105-foot-deep Bottomless Pit. Move on to the town of Horse Cave to see intricate onyx formations in Kentucky Caverns, then head to Olive Hill's Carter Caves in northeastern Kentucky and discover an underground waterfall tumbling down a 30-foot drop.

Portals to the Past

After you've explored Kentucky from top to bottom—that is, its hills and caves—what's left?

Imagine finding portals to a time far removed from traffic jams, computer crashes and all the other woes of modern life. These entry points to the past can be found throughout the Bluegrass State, but one of the finest examples is My Old Kentucky Home State Park in Bardstown. The park's centerpiece, an antebellum mansion named Federal Hill, so charmed Stephen Foster during an 1852 visit that he was inspired to write "My Old Kentucky Home."

While the 19th-century occupants of Federal Hill hosted lavish parties, their Shaker contemporaries in Pleasant Hill near Harrodsburg led a very different lifestyle. Today, the entire town, which includes 34 Federal and Georgian buildings, is a living-history museum where costumed interpreters and working artisans demonstrate the Shakers' minimalist way of living.

Recreation

In this state that offers nearly 500 miles of developed forest trails amid immense natural beauty, hiking might just be the preferred way to get around. You can trace the crest of eastern Kentucky's Pine Mountain on the 38-mile Little Shepherd Trail in Harlan. Or skirt rivers, lakes and narrow ridge tops on the Sheltowee Trace National Recreation Trail, within Daniel Boone National Forest.

Should you tire of hoofing it on your own two feet, what better place than Kentucky to saddle up for the real thing? Bring your horse and head off down any of many trails. Guided horseback riding trips are offered daily at Daniel Boone National Forest. At Land Between the Lakes National Recreation Area, you and the horse you rode in on can take advantage of riding trails and rental stalls at Wranglers Campground. You can also rent a ride at several state resort parks that provide horses as well as trails.

Like to bike? Welcome to heaven. Kentucky's renowned for its winding byways boasting postcard views, especially in the Bluegrass region, where gracious acres of horse farms vie with mossy stone fences for "most picturesque" honors. Kentucky Travel offers a free booklet detailing bike routes.

At Land Between the Lakes, mountain biking enthusiasts will find rentals and designated trails. Those who want to pick up the pace—and the mud—can try off-road driving at the park's Turkey Bay Off-Highway Vehicle Area. Bring binoculars; it's one of the Southeast's best sites for spotting bald eagles.

White water to wide waters, Kentucky's got swimming, boating and fishing covered. There's 160,000-acre Kentucky Lake, so big you can even go inland sailing. Adjacent Lake Barkley offers myriad bays and inlets ideal for exploring.

Plus, Kentucky has 14 major river systems, and most provide superb canoeing and kayaking, too. Adventuresome night owls will want to head to Woodlands Nature Station, inside Land Between the Lakes, for guided moonlight canoe trips. Or, for a really wild ride, sample the state's wealth of whitewater rafting spots. One of the best: the Cumberland River's Big South Fork, a mostly class II float through a steep-sided gorge rimmed with dense woods.

Mammoth Cave National Park

Historic Timeline

1750	Dr. Thomas Walker leads the first documented expedition through the Cumberland Gap.
1769	Daniel Boone ventures through the gap to begin settlement of the Bluegrass region.
1792	The Commonwealth of Kentucky becomes the 15th state.
1809	Abraham Lincoln is born near Hodgenville.
1853	Stephen Foster pens "My Old Kentucky Home."
1937	A devastating flood forces 200,000 Louisville citizens to evacuate their homes; some 200 die.
1939	Colonel Sanders creates his secret blend of 11 herbs and spices at his restaurant in Corbin.
1977	The Federal Surface Mining Control and Reclamation Act ensures lands ravaged by mining are returned to their original state.
1992	The 1 millionth Corvette rolls off the assembly line in Bowling Green.
2002	Horse racing legend and Triple Crown winner Seattle Slew dies in Lexington at age 28.
2008	The United States team wins the biennial Ryder Cup golf championship at Louisville's Valhalla Golf Club.

What To Pack

Temperature Averages Maximum/Minimum	JANUARY	FEBRUARY	MARCH	APRIL	MAY	JUNE	JULY	AUGUST	SEPTEMBER	OCTOBER	NOVEMBER	DECEMBER
Bowling Green	43/25	49/29	59/37	69/45	77/55	85/63	89/68	88/66	81/58	70/46	58/37	47/29
Covington	41/25	43/26	51/32	64/43	74/53	84/62	87/65	86/64	80/57	68/46	53/35	42/27
Frankfort	40/21	45/23	55/31	66/39	75/49	83/59	87/63	86/62	79/55	68/42	55/34	44/26
Lexington	43/26	45/27	53/33	65/44	76/53	85/63	88/67	87/67	81/58	69/50	54/35	44/28
Louisville	41/24	45/27	55/35	68/46	76/55	84/63	88/68	87/66	81/59	69/46	56/37	45/29
Paducah	43/27	49/32	59/39	70/47	79/56	87/65	91/69	89/67	83/60	72/48	59/40	47/31

From the records of The Weather Channel Interactive, Inc.

Good Facts To Know

ABOUT THE STATE

POPULATION: 4,339,367.

AREA: 40,408 square miles; ranks 37th.

CAPITAL: Frankfort.

HIGHEST POINT: 4,145 ft., Black Mountain.

LOWEST POINT: 257 ft., Mississippi River.

TIME ZONE(S): Eastern/Central. DST.

REGULATIONS

TEEN DRIVING LAWS: Driving is not permitted midnight-6 a.m. One unrelated passenger under the age of 20 is permitted. The minimum age for an unrestricted driver's license is 17. Phone (502) 564-1257 for more information about Kentucky driver's license regulations.

SEAT BELT/CHILD RESTRAINT LAWS: Seat belts are required for driver and all passengers ages 8 and over. Children under age 7 and between 40 and 57 inches tall are required to be in a booster seat. Children under 40 inches tall must be in a child restraint. AAA recommends the use of seat belts and appropriate child restraints for the driver and all passengers.

CELLPHONE RESTRICTIONS: Persons under 18 with an instruction permit, intermediate license or operator's license may not drive while using a personal communication device. All drivers are prohibited from texting while driving.

HELMETS FOR MOTORCYCLISTS: Required for all drivers and passengers under 21 and drivers with an instruction permit or who have had a license less than 1 year. Those 21 years and older may ride without helmets only if they can show proof that they are covered by a medical insurance policy.

RADAR DETECTORS: Permitted. Prohibited for use by commercial vehicles.

MOVE OVER LAW: Driver is required to slow down and vacate the lane nearest stopped police, fire and rescue vehicles using audible or flashing signals. Law also requires driver to use lanes further away from repair vehicles stopped roadside.

FIREARMS LAWS: Vary by state and/or county. Contact Kentucky State Police Legal Office, 919 Versailles Rd., Frankfort, KY 40601; phone (502) 782-9781.

HOLIDAYS

HOLIDAYS: Jan. 1 ■ Martin Luther King Jr. Day, Jan. (3rd Mon.) ■ Good Friday ■ Memorial Day, May (last Mon.) ■ July 4 ■ Labor Day, Sept. (1st Mon.) ■ Veterans Day (Nov. 11) ■ Thanksgiving ■ Christmas, Dec. 25.

MONEY

TAXES: Kentucky's statewide sales tax is 6 percent and statewide lodging tax is 1 percent. Local options allow for additional lodging and restaurant taxes.

VISITOR INFORMATION

INFORMATION CENTERS: State welcome centers, open daily 8-6, are on I-64W in Grayson ■ I-75N in Williamsburg ■ I-24E in Paducah (Whitehaven) ■ I-65N in Franklin ■ I-65S in Shepherdsville (Bullitt County), open daily 9-5 ■ I-24W in Hopkinsville (Christian County), open daily 9-5 ■ and I-64E in Shelbyville.

FURTHER INFORMATION FOR VISITORS:
Kentucky Department of Travel & Tourism
Department of Travel
100 Airport Rd.
2nd floor
Frankfort, KY 40601
(502) 564-4930
(800) 225-8747

NATIONAL FOREST INFORMATION:
U.S. Forest Service
Daniel Boone National Forest
1700 Bypass Rd.
Winchester, KY 40391
(859) 745-3100
(877) 444-6777 (reservations)

FISHING AND HUNTING REGULATIONS:
Kentucky Department of Fish & Wildlife Resources
#1 Sportsman's Ln.
Frankfort, KY 40601
(502) 564-3400
(800) 858-1549

RECREATION INFORMATION:
Kentucky Department of Parks
2 Hudson Hollow Rd.
Unit 1
Frankfort, KY 40601
(502) 564-2172
(800) 255-7275

 **Love the great outdoors? Find places to camp at AAA.com/campgrounds**

Kentucky Annual Events

Please call ahead to confirm event details.

 Visit **AAA.com/travelguides/events** to find AAA-listed events for every day of the year

WINTER

Dec. - Old Louisville Holiday Home Tour
Louisville / 502-635-5244
- Frontier Christmas / Maysville
606-759-7423
- Southern Lights Holiday Festival
Lexington / 859-255-5727
Jan. - Martin Luther King Jr. Holiday
Celebration / Louisville
888-568-4784
- Kentucky Bluegrass Music Kickoff
Lebanon / 270-402-3835
- Louisville Boat, RV & Sportshow
Louisville / 502-935-4141
Feb. - Kentucky Sport, Boat & Recreation
Show / Lexington / 859-566-1290
- National Farm Machinery Show and
Championship Tractor Pull / Louisville
502-367-5004
- African American Art Exhibition
Louisville / 502-584-1205

SPRING

Mar. - Humana Festival of New American
Plays / Louisville / 502-584-1265
- Blue Grass Trust Antiques and
Garden Show / Lexington
859-253-0362
- International Festival / Hopkinsville
270-885-9096
Apr. - Hillbilly Days in Pikeville / Pikeville
606-432-5504
- Rolex Kentucky Three-Day Event
Lexington / 859-254-8123
- American Quilter's Society Quilt
Show and Contest / Paducah
270-898-7903
May - Kentucky Derby / Louisville
502-636-4400
- International Bar-B-Q Festival
Owensboro / 800-489-1131
- MainStrasse Village Maifest
Covington / 859-491-0458

SUMMER

June - Shelby County Fair / Shelbyville
502-647-0064
- Kentucky Shakespeare Festival
Louisville / 502-574-9900
- Great American Brass Band Festival
Danville / 859-319-8426
July - The Louisville Blues-n-Barbecue
Festival / Louisville / 502-583-0333
- Lexington Junior League Charity
Horse Show / Lexington
859-252-8014
- Forecastle Festival / Louisville
865-523-2665
Aug. - Kentucky State Fair and Horse Show
Louisville / 502-367-5180
- Kentucky Hunter Jumper Association
Horse Show / Lexington
859-233-0492
- NSRA Street Rod Nationals
Louisville / 502-582-3732

FALL

Sept. - World Chicken Festival / London
606-878-6900
- Marion County Country Ham Days
Lebanon / 270-692-9594
- Kentucky Bourbon Festival
Bardstown / 800-638-4877
Oct. - St. James Court Art Show / Louisville
502-635-1842
- Celebration of Traditional Music
Berea / 859-985-3140
Nov. - Festival of the Mountain Masters
Harlan / 606-573-4495
- Owensboro Christmas Parade
Owensboro / 270-231-0729
- Festival of Trees and Trains
Ashland / 606-324-3175

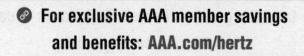

Maker's Mark Distillery, Loretto

My Old Kentucky Home
State Park, Bardstown

National Corvette Museum,
Bowling Green

Kentucky Derby Museum, Louisville

Ashland, The Henry Clay Estate, Lexington

Index: Great Experience for Members

AAA editor's picks of exceptional note

Abraham Lincoln
Birthplace National
Historical Park

Cumberland Gap
National Historical
Park

State Capitol

Shaker Village of
Pleasant Hill

See Orientation map on p. 22 for corresponding grid coordinates, if applicable.
*Indicates the GEM is temporarily closed.

For complete hotel, dining and attraction listings: AAA.com/travelguides

STAY CONNECTED

to all the things membership can do for you

- **Member discounts around you**
- **Cheapest gas nearby**
- **Diamond hotels and restaurants**
- **Travel information and reservations**
- **Roadside assistance**

**Download today.
Connect every day.
AAA.com/mobile | CAA.ca/mobile**

Kentucky Atlas Section

ROADS/HIGHWAYS

- INTERSTATE
- CONTROLLED ACCESS
- CONTROLLED ACCESS TOLL
- TOLL ROAD
- PRIMARY DIVIDED
- PRIMARY UNDIVIDED
- SECONDARY DIVIDED
- SECONDARY UNDIVIDED
- LOCAL DIVIDED
- LOCAL UNDIVIDED
- UNPAVED ROAD
- UNDER CONSTRUCTION
- TUNNEL
- PEDESTRIAN ONLY
- AUTO FERRY
- PASSENGER FERRY
- SCENIC BYWAY
- DISTANCE BETWEEN MARKERS
- EXIT NUMBER-FREE/TOLL
- INTERCHANGE FULL/PARTIAL
- WELCOME/INFORMATION CENTER
- REST AREA/ SERVICE CENTER

BOUNDARIES

- INTERNATIONAL
- STATE
- COUNTY
- TIME ZONE
- CONTINENTAL DIVIDE

ROAD SHIELDS

- INTERSTATE/BUSINESS
- U.S./STATE/COUNTY
- FOREST/INDIAN
- TRANS- CANADA
- PROVINCIAL AUTOROUTE/ KING'S HIGHWAY
- MEXICO
- HISTORIC ROUTE 66
- REFERENCE PAGE INDICATOR

AREAS OF INTEREST

- INDIAN
- MILITARY
- PARK
- FOREST
- GRASSLANDS
- HISTORIC
- INT'L/REGIONAL AIRPORT
- INCORPORATED CITY

POINTS OF INTEREST

- TOWN
- NATIONAL CAPITAL
- STATE/PROVINCIAL CAPITAL
- AAA/CAA CLUB LOCATION
- FEATURE OF INTEREST
- COLLEGE/UNIVERSITY
- CUSTOMS STATION
- HISTORIC
- LIGHTHOUSE
- MONUMENT/MEMORIAL
- STATE/PROVINCIAL PARK
- NATIONAL WILDLIFE REFUGE
- SKI AREA
- SPORTS COMPLEX
- DAM

CITIES/TOWNS are color-coded by size, showing where to find AAA Inspected and Approved lodgings or restaurants listed in the AAA TourBook guides and on AAA.com:

- ● **Red** - major destinations and capitals; many listings
- ● **Black** - destinations; some listings
- ● **Grey** - no listings

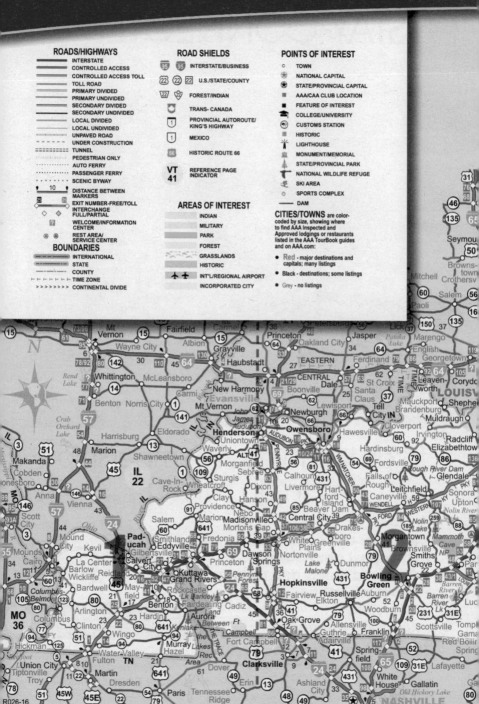

R026-16

ROAD Atlas
Travel With Someone You Trust
2020
UNITED STATES · CANADA · MEXICO

KENTUCKY

Miles 20 · 10 · 0 · 10 · 20 Miles
Kilometers 20 · 10 · 0 · 10 · 20 Kilometers
ONE INCH EQUALS APPROXIMATELY 31 MILES OR 49.89 KILOMETERS 1:1,964,160

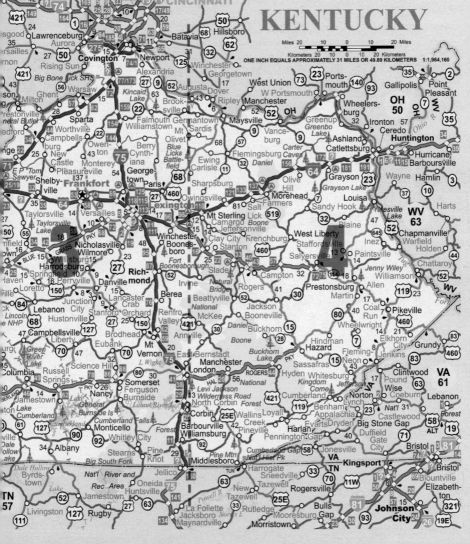

1

KENTUCKY

Miles 18.8   9.4   0   9.4   18.8 Miles
Kilometers 18.8   9.4   0   9.4   18.8 Kilometers
ONE INCH EQUALS APPROXIMATELY 21.5 MILES OR 34.6 KILOMETERS   1:1,362,240

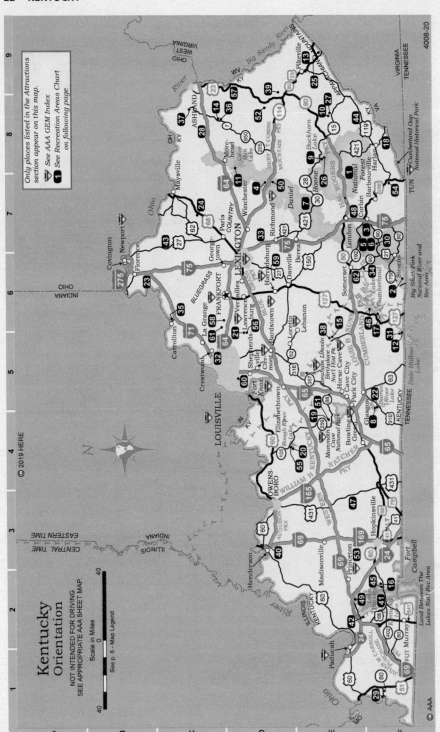

Kentucky
Orientation

NOT INTENDED FOR DRIVING
SEE APPROPRIATE AAA SHEET MAP.

See p. 6 - Map Legend

Scale in Miles

© 2019 HERE

Only places listed in the Attractions
section appear on this map.

See AAA GEM Index
See Recreation Areas Chart
on following page

Recreation Areas Chart

The map location numerals in column 2 show an area's location on the preceding map.

Find thousands of places to camp at AAA.com/campgrounds

	MAP LOCATION	CAMPING	PICNICKING	HIKING TRAILS	BOATING	BOAT RAMP	BOAT RENTAL	FISHING	SWIMMING	PET FRIENDLY	BICYCLE TRAILS	NATURE PROGS.	VISITOR CENTER	LODGE/CABINS	FOOD SERVICE
NATIONAL PARKS *(See place listings.)*															
Mammoth Cave (E-4) 52,830 acres 10 mi. w. of Cave City via SR 70. Scenic.		•	•	•	•	•		•		•	•	•	•	•	
NATIONAL FORESTS *(See place listings.)*															
Daniel Boone (D-7) 708,000 acres. Eastern Kentucky.		•	•	•	•	•	•	•		•	•		•	•	•
Big Double Creek (E-8) 3 mi. s. of Daniel Boone Pkwy. on SR 66, then 2 mi. following signs.	**1**		•	•				•				•			
Great Meadow (F-6) 6 mi. w. of Stearns on SR 92, 12 mi. s. on SR 1363, then 5 mi. s.e. via FR 137.	**2**	•	•	•				•							
Laurel River Lake (F-7) 5,600 acres off I-75 w. of Corbin.	**3**	•	•	•	•	•	•	•	•	•	•	•			
Red River Gorge Geological Area (D-7) off SR 15.	**4**	•	•	•				•		•		•		•	•
Rockcastle (E-7) 15 acres 22 mi. s.w. of London via SR 192/3497.	**5**	•	•	•	•	•		•	•	•				•	
Sawyer (F-7) 5 mi. w. of Cumberland Falls on SR 90, then 7 mi. n. on SR 896 following signs.	**6**	•	•	•	•	•		•		•					
Turkey Foot (E-7) 3 mi. n. of McKee on SR 89, then e. on FR 4 following signs for 3 mi.	**7**	•	•	•				•		•	•				
NATIONAL RECREATION AREAS															
Big South Fork National River (F-6) 125,000 acres. Equestrian camping, hunting, white-water rafting; horse trails.		•	•	•	•	•	•	•	•	•	•	•	•	•	•
Land Between the Lakes (F-2) 170,000 acres. Horseback riding, hunting; off-road vehicle trails.		•	•	•	•	•	•	•	•	•	•		•		
ARMY CORPS OF ENGINEERS															
Barren River Lake (F-4) 10,000 acres 14 mi. s. of Glasgow via US 31 and SR 252. Horse trails.	**8**	•	•	•	•	•	•	•	•	•	•	•	•	•	
Buckhorn Lake (E-8) 1,200 acres 29 mi. n.w. of Hazard via SR 15 to SR 28.	**9**	•	•	•	•	•	•	•	•	•			•	•	•
Carr Creek Lake (E-8) 32,000 acres 14 mi. e. of Hazard on SR 15.	**10**	•		•	•	•	•	•	•	•			•		
Cave Run Lake (D-7) 8,270 acres s.w. of Morehead via US 60 and SR 801.	**11**	•	•	•	•	•	•	•	•	•	•	•	•		
Dale Hollow Lake (F-5) 27,700 acres n.e. of Celina, Tenn., on SR 449 and SR 1206.	**12**	•	•	•	•	•	•	•	•	•			•	•	•
Fishtrap Lake (E-9) 15,439 acres 3 mi. s.e. of Shelbiana off US 460.	**13**	•	•	•	•	•	•	•		•		•	•		•
Grayson Lake (C-8) 1,500 acres 10 mi. s. of Grayson off SR 7.	**14**	•	•	•	•	•	•	•	•	•		•			
Green River Lake (E-6) 8,210 acres 6 mi. s. of Campbellsville via SR 55. Horse trails.	**15**	•	•	•	•	•	•	•	•	•		•	•		
Lake Barkley (F-2) 57,920 acres s. of Grand Rivers.	**16**	•	•	•	•	•	•	•	•	•	•	•	•	•	•
Lake Cumberland (F-6) 50,250 acres 15 mi. s. of Jamestown via US 127.	**17**	•	•	•	•	•	•	•	•	•	•	•	•	•	•
Martin's Fork Lake (F-8) 340 acres 13 mi. s.e. of Harlan off US 421.	**18**	•	•		•	•		•		•					•
Nolin River Lake (E-4) 5,790 acres 5 mi. n. of Brownsville via SR 259 to SR 728.	**19**	•	•	•	•	•	•	•	•	•				•	•
Rough River Lake (E-4) 5,100 acres 15 mi. s. of Harned on SR 79. Horse trails.	**20**	•	•	•	•	•	•	•	•	•		•	•	•	
Taylorsville Lake (D-5) 3,050 acres 25 mi. s.e. of Louisville via SR 155 to SR 44. Equestrian camping.	**21**	•	•	•	•	•	•	•		•	•	•			
STATE															
Barren River Lake Resort (F-5) 2,187 acres 13 mi. s.w. of Glasgow on US 31E. Golf (18 holes); tennis; horse trails.	**22**	•	•	•	•	•	•	•	•	•	•	•		•	
Big Bone Lick State Historic Site (B-6) 812 acres off SR 338. Historic. Miniature golf, tennis.	**23**	•	•	•				•	•	•		•			
Blue Licks Battlefield Resort (C-7) 1,000 acres 23 mi. s.w. of Maysville on US 68. Historic. Miniature golf.	**24**	•	•	•	•		•		•	•		•		•	

Recreation Areas Chart

The map location numerals in column 2 show an area's location on the preceding map.

Find thousands of places to camp at AAA.com/campgrounds

	MAP LOCATION	CAMPING	PICNICKING	HIKING TRAILS	BOATING	BOAT RAMP	BOAT RENTAL	FISHING	SWIMMING	PET FRIENDLY	BICYCLE TRAILS	NATURE PROGS.	VISITOR CENTER	LODGE/CABINS	FOOD SERVICE
Breaks Interstate (E-9) 4,500 acres just w. of Breaks via SR 80. Scenic. Geocaching, pedal boating; water park.	25	●	●	●	●	●	●	●	●	●	●	●	●	●	●
Buckhorn Lake Resort (E-7) 856 acres 25 mi. w. of Hazard via SR 28 to SR 1833. Miniature golf, tennis.	26		●	●	●	●	●	●	●	●				●	●
Carr Creek (E-8) 29 acres 15 mi. s.e. of Hazard on SR 15. Marina.	27	●	●		●	●	●	●	●						
Carter Caves Resort (C-8) 1,800 acres 8 mi. n.e. via US 60 and SR 182. Scenic. Canoeing, cave tours, golf (nine holes), miniature golf, tennis.	28	●	●	●				●			●		●	●	●
Columbus-Belmont State Park (F-1) 156 acres 2 blks. w. of Columbus at jct. SR 58/80/123. Historic. Miniature golf.	29	●	●							●		●		●	●
Cumberland Falls Resort (F-7) 1,776 acres 20 mi. s.w. of Corbin on SR 90 within Daniel Boone National Forest. Scenic. River rafting, tennis; horse rental.	30	●	●	●				●	●	●		●	●	●	●
Dale Hollow Lake Resort (F-5) 3,398 acres 14 mi. s.e. of Burkesville on SR1206. Golf (18 holes); horse trails.	31	●	●	●	●	●	●	●	●	●	●		●	●	●
E.P. "Tom" Sawyer (C-5) 396 acres in Louisville, n.e. on Snyder Frwy. to the W. Westport Rd. exit. Archery, tennis; dog park, playground.	32		●	●						●	●	●	●		
Fort Boonesborough State Park (D-7) 153 acres near Richmond on SR 388, off SR 627. Historic. Miniature golf.	33	●	●	●				●	●	●		●	●		
General Burnside Island (F-6) 430 acres 8 mi. s. of Somerset on US 27. Golf (18 holes).	34	●	●		●	●	●	●		●					
General Butler Resort (C-6) 791 acres 2 mi. s.e. of Carrollton on SR 227. Historic. Golf (nine holes), miniature golf, tennis.	35	●	●	●	●	●		●	●	●				●	●
Grayson Lake (D-8) 1,500 acres 15 mi. s. of Grayson on SR 7.	36	●	●	●	●	●	●	●	●	●					
Greenbo Lake Resort (C-8) 3,008 acres 16 mi. w. of Ashland on SR 1. Canoeing, miniature golf, scuba diving, tennis; horse trails.	37	●	●	●	●	●	●	●	●	●				●	
Green River Lake (E-6) 1,331 acres 5 mi. s. of Campbellsville off SR 55. Miniature golf.	38	●	●	●	●	●	●	●	●	●					●
Jenny Wiley Resort (D-9) 1,498 acres in Prestonsburg off US 23/460 on SR 3. Golf (nine holes), miniature golf; skylift.	39	●	●	●	●	●	●	●	●	●				●	●
John James Audubon State Park (D-3) 692 acres in Henderson on US 41N. Historic. Golf (nine holes), tennis.	40	●	●	●				●		●		●	●	●	●
Kenlake Resort (F-2) 1,795 acres 4 mi. e. of Aurora via US 68 and SR 94. Golf (nine holes), tennis.	41	●	●	●	●	●	●	●	●	●				●	●
Kentucky Dam Village Resort (E-2) 1,352 acres near Gilbertsville on US 641 and US 62. Golf (18 holes), miniature golf, tennis; airstrip, horse rental.	42	●	●		●	●	●	●	●	●			●	●	●
Kincaid Lake (C-7) 850 acres e. of Falmouth on SR 159. Golf (nine holes), miniature golf, tennis, volleyball.	43	●	●	●	●	●	●	●	●	●		●			
Kingdom Come (E-8) 1,727 acres near Cumberland on Old US 119. Miniature golf, paddle boats.	44	●	●	●	●	●	●	●		●		●	●		
Lake Barkley Resort (F-2) 3,700 acres 7 mi. s.w. of Cadiz off US 68. Golf (18 holes), tennis; airstrip, horse rental.	45	●	●	●	●	●	●	●	●	●			●	●	●
Lake Cumberland Resort (F-6) 3,117 acres 14 mi. s.w. of Jamestown off US 127. Golf (nine holes), miniature golf, tennis; Horse rental, horse trails.	46	●	●	●	●	●	●	●	●	●			●	●	●
Lake Malone (E-3) 349 acres 18 mi. s. of Greenville on US 181 to SR 973.	47	●	●	●	●	●		●	●	●					
Levi Jackson Wilderness Road State Park (E-7) 896 acres 4 mi. s. of London off I-75 exit 38. Historic. Miniature golf.	48	●	●	●						●	●		●		
Mineral Mound (E-2) 541 acres 4 mi. s. of Eddyville on SR 93 on Lake Barkley. Golf (18 holes)	49		●		●	●		●		●					●
Natural Bridge Resort (D-7) 2,000 acres 2.5 mi. s.e. of Slade off Mountain Pkwy. in Daniel Boone National Forest. Scenic. Tennis; skylift. Pets allowed only on Red River Gorge Trail.	50	●	●	●				●	●			●	●	●	●
Nolin Lake (E-5) 333 acres n. of Mammoth Cave National Park off SR 1827.	51	●	●	●	●	●	●		●	●	●				

Recreation Areas Chart

The map location numerals in column 2 show an area's location on the preceding map.

Find thousands of places to camp at AAA.com/campgrounds

	MAP LOCATION	CAMPING	PICNICKING	HIKING TRAILS	BOATING	BOAT RAMP	BOAT RENTAL	FISHING	SWIMMING	PET FRIENDLY	BICYCLE TRAILS	NATURE PROGS.	VISITOR CENTER	LODGE/CABINS	FOOD SERVICE
Paintsville Lake (D-8) 242 acres 4 mi. w. of Paintsville via US 460 and SR 40. Pedal-boating, volleyball.	52	•	•		•	•	•	•	•		•				
Pennyrile Forest Resort (E-3) 922 acres 7 mi. s. of Dawson Springs on SR 109N. Golf (18-hole), miniature golf, tennis; horse trails.	53	•	•	•	•		•	•	•	•			•	•	•
Pine Mountain Resort (F-7) 1,519 acres 1 mi. s. of Pineville via US 25E. Golf (nine holes), miniature golf.	54	•	•	•				•	•	•		•	•	•	•
Rough River Dam Resort (E-4) 637 acres 15 mi. s. of Harned on SR 79. Golf (nine holes), miniature golf, tennis.	55	•	•		•	•	•	•	•	•		•	•	•	
Taylorsville Lake (D-6) 2,560 acres 3 mi. e. of Taylorsville on SR 44. Equestrian camp, horse trails.	56	•	•	•	•	•	•	•		•				•	
Yatesville Lake (D-9) 808 acres 6 mi. n. of Louisa on SR 3.	57	•	•	•	•	•	•	•	•	•	•	•			
OTHER															
Guist Creek Lake (C-6) 350 acres 4 mi. e. of Shelbyville.	58	•	•		•	•		•							•
Herrington Lake (D-6) 3,500 acres 6 mi. s. of Pleasant Hill via SR 33/342.	59	•	•		•	•	•	•	•						
Jefferson Memorial Forest (D-5) 6,057 acres 1.5 mi. s. of Fairdale off SR 2055. Equestrian trails; primitive camping.	60	•	•	•				•		•		•	•	•	
Lake Shelby (C-5) 5 acres 3 mi. n. of Shelbyville on Burks Branch Rd.	61		•	•	•			•	•						
Pulaski (E-6) 468 acres w. of Somerset off SR 80. Frisbee course.	62	•	•	•	•	•		•	•	•					

ABRAHAM LINCOLN BIRTHPLACE NATIONAL HISTORICAL PARK (E-5)

Three miles south of Hodgenville on US 31E and SR 61, Abraham Lincoln Birthplace National Historical Park preserves the birthplace of the 16th U.S. president. Lincoln was born on Feb. 12, 1809, in a one-room log cabin at Sinking Spring Farm, where he lived for the first 2.5 years of his life.

In a granite and marble memorial is an early 19th-century Kentucky cabin which symbolizes the cabin in which Lincoln was born. The memorial building was completed in 1911. Above the six granite columns at the memorial building entrance are carved Lincoln's words, "With malice toward none, with charity for all." The memorial is reached by 56 steps, each representing a year of his life; a short, easy walk along a wooden boardwalk also leads to the memorial. The grounds of the park include 110 acres of the original Thomas Lincoln farm.

The visitor center has a re-created pioneer log cabin, exhibits about the family and the movie "Lincoln—The Kentucky Years." Nature trails and picnic facilities are available. The park also encompasses the Abraham Lincoln Boyhood Home, 10 miles northeast on US 31E.

Allow 1 hour minimum. Daily 8-6:45, Memorial Day-Labor Day; 8-4:45, rest of year. Closed Jan. 1, Thanksgiving and Christmas. Free. Phone (270) 358-3137.

ASHLAND (C-9) pop. 21,684, elev. 537'

Due to the rich natural resources in the area, Ashland is a major shipping and industrial center. The town, also known as the birthplace of country music's The Judds and Billy Ray Cyrus, boasts a museum and a performing arts center. In December, visit Santa and enjoy 800,000 lights during the Winter Wonderland of Lights Festival.

Ashland Area Convention and Visitors Bureau: 1509 Winchester Ave., Ashland, KY 41101. **Phone:** (606) 329-1007 or (800) 377-6249.

Self-guiding tours: Maps for a 2-mile walking or driving historical tour are available at the convention and visitors bureau.

BEST WESTERN RIVER CITIES　　606/326-0357

THREE DIAMOND
Hotel

Best Western. **AAA Benefit:** Members save up to 15% and earn bonus points!

Address: 31 Russell Plaza Dr 41101 **Location:** I-64 exit 185, 6 mi nw on US 60, then 3 mi n on US 23. **Facility:** 59 units. 3 stories, interior corridors. **Pool:** heated outdoor. **Activities:** exercise room. **Guest Services:** valet and coin laundry. **Featured Amenity:** breakfast buffet.

FAIRFIELD INN & SUITES BY MARRIOTT ASHLAND　606/928-1222

THREE DIAMOND SAVE Hotel. **Address:** 10945 Rt 60 41102

AAA Benefit: Members save 5% or more!

HAMPTON INN ASHLAND　606/928-2888

THREE DIAMOND SAVE Hotel. **Address:** 1321 Cannonsburg Rd 41102

AAA Benefit: Members save up to 15%!

HOLIDAY INN EXPRESS HOTEL & SUITES　606/929-1720

THREE DIAMOND Hotel. **Address:** 13131 Slone Ct 41101

WHERE TO EAT

BELLA FONTE-ITALIAN RESTAURANT　606/920-7682

APPROVED Italian. Casual Dining. **Address:** 1320 Carter Ave 41101

LA FINCA MEXICAN RESTAURANT　606/324-2134

APPROVED Mexican. Casual Dining. **Address:** 1201 Greenup Ave 41101

BARBOURVILLE (F-7) pop. 3,165, elev. 982'

Barbourville, on the Wilderness Road in the scenic Cumberland Valley, was one of the first settlements in southeastern Kentucky. The site was originally owned by James Barbour who donated the land in 1800 with the stipulation that half the proceeds from the sale of lots be used to erect public buildings.

The first Civil War encounter in Kentucky, a Confederate victory, took place in Barbourville Sept. 19, 1861.

BEST WESTERN WILDERNESS TRAIL INN　606/546-8500

APPROVED
Motel

 Best Western. **AAA Benefit:** Members save up to 15% and earn bonus points!

Address: 1476 S US Hwy 25 E 40906 **Location:** I-75 exit 29 (US 25E), 19 mi s. **Facility:** 43 units. 2 stories (no elevator), exterior corridors. **Pool:** outdoor.

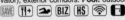

BARDSTOWN (D-5) pop. 11,700, elev. 650'
• Hotels p. 29 • Restaurants p. 29

Settled in the late 1700s, Bardstown is Kentucky's second oldest city. Its Georgian houses recall the days when Bardstown was a political and social center. A monument in Court Square marks the burial spot of steamboat inventor John Fitch.

The principal industry is distilling, due to an abundance of lime in the community's water supply; some of Kentucky's largest distilleries are in the area. Heaven Hill offers exhibits and a video presentation about the bourbon-making process, and Maker's Mark conducts tours of its complete plant *(see Loretto p. 69)*.

AAA
Life Insurance Company

Have you ever stopped to think about the countless reasons why you need life insurance?

Your why isn't just about who you're protecting, it's about what you're doing to protect them.

Whether it's a new house, a new grandchild or a new life with the one we love, life insurance can cover you for the now and whatever's next.

What's your why?

Get a free quote at AAALife.com

O'Connell Hall, on the Sisters of Charity of Nazareth's campus 3 miles north of Bardstown on US 31E, has a museum devoted to the order's history and ministries; phone (502) 348-1500.

The 🍂 Kentucky Bourbon Festival, held in mid-September, celebrates Bardstown's bourbon-making heritage. Among the festivities are a barrel relay, historical tours, art exhibits, food, activities and games.

Bardstown-Nelson County Tourist & Convention Commission: One Court Square, Suite 102, P.O. Box 867, Bardstown, KY 40004. **Phone:** (502) 348-4877 or (800) 638-4877.

Self-guiding tours: Walking tour brochures of Bardstown's historic sites are available from the tourist and convention commission.

BARDSTOWN HISTORICAL MUSEUM, 114 N. 5th St. in the restored Spalding Hall Chapel, interprets more than 200 years of area history. Displays include gifts from kings Charles X and Louis Philippe of France, Native American relics, Civil War weapons, an 1838 Kentucky long rifle, a model of a covered bridge and pioneer children's toys.

Time: Allow 30 minutes minimum. **Hours:** Mon.-Fri. 10-5, Sat. 10-4, Sun. noon-4, May-Oct.; Tues.-Sat. 10-4, Sun. noon-4, rest of year. Phone for holiday schedule. **Cost:** Donations. **Phone:** (502) 348-2999.

The Oscar Getz Museum of Whiskey History, in Spalding Hall, chronicles the history of the American whiskey industry. The collection exhibits rare documents, advertising posters and other memorabilia from pre-Colonial days through the 1960s. Also displayed are a 60-gallon copper still made in 1787 as well as whiskey bottles and containers, including an 1854 E.C. Booz bottle, the brand from which the word "booze" originated.

Time: Allow 30 minutes minimum. **Hours:** Mon.-Fri. 10-5, Sat. 10-4, Sun. noon-4, May-Oct.; Tues.-Sat. 10-4, Sun. noon-4, rest of year. Phone for holiday schedule. **Cost:** Donations. **Phone:** (502) 348-2999.

CIVIL WAR MUSEUM OF THE WESTERN THEATER, 310 E. Broadway, has artifacts and photographs from Civil War battles fought in the western theater of Georgia, Kentucky, Tennessee, Mississippi and Missouri. Exhibits display rare flags, uniforms, medical instruments, maps, artillery and weapons. Galleries are devoted to the infantry, cavalry and navy. A campsite featuring a wagon used during the conflict depicts battlefield life. The complex includes the Pioneer Village, the Women's Civil War Museum, the War Memorial of Mid-America and the Wildlife Museum.

Time: Allow 1 hour minimum. **Hours:** Daily 10-5, Mar.-Oct.; Fri.-Sun. 10-5, in Nov. Closed Thanksgiving. **Cost:** Admission, valid for 2 consecutive days, $12; $6 (ages 6-15). **Phone:** (502) 349-0291.

HEAVEN HILL DISTILLERIES BOURBON HERITAGE CENTER is at 1311 Gilkey Run Rd. Functioning as the visitor center for Heaven Hill Distilleries, the facility provides information about the history of bourbon and how it is produced. Hosts conduct 30- and 60-minute tours, which include interactive exhibits and visits to a rickhouse (where the bourbon is aged), the cistern room, the production plant and the bottling site. Guests over age 20 can sample the company's bourbons in a barrel-shaped tasting room.

Hours: Mon.-Sat. 10-5:30, Sun. noon-4, Mar.-Dec.; Tues.-Sat. 10-5, rest of year. Closed Jan. 1, Easter, Thanksgiving, Election Day, Christmas and Dec. 31. Last tour begins 1 hour before closing. **Cost:** Forty-minute Whiskey Connoisseur Tour and Tasting $20; ages 0-20 free. One-hour Mashbill Tour and Tasting $10; ages 0-20 free. Ages 0-20 are not permitted in tasting area. **Phone:** (502) 337-1000. **GT**

MY OLD KENTUCKY DINNER TRAIN departs from the Depot, 602 N. 3rd St., for a 2.5-hour round-trip ride through the Kentucky countryside in restored 1940s dining cars pulled by diesel electric engines. The meal prepared en route recaptures the experience of vintage American railroad dining. Murder mystery trips and special children's excursions also are available.

Hours: Departures Sat. at noon and 5. Also some Wed.-Fri. departures. Winter departures vary; phone ahead. **Cost:** Lunch fare $69.95; $44.95 (ages 5-12). Dinner fare $84.95; $54.95 (ages 5-12). Murder mystery trip fare $109.95; $69.95 (ages 5-12). Reservations are required. **Phone:** (502) 348-7300 or (866) 801-3463.

MY OLD KENTUCKY HOME STATE PARK is .75 mi. s.e. on US 150. The oldest part of the park's centerpiece mansion, also known as Federal Hill, was built in 1795 by Judge John Rowan, U.S. congressman and senator, state chief justice, U.S. commissioner to Mexico and cousin of Stephen Foster. Completed in 1818, the renovated home is furnished with heirlooms and old portraits. It is believed that Foster wrote "My Old Kentucky Home" here while visiting the Rowans in 1852.

In the park are a visitor center, the family cemetery, a garden and a replica of Judge Rowan's law office. Tours conducted by guides in antebellum costumes are available. An outdoor concert and drama series are presented at the park's outdoor amphitheater June through mid-August. Camping and an 18-hole golf course are available.

Time: Allow 1 hour minimum. **Hours:** Open daily 9-5. Tours daily 9:15-4:15, mid-Mar. to mid-Jan.; Wed.-Sun. 9-5, rest of year. Closed Jan. 1, Thanksgiving, Christmas Eve, Christmas, day after Christmas and Dec. 27-29 and 31. **Cost:** $14; $12 (ages 62+); $10 (ages 13-17); $9 (ages 6-12); $5 (active military with ID). **Phone:** (502) 348-3502 or (800) 323-7803. **GT** **🅰** **🏕**

The Stephen Foster Story is presented in the park's outdoor amphitheater. The musical drama captures the spirit of Foster's works. The composer's life is portrayed through his memorable compositions, which include "Camptown Races," "Oh! Susanna" and "Jeanie with the Light Brown Hair." The J. Dan Talbott Amphitheatre, in a wooded setting, seats 1,450.

Hours: Performances vary early June to mid-Aug.; phone ahead for current schedule. **Cost:** $21-$26; $19 (ages 63+); $12-$14 (ages 6-12). Children must be with an adult. Combination tickets with My Old Kentucky Home State Park are available. Reservations are recommended. **Phone:** (502) 348-5971 or (800) 626-1563.

HAMPTON INN BY HILTON   502/349-0100
THREE DIAMOND SAVE Hotel. **Address:** 985 Chambers Blvd 40004

AAA Benefit: Members save up to 15%!

SURESTAY HOTEL BY BEST WESTERN BARDSTOWN GENERAL NELSON   502/348-3977
APPROVED Motel. **Address:** 411 W Stephen Foster Ave 40004

WHERE TO EAT

BOTTLE & BOND KITCHEN AND BAR   502/252-6331
THREE DIAMOND American. Casual Dining. **Address:** 1500 Parkway Dr 40004

KURTZ RESTAURANT   502/348-8964
APPROVED Southern. Casual Dining. **Address:** 418 E Stephen Foster Ave 40004

OLD TALBOTT TAVERN   502/348-3494
APPROVED American. Casual Dining. **Address:** 107 W Stephen Foster Ave 40004

REBECCA'S PEPPERONI GRILL   502/348-4848
APPROVED Pizza Sandwiches. Casual Dining. **Address:** 966 Chambers Blvd 40004

BEREA (E-7) pop. 13,561, elev. 967'

Berea (buh-REE-uh), the "Folk Arts and Crafts Capital of Kentucky," is home to many professional craftspeople and artists who have working studios in the town. Visitors are welcome at these studios, where they can speak with the craftspeople and gain a better understanding of the processes involved in the creation of the artists' works.

A mile from the Berea exits off I-75 is a liberal arts college where students receive a tuition-free education in return for work in the school's 130 departments. Founded in 1855, Berea College only accepts students who need financial aid. Guided tours of the campus and a tour that provides an overview of the crafts program depart regularly from the Visitor Center at College Square, Center and Short streets; phone (859) 985-3018.

The Kentucky Guild of Artists and Craftsmen's Fair is held the second weekend in October; phone (859) 986-3192 for more information. *Also see Bluegrass Country.*

Berea Welcome Center: 3 Artist Cir., Berea, KY 40403. **Phone:** (859) 986-2540 or (800) 598-5263.

KENTUCKY ARTISAN CENTER is off I-75 exit 77 at 200 Artisan Way. The center is the state's showcase for Kentucky-made arts and crafts, music, literature and foods. Inside the building constructed of Kentucky limestone, exhibits feature works by artists from across the state. Complementing these exhibits are weekly demonstrations, travel information and a café offering regional specialties. **Hours:** Daily 9-6. Closed Jan. 1, Thanksgiving and Christmas. **Cost:** Free. **Phone:** (859) 985-5448. 🍴

LOG HOUSE CRAFT GALLERY is on Berea College Square at Estill (US 25) and Center sts. Part of Berea College, the gallery exhibits crafts made by students as well as those handmade by other Appalachian area artisans. Weavings, wood-crafted items, brooms, ceramics and wrought iron are among the pieces displayed.

Student-led guided tours are available Mon.-Sat. 9-5. **Hours:** Mon.-Sat. 8-7, Sun. 1-5. Closed Jan. 1, Thanksgiving and Christmas. **Cost:** Free. **Phone:** (859) 985-3226 or (800) 347-3892.

BOONE TAVERN HOTEL & RESTAURANT OF BEREA COLLEGE   859/985-3700
THREE DIAMOND
Historic Hotel

Address: 100 Main St 40404 **Location:** I-75 exit 76, 1.5 mi ne on SR 21. **Facility:** Owned and operated by the college, this 1909 hotel features lovely period detail and some custom furnishings designed and built by students. A variety of room sizes is offered; some rooms are small. 63 units. 3 stories, interior corridors. **Terms:** check-in 4 pm. **Dining:** The Restaurant at the Boone Tavern Hotel, see separate listing. **Activities:** bicycles.

SAVE ECO 🍴 ♨ CALL & BIZ
HS 🛜 ✕ 🖥 / SOME UNITS 🐾 🔒

FAIRFIELD INN & SUITES BY MARRIOTT LEXINGTON BEREA   859/985-8191
THREE DIAMOND SAVE Hotel. **Address:** 227 Paint Lick Rd 40403

AAA Benefit: Members save 5% or more!

HOLIDAY INN EXPRESS BEREA   859/985-5500
THREE DIAMOND Hotel. **Address:** 219 Paint Lick Rd 40403

WHERE TO EAT

KENTUCKY ARTISAN CENTER CAFE   859/985-5448
APPROVED American. Buffet Style. **Address:** 200 Artisan Way 40403

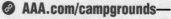

🔗 **AAA.com/campgrounds—**

For overnights under the stars

THE RESTAURANT AT THE BOONE TAVERN HOTEL
859/985-3700

⬥⬥ THREE DIAMOND

Regional American Fine Dining

$10-$27

AAA Inspector Notes: *Historic.* This restaurant is located in a hotel that was built in 1909 by Berea College. Today the dining room offers a menu that emphasizes local ingredients including Kentucky cheeses and produce. A collegiate waitstaff serves tasty fare, such as hot brown (a casserole of roast turkey in cheese sauce) and spoonbread. The Race Day Pie is loaded with chocolate, caramel and pecans. Gluten-free options are available. **Features:** full bar, Sunday brunch. **Reservations:** suggested. **Address:** 100 Main St N 40404 **Location:** I-75 exit 76, 1.5 mi ne on SR 21; in Boone Tavern Hotel & Restaurant of Berea College.

Ⓑ Ⓛ Ⓓ CALL ♿

BLUEGRASS COUNTRY (C-6)

The Bluegrass Region encompasses roughly 1,600 square miles of lush farmland in north-central Kentucky. For most visitors this land epitomizes the state—quiet farmhouse communities and rolling green pastures bounded by picturesque white and black plank fences. Rock fences, some built in the 1800s by Irish immigrants, add to the pastoral surroundings.

These pastures are seeded with the long-lived perennial for which the region is named. The grass, which produces small blue flowers during its late May blooming season, is said to take on a bluish tint; however, since most fields are constantly mowed or cropped by livestock, the blue color is rarely seen.

Color and scenic value aside, the grass—fortified with calcium and phosphorous due to limestone deposits that feed the soil—is prized for its role in producing the equine blue bloods for which the region is recognized. The Bluegrass Thoroughbred horse is world-renowned for its speed, stamina and strength.

Since the first racetrack was built in 1797, the breeding, training, racing and selling of horses—American Saddlebred horses, Standardbreds and especially Thoroughbreds—has become a lucrative industry. Some 50,000 horses are foaled each year, and many champions earn millions at big-ticket races and even more as retired studs. The wealth is apparent in the careful attention given to the construction and maintenance of horse barns. Stables, some of which resemble posh estates, feature such architectural elements as cupolas, spires and picture windows. Inside, it is not surprising to find rich woods, brass fixtures or other embellishments.

Shows and exhibitions take place year-round, and both Keeneland Race Course and The Red Mile Harness Track have spring and fall meets in Lexington. Thoroughbred racing reigns supreme, but harness races, steeplechases and horse shows also draw crowds. Thoroughbred sales take place in January, April, September and November.

Lexington *(see place listing p. 56)*, one of the world's most prominent horse centers, is the region's geographic and commercial hub. Other Bluegrass Country towns listed individually are Berea, Danville, Frankfort, Georgetown, Harrodsburg, Paris, Richmond, Versailles and Winchester.

BOWLING GREEN (E-4) pop. 58,067, elev. 499'
• Restaurants p. 32

At the time Bowling Green was settled, the area was known as the Barrens, an expanse of open prairie surrounded by forests. The first courthouse was erected in 1797, and the town was founded the following year on land donated by brothers Robert and George Moore.

Located between Confederate Tennessee and Unionist Kentucky, residents of Bowling Green at first refused to choose sides during the Civil War. On Sept. 18, 1861, however, rebel troops arrived and changed the town's neutral stance. Bowling Green was proclaimed the Confederate capital of Kentucky later that year. The Confederate army battled with disease rather than soldiers, and Union troops did not arrive until after the rebels evacuated the town.

The city is a cultural center for southern Kentucky and has a variety of industries, including automobile and clothing manufacturing, dairying, livestock raising and tobacco farming.

Bowling Green Area Convention and Visitors Bureau: 352 Three Springs Rd., Bowling Green, KY 42104. **Phone:** (270) 782-0800 or (800) 326-7465.

Self-guiding tours: The Bowling Green Civil War Discovery Trail Driving Tour features forts, memorials and other sites relating to the conflict.

In addition, several walking tours lead visitors to the city's historic sites, homes and buildings. Information is available for walking tours of the Upper East Main, College Hill and ShakeRag historic districts. The downtown Heritage Walk covers 18 markers. The 80-mile Duncan Hines Scenic Byway begins and ends at the Duncan Hines historical marker in front of the 1940 structure that Hines built as his home and office at 3098 Louisville Rd. (US 31W). Maps and brochures for all tours are available at the convention and visitors bureau and at the visitor center in the National Corvette Museum *(see attraction listing).*

Shopping: Belk, Dillard's, JCPenney and Sears are among the nearly 100 stores at Greenwood Mall, at I-65 exit 22.

THE HISTORIC RAILPARK AND TRAIN MUSEUM AT L & N DEPOT is at 401 Kentucky St. In its heyday, this 1925 depot saw more than 20 trains depart per day and to such destinations as Louisville, Ky. and Nashville, Tenn. Its museum's galleries offer such culturally and historically significant displays as Segregation & The North American Railroad as well as exhibits at which visitors may listen to passenger trains' sounds and interact with conductors and engineers. The L & N Theatre presents films and vintage news reels.

Outside the museum are five restored railcars, including an E8a diesel engine, a 1911 Presidential Office Car used to transport high-ranking officials and a 1921 Railroad Post Office Car.

Time: Allow 1 hour minimum. **Hours:** Mon.-Sat. 9-6, Sun. 11-4, May-Oct.; Tues.-Sat. 10-4, Sun. 1-4, rest of year. Closed Jan. 1, Easter, Thanksgiving and Christmas. **Cost:** $12.75; $10.75 (ages 60+); $6.75 (ages 5-12). **Phone:** (270) 745-7317. GT

KENTUCKY MUSEUM, located on the campus of Western Kentucky University at 1444 Kentucky St., relates the history of the state. Collections include furniture, paintings and decorative arts. The Civil War exhibit includes a simulated slave cabin, campsite and general store. One of Kentucky's most famous people is profiled in the Recommended by Duncan Hines exhibit. Faces and Places features more than 40 quilts and textiles, while Instruments of American Excellence exhibits a large collection of ordinary tools used by Americans. Other displays cover local genealogy, agriculture, politics and 19th-century life, including a log house on the grounds.

Guided tours are offered by appointment. **Time:** Allow 1 hour minimum. **Hours:** Tues.-Sat. 9-4. **Cost:** $11; $5 (ages 6-16 and 60+); $22 (family). **Phone:** (270) 745-2592.

LOST RIVER CAVE, jct. US 31W (Nashville Rd.) and Dishman Ln. (Cave Mill Rd.), offers a 45-minute underground boat and walking tour of a cave discovered by Native Americans 10,000 years ago. The cave, which is a constant 56°F, was a shelter for Paleo-Indians, the site of a 19th-century water-powered mill, a campsite used by both sides during the Civil War, a hiding place for outlaw Jesse James and a popular 1930s night club. A butterfly habitat can be seen in summer. Lost River Cave has 2 miles of nature trails, along which visitors can see three blue holes, sites where the underground river rises to ground level. The Nature Explore outdoor classroom includes the Nature Art Studio, Fox Hole, Thistle Theater and Busy Bee Play Area.

Time: Allow 1 hour minimum. **Hours:** Visitor center daily 8:30-6:30, mid-May through Sept. 30; daily 8:30-6, rest of year. Tours depart daily on the hour 9-5, mid-May through Sept. 30; daily on the hour 10-4, rest of year (weather permitting in winter). Closed Jan. 1, Thanksgiving and Christmas. **Cost:** Fee $19.95; $14.95 (ages 4-11); $5.95 (ages 1-3). **Phone:** (270) 393-0077. ⊠ ⛲

Get a hands-on experience in the KidZone, on the Corvette Racing Simulator and with rides in vintage Corvettes (seasonally and weather permitting). A 165-seat theater offers an orientation film, while the museum's Skydome Sinkhole Experience exhibit features the sinkhole that notoriously swallowed eight Corvettes.

Time: Allow 2 hours minimum. **Hours:** Museum open daily 8-5. Closed Jan. 1, Easter, Thanksgiving, Christmas Eve and Christmas. **Cost:** $12; $10 (ages 62+); $7 (ages 5-12); prices may vary, phone ahead. **Phone:** (270) 781-7973 or (800) 538-3883. ⊯

General Motors Bowling Green Assembly Plant is off I-65 exit 28 at Louisville Rd. and Corvette Dr. across from the National Corvette Museum. Bowling Green is the only production site for the classic American sports car, the Chevrolet Corvette. Every Corvette produced since 1982 was manufactured at the Bowling Green facility. The plant offers 1-hour, mile-long guided walking tours of portions of the assembly area.

Note: At time of publishing, tours are on hiatus and are scheduled to resume in 2019; phone ahead to confirm schedule. During the tour, cellphones, tablets, cameras, backpacks, purses and fanny packs are not permitted; shoes must have closed toes. **Hours:** Guided tours every 15 minutes Mon.-Fri. 8:30-1:45. Closed major holidays. **Cost:** $10; $5 (ages 10-16). Ages 0-9 are not permitted. Reservations are recommended. **Phone:** (270) 745-8019 or (800) 538-3883. GT

NCM Motorsports Park is off I-65 exit 28, at 505 Grimes Rd. Get behind the wheel of a Corvette for laps around the track, a driving experience or hot lap rides with a professional driver. High speed go-karts as well as touring laps in your own car, recreational racing and high-performance driver education can be found at this facility. **Hours:** Mon.-Fri. 8-5, Sat.-Sun. 8-6, Mar. Nov.; Mon.-Fri. 8-5, Dec.-Feb. Laps available Mon.-Fri. on the hour (weather and event schedule permitting) 9-4. Closed Jan. 1, Easter, Thanksgiving, Christmas Eve and Christmas. **Cost:** Spectators free. Hours and fees may vary, especially for events; phone ahead. Reservations for laps are recommended. **Phone:** (270) 467-8846.

◆ **NATIONAL CORVETTE MUSEUM** is off I-65 exit 28, across from the General Motors Bowling Green Assembly Plant. In 115,000 square feet of space, the museum showcases more than 80 'Vettes—actual models as well as concept cars—including one of the original 1953 Corvettes, the only 1983 Corvette in existence, and other rare Corvettes. Exhibits feature the cars in realistic period settings such as a 1960s Mobil station, a dealership showroom from the '60s, the legendary Route 66 and an early assembly line.

BEST WESTERN BOWLING GREEN   270/782-6933

THREE DIAMOND
Hotel

Best Western

AAA Benefit: Members save up to 15% and earn bonus points!

Address: 1940 Mel Browning St 42104 **Location:** I-65 exit 22 (Scottsville Rd), just se. **Facility:** 96 units. 3 stories, interior/exterior corridors. **Pool:** heated outdoor. **Activities:** exercise room. **Guest Services:** valet and coin laundry. **Featured Amenity:** breakfast buffet.

CANDLEWOOD SUITES
270/843-5505

THREE DIAMOND

Extended Stay Hotel

Address: 540 Wall St 42103 **Location:** I-65 exit 22 (Scottsville Rd), just nw. **Facility:** 90 efficiencies. 4 stories, interior corridors. **Pool:** heated indoor. **Activities:** exercise room. **Guest Services:** complimentary and valet laundry.

COUNTRY INN & SUITES BY RADISSON
270/781-7200

THREE DIAMOND Hotel. **Address:** 535 Wall St 42104

COURTYARD BY MARRIOTT BOWLING GREEN CONVENTION CENTER
270/783-8569

THREE DIAMOND **SAVE** Hotel. **Address:** 1010 Wilkinson Trace 42104

AAA Benefit: Members save 5% or more!

DRURY INN-BOWLING GREEN
270/842-7100

THREE DIAMOND Hotel. **Address:** 3250 Scottsville Rd 42104

FAIRFIELD INN & SUITES BY MARRIOTT BOWLING GREEN
270/599-1832

THREE DIAMOND **SAVE** Hotel. **Address:** 1832 Cave Mill Rd 42104

AAA Benefit: Members save 5% or more!

HAMPTON INN
270/842-4100

THREE DIAMOND

Hotel

AAA Benefit: Members save up to 15%!

Address: 233 Three Springs Rd 42104 **Location:** I-65 exit 22 (Scottsville Rd), 0.3 mi w. **Facility:** 131 units. 4 stories, interior corridors. **Amenities:** safes. **Pool:** outdoor. **Activities:** exercise room. **Guest Services:** valet laundry.

HILTON GARDEN INN BOWLING GREEN
270/781-6778

THREE DIAMOND **SAVE** Hotel. **Address:** 1020 Wilkinson Trace 42103

AAA Benefit: Members save up to 15%!

HOLIDAY INN EXPRESS
270/843-3200

THREE DIAMOND

Hotel

Address: 165 Three Springs Rd 42104 **Location:** I-65 exit 22 (Scottsville Rd), 0.3 mi w. **Facility:** 92 units. 3 stories, interior corridors. **Pool:** heated outdoor. **Activities:** lawn sports, picnic facilities, exercise room. **Guest Services:** valet and coin laundry.

HOLIDAY INN UNIVERSITY PLAZA
270/745-0088

THREE DIAMOND Hotel. **Address:** 1021 Wilkinson Trace 42103

HOME2 SUITES BY HILTON
270/904-2219

THREE DIAMOND **SAVE** Extended Stay Hotel. **Address:** 420 Wall St 42103

AAA Benefit: Members save up to 15%!

HYATT PLACE BOWLING GREEN
270/467-0001

THREE DIAMOND

Hotel

AAA Benefit: Members save up to 10%!

Address: 1347 Center St 42101 **Location:** Center. **Facility:** 108 units. 4 stories, interior corridors. **Pool:** outdoor. **Activities:** exercise room. **Guest Services:** valet laundry, area transportation. **Featured Amenity:** full hot breakfast.

RAMADA BOWLING GREEN
270/781-3000

APPROVED

Hotel

Address: 4767 Scottsville Rd 42104 **Location:** I-65 exit 22 (Scottsville Rd), 0.3 mi e. **Facility:** 107 units. 2 stories (no elevator), interior corridors. **Dining:** entertainment. **Pool:** outdoor. **Activities:** picnic facilities, exercise room. **Guest Services:** valet and coin laundry. **Featured Amenity:** full hot breakfast.

RED ROOF INN BOWLING GREEN
270/781-6550

APPROVED Motel. **Address:** 3140 Scottsville Rd 42104

STAYBRIDGE SUITES BOWLING GREEN
270/904-0480

THREE DIAMOND Extended Stay Hotel. **Address:** 680 Campbell Ln 42101

TOWNEPLACE SUITES BY MARRIOTT
270/782-4714

THREE DIAMOND **SAVE** Extended Stay Hotel. **Address:** 1818 Cave Mill Rd 42104

AAA Benefit: Members save 5% or more!

TRU BY HILTON BOWLING GREEN
270/904-2260

THREE DIAMOND **SAVE** Hotel. **Address:** 1864 Cave Mill Rd 42104

Members save up to 15%!

WINGATE BY WYNDHAM
270/842-3800

APPROVED

Hotel

Address: 185 Greenwood Ln 42104 **Location:** I-65 exit 22 (Scottsville Rd), 0.3 mi e. **Facility:** 69 units. 4 stories, interior corridors. **Pool:** heated indoor. **Activities:** hot tub, game room, exercise room. **Guest Services:** coin laundry. **Featured Amenity:** breakfast buffet.

WHERE TO EAT

440 MAIN RESTAURANT & BAR
270/793-0450

THREE DIAMOND American. Fine Dining. **Address:** 440 E Main Ave 42101

THE BISTRO 270/781-9646
▼▼THREE DIAMOND Mediterranean. Fine Dining. **Address:** 1129 College St 42101

BUCKHEAD KITCHEN & BAR 270/846-0110
▼▼ APPROVED American. Quick Serve. **Address:** 1760 Scottsville Rd 42104

CAMBRIDGE MARKET & CAFÉ 270/782-9366
▼▼ APPROVED Sandwiches Deli. Quick Serve. **Address:** 830 Fairview Ave 42101

CHANEY'S DAIRY BARN & RESTAURANT 270/843-5567
▼▼ APPROVED Desserts Chicken. Quick Serve. **Address:** 9191 Nashville Rd 42101

DOUBLE DOGS 270/843-9357
▼▼ APPROVED American. Casual Dining. **Address:** 1780 Scottsville Rd 42104

GARCIA'S GRILL MEXICAN RESTAURANT 270/842-6100
▼▼ APPROVED Mexican. Casual Dining. **Address:** 1689 Campbell Ln, Suite 101 42104

GENO'S ITALIAN DELI 270/904-3676
▼▼ APPROVED Italian. Quick Serve. **Address:** 1751 Scottsville Rd 42104

GRIFFS DELI 270/904-4743
▼▼ APPROVED Sandwiches Deli. Quick Serve. **Address:** 1640 Scottsville Rd 42104

HOME CAFE & MARKETPLACE 270/846-1272
▼▼ APPROVED American. Quick Serve. **Address:** 2440 Nashville Rd, Suite 108 42104

KYOTO JAPANESE STEAK HOUSE 270/796-6161
▼▼ APPROVED Japanese. Casual Dining. **Address:** 2800 Scottsville Rd, Suite 4 42103

LOST RIVER PIZZA CO. 270/746-0255
▼▼ APPROVED Pizza. Casual Dining. **Address:** 2440 Nashville Rd 42101

MARIAH'S 270/846-0020
▼▼ APPROVED American. Casual Dining. **Address:** 360 E 8th Ave 42101

MONTANA GRILLE 270/746-9746
▼▼ APPROVED Steak Barbecue. Casual Dining. **Address:** 1740 Scottsville Rd 42104

NOVO DOLCE GASTRO PUB 270/904-3300
▼▼ APPROVED American. Gastropub. **Address:** 651 31-W Bypass 42101

PUB BY NOVO 270/715-6686
▼▼ APPROVED American. Casual Dining. **Address:** 2425 Scottsville Rd 42104

SAMURAI JAPANESE STEAK & SUSHI RESTAURANT 270/782-5004
▼▼ APPROVED Japanese Sushi. Casual Dining. **Address:** 2718 Scottsville Rd 42104

STEAMER SEAFOOD 270/783-2637
▼▼ APPROVED Seafood. Casual Dining. **Address:** 801 State St 42101

WHITE SQUIRREL BREWERY 270/904-1573
▼▼ APPROVED American. Casual Dining. **Address:** 871 Broadway Ave 42101

BROOKS pop. 2,401, elev. 509'
• Part of Louisville area — see map p. 71

BAYMONT INN & SUITES 502/957-6900
▼▼ APPROVED Hotel. **Address:** 149 Willabrook Dr 40109

HAMPTON INN BY HILTON/BROOKS 502/957-5050
▼▼THREE DIAMOND **SAVE** Hotel. **Address:** 180 Willabrook Dr 40109

AAA Benefit:
Members save up to 15%!

CAMPBELLSVILLE pop. 9,108

BEST WESTERN CAMPBELLSVILLE INN 270/465-7001
▼▼ APPROVED
Hotel

Best Western.

AAA Benefit:
Members save up to 15% and earn bonus points!

Address: 1400 E Broadway 42718 **Location:** Jct SR 210, 2.1 mi e on US 68/SR 55. **Facility:** 60 units. 2 stories (no elevator), interior corridors. **Parking:** winter plug-ins. **Pool:** outdoor. **Activities:** hot tub, exercise room. **Guest Services:** coin laundry.

HOLIDAY INN EXPRESS 270/465-2727
▼▼ APPROVED Hotel. **Address:** 102 Plantation Dr 42718

WHERE TO EAT

CREEK SIDE RESTAURANT 270/465-7777
▼▼ APPROVED Southern. Casual Dining. **Address:** 1837 New Lebanon Rd 42718

GARCIA'S MEXICAN RESTAURANT & GRILL 270/465-0566
▼▼ APPROVED Mexican. Casual Dining. **Address:** 480 Campbellsville Bypass 42718

CARROLLTON (C-6) pop. 3,938, elev. 404'
• Hotels p. 34
• Part of Cincinnati area — see map p. 153

Carrollton, on a bend where the Ohio and Kentucky rivers meet, was established in 1794 as Port William. It was renamed in 1838 for Charles Carroll, a native of Maryland and a signer of the Declaration of Independence.

Carrollton/Carroll County Tourism and Convention Commission: 515 Highland Ave., P.O. Box 293, Carrollton, KY 41008. **Phone:** (502) 732-7036 or (800) 325-4290.

GENERAL BUTLER STATE RESORT PARK, 2 mi. s.e. to 1608 SR 227, is a multiuse, year-round recreation area. Facilities include basketball courts, a nine-hole golf course and tennis courts. A variety of water sports and a miniature golf course are available seasonally. The SR 227 entrance features an extensive memorial to Kentucky veterans. The park is named after the state's heralded Butler family, whose members were prominent military leaders from the Revolutionary through the Civil wars; their 19th-century home, within the park, can be toured. **Hours:** Park open daily 24 hours. House open Fri.-Sun., Memorial Day weekend-Labor Day weekend; by appointment rest of year. Phone for house hours. **Cost:** Park free. Fees are charged for house, golf and miniature golf. **Phone:** (502) 732-4384 or (866) 462-8853.

Butler-Turpin State Historic House, 2 mi. s.e. on SR 227 in General Butler State Resort Park, is the restored 1859 home of Kentucky's Butler family, which included Gen. William Orlando Butler, a hero of the Battle of New Orleans and a major general during the Mexican War, and Maj. Thomas Butler, aide-de-camp to General Andrew Jackson during the War of 1812. The Greek Revival home retains many of its original features, including woodwork, mantels and a staircase. The Butler family cemetery is located on the grounds.

Time: Allow 1 hour minimum. **Hours:** Guided house tours depart Fri.-Sun. at 1, 2 and 3, Memorial Day weekend-Labor Day weekend; by appointment rest of year. Closed major holidays. Phone ahead to confirm schedule. **Cost:** $5; $4 (senior citizens); $3 (ages 6-18). Cash only. **Phone:** (502) 732-4384 or (866) 462-8853.

HAMPTON INN BY HILTON   502/732-0700
▼▼ THREE DIAMOND SAVE Hotel. **Address:** 7 Slumber Ln 41008

AAA Benefit: Members save up to 15%!

HOLIDAY INN EXPRESS   502/732-6770
▼▼ THREE DIAMOND Hotel. **Address:** 147 Hospitality Way 41008

CAVE CITY (E-5) pop. 2,240, elev. 638'

Cave City is the center of Kentucky's cave area, which comprises 10 counties. The largest cavern is in Mammoth Cave National Park *(see place listing p. 99)*. The area also is known for its burley tobacco and dairy and beef cattle.

Cave City Convention Center & Tourism Commission: 502 Mammoth Cave St., P.O. Box 518, Cave City, KY 42127. **Phone:** (270) 773-3131.

DINOSAUR WORLD, just w. off I-65 exit 53 at 711 Mammoth Cave Rd., is an outdoor dinosaur museum with more than 150 life-size models of dinosaurs in a forested area. An indoor museum houses a collection of dinosaur eggs and raptor claws. A video presentation in the Movie Cave offers information about dinosaurs. The park also features a dinosaur-themed playground and a fossil dig with authentic fossils which may be kept upon discovery. Visitors can unearth a life-size dinosaur skeleton in the Boneyard and meet face-to-face with a mammoth herd in Mammoth Gardens.

Hours: Daily 8:30-5. Closed Thanksgiving and Christmas. **Cost:** $12.75; $10.75 (ages 60+); $9.75 (ages 3-12). **Phone:** (270) 773-4345.

FROGGETTS GUNTOWN MOUNTAIN, off I-65 exit 53 on SR 70, is an amusement park that re-creates the atmosphere of an 1880s frontier town in addition to a modern escape room and Nerf room. Featured are gun fights, music and stunt shows, and a shuttle to the top of Guntown Mountain.

Inquire about weather policies. **Hours:** Tues.-Sun. 10-6, late-May-late July and Memorial Day weekend; Sat.-Sun. 10-4:30, early Aug.-late Oct. Escape room Fri.-Sat. 6-10 (also Sat. 3-6), Sun. noon-5, in winter; otherwise varies. Phone ahead to confirm schedule. **Cost:** $15; $10 (ages 3-12). Escape room $20; $15 (ages 6-12). Reservations are required for escape room. **Phone:** (270) 773-2700, or (270) 590-1132 for reservations.

COMFORT INN & SUITES   270/773-3335
▼▼ THREE DIAMOND Hotel. **Address:** 819 Sanders St 42127

SLEEP INN & SUITES   270/773-2030
▼▼ THREE DIAMOND Hotel. **Address:** 801 Mammoth Cave St 42127

SUPER 8   270/773-3161
▼ APPROVED Hotel. **Address:** 1009 Doyle Ave 42127

WHERE TO EAT

EL MAZATLAN   270/773-7448
▼ APPROVED Mexican. Casual Dining. **Address:** 105 Gardner Ln 42127

CENTRAL CITY pop. 5,978

BEST WESTERN CENTRAL CITY   270/757-0222
▼ APPROVED Hotel

Best Western.

AAA Benefit: Members save up to 15% and earn bonus points!

Address: 627 S 2nd St 42330 **Location:** Western Kentucky Pkwy exit 58, just n. **Facility:** 37 units. 2 stories, interior corridors. **Parking:** winter plug-ins. **Pool:** heated indoor. **Activities:** exercise room. **Guest Services:** coin laundry.

DAYS INN   270/754-1222
▼ APPROVED Hotel. **Address:** 640 S 2nd St 42330

WHERE TO EAT

EL BRACERO RESTAURANT   270/757-9461
▼ APPROVED Mexican. Casual Dining. **Address:** 609 S 2nd St 42330

CLERMONT (D-5) elev. 478'
• Part of Louisville area — see map p. 71

BERNHEIM ARBORETUM AND RESEARCH FOREST is 1 mi. e. of jct. I-65 and SR 245 exit 112. The nonprofit site consists of 16,000 acres of forest and a 600-acre arboretum with three lakes, more than 40 miles of hiking trails and 16 miles of paved road for biking. Isaac W. Bernheim, a German immigrant who made his fortune in the distillery business, founded the natural area in 1929 as a gift to Kentuckians.

The arboretum features more than 8,000 labeled varieties of plants and trees, including a collection of American, Japanese and deciduous hollies. The Visitor Center, known as "a building like a tree," features a living green roof and interactive exhibits on sustainability.

More than 250 species of birds may be seen on the property, which is adorned with such nature-inspired artwork as sculptures made from metal, stone and other natural materials. Visitors may also experience life in the treetops on the Canopy Tree Walk; a nearby valley is visible from the 75-foot-high structure during winter months.

Educational programs are available. **Hours:** Daily 7-dusk. Visitor Center open daily 9-5, Mar.-Oct.; Mon.-Fri. 9-4, Sat.-Sun. 9-4:30, rest of year. Closed Jan. 1, Thanksgiving and Christmas. **Cost:** Free (Mon.-Fri.); $5 per private car, $10 per van/RV (Sat.-Sun. and holidays). **Phone:** (502) 955-8512.

JIM BEAM'S AMERICAN STILLHOUSE, 2 mi. e. of I-65 on SR 245 at 526 Happy Hollow Rd., offers a look at the history of America's first family of bourbon. A 90-minute guided walking tour through the distillery offers hands-on activities to help visitors understand the grain-to-bottle process. Self-guiding tours of the grounds include two historic exhibits on the history of bourbon making and barrel cooperage. Adults over age 21 can sample products at the end of the tour. **Hours:** Guided tours every half-hour based on availability Mon.-Sat. 9-3:30, Sun. 12:30-3. Reservations are available 48 hours in advance. Closed Jan. 1, Easter, Thanksgiving, Christmas Eve and Christmas. **Cost:** Admission free. Guided tours $14; free (ages 0-20). **Phone:** (502) 215-2295.

COLUMBIA pop. 4,452

BEST WESTERN COLUMBIA   270/384-9744

APPROVED
Motel

 Best Western. **AAA Benefit:** Members save up to 15% and earn bonus points!

Address: 710 Bomar Heights 42728 **Location:** Cumberland Pkwy exit 49, just n on SR 55, then just w. Located in a commercial area. **Facility:** 50 units. 2 stories (no elevator), exterior corridors. **Parking:** winter plug-ins. **Pool:** outdoor. **Featured Amenity:** full hot breakfast.

ANDERSON'S PIZZERIA   270/384-3333
APPROVED   Pizza. Casual Dining. **Address:** 1411 Campbellsville Rd 42728

CORBIN (F-7) pop. 7,304, elev. 1,076'

Corbin, on the Cumberland Plateau, is where Whitley, Knox and Laurel counties meet. Laurel Lake borders the western side of the city. A scenic portion of I-75 runs south from Corbin 30 miles to Jellico, Tenn., just across the state border.

Corbin Tourism & Convention Commission: 222 Corbin Center Dr., Corbin, KY 40701. **Phone:** (606) 528-8860.

BAYMONT INN & SUITES   606/523-9040
APPROVED   Hotel. **Address:** 174 Adams Rd 40701

BEST WESTERN CORBIN INN   606/528-2100
APPROVED
Motel

 Best Western. **AAA Benefit:** Members save up to 15% and earn bonus points!

Address: 2630 Cumberland Falls Hwy 40701 **Location:** I-75 exit 25, just w. **Facility:** 61 units. 2 stories (no elevator), exterior corridors. **Parking:** winter plug-ins. **Pool:** heated outdoor. **Featured Amenity:** continental breakfast.

FAIRFIELD BY MARRIOTT CORBIN   606/528-7020
THREE DIAMOND Hotel. **Address:** 25 Hwy 770 40701
AAA Benefit: Members save 5% or more!

HAMPTON INN   606/523-5696
THREE DIAMOND Hotel. **Address:** 125 Adams Rd 40701
AAA Benefit: Members save up to 15%!

HOLIDAY INN EXPRESS HOTEL & SUITES   606/523-4000
THREE DIAMOND Hotel. **Address:** 1973 Cumberland Falls Hwy 40701

WHERE TO EAT

DAVID'S STEAKHOUSE   606/528-0063
APPROVED   American. Casual Dining. **Address:** 125 W Cumberland Gap Pkwy 40701

MI CASA   606/526-0990
APPROVED   Mexican. Casual Dining. **Address:** 785 Cumberland Gap Pkwy 40701

THE WRIGLEY TAPROOM & EATERY   606/261-2008
APPROVED   American. Quick Serve. **Address:** 207 S Main St 40701

COVINGTON (B-6) pop. 40,640, elev. 515'
- Hotels p. 40 • Restaurants p. 40
- Hotels & Restaurants map & index p. 37
- Part of Cincinnati area — see map p. 153

Three bridges spanning the Ohio River connect Covington to Cincinnati. During the Civil War Covington's ties with its northern neighbor greatly divided the people's loyalty; the connection has spurred industrial ventures and trade between the two states and has made Covington a part of the Cincinnati metropolitan area.

(See map & index p. 37.)

The five- to six-block area making up MainStrasse Village is a restored 19th-century German neighborhood. Shops and restaurants are housed in renovated buildings. Of interest in the village is the Goose Girl Fountain, a life-size bronze sculpture of a German maiden carrying two geese to the market. Greek-born sculptor Eleftherios Karkadoulias destroyed the mold from which the fountain was cast, making the sculpture a unique piece.

Northern Kentucky Convention and Visitors Bureau: 50 E. RiverCenter Blvd., Suite 200, Covington, KY 41011. **Phone:** (859) 261-4677 or (800) 447-8489.

BEHRINGER-CRAWFORD MUSEUM is off I-71/75 exit 191 (Pike St./12th St.), following signs to 1600 Montague Rd. in Devou Park. The four-story museum's interactive exhibits provide a trip through Northern Kentucky's history from prehistoric mammoth fossils and ancient Indian artifacts to early settlement, the Civil War and the 21st century. Following a transportation theme in "Rivers, Roads, Rails & Runways" visitors can see a restored 1892 Kentucky streetcar, fish in the Ohio River, sit in a 1959 Buick Electra convertible to watch a drive-in movie and push buttons to activate the trains, lights and music of a miniature, mid-century community.

The museum also houses works by prominent regional artists, including primitive painter Mary Bruce Sharon, scientist/Expressionist Wolfgang Ritschel and Harlan Hubbard, whose simple, agrarian lifestyle on the Ohio River is chronicled in his paintings and books. Devou Park provides scenic views of Covington and nearby Cincinnati. **Time:** Allow 1 hour minimum. **Hours:** Tues.-Sat. 10-5, Sun. 1-5. Closed major holidays. **Cost:** $9; $8 (ages 60+); $5 (ages 3-17). Rates may change for special events. **Phone:** (859) 491-4003.

MOTHER OF GOD CHURCH is at 119 W. 6th St.; use the entrance between the church and the rectory. The Italian Renaissance-style church, built 1870-71, is enhanced by stained-glass windows imported from Bavaria in 1890 and five murals created by parishioner Johann Schmitt, some of whose works are in the Vatican. **Time:** Allow 30 minutes minimum. **Hours:** Mon.-Fri. 9:30-4:30. Closed major holidays. Phone ahead to confirm schedule. **Cost:** Free. **Phone:** (859) 291-2288.

ST. MARY'S CATHEDRAL BASILICA OF THE ASSUMPTION, 1101 Madison Ave. at 12th St., has a facade modeled after Notre Dame in Paris, France. The 1895 basilica has 82 stained-glass windows, including one of the largest stained-glass windows in the world. Four large murals on canvas painted by Covington native Frank Duveneck adorn the walls of a chapel.

Bilingual self-guiding tour brochures are available. **Time:** Allow 1 hour minimum. **Hours:** Mon.-Sat. 10-4. Guided tours are given some Sun. at 11 and daily by appointment; phone ahead to verify. Individuals can join previously scheduled 1-hour group tours Mon.-Sat.; phone to see if one is scheduled. **Cost:** Donations. Guided tour $5. **Phone:** (859) 431-2060.

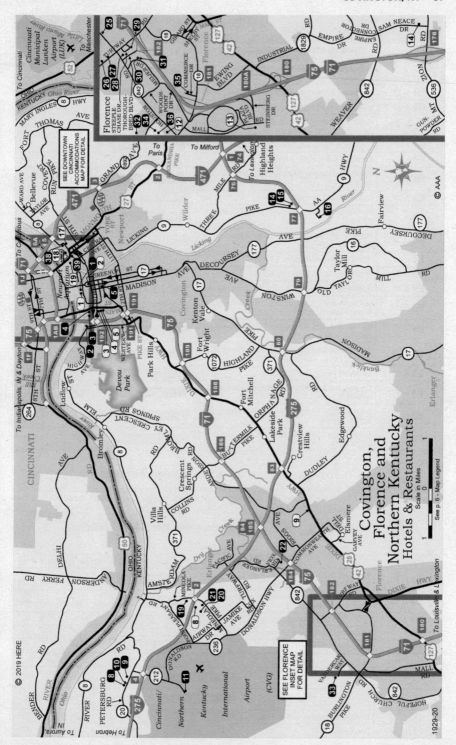

Covington, Florence and Northern Kentucky Hotels & Restaurants

✈ Airport Hotels

Map Page	CINCINNATI-NORTHERN KENTUCKY INT'L (Maximum driving distance from airport: 6.7 mi)	Designation	Member Savings	Page
21 p. 37	**Courtyard by Marriott-Cincinnati Airport, 3.7 mi**	APPROVED	✔	43
19 p. 37	Holiday Inn-Cincinnati Airport, 3.1 mi	THREE DIAMOND		43
20 p. 37	**Residence Inn by Marriott, Cincinnati Airport, 3.7 mi**	THREE DIAMOND	✔	43
22 p. 37	Wingate by Wyndham Cincinnati Airport, 4.9 mi	THREE DIAMOND		43
25 p. 37	Ashley Quarters Hotel, 5.6 mi	APPROVED		44
27 p. 37	Comfort Inn Greater Cincinnati Airport on Turfway Rd, 5.4 mi	APPROVED		44
34 p. 37	Comfort Suites Florence, 6.6 mi	THREE DIAMOND		44
36 p. 37	Fairfield Inn & Suites Cincinnati Airport South, 6.6 mi	THREE DIAMOND	✔	44
28 p. 37	**Hampton Inn by Hilton Cincinnati Airport South, 5.6 mi**	THREE DIAMOND	✔	44
29 p. 37	**Hilton Cincinnati Airport, 5.7 mi**	THREE DIAMOND	✔	44
32 p. 37	Homewood Suites by Hilton, 6.7 mi	THREE DIAMOND	✔	44
30 p. 37	**Hyatt Place Cincinnati Airport/Florence, 6.4 mi**	THREE DIAMOND	✔	44
31 p. 37	La Quinta Inn & Suites by Wyndham Cincinnati Airport Florence, 6.4 mi	THREE DIAMOND		44
26 p. 37	**SpringHill Suites by Marriott-Cincinnati Airport South, 5.2 mi**	THREE DIAMOND	✔	44
33 p. 37	Tru by Hilton Cincinnati Airport South Florence, 6.5 mi	APPROVED	✔	44
9 p. 37	Cincinnati Airport Marriott, 2.0 mi	THREE DIAMOND	✔	51
8 p. 37	**Country Inn & Suites by Radisson, Cincinnati Airport, 2.2 mi**	APPROVED	✔	51
11 p. 37	DoubleTree by Hilton Hotel Cincinnati Airport, on airport property	THREE DIAMOND	✔	51
10 p. 37	Hampton Inn Cincinnati Airport North by Hilton, 2.2 mi	THREE DIAMOND	✔	51

Covington, Florence and Northern Kentucky

This index helps you "spot" where hotels and restaurants are located on the corresponding detailed maps. Restaurant price range is a combination of lunch and/or dinner. Turn to the listing page for more information and consult display ads for special promotions.

 For more details, rates and reservations: AAA.com/travelguides/hotels

COVINGTON

Map Page	Hotels	Designation	Member Savings	Page
1 p. 37	**Embassy Suites by Hilton Cincinnati RiverCenter**	THREE DIAMOND	✔	40
2 p. 37	**Best Western Plus Cincinnati Riverfront Downtown Area**	THREE DIAMOND	✔	40
3 p. 37	Holiday Inn Cincinnati Riverfront	THREE DIAMOND		40
4 p. 37	**Courtyard by Marriott Cincinnati/Covington**	THREE DIAMOND	✔	40
5 p. 37	**Hotel Covington**	FOUR DIAMOND	✔	40

Map Page	Restaurants	Designation	Cuisine	Price Range	Page
① p. 37	10 West	APPROVED	Regional American	$12-$32	40
② p. 37	Molly Malone's Irish Pub of Covington	APPROVED	Irish	$8-$15	40
③ p. 37	Bouquet Restaurant and Winebar	THREE DIAMOND	American	$18-$50	40
④ p. 37	Dee Felice Cafe	THREE DIAMOND	Cajun	$14-$38	40

Map Page	Restaurants (cont'd)	Designation	Cuisine	Price Range	Page
⑤ p. 37	Cock & Bull Public House	APPROVED	American	$8-$17	40

HEBRON

Map Page	Hotels	Designation	Member Savings	Page
⑧ p. 37	**Country Inn & Suites by Radisson, Cincinnati Airport**	APPROVED	✔	51
⑨ p. 37	Cincinnati Airport Marriott	THREE DIAMOND	✔	51
⑩ p. 37	Hampton Inn Cincinnati Airport North by Hilton	THREE DIAMOND	✔	51
⑪ p. 37	DoubleTree by Hilton Hotel Cincinnati Airport	THREE DIAMOND	✔	51

WILDER

Map Page	Hotels	Designation	Member Savings	Page
⑭ p. 37	Holiday Inn Express and Suites Cincinnati South-Wilder	THREE DIAMOND		111
⑮ p. 37	Hampton Inn & Suites by Hilton Wilder	THREE DIAMOND	✔	111
⑯ p. 37	Comfort Inn & Suites Northern Kentucky	APPROVED		111

ERLANGER

Map Page	Hotels	Designation	Member Savings	Page
⑲ p. 37	Holiday Inn-Cincinnati Airport	THREE DIAMOND		43
⑳ p. 37	**Residence Inn by Marriott, Cincinnati Airport**	THREE DIAMOND	✔	43
㉑ p. 37	**Courtyard by Marriott-Cincinnati Airport**	APPROVED	✔	43
㉒ p. 37	Wingate by Wyndham Cincinnati Airport	THREE DIAMOND		43

Map Page	Restaurants	Designation	Cuisine	Price Range	Page
⑧ p. 37	Jo An Japanese Cuisine	APPROVED	Japanese	$9-$34	43
⑨ p. 37	Colonial Cottage Inn	APPROVED	American	$9-$17	43

FLORENCE

Map Page	Hotels	Designation	Member Savings	Page
㉕ p. 37	Ashley Quarters Hotel	APPROVED		44
㉖ p. 37	**SpringHill Suites by Marriott-Cincinnati Airport South**	THREE DIAMOND	✔	44
㉗ p. 37	Comfort Inn Greater Cincinnati Airport on Turfway Rd	APPROVED		44
㉘ p. 37	**Hampton Inn by Hilton Cincinnati Airport South**	THREE DIAMOND	✔	44
㉙ p. 37	**Hilton Cincinnati Airport**	THREE DIAMOND	✔	44
㉚ p. 37	**Hyatt Place Cincinnati Airport/Florence**	THREE DIAMOND	✔	44
㉛ p. 37	La Quinta Inn & Suites by Wyndham Cincinnati Airport Florence	THREE DIAMOND		44
㉜ p. 37	Homewood Suites by Hilton	THREE DIAMOND	✔	44
㉝ p. 37	Tru by Hilton Cincinnati Airport South Florence	APPROVED	✔	44
㉞ p. 37	Comfort Suites Florence	THREE DIAMOND		44
㉟ p. 37	**Best Western Inn Florence**	APPROVED	✔	44
㊱ p. 37	Fairfield Inn & Suites Cincinnati Airport South	THREE DIAMOND	✔	44

Map Page	Restaurants	Designation	Cuisine	Price Range	Page
⑫ p. 37	Miyoshi Japanese Restaurant	APPROVED	Japanese	$7-$25	45
⑬ p. 37	Cathay Kitchen Asian Restaurant	APPROVED	Chinese	$7-$15	45
⑭ p. 37	Buffalo Bob's Family Restaurant	APPROVED	American	$5-$42	44

NEWPORT

Map Page	Hotels	Designation	Member Savings	Page
㊳ p. 37	Aloft Newport on the Levee	THREE DIAMOND	✔	102
㊴ p. 37	Hampton Inn & Suites by Hilton Newport/Cincinnati	THREE DIAMOND	✔	102

Map Page	Restaurants	Designation	Cuisine	Price Range	Page
⑰ p. 37	Hofbrauhaus Newport	APPROVED	German	$11-$24	103
⑱ p. 37	Mitchell's Fish Market	THREE DIAMOND	Seafood	$12-$44 SAVE	103
⑲ p. 37	BB Riverboats	APPROVED	American	$35-$130	102

(See map & index p. 37.)

BEST WESTERN PLUS CINCINNATI RIVERFRONT DOWNTOWN AREA   859/581-7800

THREE DIAMOND

Hotel

Best Western PLUS

AAA Benefit: Members save up to 15% and earn bonus points!

Address: 200 Crescent Ave 41011 **Location:** Waterfront. I-71/75 exit 192, 0.6 mi nw. **Facility:** 127 units. 6 stories, interior corridors. **Amenities:** *Some:* safes. **Pool:** heated indoor. **Activities:** exercise room. **Guest Services:** valet and coin laundry. **Featured Amenity:** full hot breakfast.

COURTYARD BY MARRIOTT CINCINNATI/COVINGTON   859/491-4000

THREE DIAMOND

Hotel

COURTYARD

AAA Benefit: Members save 5% or more!

Address: 500 W 3rd St 41011 **Location:** Waterfront. I-71/75 exit 192, just e. **Facility:** 194 units. 9 stories, interior corridors. **Pool:** heated indoor. **Activities:** hot tub, exercise room. **Guest Services:** valet and coin laundry, boarding pass kiosk, area transportation.

EMBASSY SUITES BY HILTON CINCINNATI RIVERCENTER   859/261-8400

THREE DIAMOND

Hotel

EMBASSY SUITES

AAA Benefit: Members save up to 15%!

Address: 10 E RiverCenter Blvd 41011 **Location:** Waterfront. I-71/75 exit 192, 0.9 mi e on W 3rd St. **Facility:** 227 units, some two bedrooms. 8 stories, interior corridors. **Parking:** on-site (fee) and valet. **Terms:** check-in 4 pm. **Amenities:** safes. **Pool:** heated indoor. **Activities:** exercise room. **Guest Services:** complimentary and valet laundry, area transportation. **Featured Amenity:** full hot breakfast.

HOLIDAY INN CINCINNATI RIVERFRONT   859/291-4300
THREE DIAMOND Hotel. **Address:** 600 W 3rd St 41011

HOTEL COVINGTON   859/905-6600

FOUR DIAMOND

Boutique Hotel

Address: 638 Madison St 41011 **Location:** I-75 exit 192, 0.6 mi e on 5th St, then just s. **Facility:** Once a 1907 department store, this former temple to commerce has been reinvented as a stylish temple for travelers. Guest rooms have walnut veneer furniture and foyers with wood-grain tiles. 114 units. 7 stories, interior corridors. **Parking:** on-site (fee) and valet. **Amenities:** safes. **Activities:** bicycles, lawn sports, exercise room, in-room exercise equipment, massage. **Guest Services:** valet laundry, area transportation.

 **WHERE TO EAT**

| 10 WEST | 859/392-3750 |

APPROVED Regional American. Casual Dining. **Address:** 10 W RiverCenter Blvd 41011

BOUQUET RESTAURANT AND WINEBAR 859/491-7777 ③
THREE DIAMOND American. Fine Dining. **Address:** 519 Main St 41011

COCK & BULL PUBLIC HOUSE   859/581-4253 ⑤
APPROVED American. Casual Dining. **Address:** 601 Main St 41011

DEE FELICE CAFE   859/261-2365 ④
THREE DIAMOND Cajun. Casual Dining. **Address:** 529 Main St 41011

MOLLY MALONE'S IRISH PUB OF COVINGTON
859/491-6659 ②
APPROVED Irish. Casual Dining. **Address:** 112 E 4th St 41011

CRESTWOOD (C-5) pop. 4,531, elev. 784'
• Part of Louisville area — see map p. 71

YEW DELL GARDENS is e. of I-71 on SR 329, then e. on SR 146 to 6220 Old LaGrange Rd. The 60-acre site includes the home, gardens and arboretum of Theodore Klein, who operated a commercial nursery in the latter part of the 20th century. Included are more than 12,000 rare trees, shrubs and flowers, display gardens, hiking trails, a state-of-the-art greenhouse and distinctive architecture. Special events and workshops are offered throughout the year.

Time: Allow 1 hour minimum. **Hours:** Tues.-Sat. 10-4 (also Thurs. 4-dusk during the summer), Sun. noon-4, Apr.-Nov.; Tues.-Fri. 10-4, rest of year. Closed Jan. 1, Oaks and Derby days (first Fri.-Sat. in May), Thanksgiving, Christmas Eve, Christmas, day after Christmas and Dec. 27-31. **Cost:** $9; $5 (ages 55+); free (ages 0-11 and in January and February). **Phone:** (502) 241-4788 for tour reservations. GT

CUMBERLAND GAP NATIONAL HISTORICAL PARK (F-8)

> Elevations in the park range from 1,600 ft. at the Cumberland Gap to 3,513 ft. at White Rocks. Refer to AAA maps for additional elevation information.

At the convergence of Kentucky, Tennessee and Virginia, Cumberland Gap National Historical Park covers 24,000 acres of heavily forested, rugged mountains honoring the historic pass.

The gap provides a natural doorway through the mountains. It was first used by migratory animals as a seasonal thoroughfare, then by Native Americans, whose footpaths followed buffalo and deer trails. The westward movement of settlers seemed barred by the Allegheny ridge until April 1750, when Dr. Thomas Walker discovered the gap while seeking the fabled land to the west, the "Kentucke" of Native American lore.

Daniel Boone passed through with a hunting party in 1769, and in 1775 he blazed the Wilderness Road. From 1775 to 1796 the gap could only be used by those on foot or horseback, and although no wagon passed over it during this period, more than 200,000 people made their way through the gap into Kentucky and beyond.

A strategic point during the Civil War, Cumberland Gap changed hands several times without any major battles. Some of the earthwork fortifications remain.

In the 1990s, the 4,600-foot-long Cumberland Gap Highway Tunnel was built; the project also included rerouting US 25E through the tunnel and the addition of new bridges, highway interchanges and parking areas. Although the final cost of this joint effort led by the National Park Service and the Federal Highway Administration was a staggering $265 million, the construction plan alleviated traffic problems and improved motorist safety while simultaneously restoring the historic appearance of the Cumberland Gap and the Wilderness Road.

General Information and Activities

At an elevation of 2,440 feet, Pinnacle Overlook provides a view into the gap as well as views of the mountain range and parts of three states. It is accessible via a 4-mile paved road from the visitor center. No trailers or vehicles more than 20 feet long are allowed. Shuttle service may be arranged for a small fee when staff is available; reservations are required.

Still a wild area, the park offers approximately 85 miles of hiking trails ranging from relatively easy nature trails to those requiring an overnight trek. Many park features, including Sand Cave, a multicolored sandstone overhang, and White Rocks, a prominent sandstone outcropping, can be reached only by trail. Ridge Trail, a 19-mile-long route offering panoramas of the valley, approaches five primitive campsites, all accessible by foot. The Wilderness Road Campground has 160 campsites, 41 of which have hookups.

Hensley Settlement is a reconstruction of a community that was occupied 1903-51. Reminiscent of a time much earlier than that from which it actually dates, Hensley seems like a community of the late 1700s or early 1800s. The settlement sits atop a mountain in the eastern end of the park. With more than 70 acres of land under cultivation, it has several reconstructed log houses, barns and outbuildings. The site can be reached by an all-day hike or, from mid-May through Oct. 31, via a guided tour that departs the park's visitor center daily. Building interiors may be seen during the 3.5- to 4-hour trip, which includes shuttle transportation to and from the settlement. The cost is $10; $5 (ages 0-12 and senior citizens with an Interagency Senior Pass). Phone (606) 248-2817, ext. 1075, for the shuttle tour schedule; reservations are recommended.

It is not advisable to hike alone; overnight camping requires a permit. Trail guides and other information can be obtained at the visitor center. The visitor center also contains a museum, which chronicles the rich history of the gap. Throughout the year ranger-led programs suitable for the entire family introduce visitors to the historical, cultural and natural aspects of the park; phone for a schedule of events.

The park is open daily. Some parking areas close before dusk. The visitor center at the park entrance is open daily 8-5, Memorial Day-Labor Day; 9-4, rest of year; closed Christmas.

ADMISSION to the park is free.

PETS must be restricted at all times, either in vehicles or by leash, and are not allowed in public buildings.

ADDRESS inquiries to the Superintendent, Cumberland Gap National Historical Park, 91 Bartlett Park Rd., Middlesboro, KY 40965; phone (606) 248-2817.

GAP CAVE is .25 mi. s. of Middlesboro, Ky., on US 25E. Two-hour guided tours of the cave, discovered in 1750, cover a 1.5-mile route and are conducted by lantern light. Rooms and walls are covered with stalactites and stalagmites. Wildlife, including bats and salamanders, can be seen, as can the names of Civil War soldiers carved on the walls.

Note: The guided tour's path includes 183 steps; visitors are advised to wear good walking shoes. No sandals or open-toed shoes are permitted. Due to the threat of white-nose syndrome to bats, visitors should not wear clothing and footwear that has been worn in other caves unless properly decontaminated.

Time: Allow 2 hours minimum. **Hours:** Tours are given daily at 10, early Apr.-late Nov.; phone ahead for additional tour times. Tickets may be purchased at the park visitor center or at Daniel Boone parking area 30 minutes in advance of the tour. Reservations are recommended, especially on weekends. **Cost:** $8; $4 (ages 5-12 and senior citizens with an Interagency Senior Pass). Ages 0-4 are not permitted on cave tours. **Phone:** (606) 248-2817. GT

DANIEL BOONE NATIONAL FOREST
(D-7)

Elevations in the forest range from 640 ft. to nearly 2,000 ft. Refer to AAA maps for additional elevation information.

Daniel Boone National Forest runs along the Cumberland Plateau in the Appalachian foothills of eastern Kentucky. The forest encompasses more than 708,000 acres of mostly rugged terrain, including towering sandstone cliffs, steep forested ridges and narrow, low-lying ravines. Natural stone arches, waterfalls and caves are among the forest's exceptional geological features.

Visitors appreciate the recreation, scenic beauty and abundant wildlife in the forest. Popular features include Cave Run Lake, Laurel River Lake, the Red River Gorge Geological Area, Clifty Wilderness Area, Beaver Creek Wilderness and Wildlife Management Area, and the Natural Arch Scenic Area. Two state parks fall within the forest: Cumberland

Falls State Resort Park *(see Recreation Areas Chart)* and Natural Bridge Resort Park near the Red River Gorge in Slade *(see Recreation Areas Chart).*

Mature pine and hardwood trees grow on lands once cleared by logging, mining and farming. This diverse forest provides a suitable habitat for wild turkeys, quails, songbirds, white-tailed deer and other mammals as well as 23 threatened and endangered species of plants and animals. The forest also fosters the growth of a variety of rare flowering plants, including the wild white fringeless orchid and the white-haired golden rod.

Some of the recreational opportunities include camping, picnicking, hiking and boating. The approximately 290-mile Sheltowee Trace National Recreation Trail bisects the length of the forest running north to south. Hikers and other trail users are rewarded with unforgettable scenery in addition to sightings of birds and other animals. More than 600 miles of trails, along with an abundance of rivers and streams, offer quiet escapes. Mountain biking, horseback riding and off-road vehicles are allowed along designated sections of trail.

Among the highlights of the Red River Gorge National Scenic Byway are the natural geologic features, including sandstone arches carved over millions of years. Trails lead to these geological landmarks and also to picturesque waterfalls. The 11-mile Zilpo National Forest Scenic Byway runs through the forest near Cave Run Lake and provides views of the native landscape and wildlife. In the southern region of the forest, sections of the Wilderness Road Heritage Highway and the Cumberland Cultural Heritage Byway transect through the national forest.

A recreation fee is required in most areas. Kentucky state boating, fishing and hunting regulations apply. For additional information contact the Forest Supervisor's Office, Daniel Boone National Forest, 1700 Bypass Rd., Winchester, KY 40391; phone (859) 745-3100. *See Recreation Areas Chart.*

DANVILLE (D-6) pop. 16,218, elev. 973'

Settled in 1775, Danville was the capital of the Kentucky District of Virginia for many years and of the new Commonwealth of Kentucky for 3 days while the state's constitution was drawn up. The property of pioneer surgeon Dr. Ephraim McDowell has been preserved as McDowell House Museum, Apothecary and Gardens and depicts Kentucky's journey to statehood; phone (859) 236-2804 for more information.

Isaac Shelby, both the first and fifth governor of Kentucky, is buried in the Isaac Shelby Cemetery State Historic Site 5 miles south of Danville off US 127. Shelby was the chairman of the first Kentucky Constitutional Convention and served in both the American Revolution and the War of 1812.

Many of the state's landmark structures were built in Danville, including Kentucky's first college, school for the deaf, law school, log courthouse and brick courthouse as well as the first post office west of the Allegheny Mountains. Danville hosts the 🎺 Great American Brass Band Festival in June. This 3-day event includes hot air balloon races, a huge picnic on the lawns of Centre College and music by brass performers from across the country. *Also see Bluegrass Country p. 30.*

Danville-Boyle County Convention & Visitors Bureau: 105 E. Walnut St., Danville, KY 40422. **Phone:** (859) 236-7794 or (859) 236-2361.

Shopping: The historic buildings in Danville's central downtown area offer specialty shops, boutiques and restaurants.

THE GREAT AMERICAN DOLLHOUSE MUSEUM is .5 mi. w. on W. Main St. (SR 34/US 127/US 150), .2 mi. n. on St. Mildred's Ct., just e. on W. Lexington Ave., then just n. to 344 Swope Ave. More than 200 furnished dollhouses and miniature buildings are arranged as historic neighborhoods. Included in the display of miniature villages are a Shaker settlement, an old Western town, a coal mining camp and a 1900s town. **Time:** Allow 1 hour, 30 minutes minimum. **Hours:** Tues.-Sat. 11-5. Closed major holidays. **Cost:** $9; $8 (ages 60+ and military with ID); $7 (ages 4-12). **Phone:** (859) 236-1883. 🅰

HAMPTON INN BY HILTON DANVILLE   859/236-6200

THREE DIAMOND SAVE Hotel. **Address:** 100 Montgomery Way 40422

AAA Benefit: Members save up to 15%!

HOLIDAY INN EXPRESS AND SUITES   859/209-2928

THREE DIAMOND Hotel. **Address:** 200 Shannon Way 40422

DRY RIDGE pop. 2,191
• Part of Cincinnati area — see map p. 153

QUALITY INN   859/824-7121

APPROVED Hotel. **Address:** 1050 Fashion Ridge Rd 41035

ELIZABETHTOWN (D-5) pop. 28,531, elev. 708'

Elizabethtown was settled by three pioneers from Virginia in 1779. In 1797 Col. Andrew Hynes donated land for public buildings and town lots, so the settlement was named Elizabeth Town in honor of his wife. Over the years other pioneers followed, among them Thomas Lincoln, father of Abraham Lincoln. He lived in or near the town 1796-1816 and then moved to Indiana.

Costumed characters from Elizabethtown's past lead guests on a walking tour through the downtown historic district on Thursday nights June through September; phone the tourism and convention bureau for additional information about the guided tours. In December, 🎄 Freemen Lake Park is decorated with some 1 million lights.

Elizabethtown Tourism & Convention Bureau: 1030 N. Mulberry St., Elizabethtown, KY 42701. **Phone:** (270) 765-2175 or (800) 437-0092.

Self-guiding tours: Brochures outlining three self-guiding tours are available at the tourism and convention bureau. The Downtown Walking Tour covers the downtown historic district, encompassing the courthouse square and adjacent blocks. The Historic Driving Tour takes in the residential area and its many fine old homes. The Greenbelt Park Tour is made up of a series of stream-side hiking trails. Free downloadable apps are available for walking and driving tours.

HARDIN COUNTY HISTORY MUSEUM is at 201 W. Dixie Ave. The museum features permanent and changing exhibits as well as a collection of artifacts and memorabilia relating pioneer life and the history of the county, the first recorded exploration of which occurred in 1766. Civil War relics, a replica of an early log cabin, medical paraphernalia and tools used by a local doctor and an exhibit detailing the historical contributions of African-Americans born locally are displayed.

Guided tours are offered during museum hours and also by appointment. **Time:** Allow 1 hour minimum. **Hours:** Tues.-Sat. 10-2. Closed major holidays. **Cost:** Donations. **Phone:** (270) 763-8339.

HAMPTON INN BY HILTON   270/765-6663
🔷THREE DIAMOND SAVE Hotel. **Address:** 1035 Executive Dr 42701

> **AAA Benefit:** Members save up to `15%!

HILTON GARDEN INN ELIZABETHTOWN   270/900-4899
🔷THREE DIAMOND SAVE Hotel. **Address:** 203 Commerce Dr 42701

> **AAA Benefit:** Members save up to 15%!

HOLIDAY INN EXPRESS ELIZABETHTOWN NORTH
                                       270/982-9466
🔷THREE DIAMOND Hotel. **Address:** 130 The Loop 42701

LA QUINTA INN & SUITES ELIZABETHTOWN   270/765-4747
🔷THREE DIAMOND Hotel. **Address:** 210 Commerce Dr 42701

RAMADA   270/769-9683
🔷 APPROVED Hotel. **Address:** 205 Commerce Dr 42701

RED LION INN & SUITES ELIZABETHTOWN   270/769-1334
🔷THREE DIAMOND Hotel. **Address:** 107 Buffalo Creek Dr 42701

WINGFIELD INN & SUITES   270/769-3030
🔷 APPROVED
Hotel

Address: 1043 Executive Dr 42701 **Location:** I-65 exit 94, just nw. **Facility:** 123 units. 2 stories (no elevator), interior corridors. **Parking:** winter plug-ins. **Pool:** heated indoor. **Activities:** exercise room. **Guest Services:** valet and coin laundry. **Featured Amenity:** breakfast buffet.

SAVE 🍴 🛥 ♿ BIZ HS 🛜
✕ 🔌 📺 💻 / SOME UNITS 🐾

2B THAI RESTAURANT   270/766-1408
🔷 APPROVED   Thai. Casual Dining. **Address:** 3040 E Ring Rd, Suite 2 42701

BACK HOME RESTAURANT   270/769-2800
🔷 APPROVED   Southern. Casual Dining. **Address:** 251 W Dixie Ave 42701

NAMASTE INDIAN CUISINE & BAR   270/900-1011
🔷 APPROVED   Indian. Casual Dining. **Address:** 1609 N Dixie Hwy, Suite 102 42701

ERLANGER pop. 18,082
- **Hotels & Restaurants map & index p. 37**
- **Part of Cincinnati area — see map p. 153**

COURTYARD BY MARRIOTT-CINCINNATI AIRPORT
                                   859/647-9900 **21**
🔷 APPROVED
Hotel

COURTYARD **AAA Benefit:** Members save 5% or more!

Address: 3990 Olympic Blvd 41018 **Location:** I-275 exit 2, just s. **Facility:** 120 units. 4 stories, interior corridors. **Pool:** heated indoor. **Activities:** hot tub, exercise room. **Guest Services:** valet and coin laundry, boarding pass kiosk, area transportation.

SAVE 🔦 🍴 🍽 CALL ♿ 🛥
♿ BIZ HS 🛜 ✕ 🐾 🔌
💻 / SOME UNITS 📺

HOLIDAY INN-CINCINNATI AIRPORT   859/371-2233 **19**
🔷THREE DIAMOND Hotel. **Address:** 1717 Airport Exchange Blvd 41018

RESIDENCE INN BY MARRIOTT, CINCINNATI AIRPORT
                                   859/282-7400 **20**
🔷THREE DIAMOND
Extended Stay Hotel

Residence INN. **AAA Benefit:** Members save 5% or more!

Address: 2811 Circleport Dr 41018 **Location:** I-275 exit 2, just s. **Facility:** 150 units, some two bedrooms, efficiencies and kitchens. 3 stories, interior corridors. **Pool:** outdoor. **Activities:** exercise room. **Guest Services:** valet and coin laundry, area transportation.

SAVE 🔦 CALL ♿ 🛥 ♿ BIZ
🛜 ✕ 🐾 🔌 📺 💻
/ SOME UNITS 🐾 HS

WINGATE BY WYNDHAM CINCINNATI AIRPORT
                                   859/727-0144 **22**
🔷THREE DIAMOND Hotel. **Address:** 605 Viox Rd 41018

COLONIAL COTTAGE INN   859/341-4498 **9**
🔷 APPROVED   American. Casual Dining. **Address:** 3140 Dixie Hwy 41018

JO AN JAPANESE CUISINE   859/746-2634 **8**
🔷 APPROVED   Japanese. Casual Dining. **Address:** 3940 Olympic Blvd, Suite 135 41018

FLORENCE (B-6) pop. 29,951, elev. 925'
- Hotels & Restaurants map & index p. 37
- Part of Cincinnati area — see map p. 153

Before becoming known as Florence, this community tried on several names, including Crossroads, Maddentown and Connersville. One of the best known local landmarks—a water tower sporting "Florence Y'all" due to a former dispute over advertising Florence Mall— can be seen from I-75. The two-story mall offers more than 100 tenants, including Macy's and Sears.

Florence Freedom, an independent minor league baseball team, plays at UC Health Stadium, 7950 Freedom Way; phone (859) 594-4487.

ASHLEY QUARTERS HOTEL 859/525-9997 (25)
APPROVED Extended Stay Hotel. **Address:** 4880 Houston Rd 41042

BEST WESTERN INN FLORENCE 859/525-0090 (35)
APPROVED
Hotel

AAA Benefit: Members save up to 15% and earn bonus points!
Address: 7821 Commerce Dr 41042 **Location:** I-71/75 exit 181, just ne. **Facility:** 51 units. 3 stories, interior corridors. **Pool:** outdoor. **Activities:** exercise room. **Guest Services:** valet laundry.

COMFORT INN GREATER CINCINNATI AIRPORT ON TURFWAY RD 859/647-2700 (27)
APPROVED Hotel. **Address:** 7454 Turfway Rd 41042

COMFORT SUITES FLORENCE 859/488-1708 (34)
THREE DIAMOND Hotel. **Address:** 5905 Merchants St 41042

FAIRFIELD INN & SUITES CINCINNATI AIRPORT SOUTH 859/545-4828 (36)
THREE DIAMOND Hotel. **Address:** 5910 Merchants St 41042
AAA Benefit: Members save 5% or more!

HAMPTON INN BY HILTON CINCINNATI AIRPORT SOUTH 859/283-1600 (28)
THREE DIAMOND
Hotel

AAA Benefit: Members save up to 15%!
Address: 7393 Turfway Rd 41042 **Location:** I-71/75 exit 182, 0.4 mi sw. **Facility:** 116 units. 4 stories, interior corridors. **Pool:** outdoor. **Activities:** exercise room. **Guest Services:** valet laundry, area transportation. **Featured Amenity:** full hot breakfast.

HILTON CINCINNATI AIRPORT 859/371-4400 (29)
THREE DIAMOND
Hotel

AAA Benefit: Members save up to 15%!
Address: 7373 Turfway Rd 41042 **Location:** I-71/75 exit 182, 0.4 mi sw. **Facility:** 314 units. 3 stories, interior corridors. **Amenities:** safes. **Pool:** heated indoor. **Activities:** exercise room. **Guest Services:** valet laundry.

HOMEWOOD SUITES BY HILTON 859/283-2111 (32)
THREE DIAMOND Extended Stay Hotel. **Address:** 1090 Vandercar Way 41042
AAA Benefit: Members save up to 15%!

HYATT PLACE CINCINNATI AIRPORT/FLORENCE 859/647-1170 (30)
THREE DIAMOND
Hotel

AAA Benefit: Members save up to 10%!
Address: 300 Meijer Dr 41042 **Location:** I-71/75 exit 182, 0.4 mi sw. **Facility:** 126 units. 6 stories, interior corridors. **Pool:** heated indoor. **Activities:** exercise room. **Guest Services:** valet and coin laundry, area transportation. **Featured Amenity:** full hot breakfast.

LA QUINTA INN & SUITES BY WYNDHAM CINCINNATI AIRPORT FLORENCE 859/282-8212 (31)
THREE DIAMOND Hotel. **Address:** 350 Meijer Dr 41042

SPRINGHILL SUITES BY MARRIOTT-CINCINNATI AIRPORT SOUTH 859/371-3388 (26)
THREE DIAMOND
Hotel

AAA Benefit: Members save 5% or more!
Address: 7492 Turfway Rd 41042 **Location:** I-71/75 exit 182, 0.8 mi sw. **Facility:** 101 units. 4 stories, interior corridors. **Activities:** hot tub, exercise room. **Guest Services:** valet and coin laundry.

TRU BY HILTON CINCINNATI AIRPORT SOUTH FLORENCE 859/283-3000 (33)
APPROVED Contemporary Hotel. **Address:** 1080 Vandercar Way 41042
Members save up to 15%!

WHERE TO EAT

BUFFALO BOB'S FAMILY RESTAURANT 859/371-5244 (14)
APPROVED American. Casual Dining. **Address:** 9910 Berberich Dr 41042

(See map & index p. 37.)

(See map & index p. 37.)

CATHAY KITCHEN ASIAN RESTAURANT   859/282-0770   ⑬
▼▼ **APPROVED**   Chinese. Casual Dining. **Address:** 8049 Connector Dr 41042

MIYOSHI JAPANESE RESTAURANT   859/525-6564   ⑫
▼▼ **APPROVED**   Japanese. Casual Dining. **Address:** 8660 Bankers St 41042

FORT KNOX (D-5) pop. 10,124, elev. 760'

Established in 1918, Camp Knox was named in honor of Revolutionary War General Henry T. Knox, who served as Chief of Artillery for the Continental Army and later was the nation's first Secretary of War. The installation's name was changed to Fort Knox in 1932. The fort has been home to the U.S. Army Armor School and Center since the inception of the Armored Forces in 1940.

Note: All visitors over age 18 must provide photo identification in order to gain admittance to Fort Knox. Valid registration and a driver's license are required of vehicles entering the premises.

PATTON MUSEUM, 4554 Fayette Ave., is named for World War II general George S. Patton. Displays include German and Japanese war artifacts, an extensive collection of U.S. and foreign tanks and weapons, and mementos of Patton's military career, including his wartime caravan truck and the sedan in which he was fatally injured in 1945.

Armor Unit Memorial Park, adjacent to the Patton Museum, pays tribute to the units that served and protected the United States in 20th century wars. **Note:** To access the museum, visitors with no military ID card or installation entry pass must go to the Fort Knox Visitor Center, located on E. Bullion Boulevard just before the Chaffee (main) Gate, and present a valid driver's license to obtain an Automated Installation Entry pass. If your driver's license is from the states of Illinois, Minnesota, Missouri, New Mexico or Washington, please bring an additional form of ID. **Time:** Allow 1 hour minimum. **Hours:** Tues.-Sat. 10-4:30. Closed Jan. 1, Easter, Thanksgiving, Christmas Eve, Christmas and Dec. 31. **Cost:** Free. **Phone:** (502) 624-3391.

U.S. BULLION DEPOSITORY, on Gold Vault Rd., holds a large portion of the U.S. gold reserve. The 100-square-foot, 1937 treasure house is bombproof; its walls and roof are faced with huge granite blocks. At different times the vault has also held the British Crown Jewels, the Magna Carta, the Constitution of the United States and the Declaration of Independence. The depository is closed to the public.

FRANKFORT (D-6) pop. 25,527, elev. 560'
• Hotels p. 47 • Restaurants p. 47

Frankfort is surrounded by wooded hillsides and divided by the S-curve of the Kentucky River as it meanders through the Bluegrass Region. The city's north and south sections are separated not only by water but also by their historical backgrounds and architectural styles. The north section originated

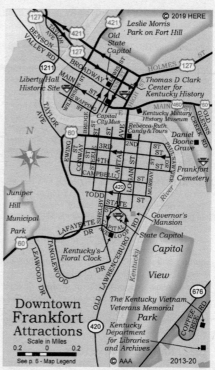

Downtown **Frankfort** Attractions
Scale in Miles
0.2   0   0.2
See p. 6 - Map Legend   © AAA   2013-20

around the time of Frankfort's founding in 1786, while the south section was developed after the new capitol was built in 1910.

The state capital, Frankfort has been Kentucky's seat of government since 1792, when it was chosen as the capital in a compromise between rivals Louisville and Lexington. As an enticement, a group of local businessmen offered land for the capitol building and grounds as well as $3,000 in gold and the nails and window glass needed for construction.

The city's oldest residential neighborhood centers on the Corner of Celebrities, bounded by Wapping, Washington, Main and Wilkinson streets. There are more than 40 sites of historical or architectural interest in the area.

In addition to state government, the rich farmlands and bourbon distilleries are strong local industries. Scenic portions of US 60 and I-64 run east from Frankfort to Lexington. *Also see Bluegrass Country p. 30.*

Frankfort-Franklin County Tourist and Convention Commission: 100 Capital Ave., Frankfort, KY 40601. **Phone:** (502) 875-8687 or (800) 960-7200.

Self-guiding tours: A self-guiding walking/driving tour map of Frankfort is available at the tourist and convention commission.

Shopping: Major shopping centers include Downtown Frankfort Shoppes and Old Capital Shoppes, on Broadway and St. Clair streets.

BUCKLEY WILDLIFE SANCTUARY is 10 mi. s. at 1305 Germany Rd.; from I-64 exit 58 take US 60E, following signs on SRs 1681, 1659 and 1964, then onto Germany Rd. This 374-acre facility of the National Audubon Society has a bird blind and three well-marked nature trails. A nature center building offers exhibits, educational programs and scheduled events. Trail booklets and maps also are available.

Pets are not permitted. **Time:** Allow 2 hours minimum. **Hours:** Trails and bird blind open Wed.-Sun. 9-5. Nature center building open by appointment. Closed major holidays. **Cost:** $4; $3 (ages 0-15). Additional fees may be charged during special events. **Phone:** (859) 873-3271.

BUFFALO TRACE DISTILLERY is off I-64 exit 58, then 5 mi. n. on US 60/421 to 113 Great Buffalo Trace. A walking tour of the distillery, where bourbon has been produced continuously since 1787, begins in the visitor center. From here visitors can see displays and a video depicting the process of distillation. Also on the tour are a warehouse where the bourbon is aged in barrels and the hand bottling house. The tour concludes with a tasting.

Time: Allow 1 hour minimum. **Hours:** Guided tours depart the visitor center hourly Mon.-Sat. 9-4, Sun. noon-3. Closed Jan. 1, Easter, Thanksgiving and Christmas. **Cost:** Free. **Phone:** (502) 696-5926 or (800) 654-8471.

FRANKFORT CEMETERY, downtown at 215 E. Main St., overlooks the city. A monument marks the graves of Daniel Boone and his wife, Rebecca. The cemetery also contains the graves of 17 Kentucky governors. A black granite wall bears the names of Kentuckians who have died defending their country from the War of 1812 through the Gulf War. Many gravestones bear quaint epitaphs. **Time:** Allow 30 minutes minimum. **Hours:** Mon.-Sat. 7:30-dusk, Sun. 8-dusk. **Cost:** Free. **Phone:** (502) 227-2403.

KENTUCKY DEPARTMENT FOR LIBRARIES AND ARCHIVES, 300 Coffee Tree Rd., houses reference materials, genealogical information about Kentuckians and public records from the state and local government. **Hours:** Library research room open Mon.-Fri. 9-4. Closed major holidays. **Cost:** Free. **Phone:** (502) 564-8300.

The Kentucky Vietnam Veterans Memorial, on a hill opposite the library and archives at 365 Vernon Cooper Ln., consists of a large sundial. The shadow of the indicator shaft falls on a granite panel on which are etched the names of Kentuckians killed in the Vietnam War. Each name appears in a place the shadow touches annually on the anniversary of that soldier's death. Behind the sundial, where the shadow never falls, are the names of veterans missing in action. **Hours:** Daily 24 hours. **Cost:** Free. **Phone:** (502) 564-9203.

LIBERTY HALL HISTORIC SITE, 202-218 Wilkinson St., consists of two historic houses situated on 4 acres of formal boxwood and perennial gardens on the banks of the Kentucky River. In order to give both of his son's equal inheritance, Sen. John Brown divided the original 4-acre site into two parcels, each with a house. Tours of both houses include changing exhibits that focus on the lives of the Brown family and the early days of Kentucky's statehood. Liberty Hall Historic Site is owned by the National Society of the Colonial Dames of America in the Commonwealth of Kentucky.

Time: Allow 1 hour minimum. **Hours:** Grounds and gardens open daily dawn-dusk. Guided house tours begin at Liberty Hall Mon.-Sat. at 1:30, mid-Mar. to mid-Nov.; otherwise by appointment. Phone ahead to confirm schedule. **Cost:** $6; $3 (ages 5-18). **Phone:** (502) 227-2560. GT

Liberty Hall, at Liberty Hall Historic Site at 218 Wilkinson St., was begun in 1796 by John Brown, a member of the Continental Congress and one of Kentucky's first two U.S. senators. Three U.S. presidents are among the dignitaries who visited Brown and his wife Margaretta at the three-story Federalist home. Period furnishings include many original Brown family items as well as Kentucky-built furniture and other early 19th-century pieces. Gardens behind the house extend to the Kentucky River. Restoration of the house is an ongoing process. **Hours:** Guided house tours daily at 1:30, mid-Mar. to mid-Nov.; otherwise by appointment. Closed Memorial Day and Labor Day. **Cost:** $6; $3 (ages 5-18). Admission included with Liberty Hall Historic Site. **Phone:** (502) 227-2560. GT

Orlando Brown House, at Liberty Hall Historic Site at 202 Wilkinson St., was designed by Gideon Shryock for the senator's second son, Orlando, for a total cost of $5,000. Little has changed over the years; the 1835 house has a floor plan similar to that of Liberty Hall. The style of the house reflects the transition from Federal to Greek Revival. Original furniture, silver, china, brass and family portraits are displayed. **Hours:** Guided house tours daily at 1:30, mid-Mar. to mid-Nov.; otherwise by appointment. Closed Memorial Day and Labor Day. **Cost:** $6; $3 (ages 5-18). Admission included with Liberty Hall Historic Site. **Phone:** (502) 227-2560. GT

SALATO WILDLIFE EDUCATION CENTER is off I-64 exit 53B; take US 127 1.5 mi. n. to US 60, then 1.5 mi. w. to 1 Sportsmans Ln. in the Kentucky Department of Fish and Wildlife Resources Headquarters Complex. The center includes indoor and outdoor exhibits focusing on Kentucky's native fish and wildlife.

Indoors, a mountain stream and native foliage are settings for butterflies, rattlesnakes, raccoons and birds in the Eastern Forest diorama, while frogs and toads occupy another area. The Living Bee Tree provides a look at honeybees busily working. Other exhibits feature venomous snakes, an aquarium with native fish and wildlife that have been successfully returned to the state.

Outdoors, paved accessible trails lead to natural exhibits housing such non-releasable animals as black bears, bobcats, bald eagles, elk, white-tail deer and buffalo. The Pea Ridge and HabiTrek trails wind through woods and fields and offer varying lengths of hikes. Fishing lakes are available onsite. **Time:** Allow 1 hour, 30 minutes minimum. **Hours:** Tues.-Fri. 9-5, Sat. 10-5, early Mar.-late Nov. Closed state holidays and Thanksgiving. **Cost:** Indoor center $5; $3 (ages 5-18). Outdoor activities free. **Phone:** (502) 564-7863 or (800) 858-1549.

STATE CAPITOL is 5 blks. s. on Capitol Ave. Set between two bluffs overlooking Frankfort, the capitol is considered to be one of the most beautiful in the country. The exterior is of Indiana limestone on a base of Vermont granite. The walls of the 1910 building are ornamented with 70 Ionic columns. The pediment over the north entrance is noteworthy, and there are several fine sculpture groups. A brochure outlining a walking tour of the capitol grounds is available.

The interior, finished in marble and accented with murals and paintings, is noted for its French influence. The rotunda and dome were copied from the Hotel des Invalides over Napoleon Bonaparte's tomb; the stairs resemble those in the Paris Grand Opéra House; and the State Reception Room is modeled after Marie Antoinette's drawing room and features original hand-carved walnut furniture and infinity mirrors.

Time: Allow 1 hour minimum. **Hours:** Guided tours depart on the hour Mon.-Fri. 9-3. Self-guiding tours of the entire building Mon.-Fri. 8-4:30. Self-guiding tours of only the main floor areas are permitted Sat. 10-2, Apr. 1-last Sat. in Oct. Call ahead to confirm schedule. **Cost:** Free. **Phone:** (502) 564-3449.

Governor's Mansion is at 704 Capital Ave. Home of Kentucky's current governor, the stately residence is patterned after the Petit Trianon on the grounds of the Palace of Versailles in France. **Time:** Allow 1 hour minimum. **Hours:** Tours are available by appointment Tues. and Thurs. at 9, 9:30, 10 and 10:30. Closed major holidays. **Cost:** Free. **Phone:** (502) 564-3449.

Kentucky's Floral Clock, on the capitol grounds, is surrounded by an illuminated reflecting pool. A garden contains thousands of plants and incorporates the name of the state. The clock has a raised 34-foot-diameter face and a minute hand that weighs 530 pounds and is more than 20 feet long. **Phone:** (502) 564-3449.

THOMAS D. CLARK CENTER FOR KENTUCKY HISTORY, at 100 W. Broadway St., features interactive displays interpreting distinct periods in Kentucky's history. The museum's permanent exhibit, A Kentucky Journey, traces the state's chronology from prehistoric times to the present. From the first Kentuckians (dating to 10,000 B.C.) through the state's frontier and antebellum days, the Civil War and its aftermath, the beginning of the new

century, the Depression era, World War II and up to the present, the exhibit depicts Kentucky's story through artifacts, technology and sounds.

The center also houses the Martin F. Schmidt Research Library, an extensive research library housing genealogy records specific to Kentucky's families, and the interactive Hall of Governors exhibit. **Time:** Allow 1 hour minimum. **Hours:** Tues.-Sat. 10-5. Library Wed.-Sat. 10-5. Closed major holidays. Phone ahead to confirm schedule. **Cost:** (includes Kentucky Military History Museum and Old State Capitol) $8; $6 (ages 6-18 and military veterans). Library free. **Phone:** (502) 564-1792.

BEST WESTERN PARKSIDE INN　　502/695-6111

 APPROVED

Hotel

 Best Western.

AAA Benefit: Members save up to 15% and earn bonus points!

Address: 80 Chenault Rd 40601 **Location:** I-64 exit 58, just nw on US 60. **Facility:** 99 units. 2 stories (no elevator), interior/exterior corridors. **Pool:** heated outdoor, heated indoor. **Activities:** exercise room. **Guest Services:** valet and coin laundry. **Featured Amenity:** continental breakfast.

FAIRFIELD INN & SUITES BY MARRIOTT FRANKFORT
502/695-8881
THREE DIAMOND Hotel. **Address:** 40 Chenault Rd 40601

AAA Benefit: Members save 5% or more!

HAMPTON INN BY HILTON　　502/223-7600
THREE DIAMOND Hotel. **Address:** 1310 US Hwy 127 S 40601

AAA Benefit: Members save up to 15%!

HOLIDAY INN EXPRESS HOTEL & SUITES　　502/352-4650
THREE DIAMOND Hotel. **Address:** 1000 Vandalay Dr 40601

WHERE TO EAT

BOURBON ON MAIN　　502/352-2720
APPROVED Sandwiches Small Plates. Casual Dining. **Address:** 103 W Main St 40601

BUDDY'S PIZZA　　502/352-2920
APPROVED Pizza. Casual Dining. **Address:** 212 W Broadway 40601

CHINA WOK　　502/695-9388
APPROVED Chinese. Casual Dining. **Address:** 111 Eastwood Shopping Center 40601

GINZA HIBACHI STEAK HOUSE & SUSHI BAR　　502/875-7578
APPROVED Japanese. Casual Dining. **Address:** 111 West Ridge Dr 40601

JIM'S SEAFOOD　　502/223-7448
APPROVED Seafood. Casual Dining. **Address:** 950 Wilkinson Blvd 40601

LA FIESTA GRANDE   502/695-8378
APPROVED   Mexican. Casual Dining. **Address:** 314 Versailles Rd 40601

SAGE GARDEN CAFE   502/352-2725
APPROVED   Sandwiches. Casual Dining. **Address:** 3690 East-West Connector Rt 676 40601

SERAFINI   502/875-5599
THREE DIAMOND Italian. Fine Dining. **Address:** 243 W Broadway St 40601

FRANKLIN pop. 8,408

BAYMONT INN & SUITES   270/598-0070
APPROVED   Motel. **Address:** 162 Anand Dr 42134

DAYS INN FRANKLIN   270/598-0163
APPROVED   Hotel. **Address:** 103 Trotters Ln 42134

HAMPTON INN   270/598-8001
THREE DIAMOND
Hotel

AAA Benefit: Members save up to 15%!

Address: 4010 Nashville Rd 42134 **Location:** I-65 exit 2, just w. **Facility:** 72 units. 3 stories, interior corridors. **Pool:** outdoor. **Activities:** exercise room. **Guest Services:** coin laundry. **Featured Amenity:** full hot breakfast.

HOLIDAY INN EXPRESS & SUITES-FRANKLIN   270/586-7626
THREE DIAMOND Hotel. **Address:** 85 Neha Dr 42134

WHERE TO EAT

BRICKYARD CAFE   270/586-9080
APPROVED   American. Casual Dining. **Address:** 205 W Cedar St 42134

GEORGETOWN (D-6) pop. 29,098, elev. 875'

Although pioneers arrived in the area as early as 1774, Georgetown's first permanent settlers, Baptist minister Elijah Craig and members of his flock, arrived in 1784 and incorporated the town of Lebanon. The territory at that time was still part of Virginia. In 1790 the Virginia legislature renamed the city George Town in honor of President George Washington.

It is believed that the first bourbon whiskey was made in Georgetown by Rev. Craig in 1789. The distillation was named for Bourbon County, Va., in which Georgetown was located. Students and faculty constructing the first building on the Georgetown College campus in 1840 reputedly put a quart of bourbon under each of the six Ionic columns that support the portico roof of this Baptist institution. Although bourbon is no longer produced in the county, the state remains the nation's largest whiskey producer.

Popular recreational activities include canoeing and bass fishing on Elkhorn Creek, walking along the Great Crossing Park Nature Trail and bicycling through the scenic countryside. Other area diversions include touring local horse farms and browsing for antiques and art in downtown, where there are many Victorian-era buildings and brick sidewalks. *Also see Bluegrass Country p. 30.*

Georgetown/Scott County Tourism Commission: 399 Outlet Center Dr., Georgetown, KY 40324. **Phone:** (502) 863-2547 or (888) 863-8600.

Self-guiding tours: Literature for a self-guiding walking tour featuring more than 200 historic buildings and homes in Georgetown is available at the tourism commission.

Shopping: Georgetown's historic downtown features boutiques and dining venues in a picturesque Victorian setting. For specialty and outlet shops such as Rue 21 and Rack Room Shoes, however, there's Factory Stores of America Outlet Center, off I-75 exit 126.

KENTUCKY HORSE PARK—see Lexington p. 59.

OLD FRIENDS is at 1841 Paynes Depot Rd. (US 62) at Dream Chase Farm. A living-history museum devoted to horse racing, the 236-acre horse farm provides a permanent retirement home for more than 130 former Thoroughbred racehorses. Ninety-minute guided tours, sometimes conducted by founder Michael Blowen, allow visitors close-up encounters with the horses, including Derby and Preakness winner Silver Charm as well as two-time Whitney winner Commentator and Belmont Stakes winner Touch Gold and Sarava. **Time:** Allow 1 hour minimum. **Hours:** Guided walking tours are given daily at 10, 1 and 3, early Mar.-early Nov.; at 11 a.m. rest of year. **Cost:** $10; $5 (ages 6-12). **Phone:** (502) 863-1775.

TOYOTA MOTOR MANUFACTURING KENTUCKY PLANT TOUR is off I-75 exit 126; take US 62 2.5 mi. e. to the visitor entrance at 1001 Cherry Blossom Way. A visitor center offers exhibits and interactive displays as well as videos and models to view. Tours of the plant, which produces the Avalon, Camry, Camry Hybrid and Venza models, last 45 minutes and begin with a short video presentation recounting the history of Toyota Motor Manufacturing in Georgetown and continue with a narrated tram tour of the stamping, body welding, plastics and assembly areas.

Note: Photo ID is required. No bags, cameras or cellphones are permitted on the tour; they should be stored in vehicles prior to entering the plant. **Time:** Allow 1 hour minimum. **Hours:** Visitor center open Mon.-Fri. 8:30-3:30 (also Thurs. 3:30-6). Tours depart at 9:30, 11:30 and 1:30 (also Thurs at 6); phone ahead to confirm schedule. Closed holidays and the third week in July. **Cost:** Free. Reservations are highly recommended. Children must at least be in the first grade to take the tour. **Phone:** (502) 868-3027 or (800) 866-4485.

BEST WESTERN PLUS GEORGETOWN CORPORATE CENTER HOTEL
502/868-0055

THREE DIAMOND
Hotel

Best Western PLUS

AAA Benefit: Members save up to 15% and earn bonus points!

Address: 132 Darby Dr 40324 **Location:** I-75 exit 126, just nw. **Facility:** 67 units, some efficiencies. 3 stories, interior corridors. **Pool:** heated indoor. **Activities:** hot tub, game room, exercise room. **Guest Services:** valet and coin laundry.

COMFORT SUITES
502/868-9500

THREE DIAMOND
Hotel

Address: 121 Darby Dr 40324 **Location:** I-75 exit 126, just w. **Facility:** 67 units, some two bedrooms. 3 stories, interior corridors. **Pool:** heated indoor. **Activities:** hot tub, exercise room. **Guest Services:** coin laundry. **Featured Amenity:** full hot breakfast.

COUNTRY INN & SUITES BY RADISSON
502/868-6800
THREE DIAMOND Hotel. **Address:** 131 Darby Dr 40324

FAIRFIELD BY MARRIOTT LEXINGTON GEORGETOWN/ COLLEGE INN
502/868-9955

THREE DIAMOND
Hotel

Fairfield

AAA Benefit: Members save 5% or more!

Address: 200 Tiger Way St 40324 **Location:** I-75 exit 126, just sw. **Facility:** 88 units. 3 stories, interior corridors. **Pool:** heated outdoor. **Activities:** hot tub, exercise room. **Guest Services:** valet and coin laundry.

HAMPTON INN BY HILTON OF GEORGETOWN
502/867-4888
APPROVED Hotel. **Address:** 128 Darby Dr 40324

AAA Benefit: Members save up to 15%!

HILTON GARDEN INN GEORGETOWN
502/863-0099
THREE DIAMOND Hotel. **Address:** 110 Grandstand Dr 40324

AAA Benefit: Members save up to 15%!

HOLIDAY INN EXPRESS LEXINGTON NORTH-GEORGETOWN
502/570-0220
THREE DIAMOND Hotel. **Address:** 140 Osborne Way 40324

HOME2 SUITES BY HILTON GEORGETOWN
502/570-4663
THREE DIAMOND Extended Stay Hotel. **Address:** 270 Tiger Way 40324

AAA Benefit: Members save up to 15%!

WHERE TO EAT

FAVA'S
502/863-4383
APPROVED Comfort Food. Casual Dining. **Address:** 159 E Main St 40324

MANCINO'S PIZZA & GRINDERS
502/863-5252
APPROVED Italian. Quick Serve. **Address:** 1611 Paris Pike 40324

GLASGOW (E-5) pop. 14,028, elev. 755'

SOUTH CENTRAL KENTUCKY CULTURAL CENTER is at 200 W. Water St. at jct. Main St. in the renovated 1928 Kentucky Pant Factory. The history of the geographic area known as the Barrens is depicted at the cultural center, also known as the Museum of the Barrens (the term "barrens" refers to an expanse of open prairie surrounded by forests).

The museum relates the history of Barren County and parts of four nearby counties. Visitors can explore a pioneer family's 19th-century log cabin, a Victorian parlor, a doctor's office and a one-room school as well as other period rooms. Local artists are featured in the Snavely Gallery. **Hours:** Mon.-Fri. 9-4, Sat. 10-3. Closed major holidays. **Cost:** Donations. **Phone:** (270) 651-9792.

HOLIDAY INN EXPRESS
270/629-2900
THREE DIAMOND Hotel. **Address:** 208 Wall St 42141

QUALITY INN
270/651-9099
APPROVED Motel. **Address:** 210 Cavalry Dr 42141

WHERE TO EAT

EL MAZATLAN
270/651-7799
APPROVED Mexican. Casual Dining. **Address:** 760 W Cherry St 42141

GRAND RIVERS pop. 382
• Restaurants p. 50

GREEN TURTLE BAY RESORT
270/362-8364

THREE DIAMOND
Vacation Rental Condominium

Address: 263 Green Turtle Bay Dr 42045 **Location:** Waterfront. I-24 exit 31 (SR 453), 3 mi s to W Commerce Ave, just e to JH O'Bryan Ave, just n to Barkley Dr, then 0.7 mi e. Located near Land Between the Lakes National Recreation Area. **Facility:** In addition to offering a fully equipped marina along the shores of Lake Barkley, this resort is set amid lovely, forested hills. The units resemble a village of tastefully designed houses. 80 condominiums. 1-2 stories (no elevator), exterior corridors. **Parking:** winter plug-ins. **Terms:** check-in 4 pm. **Dining:** 3 restaurants. **Pool:** outdoor, heated indoor. **Activities:** sauna, motor boats, self-propelled boats, marina, fishing, tennis, recreation programs in summer, playground, lawn sports, picnic facilities, trails, health club, spa. **Guest Services:** complimentary and valet laundry, area transportation.

PATTI'S INN AND SUITES
270/928-2740
APPROVED Hotel. **Address:** 1017 Dover Rd 42045

WHERE TO EAT

LITE SIDE CAFE & BAKERY   270/362-4586
APPROVED   Breakfast   Burgers.   Quick   Serve.
Address: 2115 Dover Rd 42045

PATTI'S 1880S SETTLEMENT & MR BILL'S RESTAURANT
    270/362-8844
THREE DIAMOND American. Casual Dining. **Address:** 1793 JH O'Bryan Ave 42045

HARLAN (F-8) pop. 1,745, elev. 1,197'

Originally called Mount Pleasant, Harlan was renamed in 1917 for Maj. Silas Harlan, a Kentuckian killed in 1782 in the Revolutionary War's Battle of Blue Lick.

Despite several serious clashes between labor and management during the first 3 decades of the 20th century, Harlan has developed into the coal-producing capital of Kentucky.

Harlan County Chamber of Commerce: 201 S. Main St., Harlan, KY 40831. **Phone:** (606) 573-4717.

QUALITY INN   606/573-3385
APPROVED   Hotel. **Address:** 2608 S Hwy 421 40831

HARRODSBURG (D-6) pop. 8,340, elev. 829'

Founded in 1774 by James Harrod, Harrodsburg was the first permanent English settlement west of the Allegheny Mountains. Several buildings date back to the 18th century. Probably the oldest existing group of row houses west of the Alleghenies is the 1807 Morgan Row, on S. Chiles Street. During the 19th century Harrodsburg was a popular gathering spot for those eager to partake of the local mineral springs and visit the spas that were known for their gala entertainment. *Also see Bluegrass Country p. 30.*

Harrodsburg/Mercer County Tourist Commission: 488 Price Ave., Harrodsburg, KY 40330. **Phone:** (859) 734-2364 or (800) 355-9192. *(See ad this page.)*

Self-guiding tours: Maps for a self-guiding walking and driving tour of Harrodsburg are available at the Diamond Point Welcome Center at 488 Price Ave. Among the tour's features are the 1800 Old Mud Meeting House, the first Dutch reformed church building west of the Allegheny Mountains; antebellum homes; the Bataan War Memorial, dedicated to soldiers who died in the Philippines during World War II; and other historic structures and sites associated with the springs that made Harrodsburg the "Saratoga of the South."

OLD FORT HARROD STATE PARK, downtown on S. College St., is on land colonized by Capt. James Harrod in 1774. A reproduction of the fort at this first permanent English settlement west of the Alleghenies includes replicas of Kentucky's first schoolhouse and pioneer cabins. On site are the Mansion Museum; the Lincoln Marriage Temple, with the cabin where Abraham Lincoln's parents wed; the George Rogers Clark Memorial; and the Pioneer Cemetery. The cemetery, the oldest burial ground west of the Alleghenies, contains the graves of more than 500 settlers.

Time: Allow 2 hours minimum. **Hours:** Grounds open daily. Fort open daily 9-5, Mar.-Oct.; daily 9-4:30, rest of year. Costumed artisans portray residents and demonstrate crafts mid-Apr. through Oct. 31. Closed Jan. 1-2, Thanksgiving, Christmas Eve, Christmas, day after Christmas and Dec. 27-31. **Cost:** Admission Apr.-Oct. $7; $6 (senior citizens); $4 (ages 6-12). Admission rest of year $3; $2 (ages 6-12). **Phone:** (859) 734-3314. *(See ad this page.)*

Mansion Museum, in Old Fort Harrod State Park, is one of the state's oldest Greek Revival homes; construction began in 1813. One room is devoted to the Union and Abraham Lincoln, another to the Confederacy and Jefferson Davis; both men were Kentucky natives.

Featured are the original flooring and woodwork, letters from George Washington, documents from Daniel Boone and George Rogers Clark, Native American items, musical instruments and guns. **Time:** Allow 30 minutes minimum. **Hours:** Daily 9-5:30, Mar.-Oct. **Cost:** Included with state park fee. **Phone:** (859) 734-3314.

SHAKER VILLAGE OF PLEASANT HILL, 7 mi. e. on US 68, is America's largest restored Shaker village. The village was founded in 1805 by the Shakers, members of a celibate, communal religious sect that began during the late 18th century in England. The village is an outdoor history museum preserving 34 original buildings on 3,000 acres with streams, forests and native prairies; more than one dozen buildings can be toured. All visitor services are provided in the original buildings. The structures, some dating to 1809, reflect Shaker standards of simplicity and utility. The stone Centre Family Dwelling has Shaker furniture and artifacts.

Costumed interpreters describe the society's distinctive way of life, and artisans demonstrate such heritage crafts as broom making and woodworking. Activities throughout the property include hands-on changing history displays, 40 miles of hiking and horseback riding trails, a farm experience with petting areas and chicken round-ups, organic gardens where visitors can sow seeds and wagon and hay rides. The paddle-wheel riverboat *Dixie Belle* offers 1-hour trips on the Kentucky River. In early August, the Shaker Village Craft Fair is held, and it features hand-made Shaker reproduction crafts.

Dixie Belle riverboat rides are subject to weather and river conditions. **Time:** Allow 4 hours minimum. **Hours:** Village Sun.-Thurs. 10-5, Fri.-Sat. 10-8. Riverboat trips depart from Shaker Landing Tues.-Sun. at 2 and 4, May-Oct. 31. **Cost:** Village $14; $10 (ages 62+); $7 (ages 6-12). Riverboat cruise $10; $5 (ages 6-12). **Phone:** (859) 734-5411 or (800) 734-5611. *(See ad p. 50.)*

BEAUMONT INN   859/734-3381
APPROVED Historic Country Inn. **Address:** 638 Beaumont Inn Dr 40330 *(See ad p. 50.)*

SHAKER VILLAGE OF PLEASANT HILL   859/734-5411
APPROVED Historic Country Inn. **Address:** 3501 Lexington Rd 40330

WHERE TO EAT

MAIN DINING ROOM @ BEAUMONT INN   859/734-3381
THREE DIAMOND Southern. Casual Dining. **Address:** 638 Beaumont Inn Dr 40330 *(See ad p. 50.)*

THE TRUSTEES' OFFICE   859/734-5411
APPROVED Regional American. Casual Dining. **Address:** 3501 Lexington Rd 40330

HAZARD pop. 4,456

HAMPTON INN & SUITES BY HILTON   606/439-0902
THREE DIAMOND [SAVE] Hotel. **Address:** 70 Morton Blvd 41701
AAA Benefit: Members save up to 15%!

HEBRON pop. 5,929
• Hotels & Restaurants map & index p. 37
• Part of Cincinnati area — see map p. 153

CINCINNATI AIRPORT MARRIOTT   859/586-0166 9
THREE DIAMOND [SAVE] Hotel. **Address:** 2395 Progress Dr 41048
AAA Benefit: Members save 5% or more!

COUNTRY INN & SUITES BY RADISSON, CINCINNATI AIRPORT   859/689-0700 8
APPROVED Hotel

Address: 759 Petersburg Rd 41048 **Location:** I-275 exit 4A, just e. **Facility:** 86 units. 4 stories, interior corridors. **Pool:** heated indoor. **Activities:** hot tub, exercise room. **Guest Services:** valet and coin laundry. **Featured Amenity:** breakfast buffet.

DOUBLETREE BY HILTON HOTEL CINCINNATI AIRPORT
                                 859/371-6166 11
THREE DIAMOND [SAVE] Hotel. **Address:** 2826 Terminal Dr 41048
AAA Benefit: Members save up to 15%!

HAMPTON INN CINCINNATI AIRPORT NORTH BY HILTON
                                 859/689-1960 10
THREE DIAMOND [SAVE] Hotel. **Address:** 755 Petersburg Rd 41048
AAA Benefit: Members save up to 15%!

HENDERSON (D-3) pop. 28,757, elev. 407'
• Hotels p. 52 • Restaurants p. 52

Memorials to Col. Richard Henderson and the Transylvania Co., the town's founders, are downtown. The community's location on the banks of the Ohio River attracted early industry; today Henderson is home to diverse manufacturing and service industries.

Horse racing is popular in Henderson. Ellis Park Racetrack, 3 miles north on US 41, has Thoroughbred racing mid-July through Labor Day; phone (270) 826-0608.

Note: Policies concerning admittance of children to pari-mutuel betting facilities vary. Phone for information.

The W.C. Handy Blues and Barbecue Festival, held in mid-June, celebrate the Father of the Blues in Audubon Mill Park.

Henderson County Tourist Commission: 101 N. Water St., Suite B, Henderson, KY 42420. **Phone:** (270) 826-3128.

JOHN JAMES AUDUBON STATE PARK, n. on US 41, is a memorial to John James Audubon, naturalist, ornithologist and artist, who lived in Henderson for 9 years. It is both a nature preserve and a public park with a nine-hole golf course. Nature trails provide views of 150 varieties of wildflowers. A 28-acre lake offers fishing opportunities. *See Recreation Areas Chart.* **Hours:** Park open daily dawn-dusk. Closed Christmas. **Cost:** Park free. Museum and Nature Center $6; $5 (ages 60+ and military with ID); $4 (ages 6-17); $15 (family rate, two adults and two children); free on Monday. **Phone:** (270) 826-2247.

John James Audubon Museum and Nature Center, at John James Audubon State Park, contains works and relics of the artist's life and times. Four galleries include oils, watercolors and 435 original prints from the 1839 folio edition of "The Birds of America." The Nature Center has The Observation Room overlooking a native plant garden and a woodland pond; The Discovery Center, with hands-on activities; and The Learning Center, with a naturalist and an art educator in a classroom setting.

Time: Allow 30 minutes minimum. **Hours:** Daily 10-5, mid-Mar. through Nov. 30; Thurs.-Sun. 10-5, rest of year. Closed Jan. 1, Thanksgiving, Christmas week and Dec. 31. **Cost:** Park free. Museum and Nature Center $6; $5 (ages 60+ and military with ID); $4 (ages 6-17); $15 (family rate, two adults and two children); free on Monday. **Phone:** (270) 827-1893.

COMFORT INN   270/827-8191

 APPROVED
Hotel

Address: 2820 US 41 N 42420 **Location:** On US 41, 2 mi n of Pennyrile and Audubon pkwys. **Facility:** 55 units. 3 stories, interior corridors. **Parking:** winter plug-ins. **Pool:** outdoor. **Activities:** exercise room. **Guest Services:** valet and coin laundry. **Featured Amenity: full hot breakfast.**

HOLIDAY INN EXPRESS   270/869-0533
THREE DIAMOND Hotel. **Address:** 2826 Hwy 41 N 42420

L & N BED & BREAKFAST   270/831-1100
APPROVED Historic Bed & Breakfast. **Address:** 327 N Main St 42420

SLEEP INN HENDERSON EVANSVILLE SOUTH   270/830-6500
APPROVED Hotel. **Address:** 2224 US Hwy 41 N 42420

WHERE TO EAT

COMMONWEALTH KITCHEN & BAR   270/212-2133
APPROVED American. Gastropub. **Address:** 108 2nd St 42420

FARMER & THE FRENCHMAN WINERY   270/748-1856
APPROVED American. Casual Dining. **Address:** 12522 Highway 41 S 42420

HOPKINSVILLE (F-3) pop. 31,577, elev. 534'

Agriculture and manufacturing are central to the economy of Hopkinsville. Manufacturing includes the production of automobile and truck frames, cutting tool machines, precision springs, magnetic wire, lighting fixtures and bowling balls.

Hopkinsville Community College has gained notice in academic literary circles as the home of Round Table Park. This campus feature includes a replica of a fifth-century Athenian amphitheater; a statue of Melpomene, the classical Muse of tragedy; and a full-size marble replica of the table in Winchester, England, that is alleged to be the Round Table of King Arthur.

The route of the Trail of Tears, the forced relocation of 13,000 Cherokee Indians from their tribal lands westward to a reservation in Oklahoma during the winter of 1838-39, is remembered at Trail of Tears Commemorative Park, at US 41 and Skyline Drive. Part of the Trail of Tears National Historic Trail, the park is on a campsite used by the Native Americans during the 1,200-mile march. The graves of two Cherokee chiefs who died on the trail and a heritage center with interpretive exhibits can be seen.

Hopkinsville-Christian County Convention & Visitors Bureau: 1730 E. 9th St., Hopkinsville, KY 42240. **Phone:** (270) 887-2300 or (800) 842-9959.

Self-guiding tours: A walking tour of the downtown area reflects the community's historical and architectural character. There also is a cellphone tour of the Edgar Cayce buildings and an African-American driving tour. Brochures are available at the Pennyroyal Area Museum and the convention and visitors bureau.

BEST WESTERN HOPKINSVILLE   270/886-9000

APPROVED
Hotel

Best Western
AAA Benefit: Members save up to 15% and earn bonus points!

Address: 4101 Ft Campbell Blvd 42240 **Location:** I-24 exit 81 (Pennyrile Pkwy) to exit 7, then just s. Located in a small rural town. **Facility:** 110 units. 3 stories, interior corridors. **Pool:** outdoor. **Guest Services:** valet laundry.

COMFORT SUITES   270/985-1101
THREE DIAMOND Hotel. **Address:** 210 Harvey Way 42240

HAMPTON INN & SUITES   270/886-8800
THREE DIAMOND Hotel. **Address:** 210 Richard Mills Dr 42240

AAA Benefit: Members save up to 15%!

HOLIDAY INN

THREE DIAMOND
Hotel

270/886-4413

Address: 2910 Ft Campbell Blvd 42240 **Location:** I-24 exit 81 (Pennyrile Pkwy) to exit 7, then 0.6 mi n on US 41A. Located in a small rural town. **Facility:** 101 units. 5 stories, interior corridors. **Pool:** heated indoor. **Activities:** sauna, hot tub, exercise room. **Guest Services:** valet and coin laundry. **Featured Amenity:** breakfast buffet.

LA QUINTA INN & SUITES HOPKINSVILLE   270/886-5151
THREE DIAMOND Hotel. **Address:** 345 Griffin Bell Dr 42240

TOWNEPLACE SUITES BY MARRIOTT HOPKINSVILLE
270/887-2509
THREE DIAMOND [SAVE] Extended Stay Hotel. **Address:** 220 Richard Mills Dr 42240

AAA Benefit: Members save 5% or more!

WHERE TO EAT

BISTRO ON 6TH   270/874-5357
APPROVED Sandwiches. Casual Dining. **Address:** 104 E 6th St 42240

EL BRACERO   270/886-2005
APPROVED Mexican. Casual Dining. **Address:** 200 Richard Mills Dr 42240

MAIN STREET TAVERN   270/484-5066
APPROVED American. Casual Dining. **Address:** 801 S Main St 42240

HORSE CAVE (E-5) pop. 2,311, elev. 628'

Horse Cave was named for the large cavern around which the town grew; the term "horse" was a colloquialism meaning "large." An underground river in the cavern was used to generate electricity in the late 1800s.

Self-guiding tours: A brochure featuring a walking tour of the historic buildings in Horse Cave's commercial district is available at the American Cave Museum and at businesses throughout town.

AMERICAN CAVE MUSEUM & HIDDEN RIVER CAVE is 2.5 mi. e. of I-65 exit 58 on SR 218 at 119 E. Main St. Museum exhibits, which provide information about the history and science of caves, include displays about cave formations and explorations, ground water, historical artifacts, Native Americans and aquariums containing cave animals. A set of 230 stairs leads to an underground river that flows beneath the town of Horse Cave; guided cave tours are available. Adventure tours are available by reservation.

Note: Due to the threat of White-Nose syndrome to bats, visitors should not wear clothing and footwear that has been worn in other caves unless properly decontaminated. **Time:** Allow 2 hours minimum. **Hours:** Daily 9-7, Memorial Day-Labor Day; 9-5, rest of year. Last tour departs one hour before closing. Closed Jan. 1, Thanksgiving, Christmas Eve, Christmas and Dec. 31. **Cost:** $15 (includes museum and cave tour); $10 (ages 6-15). Admission for those unable to climb stairs $7. Museum only $6. **Phone:** (270) 786-1466.

GEM KENTUCKY DOWN UNDER/MAMMOTH ONYX CAVE, off I-65 exit 58, .2 mi. s.e. on SR 218, then n. on SR 335 to 3700 L & N Turnpike Rd., is an interactive nature park that is home to both Australian wildlife and a cave filled with unusual onyx formations.

At Kentucky Down Under visitors can roam with kangaroos and other Australian animals in the Outback, hand-feed vibrant-colored birds in two walk-in aviaries, watch border collies herd sheep, participate in aboriginal culture and take part in chores at the woolshed. A nature trail, an exotic bird garden and other exhibits also are featured.

A 45-minute guided tour through Mammoth Onyx Cave allows visitors to see colorful cave formations in a constant 60°F environment.

Time: Allow 4 hours minimum. **Hours:** Kentucky Down Under and Mammoth Onyx Cave open daily 9-6, Memorial Day-Labor Day; 9-5, mid-Mar. through day before Memorial Day and day after Labor Day-Nov. 2; daily 9-4, rest of year. **Cost:** Admission $25.95; $19.95 (ages 60+, students and military with ID); $15.95 (ages 4-13). **Phone:** (270) 786-1010 or (800) 762-2869.

HOLIDAY INN EXPRESS HORSE CAVE   270/786-5000
THREE DIAMOND Hotel. **Address:** 750 Flint Ridge Rd 42749

HURSTBOURNE pop. 4,216
• Hotels & Restaurants map & index p. 87
• Part of Louisville area — see map p. 71

BAYMONT INN & SUITES LOUISVILLE EAST
502/339-1900 **41**
APPROVED Hotel. **Address:** 9400 Blairwood Rd 40222

COURTYARD BY MARRIOTT LOUISVILLE EAST
502/429-0006 **40**
THREE DIAMOND
Hotel

COURTYARD **AAA Benefit:** Members save 5% or more!

Address: 9608 Blairwood Rd 40222 **Location:** I-64 exit 15, 0.3 mi nw of Hurstbourne Pkwy. **Facility:** 151 units. 4 stories, interior corridors. **Pool:** outdoor. **Activities:** hot tub, exercise room. **Guest Services:** valet and coin laundry, boarding pass kiosk.

DRURY INN & SUITES-LOUISVILLE   502/326-4170 **38**
THREE DIAMOND Hotel. **Address:** 9501 Blairwood Rd 40222

(See map & index p. 87.)

RED ROOF INN LOUISVILLE EAST - HURSTBOURNE
502/426-7621 **39**

Motel

Address: 9330 Blairwood Rd 40222 **Location:** I-64 exit 15, 0.3 mi nw of Hurstbourne Pkwy. **Facility:** 108 units. 2 stories (no elevator), exterior corridors. **Amenities:** safes.

JEFFERSONTOWN pop. 26,595
- Hotels & Restaurants map & index p. 87
- Part of Louisville area — see map p. 71

BEST WESTERN LOUISVILLE EAST 502/499-0000 **54**

APPROVED
Hotel

 Best Western. **AAA Benefit:** Members save up to 15% and earn bonus points!

Address: 9802 Bunsen Way 40299 **Location:** I-64 exit 15, 0.4 mi s, then 0.5 mi e. **Facility:** 101 units. 5 stories, interior corridors. **Pool:** heated indoor. **Activities:** hot tub, exercise room. **Guest Services:** coin laundry. **Featured Amenity:** breakfast buffet.

COUNTRY INN & SUITES BY RADISSON-LOUISVILLE EAST
502/261-9434 **45**

APPROVED
Hotel

Address: 1241 Kentucky Mills Dr 40299 **Location:** I-64 exit 17, Just s. **Facility:** 70 units. 4 stories, interior corridors. **Pool:** heated indoor. **Activities:** hot tub, exercise room. **Guest Services:** coin laundry. **Featured Amenity:** breakfast buffet.

HAMPTON INN & SUITES BY HILTON LOUISVILLE EAST
502/809-9901 **47**

THREE DIAMOND SAVE Hotel. **Address:** 1451 Alliant Ave 40299

AAA Benefit: Members save up to 15%!

HAWTHORN SUITES BY WYNDHAM LOUISVILLE/JEFFERSONTOWN
502/261-0085 **53**

APPROVED Extended Stay Hotel. **Address:** 11762 Commonwealth Dr 40299

HILTON GARDEN INN-LOUISVILLE EAST 502/297-8066 **51**

THREE DIAMOND SAVE Hotel. **Address:** 1530 Alliant Ave 40299

AAA Benefit: Members save up to 15%!

HOLIDAY INN EXPRESS HOTEL & SUITES LOUISVILLE EAST
502/240-0035 **48**

THREE DIAMOND Hotel. **Address:** 1620 Alliant Ave 40299

HYATT PLACE LOUISVILLE-EAST 502-426-0119 **44**

THREE DIAMOND
Hotel

 HYATT PLACE **AAA Benefit:** Members save up to 10%!

Address: 701 S Hurstbourne Pkwy 40222 **Location:** I-64 exit 15, 0.8 mi n. Located in a suburban area. **Facility:** 121 units. 5 stories, interior corridors. **Parking:** winter plug-ins. **Pool:** heated outdoor. **Activities:** exercise room. **Guest Services:** valet laundry, area transportation. **Featured Amenity:** full hot breakfast.

LA QUINTA INN & SUITES LOUISVILLE 502/267-8889 **49**
THREE DIAMOND Hotel. **Address:** 1501 Alliant Ave 40299

MARRIOTT LOUISVILLE EAST 502/491-1184 **52**
FOUR DIAMOND SAVE Hotel. **Address:** 1903 Embassy Square Blvd 40299

AAA Benefit: Members save 5% or more!

MICROTEL INN BY WYNDHAM LOUISVILLE EAST
502/266-6590 **46**
APPROVED Hotel. **Address:** 1221 Kentucky Mills Dr 40299

WINGATE BY WYNDHAM 502/261-0644 **50**
THREE DIAMOND Hotel. **Address:** 12301 Alliant Ct 40299

WHERE TO EAT

BONEFISH GRILL 502/412-4666 **49**
THREE DIAMOND Seafood. Fine Dining. **Address:** 657 S Hurstbourne Pkwy 40222

BRICK HOUSE TAVERN & TAP 502/326-3182 **50**
APPROVED American. Casual Dining. **Address:** 871 S Hurstbourne Pkwy 40222

MUSSEL & BURGER BAR 502/384-4834 **51**
APPROVED Burgers. Casual Dining. **Address:** 9200 Taylorsville Rd 40299

KUTTAWA pop. 649

DAYS INN 270/388-5420
APPROVED Motel. **Address:** 139 Days Inn Dr 42055

HAMPTON INN-KUTTAWA 270/388-5777
APPROVED SAVE Hotel. **Address:** 62 Days Inn Dr 42055

AAA Benefit: Members save up to 15%!

RELAX INN & SUITES 270/388-2285
APPROVED Motel. **Address:** 224 New Circle Dr 42055

LA GRANGE (C-5) pop. 8,082, elev. 847'
- Part of Louisville area — see map p. 71

State Eastern Star Shrine, 110 Washington St., was the home of Rob Morris, founder of the Order of the Eastern Star. Visitors can see original furnishings, some of Morris' personal belongings and other relics. The shrine is open by appointment; phone (502) 222-0248.

BEST WESTERN ASHBURY INN

502/222-5500

 APPROVED

Hotel

 **AAA Benefit:** Members save up to 15% and earn bonus points!

Address: 1005 New Moody Ln 40031 **Location:** I-71 exit 22, just se. **Facility:** 100 units. 3 stories, interior corridors. **Parking:** winter plug-ins. **Pool:** outdoor. **Activities:** exercise room. **Guest Services:** coin laundry.

LAND BETWEEN THE LAKES NATIONAL RECREATION AREA (F-2)

Between Barkley and Kentucky lakes in western Kentucky and Tennessee, Land Between The Lakes National Recreation Area can be reached from I-24W exit 31 by taking SR 453 south to Woodlands Trace National Scenic Byway and following signs. The 170,000-acre wooded peninsula is managed by the USDA Forest Service.

More than 200 miles of hiking, mountain biking and horseback riding trails lead to points of natural and historic interest. Dozens of elk and bison roam a 700-acre restored prairie in the Kentucky portion of the area. Fishing, boating, camping, picnicking and hunting are popular activities. The Turkey Bay Off Highway Vehicle Area offers 100 miles of designated trails.

The recreation area is served by three visitor centers. The North Welcome Station, near Grand Rivers, and the South Welcome Station, near Dover, Tenn., provide visitor information, including trail maps. The Golden Pond Visitor Center, centrally located at Woodlands Trace and US 68/SR 80, has visitor information and maps, interpretive displays, audiovisual orientation programs and a planetarium *(see attraction listing)*.

The recreation area is accessible daily 24 hours. The North and South welcome stations are open daily 9-5, Apr.-Oct.; Wed.-Sun. 9-5 in Mar. and Nov. The Golden Pond Visitor Center is open daily 9-5, year-round. Closed Jan. 1, Thanksgiving and Christmas. Some activities free. For additional information phone (270) 924-2000 or (800) 525-7077. *See Recreation Areas Chart.*

ELK & BISON PRAIRIE is 1 mi. n. on Woodlands Trace National Scenic Byway from jct. US 68/SR 80. This 700-acre area re-creates the vast prairie that existed here 200 years ago. By prescribed burns and reintroducing plant and animal species that once thrived in the area, the grassland habitat is slowly being reestablished.

Bison, elk, wild turkeys, rabbits, raccoons, hawks, owls and songbirds can be seen. A 3.5-mile paved loop road allows guests to see the prairie from their car and visit interactive interpretive stops. **Time:** Allow 30 minutes minimum. **Hours:** Daily dawn-dusk. **Cost:** $5 (per private vehicle). **Phone:** (270) 924-2000 or (800) 525-7077.

GOLDEN POND PLANETARIUM, in the Golden Pond Visitor Center, at the jct. of Woodlands Trace National Scenic Byway and US 68/SR 80, presents shows on a 40-foot-diameter dome screen. An observatory has telescopes available for stargazing June through August. **Time:** Allow 1 hour minimum. **Hours:** Shows daily at 10, noon, 1, 2, 3 and 4. Evening laser shows Tues. and Fri.-Sat. at 5:30 and 7, June-Aug.; phone ahead to confirm schedule. Visitor Center daily 9-5. **Cost:** $5; $3 (ages 5-12). **Phone:** (270) 924-2233 or (800) 525-7077.

THE HOMEPLACE, 15 mi. s. on Woodland Trace National Scenic Byway from jct. US 68/SR 80, re-creates the lifestyle and farming practices of a mid-1800s family living between the Cumberland and Tennessee rivers. Interpreters dressed in period clothing talk with guests and perform daily activities. Buildings include 16 restored log structures, some relocated from the surrounding area. The interpretive center has an audiovisual presentation and exhibits about farm life. Special events, programs and festivals are held throughout the season.

Time: Allow 1 hour minimum. **Hours:** Daily 10-5, Apr.-Oct.; Wed.-Sun. 10-5 in Mar. and Nov. Last admission 1 hour before closing. **Cost:** $5; $3 (ages 5-12). **Phone:** (270) 924-2000, (270) 232-6457 or (800) 525-7077.

WOODLANDS NATURE STATION, n. on Woodlands Trace National Scenic Byway, then e. on Mulberry Flat Rd. following signs, has live animal exhibits, seasonal canoe and kayak rentals, trails and interpretive programming. The Nature Station, within the 5,000-acre Woodlands Nature Watch Area on Lake Barkley, enables visitors to observe wildlife in a natural setting. Special events, programs and festivals are offered weekends March through November, and bald eagle viewing excursions are available during the winter.

Time: Allow 1 hour minimum. **Hours:** Daily 10-5, Apr.-Oct.; Wed.-Sun. 10-5 in Mar. and Nov. **Cost:** $5; $3 (ages 5-12). **Phone:** (270) 924-2000, (270) 924-2299 or (800) 525-7077.

LAWRENCEBURG (D-6) pop. 10,505, elev. 774'

• Hotels p. 56

FOUR ROSES DISTILLERY is 4 mi. s. on US 127 bypass, then 1 mi. w. to 1224 Bonds Mill Rd. (SR 513). Guided 45-minute tours show how Four Roses Kentucky Straight Bourbon is produced. The brand was established in 1888, and the distillery, in a Spanish Mission-style building, has been operating since 1910. **Time:** Allow 1 hour minimum. **Hours:** Guided tours are given on the hour Mon.-Sat. 9-3, Sun. noon-3. Last tour begins at 3. Phone ahead to verify schedule. Closed Jan. 1, Easter, July 4, Thanksgiving, Christmas Eve, Christmas and Dec. 31. **Cost:** $5. **Phone:** (502) 839-3436.

BEST WESTERN LAWRENCEBURG INN 502/839-3444

APPROVED
Hotel

Best Western.

AAA Benefit: Members save up to 15% and earn bonus points!

Address: 200 Plaza Dr 40342 **Location:** Blue Grass Pkwy exit 59 (US 127), 4 mi n. **Facility:** 52 units. 2 stories, interior corridors. **Parking:** winter plug-ins. **Pool:** outdoor. **Activities:** exercise room. **Guest Services:** valet laundry. **Featured Amenity:** full hot breakfast.

LEBANON (E-6) pop. 5,539, elev. 791'

LIMESTONE BRANCH DISTILLERY is at 1280 Veterans Memorial Hwy. This craft distillery on the Kentucky Bourbon Trail presents tours offering an up-close perspective of the creative process, from mash to fermenting to distilling. A tasting bar is available at the facility, which uses as much organic and locally produced grain as possible. Visitors can access a gravel path leading to a lake, where complimentary paddleboats are available. Tasting and cocktail bar accessible to ages 21+. Photo ID is required. **Time:** Allow 1 hour, 30 minutes minimum. **Hours:** Tours on the hour Mon.-Sat. 9:30-5:30, on the half hour Sun. 11:30-5. Closed Jan. 1, Easter, Thanksgiving and Christmas. **Cost:** $8; free (ages 0-16). **Phone:** (270) 699-9004.

HAMPTON INN LEBANON 270/699-4000

APPROVED Hotel. **Address:** 1125 Loretto Rd 40033

AAA Benefit: Members save up to 15%!

LEXINGTON (D-6) pop. 295,803, elev. 967'

• Hotels p. 65 • Restaurants p. 67
• Hotels & Restaurants map & index p. 62

Kentucky's second largest city, Lexington is the commercial center of Bluegrass Country. The region is distinguished by a rich historical heritage that has centered on Thoroughbred horses and tobacco and, more recently, bourbon and hoops. Downtown Lexington is an urban tract amid rolling bluegrass pastures trimmed by miles of painted wooden fences and peppered with cupolas topping large barns. While picturesque, the pastoral scene commands a higher purpose: the horse, of course.

On the city's outskirts are hundreds of the world's most celebrated horse farms, where Thoroughbreds, Standardbreds, American Saddlebred horses and show champions are bred and trained.

Lexington is Thoroughbred Country. Even though the Kentucky Derby is held 80 miles away in Louisville, Lexington residents will remind you that many of the horses hail from the Bluegrass region. To celebrate the tradition, Lexington plays host to extravagant, black-tie galas celebrating the 2-minute race held under the Twin Spires.

The aristocracy of Lexington's Thoroughbred industry has reigned since horses were first brought to Kentucky from Virginia in the late 18th century. The city was founded in 1775, and the state's first impromptu races were held in Lexington in 1787. Two years later, the census noted more horses than humans.

The Lexington Jockey Club, the first in the country, was organized in 1894; still active, it preserves the history and integrity of breeding and racing by maintaining *The American Stud Book,* a database of all Thoroughbreds foaled in the United States, Canada and Puerto Rico. Dating to the late 1800s, it contains the records of nearly 2 million horses and the results of every Thoroughbred race in the country.

Nearly 20,000 horses are bred each year in and around Lexington. It can be argued that horses still outnumber people in Bluegrass Country, and equines are treated as well or perhaps better. And for good reason: A world-record sale in 1985 garnered $13.1 million for a horse with champion bloodlines, and a successful horse can earn millions in his racing career, not to mention stud fees.

When Man o' War (considered by many to be history's greatest racehorse) died in 1947, he was embalmed and lay in state for 3 days—the casket was lined with his black and gold racing silks. Thousands attended the funeral, and a giant bronze statue in his likeness marks his grave. Man o' War Boulevard, which circles the south side of Lexington, was named for the champion, whose 28-foot stride won 20 of the 21 races he entered.

Calumet Farm, just west on SR 60/Versailles Road, is one of the most well-known Thoroughbred farms and home to two Triple Crown, eight Preakness and eight Derby winners. Established in 1924, its 800 acres are divided by 35 miles of pristine white fencing, and the buildings are edged in devil's red, the farm's racing shade. Devotion to horses is evident in the farm's luxurious horse stalls, immaculate landscaping and six-to-one ratio of employee to horse.

Major equestrian events include Thoroughbred races at Keeneland Race Course *(see attraction listing),* founded in 1936. In April and October Thoroughbreds take to the 1.16-mile track several times per day Wednesday through Sunday. Lawn jockeys outside the Kentucky limestone buildings are painted annually in the winning team's racing colors. Spectators are allowed at Keeneland's prestigious Thoroughbred auctions, which occur several times a year.

Harness races take place July through October at The Red Mile Harness Track, said to be the country's oldest and fastest trotting track *(see attraction listing).* Steeplechases and polo matches are held at the Kentucky Horse Park.

Lexington's major crop has been tobacco, yielding one of the largest crops of burley tobacco in Kentucky. Tobacco barns, where the leaves are dried, stripped and packed, can still be seen along country roads. In addition, the city is the country's chief producer of bluegrass seed and white barley.

(See map & index p. 62.)

Lexington's business district has thrived without losing the grace or traditions of its Southern heritage. Victorian storefronts are preserved along Main Street, and restored houses line Broadway between Main and West Third streets.

Nearby is Gratz Park, fronted by such early historic properties as the three Goodlowe Houses and Hunt-Morgan House (see attraction listing). Brick paths, shady trees and a fountain make the park a welcome respite. The park was once the campus for nearby Transylvania University, said to be the oldest college west of the Allegheny Mountains. Morrison Hall, now home to administrative offices, was built in 1833 in the Greek Revival style by Gideon Shryock, who is said to have introduced the architectural style to Kentucky. Guided and self-guiding campus tours include the medical museum, the Morlan Art Gallery and the Mitchell Fine Arts Center; phone (859) 233-8120.

A statue at the old Fayette County Courthouse in the center of town honors John Hunt Morgan, a Confederate general adept at conducting guerrilla warfare. Despite his controversial tactics and a series of defeats, Morgan was considered a hero. The statue caused quite a local stir when unveiled in 1911—Hunt is shown astride a stallion instead of his best-known mount, the mare Black Bess.

Patrons of the arts appreciate the lavish interior of the 1887 Lexington Opera House at 401 W. Short St. It plays host to musical and theatrical performances; for ticket information phone (859) 233-3535.

Seven life-size bronze racehorses streak toward the finish line in the 2.5-acre Thoroughbred Park, on the corner of Main Street and Midland Avenue. Standing at a break in the rock wall, one can witness a "photo finish."

The local obsession with college basketball reaches a crescendo from late October through March, when the University of Kentucky Wildcats hit the hardwood. The eight-time national champions play at the 23,500-seat Rupp Arena at 430 W. Vine St.; phone the university ticket office, (859) 257-1818, for information about all collegiate sports.

Even though their themes may not be horse-related, three of Lexington's special events take place at some of the city's better-known horse-related sites. The ♦ Blue Grass Trust Antiques & Garden Show sets up its tent in early March at Kentucky Horse Park (see attraction listing). The last weekend in April the park is home to the ♦ Rolex Kentucky Three-Day Event. Also known as RK3DE, this event draws top horses and riders from around the world to compete in cross-country, dressage and jumping competitions. ♦ Southern Lights, celebrated mid-November through December 31, features a 4-mile driving tour past brilliantly lit seasonal displays. The route goes through the park and ends at the visitor center, where the holiday spirit continues indoors with a petting zoo, crafts and music.

Lexington is at the intersection of three scenic highways: I-64 and US 60 both run west to Frankfort (see place listing p. 45), and US 68 runs northeast to Paris (see place listing p. 106). Also see Bluegrass Country p. 30.

VisitLEX: 215 W. Main St., Suite 75, Lexington, KY 40507. **Phone:** (859) 233-7299 or (800) 845-3959.

Self-guiding tours: The Lexington Walk and the Bluegrass Country Driving Tour brochure features an approximately 2-mile-long walk that takes participants by many of Lexington's historic structures as well as a scenic driving tour past the area's famous horse farms and farmlands. The driving tour is split into three sections, varying in length from 24 to 35 miles long. Maps are provided by the convention and visitors bureau (VisitLEX).

Shopping: Two downtown areas—The Shops at Lexington Center and The Square—offer a variety of stores. Lexington Center, on W. Vine Street at Rupp Arena, has three levels of specialty shops as well as restaurants and entertainment. The Square is a block of restored 19th-century buildings on W. Main Street housing a collection of retail and specialty stores.

A variety of stores can be found at Fayette Mall, 3401 Nicholasville Rd., including Dillard's, JCPenney and Macy's. Fayette Place, an extension of the mall, features numerous eateries, shops and a cinema.

ASHLAND, THE HENRY CLAY ESTATE, 1.5 mi. s.e. at the corner of Sycamore Rd. and Richmond Rd. (E. Main St.), was the estate of "The Great Compromiser," Henry Clay, from 1806 until his death in 1852. Named for the large number of ash trees that graced the property, the stately home is surrounded by gardens and woods. The 18-room mansion is furnished with Clay family possessions.

The original house was replaced by Clay's son James in 1856 with a new structure built on the same foundation and with a similar floor plan. The interior of the two-story brick house reflects the Victorian style popular during the late 19th century. Early 19th-century outbuildings on the grounds include ice-houses, a smokehouse, a dairy cellar and privy. Also on the grounds are a carriage presented to Clay by the citizens of Newark, N.J., and a formal garden. One-hour guided tours and a 12-minute video are offered.

Time: Allow 1 hour minimum. **Hours:** Guided tours are given on the hour Tues.-Sat. 10-4, Sun. 1-4, Apr.-Nov.; Tues.-Sat. 10-4, in Mar. and in Dec. Last tour begins at 4. Closed major holidays. **Cost:** $15; $7 (ages 6-18). **Phone:** (859) 266-8581. GT

BLUE GRASS TOURS offers a guided 3-hour introduction to the Bluegrass region, highlighting renowned landmarks and historic homes of the area. Visitors explore behind the scenes at Keeneland Race Course and beyond the gates of a Thoroughbred farm in addition to viewing sites where movies such as "Secretariat," "Seabiscuit" and "Dreamer"

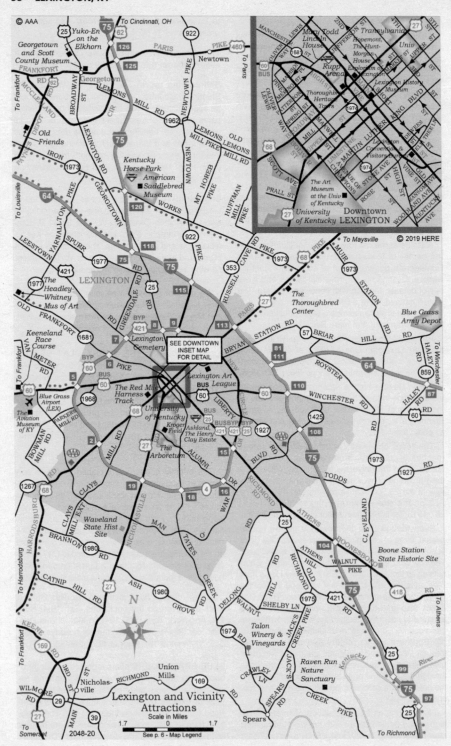

© AAA

To Cincinnati, OH

Yuko-En on the Elkhorn

Georgetown and Scott County Museum

FRANKFORT

To Frankfort

Georgetown

Newtown

To Paris

PARIS PIKE

To Louisville

Old Friends

Kentucky Horse Park

American Saddlebred Museum

WORKS

LEXINGTON

The Headley-Whitney Mus of Art

Keeneland Race Course

To Frankfort

Blue Grass Airport (LEX)

The Aviation Museum of KY

Lexington Cemetery

SEE DOWNTOWN INSET MAP FOR DETAIL

The Red Mile Harness Track

University of Kentucky

Kroger Field

The Arboretum

Ashland, The Henry Clay Estate

Lexington Art League

Waveland State Hist Site

To Harrodsburg

Union Mills

Nicholasville

WILMORE

To Somerset

Lexington and Vicinity Attractions

Scale in Miles

1.7   0   1.7

See p. 6 - Map Legend

2048-20

To Maysville

The Thoroughbred Center

Blue Grass Army Depot

To Winchester

Boone Station State Historic Site

To Athens

Talon Winery & Vineyards

Raven Run Nature Sanctuary

To Richmond

Downtown LEXINGTON

© 2019 HERE

Mary Todd Lincoln House

Hopemont, The Hunt-Morgan House

Transylvania Univ

Rupp Arena

Explorium of Lexington

Lexington History Museum

Thoroughbred Heritage Tours

Lexington Convention & Visitors Bureau

The Art Museum at the Univ of Kentucky

University of Kentucky

(See map & index p. 62.)

were filmed. A Bourbon Distillery tour is among the custom offerings.

Time: Allow 3 hours minimum. **Hours:** Tours depart daily at 9 and 1:30, Apr.-Oct. Phone ahead to confirm schedule. **Cost:** Fare $35; $32 (ages 55+); $25 (ages 0-12). Reservations are required. **Phone:** (859) 252-5744 or (800) 755-6956.

EXPLORIUM OF LEXINGTON is at 440 W. Short St. in The Square; the entrance is at the corner of W. Short and Algonquin sts. Hands-on exhibits in this children's museum's nine discovery zones cover science, nature, history, ecology and the human body.

Time: Allow 1 hour minimum. **Hours:** Mon.-Sat. 10-5, Sun. 1-5, Memorial Day-Labor Day; Tues.-Sat. 10-5, Sun. 1-5, rest of year. Closed Easter, Thanksgiving and Christmas. **Cost:** $9; $8 (ages 55+ and military with ID). Ages 0-11 must be with an adult. **Phone:** (859) 258-3253.

HORSE FARM TOURS INC. picks up visitors at several Lexington area lodgings. Guided tours of two or three Lexington area horse farms are offered as well as stops at Keeneland Race Course. Passengers also see sites featured in the movies "Seabiscuit," "Secretariat" and "Dreamer." Guides explain the sights and answer questions about the horse industry and Lexington. Some farms allow visitors to pet and photograph horses.

Time: Allow 3 hours minimum. **Hours:** Tours depart daily at 8:15 and 12:45. **Cost:** Fare $38; $36 (ages 65+); $29 (ages 0-12). Reservations are required. **Phone:** (859) 268-2906 or (800) 976-1034.

HOPEMONT, THE HUNT-MORGAN HOUSE is at 201 N. Mill St. The early 1800s Federal-style house was built by John Wesley Hunt. Prominent family members include John Hunt Morgan, the "Thunderbolt of the Confederacy," and Nobel Prize winner Thomas Hunt Morgan. The house features a fanlight doorway, a three-story cantilevered staircase, family furniture, portraits and a garden. Among the Civil War memorabilia displayed in the Alexander T. Hunt Civil War Museum, on the second floor, are documents, equipment and uniforms.

Hours: Guided tours are given Sun. and Wed.-Fri. on the hour 1-4, Sat. 10-3, mid-Mar. to mid-Nov. **Cost:** Fee $12; $6 (ages 0-12 and students with ID). **Phone:** (859) 233-3290.

KENTUCKY HORSE PARK, 9 mi. n. off I-75 exit 120, at 4089 Iron Works Pike, is a 1,200-acre facility devoted to the region's equine heritage. The Man o' War Memorial, the renowned racehorse's burial site, is at the entrance to the traditionally fenced grounds. A film about the relationship between man and horses, narrated by William Shatner, serves as an introduction to the park. Self-guiding walking tours and horse-drawn trolley rides are available.

The Breeds Barn houses multiple breeds of horses; after viewing the 25-minute Breeds Barn presentation in the show ring, visitors can meet the animals and their riders. The Hall of Champions is the

site of a 25-minute show featuring a group of championship horses, including Kentucky Derby winners Go for Gin (1994) and Funny Cide (2003). The International Museum of the Horse depicts the 50-million-year history of the horse; a circular ramp winds past displays, artifacts, trophies, paintings and carriages.

Horseback riding and pony rides are available. Another close-up opportunity comes with a visit to the Big Barn, home of the huge horses that pull the tour trolleys. The craft of horseshoeing can be seen during a stop at the Farrier Shop. An animated holiday light display brightens the park the Friday before Thanksgiving through December 31.

Hours: Park open daily 9-5, Apr.-Nov.; Wed.-Sun. 9-5, rest of year. Closed Jan. 1, day before Thanksgiving, Thanksgiving, Christmas Eve, Christmas and Dec. 31. Breeds Barn Show, Hall of Champions presentation, horse-drawn trolley and other presentations available mid-Mar. through Oct. 31. Hours may vary; phone ahead.

Cost: Admission mid-Mar. to late Oct. $20; $18 (ages 62+); $10 (ages 6-12 and military with ID). Admission rest of year $12; $11 (ages 62+); $6 (ages 6-12 and military with ID). Additional fees are charged for horse farm tours, horseback riding, pony rides and some special events. Horse-drawn trolley tours are included with park admission. **Parking:** $5; $15 (special events). **Phone:** (859) 233-4303 or (800) 678-8813.

American Saddlebred Museum, jct. I-75 exit 120 and Iron Works Pkwy. on the grounds of Kentucky Horse Park, has exhibits, video presentations and a movie tracing the history and current uses of the American Saddlebred horse, the oldest registered American breed of horse. The museum also features interactive and changing exhibits.

Time: Allow 1 hour minimum. **Hours:** Daily 9-5, Apr.-Nov.; Wed.-Sun. 9-5, rest of year. Closed Jan. 1, day before Thanksgiving, Thanksgiving, Christmas Eve and Dec. 31. **Cost:** Included with Kentucky Horse Park ticket. **Phone:** (859) 259-2746.

The International Museum of the Horse is part of Kentucky Horse Park at 4089 Iron Works Pkwy. This large, beautifully designed museum outlines the history of the first domesticated horse, the Arabian stallion, draft horses, horse-drawn vehicles and the horse as it relates to sports. Temporary international exhibits offer glimpses of the importance of horses to different cultures.

Note: Photography and video are allowed in the permanent exhibits only. **Hours:** Daily 9-5, Apr.-Nov.; Wed.-Sun. 9-5, rest of year. Closed Jan. 1, day before Thanksgiving, Thanksgiving, Christmas Eve, Christmas and Dec. 31. Phone ahead to confirm schedule. **Cost:** Admission mid-Mar. to late Oct. $20; $18 (ages 62+); $10 (ages 6-12). Admission rest of year $12; $11 (ages 65+); $6 (ages 6-12). Admission includes admittance to the Kentucky Horse

(See map & index p. 62.)

Park. **Parking:** $5; $15 (special events). **Phone:** (859) 259-4232.

LEXINGTON CEMETERY is at 833 W. Main St. Buried here are the family of Mrs. Abraham Lincoln; Henry Clay and his wife; 19th-century author and educator James Lane Allen; Col. W.C.P. Breckinridge, the "silver-tongued Orator of Kentucky"; Confederate cavalry officer Gen. John Hunt Morgan; basketball coach Adolph F. Rupp; actor Jim Varney; and 500 Confederate soldiers. Well-known as an arboretum, the cemetery has seasonal floral gardens.

Federal leader Gen. Gordon Granger and "King" Solomon, vagabond hero of the cholera plague of 1833 who was immortalized by novelist James Lane Allen, also are interred here. The cemetery embraces the nearby Lexington National Cemetery. Self-guiding walking tours are available. **Time:** Allow 2 hours minimum. **Hours:** Grounds daily 8-5. Office Mon.-Fri. 8-4, Sat. noon-4. **Cost:** Free. **Phone:** (859) 255-5522.

MARY TODD LINCOLN HOUSE at 578 W. Main St. is the first historic site to honor a first lady. Built 1803-06 as an inn, the building was purchased in 1832 by Robert Smith Todd, who renovated it for use by his family. The Todds lived in the house until 1849. The family's 16 children included Mary Todd, who would become Abraham Lincoln's wife. Mary met and married the future president after moving to Springfield, Ill. to live with her older sister; she and Lincoln visited her girlhood home several times.

Knowledgeable guides provide insight into the life of the first lady as they lead visitors through the 14-room, two-story Georgian-style brick house. The décor contains antiques interspersed with a number of Mary Todd Lincoln's possessions as well as portraits and period furnishings. Especially noteworthy are Mrs. Lincoln's porcelain perfume jars, a candelabra and a mourning jacket. A 19th-century-style garden out back contains plantings representative of the original plot. **Time:** Allow 1 hour minimum. **Hours:** Museum Mon.-Sat. 10-4, Mar. 15-Nov. 30. Guided tours depart hourly. Last tour begins 1 hour before closing. Holiday schedule varies; please phone ahead. **Cost:** $15; $6 (ages 6-17). **Phone:** (859) 233-9999.

RAVEN RUN NATURE SANCTUARY, 6 mi. s.e. on Richmond Rd., 3.5 mi. s. on US 25/421, then 5.2 mi. s. on SR 1975/Jack's Creek Pike to 3885 Raven Run Way, is a 734-acre nature sanctuary with more than 10 miles of hiking trails that traverse meadow, forest and creek ecosystems, leading to views of the Kentucky River palisades. More than 200 bird and 600 plant species may be seen. Also on the property are a historic brick house and rock fences built by pioneer farmers. A nature center has interactive exhibits about native flora and fauna and offers pamphlets outlining the area's history and wildlife.

Note: Pets of any kind are not permitted. All visitors must sign in at the nature center, located at the beginning of the trail system, upon arrival and departure. **Time:** Allow 1 hour minimum. **Hours:** Daily 9-5. Trails close 30 minutes before park closing. Hours may vary; phone ahead to confirm schedule. Closed Thanksgiving, Christmas Eve, Christmas and day after Christmas. **Cost:** Free. **Phone:** (859) 272-6105.

THE RED MILE HARNESS TRACK, 1.75 mi. s.w. on US 68 via signs at 1200 Red Mile Rd., is a 1-mile oval track for trotters and pacers with grandstand, park and clubhouse facilities. The number of world records set at this red clay track has given it the reputation as the fastest track in the world. Races are held from late July through early October. **Time:** Allow 30 minutes minimum. **Hours:** Mon.-Fri. 10-2, Sat.-Sun. 10-4. Phone ahead to confirm schedule. **Cost:** Free. **Phone:** (859) 255-0752.

THOROUGHBRED HERITAGE TOURS depart from various hotels throughout Lexington. The 3-hour, guide-narrated tours are conducted in climate-controlled vans and proceed through Bluegrass Country, offering views of Calumet Farm and other renowned bluegrass farms. Seen along the way are sites where the motion pictures "Secretariat," "Dreamer" and "Seabiscuit" were filmed. The tour includes a walk through historic Keeneland Race Track and culminates with an up-close-and-personal encounter with thoroughbreds at a private farm.

Time: Allow 3 hours minimum. **Hours:** Tours depart daily at 8:30 and 12:30. Closed Jan. 1, Thanksgiving and Christmas. **Cost:** $38; $36 (senior citizens); $30 (ages 0-11). Reservations are required. **Phone:** (859) 260-8687, or (800) 808-9533 daily 7 a.m.-9 p.m. for reservations and pick up locations. GT

UNIVERSITY OF KENTUCKY is bounded by Limestone St., Euclid Ave. and Rose St. Established in 1865, the university is the largest employer in Lexington. Guided tours of the campus depart from the visitor center in the Gatton Student Center.

Time: Allow 1 hour, 30 minutes minimum. **Hours:** Walking tours and information sessions are conducted Mon.-Sat.; phone for schedule. Closed major holidays. **Cost:** Free. Reservations are required. **Phone:** (859) 257-3595. GT

The Arboretum, on the University of Kentucky campus near Kroger Field (formerly Commonwealth Stadium), is Kentucky's Official State Botanical Garden. Its 100 acres contain a visitor center; a home demonstration garden; vegetable and herb gardens; fruit and nut gardens; The Kentucky Children's Garden; and a 2-mile walk across a sampling of Kentucky's seven physiographic landscape regions. **Time:** Allow 1 hour minimum. **Hours:** Arboretum daily dawn-dusk; closed on University of Kentucky home football game days. Visitor center Mon.-Fri. 8:30-4. Children's garden hours vary. Phone ahead to confirm schedule. **Cost:** Free. Children's garden $3; free (under age 2). **Phone:** (859) 257-6955 Mon.-Fri. 8:30-4 to schedule a tour.

(See map & index p. 62.)

The Art Museum at the University of Kentucky is on the University of Kentucky campus in Singletary Center for the Arts at jct. Rose St. and Euclid Ave. The museum's permanent collection of more than 3,900 objects features 19th- and 20th-century European and American works; photographs; decorative arts, including a collection of Tiffany glass; an Italian Baroque painting; contemporary and old master prints; African and pre-Columbian sculpture; and regional art.

The museum also features a variety of changing exhibitions. **Hours:** Tues.-Sun. noon-5 (also Fri. 5-8); closed university holidays. **Cost:** Free. A fee may be charged for some traveling exhibits (all are free Fri. 5-8). **Phone:** (859) 257-5716.

WINERIES

- **Talon Winery & Vineyards** is 10 mi. s. on SR 1974 to 7086 Tates Creek Rd. **Hours:** Mon.-Thurs. 10-7, Fri.-Sat. 10-8, Sun. noon-6, Apr.-Oct.; Mon.-Thurs. 11-6, Fri.-Sat. 11-7, Sun. 1-6, rest of year. Closed major holidays. **Phone:** (859) 971-3214. GT

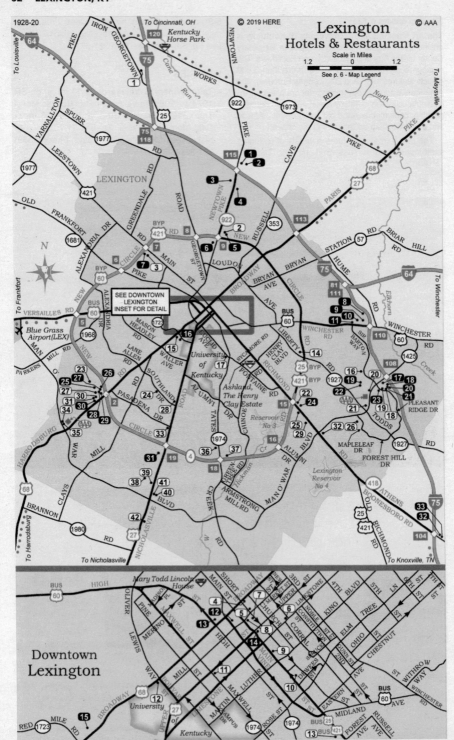

Lexington
Hotels & Restaurants

Downtown
Lexington

Lexington

This index helps you "spot" where hotels and restaurants are located on the corresponding detailed maps. Restaurant price range is a combination of lunch and/or dinner. Turn to the listing page for more information and consult display ads for special promotions.

 For more details, rates and reservations: AAA.com/travelguides/hotels

LEXINGTON

Map Page	Hotels	Designation	Member Savings	Page
1 p. 62	GLö Best Western Lexington	THREE DIAMOND	✔	66
2 p. 62	Fairfield Inn & Suites by Marriott-Lexington North	THREE DIAMOND	✔	66
3 p. 62	Embassy Suites by Hilton Lexington/UK Coldstream	THREE DIAMOND	✔	65
4 p. 62	Lexington Griffin Gate Marriott Resort & Spa	THREE DIAMOND	✔	66
5 p. 62	Courtyard by Marriott/Lexington North (See ad p. 65.)	THREE DIAMOND	✔	65
6 p. 62	Candlewood Suites	APPROVED		65
7 p. 62	Holiday Inn Express Hotel & Suites Downtown Area-Keeneland	THREE DIAMOND		66
8 p. 62	Fairfield Inn & Suites by Marriott Lexington East/I-75	THREE DIAMOND	✔	65
9 p. 62	Hampton Inn by Hilton I-75	APPROVED	✔	66
10 p. 62	Holiday Inn Express & Suites Lexington East-Winchester Road	THREE DIAMOND		66
11 p. 62	Country Inn & Suites by Radisson	THREE DIAMOND		65
12 p. 62	Hilton Lexington/Downtown	THREE DIAMOND	✔	66
13 p. 62	Hyatt Regency Lexington	THREE DIAMOND	✔	66
14 p. 62	21c Museum Hotel	FOUR DIAMOND		65
15 p. 62	SpringHill Suites by Marriott Lexington Near the University of Kentucky	THREE DIAMOND	✔	67
16 p. 62	Holiday Inn Express Hotel & Suites-Lexington Downtown at the University	THREE DIAMOND		66
17 p. 62	Hilton Garden Inn Lexington/Hamburg	THREE DIAMOND	✔	66
18 p. 62	Hyatt Place Lexington	THREE DIAMOND	✔	66
19 p. 62	Residence Inn by Marriott Lexington South/Hamburg Place	THREE DIAMOND	✔	67
20 p. 62	Homewood Suites by Hilton Lexington-Hamburg	THREE DIAMOND	✔	66
21 p. 62	Holiday Inn Lexington-Hamburg	THREE DIAMOND		66
22 p. 62	TownePlace Suites by Marriott Lexington South/Hamburg Place	THREE DIAMOND	✔	67
23 p. 62	Courtyard by Marriott Lexington South/Hamburg Place	THREE DIAMOND	✔	65
24 p. 62	DoubleTree Suites by Hilton Hotel Lexington	THREE DIAMOND	✔	65
25 p. 62	TownePlace Suites by Marriott Lexington Keeneland/Airport	THREE DIAMOND	✔	67
26 p. 62	Residence Inn by Marriott Lexington Keeneland/Airport	THREE DIAMOND	✔	67
27 p. 62	Courtyard by Marriott Lexington Keeneland/Airport	THREE DIAMOND	✔	65
28 p. 62	Hampton Inn by Hilton Keeneland Airport South	APPROVED	✔	66
29 p. 62	Fairfield by Marriott Lexington Keeneland Airport	THREE DIAMOND	✔	65
30 p. 62	Comfort Suites by Choice Hotels	APPROVED		65
31 p. 62	Embassy Suites by Hilton Lexington Green	THREE DIAMOND	✔	65
32 p. 62	Days Inn-South	APPROVED		65
33 p. 62	La Quinta Inn & Suites Lexington South/Hamburg	APPROVED		66

Map Page	Restaurants	Designation	Cuisine	Price Range	Page
① p. 62	Red State BBQ	◆ APPROVED	Barbecue	$7-$24	68
② p. 62	Tachibana	◆ APPROVED	Japanese	$7-$37	68
③ p. 62	El Mariachi Mexican Restaurant	◆ APPROVED	Mexican	$6-$18	67
④ p. 62	Shakespeare and Co.	◆ APPROVED	American	$10-$34	68
⑤ p. 62	The Village Idiot	◆ APPROVED	American	$12-$24	68
⑥ p. 62	Le Deauville	◆ APPROVED	French	$19-$36	67
⑦ p. 62	The Ruddy Duck Grille	◆ APPROVED	American	$7-$23	68
⑧ p. 62	Goodfellas Pizzeria	◆ APPROVED	Pizza	$7-$35	67
⑨ p. 62	Alfalfa Restaurant	◆ APPROVED	American	$5-$14	67
⑩ p. 62	Portofino Restaurant	◆ THREE DIAMOND	Italian	$17-$48	68
⑪ p. 62	**Joe Bologna's Restaurant & Pizzeria**	◆ APPROVED	Italian Pizza	$7-$30	67
⑫ p. 62	Tolly-Ho Restaurant	◆ APPROVED	Breakfast Burgers	$2-$14	68
⑬ p. 62	Graze	◆ THREE DIAMOND	American	$14-$25	67
⑭ p. 62	The Parkette Drive-In	◆ APPROVED	American	$5-$15	68
⑮ p. 62	Jalapeno's Restaurante Mexicano	◆ APPROVED	Mexican	$7-$18	67
⑯ p. 62	Bonefish Grill	◆ THREE DIAMOND	Seafood	$15-$34	67
⑰ p. 62	The Sage Rabbit	◆ APPROVED	American	$10-$22	68
⑱ p. 62	Double Dogs	◆ APPROVED	American	$8-$17	67
⑲ p. 62	Malone's	◆ THREE DIAMOND	Steak	$10-$100	67
⑳ p. 62	Saul Good Restaurant & Pub Hamburg	◆ APPROVED	American	$10-$26	68
㉑ p. 62	Ramsey's	◆ APPROVED	Comfort Food	$9-$14	68
㉒ p. 62	Miyako Japanese Restaurant	◆ APPROVED	Japanese Sushi	$8-$19	67
㉓ p. 62	J. Render's Southern Table & Bar	◆ APPROVED	Barbecue	$10-$24	67
㉔ p. 62	Winchell's Restaurant	◆ APPROVED	American	$12-$19	68
㉕ p. 62	Shamrock Bar & Grille	◆ APPROVED	American	$8-$13	68
㉖ p. 62	Tandoor Fine Indian Cuisine	◆ APPROVED	Indian	$13-$20	68
㉗ p. 62	Azur Restaurant & Patio	◆ THREE DIAMOND	American	$11-$36	67
㉘ p. 62	El Toro Cantina & Grill	◆ APPROVED	Mexican	$8-$19	67
㉙ p. 62	Arirang Garden-Korean Bar-B-Que	◆ APPROVED	Korean	$9-$19	67
㉚ p. 62	Sahara Mediterranean Cuisine	◆ APPROVED	Mediterranean	$5-$16	68
㉛ p. 62	Masala Indian Cuisine	◆ APPROVED	Indian Vegetarian	$10-$16	67
㉜ p. 62	Pepe's Mi Mexico	◆ APPROVED	Mexican	$7-$23	68
㉝ p. 62	Paisano's Italian Restaurant & Lounge	◆ APPROVED	Italian	$9-$22	67
㉞ p. 62	Malone's	◆ THREE DIAMOND	Steak	$15-$95	67
㉟ p. 62	Asian Wind	◆ APPROVED	Chinese	$10-$17	67
㊱ p. 62	Malone's	◆ THREE DIAMOND	American	$13-$95	67
㊲ p. 62	Merrick Inn	◆ THREE DIAMOND	American	$15-$30	67
㊳ p. 62	Saul Good Restaurant & Pub	◆ APPROVED	American	$10-$26	68
㊴ p. 62	Bella Notte	◆ APPROVED	Italian	$7-$26	67
㊵ p. 62	Honeywood	◆ THREE DIAMOND	Regional American	$11-$30	67
㊶ p. 62	Smithtown Seafood at the Summit	◆ APPROVED	Seafood	$11-$15	68
㊷ p. 62	Giuseppe's Ristorante Italiano	◆ THREE DIAMOND	Northern Italian	$19-$40	67

(See map & index p. 62.)

21C MUSEUM HOTEL 859/899-6800 **14**
FOUR DIAMOND Historic Boutique Hotel. **Address:** 167 W Main St 40507

CANDLEWOOD SUITES 859/967-1940 **6**
APPROVED Extended Stay Hotel. **Address:** 603 Adcolor Dr 40511

COMFORT SUITES BY CHOICE HOTELS 859/296-4446 **30**
APPROVED Hotel. **Address:** 3060 Fieldstone Way 40513

COUNTRY INN & SUITES BY RADISSON 859/299-8844 **11**
THREE DIAMOND Hotel. **Address:** 2297 Executive Dr 40505

COURTYARD BY MARRIOTT LEXINGTON KEENELAND/ AIRPORT 859/224-0460 **27**
THREE DIAMOND SAVE Hotel. **Address:** 3100 Wall St 40513 | **AAA Benefit:** Members save 5% or more!

COURTYARD BY MARRIOTT/LEXINGTON NORTH 859/253-4646 **5**
THREE DIAMOND Hotel | COURTYARD **AAA Benefit:** Members save 5% or more!

Address: 775 Newtown Ct 40511 **Location:** I-75/64 exit 115, 1.7 mi s on SR 922. **Facility:** 146 units, some two bedrooms. 3 stories, interior corridors. **Parking:** on-site (fee). **Pool:** heated indoor. **Activities:** hot tub, exercise room. **Guest Services:** valet and coin laundry, boarding pass kiosk. (See ad this page.)

SAVE ECO [icons] CALL [icons]
[icons] BIZ [icons]
/ SOME UNITS [icon]

COURTYARD BY MARRIOTT LEXINGTON SOUTH/HAMBURG PLACE 859/263-9090 **23**
THREE DIAMOND SAVE Hotel. **Address:** 1951 Pleasant Ridge Dr 40509 | **AAA Benefit:** Members save 5% or more!

DAYS INN-SOUTH 859/263-3100 **32**
APPROVED Motel. **Address:** 5575 Athens-Boonesboro Rd 40509

DOUBLETREE SUITES BY HILTON HOTEL LEXINGTON 859/268-0060 **24**
THREE DIAMOND SAVE Hotel. **Address:** 2601 Richmond Rd 40509 | **AAA Benefit:** Members save up to 15%!

EMBASSY SUITES BY HILTON LEXINGTON GREEN 859/271-4000 **31**
THREE DIAMOND Hotel | EMBASSY SUITES **AAA Benefit:** Members save up to 15%!

Address: 245 Lexington Green Cir 40503 **Location:** SR 4 (New Circle Rd) exit 19, just s on US 27 (Nicholasville Rd), then just w. **Facility:** 174 units. 6 stories, interior corridors. **Amenities:** safes. **Pool:** heated outdoor. **Activities:** exercise room. **Guest Services:** valet and coin laundry, area transportation. **Featured Amenity:** full hot breakfast.

SAVE [icons] CALL [icons]
[icons] BIZ [icons]
/ SOME UNITS [icon]

EMBASSY SUITES BY HILTON LEXINGTON/UK COLDSTREAM 859/455-5000 **3**
THREE DIAMOND SAVE Hotel. **Address:** 1801 Newtown Pike 40511 | **AAA Benefit:** Members save up to 15%!

FAIRFIELD BY MARRIOTT LEXINGTON KEENELAND AIRPORT 859/224-3338 **29**
THREE DIAMOND SAVE Hotel. **Address:** 3050 Lakecrest Cir 40513 | **AAA Benefit:** Members save 5% or more!

FAIRFIELD INN & SUITES BY MARRIOTT LEXINGTON EAST/ I-75 859/303-4386 **8**
THREE DIAMOND SAVE Hotel. **Address:** 2211 Elkhorn Rd 40505 | **AAA Benefit:** Members save 5% or more!

▼ See AAA listing this page ▼

(See map & index p. 62.)

FAIRFIELD INN & SUITES BY MARRIOTT-LEXINGTON NORTH
859/977-5870 **2**

THREE DIAMOND [SAVE] Hotel. **Address:** 2100 Hackney Pl 40511

AAA Benefit:
Members save 5% or more!

GLŌ BEST WESTERN LEXINGTON 859/554-8854 **1**

THREE DIAMOND

Contemporary Hotel

AAA Benefit:
Members save up to 15% and earn bonus points!

Address: 1935 Stanton Way 40511 **Location:** I-75 exit 115, just n. **Facility:** 79 units. 4 stories, interior corridors. *Bath:* shower only. **Amenities:** safes. **Pool:** heated indoor. **Activities:** exercise room. **Guest Services:** valet and coin laundry.

[SAVE] [TI+] CALL [&] [≈] [↾↾] [BIZ] [HS] [≋] [⌧] [✕] [🛏] [🍽] [☕] / SOME UNITS [🐾]

HAMPTON INN BY HILTON I-75 859/299-2613 **9**

APPROVED [SAVE] Hotel. **Address:** 2251 Elkhorn Rd 40505

AAA Benefit:
Members save up to 15%!

HAMPTON INN BY HILTON KEENELAND AIRPORT SOUTH
859/223-0088 **28**

APPROVED [SAVE] Hotel. **Address:** 3060 Lakecrest Cir 40513

AAA Benefit:
Members save up to 15%!

HILTON GARDEN INN LEXINGTON/HAMBURG
859/543-8300 **17**

THREE DIAMOND [SAVE] Hotel. **Address:** 1973 Plaudit Pl 40509

AAA Benefit:
Members save up to 15%!

HILTON LEXINGTON/DOWNTOWN 859/231-9000 **12**

THREE DIAMOND

Hotel

AAA Benefit:
Members save up to 15%!

Address: 369 W Vine St 40507 **Location:** I-75/64 exit 113, 3.3 mi sw on US 68 (Broadway Rd). Across from Rupp Arena, Triangle Park and Lexington Convention Center. **Facility:** 366 units, some two bedrooms. 3 stories, interior corridors. **Parking:** on-site (fee) and valet, winter plug-ins. **Amenities:** safes. **Pool:** heated indoor. **Activities:** hot tub, exercise room. **Guest Services:** valet laundry.

[SAVE] [✈] [TI] [🛏] [Y] CALL [&] [≈] [↾↾] [BIZ] [HS] [≋] [✕] [📹] [🍽] / SOME UNITS [🛏] [▣]

HOLIDAY INN EXPRESS & SUITES LEXINGTON EAST-WINCHESTER ROAD 859/309-0492 **10**

THREE DIAMOND Hotel. **Address:** 2255 Buena Vista Rd 40505

HOLIDAY INN EXPRESS HOTEL & SUITES DOWNTOWN AREA-KEENELAND 859/231-0656 **7**

THREE DIAMOND Hotel. **Address:** 1780 Sharkey Way 40511

HOLIDAY INN EXPRESS HOTEL & SUITES-LEXINGTON DOWNTOWN AT THE UNIVERSITY 859/389-6800 **16**

THREE DIAMOND Hotel. **Address:** 1000 Export St 40504

HOLIDAY INN LEXINGTON-HAMBURG 859/687-7008 **21**

THREE DIAMOND Hotel. **Address:** 1976 Justice Dr 40509

HOMEWOOD SUITES BY HILTON LEXINGTON-HAMBURG
859/543-0464 **20**

THREE DIAMOND [SAVE] Extended Stay Hotel. **Address:** 2033 Bryant Rd 40509

AAA Benefit:
Members save up to 15%!

HYATT PLACE LEXINGTON 859/296-0091 **18**

THREE DIAMOND

Hotel

AAA Benefit:
Members save up to 10%!

Address: 2001 Bryant Rd 40509 **Location:** I-75 exit 108, 0.3 mi w on Man O' War Blvd, just s on Pleasant Ridge Dr, 0.3 mi e on Justice Dr, then just s. **Facility:** 127 units. 6 stories, interior corridors. **Pool:** heated indoor. **Activities:** exercise room. **Featured Amenity:** full hot breakfast.

[SAVE] [TI+] [Y] CALL [&] [≈] [↾↾] [BIZ] [HS] [≋] [✕] [📹] [🛏] [🍽] / SOME UNITS [🐾]

HYATT REGENCY LEXINGTON 859/253-1234 **13**

THREE DIAMOND

Hotel

AAA Benefit:
Members save up to 10%!

Address: 401 W High St 40507 **Location:** I-75/64 exit 113, 3.3 mi sw on US 68 (Broadway Rd); center. Adjacent to Rupp Arena and Lexington Convention Center. **Facility:** 366 units. 16 stories, interior corridors. **Parking:** on-site and valet: check-in 4 pm. **Amenities:** video games, safes. **Pool:** heated indoor. **Activities:** exercise room. **Guest Services:** valet laundry.

[SAVE] [✈] [TI] [🛏] [Y] CALL [&] [≈] [↾↾] [BIZ] [≋] [✕] [🛏] [🍽]

LA QUINTA INN & SUITES LEXINGTON SOUTH/HAMBURG
859/543-1877 **33**

APPROVED Hotel. **Address:** 100 Canebrake Dr 40509

LEXINGTON GRIFFIN GATE MARRIOTT RESORT & SPA
859/231-5100 **4**

THREE DIAMOND

Resort Hotel

AAA Benefit:
Members save 5% or more!

Address: 1800 Newtown Pike 40511 **Location:** I-75/64 exit 115, 0.5 mi s on SR 922. **Facility:** An equestrian theme, reflecting the history of the region, decorates the resort's public areas. Beautiful, upscale rooms include enclosed closets and granite bathroom vanities with back-lit mirrors. 409 units. 7 stories, interior corridors. **Parking:** on-site and valet. **Terms:** check-in 4 pm. **Amenities:** safes. **Pool:** heated outdoor, heated indoor. **Activities:** sauna, hot tub, steamroom, regulation golf, tennis, exercise room, spa. **Guest Services:** valet and coin laundry, boarding pass kiosk.

[SAVE] [TI] [🛏] [Y] CALL [&] [≈] [↾↾] [BIZ] [≋] [✕] [🛏] [🍽] / SOME UNITS [🐾] [▣]

(See map & index p. 62.)

RESIDENCE INN BY MARRIOTT LEXINGTON KEENELAND/
AIRPORT   859/296-0460 26
THREE DIAMOND 〔SAVE〕 Extended   **AAA Benefit:**
Stay Hotel. **Address:** 3110 Wall St   Members save 5%
40513   or more!

RESIDENCE INN BY MARRIOTT LEXINGTON
SOUTH/HAMBURG PLACE   859/263-9979 19
THREE DIAMOND 〔SAVE〕 Extended   **AAA Benefit:**
Stay Hotel. **Address:** 2688 Pink Pigeon Members save 5%
Pkwy 40509   or more!

SPRINGHILL SUITES BY MARRIOTT LEXINGTON NEAR THE
UNIVERSITY OF KENTUCKY   859/225-1500 15
THREE DIAMOND 〔SAVE〕 Hotel. **Ad-**   **AAA Benefit:**
dress: 863 S Broadway Rd 40504   Members save 5%
                                             or more!

TOWNEPLACE SUITES BY MARRIOTT LEXINGTON
KEENELAND/AIRPORT   · 859/368-9491 25
THREE DIAMOND 〔SAVE〕 Extended   **AAA Benefit:**
Stay Hotel. **Address:** 980 Midnight   Members save 5%
Pass 40513   or more!

TOWNEPLACE SUITES BY MARRIOTT LEXINGTON SOUTH/
HAMBURG PLACE   859/263-0018 22
THREE DIAMOND 〔SAVE〕 Extended   **AAA Benefit:**
Stay Hotel. **Address:** 1790 Vendor Way Members save 5%
40509   or more!

WHERE TO EAT

ALFALFA RESTAURANT   859/253-0014 9
APPROVED American. Casual Dining. **Address:** 141
E Main St, Suite 190 40507

ARIRANG GARDEN-KOREAN BAR-B-QUE 859/269-8273 29
APPROVED Korean. Casual Dining. **Address:** 109 Mt
Tabor Rd 40517

ASIAN WIND   859/223-0060 35
APPROVED Chinese. Casual Dining. **Address:** 3735
Palomar Centre Dr, Suite 40 40513

AZUR RESTAURANT & PATIO   859/296-1007 27
THREE DIAMOND American. Casual Dining. **Address:** 3070
Lakecrest Cir, Suite 550 40513

BELLA NOTTE   859/245-1789 39
APPROVED Italian. Casual Dining. **Address:** 3715
Nicholasville Rd 40503

BONEFISH GRILL   859/233-3474 16
THREE DIAMOND Seafood. Fine Dining. **Address:** 2341 Sir
Barton Way 40509

THE CHOP HOUSE   859/268-9555
APPROVED Steak. Casual Dining. **Address:** 2640
Richmond Rd 40509

DOUBLE DOGS   859/963-4150 18
APPROVED American. Casual Dining. **Address:** 1916
Justice Dr 40509

EL MARIACHI MEXICAN RESTAURANT 859/255-0250 3
APPROVED Mexican. Casual Dining. **Address:** 125
Town Center Dr 40511

EL TORO CANTINA & GRILL   859/277-2255 28
APPROVED Mexican. Casual Dining. **Address:** 1917
Nicholasville Rd 40503

GIUSEPPE'S RISTORANTE ITALIANO 859/272-4269 42
THREE DIAMOND Northern Italian. Casual Dining. **Address:**
4456 Nicholasville Rd 40515

GOODFELLAS PIZZERIA   859/281-1101 8
APPROVED Pizza. Quick Serve. **Address:** 110 N Mill
St 40507

GRAZE   859/309-2490 13
THREE DIAMOND American. Casual Dining. **Address:** 111
Woodland Ave 40502

HONEYWOOD   859/469-8234 40
THREE DIAMOND Regional American. Casual Dining.
Address: 110 Summit at Fritz Farm 40517

JALAPENO'S RESTAURANTE MEXICANO 859/281-5171 15
APPROVED Mexican. Casual Dining. **Address:** 1030
S Broadway Rd 40504

JEAN FARRIS WINERY & BISTRO   859/263-9463
THREE DIAMOND American. Casual Dining. **Address:** 6825
Old Richmond Rd 40515

JOE BOLOGNA'S RESTAURANT & PIZZERIA
859/252-4933 11

APPROVED   **AAA Inspector Notes:** *Historic.* This
                        downtown neighborhood has undergone
Italian   some changes over the years. Originally
Pizza   a 19th-century Presbyterian church (built
Casual Dining   in 1891), the building was converted to a
$7-$30   synagogue (1912), and finally a restau-
                        rant (1989). Enjoy your pizza and locally-
brewed bourbon barrel ale while watching light filter through the
antique stained-glass windows. **Features:** beer & wine, senior
menu, happy hour. **Address:** 120 W Maxwell St 40508 **Loca-**
tion: Jct Maxwell and Jersey sts. 〔L〕〔D〕

J. RENDER'S SOUTHERN TABLE & BAR 859/296-9330 23
APPROVED Barbecue. Casual Dining. **Address:** 3191
Beaumont Centre Cir 40513

LE DEAUVILLE   859/246-0999 6
APPROVED French. Casual Dining. **Address:** 199 N
Limestone St 40507

MALONE'S   859/335-6500 36
THREE DIAMOND American. Casual Dining. **Address:** 3347
Tates Creek Rd 40502

MALONE'S   859/264-8023 19
THREE DIAMOND Steak. Casual Dining. **Address:** 1920
Pleasant Ridge Dr 40509

MALONE'S   859/977-2620 34
THREE DIAMOND Steak. Fine Dining. **Address:** 3735
Palomar Centre Dr 40513

MASALA INDIAN CUISINE   859/224-0001 31
APPROVED Indian Vegetarian. Casual Dining.
Address: 3061 Fieldstone Way, Suite 600 40513

MERRICK INN   859/269-5417 37
THREE DIAMOND American. Casual Dining. **Address:** 1074
Merrick Dr 40502

MIYAKO JAPANESE RESTAURANT   859/268-0708 22
APPROVED Japanese Sushi. Casual Dining.
Address: 2547 Richmond Rd 40509

(See map & index p. 62.)

PAISANO'S ITALIAN RESTAURANT & LOUNGE
859/277-5321 (33)
APPROVED Italian. Casual Dining. **Address:** 2417 Nicholasville Rd 40503

THE PARKETTE DRIVE-IN
859/254-8723 (14)
APPROVED American. Casual Dining. **Address:** 1230 E New Circle Rd 40505

PEPE'S MI MEXICO
859/263-2225 (32)
APPROVED Mexican. Casual Dining. **Address:** 3280 Eagle View Ln 40509

PORTOFINO RESTAURANT
859/253-9300 (10)
THREE DIAMOND Italian. Casual Dining. **Address:** 249 E Main St 40507

RAFFERTY'S RESTAURANT & BAR
859/264-8900
APPROVED American. Casual Dining. **Address:** 1865 Alysheba Way 40509

RAMSEY'S
859/264-9396 (21)
APPROVED Comfort Food. Casual Dining. **Address:** 3090 Helmsdale Pl, Suite 4 40509

RED STATE BBQ
859/233-7898 (1)
APPROVED Barbecue. Quick Serve. **Address:** 4020 Georgetown Rd 40511

THE RUDDY DUCK GRILLE
859/254-0046 (7)
APPROVED American. Casual Dining. **Address:** 131 Cheapside St 40507

THE SAGE RABBIT
859/523-2095 (17)
APPROVED American. Casual Dining. **Address:** 438 S Ashland Ave 40502

SAHARA MEDITERRANEAN CUISINE
859/224-1138 (30)
APPROVED Mediterranean. Quick Serve. **Address:** 3061 Fieldstone Way, Suite 1200 40513

SAUL GOOD RESTAURANT & PUB
859/273-4663 (38)
APPROVED American. Casual Dining. **Address:** 3801 Mall Rd, Suite 120 40503

SAUL GOOD RESTAURANT & PUB HAMBURG
859/317-9200 (20)
APPROVED American. Casual Dining. **Address:** 1808 Alysheba Way 40509

SHAKESPEARE AND CO.
859/367-0413 (4)
APPROVED American. Casual Dining. **Address:** 367 W Short St 40507

SHAMROCK BAR & GRILLE
859/269-7621 (25)
APPROVED American. Casual Dining. **Address:** 154 Patchen Dr 40517

SMITHTOWN SEAFOOD AT THE SUMMIT 859/309-0011 (41)
APPROVED Seafood. Quick Serve. **Address:** 119 Marion St 40502

TACHIBANA
859/254-1911 (2)
APPROVED Japanese. Casual Dining. **Address:** 785 Newtown Ct 40511

TANDOOR FINE INDIAN CUISINE
859/263-5771 (26)
APPROVED Indian. Casual Dining. **Address:** 3130 Mapleleaf Dr 40509

TOLLY-HO RESTAURANT
859/253-2007 (12)
APPROVED Breakfast Burgers. Quick Serve. **Address:** 606 S Broadway St 40508

THE VILLAGE IDIOT
859/252-0099 (5)
APPROVED American. Gastropub. **Address:** 307 W Short St 40507

WINCHELL'S RESTAURANT
859/278-9424 (24)
APPROVED American. Sports Bar. **Address:** 348 Southland Dr 40503

LONDON (E-7) pop. 7,993, elev. 1,244'

In the heart of the Daniel Boone National Forest, London has been a crossroads for travelers ever since settlers first ventured through the Cumberland Gap on the Wilderness Road. It now is a regional center for trade, governmental services, industry and tourism.

You are bound to have an "egg-citing" time at the 4-day celebration known as the ⬥World Chicken Festival, held in London each September. The festival honors Colonel Harland Sanders, who opened his first restaurant in nearby Corbin *(see place listing p. 35)* in the 1940s. More than 250,000 folks come each year to see the world's largest skillet, the Gospel Egg-stravaganza, the parade and live entertainment, volleyball tournament, midway-style rides and car show.

London-Laurel County Tourist Commission: 140 Faith Assembly Church Rd., London, KY 40741. **Phone:** (606) 878-6900 or (800) 348-0095.

BAYMONT INN & SUITES
606/877-1000
APPROVED Hotel. **Address:** 2075 Hwy 192 40741

COMFORT SUITES
606/877-7848
THREE DIAMOND Hotel. **Address:** 1918 W Hwy 192 Bypass 40741

COUNTRY INN & SUITES BY RADISSON
606/878-9900
THREE DIAMOND Hotel. **Address:** 2035 W Hwy 192 40741

FAIRFIELD INN & SUITES BY MARRIOTT
606/389-5640
THREE DIAMOND SAVE Hotel. **Address:** 201 Shiloh Dr 40741
AAA Benefit: Members save 5% or more!

HAMPTON INN BY HILTON LONDON-NORTH
606/864-0011
THREE DIAMOND SAVE Hotel. **Address:** 200 Alamo Dr 40741
AAA Benefit: Members save up to 15%!

HOLIDAY INN EXPRESS
606/862-0077
THREE DIAMOND Hotel. **Address:** 506 Minton Dr 40741

MICROTEL INN & SUITES BY WYNDHAM LONDON
606/877-3400
APPROVED Hotel. **Address:** 1895 W Hwy 192 40741

RED ROOF INN LONDON I-75
606/862-8844
APPROVED Hotel. **Address:** 110 Melcon Ln 40741

WHERE TO EAT

EL DORADO
606/877-2806
APPROVED Mexican. Casual Dining. **Address:** 1740 W Hwy 192 40741

GONDOLIER ITALIAN RESTAURANT AND PIZZA
606/878-1222
 APPROVED   Italian Pizza. Casual Dining. **Address:**
305 W Hwy 80 40741

SHILOH ROADHOUSE
606/864-5059
APPROVED   Steak. Casual Dining. **Address:** 218
Russel Dyche Memorial Hwy 40741

LORETTO (D-5) pop. 713, elev. 742'

MAKER'S MARK DISTILLERY, 2 mi. e. on
SR 52 to Burks Spring Rd., began opera-
tions in 1805. The visitor center is the starting point
for 60-minute guided tours. Highlights of the tour include the still house—the oldest part of the
complex—where the bourbon is made by hand; the
fermenting room, where the sour mash ferments in
deep cypress vats; one warehouse, which is more
than 100 years old, where the whisky ages; and the
bottling house, where each bottle is hand-dipped in
the distillery's signature red wax.

Hours: Tours depart Mon.-Sat. 9-3:30, Sun.
11:30-3:30. Closed Jan. 1, Easter, Thanksgiving,
Christmas Eve and Christmas. **Cost:** $14; $10 (retired military with ID); free (ages 0-20). **Phone:**
(270) 865-2099.

LOUISA pop. 2,467

BEST WESTERN PLUS LOUISA   606/638-3418
 THREE DIAMOND   Best
Hotel   Western **AAA Benefit:**
PLUS. Members save up to
15% and earn bonus
points!

 Address: 18199 Hwy 23 41230 **Location:** Jct US 23 and SR 3. **Facility:** 48
units. 3 stories, interior corridors. **Pool:**
heated indoor. **Activities:** hot tub, exercise room. **Guest Services:** coin
laundry.

SUPER 8-LOUISA   606/638-7888
APPROVED   Hotel. **Address:** 191 Falls Creek Dr 41230

Louisville

Then & Now

For 2 weeks each spring Louisville is an arena of glamour and festivity as the city anticipates and witnesses the Kentucky Oaks on the first Friday in May, where 3-year-old fillies race for a garland of lilies, and the Kentucky Derby on the first Saturday in May. The oldest continuously held horse race in the country, the Kentucky Derby pits the world's best 3-year-old Thoroughbreds in a 1.25-mile race for a purse of more than $600,000 and a chance to become the winner of the coveted Triple Crown of racing.

Louisville is much more than a horse-racing town, however: It also is a cultural and industrial center. The city is located on a plain adjacent to the falls of the Ohio River. Named in honor of Louis XVI of France, the first permanent settlement on the site was established in 1778 by Col. George Rogers Clark, accompanied by 120 soldiers and 20 families. Fort Nelson, named after Gov. Thomas Nelson of Virginia, was completed in 1782. A plaque at the corner of 7th and Main streets commemorates the establishment of the city and the fort.

AAA.com/travelguides—
more ways to look, book and save

Louisville's growth was directly related to westward expansion. The Ohio River was a conveyor of both people and commerce. The portaging of goods around the falls contributed heavily to the settlement's early economy. In 1830, when the Portland Canal opened the way for river traffic from Pittsburgh to New Orleans, Louisville was catapulted from a frontier outpost into an important station of the New Orleans commercial empire.

Louisville skyline and Ohio River

The town attracted diverse ethnic groups, with the majority of the immigrants coming from Ireland, Germany and Scotland. Together they made Louisville an industrial center and inspired its cultural and architectural growth. Well-preserved neighborhoods reflect the impact of their heritage. Victorian houses, complete with stained-glass windows and iron fences, are found in Old Louisville. Butchertown, the German settlement and meatpacking area, exemplifies the simple lifestyles of its founders.

The city is known for producing one-third of the world's supply of bourbon. From a business standpoint Louisville's location has attracted many corporate offices, including Brown-Forman Corp., Humana Inc., Papa John's International and YUM Brands, Inc. The city's facilities draw trade shows, conferences and conventions.

Louisville's downtown has undergone extensive redevelopment and represents diverse architectural styles. The Riverfront Plaza and Belvedere is an urban plaza and park; on one plaza wall

(Continued on p. 72.)

Destination Louisville

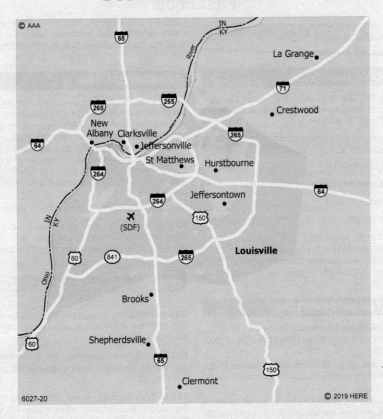

This map shows cities in the Louisville vicinity where you will find attractions, hotels and restaurants. Cities are listed alphabetically in this book on the following pages.

Fast Facts

ABOUT THE CITY

POP: 556,332 ▪ ELEV: 540 ft.

MONEY

SALES TAX: Kentucky levies a 6 percent sales tax. The city of Louisville levies an additional 9.5 percent hospitality tax on hotel rooms.

WHOM TO CALL

EMERGENCY: 911

POLICE (non-emergency): (502) 574-7111

TIME: (502) 585-5961

TEMPERATURE: (502) 581-9283

HOSPITALS: Jewish Hospital & St. Mary's Healthcare, (502) 587-4011 ▪ Norton Hospital, (502) 629-8000 ▪ Sts. Mary & Elizabeth Hospital, (502) 361-6000 ▪ University of Louisville Hospital, (502) 562-3000.

VISITOR INFORMATION

Louisville Visitor Information Center: 301 S. 4th St., Louisville, KY 40202. Phone: (502) 379-6106 or (800) 626-5646.

Contact the convention and visitors bureau at the above address to have a Louisville information packet mailed to you.

The Louisville Visitors Center, at the entrance to Fourth Street Live! and adjacent to the Hyatt Regency Louisville and Kentucky International Convention Center, provides maps, brochures, advice and directions. It is open Mon.-Sat. 10-6, Sun. noon-5; closed Jan. 1, Easter, Thanksgiving and Dec. 24-25.

The Louisville Visitors Center, at the entrance to Fourth Street Live! and adjacent to the Hyatt Regency Louisville and Kentucky International Convention Center, provides maps, brochures, advice and directions. It is open Mon.-Sat. 10-6, Sun. noon-5; closed Jan. 1, Easter, Thanksgiving and Dec. 24-25.

TRANSPORTATION

AIR TRAVEL: South of the destination near the junction of I-65 and I-264, 7 miles from downtown, Louisville International Airport (SDF) welcomes domestic and international flights. Most major passenger airlines offer airline tickets and flights daily. Cab service to the downtown area averages 15 minutes and costs $19.55. Transit Authority of River City (TARC) buses service the airport 23 times daily, 6 a.m.-11:30 p.m.; fare is $1.75.

Many hotels and motels provide courtesy car service.

RENTAL CARS: Like most large cities, Louisville has many car rental agencies. Hertz, (502) 361-0182 or (800) 654-3080, offers discounts to AAA members.

 Book and save at AAA.com/hertz

RAIL SERVICE: No passenger trains serve Louisville; look for cheap airline tickets, public transportation or low fares for rental cars.

BUSES: Greyhound Lines Inc., 7th Street and Muhammad Ali Boulevard, is the major bus line; phone (502) 561-2805.

TAXIS: Taxis are metered and charge $4.70 for the first mile and $2.25 for each additional mile. Tips range from 10 to 15 percent. Taxis must be ordered by telephone. The largest cab company is Yellow Cab, (502) 636-5511.

PUBLIC TRANSPORTATION: TARC operates buses and minibuses throughout the metropolitan area. *See Public Transportation for details.*

(Continued from p. 70.)

is a one-story stained-glass window depicting 200 years of the city's history. Kentucky Center's glass walls reflect facades of buildings which have been renovated and converted into museums, theaters, shops and restaurants. East of downtown at River Road and Zorn Avenue, The Water Tower is an example of classic industrial architecture, with a Grecian temple front and a great standpipe tower modeled after the Roman triumphal column. Also by River Road is the Patriots Peace Memorial, which commemorates fallen military personnel of the

United States. And on Bradley Avenue near Eastern Parkway is The Grotto and Garden of Our Lady of Lourdes, a contemplative spot designed to resemble its namesake shrine in France.

As it plies the waters of the Ohio, *The Belle of Louisville* is a constant reminder of the city's river history even as it offers views of the ever-evolving metropolis. Both are definitive of the Louisville that, like the bourbon it produces, is a smooth blend—a tasteful mix of new with old, big city with small town and high-tech industry with gracious living.

Find AAA Inspected & Approved
campgrounds at AAA.com/campgrounds

Must Do: AAA Editor's Picks

- Do the Derby. If you can plan ahead to attend the ◈ **Kentucky Derby** on the first Saturday in May, you'll witness a thrilling horse-racing spectacular, which also happens to be quite a party. The ◈ **Kentucky Derby Festival** precedes the race, an extravaganza featuring fireworks, concerts, sports and even a Derby Ball.

- If you can't make the Kentucky Derby, then by all means visit **Churchill Downs** (700 Central Ave.) to walk the hallowed grounds during a 30-minute guided tour. This is also the site of the ◈ **Kentucky Derby Museum** (704 Central Ave.), which showcases everything from stunning Derby hats and other fashions to exhibits about the famous Thoroughbreds that have graced the track.

- Baseball fans won't want to miss the **Louisville Slugger Museum & Factory** (800 W. Main St.), where the official bat of the major league is crafted. While some might be more inclined to view the collection of memorabilia dedicated to America's pastime, others might be curious to inspect a batting cage or observe bats being created in the onsite manufacturing facility.

- Enjoy Louisville's **parks and recreation.** For a sweeping panorama of the Ohio River, try Louisville Waterfront Park (401 River Rd.), a place with a children's play area. Or head to Cherokee Park (745 Cochran Hill Rd.), with a 2.4-mile scenic loop traveling past woodlands, meadows and rolling hills. Jefferson Memorial Forest (11311 Mitchell Hill Rd.) in Fairdale—only a 15-minute drive from downtown—offers stellar hiking, fishing and camping.

- If you're in search of an outing that appeals to all ages, you can't go wrong at the ◈ **Louisville Zoo** (1100 Trevilian Way). Playful polar bears thrill the kids, who also like hand-feeding the lorikeets, watching a bear-training demonstration or attending a giraffe feeding. You can navigate the facility by foot, or take a load off and ride the zoo's tram or train.

- The ◈ **Muhammad Ali Center** (144 N. 6th St.) pays tribute to the legendary boxer in his hometown. Interactive exhibits and multimedia presentations, including a five-screen orientation film, outline Ali's life experiences and core values. A re-creation of the Champ's training camp allows participants to practice punches on a speed bag or engage in a round of shadow boxing.

- If you're up for **learning,** Louisville is the place to go. At ◈ **Kentucky Science Center** (727 W. Main St.), you can explore math, science and technology through hands-on displays, while highlights at ◈ **Frazier History Museum** (829 W. Main St.) include such intriguing American artifacts as Daniel Boone's family Bible and President Theodore Roosevelt's "Big Stick."

- For a laid-back excursion, tour ◈ **Locust Grove** (561 Blankenbaker Ln.), a restored 1790s Georgian mansion that served as a gathering place for prominent social and political figures of the time. Just as exquisite as the home's Kentucky-crafted furniture are the meadows, gardens and woods surrounding the property, which also includes an original smokehouse and farm buildings.

- Browse for souvenirs in one of Louisville's unique shopping districts. Specialty shops and galleries dot Frankfort Avenue, also a hub for dining and entertainment. If antiques are your thing, check out the stores on East Market Street, where you'll also find artworks, home décor and upscale restaurants.

- Take a stroll through **Old Louisville,** said to be America's largest Victorian neighborhood. You can wander on your own, reserve a guided tour, or pick up a brochure for a self-guiding tour at the **Historic Old Louisville Visitors Center** (301 S. Fourth St.). Architecture buffs will delight in admiring the range of styles represented by the quaint structures, which include Queen Anne, Renaissance Revival and Chateauesque.

Kentucky Science Center

Louisville 1-day Itinerary

AAA editors suggest these activities for a great short vacation experience.

Morning

- If you'll be in Louisville on the first Saturday in May, then by all means plan to attend the Kentucky Derby, or at the very least, the Kentucky Derby Festival during the two weeks preceding the race. If you are visiting Louisville at another time, you may be able to catch another thrilling race at the legendary track, **Churchill Downs** (700 Central Ave.), which is situated in the southern portion of the city.

- Even if you don't attend a race, it's a treat to learn about the winners by taking the guided historic walking tour of Churchill Downs hosted by the adjacent ▽ **Kentucky Derby Museum** (704 Central Ave.). A behind-the-scenes tour also is available, offering sneak peeks into the press box, jockeys' quarters and millionaire's row. At the museum you can try to maintain a jockey's stance on a simulated horse, view race footage or peruse the collection of exhibits providing insight into the world of Thoroughbred racing.

- About 6 miles east of Churchill Downs (via I-65S and I-264E), the ▽ **Louisville Zoo** (1100 Trevilian Way) entertains the whole family. In addition to observing the zoo's impressive assortment of animals, there are other interesting things to do. Kids love the zoo's train while a carousel and playground delight tykes.

Afternoon

- Head to downtown Louisville, where several must-dos are within walking distance of each other on West Main Street. For stylish dishes in an artful setting, order lunch from **Proof on Main** (702 W. Main St.), which also satisfies with decadent dessert choices.

- Louisville presents first-rate facilities for those captivated by the arts and sciences. Strolling along West Main Street, you'll encounter the ▽ **Kentucky Science Center** (727 W. Main St.), enlightening guests with a vast array of interactive displays and activity centers. "The World We Create" exhibit inspires creative thinkers as it explores physical science. Just a short walk west, the ▽ **Frazier History Museum** (829 W. Main St.) holds such fascinating pieces as swords, shields and medieval weapons. Costumed interpreters and live demonstrations illustrating various techniques of using armor lend intrigue to the experience.

- Among the cluster of attractions on West Main Street, you'll come across two that represent well-crafted items unique to Kentucky. **The Kentucky Museum of Art and Craft** (715 W. Main St.) preserves the cultural heritage of the Bluegrass State. If you're a baseball fan, then you can appreciate art of a different sort at the

Churchill Downs

Louisville Slugger Museum & Factory (800 W. Main St.); this is the place where the iconic baseball bat is constructed, and you can go on a tour to see how it's done.

Evening

- Bardstown Road, just southeast of downtown, is known as the city's Restaurant Row. **Seviche-A Latin Restaurant** (1538 Bardstown Rd.) touts Nuevo Latino cuisine prepared with flair, enhanced by inventive cocktails and a modern yet cozy atmosphere with copper, leather and wood accents. For a down-home treat, try **Mark's Feed Store** (1514 Bardstown Rd.), where the barbecue consistently ranks high in area polls. Galleries, boutiques, pubs and nightspots dot the neighborhood as well.

- For a nautical endeavor, the historic steamboat *Belle of Louisville* and the riverboat *Spirit of Jefferson* offer dinner cruises (embarking at 401 W. River Rd.) on the Ohio River. Reserve a window seat if you are intent on catching the view, especially lovely at sunset.

- **Louisville Horse Trams** (801 Witherspoon St.) allows visitors to engage in evening sightseeing, with tours available after 6 p.m. You'll explore the downtown area in style via a handsome horse-drawn carriage.

- Those interested in the performing arts should check the box office at **The Kentucky Center** (501 W. Main St.). Home to the Kentucky Opera, Louisville Orchestra and Louisville Ballet, the venue also presents Broadway Across America.

Arriving
By Car

The major north-south route that bisects the city is I-65. From the north it comes from Indianapolis and enters the city via the JFK Memorial Bridge. From the south it passes through Nashville and skirts Louisville International Airport on its way into downtown. Numerous exits provide easy access to city streets. I-65 is closely paralleled north of the city by US 31. The four-lane George Rogers Clark Memorial Bridge, also known as the Second Street Bridge, crosses the Ohio River and carries US 31, a route which divides into US 31E and US 31W south of Louisville.

East-west traffic is best served by I-64. On the west it crosses the Ohio River from Indiana into Louisville on the Sherman Minton Bridge. It is a close neighbor of US 60 east of Louisville, bringing traffic from Frankfort and Lexington. In the city it hugs the riverfront, where it is called Riverside Parkway. Exits are at major city thoroughfares. The northeastern access is via I-71 from Cincinnati.

I-264 (the Henry Watterson Expressway and the Shawnee Expressway) bypasses downtown and loops around the western, southern and eastern portions of the city. Linking with short sections of I-64 and I-71, it provides a complete circuit of Louisville with interchanges at major cross routes. Farther out, the Gene Snyder Freeway (I-265) affords a bypass from US 42 to US 31W with interchanges at major highways.

Getting Around
Street System

Driving in Louisville is relatively easy with the help of a good city map. North-south address numbers start at Main Street; east-west numbering begins at 1st Street. Unless otherwise posted, the speed limit is 35 mph. Avoid rush hour traffic, 7:30-9 a.m. and 4-6 p.m., if possible.

Parking

Many downtown streets have metered parking, but be careful to check signs and meters for restricted times and limits. Commercial garage and lot parking is usually available. Rates are 50c-75c per hour. Visitors also can purchase a "Smart Card" (which works like a debit card) at the visitor's center.

Public Transportation

Transit Authority of River City (TARC) operates buses and trolleys throughout the Louisville metropolitan area. The base fare for buses is $1.75; exact change is required. Transfers from one bus route to another are free and are valid for 2 hours; remember to ask the driver for a transfer upon boarding. TARC offers discount bus fares for senior citizens and the physically impaired. The Day Tripper pass, which allows for unlimited rides for an entire day, may be purchased for $3 at the Louisville Visitors Center on the corner of 4th and Jefferson streets and at Union Station, 1000 W. Broadway.

The 4th Street Trolley travels on 4th Street from Theatre Square to the Galt House. The trolley's

George Rogers Clark Memorial Bridge

route extends further south to Breckenridge Mon.-Fri. 9-6:30. They also travel through Fourth Street Live, except during special events, when a detour route is followed. Green signs indicate stops for the 4th Street Trolley. The fare is 50 cents.

The Main Street Trolley runs a circular 3.5-mile route on Main and Market from 10th Street to Campbell Street. This trolley also provides service to Slugger Field for Louisville Bats baseball games on weeknights. Red signs indicate Main/Market Trolley stops. The fare is 50 cents.

Call the TARC Travel Center, (502) 585-1234, for information about fares, schedules and routes.

Shopping

Many of Louisville's historic buildings have been converted into shopping and dining complexes, which makes browsing for a special purchase even more interesting. Things to see by regional artists are sold at numerous galleries in **NuLu (new Louisville)**. Antique shops along **Bardstown Road** offer many choices for collectors.

Fourth Street Live!, a pedestrian mall downtown on 4th Street between Liberty Street and Muhammad Ali Boulevard, is a retail, dining and entertainment zone as well as a venue for concerts and other fun things to do. A glass ceiling over 4th Street provides protection from the elements. (SAVE) Hard Rock Cafe, 424 S. 4th St., offers a collection of rock 'n' roll merchandise.

At the intersection of Gene Snyder Freeway (I-265) and Brownsboro Road (SR 22) is **Paddock Shops,** a collection of more than 60 upscale shops and restaurants in a landscaped outdoor setting.

The Louisville area also offers three enclosed suburban malls. To the east are **Oxmoor Center** and **Mall St. Matthews,** both on Shelbyville Road. Southeast of the city is **Jefferson Mall,** at the Outer Loop east of Preston Highway. Most include major department stores, such as Dillard's, JCPenney and Old Navy.

East of the city in Shelbyville, English antiques and silver are the specialties of the **Wakefield-Scearce Galleries.**

Big Events

Louisville has much to celebrate and wastes no time doing just that through various ethnic festivals, fairs, music events, art and trade shows, and of course, horse races. For current listings of events check the local newspapers.

To Louisvillians, the ᵹ**Kentucky Derby,** held on the first Saturday in May, is not just a horse race but the last day of the ᵹ**Kentucky Derby Festival,** a 2-week event accented by picnics, banquets and dances; music events with top-name entertainment; and bicycle, balloon and steamboat races. The whole festival is kicked off in grand style by **Thunder Over Louisville,** one of the nation's premiere air shows and fireworks displays. The city comes down with Derby fever a week before the race, and its population mushrooms with the influx of tourists, all anxious to experience one of the nation's largest celebrations.

The ᵹ**National Farm Machinery Show and Championship Tractor Pull,** held at the Kentucky Exposition Center, draws crowds in mid-February. The center is also the site for the ᵹ**NSRA Street**

Rod Nationals, usually held late July-early August and said to be the world's largest street rod event with more than 11,000 pre-1949 vehicles.

Beatles fans flock to the **Abbey Road on the River Music Festival** on Memorial Day weekend when a tribute to Britain's fab four is presented. In July the **Forecastle Festival,** a music, art and activism event, draws more than 40 bands and some 50 environmental organizations to entertain and inform along the Ohio River.

In mid-August Louisville presents the ᵹ**Kentucky State Fair and Horse Show,** also held at the Exposition Center. Besides the horse show—a prestigious event for Saddlebreds—exhibits and musical entertainment also are on the fair's schedule.

WorldFest, on Labor Day weekend, features international music, dance and food. Also in September, the **IdeaFestival** attracts highly diverse thinkers from across the globe to explore and celebrate innovation, imagination and cutting-edge ideas.

Mid-September ushers in **Oktoberfest** at the German-American Club, while Butchertown's German community holds **The Original Butchertown Oktoberfest** at St. Joseph Catholic Church in late October.

The fine arts are celebrated during several fairs and festivals. Shakespearean plays are performed each summer, late May to early August, during the **Kentucky Shakespeare Festival.** Performances are free. The first weekend in October, the ᵹ**St. James Court Art Show** is held at St. James and Belgravia courts.

Step back in time to a Victorian era with holiday lights, vendors selling British fare and a parade during **Light Up Louisville** in late November.

Sports & Rec

Louisville has something to offer almost every sports enthusiast, whether adventure travel enthusiast, athlete or spectator. The parks of Louisville and Jefferson County, ranging in size from one-tenth of an acre to the 6,400-acre **Jefferson Memorial Forest** *(see Recreation Areas Chart),* offer opportunities for many adventurous things to do. For information about park facilities and events contact the Metro Parks Public Information Office, 1297 Trevilian Way, Louisville, KY 40213; phone (502) 456-8100.

With a 900-foot series of pools, waterfalls, water cannons and a wharf, **Waterfront Park,** downtown on the riverfront, connects Louisville to the Ohio River and is a fun thing to do with kids. The park features a playground and is a popular spot for concerts, picnicking, walking and jogging.

Bicycle trails wind through many of the parks, and several bicycle routes are designated along city streets. A booklet highlighting bicycle routes throughout Louisville and Jefferson County is available at most public library branches and at the visitor center at Fourth and Jefferson streets; for additional information phone (502) 574-6473. For a more unusual bicycling opportunity, however, there's **Louisville Mega Cavern,** which operates the

Waterfront Park

world's biggest indoor bicycle park with 320,000 square feet and 45 trails; phone (877) 614-6342.

Hiking is available in most of the parks, but marked hiking trails are found in Jefferson Memorial Forest, which offers hikers more than 35 miles of trails ranging from an easy .25-mile (one-way) paved walk to a strenuous 6.2-mile (one-way) trek. The forest, part of Louisville's Metro Parks system, is 16 miles south of the city in Fairdale; phone (502) 368-5404 for additional information.

Fishing is available; people between 16 and 65 must have a state fishing license. **Charlie Vettiner, Cherokee, Chickasaw, Fishermans, Iroquois, Long Run, Tom Wallace, Watterson** and **Waverly** parks have stocked lakes, and **Chickasaw, Cox, Eva Badman, Hays Kennedy, Riverview, Shawnee, Thurman Hutchins** and **Thurston** parks provide access to the Ohio River, where carp and game fish may be caught.

Golf enthusiasts can choose from any of the nine Metro Parks golf courses: **Bobby Nichols,** 4301 E. Pages Ln., (502) 937-9051; **Charlie Vettiner,** 10207 Mary Dell Ln., (502) 267-9958; **Cherokee,** 2501 Alexander Rd., (502) 458-9450; **Crescent Hill,** 3110 Brownsboro Rd., (502) 896-9193; **Iroquois,** 1501 Rundill Rd., (502) 363-9520; **Long Run,** 1605 Flat Rock Rd., (502) 245-9015; **Seneca,** 2300 Pee Wee Reese Rd., (502) 458-9298; **Shawnee,** 460 Northwestern Pkwy., (502) 776-9389; and **Sun Valley,** 6505 Bethany Ln., (502) 937-9228.

Six of these courses—**Charlie Vettiner,** Iroquois, Long Run, Seneca, Shawnee and Sun Valley—offer 18 holes. Shawnee is particularly scenic, with five holes played parallel to the Ohio River. Each course has a clubhouse and pro shop; both pull and riding carts can be rented. All courses are open daily, 30 minutes after dawn to dusk. Daily greens fees range from $9.25 to $16; discounts are available for senior citizens.

Influenced by their surroundings, visitors often want to go **horseback riding** while in Louisville. Marked horse trails ranging from 3 to 10 miles long are available at **Cherokee, Forest View, Iroquois, Seneca** and **Tom Wallace** parks. Trails also are available at five state parks: **Barren River Lake Resort, Cumberland Falls Resort, Dale Hollow Lake Resort, Lake Barkley Resort** and **Lake Cumberland Resort** (see Recreation Areas Chart) as well as **Big South Fork National River and Recreation Area.**

For **tennis** buffs the more than 150 public outdoor courts in the area are free and are available on a first-come-first-served basis, with a 1-hour time limit.

Water sports are enjoyed in the 12 outdoor pools, open mid-June to mid-August, and three indoor public pools, open year-round, as well as in area lakes and the **Ohio River.**

Spectator sports are a fun thing to do in Louisville. The **University of Louisville Cardinals** football team plays at **Papa John's Cardinal Stadium,** phone (502) 852-2779, while the college's **basketball** team schedules their games at the KFC Yum! Center downtown, phone (502) 690-9000.

The city has a AAA minor league **baseball** team, the **Louisville Bats**—the Cincinnati Reds' principal farm team—which plays April through September at **Louisville Slugger Field** on E. Main Street; phone (502) 212-2287.

Also at Slugger Field is **Louisville City FC,** or LouCity, a competing **soccer** franchise of The United Soccer League. The team's plan is to move into a new permanent 10,000-seat facility by 2020. The stadium, which would be able to expand up to 20,000 seats, will be near Adams and Campbell streets in the Butchertown neighborhood.

Besides the renowned "Run for the Roses," **Churchill Downs** offers Thoroughbred **horse racing** from late April through early July and September through November; phone (502) 636-4400.

Note: Policies concerning admittance of children to pari-mutuel betting facilities vary. Phone for information.

Performing Arts

The Louisville Fund for the Arts, started in 1949 to provide financial assistance to theater, art, music and dance, was the first of its kind in the United States. It now supports more than 12 organizations. An example of the city's enthusiasm for the arts is evident at the **Riverfront Plaza and Belvedere,** home to **The Kentucky Center** (see attraction listing p. 80).

The Tony Award-winning **Actors Theatre of Louisville,** (502) 584-1205, is in a complex at 316 W. Main St. that includes three theaters: the **Victor Jory,** a converted Victorian warehouse; the **Pamela Brown,** a modern auditorium-style structure; and the 316-seat-in-the-round **Bingham Theatre.** This resident professional troupe performs September to May. Their annual Humana Festival of New American Plays draws international attention and is held late March through early April.

Kentucky Opera; Louisville Ballet; and **Stage One: The Louisville Children's Theatre** perform at The Kentucky Center. The opera, (502) 584-4500, presents works September through February, and the ballet, (502) 583-3150, performs September through April. Stage One presents plays for children September through May; phone (502) 589-4060. Repertory dance troupes and theatrical and musical companies from throughout the country also are drawn to the center and are fun things for couples to do.

The Little Colonel Players, (502) 241-9906, the area's oldest community theater, stages its productions in Pewee Valley, while the **Derby Dinner Playhouse,** in nearby Jeffersonville, Ind., (812) 288-8281, offers Broadway plays and a buffet dinner in a theater-in-the-round setting.

The free **Kentucky Shakespeare Festival** performances from mid-June through July are a must;

phone (502) 574-9900. Enjoy a picnic in the park, then stroll over to the **Ramey Amphitheatre** at Fourth Street between Park and Magnolia. Other summer highlights are the musicals, movies and other things to see at the **Iroquois Amphitheater** in Iroquois Park; phone (502) 368-5865.

Though classic films are a given, **The Louisville Palace** (625 S. 4th St.) also features an assortment of live entertainment and special engagements inside the historic 1928 theater; phone (502) 583-4555.

The **Louisville Orchestra,** (502) 587-8681, performs September through May at The Kentucky Center. Louisville also invests in the musical talents of its young people through the **Louisville Youth Orchestra,** which performs at various locations; phone (502) 896-1851. The **Mercury Ballroom**, 622 S. 4th St., is a venue for concerts and shows; phone (502) 583-4555.

The **Chamber Music Society** sponsors concerts by international artists at the University of Louisville's School of Music; phone (502) 852-6907.

ATTRACTIONS

For a complete list of attractions, visit AAA.com/travelguides/attractions

21C MUSEUM, downtown and within the 21c Hotel at 700 W. Main St., features more than 9,000 square feet of permanent and changing exhibit space emphasizing contemporary art created by artists from around the world. Text Rain, an interactive exhibit in which visitors may interact with individual letters presented on a projection screen, is one of nine permanent museum installations. Private and public collections, pieces on loan from other museums as well as group and individual performances by live artists constitute the changing exhibits.

Time: Allow 1 hour minimum. **Hours:** Daily 24 hours. **Cost:** Free. **Phone:** (502) 217-6300 or (877) 217-6400.

AMERICAN PRINTING HOUSE FOR THE BLIND (APH) is .3 mi. e. of jct. I-64 and US 42/Mellwood Avenue at 1839 Frankfort Ave. Founded in 1858, APH is one of the largest and oldest non-profit organizations designing and manufacturing products for the visually impaired. It has been the main supplier of educational materials for blind and visually impaired students in the United States since 1879. Ninety-minute guided tours feature the braille production area, the studios where audio books are made, and a visit to an interactive museum that focuses on the international history of education for those who are blind.

Time: Allow 1 hour, 30 minutes minimum. **Hours:** Guided tours are offered Mon.-Thurs. (and select Fri.) at 10 and 2. Closed holidays, Derby Day (first Sat. in May), day after Thanksgiving and Christmas

Eve. Phone ahead to confirm schedule. **Cost:** Free. **Phone:** (800) 223-1839 for reservations. GT

The Museum of the American Printing House for the Blind is in the American Printing House for the Blind at 1839 Frankfort Ave. Among the museum's interactive exhibits are early printing equipment, an operable mechanical braille writer on which guests can write in braille and take away a copy, computer software designed for the visually impaired and an area in which visitors may compare braille to alphabets using raised letters. A copy of the book "An Essay on the Education of the Blind," published in France in 1786 and the first to include raised letters, the Book of Psalms from Helen Keller's bible and the piano used by Stevie Wonder when he was a student at the Michigan School for the Blind are displayed.

Time: Allow 1 hour, 30 minutes minimum. **Hours:** Self-guiding tours Mon.-Fri. 8:30-4:30, Sat. 10-3. Guided tours Mon.-Thurs. at 10 and 2. Closed holidays, Derby Day (first Sat. in May), day after Thanksgiving and Christmas Eve. **Cost:** Free. **Phone:** (800) 223-1839. GT

CATHEDRAL OF THE ASSUMPTION, 433 S. 5th St., between Muhammad Ali Blvd. and Liberty St., is one of America's oldest cathedrals in continuous use. Built in 1852, the interior of the imposing red brick edifice features Gothic arches, ornate columns and a vaulted ceiling with more than 8,000 24-karat gold leaf stars on a blue field, as well as a fresco of cherubs surrounding the Virgin Mary.

The sanctuary is lined with oil paintings sent to Louisville in the mid-19th century by Pope Gregory XVI. Across the street from the cathedral is the Archdiocese of Louisville History Center. **Time:** Allow 30 minutes minimum. **Hours:** Cathedral open Mon.-Sat. 9:30-4. Masses are conducted Mon.-Fri. at noon, Sat. at 5:30, Sun. at 9:30, noon and 5:30. History Center open Sun. 10:30-2. Audio tours available Mon.-Fri. Closed major holidays. **Cost:** Free. **Phone:** (502) 582-2971. GT

CHURCHILL DOWNS, at 700 Central Ave., is the historic racetrack where the Kentucky Derby is run. Racing seasons are late April through early July and late October through November; Derby Day is the first Saturday in May. A 30-minute guided walking tour of Churchill Downs is available through the Kentucky Derby Museum (weather permitting). **Phone:** (502) 636-4400.

Kentucky Derby Museum, 704 Central Ave., adjacent to Gate 1 at Churchill Downs, showcases the thoroughbred industry and the Kentucky Derby. Two floors of hats, fashion, racing artifacts and interactive exhibits share the tradition and exhilaration of Derby Day. A 360-degree high-definition film of "The Greatest Race" narrates the life of a Thoroughbred, from foal to Derby champion, while owners, trainers and jockeys relive their Derby moments in "The Winner's Stable."

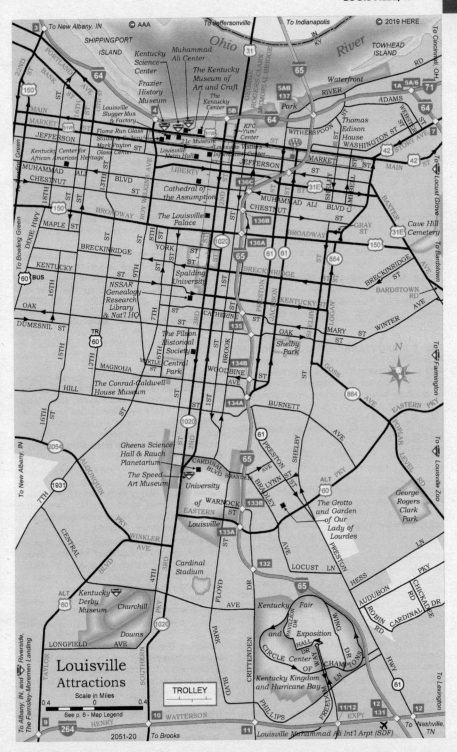

Louisville
Attractions

Scale in Miles

See p. 6 - Map Legend

TROLLEY

2051-20

Other exhibits feature race footage of every Derby since 1918, trophies, commemorative Derby glasses, riding silks and a live Thoroughbred and miniature horse. Visitors may test their Derby knowledge in an interactive trivia game and attempt to maintain a jockey's stance for 2 minutes on a mountable simulated horse. The Barn and Backside Track Tour allows guests to visit the track's stables and infield, while the Inside the Gates Tour takes visitors through the clubhouse and non-public areas of the track.

Time: Allow 2 hours minimum. **Hours:** Mon.-Sat. 8-5, Sun. 11-5, Mar. 15-Nov. 30; Mon.-Sat. 9-5, Sun. 11-5, rest of year. Closed Oaks and Derby days (first Fri.-Sat. in May), Thanksgiving, Christmas Eve and Christmas. A 30-minute guided walking tour of Churchill Downs is included with admission (weather permitting). Barn and Backside Van Tour available daily, mid-Mar. through Nov.; phone for schedule, tour rates and reservation information. Behind the Scenes Walking Tour is offered on non-race days. Other tours may vary; phone for schedule and admission.

Cost: Museum $15; $14 (ages 60+); $8 (ages 5-14); free (ages 0-4). There is an additional $11 fee for the Barn and Backside Van Tour and Behind the Scenes Walking Tour. **Phone:** (502) 637-1111 or (502) 637-7097. [🍴]

THE CONRAD-CALDWELL HOUSE MUSEUM, 1402 St. James Ct., is a Victorian Romanesque Revival mansion built in the 1890s by architect Arthur Loomis for businessman Theophilus Conrad. The carved stone exterior is complemented by the interior woodwork, which includes carved paneling and parquet floors. The surrounding neighborhood, known as Old Louisville, is noted for its turn-of-the-20th-century homes.

Time: Allow 1 hour minimum. **Hours:** Tours Wed.-Sun. at 1 and 3 (also Sat. at 11). Closed major holidays. **Cost:** $10; $7 (ages 65+ and active military with ID); $5 (ages 6-21 and students with ID). **Phone:** (502) 636-5023. [GT]

FARMINGTON is off I-264 at 3033 Bardstown Rd. Built in 1816, this 14-room Federal-style home was the center of the 550-acre hemp plantation owned by John and Lucy Speed and sustained by nearly 60 slaves. The restored house is furnished with Kentucky furniture and period antiques. A summer kitchen, springhouse, stone barn and re-created early 19th-century garden are on the 18-acre grounds.

The "Lincoln and Farmington: An Enduring Friendship" exhibit explores the friendship of Joshua Speed, one of John and Lucy's 11 children, and Abraham Lincoln, whom Joshua befriended while both young men were beginning their careers in Springfield, Ill. The two became close friends, and in 1841 Lincoln spent about 3 weeks at Farmington during a break in his relationship with Mary Todd. The exhibit's documents, letters and photographs chronicle Lincoln's visit, likely his sole experience on a slave-based plantation; an invitation to Lincoln's 1865 funeral also is displayed.

Hours: Guided tours are offered Tues.-Fri. 10-3 (also Sat. 11-1, May-Oct. 1). Closed Jan. 1, Easter, Derby Day (first Sat. in May), Thanksgiving, Christmas Eve and Christmas. Phone ahead to confirm schedule. **Cost:** Fee $9; $8 (ages 60+); $5 (ages 5-17, theater in the round show and for exhibit only). **Phone:** (502) 452-9920. [GT]

FLAME RUN GLASS STUDIO & GALLERY is at 815 W. Market St. This facility displays contemporary glass art and figures created by glass-blowing, or pipe-working, which entails a pipe or tube being used to inflate molten glass into a bubble so that it may be shaped. A gallery showcases glassworks crafted by local and international artists. Demonstrations may be seen during guided studio tours, and visitors may create their own pieces in a variety of workshops offered.

Time: Allow 1 hour minimum. **Hours:** Gallery open Mon.-Fri. 10-4, Sat. 10-5 and by appointment. "Create your own piece" workshops are available by appointment only. Closed major holidays. **Cost:** Gallery free. **Phone:** (502) 584-5353.

FRAZIER HISTORY MUSEUM is at 829 W. Main St. at 9th St. The three-story museum brings history to life for visitors through exhibits, artifacts and live performances. A world-class collection of arms, armor and related artifacts are displayed. The Frazier Collection includes such objects as Theodore Roosevelt's "big stick" rifle, a bow and arrows owned by Geronimo and Gen. George Armstrong Custer's ivory-handled Colt pistols. Other noteworthy objects include a surplus grave marker from the Battle of Little Bighorn, a first edition of *Uncle Tom's Cabin* and the arrest warrant issued for Mary Todd Lincoln.

The museum houses one of the largest collections of toy soldiers and historic miniatures on permanent public display in the world, *The Stewart Collection*. Other exhibitions feature bourbon whiskey, the Lewis and Clark expedition, Hunter S. Thompson and *White Christmas*.

The first stop on the Kentucky Bourbon Trail, the museum offers The Spirits of Kentucky display which features an in-depth look at Bourbon whiskey. The interactive and educational exhibition traces the temperance movement from 1920 until the 1933 ratification of the 21st Amendment, which repealed the 18th Amendment's ban on alcohol.

Time: Allow 2 hours minimum. **Hours:** Mon.-Sat. 9-5, Sun. noon-5. Closed Easter, Thanksgiving, Christmas Eve and Christmas. **Cost:** $12; $10 (ages 60+ and military with ID); $8 (ages 5-17 and students with ID). Additional fees for special exhibits may apply. **Parking:** $8. **Phone:** (502) 753-5663 or (866) 886-7103. [GT] [🍴]

THE KENTUCKY CENTER is on Main St. between 5th and 6th sts. Home to the Louisville Ballet, The Louisville Orchestra, PNC Broadway Across

America, Stage One Children's Theater and special events, the center also has an impressive collection of 20th-century art. Self-guiding audio tours focusing on the art collection are available.

Hours: Building open daily 7 a.m.-10 p.m. (excluding show nights). Ticket office Mon.-Sat. 10-6, Sun. noon-5. Guided tours may be arranged by appointment. **Cost:** Entrance to the building and audio tours free. Guided tours $2. Performance ticket prices and schedules vary. **Phone:** (502) 584-7777 for tickets or (800) 775-7777. [GT]

KENTUCKY CENTER FOR AFRICAN AMERICAN HERITAGE is at 1701 W. Muhammad Ali Blvd. Designed to be the state's pre-eminent center focusing on the cultural, social and artistic contributions of African-Americans, it is on the site of a restored trolley maintenance complex. Among the exhibits are those dedicated to York, the slave who played a major part in the Lewis & Clark expedition; the civil rights movement; and the role that the church has played in black culture. **Time:** Allow 1 hour minimum. **Hours:** Mon.-Fri. 9-5 (also Sat.-Sun. noon-5 for special events). Closed major holidays. **Cost:** Center free. Prices vary for exhibits and events; some are free. Phone ahead for event schedule and pricing. **Phone:** (502) 583-4100 or (502) 583-4112.

THE KENTUCKY MUSEUM OF ART AND CRAFT is at 715 W. Main St., between 7th and 8th sts. in the downtown Museum Row District. Dedicated to the advancement of contemporary local, regional and international artists, the museum features works by more than 400 craftspeople. New exhibitions are mounted every month. Most works may be purchased but must remain on display for the duration of the exhibition in which they are featured. **Time:** Allow 1 hour minimum. **Hours:** Tues.-Sat. 10-6, Sun. 10-5. **Cost:** Free. **Parking:** $6. **Phone:** (502) 589-0102.

KENTUCKY SCIENCE CENTER, 727 W. Main St., is housed in a restored, four-story, 19th-century former warehouse and features hands-on science exhibits and a four-story digital theater.

Permanent exhibits include The World Within Us, which explores the wonders of the human body; The World We Create, which celebrates how creative thinking makes scientific achievements possible; and The World Around Us, with exhibits about natural and earth sciences. Encompassing the entire first floor is the Science in Play exhibit, which is geared towards the under age 7 crowd.

Hours: Daily 9:30-5 (also Fri.-Sat. 5-9). Last admission 1 hour before closing. Closed Derby Day (first Sat. in May), Thanksgiving, Christmas Eve and Christmas. **Cost:** Exhibits only $13; $11 (ages 2-12). Movie tickets $8-$10. **Phone:** (502) 561-6100 or (800) 591-2203.

Digital Theater, in the Kentucky Science Center at 727 W. Main St., seats 225 and presents a changing series of large-format movies, including Hollywood hits, on a four-story-tall screen.

Hours: Daily 9:30-5 (also Fri.-Sat. 5-9). Closed Derby Day (first Sat. in May), Thanksgiving, Christmas Eve and Christmas. Phone ahead to confirm schedule. **Cost:** $8-$10. Movie and science center exhibits combination ticket available. **Phone:** (502) 561-6100.

KentuckyShow! is shown at The Kentucky Science Center at 727 W. Main St. This 32-minute multimedia presentation narrated by actress Ashley Judd is shown on a large high-definition screen and highlights the state's past and present, citizens, musical renown, sweeping landscapes and diverse regional cultures. It is the only production of its kind in the country to portray an entire state.

Hours: Presentations are offered daily at 2. Schedule may vary; phone ahead. Closed Derby Day (first Sat. in May), Thanksgiving, Christmas Eve and Christmas. **Cost:** Tickets $8. **Phone:** (502) 562-7800 or TTY (502) 562-0730.

LOCUST GROVE, .5 mi. w. on US 42 from jct. I-264 exit 22, then n. following signs to 561 Blankenbaker Ln., is the restored 1790 Georgian mansion of early Kentucky settlers William and Lucy Clark Croghan. Croghan was a surveying partner of frontiersman and Revolutionary War general George Rogers Clark, who also was his brother-in-law.

The farm and residence, on 55 acres, provide insights into westward expansion and the lives of the Croghans and their African-American slaves. General Clark lived at Locust Grove the last 9 years of his life. The site includes outbuildings, an 18th-century-style garden and a visitor center with exhibits. An introductory video and 45-minute tours are available.

The 1,200-square-foot gallery and permanent exhibit—A Country Worth Defending: Land & Family in Early Kentucky—focuses on the surveying work of Clark and Croghan and features a re-created 1810 log building and surveyor's office.

Hours: Mon.-Sat. 10-4:30, Sun. 1-4:30. Closed Jan. 1, Easter, Derby Day (first Sat. in May), Thanksgiving, Christmas Eve, Christmas and Dec. 31. Guided tours are given daily on the quarter hour; last tour 75 minutes before closing. Phone ahead to confirm schedule. **Cost:** Gallery and tour $9; $8 (ages 61+); $4 (ages 6-12). Gallery only free. **Phone:** (502) 897-9845. [GT]

LOUISVILLE NATURE CENTER AND BEARGRASS CREEK STATE NATURE PRESERVE is off I-264 exit 14, then following signs for the Louisville Zoo; the center is across the street from the zoo at 3745 Illinois Ave. The center offers indoor wildlife exhibits, a research library and a bird blind, a sheltered structure used to surveil the more than 150 species of resident and migratory birds inhabiting the adjacent 41-acre nature preserve. Butterfly, native wildflower and water gardens decorate the center's grounds.

The preserve features a boardwalk and more than 2 miles of hiking trails useful for viewing its 180 species of trees and shrubs as well as forest animals and a wide variety of butterfly species.

Time: Allow 1 hour minimum. **Hours:** Center and bird blind open Mon.-Sat. 9-4. Preserve open daily dawn-dusk. Closed major holidays. **Cost:** Donations. **Phone:** (502) 458-1328.

LOUISVILLE SLUGGER MUSEUM & FACTORY is downtown at 800 W. Main St. at the corner of 8th St. The first Louisville Slugger baseball bat was made by John "Bud" Hillerich in 1884. Appropriately enough, the entrance to the museum is distinguished by a 120-foot, 68,000-pound steel version of his creation. The bat, a scale model of Babe Ruth's Louisville Slugger, rests against the wall of the famous implement's manufacturing plant and headquarters.

Visitors can view collections of baseball memorabilia before moving on to the Hillerich & Bradsby Co. manufacturing facility to see bats being produced. Visitors receive a souvenir mini-bat and are able to partake in interactive exhibits and batting cages.

Time: Allow 1 hour, 30 minutes minimum. **Hours:** Mon.-Sat. 9-6 (also Thurs.-Sat. 6-8), Sun. 11-6, July 1 to mid-Aug.; Mon.-Sat. 9-5, Sun. 11-5, rest of year. Factory tours begin every 10 min. Guests should arrive no later than 1 hour before closing. Closed Thanksgiving and Christmas. **Cost:** $16; $13 (ages

60+); $9 (ages 6-12). **Phone:** (502) 588-7228 or (877) 775-8443.

LOUISVILLE ZOO is off I-264 exit 14 following signs to 1100 Trevilian Way. More than 1,500 exotic animals are presented in naturalistic indoor and outdoor habitats arranged by geographic region within the zoo's 134 acres. Exhibits feature a rare white alligator, giraffes, lions, rhinos, zebras, African and Asian elephants, a petting zoo and playgrounds.

Gorillas and pygmy hippos can be found at the Gorilla Forest; polar and grizzly bears reside at Glacier Run; the Island Village is home to orangutans, Sumatran tigers, tapirs, siamangs, penguins, Cuban crocodiles and a Komodo dragon; and the Herp-Aquarium displays rare amphibians, fish and reptiles in native settings. Lorikeet Landing, in the Australian area, features the brightly colored birds in a walk-through aviary. A tram, miniature train, ropes course, splash park, camel rides and a 1919 carousel also are on the premises.

Hours: Daily 10-5, mid-Mar. through Sept. 30; 10-4, rest of year. Zoo closes 1 hour after admission gates close. Closed Jan. 1, Thanksgiving and Christmas. **Cost:** $18.95; $12.75 (ages 3-11 and 60+). Winter admission $9.95; $6.95 (ages 3-11 and 60+). Ropes course $10. Camel rides $6. Train $5. ZooTram Shuttle $1. Carousel $3. Admission and schedule may vary; phone ahead. **Parking:** $5. **Phone:** (502) 459-2181.

MARK PAYTON GLASS CENTER, downtown at jct. 9th and Market sts. at 815 W. Market St., brings fun and education together, allowing visitors to see the procedures and techniques used to produce torch work glass creations. A self-guiding tour includes a video presentation and a chance to see flame-working, glassblowing and two galleries.

Educational workshops are available. **Time:** Allow 1 hour minimum. **Hours:** Gallery Mon.-Fri. 10-4, Sat. 10-5. Self-guiding tours Mon.-Sat. 10-3:30. Guided tours by appointment. Closed major holidays. **Cost:** Tours $7.50-$32. **Phone:** (502) 992-3270.

MUHAMMAD ALI CENTER, downtown at 144 N. 6th St. between Main St. and River Rd., is a cultural attraction and education center inspired by the ideals of the heavyweight boxing champion, humanitarian, international icon, peace activist, United Nations Messenger of Peace and Louisville native. The center's two-and-a-half levels feature exhibits that spotlight the core principles that Ali embraced: confidence, conviction, dedication, respect, giving and spirituality.

Visitors may train in an interactive boxing area, explore Ali's life inside the five-screen Orientation Theater, survey the history of the Civil Rights era, discover Ali's humanitarian timeline, participate in the Generation Ali story booth and watch Ali fight footage. Two art galleries showcase changing art and photography exhibits.

The Kentucky Center

Hours: Tues.-Sat. 9:30-5, Sun. noon-5. Last admission at 4:15. **Cost:** $14; $13 (ages 65+); $10 (military and students with ID); $9 (ages 6-12). **Phone:** (502) 584-9254.

NSSAR GENEALOGY RESEARCH LIBRARY & NATIONAL HEADQUARTERS is at 809 W. Main St. The library contains more than 58,000 materials, including genealogies and records of the Revolutionary War and Colonial periods. **Hours:** Library Mon.-Fri. 9:30-4:30 and third Sat. of the month 9-4. Closed major holidays. **Cost:** Free. **Phone:** (502) 589-1776.

 **RIVERSIDE, THE FARNSLEY-MOREMEN LANDING** is 10 mi. w. on SR 841 (Gene Snyder Frwy.) from jct. I-65 to Lower River Rd., then .1 mi. s. to 7410 Moorman Rd. This 300-acre site on the banks of the Ohio River depicts the importance of agriculture and river transportation in the nation's development. Two prosperous farm families cultivated the land and traded goods from their landing with people traveling down the river. The restored 1837 two-story red brick "I" house features a Greek Revival portico and is furnished in period with some original pieces.

The grounds include a garden, planted with vegetables, herbs and flowers similar to those the Moremen family might have grown; a reconstructed 19th-century detached kitchen; a visitors center; a sheltered pavilion; and a modern boat landing.

Time: Allow 1 hour, 30 minutes minimum. **Hours:** Visitor center Tues.-Sat. 9-5. Guided tours are given Tues.-Sat. 10-4:30, Sun. 1-4:30, Mar.-Nov.; Tues.-Sat. 10-4:30, rest of year. Last tour begins 1 hour before closing. Closed major holidays. **Cost:** Fee $6; $5 (ages 60+); $3 (ages 6-12); $15 (family rate for two adults with up to three children ages 0-17). **Phone:** (502) 935-6809.

THE SPEED ART MUSEUM, 2035 S. 3rd St., is next to the University of Louisville campus, .75 mi. w. off I-65 Eastern Pkwy. exit. Founded in 1925, the museum has works more than 6,000 years old in its collection, including art from ancient Egypt to contemporary pieces. The building, recently renovated, is considered one of the finest neoclassic structures in the South. New features include the North Building, the South Building and cinema, and the art park and piazza on the grounds.

Displays include modern and old masters paintings and sculptures, European tapestries, furniture, decorative art, American Indian objects, African cultural exhibits and contemporary works as well as a 16th-century English Renaissance room.

The Laramie L. Leatherman Art Learning Center offers hands-on exhibits. Art Sparks, the center's interactive core, contains interactive stations that educates visitors. The museum also offers special traveling exhibitions. **Hours:** Wed.-Sat. 10-5 (also

Muhammad Ali Center

Fri. 5-8), Sun. noon-5. Highlights Tour Wed.-Sun. at 1. Closed Jan. 1, first Sat. in Mar., Derby Day (first Sat. in May), July 4, Thanksgiving and Christmas. **Cost:** $18; $12 (ages 4-17, senior citizens, and students and military with ID); free (ages 0-3 and to all Sun.). **Parking:** $1.50-$5; free (after 6 p.m. and to all Sun. in metered parking spaces). **Phone:** (502) 634-2700. [T]

WHITEHALL HOUSE AND GARDENS is off I-64 exit 8; take Grinstead Dr. .2 mi. s., then 1.2 mi. e. to 3110 Lexington Rd. Built in 1855, the house was originally a two-story, eight-room brick building. In 1909 the Middleton family remodeled and expanded the building, creating a 15-room Classical Revival mansion reminiscent of an antebellum plantation house. The 10-acre grounds feature a 2-acre formal Florentine garden.

Time: Allow 1 hour minimum. **Hours:** Gardens daily dawn-dusk. Guided mansion tours are given Mon.-Fri. 10-2 and by appointment. Closed major holidays. **Cost:** Guided tour $10. **Phone:** (502) 897-2944. [GT]

ZACHARY TAYLOR NATIONAL CEMETERY, .25 mi. w. off I-264 US 42 exit at 4701 Brownsboro Rd., contains the tomb of Zachary Taylor, hero of the Mexican War and 12th president of the United States. Though born in Virginia, Taylor spent his childhood years on a farm near Louisville. **Hours:** Cemetery daily 24 hours. Office Mon.-Fri. 8-4:30. **Cost:** Free. **Phone:** (502) 893-3852.

Sightseeing

Boat Tours

The authentic 1914 stern-wheel steamboat *The Belle of Louisville*, reputedly the world's only Mississippi-style steamboat, and her sister vessel *The Spirit of Jefferson*, both docked at Louisville's 4th Street wharf, offer sightseeing, sunset, lunch and dinner cruises on the Ohio River; phone (502) 574-2992 or (866) 832-0011.

Carriage Tours

Louisville Horse Trams Inc. provides downtown horse and carriage sightseeing tours in surreys after 6 p.m. Monday through Friday (weather permitting) and Saturday and Sunday beginning at 4; phone (502) 581-0100.

Walking Tours

The city's 48-block Old Louisville neighborhood is a treasure-trove of more than 1,400 Victorian homes. The Historic Old Louisville Visitors Center at 1340 S. 4th St. in Central Park has literature for self-guiding walking tours that encompass the neighborhood's mansions; phone (502) 635-5244. This center is open Tues.-Fri. 1-5.

The Louisville Visitors Center, at Jefferson and Fourth streets across from the Kentucky International Convention Center, has maps and information about other sightseeing tours. A free 1-hour guided tour detailing the downtown civic district and the architectural features of Main Street's buildings departs May through October, weather permitting. A passport for Louisville's Urban Bourbon Trail, which consists of stops at some 26 local watering holes specializing in 50 to 165 bourbon varieties, also is available at the visitors center; the office is open Mon.-Sat. 10-5, Sun. noon-5. Phone (502) 379-6109 one day in advance for civic district tour schedule and reservations. The Main Street Visitors Center, 627 W. Main St., offers guided walking tours as well as brochures and information about the history of Main Street and its cast iron architecture; phone (502) 589-6008. The association is open Tues. and Fri. 11-3, Apr.-Nov., or by appointment; all tours are weather permitting.

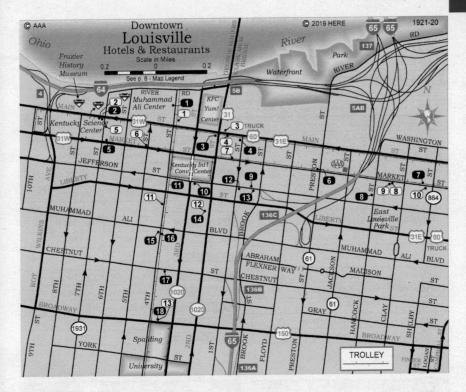

Downtown Louisville

This index helps you "spot" where hotels and restaurants are located on the corresponding detailed maps. Restaurant price range is a combination of lunch and/or dinner. Turn to the listing page for more information and consult display ads for special promotions.

 For more details, rates and reservations: AAA.com/travelguides/hotels

DOWNTOWN LOUISVILLE

Map Page	Hotels	Designation	Member Savings	Page
❶ this page	**Galt House Hotel Trademark Collection by Wyndham**	THREE DIAMOND	✔	92
❷ this page	21c Museum Hotel	FOUR DIAMOND		90
❸ this page	**Courtyard by Marriott Louisville Downtown**	THREE DIAMOND	✔	92
❹ this page	Aloft Louisville Downtown	THREE DIAMOND	✔	90
❺ this page	**Homewood Suites by Hilton Louisville Downtown**	THREE DIAMOND	✔	92
❻ this page	Residence Inn by Marriott Louisville Downtown	THREE DIAMOND	✔	93
❼ this page	**AC Hotel Louisville Downtown** *(See ad p. 91.)*	THREE DIAMOND	✔	90
❽ this page	Home2 Suites by Hilton Louisville Downtown NULU	THREE DIAMOND		92
❾ this page	Hampton Inn by Hilton Downtown	THREE DIAMOND	✔	92
❿ this page	**Louisville Marriott Downtown**	FOUR DIAMOND	✔	92
⓫ this page	**Hyatt Regency Louisville** *(See ad p. 93.)*	THREE DIAMOND	✔	92
⓬ this page	**Fairfield Inn & Suites by Marriott-Louisville Downtown**	THREE DIAMOND	✔	92
⓭ this page	**SpringHill Suites by Marriott Louisville Downtown**	THREE DIAMOND	✔	93

DOWNTOWN LOUISVILLE (cont'd)

Map Page	Hotels (cont'd)	Designation	Member Savings	Page
14 p. 85	Omni Louisville Hotel	FOUR DIAMOND		93
15 p. 85	The Seelbach Hilton Louisville	THREE DIAMOND	✔	93
16 p. 85	Embassy Suites by Hilton Louisville Downtown	FOUR DIAMOND	✔	92
17 p. 85	Hilton Garden Inn Louisville Downtown	THREE DIAMOND	✔	92
18 p. 85	The Brown Hotel (See ad p. 91.)	FOUR DIAMOND	✔	90

Map Page	Restaurants	Designation	Cuisine	Price Range	Page
1 p. 85	Jeff Ruby's	THREE DIAMOND	Steak Sushi	$22-$115	93
2 p. 85	Proof on Main	THREE DIAMOND	American	$12-$51	93
3 p. 85	Doc Crow's Southern Smokehouse & Raw Bar	APPROVED	Southern American	$9-$29	93
4 p. 85	Merle's Whiskey Kitchen	APPROVED	American	$4-$12	93
5 p. 85	Mussel & Burger Bar	THREE DIAMOND	Burgers	$10-$20	93
6 p. 85	Vincenzo's Restaurant	FOUR DIAMOND	Italian	$13-$43	94
7 p. 85	Saffron's Persian Restaurant	APPROVED	Persian	$9-$19	94
8 p. 85	Harvest	THREE DIAMOND	Regional American	$12-$50	93
9 p. 85	Toast on Market	APPROVED	American	$7-$13	94
10 p. 85	Royals Hot Chicken	APPROVED	Chicken	$7-$9	93
11 p. 85	Hard Rock Cafe	APPROVED	American	$10-$30 SAVE	93
12 p. 85	Neighborhood Services	APPROVED	American	$14-$28	93
13 p. 85	English Grill	FOUR DIAMOND	American	$23-$56	93

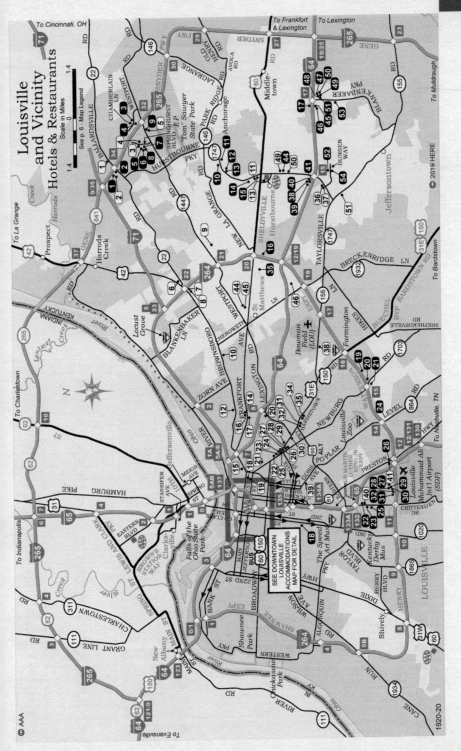

✈ Airport Hotels

Map Page	LOUISVILLE INTERNATIONAL AIRPORT (Maximum driving distance from airport: 2.6 mi)	Designation	Member Savings	Page
31 p. 87	Comfort Inn & Suites Airport/Expo, 1.0 mi	◈ APPROVED		94
27 p. 87	Crowne Plaza Louisville Airport, 0.8 mi	◈◈ THREE DIAMOND	✔	94
23 p. 87	Four Points by Sheraton Louisville Airport, 2.1 mi	◈◈ THREE DIAMOND	✔	94
30 p. 87	Hampton Inn by Hilton Louisville Airport/Fair Expo Center, 0.9 mi	◈ APPROVED	✔	94
22 p. 87	Hilton Garden Inn Louisville Airport, 2.2 mi	◈◈ THREE DIAMOND	✔	94
25 p. 87	Home2 Suites by Hilton Louisville Airport Expo Center, 2.6 mi	◈◈ THREE DIAMOND	✔	95
32 p. 87	Residence Inn by Marriott-Louisville Airport, 1.0 mi	◈◈ THREE DIAMOND	✔	95
28 p. 87	SpringHill Suites by Marriott-Louisville Airport, 0.9 mi	◈◈ THREE DIAMOND	✔	95
26 p. 87	SureStay PLUS Hotel by Best Western Louisville Airport Expo, 1.5 mi	◈ APPROVED		95
29 p. 87	Tru by Hilton Louisville Airport, 0.9 mi	◈ APPROVED	✔	95

Louisville and Vicinity

This index helps you "spot" where hotels and restaurants are located on the corresponding detailed maps. Restaurant price range is a combination of lunch and/or dinner. Turn to the listing page for more information and consult display ads for special promotions.

 For more details, rates and reservations: AAA.com/travelguides/hotels

LOUISVILLE

Map Page	Hotels	Designation	Member Savings	Page
1 p. 87	Hilton Garden Inn Louisville Northeast	◈◈ THREE DIAMOND	✔	94
2 p. 87	Drury Inn & Suites Louisville North	◈◈ THREE DIAMOND		94
3 p. 87	Holiday Inn Express Louisville Northeast	◈◈ THREE DIAMOND		95
4 p. 87	Hampton Inn by Hilton Louisville Northeast	◈◈ THREE DIAMOND	✔	94
5 p. 87	TownePlace Suites by Marriott Louisville Northeast	◈◈ THREE DIAMOND	✔	95
6 p. 87	Fairfield Inn & Suites Louisville Northeast	◈◈ THREE DIAMOND	✔	94
7 p. 87	Residence Inn by Marriott-Louisville NE	◈◈ THREE DIAMOND	✔	95
8 p. 87	Courtyard by Marriott-Louisville NE	◈◈ THREE DIAMOND	✔	94
9 p. 87	Aloft Louisville East	◈◈ THREE DIAMOND	✔	94
10 p. 87	Embassy Suites by Hilton Louisville East	◈◈ THREE DIAMOND	✔	94
11 p. 87	SpringHill Suites by Marriott Louisville Hurstbourne/North	◈◈ THREE DIAMOND	✔	95
12 p. 87	Home2 Suites by Hilton Louisville East/Hurstbourne	◈◈ THREE DIAMOND	✔	95
13 p. 87	Hampton Inn Louisville East/Hurstbourne	◈◈ THREE DIAMOND	✔	94
14 p. 87	Homewood Suites Louisville East	◈◈ THREE DIAMOND	✔	95
15 p. 87	Residence Inn by Marriott Louisville East	◈◈ THREE DIAMOND	✔	95
16 p. 87	Residence Inn by Marriott Louisville East/Oxmoor	◈◈ THREE DIAMOND	✔	95
17 p. 87	Staybridge Suites Louisville East	◈◈ THREE DIAMOND		95
18 p. 87	Central Park Bed & Breakfast	◈◈ THREE DIAMOND		94
19 p. 87	Wingate by Wyndham Fair & Expo Center	◈◈ THREE DIAMOND	✔	96
20 p. 87	Holiday Inn Express Louisville Airport Expo Center	◈◈ THREE DIAMOND	✔	95
21 p. 87	Red Roof Inn Louisville Fair And Expo	◈ APPROVED	✔	95
22 p. 87	Hilton Garden Inn Louisville Airport	◈◈ THREE DIAMOND	✔	94
23 p. 87	Four Points by Sheraton Louisville Airport	◈◈ THREE DIAMOND	✔	94
24 p. 87	Candlewood Suites Louisville Airport	◈ APPROVED		94
25 p. 87	Home2 Suites by Hilton Louisville Airport Expo Center	◈◈ THREE DIAMOND	✔	95

LOUISVILLE (cont'd)

Map Page	Hotels (cont'd)	Designation	Member Savings	Page
26 p. 87	SureStay PLUS Hotel by Best Western Louisville Airport Expo	APPROVED		95
27 p. 87	**Crowne Plaza Louisville Airport**	THREE DIAMOND	✔	94
28 p. 87	SpringHill Suites by Marriott-Louisville Airport	THREE DIAMOND	✔	95
29 p. 87	Tru by Hilton Louisville Airport	APPROVED	✔	95
30 p. 87	Hampton Inn by Hilton Louisville Airport/Fair Expo Center	APPROVED	✔	94
31 p. 87	Comfort Inn & Suites Airport/Expo	APPROVED		94
32 p. 87	Residence Inn by Marriott-Louisville Airport	THREE DIAMOND	✔	95

Map Page	Restaurants	Designation	Cuisine	Price Range	Page
1 p. 87	The Joy Luck	APPROVED	Asian	$9-$27	96
2 p. 87	Mitchell's Fish Market	THREE DIAMOND	Seafood	$12-$44 SAVE	96
3 p. 87	Cuvee Wine Table	APPROVED	Small Plates	$7-$15	96
4 p. 87	Fuji Japanese Steakhouse	APPROVED	Japanese	$8-$34	96
5 p. 87	Martin's Bar-B-Que Joint	APPROVED	Barbecue	$6-$18	96
6 p. 87	Con Huevos	APPROVED	Mexican	$8-$14	96
7 p. 87	Noosh Nosh	APPROVED	American	$7-$19	97
8 p. 87	Shady Lane Cafe	APPROVED	American	$6-$14	97
9 p. 87	Napa River Grill	THREE DIAMOND	Regional American	$12-$30	97
10 p. 87	Mesh	THREE DIAMOND	American	$13-$38	96
11 p. 87	Brasserie Provence	THREE DIAMOND	French	$12-$50	96
12 p. 87	Pat's Steak House	APPROVED	Steak	$20-$47	97
13 p. 87	Z's Oyster Bar & Steakhouse	THREE DIAMOND	Steak	$15-$75	97
14 p. 87	Con Huevos	APPROVED	Mexican	$8-$14	96
15 p. 87	Butchertown Grocery	THREE DIAMOND	American	$16-$65	96
16 p. 87	Irish Rover Restaurant	APPROVED	Irish	$7-$19	96
17 p. 87	Fork & Barrel	THREE DIAMOND	American	$15-$36	96
18 p. 87	Feast	APPROVED	Barbecue	$9-$20	96
19 p. 87	Rye	THREE DIAMOND	American	$12-$48	97
20 p. 87	Le Moo	APPROVED	American	$18-$99	96
21 p. 87	Ciao Ristorante	APPROVED	Italian	$13-$28	96
22 p. 87	Molly Malone's Irish Pub & Restaurant	APPROVED	Irish	$10-$20	96
23 p. 87	Jack Fry's	APPROVED	American	$11-$48	96
24 p. 87	Homemade Ice Cream and Pie Kitchen Deli	APPROVED	Deli Breads/ Pastries	$5-$8	96
25 p. 87	Gralehaus	APPROVED	Southern	$6-$13	96
26 p. 87	The Fat Lamb Modern Kitchen & Bar	THREE DIAMOND	American	$13-$41	96
27 p. 87	Stevens & Stevens Deli	APPROVED	Deli	$6-$8	97
28 p. 87	Ditto's Grill	APPROVED	American	$11-$42	96
29 p. 87	Lilly's	THREE DIAMOND	American	$12-$34	96
30 p. 87	The Eagle	APPROVED	Southern Chicken	$7-$20	96
31 p. 87	Seviche-A Latin Restaurant	THREE DIAMOND	Latin American	$21-$35	97
32 p. 87	Mark's Feed Store	APPROVED	Barbecue	$7-$23	96
34 p. 87	Uptown Cafe	APPROVED	American	$10-$30	97
35 p. 87	Superchefs	APPROVED	American	$6-$17	97
36 p. 87	Shalimar Restaurant	APPROVED	Northern Indian	$10-$17	97
37 p. 87	BoomBozz Craft Pizza & Taphouse	APPROVED	Pizza Sandwiches	$8-$23	96
38 p. 87	Queen of Sheba	APPROVED	Ethiopian	$7-$15	97
39 p. 87	Couvillion	THREE DIAMOND	Cajun	$4-$26	96
40 p. 87	Cardinal Hall of Fame Cafe	APPROVED	American	$8-$25	96

Map Page	Restaurants (cont'd)	Designation	Cuisine	Price Range	Page
㊶ p. 87	Mirage Mediterranean Restaurant	APPROVED	Mediterranean	$7-$16	96

ST. MATTHEWS

Map Page	Hotel	Designation	Member Savings	Page
㉟ p. 87	Hilton Garden Inn Louisville Mall of St Matthews	THREE DIAMOND	✔	109

Map Page	Restaurants	Designation	Cuisine	Price Range	Page
㊹ p. 87	Del Frisco's Restaurant	APPROVED	Steak	$22-$50	109
㊺ p. 87	Equus Restaurant	THREE DIAMOND	New American	$14-$39	109
㊻ p. 87	Wild Eggs	APPROVED	American	$8-$15	109

HURSTBOURNE

Map Page	Hotels	Designation	Member Savings	Page
㊳ p. 87	Drury Inn & Suites-Louisville	THREE DIAMOND		53
㊴ p. 87	**Red Roof Inn Louisville East - Hurstbourne**	APPROVED	✔	54
㊵ p. 87	**Courtyard by Marriott Louisville East**	THREE DIAMOND	✔	53
㊶ p. 87	Baymont Inn & Suites Louisville East	APPROVED		53

JEFFERSONTOWN

Map Page	Hotels	Designation	Member Savings	Page
㊹ p. 87	**Hyatt Place Louisville-East**	THREE DIAMOND	✔	54
㊺ p. 87	**Country Inn & Suites by Radisson-Louisville East**	APPROVED	✔	54
㊻ p. 87	Microtel Inn by Wyndham Louisville East	APPROVED		54
㊼ p. 87	Hampton Inn & Suites by Hilton Louisville East	THREE DIAMOND	✔	54
㊽ p. 87	Holiday Inn Express Hotel & Suites Louisville East	THREE DIAMOND		54
㊾ p. 87	La Quinta Inn & Suites Louisville	THREE DIAMOND		54
㊿ p. 87	Wingate by Wyndham	THREE DIAMOND		54
(51) p. 87	Hilton Garden Inn-Louisville East	THREE DIAMOND	✔	54
(52) p. 87	Marriott Louisville East	FOUR DIAMOND	✔	54
(53) p. 87	Hawthorn Suites by Wyndham Louisville/Jeffersontown	APPROVED		54
(54) p. 87	**Best Western Louisville East**	APPROVED	✔	54

Map Page	Restaurants	Designation	Cuisine	Price Range	Page
㊾ p. 87	Bonefish Grill	THREE DIAMOND	Seafood	$15-$32	54
㊿ p. 87	Brick House Tavern & Tap	APPROVED	American	$10-$38	54
(51) p. 87	Mussel & Burger Bar	APPROVED	Burgers	$10-$20	54

DOWNTOWN LOUISVILLE

- **Restaurants p. 93**
- **Hotels & Restaurants map & index p. 85**

21C MUSEUM HOTEL 502/217-6300 ②

FOUR DIAMOND Boutique Contemporary Hotel. **Address:** 700 W Main St 40202

AC HOTEL LOUISVILLE DOWNTOWN 502/568-6880 ⑦

THREE DIAMOND

Hotel

AAA Benefit: Members save 5% or more!

Address: 727 E Market St 40202 **Location:** I-65 exit 136C, to Brook St, then E Market St. **Facility:** 156 units. 5 stories, interior corridors. **Parking:** on-site (fee) and valet. **Amenities:** safes. **Activities:** exercise room. **Guest Services:** valet and coin laundry. *(See ad p. 91.)*

SAVE CALL BIZ HS

ALOFT LOUISVILLE DOWNTOWN 502/583-1888 ④

THREE DIAMOND SAVE Boutique Contemporary Hotel. **Address:** 102 W Main St 40202

AAA Benefit: Members save 5% or more!

THE BROWN HOTEL 502/583-1234 ⑱

FOUR DIAMOND

Historic Hotel

Address: 335 W Broadway 40202 **Location:** I-65 exit 136C (Jefferson St) southbound; exit 136A (Broadway) northbound, 1 mi s on 4th St; corner of 4th St and Broadway. **Facility:** Built in 1923, this restored hotel features marble floors, elaborate plaster ceilings, chandeliers and intricately carved European antique furniture. Rooms have a handsome décor. 293 units, some two bedrooms. 16 stories, interior corridors. **Parking:** on-site (fee) and valet. **Terms:** check-in 4 pm. **Amenities:** safes. **Dining:** 2 restaurants, also, English Grill, see separate listing. **Activities:** exercise room. **Guest Services:** valet laundry, boarding pass kiosk, area transportation. Affiliated with Preferred Hotels & Resorts. *(See ad p. 91.)*

SAVE BIZ HS / SOME UNITS

▼ See AAA listing p. 90 ▼

AC HOTEL LOUISVILLE DOWNTOWN

NuLu District, near Churchill Downs

Our AC Hotel reflects the soul of the city while offering trendy accommodations.

Great location for horse lovers, fans of the Urban Bourbon Trail & anyone looking for an upscale Louisville hotel.

Enjoy a Spanish twist on breakfast, serve up tapas & handcrafted cocktails in our AC Lounge.

502.568.6880
www.achotellouisville.com
727 East Market Street, Louisville, KY

▼ See AAA listing p. 90 ▼

ℬREATHTAKING

"Top 10 Hotels in the South"

"I love a grand hotel. I adore sweeping into a lavish lobby that looks as though it came straight from a 1930's movie set. Few places offer such sparkling accommodations."
– SOUTHERN LIVING MAGAZINE

The BROWN HOTEL

Complimentary Airport Shuttle. Complimentary Wireless Internet.
(888) 888-5252 • Fourth & Broadway • Louisville, KY 40202

AAA Members
Up to 15% Off

HISTORIC HOTELS of AMERICA
NATIONAL TRUST FOR HISTORIC PRESERVATION

LIFESTYLE
Preferred
HOTELS & RESORTS

*Discount off prevailing rate. Subject to availability. Excludes special events. Not available for group or promotional rates. AAA card required at check-in. Visit us at www.aaa.com and www.brownhotel.com

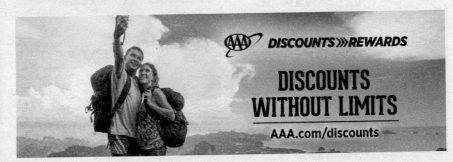

(See map & index p. 85.)

COURTYARD BY MARRIOTT LOUISVILLE DOWNTOWN
502/562-0200 **3**

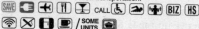

Hotel

COURTYARD'

AAA Benefit: Members save 5% or more!

Address: 100 S 2nd St 40202 **Location:** I-65 exit 136B (Brooks St) northbound; exit 136C (Jefferson St) southbound, just w, then just n. **Facility:** 140 units. 8 stories, interior corridors. **Parking:** on-site (fee). **Amenities:** safes. **Pool:** heated indoor. **Activities:** exercise room. **Guest Services:** valet and coin laundry, boarding pass kiosk, area transportation.

EMBASSY SUITES BY HILTON LOUISVILLE DOWNTOWN
502/813-3800 **16**

FOUR DIAMOND

Historic Boutique Hotel

EMBASSY SUITES **AAA Benefit:** Members save up to 15%!

Address: 501 S Fourth St 40202 **Location:** I-65 exit 136C (Muhammad Ali Blvd), 0.3 mi w, then just s. **Facility:** Built in 1907 as a department store, this building has been reincarnated as a sparkling new hotel featuring spacious, modern guest rooms appointed with dark hardwood furniture and silken white linens. 304 units. 7 stories, interior corridors. **Parking:** valet only. **Amenities:** safes. **Pool:** heated indoor. **Activities:** game room, exercise room. **Guest Services:** valet and coin laundry. **Featured Amenity: full hot breakfast.**

FAIRFIELD INN & SUITES BY MARRIOTT-LOUISVILLE DOWNTOWN
502/569-3553 **12**

THREE DIAMOND

Hotel

Fairfield **AAA Benefit:** Members save 5% or more!

Address: 100 E Jefferson St 40202 **Location:** I-65 exit 136B (Brooks St), just w. **Facility:** 140 units. 6 stories, interior corridors. **Parking:** on-site (fee). **Pool:** indoor. **Activities:** exercise room. **Guest Services:** valet and coin laundry. **Featured Amenity: full hot breakfast.**

GALT HOUSE HOTEL TRADEMARK COLLECTION BY WYNDHAM
502/589-5200 **1**

THREE DIAMOND

Hotel

Address: 140 N 4th St 40202 **Location:** Waterfront. I-64 exit 5B (3rd St), 0.5 mi w. **Facility:** 1239 units, some two bedrooms. 18-25 stories, interior corridors. **Parking:** on-site (fee) and valet. **Amenities:** Some: safes. **Dining:** 6 restaurants. **Pool:** outdoor. **Activities:** sauna, health club, spa. **Guest Services:** valet laundry, boarding pass kiosk.

HAMPTON INN BY HILTON DOWNTOWN
502/585-2200 **9**

THREE DIAMOND Hotel. **Address:** 101 E Jefferson St 40202

AAA Benefit: Members save up to 15%!

HILTON GARDEN INN LOUISVILLE DOWNTOWN
502/584-5175 **17**

THREE DIAMOND Hotel. **Address:** 350 W Chestnut St 40202

AAA Benefit: Members save up to 15%!

HOME2 SUITES BY HILTON LOUISVILLE DOWNTOWN NULU
502/561-0460 **8**

THREE DIAMOND Extended Stay Hotel. **Address:** 240 S Hancock St 40202

HOMEWOOD SUITES BY HILTON LOUISVILLE DOWNTOWN
502/589-2000 **5**

THREE DIAMOND

Extended Stay Hotel

HOMEWOOD SUITES BY HILTON **AAA Benefit:** Members save up to 15%!

Address: 635 Market St 40202 **Location:** Jct of W Market and S 7th sts. **Facility:** 133 efficiencies. 8 stories, interior corridors. **Parking:** on-site (fee) and valet. **Terms:** check-in 4 pm. **Pool:** indoor. **Activities:** exercise room. **Guest Services:** valet and coin laundry.

HYATT REGENCY LOUISVILLE
502/581-1234 **11**

THREE DIAMOND

Hotel

HYATT REGENCY' **AAA Benefit:** Members save up to 10%!

Address: 320 W Jefferson St 40202 **Location:** At 3rd and Jefferson sts. **Facility:** 393 units. 20 stories, interior corridors. **Parking:** on-site (fee) and valet. **Terms:** check-in 4 pm. **Amenities:** safes. **Dining:** 2 restaurants. **Pool:** heated indoor. **Activities:** tennis, exercise room, in-room exercise equipment. **Guest Services:** valet laundry, boarding pass kiosk. *(See ad p. 93.)*

LOUISVILLE MARRIOTT DOWNTOWN
502/627-5045 **10**

FOUR DIAMOND

Hotel

MARRIOTT **AAA Benefit:** Members save 5% or more!

Address: 280 W Jefferson St 40202 **Location:** At 2nd and Jefferson sts. **Facility:** This hotel has excellent paneling, artwork and ceiling enhancements in its lobby and ballrooms. Rooms have a cool color scheme with upscale furnishings and an enhanced television package. 620 units. 17 stories, interior corridors. **Parking:** on-site (fee) and valet. **Terms:** check-in 4 pm. **Pool:** heated indoor. **Activities:** hot tub, exercise room, massage. **Guest Services:** valet and coin laundry, boarding pass kiosk.

(See map & index p. 85.)

OMNI LOUISVILLE HOTEL   502/656-7220   **14**
FOUR DIAMOND Hotel. **Address:** 400 S 2nd St 40202

RESIDENCE INN BY MARRIOTT LOUISVILLE DOWNTOWN
502/589-8998   **6**

| **THREE DIAMOND** SAVE Extended Stay Hotel. **Address:** 333 E Market St 40202 | **AAA Benefit:** Members save 5% or more! |

THE SEELBACH HILTON LOUISVILLE   502/585-3200   **15**

| **THREE DIAMOND** SAVE Historic Hotel. **Address:** 500 4th St 40202 | **AAA Benefit:** Members save up to 15%! |

SPRINGHILL SUITES BY MARRIOTT LOUISVILLE DOWNTOWN
502/569-7373   **13**

| **THREE DIAMOND** Hotel | SPRINGHILL SUITES MARRIOTT | **AAA Benefit:** Members save 5% or more! |

Address: 132 E Jefferson St 40202 **Location:** I-65 exit 136B (Brooks St), just w. **Facility:** 198 units. 9 stories, interior corridors. **Parking:** on-site (fee). **Pool:** heated indoor. **Activities:** exercise room. **Guest Services:** valet and coin laundry. **Featured Amenity:** breakfast buffet.

SAVE 🍴↑ CALL 🚭 🏊 ♿ BIZ
HS 📶 ✕ 🛗 🖥 🖨

WHERE TO EAT

DOC CROW'S SOUTHERN SMOKEHOUSE & RAW BAR
502/587-1626   **3**
APPROVED Southern American. Gastropub. **Address:** 127 W Main St 40202

ENGLISH GRILL   502/583-1234   **13**
FOUR DIAMOND
American Fine Dining
$23-$56
AAA Inspector Notes: *Historic.* This restaurant's seasonal menu features sophisticated, imaginative preparations. Start with an appetizer of shrimp and grits or a Caesar salad prepared tableside. Good entrée choices include the rack of lamb with dried cherry reduction, the Verlasso salmon and the Berkshire pork chop with collard greens. For dessert, try the restaurant's version of bananas Foster, a dessert prepared tableside and topped with flaming bourbon. **Features:** full bar. **Reservations:** suggested. Semiformal attire. **Address:** 335 W Broadway 40202 **Location:** I-65 exit 136C (Jefferson St) southbound; exit 136A (Broadway) northbound, 1 mi s on 4th St; corner of 4th St and Broadway; in The Brown Hotel. **Parking:** valet only. **D**

HARD ROCK CAFE   502/568-2202   **11**
APPROVED SAVE American. Casual Dining. **Address:** 424 S 4th St 40202

HARVEST   502/384-9090   **8**
THREE DIAMOND Regional American. Casual Dining. **Address:** 624 E Market St 40202

JEFF RUBY'S   502/584-0102   **1**
THREE DIAMOND Steak Sushi. Fine Dining. **Address:** 325 W Main St 40202

MERLE'S WHISKEY KITCHEN   502/290-8888   **4**
APPROVED American. Casual Dining. **Address:** 122 W Main St 40202

MUSSEL & BURGER BAR   502/749-6451   **5**
THREE DIAMOND Burgers. Gastropub. **Address:** 113 S 7th St 40202

NEIGHBORHOOD SERVICES   502/313-6664   **12**
APPROVED American. Casual Dining. **Address:** 400 S 2nd St 40202

PROOF ON MAIN   502/217-6360   **2**
THREE DIAMOND American. Casual Dining. **Address:** 702 W Main St 40202

ROYALS HOT CHICKEN   502/919-7068   **10**
APPROVED Chicken. Quick Serve. **Address:** 736 E Market St 40202

▼ See AAA listing p. 92 ▼

(See map & index p. 85.)

SAFFRON'S PERSIAN RESTAURANT 502/584-7800 ⑦
▼ APPROVED Persian. Casual Dining. **Address:** 131 W Market St 40202

TOAST ON MARKET 502/569-4099 ⑨
▼ APPROVED American. Casual Dining. **Address:** 620 E Market St 40202

VINCENZO'S RESTAURANT 502/580-1350 ⑥
▼ FOUR DIAMOND **AAA Inspector Notes:** *Historic.* This restaurant is located in an imposing, classically designed former-bank building built in 1860. The restaurant has sophisticated décor, including a large, open entry area, upscale table settings and intimate lighting. The style of service is very formal and many dishes are prepared tableside. A specialty entrée is the "Veal Madeira."
Italian
Fine Dining
$13-$43
Features: full bar. **Reservations:** suggested. Semiformal attire. **Address:** 150 S 5th St 40202 **Location:** Corner of 5th and Market sts. **Parking:** valet and street only. Ⓛ Ⓓ

LOUISVILLE
• Restaurants p. 96
• Hotels & Restaurants map & index p. 87

ALOFT LOUISVILLE EAST 502/429-9901 ⑨
▼ THREE DIAMOND SAVE Hotel. **Address:** 10700 Westport Rd 40241
AAA Benefit:
Members save 5% or more!

CANDLEWOOD SUITES LOUISVILLE AIRPORT 502/357-3577 ㉔
▼ APPROVED Extended Stay Hotel. **Address:** 1367 Gardiner Ln 40213

CENTRAL PARK BED & BREAKFAST 502/638-1505 ⑱
▼ THREE DIAMOND Historic Bed & Breakfast. **Address:** 1353 S 4th St 40208

COMFORT INN & SUITES AIRPORT/EXPO 502/375-2233 ㉛
▼ APPROVED Hotel. **Address:** 653 Phillips Ln 40209

COMFORT SUITES LOUISVILLE AIRPORT 502/964-0740
▼ THREE DIAMOND Hotel. **Address:** 6535 Paramount Park Dr 40213

COURTYARD BY MARRIOTT-LOUISVILLE NE 502/429-9293 ⑧
▼ THREE DIAMOND
Hotel
COURTYARD **AAA Benefit:** Members save 5% or more!
Address: 10200 Champion Farms Dr 40241 **Location:** I-265 exit 32, 0.7 mi w on Westport Rd, then just n. **Facility:** 114 units. 4 stories, interior corridors. **Pool:** heated indoor. **Activities:** hot tub, exercise room. **Guest Services:** valet and coin laundry, boarding pass kiosk.
SAVE 🛏 🍽 CALL ⚬ 👪 BIZ 🛜 ✖ 🐾 ⦿ ⊟ ⊡

CROWNE PLAZA LOUISVILLE AIRPORT 502/367-2251 ㉗
▼ THREE DIAMOND
Hotel
Address: 830 Phillips Ln 40209 **Location:** I-264 exit 11 (Fairgrounds/Expo Center Main Gate). **Facility:** 588 units, some two and three bedrooms. 6-8 stories, interior corridors. **Pool:** heated indoor. **Activities:** exercise room. **Guest Services:** valet laundry, area transportation.
SAVE ⊞ 🍽 👪 🍽 CALL ⚬ ⊠ 👪 BIZ HS 🛜 ✖ ⊡
/SOME UNITS 🐾 ⊟

DRURY INN & SUITES LOUISVILLE NORTH 502/425-5500 ②
▼ THREE DIAMOND Hotel. **Address:** 9597 Brownsboro Rd 40241

EMBASSY SUITES BY HILTON LOUISVILLE EAST 502/426-9191 ⑩
▼ THREE DIAMOND SAVE Hotel. **Address:** 9940 Corporate Campus Dr 40223
AAA Benefit: Members save up to 15%!

FAIRFIELD INN & SUITES LOUISVILLE NORTHEAST 502/637-1200 ⑥
▼ THREE DIAMOND SAVE Hotel. **Address:** 10110 Champions Farm Dr 40241
AAA Benefit: Members save 5% or more!

FOUR POINTS BY SHERATON LOUISVILLE AIRPORT 502/753-5555 ㉓
▼ THREE DIAMOND
Hotel
FOUR POINTS BY SHERATON **AAA Benefit:** Members save 5% or more!

Address: 2850 Crittenden Dr 40209 **Location:** I-65 exit 132, 0.6 mi s. **Facility:** 117 units, some two bedrooms. 6 stories, interior corridors. **Amenities:** safes. **Pool:** heated indoor. **Activities:** exercise room. **Guest Services:** valet and coin laundry, area transportation.
SAVE ⊞ 🍽 ⦿ CALL ⚬ 🐾
👪 BIZ HS 🛜 ✖ ⊟ ⊡
/SOME UNITS 🐾

HAMPTON INN BY HILTON LOUISVILLE AIRPORT/FAIR EXPO CENTER 502/366-8100 ㉚
▼ APPROVED SAVE Hotel. **Address:** 800 Phillips Ln 40209
AAA Benefit: Members save up to 15%!

HAMPTON INN BY HILTON LOUISVILLE NORTHEAST 502/327-8880 ④
▼ THREE DIAMOND SAVE Hotel. **Address:** 4100 Hampton Lake Way 40241
AAA Benefit: Members save up to 15%!

HAMPTON INN LOUISVILLE EAST/HURSTBOURNE 502/426-1822 ⑬
▼ THREE DIAMOND SAVE Hotel. **Address:** 1150 Forest Bridge Road Building B 40223
AAA Benefit: Members save up to 15%!

HILTON GARDEN INN LOUISVILLE AIRPORT 502/637-2424 ㉒
▼ THREE DIAMOND SAVE Hotel. **Address:** 2735 Crittenden Dr 40209
AAA Benefit: Members save up to 15%!

HILTON GARDEN INN LOUISVILLE NORTHEAST 502/423-0018 ①
▼ THREE DIAMOND SAVE Hotel. **Address:** 9850 Park Plaza Ave 40241
AAA Benefit: Members save up to 15%!

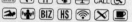

(See map & index p. 87.)

HOLIDAY INN EXPRESS LOUISVILLE AIRPORT EXPO CENTER
502/456-4411 **20**

THREE DIAMOND
Hotel

Address: 1921 Bishop Ln 40218 **Location:** I-264 exit 15 eastbound; exit 15B westbound, 0.3 mi s. **Facility:** 150 units. 4 stories, interior corridors. **Amenities:** safes. **Pool:** outdoor. **Activities:** exercise room. **Guest Services:** complimentary laundry. **Featured Amenity: full hot breakfast.**

SAVE ⬦ CALL ⬦ ⬦ ⬦ BIZ
⬦ ⬦ ⬦ ⬦ ⬦

HOLIDAY INN EXPRESS LOUISVILLE NORTHEAST
502/814-0004 **3**

THREE DIAMOND Hotel. **Address:** 3711 Chamberlain Ln 40241

HOLIDAY INN LOUISVILLE AIRPORT SOUTH
502/966-0000

THREE DIAMOND Hotel. **Address:** 6551 Paramount Park Dr 40213

HOME2 SUITES BY HILTON LOUISVILLE AIRPORT EXPO CENTER
502/916-3800 **25**

THREE DIAMOND SAVE Extended Stay Hotel. **Address:** 3000 Crittenden Dr 40209

AAA Benefit: Members save up to 15%!

HOME2 SUITES BY HILTON LOUISVILLE EAST/HURSTBOURNE
502/326-3824 **12**

THREE DIAMOND SAVE Extended Stay Hotel. **Address:** 1150 Forest Bridge Rd, Building A 40223

AAA Benefit: Members save up to 15%!

HOMEWOOD SUITES LOUISVILLE EAST
502/429-9070 **14**

THREE DIAMOND SAVE Extended Stay Hotel. **Address:** 9401 Hurstbourne Trace 40222

AAA Benefit: Members save up to 15%!

RED ROOF INN LOUISVILLE FAIR AND EXPO
502/456-2993 **21**

APPROVED
Hotel

Address: 3322 Red Roof Inn Pl 40218 **Location:** I-264 exit 15 eastbound; exit 15B westbound, 0.3 mi s. **Facility:** 110 units. 3 stories, exterior corridors. **Amenities:** safes. **Guest Services:** coin laundry.

SAVE ⬦ HS ⬦ ⬦ ⬦
/SOME UNITS ⬦ ⬦ ⬦ ⬦

RESIDENCE INN BY MARRIOTT-LOUISVILLE AIRPORT
502/363-8800 **32**

THREE DIAMOND SAVE Extended Stay Hotel. **Address:** 700 Phillips Ln 40209

AAA Benefit: Members save 5% or more!

RESIDENCE INN BY MARRIOTT LOUISVILLE EAST
502/425-1821 **15**

THREE DIAMOND SAVE Extended Stay Hotel. **Address:** 120 N Hurstbourne Pkwy 40222

AAA Benefit: Members save 5% or more!

RESIDENCE INN BY MARRIOTT LOUISVILLE EAST/OXMOOR
502/409-8071 **16**

THREE DIAMOND SAVE Extended Stay Contemporary Hotel. **Address:** 401 Bullitt Ln 40222

AAA Benefit: Members save 5% or more!

RESIDENCE INN BY MARRIOTT-LOUISVILLE NE
502/412-1311 **7**

THREE DIAMOND
Extended Stay Hotel

Residence INN **AAA Benefit:** Members save 5% or more!

Address: 3500 Springhurst Commons Dr 40241 **Location:** I-265 exit 32, 0.7 mi w on Westport Rd, then just n. **Facility:** 102 units, some two bedrooms, efficiencies and kitchens. 4 stories, interior corridors. **Pool:** hot tub, exercise room. **Guest Services:** valet and coin laundry. **Featured Amenity: breakfast buffet.**

SAVE ⬦ CALL ⬦ ⬦ ⬦ BIZ
⬦ ⬦ ⬦ ⬦ ⬦ ⬦ /SOME UNITS ⬦

SPRINGHILL SUITES BY MARRIOTT-LOUISVILLE AIRPORT
502/361-9009 **28**

THREE DIAMOND SAVE Hotel. **Address:** 820 Phillips Ln 40209

AAA Benefit: Members save 5% or more!

SPRINGHILL SUITES BY MARRIOTT LOUISVILLE HURSTBOURNE/NORTH
502/326-3895 **11**

THREE DIAMOND SAVE Hotel. **Address:** 10101 Forest Green Blvd 40223

AAA Benefit: Members save 5% or more!

STAYBRIDGE SUITES LOUISVILLE EAST
502/244-9511 **17**

THREE DIAMOND Extended Stay Hotel. **Address:** 11711 Gateworth Way 40299

SURESTAY PLUS HOTEL BY BEST WESTERN LOUISVILLE AIRPORT EXPO
502/368-0007 **26**

APPROVED Hotel. **Address:** 4125 Preston Hwy 40213

TOWNEPLACE SUITES BY MARRIOTT LOUISVILLE AIRPORT
502/749-6634

THREE DIAMOND SAVE Extended Stay Hotel. **Address:** 6601 Paramount Park Dr 40213

AAA Benefit: Members save 5% or more!

TOWNEPLACE SUITES BY MARRIOTT LOUISVILLE NORTHEAST
502/339-5410 **5**

THREE DIAMOND SAVE Extended Stay Hotel. **Address:** 10110 Champions Farm Dr 40241

AAA Benefit: Members save 5% or more!

TRU BY HILTON LOUISVILLE AIRPORT
502/792-8800 **29**

APPROVED SAVE Hotel. **Address:** 810 Phillips Ln 40209

Members save up to 15%!

🔗 **What's for dinner?**

AAA.com/travelguides/restaurants

(See map & index p. 87.)

WINGATE BY WYNDHAM FAIR & EXPO CENTER
502/473-0000 [19]

THREE DIAMOND | **Motel** | Address: 3200 Kemmons Dr 40218 Location: I-264 exit 15, 0.3 mi s to Goldsmith Ln, 0.5 mi e to Kemmons Dr, then 1 blk n. Facility: 107 units. 5 stories, interior corridors. Pool: heated outdoor. Guest Services: coin laundry. Featured Amenity: full hot breakfast.

/SOME UNITS

WHERE TO EAT

BOOMBOZZ CRAFT PIZZA & TAPHOUSE 502/491-4111 [37]
APPROVED Pizza Sandwiches. Casual Dining. Address: 1890 S Hurstbourne Pkwy 40220

BRASSERIE PROVENCE 502/883-3153 [11]
THREE DIAMOND French. Casual Dining. Address: 150 N Hurstbourne Pkwy 40222

BUTCHERTOWN GROCERY 502/742-8315 [15]
THREE DIAMOND American. Casual Dining. Address: 1076 E Washington St 40206

CARDINAL HALL OF FAME CAFE 502/635-8686 [40]
APPROVED American. Sports Bar. Address: 2745 Crittenden Dr 40209

CIAO RISTORANTE 502/690-3532 [21]
APPROVED Italian. Casual Dining. Address: 1201 Payne St 40204

CON HUEVOS 502/384-3744 [14]
APPROVED Mexican. Quick Serve. Address: 2339 Frankfort Ave 40206

CON HUEVOS 502/384-3744 [6]
APPROVED Mexican. Quick Serve. Address: 4938 US-42 40222

COUVILLION 502/365-1813 [39]
THREE DIAMOND Cajun. Casual Dining. Address: 1318 McHenry St 40217

CUVEE WINE TABLE 502/242-5200 [3]
APPROVED Small Plates. Casual Dining. Address: 3598 Springhurst Blvd 40241

DITTO'S GRILL 502/581-9129 [28]
APPROVED American. Casual Dining. Address: 1114 Bardstown Rd 40204

THE EAGLE 502/498-8420 [30]
APPROVED Southern Chicken. Casual Dining. Address: 1314 Bardstown Rd 40204

EL NOPAL
APPROVED Mexican. Casual Dining.
LOCATIONS:
Address: 9451 Westport Rd 40241 Phone: 502/327-6551
Address: 4214 Outer Loop 40219 Phone: 502/968-2566
Address: 3945 Taylorsville Rd 40220 Phone: 502/459-9061

EL NOPAL 502/961-9851
APPROVED Mexican. Casual Dining. Address: 11336 Preston Hwy 40229

THE FAT LAMB MODERN KITCHEN & BAR
502/409-7499 [26]
THREE DIAMOND American. Casual Dining. Address: 2011 Grinstead Dr 40204

FEAST 502/749-9900 [18]
APPROVED Barbecue. Quick Serve. Address: 909 E Market St 40206

FORK & BARREL 502/907-3675 [17]
THREE DIAMOND American. Casual Dining. Address: 2244 Frankfort Ave 40206

FUJI JAPANESE STEAKHOUSE 502/339-1978 [4]
APPROVED Japanese. Casual Dining. Address: 3576 Springhurst Blvd 40241

GANDER, AN AMERICAN GRILL 502/915-8484
APPROVED American. Casual Dining. Address: 111 S English Station Rd 40233

GRALEHAUS 502/454-7075 [25]
APPROVED Southern. Quick Serve. Address: 1001 Baxter Ave 40204

HOMEMADE ICE CREAM AND PIE KITCHEN DELI
502/618-3380 [24]
APPROVED Deli Breads/Pastries. Quick Serve. Address: 1041 Bardstown Rd 40204

THE HUNGRY PELICAN 502/239-7145
APPROVED Seafood. Casual Dining. Address: 5412 Bardstown Rd 40291

IRISH ROVER RESTAURANT 502/899-3544 [16]
APPROVED Irish. Gastropub. Address: 2319 Frankfort Ave 40206

JACK FRY'S 502/452-9244 [23]
APPROVED American. Casual Dining. Address: 1007 Bardstown Rd 40204

THE JOY LUCK 502/618-1601 [1]
APPROVED Asian. Casual Dining. Address: 9850 Von Allmen Ct 40241

LE MOO 502/458-8888 [20]
APPROVED American. Casual Dining. Address: 2300 Lexington Rd 40206

LILLY'S 502/451-0447 [29]
THREE DIAMOND American. Fine Dining. Address: 1147 Bardstown Rd 40204

MARK'S FEED STORE 502/458-1570 [32]
APPROVED Barbecue. Casual Dining. Address: 1514 Bardstown Rd 40205

MARTINI ITALIAN BISTRO 502/394-9797
APPROVED Italian. Casual Dining. Address: 4021 Summit Plaza Dr 40241

MARTIN'S BAR-B-QUE JOINT 502/242-4666 [5]
APPROVED Barbecue. Quick Serve. Address: 3408 Indian Lake Dr 40241

MESH 502/632-4421 [10]
THREE DIAMOND American. Casual Dining. Address: 3608 Brownsboro Rd 40207

MIRAGE MEDITERRANEAN RESTAURANT
502/363-7788 [41]
APPROVED Mediterranean. Casual Dining. Address: 4100 Preston Hwy 40213

MITCHELL'S FISH MARKET 502/412-1818 [2]
THREE DIAMOND SAVE Seafood. Casual Dining. Address: 4031 Summit Plaza Dr 40241

MOLLY MALONE'S IRISH PUB & RESTAURANT
502/473-1222 [22]
APPROVED Irish. Casual Dining. Address: 933 Baxter Ave 40204

(See map & index p. 87.)

NAPA RIVER GRILL   502/423-5822 (9)
THREE DIAMOND Regional American. Casual Dining.
Address: 1211 Herr Ln 40222

NOOSH NOSH   502/205-2888 (7)
APPROVED American. Casual Dining. **Address:** 4816
Brownsboro Center 40207

PAT'S STEAK HOUSE   502/893-2062 (12)
APPROVED Steak. Casual Dining. **Address:** 2437
Brownsboro Rd 40206

QUEEN OF SHEBA   502/459-6301 (38)
APPROVED Ethiopian. Casual Dining. **Address:** 2804
Taylorsville Rd 40205

RYE   502/749-6200 (19)
THREE DIAMOND American. Casual Dining. **Address:** 900
E Market St 40206

SEVICHE-A LATIN RESTAURANT   502/473-8560 (31)
THREE DIAMOND Latin American. Fine Dining. **Address:**
1538 Bardstown Rd 40205

SHADY LANE CAFE   502/893-5118 (8)
APPROVED American. Quick Serve. **Address:** 4806
Brownsboro Center 40207

SHALIMAR RESTAURANT   502/493-8899 (36)
APPROVED Northern Indian. Casual Dining. **Address:**
1850 S Hurstbourne Pkwy 40220

STEVENS & STEVENS DELI   502/584-3354 (27)
APPROVED Deli. Quick Serve. **Address:** 1114
Bardstown Rd 40204

SUPERCHEFS   502/409-8103 (35)
APPROVED American. Casual Dining. **Address:** 1702
Bardstown Rd 40205

UPTOWN CAFE   502/458-4212 (34)
APPROVED American. Casual Dining. **Address:** 1624
Bardstown Rd 40205

Z'S OYSTER BAR & STEAKHOUSE   502/429-8000 (13)
THREE DIAMOND Steak. Fine Dining. **Address:** 101
Whittington Pkwy 40222

Nearby Indiana

CLARKSVILLE pop. 21,724, elev. 456'
• Part of Louisville area — see map p. 71

Clarksville was established in 1783 on land granted
to Col. George Rogers Clark and his men, who de-
fended the territory from British assaults 1778-79.
Clark strategically positioned an outpost at the head of
an unnavigable section of the Ohio River—2.5 miles of
cascading rapids, or cataract falls, created by rock
reefs. Though they provided a natural defense, the
falls of the Ohio impeded early commerce. Goods had
to be portaged around until the Portland Canal was
completed at Louisville in 1830.

In 1803 Clark's brother William met up with Corps of
Discovery co-commander Meriwether Lewis in Clarksville to make final preparations for the historic expedition to the Pacific Ocean. The Lewis and Clark Park,
off Harrison Avenue, features interpretive panels detailing the journey; a half-scale replica of the keelboat
the explorers used also is on the grounds.

Falls of the Ohio National Wildlife Conservation
Area, more than 1,400 acres of river bottom between Indiana and Kentucky, contains a coral reef of
great geologic importance. Overlooking the conservation area is Falls of the Ohio State Park.

Shopping: Green Tree Mall, on SR 131, is anchored by Dillard's, JCPenney and Sears.

BEST WESTERN GREEN TREE INN   812/288-9281
APPROVED
Motel

BW **Best Western.** **AAA Benefit:** Members save up to 15% and earn bonus points!

Address: 1425 Broadway St 47129 **Location:** I-65 exit 4, just w. **Facility:** 102
units. 1 story, exterior corridors. **Parking:**
winter plug-ins. **Activities:** exercise
room. **Guest Services:** coin laundry.

CANDLEWOOD SUITES LOUISVILLE NORTH
                                      812/284-6113
APPROVED
Extended Stay
Hotel

Address: 1419 Bales Ln 47129 **Location:** I-65 exit 4, just w, then just n on
Broadway St. **Facility:** 104 efficiencies.
4 stories, interior corridors. **Pool:** heated
indoor. **Activities:** exercise room. **Guest
Services:** complimentary and valet
laundry.

HAMPTON INN BY HILTON LOUISVILLE NORTH
                                      812/280-1501
THREE DIAMOND [SAVE] Hotel. **Address:** 1501 Broadway St 47129

AAA Benefit: Members save up to 15%!

**HOME2 SUITES BY HILTON CLARKSVILLE LOUISVILLE
NORTH**   812/920-1880
THREE DIAMOND [SAVE] Extended
Stay Hotel. **Address:** 1624 Leisure Way
47129

AAA Benefit: Members save up to 15%!

RADISSON HOTEL LOUISVILLE NORTH   812/283-4411
APPROVED Hotel. **Address:** 505 Marriott Dr 47129

**SUBURBAN EXTENDED STAY HOTEL LOUISVILLE
NORTH-CLARKSVILLE**   812/283-9696
APPROVED Extended Stay Hotel. **Address:** 1620 Lei-
sure Way 47129

WHERE TO EAT

SEÑOR IGUANAS   812/280-8555
APPROVED Mexican. Casual Dining. **Address:** 1415
Broadway St 47129

JEFFERSONVILLE pop. 44,953, elev. 844'

- Hotels p. 98 • Restaurants p. 98
- Part of Louisville area — see map p. 71

In 1834 James Howard launched his first steamboat, the *Hyperion,* at Jeffersonville. For nearly a century the Howard family turned out some of the finest ships on American rivers, and shipbuilding remains a major component in Jeffersonville's economy. The town promotes its river heritage through preservation of the historic commercial architecture along the scenic Ohio River.

Clark-Floyd Counties Convention and Tourism Bureau: 315 Southern Indiana Ave., Jeffersonville, IN 47130-3218. **Phone:** (812) 282-6654 or (800) 552-3842.

HOWARD STEAMBOAT MUSEUM AND MANSION is at 1101 E. Market St. Riverboat history is depicted through craft models and tools used to build boats in the Howard Shipyards (1834-1941) on Ohio River. Housed in 1894 Victorian mansion built for shipyard founder James Howard, the museum also contains original family furnishings. Highlights include paddlewheel from the Delta Queen, a three-story walnut staircase, brass chandeliers and leaded and stained glass windows.

Time: Allow 1 hour minimum. **Hours:** Guided tours are given Tues.-Sat. 10-4, Sun. 1-4. Last tour begins 1 hour before closing. Closed major holidays. **Cost:** $7; $6 (ages 65+); $5 (students ages 6+); free (children 0-5). **Parking:** Free. **Phone:** (812) 283-3728. [GT]

FAIRFIELD INN & SUITES BY MARRIOTT LOUISVILLE NORTH
812/280-8220
[APPROVED] [SAVE] Hotel. **Address:** 619 N Shore Dr 47130
AAA Benefit: Members save 5% or more!

HAWTHORN SUITES BY WYNDHAM LOUISVILLE NORTH
812/280-8200
[APPROVED] Extended Stay Hotel. **Address:** 703 North Shore Dr 47130

SHERATON LOUISVILLE RIVERSIDE HOTEL
812/284-6711
[THREE DIAMOND] Hotel
SHERATON
AAA Benefit: Members save 5% or more!

Address: 700 W Riverside Dr 47130 **Location:** Waterfront. I-65 exit 1, just w. **Facility:** 180 units. 10 stories, interior corridors. **Amenities:** safes. **Dining:** 2 restaurants. **Pool:** heated indoor. **Activities:** hot tub, exercise room. **Guest Services:** valet laundry, area transportation. **Featured Amenity:** breakfast buffet.

/ SOME UNITS

TOWNEPLACE SUITES BY MARRIOTT LOUISVILLE NORTH
812/914-4100
[THREE DIAMOND] [SAVE] Extended Stay Hotel. **Address:** 301 W Maple St 47130
AAA Benefit: Members save 5% or more!

WHERE TO EAT

BUCKHEAD MOUNTAIN GRILL 812/284-2919
[APPROVED] American. Casual Dining. **Address:** 707 W Riverside Dr 47130

KINGFISH RESTAURANT 812/284-3474
[APPROVED] Seafood. Casual Dining. **Address:** 601 W Riverside Dr 47130

THE RED YETI 812/288-5788
[APPROVED] American. Casual Dining. **Address:** 256 Spring St 47130

NEW ALBANY pop. 36,372, elev. 442'

- Part of Louisville area — see map p. 71

New Albany is across the Ohio River from Louisville. Local shipbuilders of the 19th century produced speed record-setting steamships, including the *Robert E. Lee* and the *City of Louisville.*

CARNEGIE CENTER FOR ART & HISTORY is at 201 E. Spring St. Completed in 1904 with funds from Andrew Carnegie, the now-restored neoclassical building originally served as a public library. The Ordinary People, Extraordinary Courage exhibit consists of photographs, newspaper articles and other artifacts related to the Underground Railroad, culminating in a feature-length video program. Remembered: The Life of Lucy Higgs Nichols describes the life and accomplishments of the escaped slave who became a nurse with the 23rd Indiana Regiment during the Civil War.

The George W. Morrison Gallery features historically important Southern Indiana paintings, including many by 19th-century painter George Morrison. Educational programs and changing art exhibits are offered throughout the year. **Time:** Allow 1 hour minimum. **Hours:** Tues.-Sat. 10-5:30. Closed major holidays. **Cost:** Free. **Phone:** (812) 944-7336.

CULBERTSON MANSION STATE HISTORIC SITE is 9 blks. e. at 914 E. Main St. Visitors are taken on a guided tour of this French Second Empire-style mansion, which was owned by 19th-century entrepreneur and philanthropist William S. Culbertson. Furnished in period, the 1869 house has such Victorian effects as hand-painted ceilings, Italian marble fireplaces and elaborate woodwork, including a three-story mahogany and rosewood staircase.

Time: Allow 1 hour, 15 minutes minimum. **Hours:** Tours are given on the hour Tues.-Sat. 9-5, Sun. 1-5, Apr.-Dec.; Mon.-Fri. 9-5, rest of year. Last tour begins 1 hour before closing. Closed on state holidays. Phone ahead to confirm schedule. **Cost:** $10; $8 (ages 60+); $5 (ages 0-17). **Phone:** (812) 944-9600. [GT]

HOLIDAY INN EXPRESS NEW ALBANY 812/944-4600
[THREE DIAMOND] Hotel. **Address:** 506 W Spring St 47150

BROOKLYN AND THE BUTCHER   812/590-2646
THREE DIAMOND New Steak. Fine Dining. **Address:** 148 E
Market St 47150

THE EXCHANGE PUB + KITCHEN   812/948-6501
APPROVED American. Casual Dining. **Address:** 118
W Main St 47150

MARK'S FEED STORE   812/949-7427
APPROVED Barbecue. Casual Dining. **Address:** 3827
Charlestown Rd 47150

NEW ALBANIAN BREWING CO, PIZZERIA & PUB
                                            812/944-2577
APPROVED Pizza. Brewpub. **Address:** 3312 Plaza Dr
47150

This ends the Louisville section and resumes
the alphabetical city listings for Kentucky.

MADISONVILLE (E-3) pop. 19,591, elev. 513'

GOVERNOR RUBY LAFFOON'S BIRTHPLACE,
107 Union St., is a restored log cabin furnished as it
was when the former governor lived there in the late
1800s. Also on the grounds is the Historical Society
and Museum, which displays old photographs, Civil
War items and other artifacts relating to the period.
Time: Allow 1 hour minimum. **Hours:** Mon.-Fri. 1-5,
Apr.-Oct.; noon-4, rest of year. Closed major holidays. **Cost:** Donations. **Phone:** (270) 821-3986.

BAYMONT INN & SUITES MADISONVILLE INN   270/821-2121
APPROVED Hotel. **Address:** 1891 Lantaff Blvd 42431

COMFORT INN & SUITES   270/825-3535
THREE DIAMOND Hotel. **Address:** 545 Powell Dr 42431

HAMPTON INN & SUITES BY HILTON   270/825-2226
THREE DIAMOND SAVE Hotel. **Ad-** | **AAA Benefit:**
dress: 201 Ruby Dr 42431 | Members save up to
                                          | 15%!

NU9VE CANTINA AND STEAKHOUSE   270/245-2355
APPROVED Mexican. Casual Dining. **Address:** 1002
Main St 42431

MAMMOTH CAVE NATIONAL PARK (E-4)

Elevations in the park range from 450 ft. at
river level to 950 ft. at Mammoth Cave Ridge.

Northeast of Bowling Green, northwest of Park City
and 10 miles west of Cave City via SR 70, Mammoth
Cave National Park occupies 52,830 acres. Much of
the park is in its natural state, providing shelter to a
large variety of birds and other wildlife.

A tributary of the Ohio River, the scenic Green
River traverses this well-forested, rugged terrain for
25 miles. More than 80 miles of back-country trails,

all of which can be used for hiking and some available for horseback riding and mountain biking, run
along the river's bluffs, ridges and valleys. Biking
trails also are available. In the northwestern section
of the park is the 7-mile-long Nolin River. Several
scenic driving tour routes wind through the park.

Within the park is Mammoth Cave, which has
yielded archeological evidence of humans approximately 5,000 years ago. During the War of 1812 the
cave furnished saltpeter used to manufacture
gunpowder.

Mammoth Cave contains more than 400 miles of
underground passages charted on five levels. Said
to be the longest cave system known, it was hol-
lowed out by the seepage of ground water and the
flow of underground streams. The cave contains diverse passageways, some of which contain remnants of 5,000-year-old stick cane torches, woven
sandals and names written on the cave walls by
guides during the 19th century using candle smoke.

General Information and Activities

Informal campfire programs are held at the amphitheater nightly during the summer and as scheduled in the spring and fall. During the summer and
other months of heavy visitation, park interpreters
conduct nature walks. The Green and Nolin rivers
provide 31 miles of fishing and canoeing waters.

Camping and picnicking facilities are near the
visitor center and at Houchin Ferry. Free permits for
back-country camping can be obtained at the visitor
center. Food is available at the camp store.

The park and self-guiding nature trails are open
year-round. The visitor center is open daily 8-6:30,
June-Aug.; 8:30-4:30, rest of year. Closed
Christmas. Phone (270) 758-2180 daily 9-4:15. *See
Recreation Areas Chart.*

ADMISSION to the park is free. Fees are charged
for cave tours and camping.

PETS are permitted in the park only if leashed,
crated or otherwise physically restricted at all times.
No pets, with the exception of designated service
animals, are allowed in the cave or visitor center;
kennels are available.

ADDRESS inquiries to the Superintendent, Mammoth Cave National Park, Mammoth Cave Pkwy.,
P.O. Box 7, Mammoth Cave, KY 42259.

MAMMOTH CAVE, about 10 mi. w. of Cave City and
8 mi. n.w. of Park City off I-65, has more than 400
miles of known passageways with an average temperature of 54°F; bring a light jacket. Some underground rooms are as wide as 200 feet; the tallest
dome is 192 feet high; the deepest pit is 105 feet.
Guided cave tours, ranging from 1.25 to 6 hours, vary
in degree of difficulty. Visitors should select the tour
that best suits their physical abilities and dress appropriately. The cave is inhabited by creatures who have
adapted to the darkness, including fish, cave crickets
and eyeless crayfish. Tour schedules are available at
the visitor center, from which all tours depart.

Wear sturdy shoes with good traction; some passages are wet and slippery. **Hours:** Guided tours are conducted daily year-round; phone ahead to verify schedule. Closed Christmas. **Cost:** Entrance to the park is free. Guided tour fees range from $7-$55; $5-$20 (ages 6-12); $3.50-$27.50 (senior citizens with Golden Age Passport); free (ages 0-5). Ages 0-5 are not permitted on some tours. Reservations are recommended. **Phone:** (270) 758-2180 for park information, or (877) 444-6777 for the reservation service.

MAYSVILLE (C-7) pop. 9,011, elev. 524'

Maysville, first known as Limestone, is on the south bank of the Ohio River; the city was renamed and incorporated in 1792. The influence of the river trade during the 1800s is evident in Maysville's architecture—the iron grillwork of the row houses along Third Street is reminiscent of New Orleans. In front of the old county courthouse is Old Tip, a cannon used in the Battle of Tippecanoe during the War of 1812.

The history of Maysville is depicted through a series of murals painted on the city's floodwall. Beginning near Limestone Landing with an illustration of a 17th-century Native American hunting party, the murals progress to show visits by the Marquis de Lafayette and Henry Clay, the Underground Railroad, mid-19th- and early 20th-century street scenes and the grandstand at an annual fair. A 2007 addition pays homage to actress and singer Rosemary Clooney, born in Maysville in 1928.

Maysville-Mason County Convention & Visitors Bureau: 216 Bridge St., Maysville, KY 41056. **Phone:** (606) 564-9419 or (888) 875-6297.

Self-guiding tours: Brochures outlining a walking tour are available from the visitors bureau.

KENTUCKY GATEWAY MUSEUM CENTER is at 215 Sutton St., in the downtown historic district. The museum, housed in the 1881 town library, features dioramas depicting the earliest settlement of Maysville, a map collection, slides of area scenes and architecture, exhibits about area agriculture and industry, an art gallery, a rotating exhibit gallery and a genealogical research library. The Kathleen Savage Browning Miniatures Collection is housed in 3,200 square feet of exhibit space and contains thousands of one-twelfth scale homes, mansions and vignettes. An adjacent pioneer graveyard dates to 1800.

Time: Allow 1 hour minimum. **Hours:** Tues.-Fri. 10-4, Sat. 10-3. Closed major holidays. **Cost:** Museum $10; $2 (students with ID and children). Genealogical research library $10. **Phone:** (606) 564-5865.

NATIONAL UNDERGROUND RAILROAD MUSEUM, 38 W. 4th St., is in the Bierbower House, a mid-19th-century "safe house" where runaway slaves were concealed. Maysville was on one of the main escape routes used by fugitive slaves as they

headed north to freedom. The museum features historical artifacts, records and documents depicting life on the Underground Railroad. Of note is "Sampson," an original Parker Tobacco Press.

Time: Allow 1 hour minimum. **Hours:** Wed. and Fri.-Sat. 10-3, Mar.-Oct. (weather permitting). Closed major holidays. Phone ahead to confirm schedule. **Cost:** $5; $4 (students with ID); $3 (ages 6-12). **Phone:** (606) 564-3200.

FRENCH QUARTER INN   606/564-8000
▽▽ **APPROVED**   Hotel. **Address:** 25 E McDonald Pkwy 41056

HAMPTON INN BY HILTON   606/759-0600
▽▽ **APPROVED** SAVE Hotel. **Address:** 503 Market Place Dr 41056   **AAA Benefit:** Members save up to 15%!

WHERE TO EAT

CAPRONI'S ON THE RIVER   606/564-4321
▽▽ **APPROVED**   Italian. Casual Dining. **Address:** 320 Rosemary Clooney St 41056

CHANDLER'S ON MARKET   606/564-6385
▽▽ **APPROVED**   American. Casual Dining. **Address:** 212 Market St 41056

DESHA'S   606/564-9275
▽▽ **APPROVED**   American. Casual Dining. **Address:** 1166 US 68 41056

PASQUALE'S RESTAURANT   606/564-4039
▽▽ **APPROVED**   Pizza. Casual Dining. **Address:** 786 US 68 41056

MIDDLESBORO

HOLIDAY INN EXPRESS   606/248-6860
▽▽ **THREE DIAMOND** Hotel. **Address:** 1252 N 12th St 40965

SLEEP INN & SUITES   606/576-7829
▽▽ **APPROVED**   Hotel. **Address:** 1260 N 12th St 40965

MONTICELLO pop. 6,188

BEST WESTERN LAKE CUMBERLAND INN
606/340-8687
▽▽ **APPROVED**
Hotel   BW Best Western   **AAA Benefit:** Members save up to 15% and earn bonus points!

Address: 2030 E Hwy 90 Bypass 42633 **Location:** SR 90 and 1275, just e. Located in a rural area. **Facility:** 60 units. 3 stories, interior corridors. **Parking:** winter plug-ins. **Pool:** heated indoor. **Activities:** exercise room. **Guest Services:** coin laundry. **Featured Amenity:** continental breakfast.

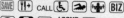

MOREHEAD (D-8) pop. 6,845, elev. 712'

In 1911 Morehead furnished the locale for the first of Cora Wilson Stewart's "moonlight schools." A forerunner of modern adult education, these schools enrolled students from 18 to 86, held classes on moonlit nights, taught the basics—reading and writing—and within 2 years largely eliminated illiteracy in eastern Kentucky.

The little schoolhouse in which Stewart began her teaching career stands next to the public library on First Street in tribute to the dynamic impact on national and international education that began in this small community.

At the northern end of Daniel Boone National Forest *(see place listing p. 41)* and close to Cave Run Lake, the Morehead area provides many recreational opportunities, including trails for hiking, bicycling and horseback riding, and a sanctuary for Canada geese.

Morehead Tourism Commission: 111 E. First St., Morehead, KY 40351. **Phone:** (606) 780-4342 or (855) 270-8733.

BEST WESTERN EAGLES INN   606/784-5796

Hotel

AAA Benefit: Members save up to 15% and earn bonus points!

Address: 110 Toms Dr 40351 **Location:** I-64 exit 137 (SR 32), just sw. **Facility:** 49 units. 2 stories, interior corridors. **Pool:** heated indoor. **Activities:** exercise room. **Guest Services:** coin laundry.

COMFORT INN & SUITES   606/780-7378

THREE DIAMOND

Hotel

Address: 2650 Kentucky 801 N 40351 **Location:** I-64 exit 133, just s. **Facility:** 65 units. 3 stories, interior corridors. **Pool:** heated outdoor. **Activities:** exercise room. **Guest Services:** coin laundry. **Featured Amenity:** full hot breakfast.

HAMPTON INN BY HILTON-MOREHEAD   606/780-0601

THREE DIAMOND **SAVE** Hotel. **Address:** 500 Hampton Way 40351

AAA Benefit: Members save up to 15%!

MURRAY (F-2) pop. 17,741, elev. 480'
• Restaurants p. 102

Murray is the home of Murray State University, which has a wide variety of facilities open to the public. The Clara M. Eagle Gallery presents changing exhibits of fine arts and crafts in a range of styles and media. The Wrather-West Kentucky Museum contains university and Jackson Purchase

memorabilia. The Curris Center on Chestnut Street serves as a student and conference center as well as a community gathering place.

The MSU Libraries house reference sources, government documents and historical materials about the area in addition to some Jesse Stuart manuscripts, first editions and items related to the Kentuckian's career as a writer and educator. The libraries are open daily 7 a.m.-9 p.m. Also on the MSU campus is the CFSB Center, which hosts sporting events and concerts throughout the year.

One mile west of the campus on MSU's 254-acre University Farm is the Bill Cherry Agricultural Exposition Center, used for such events as rodeos, concerts, horse shows, circuses, motorcycle races and various exhibitions.

In town, Playhouse in the Park offers a variety of productions in the 1907 Freight Depot in the city park. In addition Murray is convenient to nearby Kentucky Lake and Lake Barkley Park *(see Land Between the Lakes National Recreation Area p. 55).*

Murray Convention & Visitors Bureau: 206 S. 4th St., P.O. Box 321, Murray, KY 42071. **Phone:** (270) 759-2199 or (800) 651-1603.

BEST WESTERN UNIVERSITY INN   270/753-5353

APPROVED

Motel

AAA Benefit: Members save up to 15% and earn bonus points!

Address: 1503 N 12th St 42071 **Location:** 1.9 mi n on US 641. **Facility:** 72 units. 2 stories (no elevator), exterior corridors. **Parking:** winter plug-ins. **Terms:** check-in 4 pm. **Pool:** outdoor. **Activities:** exercise room. **Guest Services:** valet laundry.

HAMPTON INN & SUITES BY HILTON   270/767-2226

THREE DIAMOND **SAVE** Hotel. **Address:** 1415 Lowes Dr 42071

AAA Benefit: Members save up to 15%!

HOLIDAY INN EXPRESS HOTEL & SUITES   270/759-4449

THREE DIAMOND Hotel. **Address:** 1504 N 12th St 42071

QUALITY INN   270/759-5910

APPROVED

Hotel

Address: 1210 N 12th St 42071 **Location:** 1.8 mi n on US 641. **Facility:** 58 units. 2 stories (no elevator), interior corridors. **Pool:** heated indoor. **Activities:** hot tub, limited exercise equipment. **Guest Services:** valet laundry. **Featured Amenity:** continental breakfast.

SPRINGHILL SUITES BY MARRIOTT MURRAY   270/917-8000

THREE DIAMOND Hotel. **Address:** 1512 N 12th St 42071

JASMINE-THAI CUISINE & SUSHI BAR   270/761-8424
▼▼ APPROVED   Thai. Casual Dining. **Address:** 506 N
12th St, Suite E 42071

LOS PORTALES   270/767-0315
▼▼ APPROVED   Mexican. Casual Dining. **Address:** 1506
Lowes Dr 42071

MUGSY'S HIDEOUT   270/767-0020
▼▼ APPROVED   Pizza. Casual Dining. **Address:** 410 Main
St 42071

NEWPORT (B-6) pop. 15,273, elev. 508'
- Hotels & Restaurants map & index p. 37
- Part of Cincinnati area — see map p. 153

Named after Admiral Christopher Newport, the commander of the first English settlement at Jamestown, Virginia, in 1603, Newport's location at the confluence of the Ohio and Licking rivers was a natural stopping point for pioneers heading west. Founded in 1795, Newport and its neighbor Cincinnati grew and prospered as a result of riverboat traffic along the Ohio.

The early 20th century, however, saw a change in the city's character. Coinciding with the invention of the Thompson machine gun ("Tommy Gun") by Newport native John Thompson, the city became a haven for gangsters in the 1920s. Gambling halls, glitzy nightclubs and prostitution followed and earned Newport the nickname "Sin City" from the 1940s through the '80s.

Reform, coupled with renovation and redevelopment, has transformed the city. The East Row Historic District is graced with tree-lined streets and elegant 19th-century homes, and the riverfront has been revived with the addition of trendy shopping and entertainment areas and the Newport Aquarium (see attraction listing).

The city's Levee District is home to the World Peace Bell, which was the world's largest free-swinging bell 2000-2016. One of 20 worldwide, the bell within the transparent Freedom Tower, 425 York St., commemorates the 50th anniversary of the 1948 Universal Declaration of Human Rights and rings each morning around noon and during special occasions. Guided tours are available for a fee Mon.-Fri. 10-4; phone (859) 655-7700. Also nearby are the Northern Kentucky Firefighters Memorial and a scaled version of the two World Trade Center towers, honoring Sept. 11, 2001, and the valor of firefighters.

Shopping: Newport on the Levee, 1 Levee Way on the banks of the Ohio River, is an entertainment district featuring shopping, dining and clubs.

NEWPORT AQUARIUM, off I-471 exit 5 (SR 8), then w. following signs to the Newport on the Levee complex, displays thousands of aquatic creatures from every continent and ocean. Canyon Falls is home to Asian small-clawed otters while Turtle Canyon features a diverse collection of more than 14 species of turtles spanning three continents—from the Galapagos tortoise, said to be the largest tortoise species in the world, to the Egyptian tortoise, reputedly the smallest tortoise species in the Northern Hemisphere. A turtle corral allows guests to touch multiple species of turtles. Surrounded by Sharks takes guests through the underwater tunnels of a 385,000-gallon tank filled with six shark species, four rare and exotic shark rays, 300 fish and Denver, a nearly 200-pound loggerhead sea turtle.

In the Frog Bog exhibit, kids can crawl through a play area designed to introduce them to more than 20 different species of frogs from around the world. The Jellyfish Gallery features walk-around tanks and interactive games as a means of learning about the various species.

Gator Alley is a swampland showcasing eight species of crocodilians from four continents, including Mighty Mike, one of the biggest American alligators outside of Florida. Other exhibits include Shark Central, a touch tank where visitors can pet a shark; Shore Gallery, with a touch pool populated by starfish, crabs and urchins; Dangerous & Deadly, inhabited by piranhas, poison dart frogs and puffer fish; and Kroger Penguin Palooza. African penguin encounters as well as the Backstage Animal Experience showing the inner workings of the aquarium are available for additional fees. A coral reef, five acrylic tunnels, murals and the Shark Ray Bay theater showcasing dive shows daily also are featured. Ring of Fire: World of the Octopus gives visitors a peek into the world of the shape-shifting, color-changing giant Pacific octopus and his underwater home of towering volcanoes along the Pacific Ring of Fire.

Time: Allow 2 hours minimum. **Hours:** Daily 9-7, late May-early Sept.; daily 10-6, rest of year. Penguin encounter and behind-the-scenes tour are available daily. **Cost:** $24.99; $17.99 (ages 2-12). Penguin encounter additional $26.99. Behind-the-scenes tour additional $14.99. **Parking:** $0-$5. **Phone:** (859) 261-7444 or (800) 406-3474. 🍴

ALOFT NEWPORT ON THE LEVEE   859/916-5306 38
▼▼ THREE DIAMOND [SAVE] Boutique   **AAA Benefit:**
Contemporary Hotel. **Address:** 201 E   Members save 5%
3rd St 41071   or more!

HAMPTON INN & SUITES BY HILTON NEWPORT/CINCINNATI
                                   859/415-0678 39
▼▼ THREE DIAMOND [SAVE] Hotel. **Ad-**   **AAA Benefit:**
dress: 275 Columbia St 41071   Members save up to
                                         15%!

BB RIVERBOATS   859/261-8500 19
▼▼ APPROVED   American. Buffet Style. **Address:** 101
Riverboat Row 41071

(See map & index p. 37.)

HOFBRAUHAUS NEWPORT   859/491-7200   (17)
APPROVED   German. Casual Dining. **Address:** 200 E 3rd St 41071

MITCHELL'S FISH MARKET   859/291-7454   (18)
THREE DIAMOND [SAVE] Seafood. Casual Dining. **Address:** 1 Levee Way, Suite 2129 41071

OAK GROVE pop. 7,489

CANDLEWOOD SUITES FORT CAMPBELL - OAK GROVE   270/605-9300
THREE DIAMOND Extended Stay Hotel. **Address:** 12885 Fort Campbell Blvd 42262

HAMPTON INN OAK GROVE FORT CAMPBELL   270/640-7299
THREE DIAMOND [SAVE] Hotel. **Ad-dress:** 164 Naomi Ln 42262

AAA Benefit: Members save up to 15%!

HOLIDAY INN EXPRESS   270/439-0022
THREE DIAMOND Hotel. **Address:** 12759 Ft Campbell Blvd 42262

SLEEP INN & SUITES   270/640-7170
THREE DIAMOND Hotel. **Address:** 220 Auburn St 42262

OWENSBORO (D-3) pop. 57,265, elev. 400'
• Restaurants p. 104

The largest city in western Kentucky, Owensboro is on the banks of the Ohio River. Agriculture and industry play important roles in the economy. The agricultural basis centers on the production of corn, soybeans and tobacco. Industrial plants produce a diversity of manufactured products.

Known as Kentucky's Festival City as well as being designated a sports town, Owensboro holds more than 20 annual festivals and events. The Edge Ice Center, 1400 Hickman Ave., features ice skating, while the Diamond Lake Resort, west of town off SR 56, has 157 acres for fishing, camping and pedal-boating.

Located 4 miles west of Owensboro, Ben Hawes Park offers an archery range, nine- and 18-hole golf courses, and hiking and mountain bike trails among the recreational facilities available on its 297 acres; phone (270) 687-7134.

Owensboro-Daviess County Convention & Visitors Bureau: 215 E. 2nd St., Owensboro, KY 42303. **Phone:** (270) 926-1100 or (800) 489-1131.

Shopping: Towne Square Mall, south of the bypass at 5000 Frederica St., numbers JCPenney and Macy's among its more than 60 stores. Downtown Owensboro, along 2nd and 3rd streets, includes antique, gift, coffee and candy shops as well as bistros.

INTERNATIONAL BLUEGRASS MUSIC MUSEUM is downtown at the jct. of E. 2nd and Daviess sts. at 207 E. 2nd St. The entrance is at 117 Daviess St. The museum is home to exhibits and galleries documenting the origins and practitioners of bluegrass music, an art form dating to the 1940s. The Hall of Honor focuses on originators such as Bill Monroe,

considered the father of bluegrass, as well as individuals whose efforts fostered the music's popularity. Interactive features allow visitors to compare and contrast traditional and current styles.

Time: Allow 1 hour minimum. **Hours:** Tues.-Sat. 10-5, Sun. 1-4. Closed Jan. 1, Easter, Memorial Day, July 4, Labor Day, Thanksgiving and Christmas. **Cost:** $12; $10 (senior citizens and military with ID); $8 (students with ID); free (ages 0-6). Reservations are required for tours. **Phone:** (270) 926-7891 or (888) 692-2656. [GT]

WESTERN KENTUCKY BOTANICAL GARDEN is 2 mi. w. on 2nd Street, then just n. to 25 Carter Rd. Now expanded to 12 acres, nine themed gardens showcase an extensive collection of daylilies, irises and roses as well as ornamental and perennial grasses. An early 20th-century doctor's building is adjacent to the Herb Garden, which features herbs and plants used medicinally at the time. A symbolic Japanese memorial garden is arranged with hollies, lattice fences and stone lanterns. A 21-foot stainless-steel basket sculpture which acts as a sundial and a solar smart flower which traps solar energy to use as electricity are the garden's recent additions.

Time: Allow 1 hour minimum. **Hours:** Daily 9-6, mid-Mar. to mid-Nov.; Mon.-Fri. 9-3, Sat.-Sun. by appointment, rest of year. Closed major holidays. **Cost:** $5; $3 (ages 65+); $1 (children). **Phone:** (270) 993-1234. [GT]

BEST WESTERN PLUS OWENSBORO   270/689-0939

THREE DIAMOND
Hotel

Best Western PLUS

AAA Benefit: Members save up to 15% and earn bonus points!

Address: 1018 Goetz Dr 42301 **Location:** US 60 Bypass exit 14. **Facility:** 63 units. 3 stories, interior corridors. **Pool:** heated indoor. **Activities:** exercise room. **Guest Services:** valet and coin laundry.

COMFORT SUITES OWENSBORO   270/926-7675
APPROVED Hotel. **Address:** 230 Salem Dr 42303

COURTYARD BY MARRIOTT   270/685-4140
THREE DIAMOND [SAVE] Hotel. **Address:** 3120 Highland Pointe Dr 42303

AAA Benefit: Members save 5% or more!

FAIRFIELD BY MARRIOTT OWENSBORO   270/688-8887

THREE DIAMOND   Fairfield   **AAA Benefit:** Members save 5% or more!
Hotel

Address: 800 Salem Dr 42303 **Location:** US 60 Bypass exit 14, just s. **Facility:** 100 units. 4 stories, interior corridors. **Pool:** heated indoor. **Activities:** hot tub, exercise room. **Guest Services:** valet and coin laundry. **Featured Amenity:** continental breakfast.

HAMPTON INN & SUITES BY HILTON DOWNTOWN/WATERFRONT   270/685-2005

THREE DIAMOND Hotel. **Address:** 401 2nd St 42301   **AAA Benefit:** Members save up to 15%!

HAMPTON INN BY HILTON OWENSBORO SOUTH   270/926-2006

THREE DIAMOND Hotel. **Address:** 615 Salem Dr 42303   **AAA Benefit:** Members save up to 15%!

HOLIDAY INN OWENSBORO RIVERFRONT   270/683-1111

THREE DIAMOND Hotel. **Address:** 701 W 1st St 42301

TOWNEPLACE SUITES BY MARRIOTT   270/594-1002

THREE DIAMOND Extended Stay Hotel. **Address:** 3365 Hayden Rd 42303   **AAA Benefit:** Members save 5% or more!

WINGFIELD INN & SUITES   270/685-2433

APPROVED   **Address:** 3220 W Parrish Ave 42301 **Location:** US 60 Bypass exit 11, just n. **Facility:** 70 units. 2 stories, interior corridors. **Parking:** winter plug-ins. **Terms:** check-in 4 pm. **Pool:** outdoor. **Activities:** limited exercise equipment. **Guest Services:** valet and coin laundry. **Featured Amenity:** breakfast buffet.
Hotel

WHERE TO EAT

BILL'S RESTAURANT   270/852-8120

APPROVED   American. Casual Dining. **Address:** 420 Frederica St 42301

THE BRIARPATCH   270/685-3329

APPROVED   American. Casual Dining. **Address:** 2760 Veach Rd 42303

CITY WALK OF OWENSBORO   270/478-4958

APPROVED   American. Casual Dining. **Address:** 222 Allen St 42303

COLBY'S FINE FOOD & SPIRITS   270/685-4239

APPROVED   American. Casual Dining. **Address:** 204 W 3rd St 42303

THE FAMOUS BISTRO   270/686-8202

APPROVED   Italian. Casual Dining. **Address:** 102 W Second St 42303

FETTA   270/926-0005

APPROVED   Pizza. Casual Dining. **Address:** 118 St Ann St 42303

THE MILLER HOUSE RESTAURANT   270/685-5878

APPROVED   Southern American. Casual Dining. **Address:** 301 E 5th St 42303

MOONLITE BAR-B-QUE INN   270/684-8143

APPROVED
Regional Barbecue Casual Dining
$5-$20

AAA Inspector Notes: *Classic.* Established in the 1940s, this friendly restaurant has a stone fireplace and bucolic artwork that provides a rustic ambience. The buffet's lineup of pork, beef, chicken, ribs, fresh vegetables and homemade desserts is this spot's main draw. However, you can also order from the menu. One unusual dish featured is Kentucky barbecued mutton. On Thursday and Friday evenings, you can also enjoy the "fiddler dinner," which is fried catfish. **Features:** beer & wine, Sunday brunch. **Address:** 2840 W Parrish Ave 42301 **Location:** US 60 Bypass, 0.5 mi e.

NIKO'S ITALIAN CUISINE   270/852-1618

APPROVED   Italian. Casual Dining. **Address:** 2200 E Parish Ave 42303

OLD HICKORY BAR-B-QUE   270/926-9000

APPROVED   Barbecue. Casual Dining. **Address:** 338 Washington Ave 42301

REAL HACIENDA MEXICAN RESTAURANT   270/684-5595

APPROVED   Mexican. Casual Dining. **Address:** 3023 Highland Pointe Dr 42303

PADUCAH (E-2) pop. 25,024, elev. 344'
• Hotels p. 106 • Restaurants p. 106

Paducah (puh-DOO-ka), at the confluence of the Ohio and Tennessee rivers, was named by its founder, Gen. William Clark—of Lewis and Clark expedition fame—who named the settlement after the Padouca Indian Nation. A statue at Jefferson and 19th streets crafted by noted sculptor Lorado Taft honors the legendary and peaceful Chickasaw Indian leader Chief Paduke.

A series of colorful floodwall murals painted by internationally recognized artist Robert Dafford and the Dafford Murals Team give an account of the city's history; the murals are downtown between Kentucky Avenue and Jefferson Street.

A memorial statue of Alben W. Barkley, a native son who served as U.S. vice president under Harry Truman 1949-53, is at 28th Street and Jefferson Boulevard. Also notable is the city hall at 300 S. 5th St.; the building, a replica of the U.S. embassy in New Delhi, India, was designed by noted architect Edward Durell Stone.

Bob Noble Park, 3 miles northwest on US 60, has a medieval gate, winding driveways, a lake with a fountain, an outdoor theater, a swimming pool, picnic tables, a children's playground, a jogging trail, a skate park, disc golf course, tennis courts and a basketball court; phone (270) 444-8508.

Quilters from around the country converge on Paducah in late April for the American Quilter's Society Quilt Show & Contest. More than 500 quilts are displayed at the event, which also features vendor booths, a quilt making school, an auction and awards. Paintings, jewelry and other arts and crafts can be found in the colorful studios and galleries lining the streets of the 26-block LowerTown Fine Arts District, located in one of Paducah's oldest neighborhoods. The Carson Center for the Performing Arts, 100 Kentucky Ave., offers traveling Broadway hits, theater, dance and musicals. Historic restoration in downtown Paducah is evident in the Historic Market House Square area. The Market House Theatre, 141 Kentucky Ave., hosts plays and musicals with local actors.

The Hotel Metropolitan, 724 Jackson St., was run by an African-American woman, Maggie Steed, in 1909; the hotel closed in 1996. The hotel has attracted such distinguished guests as musicians Louis Armstrong, Cab Calloway, Duke Ellington and B.B. King, Major League Baseball Hall of Famers James "Cool Papa" Bell, Josh Gibson and Leroy "Satchel" Paige and U.S. Supreme Court Justice Thurgood Marshall. The building now houses a museum with permanent exhibits focusing on African-American heritage, area history and the hotel's prominent guests; its rooms are furnished in varying periods to depict how they may have looked during the hotel's operation. Tours are available by appointment; phone (270) 443-7918.

Paducah Convention & Visitors Bureau: 128 Broadway, Paducah, KY 42001. **Phone:** (270) 443-8783 or (800) 723-8224.

Shopping: Kentucky Oaks Mall, with more than 100 shops, including Best Buy, Dillard's, JCPenney and Old Navy, is at I-24 exit 4. The historic downtown, midtown and southside areas offer antique shopping and specialty boutiques.

NATIONAL QUILT MUSEUM OF THE UNITED STATES is at 215 Jefferson St. The museum's permanent collection of more than 500 contemporary quilts and fiber art is one of the country's largest. Three climate-controlled galleries celebrate the fabric medium and rotate more than 150 quilts of extraordinary and pictorial design, including a selection from the award-winning collection as well as changing exhibits featuring antique and thematic quilts. Another gallery displays to-scale miniature quilts, all 24 inches or smaller in size. The museum lobby's eight stained-glass windows are highlighted with designs inspired by quilt patterns.

A self-guiding tour delves into the origins of the quilts and their creators and explores traditional quilting styles and techniques. Activities, events and workshops are offered for experienced and novice quilters.

Guided tours are available by appointment. **Time:** Allow 1 hour minimum. **Hours:** Mon.-Sat. 10-5, Sun. 1-5, Mar.-Nov.; Mon.-Sat. 10-5, rest of year. Closed Jan. 1, Easter, Thanksgiving, Christmas Eve and Christmas. **Cost:** $12; $11 (ages 62+); $5 (full-time students with ID); free (ages 0-12 with adult). **Phone:** (270) 442-8856.

PADUCAH RAILROAD MUSEUM is at 200 Washington St. The museum offers a large collection of vintage railroad artifacts including tools, photographs, maps, signals, communication and dispatching equipment, a locomotive simulator and a large model train layout. **Time:** Allow 30 minutes minimum. **Hours:** Wed.-Fri. noon-4, Sat. 10-4, Mar.-Dec.; otherwise by appointment. Closed major holidays. **Cost:** $6; $3 (ages 0-12). **Phone:** (270) 908-6451.

RIVER DISCOVERY CENTER, 117 S. Water St., features interactive displays including a boat simulator; 24 Hours on the River; a river boat timeline; a rain table; a lock and dam; a dredge model; river habitats including turtles and other wildlife; a 16-minute river film; a Civil War exhibit; and a restored 1920s calliope. In a renovated two-story, brick, 1843 antebellum structure built to house a bank, the museum overlooks the confluence of the Ohio and Tennessee rivers.

Time: Allow 1 hour minimum. **Hours:** Mon.-Sat. 9:30-5, Sun. 1-5, Apr.-Nov.; Mon.-Sat. 9:30-5, rest of year. Closed Thanksgiving and Christmas. **Cost:** $8; $7 (ages 60+); $5 (ages 0-12); free (active military with ID). **Phone:** (270) 575-9958.

WHITEHAVEN, jct. I-24 and US 45 exit 7, at 1845 Lone Oak Rd., is an 1860s mansion remodeled in 1903 in the Classical Revival style. Restored to late 19th-century grandeur, the house serves as a state welcome center and rest area. It contains a collection of Vice President Alben Barkley's memorabilia, including the first U.S. vice presidential flag.

Hours: Welcome center open for travel information Mon.-Sat. 8-4:30. Guided tours are offered daily 1-4, based on personnel availability. Rest area and lobby open daily 24 hours. Closed Jan. 1, Thanksgiving, day after Thanksgiving, Christmas Eve, Christmas, day after Christmas and Dec. 31. **Cost:** Free. **Phone:** (270) 554-2077.

WILLIAM CLARK MARKET HOUSE MUSEUM is at 121 S. 2nd St. in the center of the 1905 Market House. The museum displays artifacts from Paducah's past, including a complete 1877 drugstore with gingerbread woodwork, Civil War artifacts including a quilt made by Mrs. Robert E. Lee, furniture used by Ulysses S. Grant and the Lincolns, and highlights from landmark businesses and notable Paducah natives including Vice President Alben W. Barkley and John T. Scopes. A short film about the 1937 flood also is available. **Time:** Allow 30 minutes minimum. **Hours:** Tues.-Sat. 10-4, Mar. 1-Dec. 15. Closed major holidays. **Cost:** $5; $1 (ages 0-11). **Phone:** (270) 443-7759.

BEST WESTERN PADUCAH INN 270/443-2323

▼▼ THREE DIAMOND

Hotel

Best Western.

AAA Benefit: Members save up to 15% and earn bonus points!

Address: 2960 Husband Rd 42003 **Location:** I-24 exit 11, just ne. **Facility:** 50 units. 2 stories (no elevator), interior corridors. **Parking:** winter plug-ins. **Pool:** outdoor. **Activities:** exercise room. **Guest Services:** valet and coin laundry. **Featured Amenity:** full hot breakfast.

SAVE ⊞ CALL 🚭 🛁 ⚕ BIZ

HS 📶 ✕ 🖥 📷 🖥

CANDLEWOOD SUITES 270/442-3969
▼▼ THREE DIAMOND Extended Stay Hotel. **Address:** 3940 Coleman Crossing Cir 42001

COUNTRY INN & SUITES BY RADISSON 270/442-2201
▼▼ APPROVED Hotel. **Address:** 145 McBride Ln 42001

COURTYARD BY MARRIOTT 270/442-3600
▼▼ THREE DIAMOND SAVE Hotel. **Address:** 3835 Technology Dr 42001

AAA Benefit: Members save 5% or more!

DRURY INN 270/443-3313
▼▼ THREE DIAMOND Hotel. **Address:** 3975 Hinkleville Rd 42001

DRURY SUITES 270/441-0024
▼▼ THREE DIAMOND Hotel. **Address:** 2930 James Sanders Blvd 42001

FAIRFIELD INN & SUITES BY MARRIOTT 270/442-1700
▼▼ THREE DIAMOND SAVE Hotel. **Address:** 3950 Coleman Crossing Cir 42001

AAA Benefit: Members save 5% or more!

HAMPTON INN & SUITES 270/442-0200
▼▼ THREE DIAMOND SAVE Hotel. **Address:** 3901 Coleman Crossing Cir 42001

AAA Benefit: Members save up to 15%!

HOLIDAY INN EXPRESS 270/442-8874
▼▼ THREE DIAMOND Hotel. **Address:** 3996 Hinkleville Rd 42001

HOLIDAY INN RIVERFRONT PADUCAH 270/366-7614
▼▼ THREE DIAMOND Hotel. **Address:** 600 N 4th St 42001

HOMEWOOD SUITES BY HILTON PADUCAH 270/443-0009
▼▼ THREE DIAMOND SAVE Extended Stay Hotel. **Address:** 3925 Coleman Crossing Cir 42001

AAA Benefit: Members save up to 15%!

LA QUINTA INN & SUITES PADUCAH 270/443-4800
▼▼ THREE DIAMOND Hotel. **Address:** 3960 Coleman Crossing Cir 42001

PEAR TREE INN BY DRURY 270/444-7200
▼▼ APPROVED Hotel. **Address:** 5006 Hinkleville 42001

RESIDENCE INN BY MARRIOTT 270/444-3966
▼▼ THREE DIAMOND SAVE Extended Stay Hotel. **Address:** 3900 Coleman Crossing Cir 42001

AAA Benefit: Members save 5% or more!

WHERE TO EAT

BACKWOODS BAR-B-QUE 270/441-7427
▼▼ APPROVED Barbecue. Casual Dining. **Address:** 5172 Hinkleville Rd 42001

CYNTHIA'S 270/443-3319
▼▼ THREE DIAMOND American. Casual Dining. **Address:** 125 Market House Square 42001

DOE'S EAT PLACE 270/443-9006
▼▼ APPROVED Steak. Casual Dining. **Address:** 136 Broadway St 42001

FLAMINGO ROW 270/442-0460
▼▼ APPROVED Caribbean. Casual Dining. **Address:** 2640 Perkins Creek Dr 42001

FREIGHT HOUSE 270/908-0006
▼▼ THREE DIAMOND Southern American. Casual Dining. **Address:** 330 S 3rd St 42003

ITALIAN GRILL ON BROADWAY 270/443-5222
▼▼ THREE DIAMOND Italian. Casual Dining. **Address:** 314 Broadway St 42001

JASMINE 270/442-0000
▼▼ APPROVED Thai Sushi. Casual Dining. **Address:** 451 Jordan Dr 42001

KIRCHHOFF'S DELI & BAKERY 270/442-7117
▼▼ APPROVED Breads/Pastries. Deli. Quick Serve. **Address:** 118 Market House Square 42001

MAX'S BRICK OVEN CAFE 270/575-3473
▼▼ APPROVED Mediterranean. Casual Dining. **Address:** 112 Market House Square 42001

PADUCAH BEER WERKS 270/933-1265
▼▼ APPROVED Pizza. Casual Dining. **Address:** 301 N 4th St 42001

RAFFERTY'S RESTAURANT & BAR 270/442-1014
▼▼ APPROVED American. Casual Dining. **Address:** 3970 Hinkleville Rd 42001

THE STATION BURGER CO. 270/408-3473
▼▼ APPROVED Burgers. Quick Serve. **Address:** 3500 James Sanders Blvd 42001

STRICKLAND'S SEAFOOD 270/538-3474
▼▼ APPROVED Seafood. Casual Dining. **Address:** 548 N 32nd St 42001

TRIBECA MEXICAN CUISINE 270/444-3960
▼▼ APPROVED Mexican. Casual Dining. **Address:** 127 Market House Square 42001

PARIS (C-7) pop. 8,553, elev. 847'

Paris, seat of Bourbon County, was first settled in 1776. Both the town and the county were named in appreciation for French aid during the Revolution, one for the capital of France and the other for the French ruling house. One of Kentucky's earliest distilleries named the liquor it produced for the county. Later "bourbon" was applied to any corn whiskey made with this distillery's formula.

The Duncan Tavern, 323 High St, has been in continuous use as a tavern or boarding house since its construction in 1788, four years prior to Kentucky being admitted into the union as the fifteenth state. Frontiersmen and pioneers Daniel Boone, Simon

Kenton and Michael Stoner, as well as statesman Samuel Adams, were among the prominent visitors to the three-story stone building. The attached Anne Duncan house, built in 1801, features a genealogical library. The library is open and guided tours of the tavern are offered April through mid-December; phone (859) 987-1788.

Nearby horse farms include Denali Stud, Hillcroft Farm, Indian Creek Farm and Claiborne Farm, the spot where Triple Crown winner Secretariat is buried. They can be visited by appointment only. *Also see Bluegrass Country p. 30.*

Paris-Bourbon County Chamber of Commerce: 525 High St., Paris, KY 40361. **Phone:** (859) 987-3205.

CANE RIDGE MEETING HOUSE is 9 mi. e. via US 460 to SR 537/1655 Cane Ridge Rd. Built of blue ash logs by Scots-Irish pioneers in 1791, it was the site of an 1801 revival that led to the 1804 dissolution of the Springfield Presbytery. From this act came a new movement, the precursor to several modern-day churches including the Christian Church (Disciples of Christ), the Christian Churches and the Churches of Christ. The meeting house is encased in a limestone superstructure for preservation and unrestricted access.

The grounds include a small museum with historical items and a pioneer cemetery. **Time:** Allow 1 hour minimum. **Hours:** Mon.-Sat. 9-5, Sun. 1-5, Apr.-Oct.; by appointment, rest of year. **Cost:** Donations. **Phone:** (859) 987-5350.

BEST WESTERN PARIS INN   859/987-0779

 APPROVED

Hotel

BW Best Western. **AAA Benefit:** Members save up to 15% and earn bonus points!

Address: 2011 Alverson Dr 40361 **Location:** Jct US 27/68 Bypass, just w. **Facility:** 49 units. 2 stories (no elevator), interior/exterior corridors. **Parking:** winter plug-ins. **Pool:** outdoor.

WHERE TO EAT

PARADISE CAFE   859/987-8383
APPROVED Asian. Casual Dining. **Address:** 731 Main St 40361

PARK CITY (E-5) pop. 537, elev. 650'

HISTORIC DIAMOND CAVERNS, 1.2 mi. n. on SR 255 (Mammoth Cave Pkwy.) off I-65 exit 48, is one of the nation's oldest show caves. The caverns, with a constant temperature of 58°F, contain stalactite and stalagmite formations and drapery and flowstone deposits. One-hour, .5-mile guided tours are offered.

Note: The guided tour's paths contain more than 350 stair steps; visitors are advised to wear good walking shoes. **Hours:** Tours offered daily 9-5, Mar. 15-Labor Day; 9-4, day after Labor Day-Oct. 31; 10-4, rest of year. Closed Thanksgiving, Christmas Eve and Christmas. **Cost:** Fee $20; $10 (ages 4-12). **Phone:** (270) 749-2233.

PIKEVILLE (E-9) pop. 6,903, elev. 679'

Pikeville, county seat to the state's largest county, is named for Gen. Zebulon M. Pike, a U.S. Army officer and explorer who discovered Pike's Peak in Colorado. A statue dedicated to Col. James A. Garfield, Union Army officer and 20th president of the United States, can be viewed in the Pikeville City Park.

The town is home to the Pikeville Cut-Through and Scenic Overlook, purportedly the second largest earth-moving project north of the Panama Canal. It took some 14 years to physically re-route the river and the railroad system to relieve the town from flooding when it was completely underwater 1957-77.

Pike County Tourism CVB: 831 Hambley Blvd., P.O. Box 1497, Pikeville, KY 41502-1497. **Phone:** (606) 432-5063 or (800) 844-7453.

Self-guiding tours: A map for a self-guiding driving tour outlining the Hatfield-McCoy feud sites is available at the tourism office. The two families feuded 1863-1891, and the tour highlights some of the places where actual events took place. One of the sites along the tour is the Historic Dills Cemetery, a resting place for several of the McCoy family members as well as the first integrated cemetery in eastern Kentucky.

BIG SANDY HERITAGE CENTER MUSEUM is at 172 Division St. The museum, in Pikeville's railroad depot, has exhibits that relate the history of this eastern Kentucky area. Visitors can see an 1860s log home, Civil War artifacts, early 20th-century railroad memorabilia and a tool collection. **Hours:** Thurs.-Sat. 9-4:30. Closed major holidays. **Cost:** $5; $3 (ages 5-14). **Phone:** (606) 766-1025.

HILTON GARDEN INN PIKEVILLE   606/766-2000
THREE DIAMOND SAVE Hotel. **Address:** 849 Hambley Blvd 41501

AAA Benefit: Members save up to 15%!

THE LANDMARK HOTEL   606/432-2545
APPROVED Hotel. **Address:** 190 S Mayo Tr 41502

PIKEVILLE HAMPTON INN   606/432-8181
THREE DIAMOND SAVE Hotel. **Address:** 831 Hambley Blvd 41501

AAA Benefit: Members save up to 15%!

WHERE TO EAT

THE BLUE RAVEN   606/509-2583
APPROVED American. Casual Dining. **Address:** 211 Main St 41501

CHIRICO'S RISTORANTE 606/432-7070
APPROVED Italian. Casual Dining. **Address:** 235 Main St 41501

PRINCETON (E-2) pop. 6,329, elev. 455'

ADSMORE HOUSE AND GARDENS, 304 N. Jefferson St., is the former residence of four generations of the Smith-Garrett family. Purchased in the early 1900s, the family added several Federal-style touches to this 1850s brick mansion, including a columned portico. The rooms in the manor include original furnishings and are decorated according to specific periods in the residents' lives, such as the marriage of one of the family members in 1907. Seven other decorative themes are presented during the year.

Time: Allow 1 hour minimum. **Hours:** Guided tours by costumed interpreters are given Tues.-Sat. 11-4, Mar.-Dec.; schedule varies rest of year. Closed Christmas Eve and Christmas. **Cost:** $10; $8 (ages 65+); $2 (ages 6-12). **Phone:** (270) 365-3114. GT

RADCLIFF pop. 21,688

CANDLEWOOD SUITES RADCLIFF-FORT KNOX
270/351-3333
THREE DIAMOND Extended Stay Hotel. **Address:** 40 Bourbon St 40160

HAMPTON INN & SUITES BY HILTON RADCLIFF/FORT KNOX
270/351-5777
THREE DIAMOND SAVE Hotel. **Address:** 50 Bourbon St 40160

AAA Benefit: Members save up to 15%!

HOLIDAY INN EXPRESS RADCLIFF-FORT KNOX
270/352-4329
THREE DIAMOND Hotel. **Address:** 30 Bourbon St 40160

WHERE TO EAT

COLTON'S STEAKHOUSE & GRILL 270/319-4939
APPROVED Steak. Casual Dining. **Address:** 3050 S Dixie Hwy 40160

RICHMOND (D-7) pop. 31,364, elev. 937'

Named after the capital of Virginia, Richmond was the scene of a decisive Confederate victory in Kentucky. This major Civil War battle, waged Aug. 29-30, 1862, pitted Gen. William Nelson's Union forces against Gen. Kirby Smith's Confederate troops. Although the conflict originated 6 miles south of Richmond, a sharply contested retreat through the town left many buildings scarred.

Richmond is a farming, cattle ranching and industrial center as well as the home of Eastern Kentucky University. Arnim D. Hummel Planetarium, on the university's campus, offers shows on the first Saturday of the month; phone (859) 622-1547 for information.

The downtown area includes three historic districts comprising a number of 19th-century houses. *Also see Bluegrass Country p. 30.*

Richmond Tourism and Visitors Center: 531 W. Main S., Richmond, KY 40475. **Phone:** (800) 866-3705.

Self-guiding tours: Downtown walking tour brochures and a Civil War audio driving tour are available at the visitors center.

FORT BOONESBOROUGH STATE PARK, off SR 627 to SR 388, contains a re-creation of the fort built by Daniel Boone in 1775. Artisans demonstrate 18th-century trades and skills, April through October. Films shown in the orientation blockhouse depict the pioneers' struggle at the fort. The Kentucky Museum offers insight into the lives of the families who lived in the area in the 1900s. Riverside interpretive trails pass native plants and unusual geological sites. Picnicking, camping, fishing, swimming and a miniature golf course are available. *See Recreation Areas Chart.*

Time: Allow 1 hour minimum. **Hours:** Park open daily dawn-dusk. Fort open Wed.-Sun. 9-5, Apr.-Oct.; Fri.-Sun. 10-4, rest of year. Closed Christmas-Jan. 1. Phone ahead to confirm schedule. **Cost:** Park free. Fort tour (includes admission to Kentucky River Museum) $8; $5 (ages 6-12). **Phone:** (859) 527-3131.

WHITE HALL STATE HISTORIC SITE is off I-75 exit 95, w. .25 mi. on SR 627 to White Hall State Shrine Rd., then following signs for 2 mi. An imposing 44-room estate house in two architectural styles, White Hall was the home of emancipationist Cassius Marcellus Clay. The site, which is near the Kentucky River, covers 13 acres.

The first section, Clermont, was built by Clay's father in 1798 in a Georgian design. During the 1860s Cassius Clay annexed an Italianate front and side addition to the house, more than doubling the home's size. White Hall was the first house in the area to have central heating and indoor plumbing. Guides conduct 1-hour tours of the home.

Time: Allow 1 hour minimum. **Hours:** Guided tours are given on the hour Wed.-Sat. 10-4, Sun. noon-4, Apr.-Oct.; by appointment rest of year. Phone ahead to confirm schedule. **Cost:** $10; $8 (62+ and military with ID); $5 (ages 6-12). Phone ahead for admission cost during special events. **Phone:** (859) 623-9178. GT

BEST WESTERN RICHMOND HOTEL 859/623-9220
APPROVED
Hotel

BW Best Western. **AAA Benefit:** Members save up to 15% and earn bonus points!

Address: 100 Eastern Bypass 40475 **Location:** I-75 exit 87, just e. **Facility:** 80 units. 2 stories (no elevator), interior corridors. **Parking:** winter plug-ins. **Pool:** heated indoor. **Activities:** hot tub, exercise room. **Guest Services:** valet laundry.

HAMPTON INN BY HILTON RICHMOND   859/626-1002
THREE DIAMOND SAVE Hotel. **Address:** 1099 Barnes Mill Rd 40475

AAA Benefit: Members save up to 15%!

HOLIDAY INN EXPRESS HOTEL & SUITES   859/624-4055
THREE DIAMOND Hotel. **Address:** 1990 Colby Taylor Dr 40475

TOWNEPLACE SUITES   859/353-4860
THREE DIAMOND SAVE Extended Stay Hotel. **Address:** 2018 Colby Taylor Dr 40475

AAA Benefit: Members save 5% or more!

TRU BY HILTON RICHMOND   859/544-6312
THREE DIAMOND   SAVE

Contemporary Hotel. **Address:** 1020 Amberly Way 40475

Members save up to 15%!

WHERE TO EAT

CASA FIESTA   859/623-8582
APPROVED Mexican. Casual Dining. **Address:** 240 Eastern Bypass 40475

MADISON GARDEN BAR & GRILL   859/623-9720
APPROVED American. Casual Dining. **Address:** 152 N Madison Ave 40475

ST. MATTHEWS pop. 17,472
• Hotels & Restaurants map & index p. 87
• Part of Louisville area — see map p. 71

HILTON GARDEN INN LOUISVILLE MALL OF ST MATTHEWS
502/690-3325   35
THREE DIAMOND SAVE Hotel. **Address:** 400 Sherburn Ln 40207

AAA Benefit: Members save up to 15%!

WHERE TO EAT

DEL FRISCO'S RESTAURANT   502/897-7077   44
APPROVED Steak. Casual Dining. **Address:** 4107 Oechsli Ave 40207

EQUUS RESTAURANT   502/897-9721   45
THREE DIAMOND New American. Fine Dining. **Address:** 122 Sears Ave 40207

WILD EGGS   502/893-8005   46
APPROVED American. Casual Dining. **Address:** 3985 Dutchmans Ln 40207

SHELBYVILLE pop. 14,045

ECONO LODGE   502/633-5771
APPROVED Hotel. **Address:** 100 Howard Dr 40065

RAMADA   502/633-9933
APPROVED Hotel. **Address:** 251 Breighton Cir 40065

WHERE TO EAT

CATTLEMAN'S ROADHOUSE   502/647-5959
APPROVED American. Casual Dining. **Address:** 221 Breighton Cir 40065

FIREFRESH BBQ   502/647-7675
APPROVED Barbecue. Casual Dining. **Address:** 81 Jeanie Dr 40065

KEN-TEX BAR-B-Q   502/633-2463
APPROVED Barbecue. Quick Serve. **Address:** 1163 Mount Eden Rd 40065

SHEPHERDSVILLE (D-5) pop. 11,222, elev. 443'
• Restaurants p. 110
• Part of Louisville area — see map p. 71

Founded in 1793, Shepherdsville is the oldest town in Bullitt County and has served as its county seat since its inception in 1796. It is named after Adam Shepherd, a Maryland native who regularly visited the area to tend to his father's interests, which included land grants and surveying. Shepherd built a mill and store and also designed the streets of the town, part of a 900-acre area he owned just north of the Salt River.

The salt production industry—the state's first—was Shepherdsville's focus in its earliest days. The area's abundance of salt was the result of a receding shallow ocean which covered Kentucky more than 350 million years ago. Those who continued westward utilized the salt to preserve meats and other foods on their journeys. Mineral water from the Paroquet Springs spa, which opened in 1836, was said to have medicinal value; sufferers of a variety of ailments traveled to the town to drink and bathe in the spa's water. The iron-smelting industry also was prominent in Shepherdsville from 1830-80. The Belmont Iron Furnace, 3 miles south off SR 61, supplied much of the pig iron used during this time. It is one of the state's last remaining standing furnaces.

Shepherdsville Country Music Show, off I-65 exit 117 on SR 44, features live bluegrass and country music performed by local musicians. The bluegrass show is offered on Fridays from October through late April; the country show is held on Saturdays throughout the year. Phone (502) 543-6551 for show schedules and reservations.

Shepherdsville/Bullitt County Tourist & Convention Commission: 142 Buffalo Run Rd., Shepherdsville, KY 40165. **Phone:** (502) 543-8687 or (800) 526-2068.

BEST WESTERN SHEPHERDSVILLE   502/543-7097
APPROVED
Hotel

 Best Western. **AAA Benefit:** Members save up to 15% and earn bonus points!

Address: 211 S Lakeview Dr 40165 **Location:** I-65 exit 117 (SR 44 W), just se. **Facility:** 84 units. 2 stories, interior corridors. **Parking:** winter plug-ins. **Pool:** outdoor. **Activities:** exercise room. **Guest Services:** coin laundry. **Featured Amenity:** full hot breakfast.

COMFORT INN LOUISVILLE SOUTH   502/955-5566
APPROVED Hotel. **Address:** 191 Brenton Way 40165

COUNTRY INN & SUITES BY RADISSON, LOUISVILLE SOUTH
502/543-8400
 APPROVED Hotel. **Address:** 400 Paroquet Springs Dr 40165

FAIRFIELD BY MARRIOTT LOUISVILLE SOUTH 502/955-5533
APPROVED SAVE Hotel. **Address:** 362 Brenton Way 40165

AAA Benefit:
Members save 5% or more!

HOLIDAY INN EXPRESS HOTEL & SUITES
502/955-4984
 THREE DIAMOND

Hotel

Address: 365 Brenton Way 40165 **Location:** I-65 exit 121, just e. **Facility:** 67 units. 3 stories, interior corridors. **Parking:** winter plug-ins. **Pool:** heated indoor. **Activities:** exercise room. **Guest Services:** valet and coin laundry. **Featured Amenity:** breakfast buffet.

SLEEP INN & SUITES-LOUISVILLE SOUTH 502/921-1001
APPROVED Hotel. **Address:** 130 Spring Pointe Dr 40165

WHERE TO EAT

ISAAC'S CAFE 502/543-3966
APPROVED Sandwiches. Quick Serve. **Address:** 1701 Clermont Rd 40165

TUMBLEWEED SOUTHWEST GRILL 502/955-5747
APPROVED Southwestern. Casual Dining. **Address:** 380 Brenton Way 40165

SOMERSET (E-6) pop. 11,196, elev. 971'

Drawing many settlers from Somerset County, N.J., this community came together in the late 18th century. Two Civil War battles—Mill Springs and Dutton's Hill—occurred nearby. However, due to the creation of Lake Cumberland circa 1950, the area is now best known for recreation. Tubing, fishing, camping and hiking are popular pastimes.

BEST WESTERN MID-TOWN INN & SUITES
606/677-9000
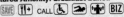 **APPROVED**

Hotel

Best Western. **AAA Benefit:** Members save up to 15% and earn bonus points!

Address: 103 Jefferson Dr 42501 **Location:** Jct SR 80, 2 mi s on US 27; at traffic light 14. **Facility:** 61 units. 4 stories, interior corridors. **Pool:** heated indoor. **Activities:** exercise room.

COUNTRY INN & SUITES BY RADISSON 606/679-3711
APPROVED Hotel. **Address:** 515 N Hwy 27 42501

COURTYARD BY MARRIOTT SOMERSET 606/679-0090
THREE DIAMOND SAVE Hotel. **Address:** 2254 S Hwy 27 42501

AAA Benefit:
Members save 5% or more!

HAMPTON INN BY HILTON 606/676-8855
 THREE DIAMOND SAVE Hotel. **Address:** 4141 S Hwy 27 42501

AAA Benefit:
Members save up to 15%!

HOLIDAY INN EXPRESS & SUITES 606/425-4444
THREE DIAMOND Hotel. **Address:** 50 Stevie Lynn Dr 42503

WHERE TO EAT

AMON'S SUGAR SHACK 606/678-4392
APPROVED Breads/Pastries Sandwiches. Quick Serve. **Address:** 1900 S Hwy 27 42503

EL CHARRO MEXICAN RESTAURANT 606/678-2883
APPROVED Mexican. Casual Dining. **Address:** 2835 S Hwy 27 42501

STEARNS (F-6) pop. 1,416, elev. 1,351'

BIG SOUTH FORK SCENIC RAILWAY, 1 mi. w. of US 27 on SR 92, offers a scenic 16-mile tour along Big South Fork, a branch of the Cumberland River, in enclosed and open-air excursion cars. There is a stopover in Blue Heron *(see attraction listing),* an abandoned coal mine company town that has been restored by the National Park Service. The line originally was used by the Stearns Coal & Lumber Co. to transport logs and coal. The 90-minute Run to the Gorge excursion is offered in November.

Time: Allow 3 hours, 30 minutes minimum. **Hours:** Departures Wed.-Fri. at 11, Sat. at 11 and 2:30, Sun. at 12:30, May-Sept. (also Sun. at 11 and 2:30, Mon. at 11 on Memorial Day and Labor Day weekends); Tues.-Fri. at 11, Sat. at 11 and 2:30, Sun. at 12:30, in Oct.; Thurs.-Fri. at 11, Sat. at 11 and 2:30, in Apr. Run to the Gorge rides (1.5-hour duration) depart Thurs.-Sat. at 1, Nov. 1-18 and 27-30. Phone for information about Halloween and Christmas departures. Closed Thanksgiving.

Cost: Fare (includes train, mining town and The McCreary County Museum at Stearns) $28; $25 (ages 60+); $18 (ages 3-12). **Phone:** (606) 376-5330 or (800) 462-5664.

VERSAILLES (D-6) pop. 8,568, elev. 895'

Established in 1792, the streets of Versailles (ver-SALES) are lined with shady trees and Victorian-style homes and buildings. The city is the county seat of Woodford County, which is known for its horse farms.

The Bluegrass Scenic Railroad & Museum, 2 miles west on US 62 in Woodford County Park, offers weekend train rides through the rolling Bluegrass Region on the old Louisville Southern Mainline. The museum is dedicated to the reconstruction, restoration and preservation of railroad arts and artifacts; phone (859) 873-2476. *Also see Bluegrass Country p. 30.*

Woodford County Chamber of Commerce: 141 N. Main St., Versailles, KY 40383. **Phone:** (859) 873-5122.

NOSTALGIA STATION TOY AND TRAIN MUSEUM, 279 Depot St., is a model train museum housed in a restored 1911 railroad station. Exhibits include a reproduction of a 1926 standard gauge Lionel store display as well as children's toys and railroad memorabilia. A late 1950s Lionel store display includes accessories authentic to the original layout. **Time:** Allow 1 hour minimum. **Hours:** Wed.-Sat. 10-5. Closed major holidays. **Cost:** $5; $4 (ages 61+). **Phone:** (859) 873-2497.

WOODFORD RESERVE DISTILLERY is 6 mi. w. on US 60, s.w. on Grassy Springs Rd. (CR 3360), then w. on McCracken Pike to entrance. Guided tours of this restored 1812 facility show visitors the traditional method of making Kentucky straight bourbon whiskey. Tours through the distillery's limestone buildings, some more than a century old, include a look at the cypress fermentors, old-fashioned copper pot stills and charred-oak barrels.

A short film about the site's history is shown at the visitor center, which also has exhibits, artifacts and photographs. The distillery produces the super-premium Woodford Reserve Bourbon.

Time: Allow 1 hour, 30 minutes minimum. **Hours:** Visitors center Mon.-Sat. 9-5, Sun. noon-4:30, Mar.-Dec.; Mon.-Sat. 9-5, rest of year. Tours are given on the hour Mon.-Sat. at 10-3, Sun. 1-3, Mar.-Dec.; Mon.-Sat. at 10-3, rest of year. Closed major holidays. **Cost:** Fee $15-$30. Reservations are recommended. **Phone:** (859) 879-1812. GT

WILDER pop. 3,035
- Hotels & Restaurants map & index p. 37
- Part of Cincinnati area — see map p. 153

COMFORT INN & SUITES NORTHERN KENTUCKY
859/441-3707 16
APPROVED Hotel. **Address:** 10 Country Dr 41076

HAMPTON INN & SUITES BY HILTON WILDER
859/441-3049 15
THREE DIAMOND SAVE Hotel. **Address:** 10 Hampton Ln 41076

AAA Benefit: Members save up to 15%!

HOLIDAY INN EXPRESS AND SUITES CINCINNATI SOUTH-WILDER
859/815-8855 14
THREE DIAMOND Hotel. **Address:** 8 Hampton Ln 41076

WILLIAMSBURG pop. 5,245, elev. 951'

HAMPTON INN WILLIAMSBURG
606/549-3775
THREE DIAMOND SAVE Hotel. **Address:** 530 Hwy 92 W 40769

AAA Benefit: Members save up to 15%!

WINCHESTER (D-7) pop. 18,368, elev. 995'
Founded in 1793, Winchester was named after the former Virginia home of frontiersman John Baker who donated 66 acres of land for the town's creation. The town was given distinction by Henry Clay, "The Great Compromiser," when he made both his first and last Kentucky speeches in the city.

Early on, Winchester became the marketing center of the agricultural inner Bluegrass Region. Industrial enterprises and manufacturing supplement the economy. *Also see Bluegrass Country p. 30.*

Of interest off SR 1924 is the Civil War Fort at Boonesboro. Built by Union soldiers in 1863, the earthwork fortification was used to defend the ford and ferry at Boonesboro. Today visitors can hike the scenic trail with views of the Kentucky River and see a mural depicting the history of the river. Guided tours are offered by appointment; phone (859) 744-0556. Located on 240 acres of land, the Lower Howard's Creek Nature Preserve offers guided tours of its environment of native flora and fauna; phone (859) 744-4888.

Winchester/Clark County Tourism Commission: 2 S. Maple St., Winchester, KY 40391. **Phone:** (859) 744-0556 or (800) 298-9105.

Self-guiding tours: The tourism commission offers guided tours as well as maps and brochures outlining driving and walking tours of area points of interest. One of Kentucky's first guided cellphones tours is offered; highlights include the history of downtown and the Civil War Fort at Boonesboro; phone (859) 592-9166.

BEST WESTERN WINCHESTER HOTEL   859/744-7210
APPROVED
Motel

Best Western. **AAA Benefit:** Members save up to 15% and earn bonus points!

Address: 1307 W Lexington Ave 40391 **Location:** I-64 exit 94 (US 60), 0.9 mi se. **Facility:** 46 units, some efficiencies. 2 stories (no elevator), exterior corridors. **Parking:** winter plug-ins. **Pool:** outdoor. **Featured Amenity:** breakfast buffet.

SAVE / SOME UNITS

HAMPTON INN BY HILTON   859/745-2000
THREE DIAMOND SAVE Hotel. **Address:** 1025 Early Dr 40391

AAA Benefit: Members save up to 15%!

WHERE TO EAT

GAUNCE'S DELI & CAFE   859/744-8664
APPROVED Deli. Quick Serve. **Address:** 853 Bypass Rd 40391

GIOVANNI'S   859/745-2991
APPROVED Italian Pizza. Quick Serve. **Address:** 728 Boone Ave 40391

Cincinnati

Ohio

Like the proverbial coin, there are two sides to Ohio. On one side you have the "three C's"—Cleveland, Cincinnati and Columbus. These major metropolitan areas offer big-city attractions: top-notch art museums, child-friendly science centers, world-class zoos, pro sports teams, ethnic festivals and razzle-dazzle annual events. It's a prominent facet of the Buckeye State.

But flip the coin and you'll discover the small towns and family-owned farms of Middle America. Here the reminders of a simpler time are evident in painstakingly restored historic villages and Amish-populated rural areas. Craft demonstrations, barn raisings and horse-drawn buggies are more characteristic of this side. Question: Which is the "real" Ohio? Answer: Both.

"Our position in the nation," one 19th-century historian wrote of his adopted state, "is peculiarly felicitous as to soil, climate and productions, and it will be our own fault if we

Amish life

are not the happiest people in the Union." And to many early settlers, success in this new frontier likely seemed guaranteed. As immigrants pushed westward along the Ohio River, river towns boomed. This wave of settlement came after the Revolutionary War, and Ohio became the first state to be carved from the Northwest Territory.

Due to an advantageous location on the Ohio River, Cincinnati became the first industrial city in what was then—before the era of westward expansion—considered the American West. By the late 19th century it was Cleveland's turn to boom. Proximity to coal fields in West Virginia and Pennsylvania and iron mines in Minnesota transformed this Great Lakes port into one of America's leading manufacturing centers. Recent decades have unfortunately not been as prosperous for this corner of the so-called "rust belt." It does, however, offer its share of tourist-worthy fare.

The Cleveland Museum of Art has ancient Egyptian statues as well as Impressionist masterpieces, while the dinosaur skeletons at the Cleveland Museum of Natural History include a looming example known as "Lucy." And standing on the Lake Erie shoreline is the eye-popping glass-and-steel monument to a 4/4 backbeat: the Rock and Roll Hall of Fame. You'll probably find at least a few of your faves among hall of fame inductees that range from Alice Cooper to ZZ Top.

The Simple Life

On the other side of the Ohio coin are rustic locales that hark back to a time when life was less complicated and moved at a slower pace. Surrender to nostalgia at Roscoe Village in Coshocton, a restored 1830s canal town where costumed interpreters demonstrate skills like candle dipping and tin punching. Hale Farm and Village, near Bath, and Historic Sauder Village, in Archbold, are other places to experience living history.

These restored villages carefully re-create the past, but if it's the real thing you're after, visit Amish country. The Amish and Mennonites of eastern Ohio shun modern conveniences, continuing a farming tradition that beguiles anyone who's ever bemoaned the harried pace of contemporary life. Berlin is a good place to hop on a buggy, relax and get a taste of how the Amish handle their day. So flip a coin; either way you win.

Recreation

Resorts along sandy stretches of Lake Erie beach offer activities for powerboaters and fans of other personal watercraft, and charter boats embark on fishing trips and diving excursions to shipwreck sites. When temperatures drop and the water freezes, ice shanty camps set up off the west shore of Put-in-Bay between Rattlesnake and Middle Bass islands.

Mohican State Park, near Mansfield, encompasses both the meandering Clear Fork River and dramatic Clear Fork Gorge. The river teems with brown trout, creating a paradise for fishing. The lower section of the river is the most accessible; a trail that follows the magnificent gorge (more than 1,000 feet wide and 300 feet deep) passes two waterfalls, offering both spectacular scenery and easy access for anglers.

In southern Ohio, Hocking State Forest has a climbing and rappelling area that challenges daredevils and those in enviable shape with formidable cliffs and sheer rock faces; the climbs range in height from 20 to 120 feet. Less adventurous outdoor enthusiasts can head to Hocking Hills State Park, where a concrete trail—accessible to the physically impaired and suitable for young kids—snakes past sandstone cliffs, carved gorges and a 90-foot waterfall on its way to Ash Cave.

Cleveland's 100-mile chain of metropolitan parks, known as the "Emerald Necklace," offers places to **hike, boat, golf** and go

horseback riding and **in-line skating** during warm weather. Winter activities include **tobogganing, cross-country skiing, sledding** and **ice fishing**. Cleveland Metroparks' Lakefront Reservation includes Edgewater Park, which is close to downtown and has two beaches, a **fishing** pier and boat ramps; scuba divers can explore a freshwater reef created by remnants of demolished Cleveland Municipal Stadium.

Go **biking,** hiking or cross-country skiing along the Ohio and Erie Canal Towpath Trail. Running the 22-mile length of Cuyahoga Valley National Park from Cleveland to Akron, it passes locks, spillways, an aqueduct and historic homes.

If you'd rather ride in a golf cart than lace up a pair of hiking boots, head for The Golf Center at Kings Island, in Mason (right outside Cincinnati). Take your pick of two courses: the Bruin is easy on duffers, while the challenging Grizzly is a championship layout designed in part by the Golden Bear himself, Jack Nicklaus. And for those not interested in following a little white ball, Kings Island has a day's worth of theme park thrill rides, roller coasters and other family-friendly diversions.

Hocking Hills State Park, Logan

Historic Timeline

1788	Marietta becomes the first permanent American settlement in the Northwest Territory.
1833	The nation's first interracial, coeducational college is founded in Oberlin.
1886	Trade union leaders establish the American Federation of Labor at a meeting in Columbus.
1904	Orville and Wilbur Wright begin to perfect their airplane at Huffman Prairie Flying Field in Dayton.
1920	The American Professional Football Association (later renamed the National Football League) is founded in Canton.
1967	Carl Stokes is elected mayor of Cleveland, making him the first African-American mayor of a major U.S. city.
1969	Neil Armstrong of Wapakoneta becomes the first person to walk on the moon.
1970	Four students are killed by National Guardsmen during anti-war demonstrations at Kent State University.
1998	Ohioan John Glenn (the first American to orbit the Earth) flies aboard *Discovery,* becoming the oldest person to fly in space.
1999	Rep. Stephanie Tubbs Jones (Cleveland) begins serving as the first African-American woman to represent Ohio in Congress.
2006	Voters pass Issue 5 to enact Ohio's Smoke-Free Workplace Act.

What To Pack

Temperature Averages Maximum/Minimum	JANUARY	FEBRUARY	MARCH	APRIL	MAY	JUNE	JULY	AUGUST	SEPTEMBER	OCTOBER	NOVEMBER	DECEMBER
Cincinnati	39/22	44/26	55/34	65/43	75/53	83/62	87/66	85/64	79/57	68/45	55/36	44/27
Cleveland	33/19	36/21	46/29	57/38	69/48	77/58	81/62	79/61	72/54	61/44	49/35	37/25
Columbus	36/20	41/23	53/32	64/40	74/51	82/60	86/64	84/62	78/55	67/43	53/34	41/25
Dayton	35/21	40/24	51/32	63/42	74/53	83/63	87/67	85/65	79/57	66/45	52/36	40/26
Toledo	33/22	38/24	48/33	61/42	74/53	83/63	87/68	84/66	77/59	64/48	51/38	38/27
Youngstown	32/16	36/17	46/25	58/35	69/45	78/54	82/58	80/55	73/49	62/38	49/31	38/22

From the records of The Weather Channel Interactive, Inc.

Good Facts To Know

ABOUT THE STATE

POPULATION: 11,536,504.

AREA: 44,826 square miles; ranks 34th.

CAPITAL: Columbus.

HIGHEST POINT: 1,550 ft., Campbell Hill, Bellefontaine.

LOWEST POINT: 433 ft., Ohio River.

TIME ZONE(S): Eastern. DST.

GAMBLING

MINIMUM AGE FOR GAMBLING: 18 (lottery), 21 (casino).

REGULATIONS

TEEN DRIVING LAWS: No more than one passenger permitted for drivers for the first 12 months (family exempt). Driving is not permitted 12 a.m.-6 a.m. for the first 12 months; and 1 a.m.-5 a.m. for over the second 12 months (work or school functions exempt). Minimum age for an unrestricted driver's license is 18. For more information about Ohio driver's license laws phone (614) 752-7600.

SEAT BELT CHILD RESTRAINT LAWS: Seat belts are required for driver and front-seat passengers ages 15 and over. Children ages 8-14 are required to be in either a child restraint or seat belt. Children ages 4-7, over 40 pounds and under 57 inches are required to be in a booster seat. Child restraints are required for children under age 4 or less than 40 lbs. AAA recommends the use of seat belts and appropriate child restraints for the driver and all passengers.

CELLPHONE RESTRICTIONS: Text messaging while driving is prohibited. Temporary instruction permit holders under age 18 and probationary license holders are prohibited from using any type of wireless device while driving. The use of handheld cellphones while driving is prohibited in several municipalities, including Beachwood, Brooklyn, Marietta, North Olmsted, North Royalton, South Euclid, Walton Hills and Woodmere.

HELMETS FOR MOTORCYCLISTS: Required for riders under age 18, all drivers during their first year of licensure and all passengers of riders required to wear a helmet.

RADAR DETECTORS: Permitted. Prohibited for use by commercial vehicles.

MOVE OVER LAW: Driver is required to slow down and vacate the lane nearest stopped police, fire, rescue and road maintenance vehicles using audible or flashing signals. The law includes recovery vehicles such as tow trucks, municipal vehicles and road maintenance vehicles.

FIREARMS LAWS: Vary by state and/or county. Contact the Ohio Highway Patrol/State Police at 1970 W. Broad St., Columbus, OH 43223; phone (614) 466-2660.

HOLIDAYS

HOLIDAYS: Jan. 1 ▪ Martin Luther King Jr. Day, Jan. (3rd Mon.) ▪ Washington's Birthday/Presidents Day, Feb. (3rd Mon.) ▪ Memorial Day, May (last Mon.) ▪ July 4 ▪ Labor Day, Sept. (1st Mon.) ▪ Columbus Day, Oct. (2nd Mon.) ▪ Veterans Day, Nov. 11 ▪ Thanksgiving ▪ Christmas, Dec. 25.

MONEY

TAXES: The state sales and use tax rate is 5.75 percent. Counties and regional transit authorities may levy additional sales and use taxes. Local options also allow lodgings taxes up to 10.5 percent.

VISITOR INFORMATION

INFORMATION CENTERS: Welcome centers are off I-90 westbound 1 mile w. of the Pennsylvania line near Conneaut ▪ I-71 north- and southbound 2 miles n. of SR 123 interchange near Lebanon ▪ I-80 westbound 1 mile w. of the Pennsylvania line near Hubbard ▪ I-70 westbound 5 miles w. of St. Clairsville ▪ I-77 northbound 6 miles n. of Marietta ▪ I-75 north- and southbound 1 mile s. of US 6 interchange near Bowling Green ▪ I-70 eastbound 3 miles e. of the Indiana line near New Paris ▪ I-75 northbound near Monroe ▪ and on US 23 northbound 15 miles n. of the Kentucky line.

FURTHER INFORMATION FOR VISITORS:
Discover Ohio, Ohio Office of Tourism
77 S. High St.
Columbus, OH 43216
(614) 466-8844
(800) 282-5393

NATIONAL FOREST INFORMATION:
Forest Supervisor, Wayne National Forest
13700 US 33
Nelsonville, OH 45764
(740) 753-0101 (information)
(877) 444-6777 (reservations)

FISHING AND HUNTING REGULATIONS:
Division of Wildlife, Dept. of Natural Resources
2045 Morse Rd., Building G
Columbus, OH 43229-6693
(614) 265-6565
(800) 945-3543

RECREATION INFORMATION:
Division of Parks and Recreation
Department of Natural Resources
2045 Morse Rd., Building C
Columbus, OH 43229-6693
(614) 265-6561

Ohio Annual Events

Please call ahead to confirm event details.

 Visit **AAA.com/travelguides/events** to find AAA-listed events for every day of the year

WINTER

Dec. - Holiday Lantern Tours / Bath
330-666-3711
- Christmas Festival and Horse-Drawn Carriage Parade / Lebanon
513-932-1100
- Christmas in the Village / Canal Winchester / 614-834-9915

Jan. - A Taste of Wine and Jazz / Greenville
937-547-0908
- Cincinnati Travel, Sports and Boat Show / Cincinnati / 513-281-0022
- Mohican Winterfest / Loudonville
419-994-4789

Feb. - Honoring Our Native Heritage Powwow / Lima / 419-238-0197
- Fairytales and Frogs at the Zoo Cleveland / 216-661-6500
- Ski Carnival at Snow Trails Mansfield / 800-644-6754

SPRING

Mar. - St. Patrick's Day Parade / Dublin
614-792-7666
- Cincinnati Home & Garden Show and The Garden Market / Cincinnati
513-281-0022
- St. Patrick's Day Parade / Cleveland
216-556-5183

Apr. - I-X Indoor Amusement Park Cleveland / 800-897-3942
- Equine Affaire / Columbus
740-845-0085

May - Appalachian Festival / Cincinnati
513-251-3378
- Taste of Cincinnati / Cincinnati
513-579-3197
- Main Street Port Clinton Walleye Festival / Port Clinton / 419-732-3171

SUMMER

June - Avon Heritage Duck Tape Festival Avon / 866-818-1116
- Washboard Music Festival / Logan
740-380-2752
- Tri-C JazzFest / Cleveland
216-987-4444

July - Jazz and Rib Fest / Columbus
614-645-3800
- Red, White and Boom / Columbus
614-823-7151
- Ohio State Fair / Columbus
614-644-4000

Aug. - Carnation Festival / Alliance
330-823-6260
- Dublin Irish Festival / Dublin
614-410-4545
- Flag City BalloonFest / Findlay
419-422-3315

FALL

Sept. - Columbus Oktoberfest / Columbus
614-444-5908
- Oktoberfest Zinzinnati / Cincinnati
513-579-3191

Oct. - HallZOOween / Cincinnati
513-281-4700
- Circleville Pumpkin Show / Circleville
740-474-8973

Nov. - Dickens Victorian Village / Cambridge
740-421-4956
- Wildlights at the Columbus Zoo and Aquarium / Powell / 614-645-3550
- Dayton Holiday Festival / Dayton
937-224-1518

Deeds Carillon at Carillon Historical Park, Dayton

Everett Road Covered Bridge, Cuyahoga Valley National Park

Ash Cave in Hocking Hills State Park, Logan

Lanterman's Mill in Mill Creek Park, Youngstown

Toledo

Index: Great Experience for Members

AAA editor's picks of exceptional note

Hale Farm and
Village

Cleveland Museum of
Natural History

Cuyahoga Valley
National Park

Hocking Hills State
Park

See Orientation map on p. 128 for corresponding grid coordinates, if applicable.
*Indicates the GEM is temporarily closed.

STAY CONNECTED

to all the things membership can do for you

- **Member discounts around you**
- **Cheapest gas nearby**
- **Diamond hotels and restaurants**
- **Travel information and reservations**
- **Roadside assistance**

Download today.
Connect every day.
AAA.com/mobile | CAA.ca/mobile

Ohio

Atlas Section

ROADS/HIGHWAYS
- INTERSTATE
- CONTROLLED ACCESS
- CONTROLLED ACCESS TOLL
- TOLL ROAD
- PRIMARY DIVIDED
- PRIMARY UNDIVIDED
- SECONDARY DIVIDED
- SECONDARY UNDIVIDED
- LOCAL DIVIDED
- LOCAL UNDIVIDED
- UNPAVED ROAD
- UNDER CONSTRUCTION
- TUNNEL
- PEDESTRIAN ONLY
- AUTO FERRY
- PASSENGER FERRY
- SCENIC BYWAY
- DISTANCE BETWEEN MARKERS
- EXIT NUMBER-FREE/TOLL
- INTERCHANGE FULL/PARTIAL
- WELCOME/INFORMATION CENTER
- REST AREA/ SERVICE CENTER

ROAD SHIELDS
- INTERSTATE/BUSINESS
- U.S./STATE/COUNTY
- FOREST/INDIAN
- TRANS-CANADA
- PROVINCIAL AUTOROUTE/ KING'S HIGHWAY
- MEXICO
- HISTORIC ROUTE 66
- VT 41 REFERENCE PAGE INDICATOR

BOUNDARIES
- INTERNATIONAL
- STATE
- COUNTY
- TIME ZONE
- CONTINENTAL DIVIDE

POINTS OF INTEREST
- TOWN
- NATIONAL CAPITAL
- STATE/PROVINCIAL CAPITAL
- AAA/CAA CLUB LOCATION
- FEATURE OF INTEREST
- COLLEGE/UNIVERSITY
- CUSTOMS STATION
- HISTORIC
- LIGHTHOUSE
- MONUMENT/MEMORIAL
- NATIONAL WILDLIFE REFUGE
- STATE/PROVINCIAL PARK
- SKI AREA
- SPORTS COMPLEX
- DAM

AREAS OF INTEREST
- INDIAN
- MILITARY
- PARK
- FOREST
- GRASSLANDS
- HISTORIC
- INT'L/REGIONAL AIRPORT
- INCORPORATED CITY

CITIES/TOWNS are color-coded by size, showing where to find AAA Inspected and Approved lodgings or restaurants listed in the AAA TourBook guides and on AAA.com:
- Red - major destinations and capitals; many listings
- Black - destinations; some listings
- Grey - no listings

Use these detailed driving maps to plan your stops and find your way. For complete route planning, purchase the latest AAA Road Atlas at participating AAA/CAA offices, and use the free online TripTik Travel Planner at AAA.com/maps

Atlas ROAD 2020

Southern OHIO

1:855,360
Scale in Miles

Scale in Kilometers

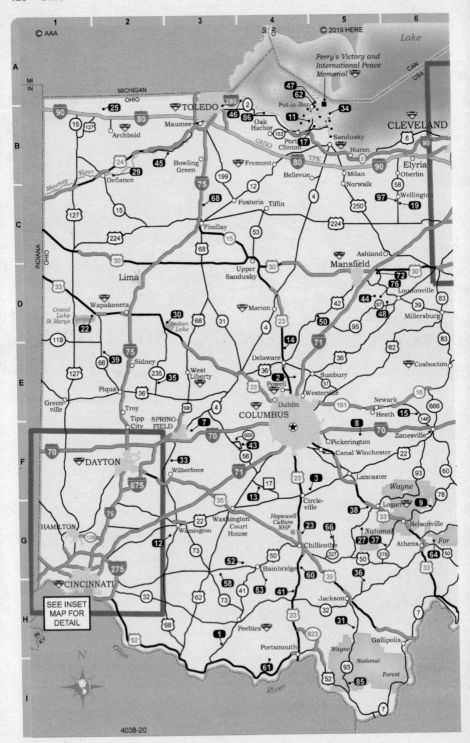

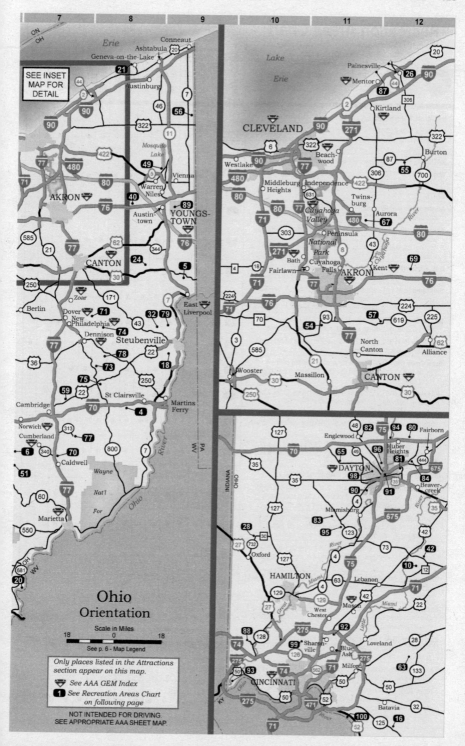

Ohio
Orientation

Scale in Miles

18   0   18

See p. 6 - Map Legend

Only places listed in the Attractions section appear on this map.

See AAA GEM Index

See Recreation Areas Chart on following page

NOT INTENDED FOR DRIVING
SEE APPROPRIATE AAA SHEET MAP.

Recreation Areas Chart

The map location numerals in column 2 show an area's location on the preceding map.

🔗 **Find thousands of places to camp at AAA.com/campgrounds**

	MAP LOCATION	CAMPING	PICNICKING	HIKING TRAILS	BOATING	BOAT RAMP	BOAT RENTAL	FISHING	SWIMMING	PET FRIENDLY	BICYCLE TRAILS	WINTER SPORTS	VISITOR CENTER	LODGE/CABINS	FOOD SERVICE
NATIONAL PARKS *(See place listings.)*															
Cuyahoga Valley (C-11) Northeastern Ohio. 33,000 acres. Cross-country skiing, downhill skiing, golf, ice fishing, snowshoeing; horse trails.		•	•	•				•		•	•	•	•	•	•
NATIONAL FORESTS *(See place listings.)*															
Wayne (F-6) 241,000 acres. Southeastern Ohio. Hunting; horse rental.		•	•	•	•	•		•	•	•	•				
STATE															
Adams Lake (H-3) 96 acres 1 mi. n.e. of West Union on SR 41. Boats with electric motors only.	❶		•	•	•	•		•							
Alum Creek (E-4) 8,017 acres 7 mi. s.e. of Delaware off SRs 36 and 37, 1 mi. w. of jct. I-71. Cross-country skiing, disc golf, hunting, ice-skating, sledding, snowmobiling; dog park, horse trails.	❷	•	•	•	•	•	•	•	•	•	•	•	•		
A.W. Marion (F-5) 454 acres 5 mi. e. of Circleville off US 22. Hunting, ice-skating, sledding. Boats with electric motors only.	❸	•	•	•	•	•	•	•	•	•	•				•
Barkcamp (E-8) 1,112 acres 1 mi. e. of Belmont off SR 149. Nature programs. Cross-country skiing, hunting, ice-skating, sledding, snowmobiling; horse trails. Boats with electric motors only.	❹	•	•	•	•	•		•	•	•	•	•			
Beaver Creek (D-9) 2,722 acres 8 mi. n. of East Liverpool off SR 7. Canoeing, hunting, sledding; wildlife education center.	❺	•	•	•	•			•		•	•	•			
Blue Rock (F-7) 350 acres 12 mi. s.e. of Zanesville off SR 60 on CR 45. Ice-skating, sledding. Boats with electric motors only.	❻	•	•	•	•	•		•	•	•					•
Buck Creek (F-3) 4,030 acres 4 mi. e. of Springfield on SR 4. Cross-country skiing, disc golf, hunting, sledding, snowmobiling; horse trail.	❼	•	•	•	•	•		•	•	•	•			•	•
Buckeye Lake (F-5) 3,557 acres 9 mi. s. of Newark off SR 13. Hunting, iceboating, ice fishing, ice-skating; beaches.	❽		•		•	•		•	•	•	•				
Burr Oak (G-6) 3,256 acres 6 mi. n.e. of Glouster off SR 13. Nature programs. Hunting, ice fishing, ice-skating, sledding; horse trails.	❾	•	•	•	•	•	•	•	•	•	•			•	•
Caesar Creek (G-12) 6,571 acres on SR 73 6 mi. w. of jct. I-71. Historic. Cross-country skiing, hunting, ice fishing; horse trails, marina. Food service is seasonal.	❿	•	•	•	•	•	•	•	•	•	•	•			•
Catawba Island (B-4) 10 acres in Catawba off SR 53.	⓫		•		•	•		•	•	•	•				
Cowan Lake (G-2) 1,775 acres 5 mi. s. of Wilmington off US 68. Nature programs. Cross-country skiing, hunting, sledding; bicycle rental, cottages. Food service is seasonal.	⓬	•	•	•	•	•	•	•	•	•	•			•	•
Deer Creek (F-4) 3,614 acres 7 mi. s. of Mount Sterling on SR 207. Nature programs. Golf (18 holes), hunting, ice fishing, ice-skating, snowmobiling; bicycle rental, horse trails.	⓭	•	•	•	•	•	•	•	•	•	•	•	•	•	•
Delaware (D-4) 3,145 acres 6 mi. n. of Delaware on US 23. Cross-country skiing, disc golf, hunting, ice fishing, ice-skating; yurt rentals.	⓮	•	•	•	•	•	•	•	•	•	•	•	•	•	•
Dillon (E-6) 3,845 acres 5 mi. n.w. of Zanesville off SR 146. Disc golf, hunting, ice-skating, sledding; archery range, cottage rentals.	⓯	•	•	•	•	•	•	•	•	•	•	•		•	
East Fork (I-12) 7,030 acres 4 mi. s.e. of Amelia off SR 125. Cross-country skiing, hunting, ice fishing, ice-skating, sledding; horse trails. Food service is seasonal.	⓰	•	•	•	•	•	•	•	•	•	•	•			•
East Harbor (B-4) 1,831 acres 8 mi. e. of Port Clinton off SR 269. Nature programs. Cross-country skiing, disc golf, hunting, ice-boating, ice fishing, ice-skating, snowmobiling.	⓱	•	•	•	•	•	•	•	•	•	•	•	•		•
Fernwood State Forest (E-9) 3,023 acres n. of SR 151 in New Philadelphia. Hunting.	⓲	•	•	•				•		•					
Findley (C-6) 931 acres 3 mi. s. of Wellington on SR 58. Nature programs. Cross-country skiing, disc golf (18 holes), hunting, ice fishing, ice-skating; bicycle, canoe, kayak and rowboat rentals. Boats with electric motors only.	⓳	•	•	•	•	•	•	•	•	•	•	•			•

Recreation Areas Chart

The map location numerals in column 2 show an area's location on the preceding map.

Find thousands of places to camp at AAA.com/campgrounds

	MAP LOCATION	CAMPING	PICNICKING	HIKING TRAILS	BOATING	BOAT RAMP	BOAT RENTAL	FISHING	SWIMMING	PET FRIENDLY	BICYCLE TRAILS	WINTER SPORTS	VISITOR CENTER	LODGE/CABINS	FOOD SERVICE
Forked Run (H-7) 791 acres 3 mi. s.w. of Reedsville off SR 124. Nature programs in summer. Disc golf, hunting, sledding.	20	•	•	•	•	•	•	•	•	•	•		•	•	•
Geneva (A-8) 698 acres on the shore of Lake Erie at Geneva-on-the-Lake. Cross-country skiing, hunting, ice fishing, snowmobiling; marina.	21	•	•	•	•	•	•		•	•	•	•	•	•	•
Grand Lake St. Marys (D-1) 14,000 acres 2 mi. w. of St. Marys on SR 703. Nature programs. Cross-country skiing, hunting, snowmobiling; dog park.	22	•	•	•	•	•	•	•	•	•	•	•			
Great Seal (G-4) 1,864 acres 3 mi. n.e. of Chillicothe on Marietta Pike. Cross-country skiing, disc golf, hunting; horse trails.	23	•	•	•							•	•	•	•	
Guilford Lake (C-8) 488 acres 6 mi. n.w. of Lisbon off SR 172. Hunting, ice fishing, ice-skating.	24	•	•	•	•	•	•		•	•	•		•		
Harrison Lake (B-2) 247 acres 4 mi. s. of Fayette off SR 66. Cross-country skiing, ice fishing, sledding. No wake boating.	25	•	•	•	•	•	•	•	•	•	•		•		•
Headlands Beach (A-12) 125 acres .3 mi. w. off SR 44 at 9601 Headlands Rd. in Mentor. Cross-country skiing, sledding.	26		•	•	•				•	•		•	•		
Hocking Hills (G-5) 2,356 acres 10 mi. s.w. of US 33 on SR 664. Nature programs. Ice fishing; pool.	27	•	•	•				•	•	•			•	•	
Hueston Woods (G-10) 3,596 acres 5 mi. n. of Oxford off SR 732. Nature programs. Cross-country skiing, disc golf (36 holes), golf (18 holes), hunting, ice-skating, sledding; bicycle rental, dog park, horse trails.	28	•	•	•	•	•	•	•	•	•	•	•	•	•	•
Independence Dam (B-2) 525 acres 4 mi. e. of Defiance on SR 424. Cross-country skiing, ice-skating, sledding.	29	•	•	•	•	•		•			•		•		
Indian Lake (D-3) 6,452 acres 2 mi. n. of Lakeview on SR 235. Nature programs. Cross-country skiing, hunting, iceboating, ice fishing, ice-skating, snowmobiling; beach.	30	•	•	•	•	•	•	•	•	•	•		•	•	
Jackson Lake (H-5) 334 acres 2 mi. w. of Oak Hill on SR 279. Ice fishing, ice-skating, sledding.	31	•	•					•	•	•			•		
Jefferson Lake (D-8) 945 acres 16 mi. n.w. of Steubenville off SR 43. Cross-country skiing, hunting, ice fishing, ice-skating; horse trails.	32	•	•					•	•	•			•		
John Bryan (F-3) 750 acres 2 mi. e. of Yellow Springs on SR 370. Cross-country skiing, disc golf, sledding.	33	•	•	•	•			•			•	•	•		
Kelleys Island (B-5) 677 acres. Scenic. Cross-country skiing, hunting, ice fishing, ice-skating. Kayak rentals.	34	•	•	•	•	•		•	•	•	•	•			
Kiser Lake (E-3) 927 acres 17 mi. n.w. of Urbana on SR 235. Hunting, iceboating, ice fishing, ice-skating, sledding; horse trails.	35	•	•	•	•	•	•	•	•		•		•	•	
Lake Alma (G-5) 350 acres 3 mi. n.e. of Wellston on SR 349. Cross-country skiing, hunting, ice fishing, ice-skating; dog swim area.	36	•	•	•	•	•	•	•	•	•	•	•	•	•	•
Lake Hope (G-5) 3,223 acres 12 mi. n.e. of McArthur on SR 278. Nature programs. Cross-country skiing, hunting, ice fishing, ice-skating; cottage rentals, horse trails.	37	•	•	•	•	•	•	•	•	•	•		•	•	•
Lake Logan (G-5) 719 acres 4 mi. w. of Logan off SR 664. Hunting, ice fishing, ice-skating, sledding. Boat speed limit 10 miles per hour or less.	38		•	•	•	•	•	•				•	•		
Lake Loramie (E-2) 2,080 acres 3 mi. s.e. of Minster off SR 66. Cross-country skiing, hunting, iceboating, ice fishing, ice-skating, snowmobiling.	39	•	•	•	•	•	•	•	•	•	•		•	•	
Lake Milton (C-8) 1,685 acres 1 mi. s. of I-76 off SR 534. Cross-country skiing, hunting, ice fishing, snowmobiling.	40		•	•	•	•		•				•	•		
Lake White (H-4) 444 acres 2 mi. s.w. of Waverly on SR 104. **Note:** At press time, part of the park was closed. Phone ahead for updates.	41		•		•	•		•	•	•					
Little Miami (G-12) 813 acres n. of Corwin. Scenic. Canoeing, cross-country skiing; horse trails.	42		•	•	•			•		•	•	•			

Recreation Areas Chart

The map location numerals in column 2 show an area's location on the preceding map.

Find thousands of places to camp at AAA.com/campgrounds

	MAP LOCATION	CAMPING	PICNICKING	HIKING TRAILS	BOATING	BOAT RAMP	BOAT RENTAL	FISHING	SWIMMING	PET FRIENDLY	BICYCLE TRAILS	WINTER SPORTS	VISITOR CENTER	LODGE/CABINS	FOOD SERVICE
Madison Lake (F-4) 186 acres 3 mi. e. of London off SR 665. Hunting, sailboating.	43		•	•	•	•		•	•						
Malabar Farm (D-5) 917 acres. Nature programs. Cross-country skiing, ice-skating, sledding; horse trails.	44	•	•	•				•		•		•	•	•	•
Mary Jane Thurston (B-2) 555 acres 2 mi. w. of Grand Rapids on SR 65. Cross-country skiing, ice fishing, ice-skating, sledding.	45	•	•		•	•				•	•				•
Maumee Bay (B-3) 1,450 acres 8 mi. e. of Toledo, then 3 mi. n. off SR 2. Cross-country skiing, golf (18 holes), hunting, ice-skating, sledding; bicycle rental, cottage rental, nature center, yurt rental.	46	•	•	•				•	•	•	•	•	•	•	•
Middle Bass Island (A-4) 124 acres on Middle Bass Island. Marina.	47	•	•		•	•		•		•					
Mohican (D-5) 1,110 acres. Nature programs. Scenic. Snowmobiling; cottage rentals, horse trails.	48	•	•	•				•	•	•		•	•	•	•
Mosquito Lake (B-8) 11,811 acres at 1439 SR 305 in Cortland. Hunting, iceboating, ice fishing, ice-skating, snowmobiling; dog park, horse trails, yurt rentals.	49	•	•	•	•	•	•	•	•	•	•	•			•
Mount Gilead (D-5) 210 acres 1 mi. e. of Mount Gilead on SR 95. Cross-country skiing, ice fishing, ice-skating, sledding; amphitheater. **Note:** Work is being done on the dam; the lake and hiking trails near it are currently closed.	50	•	•	•				•	•		•		•	•	
Muskingum River (F-7) 120 acres along 80 miles of the Muskingum River extending from Devola to Ellis Locks.	51	•	•	•	•	•	•	•		•					
Paint Creek (G-3) 10,200 acres 17 mi. e. of Hillsboro on US 50. Nature programs. Hunting, rock climbing, sledding; horse trails.	52	•	•	•	•	•	•	•	•	•	•	•	•	•	•
Pike Lake (H-4) 613 acres 7 mi. s.e. of Bainbridge. Nature programs. Disc golf (18 holes), hunting, ice fishing, ice-skating, sledding; cottage rentals.	53	•	•	•		•	•	•	•	•		•	•	•	
Portage Lakes (D-11) 2,500 acres in Akron on SR 93. Cross-country skiing, hunting; dog park.	54		•	•	•	•		•	•	•		•			
Punderson (B-12) 996 acres 2 mi. e. of Newbury off SR 87. Nature programs. Cross-country skiing, disc golf, golf (18 holes), hunting, snowmobiling, tennis; cottage rentals.	55	•	•	•				•	•	•		•	•	•	•
Pymatuning (B-9) 17,500 acres 6 mi. s.e. of Andover off US 85. Nature programs. Cross-country skiing, hunting, iceboating, ice fishing, ice-skating; cottage and yurt rentals.	56	•	•	•	•	•	•	•	•	•		•	•	•	•
Quail Hollow (D-11) 700 acres 2 mi. n. of Hartville on Congress Lake Rd. Nature programs. Cross-country skiing, ice-skating, sledding; horse trails.	57	•	•	•					•		•	•	•	•	
Rocky Fork (H-3) 3,464 acres 3 mi. e. of Hillsboro off SR 124. Disc golf, hunting, sledding.	58	•	•	•	•	•	•	•	•	•		•	•	•	•
Salt Fork (E-7) 20,181 acres 7 mi. n.e. of Cambridge on US 22. Nature programs. Cross-country skiing, golf (18 holes), hunting, ice fishing, snowmobiling; bicycle rental, cottage rentals, horse trails.	59	•	•	•	•	•	•	•	•	•	•	•	•	•	•
Scioto Trail (G-4) 248 acres 10 mi. s. of Chillicothe off US 23. Cross-country skiing, hunting, ice fishing, ice-skating, sledding. Boats with electric motors.	60	•	•	•	•	•	•	•	•	•	•	•	•		
Shawnee (I-4) 1,168 acres 8 mi. w. of Portsmouth on SR 125. Nature programs. Golf (18 holes), hunting, miniature golf; canoe rentals, cottage rentals, horse trails, paddleboat rentals.	61	•	•	•	•	•	•	•	•	•	•	•		•	•
South Bass Island (A-4) 35 acres on South Bass Island by summer ferry. Ice fishing, ice-skating; cottage and kayak rentals.	62	•	•					•		•		•			•
Stonelick (I-12) 1,258 acres 1 mi. s. of Edenton off SR 727. Cross-country skiing, hunting, iceboating, ice fishing, ice-skating, sledding; bicycle rental. Boats with electric motors only.	63	•	•	•		•		•	•	•	•	•			
Strouds Run (G-6) 2,606 acres 8 mi. n.e. of Athens off US 50A on CR 20. Cross-country skiing, hunting, sledding; horse trails.	64	•	•	•	•	•		•	•	•		•			•
Sycamore (F-11) 2,384 acres 1 mi. w. of Trotwood on SR 49. Hunting, snowmobiling; horse trails.	65	•	•	•				•		•		•	•		

Recreation Areas Chart

The map location numerals in column 2 show an area's location on the preceding map.

Find thousands of places to camp at AAA.com/campgrounds

	MAP LOCATION	CAMPING	PICNICKING	HIKING TRAILS	BOATING	BOAT RAMP	BOAT RENTAL	FISHING	SWIMMING	PET FRIENDLY	BICYCLE TRAILS	WINTER SPORTS	VISITOR CENTER	LODGE/CABINS	FOOD SERVICE
Tar Hollow (G-5) 634 acres 10 mi. s. of Adelphi off SR 327. Hunting; bicycle rental. Boats with electric motors only.	66	•	•	•	•	•	•	•	•	•	•	•		•	
Tinker's Creek (C-12) 369 acres 2 mi. w. of SR 43 on Aurora-Hudson Rd. near Portage. Cross-country skiing, ice fishing.	67		•	•				•				•			
Van Buren (C-3) 296 acres 1 mi. e. of Van Buren on Township Rd. 218. Bow hunting, cross-country skiing, disc golf, ice fishing, ice-skating; horse trails.	68	•	•	•	•	•		•		•		•	•		
West Branch (C-12) 8,002 acres 5 mi. e. of Ravenna off SR 5. Nature programs. Cross-country skiing, hunting, iceboating, ice fishing, snowmobiling; horse trails.	69	•	•	•	•	•	•	•	•	•	•	•			•
Wolf Run (F-7) 1,363 acres 1 mi. e. of Belle Valley off I-77. Cross-country skiing, hunting, scuba diving, sledding.	70	•	•	•	•	•		•	•	•		•			
MUSKINGUM WATERSHED CONSERVANCY DISTRICT															
Atwood Lake (D-8) 4,536 acres 2 mi. s.e. of New Cumberland off SR 212. Nature programs. Hunting; beach, playground.	71	•	•	•	•	•	•	•	•	•			•	•	•
Charles Mill Lake (D-6) 3,347 acres 9 mi. e. of Mansfield on SR 430. Nature programs. Hunting.	72	•	•	•	•	•	•	•	•	•				•	•
Clendening Lake (E-8) 6,550 acres 3 mi. n. of Freeport off SR 800. Hunting.	73	•	•		•	•	•	•						•	•
Leesville Lake (D-8) 3,625 acres 4 mi. s. of Sherrodsville off SR 212. Hunting.	74	•	•	•	•	•	•	•		•				•	•
Piedmont Lake (E-7) 6,642 acres 2 mi. s.e. of Smyrna off SR 800. Hunting.	75	•	•	•	•	•	•	•		•				•	•
Pleasant Hill Lake (D-6) 2,195 acres 3 mi. s.w. of Perrysville on SR 95. Nature programs. Hunting; horse trails.	76	•	•	•	•	•	•	•	•	•			•	•	•
Seneca Lake (F-7) 7,613 acres 3 mi. s.e. of Senecaville off SR 574. Nature programs.	77	•	•	•	•	•	•	•	•	•				•	•
Tappan Lake (E-8) 7,597 acres 12 mi. n.w. of Cadiz off US 250. Nature programs. Hunting.	78	•	•	•	•	•	•	•	•	•				•	•
OTHER															
Austin Lake Park (D-9) 1,300 acres n. of Steubenville on SR 152. Dog water park.	79	•	•	•	•	•		•	•	•					
Carriage Hill MetroPark (F-12) 944 acres just n. of SR 201 on E. Shull Rd. in Huber Heights. Bird-watching, cross-country skiing, sledding; horse trails.	80	•	•	•				•		•		•	•		
Eastwood MetroPark (F-12) 437 acres 1 mi. off SR 4 on Harshman Rd. in Dayton. Bird-watching, canoeing, cross-country skiing, kayaking, water activities, wildlife viewing; playground.	81		•	•	•	•		•		•	•	•			
Englewood MetroPark (F-11) 1,956 acres just e. of Englewood off US 40. Bird-watching, canoeing, cross-country skiing, disc golf, kayaking, sledding; horse trails.	82	•	•	•	•			•		•	•	•			
Germantown MetroPark (G-11) 1,665 acres just w. of SR 4 in Germantown. Bird-watching, canoeing, cross-country skiing, kayaking, sledding, wildlife viewing; backpacking trail.	83	•	•	•	•			•		•	•	•			
Huffman MetroPark (F-12) 283 acres w. of Wright-Patterson Air Force Base off SR 4 on Lower Valley Pike. Bird-watching, canoeing, cross-country skiing, kayaking, mountain biking.	84		•	•	•	•		•		•	•	•			
Lake Vesuvius (I-5) 200 acres 6 mi. n. of Ironton off SR 93.	85	•	•	•	•			•	•	•	•		•		
Magee Marsh Wildlife Area (B-4) 2,200 acres 2 mi. w. of SR 19 on SR 2 in Oak Harbor. Bird-watching, hunting.	86		•	•				•	•	•			•		
Mentor Lagoons Nature Preserve & Marina (A-12) 450 acres just w. off SR 283. Bird-watching.	87		•	•	•	•		•		•					
Miami Whitewater Forest (H-10) n.w. of Cincinnati off I-74. Golf (18 holes), disc golf, wildlife viewing; bicycle rental, kayak ramp, horse trails, playground, water playground.	88	•	•	•	•	•	•	•		•	•		•		•
Mill Creek Park (C-9) 2,882 acres s. of Mahoning Ave. off Glenwood Ave. Cross-country skiing, golf, sledding, tennis; boardwalk, nature center.	89			•	•						•	•	•		

Recreation Areas Chart

The map location numerals in column 2 show an area's location on the preceding map.

Find thousands of places to camp at AAA.com/campgrounds

	MAP LOCATION	CAMPING	PICNICKING	HIKING TRAILS	BOATING	BOAT RAMP	BOAT RENTAL	FISHING	SWIMMING	PET FRIENDLY	BICYCLE TRAILS	WINTER SPORTS	VISITOR CENTER	LODGE/CABINS	FOOD SERVICE
Possum Creek MetroPark (F-11) 556 acres just e. of SR 4 on Frytown Rd. in Dayton. Cross-country skiing; children's activities, a farm, horse trails.	90	•	•	•	•	•				•		•		•	
Riverscape MetroPark (F-12) 1.4 acres on Monument Ave. in Dayton. Canoeing, cross-country skiing, ice-skating, in-line skating.	91		•	•				•			•	•	•		•
Sharon Woods (H-11) n.e. of Cincinnati off I-270 Cleveland Avenue exit. Golf; bicycle rental, playground, water playground.	92		•	•	•	•	•	•		•	•	•	•		•
Shawnee Lookout (I-10) w. of Cincinnati via US 50. Nature programs. Cross-country skiing, golf (18 holes), ice fishing, ice-skating, sledding; playground.	93		•	•	•	•		•		•		•	•		•
Taylorsville MetroPark (F-12) 1,312 acres just n. of I-70 on US 40 in Vandalia. Bird-watching, canoeing, cross-country skiing, kayaking, sledding, wildlife viewing.	94	•	•	•	•			•		•	•	•			
Twin Creek MetroPark (G-11) 1,000 acres off SR 4 in Germantown on Eby Rd. Historic. Bird-watching, canoeing, cross-country skiing, kayaking, wildlife viewing; horse trails.	95	•	•	•	•					•		•			
Wegerzyn Gardens MetroPark (F-12) just off Siebenthaler Ave. Bird-watching, cross-country skiing, wildlife viewing; gardens. Pets are not permitted in the gardens.	96		•	•						•		•	•		
Wellington Reservation (C-5) 550 acres at 535 Jones Rd. in Wellington. Paddleboat rental, playground.	97		•	•	•	•	•	•				•		•	
Wesleyan MetroPark (F-11) 55 acres on Wesleyan Rd. in Dayton. Cross-country skiing, sledding, wildlife viewing; playground.	98		•	•						•		•	•		
Winton Woods (H-10) n. of Cincinnati off Winton Road. Cross-country skiing, disc golf, golf (18 holes), ice fishing, ice-skating, sledding; bicycle rental, horse rental, playground, water playground.	99	•	•	•	•	•	•	•		•	•	•	•	•	•
Woodland Mound (I-11) 1,066 acres off I-275 Beechmont Ave. exit (SR 125) from Anderson Township, 2 mi. w., then s. on Nordyke Rd. Nature programs. Cross-country skiing, disc golf, golf (18 holes), ice-skating; butterfly garden, water playground.	100	•	•	•	•	•		•			•	•	•		•

Love the Great Outdoors?

For getaways off the beaten path, visit AAA.com/campgrounds or AAA.com/maps and choose from thousands of AAA-listed places to camp across the U.S. and Canada.

Look for locations with the trusted mark of approval.

Inspected & Approved

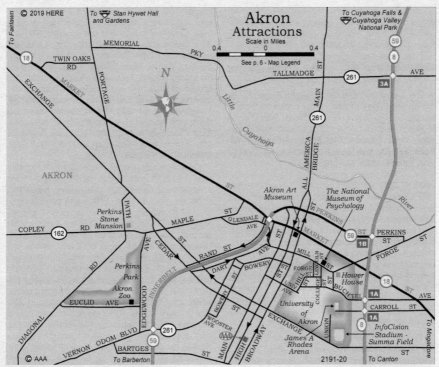

Akron
Attractions
Scale in Miles
0.4   0   0.4
See p. 6 - Map Legend

AKRON (C-7) pop. 199,110, elev. 873'
• Hotels p. 136 • Restaurants p. 137

The center of global rubber empires, Akron once led the world in the manufacturing of rubber products. Although local production is now minimal, Akron is still the corporate home of Goodyear. Akron also is a merchandising center—a vital distribution gateway between the industrial East and Midwest.

From the standpoint of scientific research, Akron is perhaps the nation's fastest growing city. The Firestone and Goodyear laboratories specialize in research involving rubber and plastics. Bridgestone Americas Center for Research and Technology is one of the leading labs in the field of polymers. The original space suits worn by U.S. astronauts were made and fitted at B.F. Goodrich. The University of Akron's College of Polymer Science and Polymer Engineering has gained renown for its work in combining molecules through chemical reactions.

The Akron area offers a variety of cultural and sporting activities, including events at The University of Akron's E.J. Thomas Hall. The Akron Civic Theatre, with its opulent design and ceiling replete with blinking stars and floating clouds, is one of the few remaining "atmospheric" theaters. Guided tours are offered monthly on the third Tuesday; phone (330) 535-3179.

The 1837 Greek Revival Perkins Stone Mansion, 550 Copley Rd., was home to Simon Perkins, the son of Akron founder Gen. Simon Perkins; he lived in the house with his wife and 11 children. Perkins and John Brown (who later became the famed abolitionist) were partners in the wool company Perkins and Brown for 10 years; Brown lived across the street 1844-46. Tours of both houses are available Wed.-Sat. 1-4, Apr.- Dec.; phone (330) 535-1120.

April through September, the Akron Rubber-Ducks, the AA minor league baseball team affiliated with the Cleveland Indians, plays at state-of-the-art Canal Park, on the corner of S. Main and W. Exchange streets.

In July Derby Downs is home to the annual All-American Soap Box Derby championship race. August brings the Bridgestone Invitational World Series of Golf.

Goodwill Industries of Akron, 570 E. Waterloo Rd., offers tours of its rehabilitation training facility; phone (330) 724-6995.

Akron/Summit Convention and Visitors Bureau: 77 E. Mill St., Akron, OH 44308. **Phone:** (330) 374-7560 or (800) 245-4254.

Shopping: Chapel Hill Mall, at Howe and Brittain roads, features JCPenney. Stagecoach Antiques, 449 W. Market St., has been around since the 1940s and is a nice place to go antiquing.

AKRON ART MUSEUM, One S. High St. at jct. E. Market St., occupies a late 19th-century brick Italian Renaissance Revival structure—formerly the post office—and the 2007 John S. and James L. Knight Building, which integrates part of the historic building. The museum's permanent collection presents a distinctive look at regional, national and international art from 1850 to the present, with a strong focus on paintings, sculpture and photography. Artists represented include Chuck Close, Childe Hassam and Andy Warhol. Nearly a dozen changing exhibits are presented each year.

The 1-acre Bud and Susie Rogers Garden is on the grounds. **Time:** Allow 1 hour minimum. **Hours:** Museum Tues.-Sun. 11-5 (also Thurs. 5-9). Garden Mon.-Fri. 9-6, Sat.-Sun. 10-5. Closed major holidays. **Cost:** Museum $10; $8 (ages 65+ and students with ID); free (ages 0-17 and Thurs.). Garden free. **Phone:** (330) 376-9185. ⓘ

AKRON ZOO is at 505 Euclid Ave. Among the zoo's 700 animals are red pandas, Humboldt penguins, snow leopards, jaguars and three species of lemurs. The interactive Tiger Valley exhibit includes Sumatran tigers, sloth bears and lions. Grizzly Ridge features grizzly bears, bald eagles, otters, red wolves, coyotes and an aviary. Komodo dragons and Galapagos tortoises are among the favorites at Komodo Kingdom. Children may feed the animals at the Ohio Farmyard Encounter or take a train ride. The Lehner Family Zoo Gardens include more than 7,000 plants and flowers. The zoo is decked out in holiday lights during the Wild Lights event in December.

Time: Allow 3 hours minimum. **Hours:** Daily 10-5, Apr.-Oct.; 11-4, rest of year. **Cost:** May-Oct. $12; $10 (ages 65+); $9 (ages 2-14). Rest of year $7. **Parking:** $3. **Phone:** (330) 375-2550 or (330) 375-2525. GT ⌂

THE NATIONAL MUSEUM OF PSYCHOLOGY is at the Drs. Nicholas and Dorothy Cummings Center for the History of Psychology, 73 S. College St., on The University of Akron campus. This museum is loaded with displays, hands-on exhibits and video clips of psychological tests, turn-of-the-century scientific instruments and visual illusions. **Note:** The museum is closed through part of 2018 for an expansion project. Phone ahead for further details. **Hours:** Tues.-Sat. 11-4 (also Thurs. 4-8 p.m.). Closed major and state holidays. **Cost:** $10; $5 (students). **Phone:** (330) 972-7285.

STAN HYWET HALL & GARDENS, 714 N. Portage Path, is considered one of the finest examples of Tudor Revival architecture in the country. It was built 1912-15 for Frank A. Seiberling, co-founder of Goodyear and founder of Seiberling Rubber companies. The 65-room manor house contains art treasures from around the world. Features include an impressive music room and the three-story Great Hall. The Gate Lodge near the front gate was originally the estate superintendent's home. It was in the Gate Lodge that the first discussion of what would become Alcoholics Anonymous took place. An exhibit highlights the historic event.

Self-guiding and 1.25-hour guided tours are offered. The 1.5-hour Nooks & Crannies Manor House Tour takes visitors to additional areas of the house, including the domestic and service areas. The property also offers a restored English garden, a Japanese garden, a lagoon and scenic vistas. The 2.5-hour Grand Estate Tour includes the house and garden. The Corbin Conservatory houses a tropical garden, "Garden Under Glass." **Time:** Allow 1 hour minimum. **Hours:** Tues.-Sun. (also Memorial Day and Labor Day) 10-6; last admission 1 hour, 30 minutes before closing. Self-guiding grounds tours 10-6. Self-guiding house tours 11-4:30. Guided house tour departs on the hour 11-4. Nooks & Crannies Tour departs Tues.-Sun. at 11:30, 1:30 and 3:30. Grand Estate Tour departs Tues.-Sun. at 12:30, May-Sept. Closed major holidays.

Cost: Grounds (includes Gate Lodge and conservatory) $12; $6 (military with ID); $5 (ages 6-17 and college students with ID). Self-guiding house tour (includes grounds, Gate Lodge and conservatory) $15; $7.50 (military with ID); $6 (ages 6-17 and college students with ID). Guided house tour (includes grounds, Gate Lodge and conservatory) $19; $9.50 (military with ID); $8 (ages 6-17 and college students with ID). Nooks & Crannies Tour (includes grounds, Gate Lodge and conservatory) $28; $14 (military with ID); $10 (ages 6-17 and college students with ID). Grand Estate Tour (includes guided house tour and guided historic garden tour) $24; $12 (military with ID); $10 (ages 6-17 and college students with ID). Senior citizens receive a 50 percent discount Tues. only. Ages 0-15 must be accompanied by an adult in the house. **Phone:** (330) 836-5533. GT ⓘ

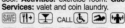

HOLIDAY INN EXPRESS & SUITES AKRON SOUTH
330/644-5600
APPROVED Hotel. **Address:** 898 Arlington Ridge E 44312

RESIDENCE INN BY MARRIOTT AKRON SOUTH GREEN
330/644-2111
THREE DIAMOND [SAVE] Extended Stay Hotel. **Address:** 897 Arlington Ridge E 44312

AAA Benefit:
Members save 5% or more!

WHERE TO EAT

BRICCO
330/475-1600
APPROVED Italian. Casual Dining. **Address:** 1 W Exchange St 44308

KEN STEWART'S GRILLE
330/867-2555
THREE DIAMOND American. Fine Dining. **Address:** 1970 W Market St 44313

LUIGI'S
330/253-2999
APPROVED Italian. Casual Dining. **Address:** 105 N Main St 44308

TRECASO'S MARY COYLE ICE CREAM & ITALIAN CUISINE
330/253-1511
APPROVED Italian. Casual Dining. **Address:** 780 W Market St 44303

VACCARO'S TRATTORIA
330/666-6158
THREE DIAMOND Italian. Fine Dining. **Address:** 1000 Ghent Rd 44333

ALLIANCE (D-12) pop. 22,322, elev. 1,158'

The Carnation City is home to the University of Mount Union (formerly Mount Union College), a small liberal arts school. The showpiece of this beautiful campus—definitely worth driving through if you're in the area—is the five-story brick Chapman Hall. If you follow NCAA Division III football, you know about the Purple Raiders. The team holds 12 national titles, more than any other team in any division.

THE COLLEGE INN
330/823-3332
APPROVED American. Quick Serve. **Address:** 935 W State St 44601

ARCHBOLD (B-2) pop. 4,346, elev. 732'

In a region once known as the Great Black Swamp, Archbold is surrounded by fertile farmland. About 5 miles northwest of town is the 321-acre Goll Woods State Nature Preserve, an old-growth woods reminiscent of the Great Black Swamp; go north on SR 66 for 1.5 miles to Township Road F, then west for 3 miles to Township Road 26 and go south about a quarter-mile.

Archbold is home to one of the country's largest furniture manufacturers, Sauder Woodworking, and to ConAgra Foods, makers of such brands as La Choy, Healthy Choice and Chef Boyardee.

Archbold Area Chamber of Commerce: 300 N. Defiance St., P.O. Box 102, Archbold, OH 43502. **Phone:** (419) 445-2222.

Shopping: Defiance Street (SR 66) offers independent shops and boutiques and an old-fashioned "Main Street" atmosphere. Sauder Furniture Store & Outlet, on the grounds of Historic Sauder Village, sells the local company's line of ready-to-assemble furniture.

HISTORIC SAUDER VILLAGE is on SR 2, .5 mi. e. of SR 66. This living-history village tells the story of the early settlers of Ohio's Great Black Swamp. The village includes more than 40 historic homes and shops. Costumed guides bring history to life in the homes, schools, barbershop, doctor's office and more.

There are cooking, farming and other period demonstrations that change with the season. Working craftspeople include a potter, glassblower, blacksmith, woodworker, spinner, weaver, cooper, broom maker and tinsmith. The village also includes a turn-of-the-20th-century homestead with a barn and animals, a Native American village, a pioneer settlement area and a museum. At Little Pioneers Homestead children can "play pioneer" in the cabin, barn and garden. Carriage and train rides are available. The village also hosts many events during the season.

Time: Allow 4 hours minimum. **Hours:** Tues.-Sat. and Mon. holidays 10-5, Sun. noon-4, Memorial Day-Labor Day; Tues.-Fri. 10-3:30, Sat. 10-5, Sun. noon-4, late Apr.-day before Memorial Day and day after Labor Day-late Oct. **Cost:** $18; $16 (ages 60+ and inactive or retired military with ID); $12 (ages 6-16); free (active military with ID, active military families Memorial Day-Labor Day, ages 0-5 and ages 6-16 every Sun.). **Phone:** (419) 446-2541 or (800) 590-9755.

SAUDER HERITAGE INN
419/445-6408
THREE DIAMOND Hotel. **Address:** 22611 SR 2 43502

WHERE TO EAT

BARN RESTAURANT
419/445-2231
APPROVED Comfort Food. Casual Dining. **Address:** 22611 SR 2 43502

ASHLAND (C-6) pop. 20,362, elev. 1,076'
• Hotels p. 138 • Restaurants p. 138

Founded in 1815 and situated in the rolling hills of mainly agricultural Ashland County, Ashland maintains a prosperous economy thanks to light industry and its location off I-71 approximately halfway between Cleveland and Columbus. The city is home to the 6,000-student Ashland University, the Ashbrook Center and Ashland Theological Seminary.

During the summer months, a variety of free concerts are performed Thursdays and Sundays at the Guy Chase Myers Memorial Band Shell. The city also serves as a base for visitors to Charles Mill Lake and Pleasant Hill Lake recreational areas, Mohican State Park and Malabar Farm State Park, all of which lie in towns within 20 miles south of Ashland. *See Recreation Areas Chart.*

Ashland Area Convention & Visitors Bureau: 211 Claremont Ave., Ashland, OH 44805. **Phone:** (419) 281-4584, ext. 101 or (877) 581-2345, ext. 101.

HAMPTON INN & SUITES BY HILTON ASHLAND
419/903-0900
THREE DIAMOND SAVE Hotel. **Address:** 2055 E Main St 44805

AAA Benefit: Members save up to 15%!

HOLIDAY INN EXPRESS HOTEL & SUITES-ASHLAND
419/281-2900
APPROVED Hotel. **Address:** 1392 Enterprise Pkwy 44805

WHERE TO EAT

JAKE'S RESTAURANT   419/281-5253
APPROVED American. Casual Dining. **Address:** 1040 Sugarbush Dr 44805

ASHTABULA (A-8) pop. 19,124, elev. 647'

Moses Cleaveland's 1796 discovery of a harbor in northeast Ohio on Lake Erie led to the settlement of Ashtabula, a major coal and iron port. In addition to its role as a manufacturing center, the city also is a waterfront resort and home to a 1,500-student regional campus of Kent State University.

Walnut Beach, on Lake Erie at Walnut Boulevard and Lake Avenue, is a municipal park with a white sand beach, tennis courts, a playground and picnic facilities; food is available. Lake Shore Park, northeast of Walnut Beach on SR 531, has a boat ramp, picnic area, playground and concessions. The parks close at dusk.

Nearby countryside offers opportunities for scenic drives visiting the county's covered bridges. In late August 2008 a dedication ceremony took place for the county's 17th bridge, which, at 613 feet, makes it the nation's longest covered bridge. The structure—Smolen-Gulf Bridge, Ashtabula County Highway 25—spans the Ashtabula River and was named for former Ashtabula County engineer and longtime covered bridge advocate John Smolen.

The 43-mile Western Reserve Greenway trail begins in Ashtabula and heads south to Warren. The trail offers opportunities for biking, hiking and horseback riding.

Self-guiding tours: Brochures outlining Ashtabula County's scenic charms—five self-guiding driving tours featuring Western Reserve architecture, 18 covered bridges, more than 60 quilt barns and nearly two dozen wineries—are available from the Ashtabula County Convention and Visitors Bureau in Austinburg. Quilt barns display colorful quilt patterns on barn exteriors for passersby to enjoy; they celebrate the area's quilting and rural heritage.

Shopping: Historic Ashtabula Harbor District, 5 miles north of I-90 on SR 11, then 1 mile west on SR 531, features specialty shops.

HUBBARD HOUSE UNDERGROUND RAILROAD MUSEUM is at jct. Walnut Blvd. and Lake Ave. The 1840s brick house was an important stop on the Underground Railroad, the network of abolitionist-run safe houses that helped slaves escape to freedom before the Civil War. Fugitive slaves waited in the house until a ship arrived to take them to Canada. The house, furnished in period, contains exhibits relating to the Underground Railroad, the Civil War and local history.

Time: Allow 30 minutes minimum. **Hours:** Fri.-Sun. 1-5, Memorial Day weekend-Labor Day; by appointment rest of year (10 people minimum). Last tour begins 30 minutes before closing. Closed major holidays. Phone ahead to confirm schedule. **Cost:** $5; $4 (senior citizens); $3 (ages 6-16). Cash only. **Phone:** (440) 964-8168. GT

BASCULE BRIDGE GRILLE & WINE BAR   440/964-0301
THREE DIAMOND New American. Casual Dining. **Address:** 1006 Bridge St 44004

HIL-MAK SEAFOOD RESTAURANT   440/964-3222
APPROVED Seafood. Casual Dining. **Address:** 449 Lake Ave 44004

ATHENS (G-6) pop. 23,832, elev. 650'

Athens is best known as the home of Ohio University, which was founded in 1804. It was the first public institution for higher learning in the Northwest Territory, and there are now more than 17,000 undergraduate students enrolled. Guided tours of the university campus can be arranged by phoning the admissions office at (740) 593-4100.

Athens County Convention and Visitors Bureau: 667 E. State St., Athens, OH 45701. **Phone:** (740) 592-1819 or (800) 878-9767.

HAMPTON INN ATHENS   740/593-5600
THREE DIAMOND SAVE Hotel. **Address:** 986 E State St 45701

AAA Benefit: Members save up to 15%!

THE OHIO UNIVERSITY INN & CONFERENCE CENTER
740/593-6661
THREE DIAMOND Hotel. **Address:** 331 Richland Ave 45701

WHERE TO EAT

LUI-LUI RESTAURANT   740/594-8905
APPROVED Thai. Casual Dining. **Address:** 8 Station St 45701

RESTAURANT SALAAM   740/594-3800
APPROVED Mediterranean. Casual Dining. **Address:** 21 Washington 45701

SHADE ON STATE STREET   740/566-1009
APPROVED American. Casual Dining. **Address:** 994 E State St 45701

AURORA (C-11) pop. 15,548, elev. 1,129'
• Hotels & Restaurants map & index p. 194
• Part of Cleveland area — see map p. 177

Founded in 1799, Aurora was originally settled by Revolutionary War veteran Capt. Ebenezer Sheldon during the land grant period resulting from the Northwest Territory Ordinance of 1787. Between 1855 and 1910 Aurora established itself as the largest cheese center in the United States. Today with its diverse economy and a growing cultural community, Aurora maintains its Western Reserve style, heritage and history.

Aurora Chamber of Commerce & Visitors Bureau: 9 E. Garfield Rd., #101, Aurora, OH 44202. **Phone:** (330) 562-3355.

Shopping: Aurora Farms Premium Outlets, on SR 43 at 549 S. Chillicothe Rd., is comprised of 70 outlet stores and specialty and antique shops in a village setting.

AURORA INN HOTEL AND EVENT CENTER
330/562-0767   91
THREE DIAMOND Boutique Hotel. **Address:** 30 Shawnee Tr 44202

WHERE TO EAT

CAFE TOSCANO   330/995-2333   62
APPROVED   Italian. Fine Dining. **Address:** 215 W Garfield Rd 44202

THE CUTTING BOARD   330/562-0767   61
APPROVED   American. Casual Dining. **Address:** 30 Shawnee Tr 44202

AUSTINBURG (A-8) pop. 516, elev. 810'

Ashtabula County Convention and Visitors Bureau: 1850 Austinburg Rd., Austinburg, OH 44010. **Phone:** (440) 275-3202 or (800) 337-6746.

HAMPTON INN BY HILTON ASHTABULA   440/275-2000
THREE DIAMOND SAVE Hotel. **Address:** 2900 GH Dr 44010

AAA Benefit:
Members save up to 15%!

HOLIDAY INN EXPRESS HOTEL & SUITES   440/275-2020
THREE DIAMOND Hotel. **Address:** 1831 Austinburg Rd 44010

AUSTINTOWN (C-8) pop. 29,677, elev. 1,129'

Austintown lies about 10 miles west of Youngstown. The highlight of its park system is 206-acre Township Park, 6000 Kirk Rd., which is home to Yeager Pond, an observation deck and a variety of wildlife and habitats in addition to recreational offerings like hiking and cross-country skiing.

AUSTINTOWN/YOUNGSTOWN SUPER 8   330/793-7788
APPROVED   Motel. **Address:** 5280 76 Dr 44515

FAIRFIELD BY MARRIOTT   330/505-2173
THREE DIAMOND SAVE Hotel. **Address:** 801 N Canfield-Niles Rd 44515

AAA Benefit:
Members save 5% or more!

HAMPTON INN YOUNGSTOWN WEST I-80   330/544-0660
THREE DIAMOND SAVE Hotel. **Address:** 880 N Canfield-Niles Rd 44515

AAA Benefit:
Members save up to 15%!

HOLIDAY INN EXPRESS & SUITES   330/505-5700
THREE DIAMOND Hotel. **Address:** 5555 Cerni Pl 44515

HOME2 SUITES BY HILTON   330/505-9935
THREE DIAMOND SAVE Extended Stay Hotel. **Address:** 5580 Interstate Blvd 44515

AAA Benefit:
Members save up to 15%!

QUALITY INN   330/544-2378
APPROVED   Hotel. **Address:** 870 N Canfield Niles Rd 44515

SLEEP INN   330/544-5555
APPROVED
Hotel
Address: 5555 Interstate Blvd 44515 **Location:** I-80 exit 223, just s on SR 46. **Facility:** 57 units. 3 stories, interior corridors. **Pool:** heated indoor. **Featured Amenity:** continental breakfast.
SAVE CALL BIZ / SOME UNITS HS

AVON pop. 21,193
• Hotels & Restaurants map & index p. 194
• Part of Cleveland area — see map p. 177

CAMBRIA HOTEL & SUITES CLEVELAND/AVON
440/695-1270   65
THREE DIAMOND Hotel. **Address:** 35600 Detroit Rd 44011

FAIRFIELD INN & SUITES BY MARRIOTT   440/934-7445
THREE DIAMOND SAVE Hotel. **Address:** 39050 Colorado Ave 44011

AAA Benefit:
Members save 5% or more!

RESIDENCE INN BY MARRIOTT CLEVELAND/AVON AT THE EMERALD EVENT CENTER   440/937-0909   64
THREE DIAMOND SAVE Extended Stay Hotel. **Address:** 33040 Just Imagine Dr 44011

AAA Benefit:
Members save 5% or more!

WHERE TO EAT

NEMO GRILLE   440/934-0061
THREE DIAMOND Seafood Steak. Casual Dining. **Address:** 36796 Detroit Rd 44011

STRIP STEAK HOUSE   440/934-9900
THREE DIAMOND Steak. Fine Dining. **Address:** 36840 Detroit Rd 44011

WINKING LIZARD TAVERN   440/937-7612
APPROVED   American. Casual Dining. **Address:** 2125 Center Rd 44011

BAINBRIDGE (G-4) pop. 860, elev. 735'

Once the land of the Shawnee, Bainbridge was founded in 1805 by surveyor Nathaniel Massie, a wealthy landowner from Chillicothe. This rural trade center became known as the "cradle of American dentistry" after the profession's first school was established by Dr. John Harris in 1827.

Two scenic routes to Bainbridge are US 50 from the east and SR 41 from the south. The town is in the Appalachian plateau, and nearby Pike Lake State Park *(see Recreation Areas Chart)* offers a variety of recreational opportunities for summer and winter outdoor enthusiasts.

BARBERTON pop. 26,550

CASA DEL RANCHERO   330/753-8494
APPROVED Mexican. Casual Dining. **Address:** 562 W Tuscarawas Ave 44203

DEVORE'S HOPOCAN GARDENS   330/825-9923
APPROVED Chicken. Casual Dining. **Address:** 4396 Hopocan Ave 44203

FA-RAYS   330/745-6091
APPROVED American. Casual Dining. **Address:** 1115 Wooster Rd W 44203

GREEN DIAMOND GRILLE & PUB   330/745-1900
APPROVED American. Sports Bar. **Address:** 125 2nd St NW 44203

BATAVIA (I-12) pop. 1,509, elev. 594'
• Hotels & Restaurants map & index p. 166
• Part of Cincinnati area — see map p. 153

Clermont County Convention & Visitors Bureau: 410 E. Main St., P.O. Box 100, Batavia, OH 45103. **Phone:** (513) 732-3600.

COMFORT INN & SUITES EASTGATE   513/947-0100 **81**
APPROVED Hotel. **Address:** 4421 Aicholtz Rd 45245

FAIRFIELD BY MARRIOTT CINCINNATI EASTGATE
                                                                     513/947-9402 **79**
THREE DIAMOND SAVE Hotel. **Address:** 4521 Eastgate Blvd 45245 | **AAA Benefit:** Members save 5% or more!

HAMPTON INN BY HILTON-CINCINNATI EASTGATE
                                                                     513/752-8584 **80**
THREE DIAMOND SAVE Hotel. **Address:** 858 Eastgate North Dr 45245 | **AAA Benefit:** Members save up to 15%!

HOLIDAY INN & SUITES CINCINNATI EASTGATE
                                                                     513/752-4400 **78**
THREE DIAMOND   Hotel

Address: 4501 Eastgate Blvd 45245 **Location:** I-275 exit 63A (SR 32), 0.4 mi e to Eastgate Mall exit, then just n. **Facility:** 212 units, some two bedrooms. 6 stories, interior corridors. **Pool:** heated indoor. **Activities:** hot tub, exercise room. **Guest Services:** complimentary and valet laundry. **Featured Amenity:** full hot breakfast.

BAN THAI RESTAURANT   513/752-3200 **69**
APPROVED Thai. Casual Dining. **Address:** 792 Eastgate South Dr, Suite 300 45245

GOLD STAR CHILI
APPROVED American. Quick Serve.
LOCATIONS:
Address: 2792 Williamsburg-Batavia Pike 45103 **Phone:** 513/724-2547
Address: 4601 Eastgate Blvd 45245 **Phone:** 513/752-0108

HIGHWAY 55 BURGERS   513/943-0102 **70**
APPROVED Burgers. Casual Dining. **Address:** 4450 Eastgate Blvd 45245

SKYLINE CHILI   513/752-4040
APPROVED American. Quick Serve. **Address:** 856 Eastgate South Dr 45245

BATH (C-10) elev. 1,122'

HALE FARM AND VILLAGE is at 2686 Oak Hill Rd. A number of historic structures can be explored on the 90-acre farm in the Cuyahoga Valley. This working farm and restored village simulates the sights, sounds and smells of Wheatfield Village, a fictional re-creation representing bustling 19th-century Western Reserve townships. Artisans demonstrate basket making, brick making, broom making, candle making, glassblowing, spinning, weaving and other activities of the mid-1800s. Visitors can see cattle, horses, sheep, pigs and chickens.

Visitors can join in daily hands-on programs involving farm chores and historic crafts and trades. **Time:** Allow 3 hours minimum. **Hours:** Wed.-Sun. 10-5, June-Aug.; Sat.-Sun. 10-5, Sept.-Oct.; by appointment rest of year. **Cost:** $10; $5 (ages 3-12). **Phone:** (330) 666-3711 or (800) 589-9703.

BEACHWOOD (B-11) pop. 11,953, elev. 1,188'
• Hotels & Restaurants map & index p. 194
• Part of Cleveland area — see map p. 177

MALTZ MUSEUM OF JEWISH HERITAGE is off I-271 Chagrin Blvd. exit, 1 mi. w. on Chagrin Blvd., then .6 mi. n. to 2929 Richmond Rd. The structure was built with Golden Jerusalem limestone, which was mined and hand-chiseled in southern Israel. In the lobby, a timeline introduces visitors to key events in world history, but it may not always be on view. Artwork, artifacts, films, interactive exhibits, oral histories and photographs are all put to use telling stories about Cleveland history, Jewish heritage and the corrosive effects of hate and intolerance. A 7-minute orientation film is shown in a 60-seat theater.

Each of seven themed areas is dedicated to sharing a piece of the main story—from immigration to assimilation—and all the culture, religion, joys and heartaches that accompanied the process are woven throughout. An emphasis is placed on Cleveland's Jewish immigrants, the role they played in the

(See map & index p. 194.)

city's history and how they were affected by the atrocities of World War II. A highlight of the facility is the Temple-Tifereth Israel Gallery, where Judaica is displayed, including textiles, sacred objects, works of art and Israeli stamps. Special exhibitions from museums around the country, as well as those created in-house, are presented year-round.

Time: Allow 2 hours minimum. **Hours:** Tues.-Sun. 11-5 (also Wed. 5-9). Closed major holidays. **Cost:** $12; $10 (ages 12-18, ages 60+ and college students with ID); $5 (ages 5-11). **Phone:** (216) 593-0575. GT ☐ Green Road, 24

ALOFT CLEVELAND BEACHWOOD   216/595-0900   37
THREE DIAMOND SAVE Hotel. Address: 1010 Eaton Blvd 44122
AAA Benefit: Members save 5% or more!

COURTYARD BY MARRIOTT CLEVELAND BEACHWOOD   216/765-1900   33
THREE DIAMOND SAVE Hotel. Address: 3695 Orange Pl 44122
AAA Benefit: Members save 5% or more!

DOUBLETREE BY HILTON HOTEL-CLEVELAND EAST/BEACHWOOD   216/464-5950   32
THREE DIAMOND SAVE Hotel. Address: 3663 Park East Dr 44122
AAA Benefit: Members save up to 15%!

EMBASSY SUITES BY HILTON CLEVELAND - BEACHWOOD   216/765-8066   35
THREE DIAMOND Hotel
AAA Benefit: Members save up to 15%!
Address: 3775 Park East Dr 44122 **Location:** I-271 exit 29, just w on Chagrin Blvd, then just s. **Facility:** 216 units. 4 stories, interior corridors. **Terms:** check-in 4 pm. **Amenities:** safes. **Pool:** heated indoor. **Activities:** hot tub, exercise room. **Guest Services:** valet and coin laundry, area transportation. **Featured Amenity:** breakfast buffet.

FAIRFIELD INN & SUITES BY MARRIOTT   216/831-3300   34
APPROVED Hotel   Fairfield
AAA Benefit: Members save 5% or more!
Address: 3750 Orange Pl 44122 **Location:** I-271 exit 29, just e on Chagrin Blvd, then just s. **Facility:** 158 units. 4 stories, interior corridors. **Pool:** heated indoor. **Activities:** hot tub, exercise room. **Guest Services:** valet and coin laundry. **Featured Amenity:** full hot breakfast.

HAMPTON INN & SUITES BY HILTON CLEVELAND-BEACHWOOD   216/831-3735   36
THREE DIAMOND SAVE Hotel. Address: 3840 Orange Pl 44122
AAA Benefit: Members save up to 15%!

HOME2 SUITES BY HILTON   216/755-7310   30
THREE DIAMOND SAVE Extended Stay Contemporary Hotel. Address: 3589 Park East Dr 44122
AAA Benefit: Members save up to 15%!

HOMEWOOD SUITES BY HILTON   216/464-9600   29
THREE DIAMOND SAVE Extended Stay Hotel. Address: 25725 Central Pkwy 44122
AAA Benefit: Members save up to 15%!

RESIDENCE INN BY MARRIOTT CLEVELAND-BEACHWOOD   216/831-3030   31
THREE DIAMOND Extended Stay Hotel   Residence INN.
AAA Benefit: Members save 5% or more!
Address: 3628 Park East Dr 44122 **Location:** I-271 exit 29, just w on Chagrin Blvd, then just s. **Facility:** 174 units, some two bedrooms, efficiencies and kitchens. 4 stories, interior corridors. **Terms:** check-in 4 pm. **Pool:** heated outdoor. **Activities:** hot tub, exercise room. **Guest Services:** valet and coin laundry.

WHERE TO EAT

CHOOLAAH INDIAN BBQ   216/350-3136   33
APPROVED Indian. Quick Serve. Address: 27100 Chagrin Blvd 44122

MOXIE THE RESTAURANT   216/831-5599   30
THREE DIAMOND American. Fine Dining. Address: 3355 Richmond Rd 44122

RED, THE STEAKHOUSE   216/831-2252   31
THREE DIAMOND Steak. Fine Dining. Address: 3355 Richmond Rd 44122

RISTORANTE GIOVANNI'S   216/831-8625   32
THREE DIAMOND Northern Italian Fine Dining $15-$70
AAA Inspector Notes: This upscale restaurant has a quiet, intimate décor featuring subtly-coordinated draperies and carpet, wine racks on the walls and a formally-attired waitstaff. Popular with suburban Cleveland baby boomers, the menu has a strong focus on local meats, as well as pasta and seafood dishes. The nightly specials always particularly interesting. **Features:** full bar, happy hour. **Reservations:** suggested. **Address:** 25550 Chagrin Blvd 44122 **Location:** I-271 exit 29, 0.3 mi w; in Chagrin Richmond Building. **Parking:** on-site and valet. L D

SHUHEI   216/464-1720   34
THREE DIAMOND Japanese Sushi. Casual Dining. Address: 23360 Chagrin Blvd 44122

YOURS TRULY RESTAURANT   216/464-4848
APPROVED American. Casual Dining. Address: 25300 Chagrin Blvd 44122

BEAVERCREEK (F-12) pop. 45,193, elev. 876'
• Hotels & Restaurants map & index p. 242

Greene County Convention and Visitors Bureau: 1221 Meadow Bridge Dr., Suite A, Beavercreek, OH 45434. **Phone:** (937) 429-9100 or (800) 733-9109.

COURTYARD BY MARRIOTT BEAVERCREEK
937/429-5203 **38**
THREE DIAMOND SAVE Hotel. **Address:** 2777 Fairfield Commons Blvd 45431
AAA Benefit: Members save 5% or more!

HILTON GARDEN INN DAYTON/BEAVERCREEK
937/458-2650 **37**
THREE DIAMOND SAVE Hotel. **Address:** 3520 Pentagon Park Blvd 45431
AAA Benefit: Members save up to 15%!

RESIDENCE INN BY MARRIOTT BEAVERCREEK
937/427-3914 **39**
THREE DIAMOND SAVE Extended Stay Hotel. **Address:** 2779 Fairfield Commons Blvd 45431
AAA Benefit: Members save 5% or more!

SPRINGHILL SUITES BY MARRIOTT DAYTON BEAVERCREEK
937/429-9090 **40**
THREE DIAMOND SAVE Hotel. **Address:** 2663 Fairfield Commons Dr 45431
AAA Benefit: Members save 5% or more!

WHERE TO EAT

ACE ASIAN CAFE
937/320-0002 **24**
APPROVED Asian. Casual Dining. **Address:** 4394 Juniper Way 45440

CITY BARBEQUE
937/320-0000
APPROVED Barbecue. Quick Serve. **Address:** 2330 N Fairfield Rd 45431

PASHA GRILL
937/429-9000 **23**
THREE DIAMOND Turkish. Casual Dining. **Address:** 72 Plum St 45440

PIES & PINTS
937/429-7437 **22**
APPROVED Pizza. Casual Dining. **Address:** 52 Plum St 45440

THE PUB AT BEAVERCREEK
937/320-1199 **21**
APPROVED British. Gastropub. **Address:** 39 Greene Blvd 45440

BELLEVUE (B-5) pop. 8,202, elev. 743'

Located in the corner of four counties, Bellevue was established over a vast subterranean ground waterway system that underlies this area of Ohio. The city remains an important railroad center and has a diversified manufacturing economy while continuing to flourish as an agricultural region noted for its corn, grains and soy beans.

SORROWFUL MOTHER SHRINE is 6 mi. s. of US 20/18 to 4106 SR 269 N. The shrine includes 120 acres of lawns, flower gardens and woods. A mile-long trail leads to grottoes and an outdoor Way of the Cross. **Hours:** Grounds open daily dawn-dusk. Mass daily at 11 (also Sat. at 4, Sun. at 9 a.m.). **Cost:** Free. **Phone:** (419) 483-3435.

BERLIN (D-7) pop. 898, elev. 954'

Berlin, in the heart of Amish country, offers visitors a chance to view a lifestyle different from their own. The Amish have maintained their simplified way of life, rejecting many modern conveniences. The area has charming country roads on which Amish families travel in horse-drawn buggies.

Shopping: Crafts, antiques and homemade foods can be bought from the Amish at roadside stands or in area shops. The Wendell August Forge is 3 miles north of Berlin on SR 62 and then just east on CR 672; the shop features forged aluminum, bronze, pewter, copper and silver items.

AMISH HEARTLAND GROUP TOURS departs from multiple locations in and near Berlin; specific locations are provided at time of reservation. The 3-hour Amish Backroads Tour covers 28 miles of Amish backroads. The 1.5-hour Amish Organic Farm Tour offers a backroad buggy tour, while the 1-hour Amish Home Tour includes a buggy ride and homemade cookies. Visitors can also experience meals in Amish homes. **Hours:** Mon.-Fri. 9-3. **Cost:** $30-$75. Reservations are required. **Phone:** (330) 893-3248. GT

A TASTE OF THE BACKROAD TOUR departs from Berlin Grande Hotel at 4787 CR 366. Passengers travel the back roads in an 11-passenger air-conditioned high-top sightseeing van. You'll learn about the Amish way of life on this 2.5-hour sightseeing tour that includes stops to visit two Amish crafters. **Hours:** Tours depart Tues.-Sat. at 11 and 2:30. **Cost:** $45; free (ages 0-11. Reservations are required. **Phone:** (330) 340-7343. GT

"BEHALT" AT THE AMISH & MENNONITE HERITAGE CENTER is .75 mi. e. on SR 39, then 1 mi. n. on CR 77. This 265-foot cyclorama, by international artist Heinz Gaugel, illustrates the heritage of the Amish and Mennonite people. Also on the grounds are a one-room schoolhouse and a pioneer barn with an original Conestoga wagon. A video presentation about the local community is shown.

Time: Allow 1 hour minimum. Hours: Mon.-Sat. 9-5, Mar.-Nov.; 9:30-4:30, rest of year. Cost: Cyclorama $8.75; $4.25 (ages 6-12). Combined cyclorama, barn and schoolhouse $12.50; $8 (ages 6-12). Phone to confirm admission. Phone: (330) 893-3192.

BERLIN GRANDE HOTEL 330/403-3050

THREE DIAMOND Hotel

Address: 4787 Township Rd 366 44610 Location: SR 39, just n on US 62. Facility: 102 units. 4 stories, interior corridors. Pool: heated indoor. Activities: hot tub, exercise room. Guest Services: complimentary and valet laundry. Featured Amenity: breakfast buffet.

SAVE ⬦ CALL ⬦ ⬦ ⬦ BIZ
⬦ ⬦ ⬦ ⬦ ⬦ / SOME UNITS ⬦

COMFORT SUITES BERLIN HOTEL AND CONFERENCE CENTER 330/893-7400
THREE DIAMOND Hotel. Address: Twp Rd 366 44610

WHERE TO EAT

FARMSTEAD RESTAURANT 330/893-4600
APPROVED American. Casual Dining. Address: 4757 Township Rd 366 44610

BLUE ASH (H-11) pop. 12,114, elev. 846'
• Restaurants p. 144
• Hotels & Restaurants map & index p. 166
• Part of Cincinnati area — see map p. 153

The Blue Ash Bicentennial Veterans Memorial is downtown at Hunt and Cooper roads. Created for the town's 1991 bicentennial celebration, the memorial consists of 10 life-size statues of members of the armed forces representing America's major wars from the American Revolution to the Persian Gulf War. Behind each statue flies a U.S. flag from the corresponding era.

THE BLU HOTEL, AN ASCEND HOTEL COLLECTION MEMBER 513/530-5999
THREE DIAMOND Hotel. Address: 11349 Reed Hartman Hwy 45241

COMFORT INN 513/791-3535
APPROVED Hotel. Address: 4640 Creek Rd 45242

COURTYARD BY MARRIOTT CINCINNATI BLUE ASH 513/733-4334

THREE DIAMOND Hotel | COURTYARD AAA Benefit: Members save 5% or more!

Address: 4625 Lake Forest Dr 45242 Location: I-275 exit 47, 2.4 mi s; I-71 exit 15, 1 mi w on Pfeiffer Rd, then just n on Reed Hartman Hwy. Facility: 149 units. 2-3 stories, interior corridors. Pool: heated indoor. Activities: exercise room. Guest Services: valet and coin laundry, boarding pass kiosk.

SAVE ECO ⬦ CALL ⬦ ⬦ ⬦
BIZ ⬦ ⬦ ⬦ ⬦

/ SOME UNITS ⬦

EMBASSY SUITES BY HILTON HOTEL-CINCINNATI NORTHEAST 513/733-8900

THREE DIAMOND Hotel | EMBASSY SUITES AAA Benefit: Members save up to 15%!

Address: 4554 Lake Forest Dr 45242 Location: I-275 exit 47, 2.3 mi s; I-71 exit 15, 1 mi w on Pfeiffer Rd. Facility: 238 units. 5 stories, interior corridors. Terms: check-in 4 pm. Amenities: safes. Pool: heated indoor. Activities: exercise room. Guest Services: valet and coin laundry, area transportation. Featured Amenity: full hot breakfast.

SAVE ⬦ ⬦ CALL ⬦ ⬦ ⬦
BIZ ⬦ ⬦ ⬦ ⬦ ⬦ / SOME UNITS ⬦

HAWTHORN SUITES BY WYNDHAM 513/733-0100
APPROVED Extended Stay Hotel. Address: 10665 Techwood Cir 45242

HILTON GARDEN INN CINCINNATI/BLUE ASH 513/469-6900
THREE DIAMOND SAVE Hotel. Address: 5300 Cornell Rd 45242 | AAA Benefit: Members save up to 15%!

HOLIDAY INN EXPRESS HOTEL & SUITES 513/985-9035
APPROVED Hotel. Address: 4660 Creek Rd 45242

HYATT PLACE CINCINNATI/BLUE ASH 513/489-3666

THREE DIAMOND Hotel | HYATT PLACE AAA Benefit: Members save up to 10%!

Address: 11435 Reed Hartman Hwy 45241 Location: I-275 exit 47, 0.8 mi s. Facility: 125 units. 6 stories, interior corridors. Pool: heated indoor. Activities: exercise room. Guest Services: valet laundry. Featured Amenity: full hot breakfast.

SAVE CALL ⬦ ⬦ ⬦ BIZ ⬦
⬦ ⬦ ⬦ / SOME UNITS ⬦ HS

SONESTA ES SUITES CINCINNATI BLUE ASH 513/530-5060

THREE DIAMOND Extended Stay Hotel

Address: 11401 Reed Hartman Hwy 45241 Location: I-275 exit 47, 0.8 mi s. Facility: 118 units, some two bedrooms, efficiencies and kitchens. 2 stories (no elevator), interior/exterior corridors. Pool: heated outdoor. Activities: tennis, exercise room. Guest Services: valet and coin laundry. Featured Amenity: breakfast buffet.

SAVE CALL ⬦ ⬦ ⬦ BIZ ⬦
⬦ ⬦ ⬦ ⬦ / SOME UNITS ⬦

SPRINGHILL SUITES BY MARRIOTT 513/793-1000
THREE DIAMOND SAVE Hotel. Address: 4650 Creek Rd 45242 | AAA Benefit: Members save 5% or more!

WINGATE BY WYNDHAM CINCINNATI BLUE ASH 513/733-1142
THREE DIAMOND Hotel. Address: 4320 Glendale-Milford Rd 45242

(See map & index p. 166.)

WHERE TO EAT

BROWN DOG CAFE 513/794-1610 ㊼
THREE DIAMOND American. Fine Dining. **Address:** 4335 Glendale-Milford Rd 45242

FIREHOUSE GRILL 513/733-3473 ㊻
APPROVED American. Casual Dining. **Address:** 4785 Lake Forest Dr 45242

PARKER'S BLUE ASH TAVERN 513/891-8300 ㊿
THREE DIAMOND Steak. Casual Dining. **Address:** 4200 Cooper Rd 45242

SAMMY'S CRAFT BURGERS & BEERS 513/745-9484 ㊺
APPROVED Burgers. Casual Dining. **Address:** 4767 Creek Rd 45242

SENATE 513/769-0099 ㊽
APPROVED American. Gastropub. **Address:** 1100 Summit Ave 45242

SLATT'S PUB 513/791-2223 (51)
APPROVED American. Casual Dining. **Address:** 4858 Cooper Rd 45242

TAHONA KITCHEN & BAR 513/777-8226 ㊾
APPROVED Mexican. Casual Dining. **Address:** 1100 Summit Pl, Suite B 45242

BOARDMAN pop. 35,376

HOLIDAY INN-BOARDMAN 330/726-1611
THREE DIAMOND Hotel. **Address:** 7410 South Ave 44512

WHERE TO EAT

ALADDIN'S EATERY 330/629-6450
APPROVED Lebanese. Casual Dining. **Address:** 7325 South Ave Extension 44512

MAGIC TREE PUB & EATERY 330/629-2667
APPROVED American. Casual Dining. **Address:** 7463 South Ave 44512

BOWLING GREEN (B-3) pop. 30,028, elev. 696'

The magnificent late 19th-century Wood County Courthouse at E. Court and N. Prospect St. is a must-see if you're visiting or just passing through Bowling Green. A highlight of the structure is the 185-foot granite clock tower.

The city is probably best known as the home of Bowling Green State University, founded in 1910 and now home to more than 20,000 students on its main campus. The northwest entrance to the campus (Poe Road at N. College Dr.) features a piece of public art entitled "The People." A team of art students created a design to depict silhouettes of the people of the area engaged in their professions and everyday activities. Bowling Green buildings and landmarks and the Great Black Swamp are represented as well.

Simpson Garden Park, 1291 Conneaut Ave., features a variety of themed gardens. It's open daily dawn-dusk.

Figure skater Scott Hamilton, who grew up in Bowling Green, frequented BGSU Ice Arena. The facility offers public skating; for schedule information phone (419) 372-2264.

Bowling Green Convention & Visitors Bureau: 130 S. Main St., Bowling Green, OH 43402. **Phone:** (419) 353-9445 or (800) 866-0046.

Self-guiding tours: Information and brochures about themed self-guiding tours are available at the convention and visitors bureau.

SNOOK'S DREAM CARS is off I-75 exit 179, .5 mi. e. on SR 6, then just n. to 13920 County Home Rd. The museum houses more than two dozen antique and classic cars from the 1930s through 1960s. A replica of a 1940s Texaco filling station is included, as are hundreds of automobile-related collectibles. **Time:** Allow 1 hour minimum. **Hours:** Mon.-Fri. 8-5, Sat.-Sun. by appointment. **Cost:** $8; $6 (ages 65+); $5 (ages 0-12). **Phone:** (419) 353-8338.

BEST WESTERN FALCON PLAZA 419/352-4671
APPROVED
Motel

Best Western. **AAA Benefit:** Members save up to 15% and earn bonus points!

Address: 1450 E Wooster St 43402 **Location:** I-75 exit 181, 1 mi w. Opposite Bowling Green State University. **Facility:** 85 units. 2 stories (no elevator), interior/exterior corridors. **Parking:** winter plug-ins. **Activities:** hot tub, exercise room.

SAVE BIZ

FAIRFIELD INN & SUITES BY MARRIOTT BOWLING GREEN 419/352-0033
THREE DIAMOND SAVE Hotel. **Address:** 1544 E Wooster St 43402

AAA Benefit: Members save 5% or more!

HAMPTON BY HILTON BOWLING GREEN 419/353-3464
THREE DIAMOND SAVE Hotel. **Address:** 142 Campbell Hill Rd 43402

AAA Benefit: Members save up to 15%!

HOLIDAY INN EXPRESS & SUITES BOWLING GREEN 419/353-5500
THREE DIAMOND Hotel. **Address:** 2150 E Wooster St 43402

WHERE TO EAT

EASYSTREET CAFE 419/353-0988
APPROVED American. Casual Dining. **Address:** 104 S Main St 43402

EL ZARAPE 419/353-0937
APPROVED Mexican. Casual Dining. **Address:** 1616 E Wooster St 43402

BROOKLYN pop. 11,169
- Hotels & Restaurants map & index p. 194
- Part of Cleveland area — see map p. 177

EXTENDED STAY AMERICA CLEVELAND-BROOKLYN
216/267-7799
 APPROVED Extended Stay Hotel. **Address:** 10300 Cascade Crossing 44144

HAMPTON INN-CLEVELAND AIRPORT/TIEDEMAN RD
216/929-8400
 THREE DIAMOND
Hotel

 AAA Benefit: Members save up to 15%!

Address: 10305 Cascade Crossing 44144. **Location:** I-480 exit 13, just s, then just e. **Facility:** 81 units. 4 stories, interior corridors. **Terms:** check-in 4 pm. **Pool:** heated indoor. **Activities:** hot tub, exercise room. **Guest Services:** valet and coin laundry, area transportation. **Featured Amenity:** breakfast buffet.

[SAVE] [✈] CALL [♿] [🚐] [👶] [BIZ]
[📶] [✕] [🔌] [🍴] [💻]

BROOK PARK pop. 19,212
- Hotels & Restaurants map & index p. 194
- Part of Cleveland area — see map p. 177

BEST WESTERN AIRPORT INN & SUITES CLEVELAND
216/267-9364
 APPROVED
Hotel

Best Western. **AAA Benefit:** Members save up to 15% and earn bonus points!

Address: 16501 Snow Rd 44142 **Location:** I-71 exit 237, just e. **Facility:** 64 units, some efficiencies. 3 stories, interior corridors. **Terms:** check-in 4 pm. **Pool:** heated indoor. **Activities:** exercise room. **Guest Services:** valet and coin laundry.

[SAVE] [✈] [🍴] CALL [♿] [🚐] [👶]
[BIZ] [📶] [✕] [🔌] [🍴] [💻]
/ SOME UNITS [🐾]

BRUNSWICK pop. 34,255
- Hotels & Restaurants map & index p. 194

COZUMEL 330/220-3335
 APPROVED Mexican. Casual Dining. **Address:** 625 Pearl Rd 44212

FATBOB PIZZA 330/273-5455
 APPROVED Pizza. Casual Dining. **Address:** 1739 Pearl Rd 44212

MUCHO BUENO'S 330/273-6294
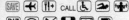 **APPROVED** Mexican. Casual Dining. **Address:** 1421 Town Center Blvd 44212

RITO'S 330/220-3103
APPROVED Breads/Pastries. Quick Serve. **Address:** 1930 Pearl Rd 44212

BURTON (B-12) pop. 1,455, elev. 1,310'

Burton, the oldest settlement in the Western Reserve, was founded in 1798. The town retains its historic charm, being built around a typical New England town park, with school, church and several lovely 19th-century homes. The town is on the western edge of the fourth largest Amish community in the world, and horse-drawn buggies can be seen traveling around the square. The square is also home to the Burton Log Cabin, a working sugar house. It was built in 1931 and several additions were added through 1962. During the maple sugaring season, sap is collected from nearby trees and then boiled to make maple syrup. Maple candy is made year-round. The gift shop sells maple products made on-site.

Burton is the home of The Great Geauga County Fair, Ohio's oldest fair. The fair was founded in 1823 and is held Thursday through Monday every Labor Day weekend. More than 2,000 exhibitors enter more than 13,000 exhibits to intrigue and delight more than 200,000 visitors. For more information phone (440) 834-1846.

RED MAPLE INN BED & BREAKFAST 440/834-8334
THREE DIAMOND
Bed & Breakfast

Address: 14707 S Cheshire St 44021 **Location:** Just e of Park Cir on SR 168 and 700. **Facility:** This inn offers a quiet retreat in a well-preserved Western Reserve village. The property has Amish-made furniture, charming rustic décor and serene views of hilly farmland. Some rooms have a balcony. 18 units. 2 stories, interior corridors. **Activities:** game room, exercise room. **Guest Services:** valet laundry. **Featured Amenity:** continental breakfast.

[SAVE] CALL [♿] [👶] [📶] [✕] [💻]
/ SOME UNITS [🔌] [🍴]

CALDWELL (F-7) pop. 1,748, elev. 744'
- Hotels p. 146 • Restaurants p. 146

NOBLE COUNTY HISTORICAL SOCIETY is at 419 West St., on the courthouse square. Guided tours are offered of this 1882 brick and stone structure that once served as the county jail and jailer's residence. Exhibits chronicle the history of the building as well as other topics of local history, including agriculture, medical practices and the oil industry. The story of the 1925 crash of the airship USS *Shenandoah* in Noble County also is featured.

A research library is included. **Time:** Allow 30 minutes minimum. **Hours:** Mon. and Wed.-Thurs. 10:30-4:30. **Cost:** Donations. **Phone:** (740) 732-5288. [GT]

BEST WESTERN CALDWELL INN 740/732-7599

 APPROVED
Hotel

 Best Western.
AAA Benefit: Members save up to 15% and earn bonus points!

Address: 44128 Fairground Rd 43724 **Location:** I-77 exit 25, just e. **Facility:** 52 units. 2 stories, interior corridors. **Parking:** winter plug-ins. **Pool:** heated indoor. **Activities:** exercise room. **Guest Services:** valet laundry. **Featured Amenity: full hot breakfast.**

SAVE 🍴 CALL ♿ 🛄 🐾 BIZ
📶 🔋 🛏 💻

COMFORT INN & SUITES 740/732-2625

THREE DIAMOND
Hotel

Address: 44380 W Hills Ln 43724 **Location:** I-77 exit 25, just w. **Facility:** 76 units. 3 stories, interior corridors. **Pool:** heated indoor. **Activities:** hot tub, exercise room. **Guest Services:** coin laundry. **Featured Amenity: full hot breakfast.**

SAVE CALL ♿ 🐾 BIZ 📶
✕ 🔋 🛏 💻

MICROTEL INN & SUITES BY WYNDHAM 740/732-4200

APPROVED Hotel. **Address:** 44266 Fairground Rd 43724

WHERE TO EAT

LORI'S FAMILY RESTAURANT 740/732-4711

APPROVED American. Casual Dining. **Address:** 17020 McConnelsville Rd 43724

CAMBRIDGE (E-7) pop. 10,635, elev. 800'

Cambridge was the boyhood home of actor William Boyd, born in nearby Hendrysburg in 1895, who became famous for his film and television role as Hopalong Cassidy.

The Guernsey County Historical Society Museum, 218 N. 8th St., is a restored early 19th-century house containing Cambridge memorabilia from the town's beginning through the present; phone (740) 439-5884.

Nearby parks, including Salt Fork, Senecaville Lake and Wolf Run offer recreational activities throughout the year. *See Recreation Areas Chart.*

The holidays are particularly festive in downtown Cambridge. From November 1 to early January the Dickens Victorian Village is set up along Wheeling Avenue. Ninety-three scenes populated by handcrafted mannequins dressed in period clothing are set up at each lamppost and bench between 6th and 11th streets; they depict Dickens-era activities and some of his literary characters, including Bob Cratchit and Tiny Tim. Downtown retailers have brochures available. For more holiday merriment, stop by the 1881 Guernsey County Courthouse on an evening from early November to early January; each night it is lit with 30,000 lights set to holiday music.

Cambridge/Guernsey County Visitors & Convention Bureau: 627 Wheeling Ave., Suite 200, Cambridge, OH 43725. **Phone:** (740) 432-2022 or (800) 933-5480.

BAYMONT INN & SUITES 740/439-1505

APPROVED Motel. **Address:** 61595 Southgate Pkwy 43725

CAMBRIDGE HAMPTON INN BY HILTON 740/439-0600

APPROVED SAVE Hotel. **Address:** 8775 Georgetown Rd 43725

AAA Benefit: Members save up to 15%!

COMFORT INN 740/435-3200

APPROVED
Hotel

Address: 2327 Southgate Pkwy 43725 **Location:** I-70 exit 178, just n on SR 209. **Facility:** 70 units. 3 stories, interior corridors. **Parking:** winter plug-ins. **Amenities:** safes. **Pool:** heated indoor. **Activities:** hot tub, exercise room. **Guest Services:** valet and coin laundry. **Featured Amenity: full hot breakfast.**

SAVE 🍴 CALL ♿ 🐾 📶
✕ 🔋 🛏 💻
/ SOME UNITS 🐾 HS

FAIRFIELD INN & SUITES BY MARRIOTT 740/435-8700

THREE DIAMOND SAVE Hotel. **Address:** 8700 Dozer Rd 43725

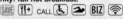

AAA Benefit: Members save 5% or more!

HOLIDAY INN EXPRESS & SUITES 740/421-4988

THREE DIAMOND Hotel. **Address:** 2035 Southgate Pkwy 43725

MICROTEL INN & SUITES BY WYNDHAM 740/435-8080

APPROVED Hotel. **Address:** 8779 Georgetown Rd 43725

SLEEP INN & SUITES 740/435-0035

THREE DIAMOND
Hotel

Address: 2307 Southgate Pkwy 43725 **Location:** I-70 exit 178, just n on SR 209. **Facility:** 71 units. 3 stories, interior corridors. **Parking:** winter plug-ins. **Pool:** heated indoor. **Activities:** limited exercise equipment. **Guest Services:** valet and coin laundry. **Featured Amenity: full hot breakfast.**

SAVE 🍴 CALL ♿ 🐾 BIZ 📶
✕ 🔋 🛏 💻
/ SOME UNITS 🐾 HS

WHERE TO EAT

BEAR'S DEN RESTAURANT 740/432-5285

APPROVED American. Casual Dining. **Address:** 13320 E Pike Rd 43725

THE FORUM 740/439-2777

APPROVED American. Casual Dining. **Address:** 2205 Southgate Pkwy 43725

THEO'S RESTAURANT 740/432-3878

APPROVED American. Casual Dining. **Address:** 632 Wheeling Ave 43725

CANAL WINCHESTER (F-5) pop. 7,101, elev. 761'

- Hotels & Restaurants map & index p. 222
- Part of Columbus area — see map p. 205

SLATE RUN LIVING HISTORICAL FARM is at 1375 Winchester Southern Rd. (SR 674N). This 1880s working farm includes restored buildings and employs the methods of the late 19th century. A self-guiding tour allows visitors to see farm routines that change with the seasons. Work may include planting or harvesting; making cider, soap or toys; and such daily chores as sewing, cooking and milking.

Time: Allow 1 hour, 30 minutes minimum. **Hours:** Tues.-Sat. 9-4 (also Fri.-Sat. 4-6), Sun. 11-6, June-Aug.; Tues.-Sat. 9-4, Sun. 11-4 Apr.-May and Sept.-Oct.; Wed.-Sat. 9-4, Sun. 11-4, rest of year. Activities are reduced and some buildings may be closed Jan.-Mar.; phone to confirm. **Cost:** Free. **Phone:** (614) 833-1880. 👫

BEST WESTERN CANAL WINCHESTER INN-COLUMBUS SOUTH EAST   614/834-4790   86

 APPROVED
Hotel

Best Western. AAA Benefit: Members save up to 15% and earn bonus points!

Address: 6323 Prentiss School Dr 43110 **Location:** US 33 exit 135 (Canal Winchester), just sw. **Facility:** 59 units. 2 stories (no elevator), interior corridors. **Parking:** winter plug-ins. **Pool:** heated indoor. **Guest Services:** valet laundry. **Featured Amenity:** continental breakfast.

SAVE 🍴 🏊 BIZ 🛜 ✕ 🛎
🖥 🖨

 **WHERE TO EAT**

BREWDOG DOGTAP   614/908-3051   86
 APPROVED   American. Casual Dining. **Address:** 96 Gender Rd 43110

SKYLINE CHILI   614/920-0782
APPROVED   American. Quick Serve. **Address:** 6290 Prentiss School Pl 43110

CANFIELD pop. 7,515

COURTYARD BY MARRIOTT YOUNGSTOWN CANFIELD
330/533-6880
THREE DIAMOND SAVE Hotel. **Address:** 4173 Westford Pl 44406
AAA Benefit: Members save 5% or more!

HAMPTON INN & SUITES BY HILTON   330/702-1900
THREE DIAMOND SAVE Hotel. **Address:** 6690 Ironwood Blvd 44406
AAA Benefit: Members save up to 15%!

CANTON (D-7) pop. 73,007, elev. 1,052'

- Hotels p. 148 • Restaurants p. 149

Canton derived its name from the wealthy estate near Baltimore, where Bezaleel Wells lived before settling in Ohio around 1805. Although Canton grew into a major industrial center, the city maintains an informal neatness dating from the 19th century, when immigrant Swiss and German watchmakers influenced city planning.

Canton was the home of President William McKinley. He attended the Church of the Savior United Methodist at Cleveland Avenue and W. Tuscarawas Street. Four memorial windows presented by Mrs. McKinley adorn the structure.

In 1918, after delivering a speech in Canton, one-time Socialist presidential candidate Eugene V. Debs was arrested for violating the Espionage Act of 1917.

Visit Canton/Stark County Convention & Visitors Bureau: 222 Market Ave. N., Canton, OH 44702. **Phone:** (330) 454-1439 or (800) 552-6051.

Shopping: A major shopping complex is Belden Village Mall, off I-77 Everhard Rd. exit. Its stores include Dillard's, Macy's and Sears.

THE CULTURAL CENTER FOR THE ARTS is at 1001 Market Ave. N. The center presents performances by the Players Guild Theatre and is home to the Canton Ballet and Voices of Canton. Within the center is the Canton Museum of Art *(see attraction listing)*, which offers multimedia exhibitions with an emphasis on Ohio artists. **Phone:** (330) 452-4096 for the cultural center, (330) 455-7220 for ballet information, (330) 453-7617 for theater tickets, or (330) 455-1000 for Voices of Canton.

Canton Museum of Art is at 1001 Market Ave. N. in The Cultural Center for the Arts. The permanent collection's focus is on American watercolors since the 19th century as well as contemporary ceramics. Winslow Homer, Edward Hopper, Maurice Prendergast, Andy Warhol and Andrew Wyeth works are part of the collection, as are ceramics by Toshiko Takaezu, Don Reitz and Don Pilcher. The museum also presents more than 15 changing exhibits through the year.

Time: Allow 1 hour minimum. **Hours:** Tues.-Thurs. 10-8, Fri.-Sat. 10-5, Sun. 1-5. **Cost:** $8; $6 (ages 13-18, ages 60+ and college students with ID). **Phone:** (330) 453-7666.

FANNIE MAY & HARRY LONDON CHOCOLATE FACTORY—see North Canton p. 280.

FIRST LADIES NATIONAL HISTORIC SITE is at 205 and 331 Market Ave. S. Memorabilia and personal effects of First Lady Ida Saxton McKinley can be seen in the carefully restored Saxton McKinley House.

The Education and Research Center, at 205 Market Ave. S., contains a research library, exhibits and a small theater. Through changing exhibits, the museum highlights the roles of the First Lady—from director of social affairs to Presidential liaison, policy advocate, political reformer and keeper of "the people's house"—and details achievements and the manner in which each interpreted and personalized her role.

Guided tours of the site, which begin at the Education and Research Center, are led by volunteer docents. Tour size is limited. **Time:** Allow 1 hour, 30 minutes minimum. **Hours:** Tours are offered Tues.-Sat. at 9:30, 10:30, 12:30, 1:30 and 2:30 (also Sun. at 12:30, 1:30 and 2:30, June-Aug.). Closed major holidays. **Cost:** $7; $6 (ages 62+); $5 (ages 0-17). Reservations are recommended. **Phone:** (330) 452-0876, ext. 320. GT

PRO FOOTBALL HALL OF FAME is at 2121 George Halas Dr. N.W., at jct. I-77 and US 62. The hall presents films and memorabilia of professional football history; teams and individual stars are highlighted. The Super Bowl Theatre rotates 180 degrees to offer its audience two separate video presentations. Exhibits showcase football history's defining moments as well as the sport's current thrills. The Hall of Fame Gallery is where you'll get to see a bronze bust of each enshrined member as well as learn about each inductee from touch-screen kiosks.

The Hunt/Casterline Pro Football Hall of Fame Card Collection, a recent addition to the attraction, features what is said to be the world's most valuable collection of its kind. An induction ceremony, parades, an exhibition football game and other events are held late July to early September during the Pro Football Hall of Fame Enshrinement Festival.

The hall of fame campus is undergoing a major expansion, the majority of which is expected to be completed by 2019. **Time:** Allow 2 hours minimum. **Hours:** Daily 9-8, Memorial Day weekend-Labor Day; 9-5, rest of year. One-hour guided tours are offered 11-2. **Cost:** $26; $22 (ages 65+); $19 (ages 6-12). Guided tour $10 (per person). **Parking:** $10. **Phone:** (330) 456-8207. GT ⑪

COMFORT INN-HALL OF FAME 330/492-1331
APPROVED Hotel. **Address:** 5345 Broadmoor Cir NW 44709

COURTYARD BY MARRIOTT 330/494-6494
THREE DIAMOND SAVE Hotel. **Address:** 4375 Metro Cir NW 44720
AAA Benefit: Members save 5% or more!

FAIRFIELD INN & SUITES BY MARRIOTT 330/493-7373
APPROVED SAVE Hotel. **Address:** 5285 Broadmoor Cir NW 44709
AAA Benefit: Members save 5% or more!

FAIRFIELD INN & SUITES BY MARRIOTT-CANTON SOUTH 330/484-0300

THREE DIAMOND
Hotel

 Fairfield **AAA Benefit:** Members save 5% or more!

Address: 4025 Greentree Ave SW 44706 **Location:** I-77 exit 101, just e. Located in a semi-rural area. **Facility:** 99 units. 4 stories, interior corridors. **Parking:** winter plug-ins. **Pool:** heated indoor. **Activities:** exercise room. **Guest Services:** valet and coin laundry.
SAVE CALL ⑤ 🐎 🔟 BIZ HS 🛜 ✖ 🔋 📷 📠

GERVASI VINEYARD 330/497-1000
FOUR DIAMOND
Boutique Hotel

Address: 1700 55th St NE 44721 **Location:** Jct 55th St, 0.7 mi e. **Facility:** This hotel is an upscale Tuscan-inspired resort winery featuring excellent, estate-produced wines, private winery tours, tastings and pairings, boutique shopping and luxurious villa suites. 48 units, some two bedrooms, kitchens and houses. 1-2 stories (no elevator), interior corridors. *Bath:* shower only. **Amenities:** safes. **Dining:** The Bistro at Gervasi Vineyard, The Crush House, see separate listings, entertainment. **Activities:** recreation programs, bicycles, lawn sports, massage. **Guest Services:** valet laundry. **Featured Amenity:** continental breakfast.
SAVE ⑪ 🔟 🍸 CALL ⑤ HS 🛜 ✖ 🔋 📷 📠

HAMPTON INN & SUITES BY HILTON CANTON 330/491-4335
THREE DIAMOND SAVE Hotel. **Address:** 5256 Broadmoor Cir NW 44709
AAA Benefit: Members save up to 15%!

HOLIDAY INN CANTON 330/494-2770
THREE DIAMOND Hotel. **Address:** 4520 Everhard Rd NW 44718

HOME2 SUITES BY HILTON CANTON 330/491-9714
THREE DIAMOND SAVE Extended Stay Hotel. **Address:** 5244 Broadmoor Cir NW 44709
AAA Benefit: Members save up to 15%!

HYATT PLACE CANTON 330/244-1700
THREE DIAMOND
Hotel

HYATT PLACE **AAA Benefit:** Members save up to 10%!

Address: 5421 Whipple Ave NW 44720 **Location:** I-77 exit 109 southbound; exit 109B northbound, just e. **Facility:** 105 units. 4 stories, interior corridors. **Parking:** winter plug-ins. **Pool:** heated indoor. **Activities:** hot tub, exercise room. **Guest Services:** valet and coin laundry, area transportation. **Featured Amenity:** full hot breakfast.
SAVE ⊁ ⑪ 🍸 CALL ⑤ 🐎 🔟 BIZ HS 🛜 ✖ 🔋 📷 / SOME UNITS 🐾

QUALITY INN HALL OF FAME
330-956-5056

APPROVED
Hotel

Address: 3970 Convenience Cir NW 44718 **Location:** I-77 exit 109, just e on Everhard Rd, then just s on Whipple Ave. **Facility:** 59 units. 3 stories (no elevator), interior corridors. **Activities:** exercise room. **Guest Services:** coin laundry. **Featured Amenity:** full hot breakfast.

RED ROOF INN CANTON
330-499-1970

APPROVED
Motel

Address: 5353 Inn Circle Ct NW 44720 **Location:** I-77 exit 109, just w on Everhard Rd. **Facility:** 108 units. 2 stories (no elevator), exterior corridors. **Amenities:** safes.

RESIDENCE INN BY MARRIOTT
330/493-0004

THREE DIAMOND Extended Stay Hotel. **Address:** 5280 Broadmoor Cir NW 44709

AAA Benefit: Members save 5% or more!

STAYBRIDGE SUITES CANTON
330/966-6620

THREE DIAMOND Extended Stay Hotel. **Address:** 3879 Everhard Rd NW 44709

WHERE TO EAT

BAKER'S CAFE 330/454-0528
APPROVED Steak. Casual Dining. **Address:** 1927 Stark Ave SW 44706

BENDER'S RESTAURANT 330/453-8424
THREE DIAMOND Seafood. Gastropub. **Address:** 137 Court Ave SW 44702

THE BISTRO AT GERVASI VINEYARD 330/497-1000
THREE DIAMOND Northern Italian. Fine Dining. **Address:** 1700 55th St NE 44721

THE BISTRO OF OAKWOOD 330/915-8173
APPROVED American. Casual Dining. **Address:** 2664 Easton St NE 44721

BROWN DERBY ROADHOUSE 330/494-4413
APPROVED Steak Seafood. Casual Dining. **Address:** 4670 Everhard Rd 44718

BURNTWOOD TAVERN 234/209-9746
APPROVED American. Casual Dining. **Address:** 4320 Everhard Rd NW 44718

THE CRUSH HOUSE 330/497-1000
APPROVED American. Casual Dining. **Address:** 1700 55th St NE 44721

DON QUIJOTE RESTAURANT 330/978-2273
THREE DIAMOND Spanish. Casual Dining. **Address:** 4695 Dressler Rd 44718

FAT HEAD'S BREWERY 330/244-8601
APPROVED Sandwiches. Brewpub. **Address:** 3885 Everhard Rd NW 44709

JOHN'S BAR & GRILLE 330/454-1259
APPROVED American. Casual Dining. **Address:** 2749 Cleveland Ave NW 44709

LA PIZZARIA 330/477-4700
APPROVED Italian. Casual Dining. **Address:** 3656 Dressler Rd NW 44718

PAPA BEAR'S ITALIAN RESTAURANT 330/493-0714
APPROVED Italian Pizza. Casual Dining. **Address:** 4990 Dressler Rd NW 44718

THE RAIL 330/497-7550
APPROVED Burgers. Casual Dining. **Address:** 4347 Belden Village Mall 44718

SAMANTHA'S SUNNY CORNER RESTAURANT 330/493-0523
APPROVED Comfort Food. Casual Dining. **Address:** 4205 Hills and Dales Rd NW 44708

SNORKY'S ON THIRD 330/409-0343
APPROVED American. Brewpub. **Address:** 120 3rd St NW 44702

TLAQUEPAQUE 330/649-9109
APPROVED Mexican. Casual Dining. **Address:** 4460 Dressler Rd 44718

WINKING LIZARD TAVERN 330/497-1133
APPROVED American. Casual Dining. **Address:** 5710 Fulton Dr NW 44718

CELINA pop. 10,400

BEST WESTERN-CELINA
419/586-4919

APPROVED
Hotel

Best Western AAA Benefit: Members save up to 15% and earn bonus points!

Address: 2020 Holiday Dr 45822 **Location:** Jct SR 29 and Havemann Rd, just n; e of downtown. **Facility:** 52 units. 2 stories, interior corridors. **Parking:** winter plug-ins. **Pool:** heated indoor. **Activities:** hot tub, exercise room.

WHERE TO EAT

BELLA'S ITALIAN GRILLE 419/586-9545
APPROVED Italian. Casual Dining. **Address:** 1081 W Bank Rd 45822

CJ'S HIGHMARKS 419/586-5552
APPROVED American. Casual Dining. **Address:** 1211 Irmscher Blvd 45822

C-TOWN WINGS 419/942-9464
APPROVED Wings Sandwiches. Casual Dining. **Address:** 1903 Havemann Rd 45822

AAA.com/ TourBook Comments

Let Your Voice Be Heard

CENTERVILLE pop. 23,999

• Hotels & Restaurants map & index p. 242

HOLIDAY INN EXPRESS & SUITES DAYTON/CENTERVILLE
937/424-5757 **43**
◊ **APPROVED** Hotel. **Address:** 5655 Wilmington Pike
45459

HOLIDAY INN EXPRESS & SUITES DAYTON/SOUTH I-675
937/938-9550 **44**
◊ **THREE DIAMOND** Hotel. **Address:** 7701 Washington Village
Dr 45459

HOME2 SUITES BY HILTON DAYTON-CENTERVILLE
937/988-0050 **45**
◊ **THREE DIAMOND** ⓢ Extended   **AAA Benefit:**
Stay Hotel. **Address:** 5161 Cornerstone   Members save up to
North Blvd 45440   15%!

WHERE TO EAT

CHAPPY'S SOCIAL HOUSE   937/439-9200 **31**
◊ **APPROVED** Comfort Food. Casual Dining. **Address:**
7880 Washington Village Dr 45459

THE CHOP HOUSE   937/291-1661
◊ **APPROVED** Steak Seafood. Casual Dining. **Address:**
7727 Washington Village Dr 45459

CITY BARBEQUE   937/312-1350
◊ **APPROVED** Barbecue. Quick Serve. **Address:** 5 E
Franklin St 45459

THE FAMOUS RESTAURANT   937/951-2422 **34**
◊ **APPROVED** Comfort Food. Casual Dining. **Address:**
953 S Main St 45459

J. ALEXANDER'S REDLANDS GRILL   937/435-4441 **32**
◊ **THREE DIAMOND** American. Casual Dining. **Address:** 7970
Washington Village Dr 45459

THE PARAGON SUPPER CLUB   937/433-1234 **33**
◊ **APPROVED** Steak Seafood. Casual Dining. **Address:**
797 Miamisburg-Centerville Rd 45459

SKYLINE CHILI
◊ **APPROVED** American. Quick Serve.
LOCATIONS:
Address: 945 S Main St 45458 **Phone:** 937/436-7430
Address: 8906 Kingsridge Dr 45458 **Phone:** 937/434-3952

CHERRY GROVE pop. 4,378

• Hotels & Restaurants map & index p. 166
• Part of Cincinnati area — see map p. 153

BEST WESTERN CLERMONT   513/528-7702 **84**
◊ **APPROVED**
     Motel

ⒷⓌ **Best Western.** **AAA Benefit:** Members save up to 15% and earn bonus points!

Address: 4004 Williams Dr 45255 **Location:** I-275 exit 65, just w, then just s. **Facility:** 96 units. 2 stories (no elevator), exterior corridors. **Pool:** outdoor. **Activities:** exercise room. **Guest Services:** valet and coin laundry. **Featured Amenity:** breakfast buffet.

WHERE TO EAT

GOLD STAR CHILI   513/474-4916
◊ **APPROVED** American. Quick Serve. **Address:** 8467
Beechmont Ave 45255

SKYLINE CHILI   513/528-6611
◊ **APPROVED** American. Quick Serve. **Address:** 440
Ohio Pike 45255

CHILLICOTHE (G-4) pop. 21,901, elev. 632'

Founded in 1796, Chillicothe served as capital of the Northwest Territory and was governed by Gen. Arthur St. Clair 1800-02. The city was host to the state's first constitutional convention in 1802, and Chillicothe was Ohio's first capital. Today it is an industrial center surrounded by a productive agricultural region.

Chillicothe is at the junction of two scenic highways. A picturesque portion of SR 159 runs 34 miles southwest from Lancaster, while an impressive portion of US 50 runs 19 miles northeast from Bainbridge.

At 90 W. Sixth St. you'll find the Lucy Hayes Heritage Center, which was the birthplace and childhood home of First Lady Lucy Ware Webb Hayes, who was born Aug. 28, 1831. In 1852 she married Rutherford B. Hayes, who was later elected the nation's president in 1877. The restored house has period furnishings and photos of the family, but there are no items that belonged to them. Tours are given Fri.-Sat. 1-4, Apr.-Sept.; other times by appointment. Phone (740) 775-5829.

Ross-Chillicothe Convention and Visitors Bureau: 230 N. Plaza Blvd., Chillicothe, OH 45601. **Phone:** (740) 702-7677 or (800) 413-4118.

ADENA MANSION & GARDENS is off Pleasant Valley Rd., just n.w. of jct. US 35 and SR 104 at 847 Adena Rd. Adena once belonged to Thomas Worthington, sixth governor of Ohio. Furnished in period, the Georgian stone mansion was completed in 1807. A 12,500-square-foot visitor center offers interactive exhibits about early 1800s life in Ohio; five outbuildings and formal gardens are on the grounds. An overlook provides a view of the hills that are reproduced on the state seal. The mansion may only be seen via a guided tour.

Hours: Grounds open Wed.-Sat. 9-5, Sun. noon-5, Apr.-Oct. Guided mansion tours depart Wed.-Sat. at 9:30, 10:30, 11:30, 1:30, 2:30 and 3:30, Sun. at 12:30, 1:30, 2:30 and 3:30. Phone ahead to confirm schedule. **Cost:** $10; $9 (senior citizens); $5 (ages 6-12). Rates may vary (including during special events); phone ahead. **Phone:** (740) 772-1500 or (800) 319-7248. **GT**

HOPEWELL CULTURE NATIONAL HISTORICAL PARK—see place listing p. 259.

BEST WESTERN ADENA INN   740/775-7000

Address: 1250 N Bridge St 45601 **Location:** US 35 exit Bridge St, 0.8 mi n. **Facility:** 42 units. 2 stories (no elevator), interior corridors. **Parking:** winter plug-ins. **Pool:** outdoor. **Featured Amenity:** full hot breakfast.

CHRISTOPHER INN & SUITES   740/774-6835

APPROVED   Hotel. **Address:** 30 N Plaza Blvd 45601

FAIRFIELD BY MARRIOTT   740/771-9090

THREE DIAMOND SAVE Hotel. **Address:** 300 N Plaza Blvd 45601

HAMPTON INN & SUITES BY HILTON   740/773-1616

THREE DIAMOND SAVE Hotel. **Address:** 100 N Plaza Blvd 45601

WHERE TO EAT

DAKOTA'S ROADHOUSE   740/772-7427

APPROVED   Steak. Casual Dining. **Address:** 28 Stoneridge Dr 45601

THE OLD CANAL SMOKEHOUSE   740/779-3278

APPROVED   Barbecue. Casual Dining. **Address:** 94 E Water St 45601

THE POUR HOUSE AT MACHINERY HALL   740/771-4770

APPROVED   American. Brewpub. **Address:** 25 E 2nd St 45601

SUMBURGER DRIVE IN   740/772-1055

APPROVED   Burgers. Casual Dining. **Address:** 1487 N Bridge St 45601

Cincinnati

Then & Now

Winston Churchill called Cincinnati "the most beautiful of America's inland cities." Its location has much to do with its aesthetic appeal and stable business community. On the Ohio River's north shore, the downtown section is in a basin surrounded by hills.

Cincinnati was platted in 1788 by three land speculators. In 1789 Fort Washington was built to protect the settlers from the Native Americans, but the area only became open for further settlement with the defeat of the Ohio Indians at Fallen Timbers in 1794. Cincinnati's accessibility increased in 1811 with the arrival of the *New Orleans,* the first steamboat to reach its shores.

The construction of the Miami and Erie canals in the late 1820s provided farmers with transportation to the city where they could market their produce. Businessmen created new industries to process raw products into marketable whiskey, pork and flour. Plagued by religious and political conflicts, many Germans immigrated in the 1830s, followed in the 1840s by Irish driven from their country by the potato famine.

AAA.com/travelguides—
more ways to look, book and save

By 1850 Cincinnati was the world's largest pork-packing center, a status that brought the nickname Porkopolis. The South became the city's major market. This caused residents' loyalties to be divided with the approach of the Civil War, but the city eventually supported the Union forces. For a long time it had been a major stop on the Underground Railroad.

Following the war, Cincinnati experienced another burst of prosperity as the resumption of trade between North and South created heavy river commerce. In the 1870s Cincinnati businessmen arranged for the building of a railroad to reach their southern markets.

Cincinnati riverfront

Modern Cincinnati attracts many companies, including many corporate headquarters and Fortune 500 companies like Kroger, Macy's, Procter & Gamble and Convergys. Fountain Square is the hub. Centered on the historic 1871 Tyler Davidson Fountain, which tops a large underground garage, the square is surrounded by modern office buildings, hotels, shops and restaurants.

Cincinnati is also home to the 45,000-student University of Cincinnati, founded in 1819, and 7,000-student Xavier University, founded in 1831.

It's not all business in Cincinnati, though. Washington Park offers abundant green space and performance areas. The riverfront is a great destination for finding fun things to do outdoors. Bicentennial Commons at Sawyer Point features playgrounds, a skating pavilion, and tennis and volleyball courts as well as two performance venues and plaques

(Continued on p. 154.)

Destination Cincinnati

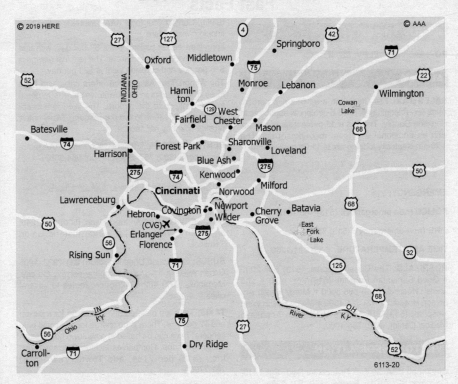

This map shows cities in the Cincinnati vicinity where you will find attractions, hotels and restaurants. Cities are listed alphabetically in this book on the following pages.

Fast Facts

ABOUT THE CITY

POP: 296,943 ▪ **ELEV:** 820 ft.

MONEY

SALES TAX: The Cincinnati area has a 7 percent sales tax. A lodging tax of 13.5 percent is applicable in Hamilton County. There is a 12 percent rental car tax with an additional 9 percent recoupment tax. The northern Kentucky lodging tax is 11.24 percent.

WHOM TO CALL

EMERGENCY: 911

POLICE (non-emergency): (513) 765-1212

FIRE (non-emergency): (513) 765-1212

TIME AND TEMPERATURE: (513) 721-1700

HOSPITALS: The Christ Hospital, (513) 585-2000 ▪ Good Samaritan Hospital, (513) 862-1400 ▪ The Jewish Hospital, (513) 686-3000 ▪ Mercy Health Anderson Hospital, (513) 624-4500 ▪ Mercy Health West Hospital, (513) 215-5000 ▪ UC Health Academic Medical Center, (513) 584-1000.

VISITOR INFORMATION

Cincinnati USA: 50 East Rivercenter Blvd., Suite 810, Covington, KY 41011. **Phone:** (859) 581-2260, (513) 534-5877 (Visitor Center) or (800) 543-2613.

The visitor center is on Fountain Square at 511 Walnut St. and is open Thurs.-Sun. 11-5.

TRANSPORTATION

AIR TRAVEL: Major passenger airlines serve the Cincinnati/Northern Kentucky International Airport (CVG). Contact your local AAA travel advisor for help finding cheap airfare.

Long-term airport parking costs $9 per day, with free shuttle service to the terminals. The terminal garage is $16 per day and curbside valet is $25 per day.

The Airport Taxi Association offers cabs with fixed fares from the airport to downtown (fare is metered from downtown to the airport). The fixed fare is approximately $34 (one to five passengers). Many hotels provide courtesy car service.

RENTAL CARS: Hertz offers discounts to AAA members; phone (859) 767-3535 or (800) 654-3080.

 Book and save at AAA.com/hertz

RAIL SERVICE: The Amtrak station, (800) 872-7245, is at 1301 Western Ave. inside historic Union Terminal.

BUSES: Greyhound Lines Inc., (800) 231-2222, 1005 Gilbert Ave., is the major company serving the city. Megabus, (877) 462-6342, offers routes to several cities.

TAXIS: Taxis are metered and charge $4 for a pickup and $2 per mile. There is no charge for additional passengers. Taxis can be hailed at downtown hotels or ordered by phone. Companies include Cincinnati Taxi Inc., (513) 666-2184, and Towne Taxi, (513) 761-7700.

PUBLIC TRANSPORTATION: Metro operates buses throughout the metropolitan area. The base fare is $1.75. Exact change is required, and zone and transfer charges are additional. Signs at many bus stops list the numbers of the routes that stop there.

For route and schedule information phone (513) 621-4455, Mon.-Fri. 6:30 a.m.-6 p.m. Information also is available at Mercantile Way Arcade, 120 E. Fourth St., Mon.-Fri. 7-5:30; phone (513) 632-7699.

(Continued from p. 152.)

relating tidbits of Cincinnati history. Yeatman's Cove is adorned with the Serpentine Wall, which runs along the river. A 30-foot steamboat paddle wheel that blows steam and plays music is a monument acknowledging the city's riverboat heritage.

The Newport Southbank Bridge, known as the Purple People Bridge thanks to a distinctive paint choice, is a pedestrian bridge linking the Cincinnati riverfront with Newport, Ky., and a nice place to watch river traffic. Smale Riverfront Park enhances the riverfront with a promenade, playground, carousel, gardens, interactive fountains, an event stage and a monument to the Black Brigade.

There are many fun places to go for indoor entertainment, too, including the complex at the Cincinnati Museum Center at Union Terminal, a beautiful restored Art Deco-style train station. One stop offers the Cincinnati History Museum, the Cincinnati History Library and Archives, the Duke Energy Children's Museum, the Museum of Natural History & Science and the Robert D. Lindner Family OMNIMAX Theater.

For fans of the performing arts who are looking for fun things to do, Cincinnati offers venues both large and small. Catch the Cincinnati Ballet, Broadway shows and children's theater at The Aronoff Center for the Arts downtown.

A trio of sports venues parallels the Ohio River. The Reds play baseball at Great American Ball Park, football's Bengals compete in the Paul Brown Stadium and hockey and other events take place at U.S. Bank Arena.

Must Do: AAA Editor's Picks

- Clip-clop through downtown on a **horse-drawn carriage ride** offered by one of the companies stationed near Fountain Square (Fifth and Vine sts.), Cincinnati's entertainment hub where you'll find plenty of things to do. Don't forget to snap some photos of the iconic 1871 Tyler Davidson Fountain before or after your tour.

- Pay a visit to the **Cincinnati Museum Center at Union Terminal** (1301 Western Ave.), home to three stellar museums and a state-of-the-art theater. Learn about the Queen City's past at the **Cincinnati History Museum,** stroll through prehistoric landscapes at the **Museum of Natural History & Science,** let the kids take charge at the **Duke Energy Children's Museum** and become immersed in breathtaking films at the **Robert D. Lindner Family OMNIMAX Theater.**

- Meet all sorts of fascinating creatures—from Bengal tigers to horned puffins to dart frogs—in a beautiful garden setting at the **Cincinnati Zoo and Botanical Garden** (3400 Vine St.). Be sure to check the schedule for the always-amusing shows and feedings, and if you happen to be visiting during the holiday season, don't miss the spectacular **PNC Festival of Lights** event.

- See a Reds—the world's first pro baseball team—**ballgame** or go on **Great American Ball Park Tours'** (100 Joe Nuxhall Way) guided behind-the-scenes tour of the Reds' 42,271-seat stadium.

- Reflect on Cincinnati's role in the fight for freedom at the **National Underground Railroad Freedom Center** (50 E. Freedom Way). Interactive exhibits, professional displays, special-effects films and a children's gallery portray the history of slavery in North America, focusing on the secret network followed by thousands of fugitive slaves seeking liberty.

- Shop 'til you drop, then linger over food or drinks in **Mount Adams** (just north of downtown), one of Cincinnati's most exclusive residential and business districts. Reminiscent of San Francisco, this hip, architecturally stunning hilltop community features narrow streets and an eclectic mix of places to eat, bars and specialty stores. Many restaurant decks afford panoramas of downtown, the Ohio River and parts of Kentucky.

- Explore **Eden Park** (950 Eden Park Dr.), a lovely 186-acre green space linked to Mount Adams by the Art Deco-style Ida Street Viaduct. Walk or jog along worn paths and soak up views of the lakes, gardens, memorial tree groves and other landmarks; peruse 6,000 years' worth of captivating art and artifacts at the **Cincinnati Art Museum** (953 Eden Park Dr.); enter greenhouses filled with tropical and desert plants, orchids and bonsai at **Krohn Conservatory** (1501 Eden Park Dr.); or watch a modern American or European drama at **Playhouse in the Park** (962 Mt. Adams Cir.).

- Get tickets to see a show at either the **Aronoff Center for the Arts** (650 Walnut St.) or **Music Hall** (1241 Elm St.)—stylistically different but equally lovely buildings. The pair houses many of the city's music, theater and dance companies.

- Eyeball some world-class pieces at the **Taft Museum of Art** (316 Pike St.). Displayed in an 1820 Palladian mansion that's a work of art in itself, the museum's outstanding collection includes sculpture, Chinese porcelains, old masters paintings, European decorative arts, antique watches and more.

- Brave The Beast and the Diamondback, two roller coasters guaranteed to make you scream, or perhaps the Banshee, the world's longest inverted roller coaster. **Kings Island** in nearby Mason (6300 Kings Island Dr.) is a destination that thrills families not only with hair-raising rides but also with live stage shows, animatronic dinosaurs, a Peanuts-themed kiddie area, and a water park featuring slides, wave pools and tropical lagoons.

Tyler Davidson Fountain

Arriving
By Car

Cincinnati straddles I-75, one of the nation's major north-south routes, shuttling traffic from the Canadian border to the north and Florida's Gulf Coast to the south. A shorter artery, I-71, angles through the city, providing a fast route from Louisville, central Ohio and Lake Erie cities.

Both routes join in the Kentucky suburbs to cross the river via the Brent Spence Bridge. From the north they follow separate alignments to the river but are connected across Ohio suburban areas by the Norwood Lateral Expressway (SR 562) and the Ronald Reagan Cross County Highway (SR 126).

I-71 and I-75 provide good access from I-70, a major transcontinental route that bisects Ohio some 55 miles north of the city, and each interchanges with primary city streets.

US 50 and scenic US 52 funnel east-west travelers to the city from the Indiana and Ohio countrysides; these older roads accommodate mostly local traffic. US 52 offers a scenic trip along the Ohio River east of Cincinnati.

I-74 is the principal link from the west, collecting traffic from some of the nation's busiest thoroughfares, I-80 and I-70, as well as highways from the Chicago area. SR 32 (Appalachian Highway) is a good route from rural areas east of the city.

I-275 (Circle Freeway) swings in a full orbit through the Ohio, Kentucky and Indiana environs. It provides a complete bypass of the city proper and interchanges with all major intersecting routes for easy access to downtown. I-471 offers an additional spur

Findlay Market

from the Kentucky portion of this circumferential highway into downtown via the Daniel Carter Beard Bridge (colloquially known as the Big Mac Bridge).

Getting Around
Street System

With the aid of a good city map, driving in Cincinnati is relatively easy. The downtown area is laid out in a grid pattern with streets running either north-south or east-west. The numbered streets run east-west beginning with 2nd Street near the Ohio River; named north-south streets intersect them. East-west address numbers start at Vine Street.

Unless otherwise posted, the speed limit on most streets is 25 or 30 mph. Rush-hour traffic, 7-9 a.m. and 3-6 p.m., should be avoided. Right turns on red are permitted unless otherwise posted.

Parking

Metered parking is found on many downtown streets; be sure to check signs and meters for restricted times and limits. There are several commercial garages and lots, and most hotels provide parking for guests. Municipal garage rates vary but generally are $2 for the first 2 hours, $1 for each additional hour up to $15 per day.

Shopping

Whether you are looking for designer fashions or clothing from grandmother's attic, it can be found in Cincinnati's array of department stores, boutiques and specialty shops. Downtown offers Brooks Brothers, Macy's, Saks Fifth Avenue and Tiffany & Co.

Trendsetters will want to plan a trip to **Mount Adams,** a San Francisco-style hillside shopping and dining destination. Novelty shops and fashion boutiques are scattered among local restaurants, nightspots and parks. Collegiate-style attire is found in **Clifton,** where many shops cater to University of Cincinnati students.

Consumer frenzy also can be satisfied at shopping malls, including **Eastgate Mall,** I-275 exit 63B; **Florence Mall,** in Florence, Ky.; **Kenwood Towne Centre,** off I-71N exit 12 or I-71S exit 11 at 7875 Montgomery Rd.; **Northgate Mall,** I-275 exit 33; and **Tri-County Mall,** I-275 exit 42. **Rookwood Commons & Pavilion,** off I-71 exit 6, houses around 45 upscale shops, and **Crestview Hills Town Center** in Crestview Hills, Ky., offers 300,000 square feet of shops and places to eat.

Bargain hunters will love the **Cincinnati Premium Outlets** only 30 miles north of downtown. Die-hard discount shoppers can travel 60 miles northeast to SAVE **Tanger Outlets** in Jeffersonville, Ohio (8000 Factory Shops Blvd.).

Findlay Market, Race and Elder streets, is an open-air marketplace that is a Cincinnati tradition. In operation since 1852, it offers a variety of ethnic foods within an old world atmosphere.

Big Events

May is a busy event month. The **Cincinnati Flying Pig Marathon,** held the first weekend of the month, draws runners of all abilities, and entertainment and events are offered, too. The **Appalachian Festival,** held at **Coney Island,** is said to be the largest craft show in the nation.

During two weekends in May, the city's renowned music community celebrates **May Festival,** the oldest continuing festival of choral and orchestral music in the United States. The tradition began in 1873; performances consist of a 150-voice chorus accompanied by the Cincinnati Symphony and joined by top-name guest conductors and opera singers.

Restaurateurs show off their talents on Memorial Day weekend during the **Taste of Cincinnati,** a sidewalk smorgasbord along **Fifth Street at Fountain Square.**

Cincinnati heralds the summer season with its **Summerfair** in early summer. More than 300 artists gather at Coney Island and display their works, while musicians perform classical, pop, country and jazz music.

Summer also offers music festivals. The 3-day **Bunbury Music Festival** in June features alternative music acts at **Sawyer Point** and **Yeatman's Cove.** The **Cincinnati Music Festival** in July offers 2 days of hip hop, R&B, jazz and soul music at **Paul Brown Stadium.** The summer draws to a close in September with Cincinnati's **Riverfest** on the Sunday of Labor Day. In honor of their river heritage, more than 500,000 people gather along the riverfront in both Ohio and Kentucky to watch water skiing, sky diving and air shows, and enjoy riverboat cruises. The festival climaxes with a spectacular fireworks display accompanied by a soundtrack broadcast by radio station WEBN (102.7 FM).

Another major end-of-summer event is the **Green Township Harvest Home Fair,** held the weekend following Labor Day in nearby Cheviot. A parade marks the traditional kickoff for what is dubbed "the biggest little fair in Ohio." Fairgoers can view horse, artwork and flower shows or attend a 4-H auction, among other fun things to do. Food, drink and stage entertainment are available.

With more than half the city's population of German ancestry, it is little wonder ⚜ **Oktoberfest Zinzinnati** is celebrated with almost as much vigor as its counterpart in Munich, Germany. Attracting more than 500,000 people, it is said to be the largest such celebration in the country. During a mid-September weekend, six blocks of downtown around Fountain Square are transformed into a German biergarten, complete with music, dancing, singing and, of course, lots of sauerkraut and beer. Be sure to take part in one of the world's largest chicken dances.

Coney Island celebrates autumn with its **Fall-O-Ween Festival,** held several weekends in October.

At the ⚜ **PNC Festival of Lights at the Cincinnati Zoo and Botanical Garden,** more than 2 million lights bedeck the grounds from late November

Sawyer Point

to early January. Visitors and locals alike enjoy ice-skating at the ice rink on Fountain Square from November through February. Another festive winter event is **Holiday Junction featuring the Duke Energy Holiday Trains** display at the **Cincinnati Museum Center at Union Terminal.** This is one of the largest portable train models in the world with 1,000 feet of track.

Sports & Rec

Cincinnati's city parks, Hamilton County's 17 parks and several state parks are easily accessible to Cincinnati visitors looking for adventurous things to do. Among these choices, the sports-minded can find facilities for almost any activity. Many of the parks have **tennis** courts, **camping** sites and lakes for **boating, fishing** and **swimming.**

Bicycling fans can rent a bike at **Smale Riverfront Park's** Cincinnati Bike Center (120 E. Mehring Way); phone (513) 282-4260. Red Bike has many bike rental locations throughout Cincy and northern Kentucky; phone (513) 621-2453.

Hiking trails are plentiful, especially at **Mount Airy Forest. Eden Park,** 186 acres off Gilbert Avenue between Elsinore and Morris, offers picnic facilities, lakes for **ice-skating** and an **exercise course.** An enjoyable activity is a stroll along the riverfront at **Bicentennial Commons at Sawyer Point** or **Yeatman's Cove Park.** For information about city park facilities phone (513) 352-4080.

There are many **golf** courses in the area, including seven city-owned and seven county-owned courses. The most well-known course is **The Golf**

Center at Kings Island, (513) 398-7700, with two Jack Nicklaus-designed courses.

For those more interested in spectator sports, the city has much to offer. When in the Queen City, if your favorite **baseball** team is not the **Cincinnati Reds,** it is best to keep that fact under your hat. World Series winners in 1919, 1940, 1975, 1976 and 1990 and National League division champs in 2012, the Big Red Machine has a large following. The Reds play at **Great American Ball Park** *(see attraction listing p. 162)*; for ticket and schedule information phone (513) 765-7000.

When all eyes turn from the diamond to the gridiron, **football's Cincinnati Bengals** become the city's stars. The team plays at **Paul Brown Stadium,** which opened in 2000. They gained a lofty status when they captured the 1981 and 1988 American Football Conference championships. For ticket and schedule information phone (513) 621-8383 or (866) 621-8383.

Hockey fans can head to **U.S. Bank Arena** October through March to root for the ECHL's two-time Kelly Cup winner **Cincinnati Cyclones;** phone (513) 421-7825 for ticket information. Tennis fans won't want to miss the **Western & Southern Open** in August in nearby Mason; phone (513) 651-0303 or (800) 745-3000 for ticket information.

Perhaps because of Cincinnati's proximity to Kentucky, **horse racing** events are popular. **Belterra Park,** (513) 232-8000, at 6301 Kellogg Ave., offers Thoroughbred racing late April through Labor Day and simulcast racing daily year-round. **Miami Valley Gaming,** about 30 miles northeast in Lebanon at 6000 SR 63, features live harness racing early

Great American Ball Park

January to early May and simulcast racing daily year-round; phone (513) 934-7070 or (855) 946-6847. **Turfway Park,** about 10 miles south off I-75 exit 182 at 7500 Turfway Rd. in Florence, Ky., is the scene of Thoroughbred racing September to mid-October and December through March; phone (859) 371-0200 or (800) 733-0200 for dates. The **Kentucky Speedway,** in nearby Sparta, Ky., hosts **automobile racing** June through September; phone (859) 578-2300 or (888) 652-7223 for ticket information.

Note: Policies vary concerning admittance of children to pari-mutuel betting facilities. Phone for information.

Performing Arts

The city's premier arts and entertainment destination is the **Aronoff Center for the Arts,** 650 Walnut St. between 6th and 7th streets; phone (513) 721-3344 or (513) 621-2787 for tickets. The center's three theaters present more than 10,000 exhibits and performances throughout the year, including Broadway shows and children's theater. In addition, the center is the main performance hall for the **Cincinnati Ballet;** phone (513) 621-5219 for information or (513) 621-5282 for tickets.

Other professional theaters include **Playhouse in the Park,** (513) 421-3888, with its two theaters, the **Robert S. Marx** and the **Thompson Shelterhouse,** on Mount Adams Circle in Eden Park. These stages present modern American and European plays September through June.

The **Ensemble Theatre of Cincinnati,** (513) 421-3555, downtown at 1127 Vine St., presents live theatrical shows from September through May. Performances of new plays and well-known modern works are given Tuesday through Saturday evenings and Sunday afternoons.

The **Cincinnati Shakespeare Company,** at 719 Race St., performs eight to nine classic plays as well as some free traveling performances throughout the summer months; phone (513) 381-2273 for additional information.

Music Hall, 1241 Elm St., was built by philanthropic leaders in 1878 and is fondly referred to as the Grand Dame of the Queen City. The interior of the red brick building is adorned with crystal chandeliers. The hall is a fitting home to the **Cincinnati Pops Orchestra** and the **Cincinnati Symphony Orchestra;** phone (513) 381-3300. The **Cincinnati Opera,** America's second oldest opera company, also performs in Music Hall; its mid-June to late July season includes grand operas, operettas and musicals. Phone (513) 241-2742 for more information.

The **University of Cincinnati's College-Conservatory of Music** at Jefferson Avenue and Corry Boulevard makes impressive contributions to the area's music scene. A prominent music school, the 1,400-student college offers a variety of performing arts entertainment, ranging from opera and musical theater to dance and drama. If you're looking for things for couples to do, the conservatory

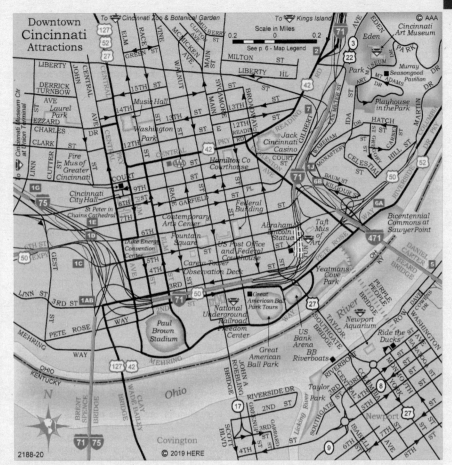

Downtown Cincinnati Attractions

2188-20 © 2019 HERE

offers more than 1,000 performances a year and many of them are free; phone (513) 556-4183 for schedule and ticket information.

Concerts by popular entertainers and groups are often held at the **Riverbend Music Center,** (513) 232-6220, the summer home of the Cincinnati Symphony and the Cincinnati Pops Orchestra. The **Cincinnati Gardens,** (513) 631-7793, and the **U.S. Bank Arena,** (513) 421-4111, also host many entertainment and sporting events.

ATTRACTIONS

For a complete list of attractions, visit AAA.com/travelguides/attractions

AMERICAN SIGN MUSEUM is at 1330 Monmouth Ave. in the Camp Washington neighborhood. This impressive collection of 19th- and 20th-century American signs features an array of themes and is very well organized. Visitors will journey through the history of signage and learn all about the types of signs that have

graced walls and buildings over the years, including gold leaf on glass signs, non-illuminated painted signs, plastic signs and neon signs.

The collection also includes equipment, materials and tools as well as architectural models, archival material, artwork, photographs and sales samples. **Hours:** Wed.-Sat. 10-4, Sun. noon-4. Guided 1-hour tours offered Wed.-Sat. at 11 and 2, Sun. at 2. **Cost:** $15; $10 (ages 65+ and active duty military and students with ID); free (ages 0-12 with adult). **Phone:** (513) 541-6366. GT

CINCINNATI ART MUSEUM is off I-71 exit 2 at 953 Eden Park Dr., following signs to Eden Park. The museum's more than 67,000 objects showcase visual arts from major civilizations over the past 6,000 years through sculpture, paintings, prints, photographs, textiles and decorative arts. Masterpieces from such artists as Claude Monet, Pablo Picasso and Vincent van Gogh are on display as well as artifacts from Ancient Egypt, Rome and Greece. Asian, African and Native American works of art also are included.

The Cincinnati Wing features more than 500 works of art by, for and about Cincinnatians from 1788 to the present. **Hours:** Tues.-Sun. 11-5 (also Thurs. 5-8 p.m.). Closed Thanksgiving and Christmas. **Cost:** Free. **Phone:** (513) 721-2787 or (877) 472-4226.

CINCINNATI MUSEUM CENTER AT UNION TERMINAL is off I-75 at Ezzard Charles Dr. to 1301 Western Ave. The center hosts traveling exhibitions and is home to Cincinnati History Museum; Duke Energy Children's Museum; Museum of Natural History & Science; Cincinnati Historical Society Library; and Robert D. Lindner Family OMNIMAX Theater. The restored Art Deco-style train station was a major departure point for troops during World War II. The building features several large mosaic tile murals created in the 1930s.

Time: Allow 2 hours minimum. **Hours:** Mon.-Sat. 10-5, Sun. 11-6 (closes at 3 on Christmas Eve). **Cost:** (includes Cincinnati History Museum, Museum of Natural History and Science, and Duke Energy Children's Museum) $14.50; $13.50 (ages 60+); $10.50 (ages 3-12); $5.50 (ages 1-2). Phone for special exhibition pricing. **Parking:** $6 (per vehicle); $4 (after 4:30). **Phone:** (513) 287-7000, (800) 733-2077 or TTY (800) 750-0750. GT

Cincinnati History Museum is on the grounds of Cincinnati Museum Center at Union Terminal at 1301 Western Ave. Exhibits relate the history of Cincinnati and include a re-creation of the 1850s Public Landing, with a 94-foot side-wheel steamboat that can be boarded; vintage automobiles; a 1920s streetcar; and an S-scale model of the city 1900-40, complete with working trains and trolleys. A research library contains local historical items. **Hours:** Daily 10-5 (closes at 3 p.m. on Christmas Eve). **Cost:** (includes Cincinnati Museum Center, Museum of Natural History and Science, and Duke Energy Children's Museum) $14.50; $13.50 (ages 60+); $10.50 (ages 3-12); $5.50 (ages 1-2). **Phone:** (513) 287-7000, (800) 733-2077 or TTY (800) 750-0750.

Duke Energy Children's Museum is on the grounds of Cincinnati Museum Center at Union Terminal at 1301 Western Ave. The museum's 10 hands-on exhibit areas are designed for infants to 10-year-olds. Kids can explore a two-story tree house in The Woods, explore the power of simple machines in the Energy Zone, discover how a community works in Kids' Town, and practice proper oral health while climbing into a giant mouth in Inside the Grin. Also included is an indoor play area for infants and toddlers.

Hours: Mon.-Sat. 10-5, Sun. 11-6 (closes at 3 on Christmas Eve). **Cost:** (includes Cincinnati Museum Center, Cincinnati History Museum and Museum of Natural History and Science) $14.50; $13.50 (ages 60+); $10.50 (ages 3-12); $5.50 (ages 1-2). **Parking:** $6 (per vehicle); $4 (after 4:30). **Phone:** (513) 287-7000, (800) 733-2077 or TTY (800) 750-0750.

Museum of Natural History & Science is on the grounds of Cincinnati Museum Center at Union Terminal at 1301 Western Ave. Permanent and changing exhibits include a replica of a limestone cavern with underground waterfalls and 500 feet of trails, dinosaur fossils, a hands-on discovery center for children and an Ice Age trail that re-creates a prehistoric environment. **Hours:** Daily 10-5 (closes at 3 p.m. Christmas Eve). **Cost:** (includes Cincinnati Museum Center, Cincinnati History Museum and Duke Energy Children's Museum) $14.50; $13.50 (ages 60+); $10.50 (ages 3-12); $5.50 (ages 1-2). **Phone:** (513) 287-7000, (800) 733-2077 or TTY (800) 750-0750.

Robert D. Lindner Family OMNIMAX Theater, on the grounds of Cincinnati Museum Center at Union Terminal at 1301 Western Ave., features a 5-story dome screen and a digital state-of-the art sound system. **Hours:** Fri.-Sat. 10-9, Sun.-Thurs. 10-5 (closes at 3 p.m. on Christmas Eve). Phone ahead to confirm schedule. **Cost:** $9; $8 (ages 60+); $7 (ages 3-12). **Phone:** (513) 287-7000, (800) 733-2077 or TTY (800) 750-0750.

CINCINNATI ZOO AND BOTANICAL GARDEN is reached via I-75 exit 6, following signs to 3400 Vine St. In a garden setting, the zoo houses some of the world's rarest animals, including cheetahs, elephants and manatees. Nearly two dozen areas include Manatee Springs, where the residents include manatees, alligators and crocodiles; the Jungle Trail's orangutans; Elephant Reserve; Giraffe Ridge and Lords of the Arctic, featuring an underwater view of two polar bears. In Night Hunters, observe the behaviors of clouded leopards, vampire bats and a Burmese python. Come face-to-face with the zoo's big cats at Cat Canyon, home to tigers, snow leopards and cougars. At Spaulding Children's Zoo kids can have close encounters with gentle creatures. Africa Habitat offers open-air views of a sprawling savanna, African painted dogs, African lions, giraffes and meerkats. Africa's newest addition is Hippo Cove, where visitors are treated to underwater views of the famous baby hippo Fiona and her mother, Bibi. Train rides, a carousel and a 4-D theater are available year-round, and in summer, animal encounters where birds fly and cheetahs run at top speeds are offered.

More than 3,000 varieties of plants grace the 75-acre grounds. Themed gardens include a butterfly garden, an African violet garden, a rain garden and an endangered plant species garden. Seasons determine the types of items you'll see; for instance, the more than 100,000 spring tulips are a highlight and in winter fruits and berries set the holiday tone. A botanical center offers interactive children's displays.

Brochures for themed self-guiding tours can be picked up at the Harold C. Schott Education Center. **Time:** Allow 3 hours minimum. **Hours:** Daily 10-6, Memorial Day-Labor Day; 10-5, rest of year. Phone ahead to confirm schedule. **Cost:** Zoo $19; $13

(ages 2-12 and 62+). Theater $5. Train ride $4. Carousel $3. Combination tickets are available. Phone to confirm prices. **Parking:** $10. **Phone:** (513) 281-4700 or (800) 944-4776.

CONEY ISLAND is off I-275 exit 72 at 6201 Kellogg Ave. The park offers a huge range of recreational activities. Visitors can swim in Sunlite Adventure, which features Sunlite Pool, Typhoon Tower and four waterslides. There are 26 classic rides as well as live shows and miniature golf.

Time: Allow 2 hours minimum. **Hours:** Sunlite Adventure open daily 10-8 and rides open daily 11-8 (also Fri.-Sun. 8-9 p.m.), Memorial Day-Labor Day. **Cost:** Sunlite Adventure and rides $25.95; $20.95 (ages 62+); $13.95 (ages 2-7). Admission after 4 p.m. $16.95. Sunlite Adventure only $17.50; $14 (ages 62+); $9.50 (ages 2-7). Sunlite Adventure admission after 4 p.m. $11.50. All-day ride bracelet $15.50; $7.95 (ages 2-7). All-day ride bracelet after 4 p.m. $10.50. Phone to verify rates. **Parking:** $8. **Phone:** (513) 232-8230. 🖮

GREAT AMERICAN BALL PARK TOURS departs from 100 Joe Nuxhall Way at jct. Second St. Tour access includes the press box, dugout, Crosley Terrace and various seating areas. Afterward visitors can take a self-guiding tour of the Cincinnati Reds Hall of Fame.

Access areas may vary based on stadium availability. **Time:** Allow 1 hour, 45 minutes minimum. **Hours:** In-season tours depart game days Mon.-Fri. at 11, noon and 1, Sat. at 10:30, 11, 11:30, noon, 12:30 and 1; non-game days Sun.-Fri. at 11:30 and

1:30, Sat. at 11:30, 12:30, 1:30 and 2:30. Tours are not given when an early afternoon game is scheduled. Phone for off-season (Oct.-Mar.) schedule. Phone ahead to confirm schedule. **Cost:** $20; $17 (students, senior citizens and active military); free (ages 0-4). Reservations are recommended. **Parking:** $5-$10. **Phone:** (513) 765-7923. [GT]

HERITAGE VILLAGE MUSEUM—see Sharonville p. 292.

KINGS ISLAND—see Mason p. 270.

KROHN CONSERVATORY is off I-71 Reading Rd. exit, then 1 mi. e. to 1501 Eden Park Dr., following signs. The Art Deco-styled greenhouse features six collections, including seasonal floral displays among citrus trees in the Floral House. Bromeliads and ferns as well as papaya, vanilla and guava plants tempt the senses in the Tropical House, and each week a different species of orchid blooms in the Orchid House. Palms thrive in the Palm House's tropical rain forest setting, complete with a waterfall, while the Desert House displays yuccas, agaves, cacti, and aloes.

A bonsai collection also is included. **Time:** Allow 1 hour minimum. **Hours:** Tues.-Sun.10-5, with extended hours during special shows and exhibits. **Cost:** $7; $4 (ages 5-12). Additional fees may be charged for special exhibitions. **Phone:** (513) 421-4086.

NATIONAL UNDERGROUND RAILROAD FREEDOM CENTER is at 50 E. Freedom Way. Located on the banks of the Ohio River, which once marked the border between slave and free states, this 158,000-square-foot facility houses a collection that tells about slavery in America, highlighting the role of the Underground Railroad. The perseverance, courage and multicultural cooperation that led to the freedom of so many is celebrated with interactive exhibits and multimedia. The center also addresses modern abolition, connecting the past to the present.

Visitors see an actual 1830 two-story log slave pen, with wrought-iron shackles intact, which was moved from Kentucky. Professional displays and interactive, thought-provoking exhibits trace 300 years of slavery in North America. A series of five powerful short films is shown. One gallery is geared toward children. **Time:** Allow 1 hour minimum. **Hours:** Tues.-Sat. 10-5, Sun.-Mon. noon-5. **Cost:** $15; $13 (ages 60+); $10.50 (ages 3-12). Prices may vary; phone ahead. **Parking:** $3 per hour ($9 daily maximum). **Phone:** (513) 333-7500 or (877) 648-4838.

SPRING GROVE CEMETERY & ARBORETUM is off I-75 exit 6, .3 mi. w. on Mitchell Ave., then .3 mi. s. to 4521 Spring Grove Ave. A National Historic Landmark, this 733-acre cemetery was founded in the 1840s and is the burial site of numerous notable persons, including governors, business leaders, Revolutionary War soldiers and Civil War generals. The grounds contain 15 lakes, a waterfall, 1,000 labeled trees and shrubs, and a 10-acre woodland. Historical

Taft Museum of Art

information brochures and maps for a 33-stop self-guiding tour that highlights the history, art and architecture of the facility are available from the office. Special event tours are held throughout the year.

Time: Allow 1 hour minimum. **Hours:** Grounds daily 8-6 (also Mon. and Thurs. 6-8 p.m., May-Aug.). Guided tours are available by appointment. Phone for special event tour schedule. Phone ahead to confirm schedule. **Cost:** Free. Grounds tour $5; $4 (ages 55+); free (ages 0-12). **Phone:** (513) 681-7526. [GT]

TAFT MUSEUM OF ART is at 316 Pike St. The 1820 Palladian-style mansion, once the home of art patrons Charles and Anna Taft, features landscape murals by Robert S. Duncanson, a noted 19th-century African-American artist. Twelve rooms display impressive visual arts. A permanent collection boasts old masters paintings, more than 200 Chinese porcelains from the Ming and Qing dynasties, medieval and Renaissance European art, Italian Renaissance ceramics and intricate watches crafted by 17th- through 19th-century watchmakers.

The Dutch Masters collection includes works by Rembrandt, Pieter de Hooch and Jan Steen. Landscapes by Thomas Gainsborough and portraits by Joshua Reynolds and John Singer Sargent are highlights. Changing exhibitions and special events are presented. A formal garden graces the grounds.

Time: Allow 2 hours minimum. **Hours:** Wed.-Fri. 11-4, Sat.-Sun. 11-5. Food is available Wed.-Fri. 11-4, Sat.-Sun. 11-5. **Cost:** $12; $10 (senior citizens); free (ages 0-17 and on Sun.). Prices may vary; phone ahead. **Phone:** (513) 241-0343. [GT] [†]

WILLIAM HOWARD TAFT NATIONAL HISTORIC SITE is at 2038 Auburn Ave. The Greek Revival brick house is the birthplace and boyhood home of the 27th president and 10th chief justice of the United States. Four rooms are furnished to reflect the Taft's family life 1851-77. Other rooms have exhibits depicting the Taft family and the president's devotion to his public career. Tours begin in the Taft Education center next door.

Hours: Grounds open daily 8:30-4:45. Guided tours depart every 30 minutes. Last tour begins 30 minutes before closing. **Cost:** Free. **Phone:** (513) 684-3262. [GT]

Sightseeing
Carriage Tours

A guided tour is a good way to become familiar with the city. For those who would like to take a trip through the downtown area in 18th- and 19th-century style, horse-drawn carriage tours leave from Fountain Square (Fifth and Vine streets).

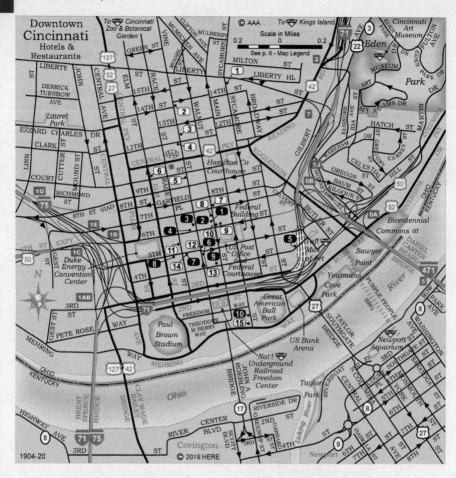

Downtown Cincinnati
Hotels & Restaurants

1904-20 © 2019 HERE

Downtown Cincinnati

This index helps you "spot" where hotels and restaurants are located on the corresponding detailed maps. Restaurant price range is a combination of lunch and/or dinner. Turn to the listing page for more information and consult display ads for special promotions.

 For more details, rates and reservations: AAA.com/travelguides/hotels

DOWNTOWN CINCINNATI

Map Page	Hotels	Designation	Member Savings	Page
1 this page	**21c Museum Hotel Cincinnati**	⬥ FOUR DIAMOND	✔	171
2 this page	Hampton Inn & Suites by Hilton Cincinnati Downtown	⬥ THREE DIAMOND	✔	171
3 this page	Homewood Suites by Hilton Cincinnati Downtown	⬥ THREE DIAMOND	✔	171
4 this page	The Cincinnatian Hotel, Curio Collection by Hilton	⬥ FOUR DIAMOND	✔	171
5 this page	Residence Inn by Marriott Cincinnati Downtown/ The Phelps	⬥ THREE DIAMOND	✔	172
6 this page	**The Westin Cincinnati**	⬥ THREE DIAMOND	✔	172
7 this page	**Hilton Cincinnati Netherland Plaza**	⬥ FOUR DIAMOND	✔	171
8 this page	**Hyatt Regency Cincinnati**	⬥ THREE DIAMOND	✔	172
9 this page	Renaissance Cincinnati Downtown	⬥ FOUR DIAMOND	✔	172
10 this page	AC Hotel by Marriott Cincinnati at the Banks	⬥ THREE DIAMOND	✔	171

Map Page	Restaurants	Designation	Cuisine	Price Range	Page
① p. 164	Nicola's	▨ FOUR DIAMOND	Italian	$26-$38	172
② p. 164	The Eagle OTR	▨ APPROVED	Southern American	$7-$19	172
③ p. 164	Senate	▨ APPROVED	American	$11-$27	172
④ p. 164	Taste of Belgium: Bistro on Vine	▨ APPROVED	Belgian	$6-$24	172
⑤ p. 164	Scotti's Italian Restaurant	▨ APPROVED	Italian	$8-$33	172
⑥ p. 164	Washington Platform Saloon & Restaurant	▨ APPROVED	American	$17-$32	172
⑦ p. 164	Jeff Ruby's Steakhouse	▨ THREE DIAMOND	Steak	$20-$115	172
⑧ p. 164	Nicholson's Tavern & Pub	▨ APPROVED	Scottish	$11-$29	172
⑨ p. 164	Boca Restaurant	▨ FOUR DIAMOND	New American	$16-$76	172
⑩ p. 164	Nada	▨ THREE DIAMOND	Mexican	$12-$24	172
⑪ p. 164	Maplewood Kitchen and Bar	▨ APPROVED	American	$11-$24	172
⑫ p. 164	Via Vite	▨ THREE DIAMOND	Italian	$17-$33	172
⑬ p. 164	McCormick & Schmick's	▨ THREE DIAMOND	Seafood	$11-$50	172
⑭ p. 164	Orchids at Palm Court	▨ FIVE DIAMOND	American	$40-$94	172
⑮ p. 164	Moerlein Lager House	▨ APPROVED	American	$12-$29	172

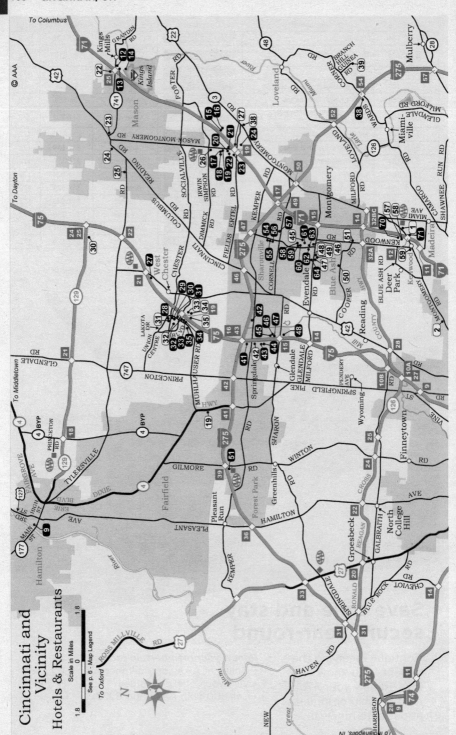

Cincinnati and
Vicinity
Hotels & Restaurants

See p. 6 - Map Legend

Scale in Miles

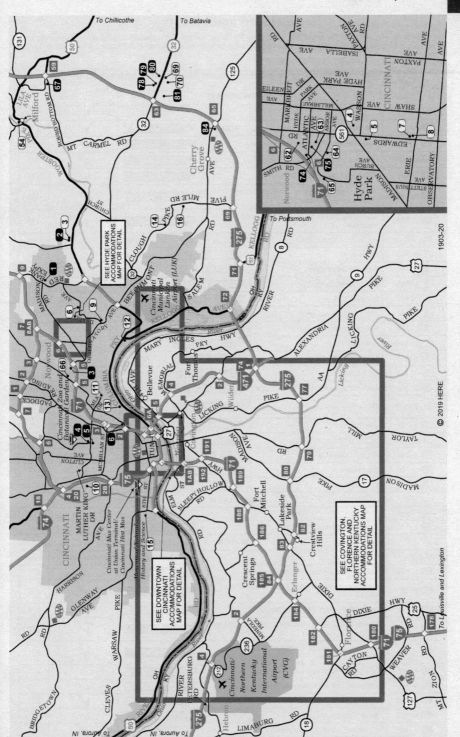

Cincinnati and Vicinity

This index helps you "spot" where hotels and restaurants are located on the corresponding detailed maps. Restaurant price range is a combination of lunch and/or dinner. Turn to the listing page for more information and consult display ads for special promotions.

 For more details, rates and reservations: AAA.com/travelguides/hotels

CINCINNATI

Map Page	Hotels	Designation	Member Savings	Page
1 p. 166	**The Summit, A Dolce Hotel** *(See ad p. 173.)*	THREE DIAMOND	✔	173
2 p. 166	**Best Western Premier Mariemont Inn**	THREE DIAMOND	✔	172
3 p. 166	Hilton Garden Inn Cincinnati Midtown	THREE DIAMOND	✔	173
4 p. 166	**Graduate Cincinnati**	THREE DIAMOND	✔	173
5 p. 166	Hampton Inn & Suites by Hilton Cincinnati/ Uptown-University Area	THREE DIAMOND	✔	173
6 p. 166	**SpringHill Suites by Marriott Cincinnati Midtown**	THREE DIAMOND	✔	173

Map Page	Restaurants	Designation	Cuisine	Price Range	Page
1 p. 166	Embers	THREE DIAMOND	Steak Seafood	$28-$58	174
2 p. 166	Revolution Rotisserie	APPROVED	Chicken	$9-$18	174
3 p. 166	The Quarter Bistro	THREE DIAMOND	American	$13-$34	174
4 p. 166	Bonefish Grill	THREE DIAMOND	Seafood	$10-$26	174
5 p. 166	Wild Ginger Asian Bistro	APPROVED	Asian	$9-$24	174
6 p. 166	Bangkok Bistro	APPROVED	Thai	$13-$20	174
7 p. 166	Arthur's Cafe	APPROVED	American	$8-$14	174
8 p. 166	Tellers of Hyde Park	THREE DIAMOND	American	$11-$35	174
9 p. 166	Zip's Cafe	APPROVED	American	$6-$13	174
10 p. 166	Camp Washington Chili Inc	APPROVED	American	$4-$7	174
11 p. 166	O Pie O	APPROVED	Desserts Sandwiches	$6-$14	174
12 p. 166	The Precinct	THREE DIAMOND	Steak Seafood	$22-$115	174
13 p. 166	Le Bar a Boeuf	THREE DIAMOND	French	$11-$26	174
14 p. 166	Clough Crossings	APPROVED	American	$10-$26	174
15 p. 166	Primavista	THREE DIAMOND	Northern Italian	$17-$37	174
16 p. 166	El Coyote	APPROVED	Tex-Mex	$13-$42	174

HAMILTON

Map Page	Hotel	Designation	Member Savings	Page
9 p. 166	**Courtyard by Marriott Hamilton**	THREE DIAMOND	✔	257

MASON

Map Page	Hotels	Designation	Member Savings	Page
12 p. 166	Comfort Suites-Mason-Kings Island	THREE DIAMOND		271
13 p. 166	Residence Inn by Marriott Cincinnati Northeast/ Mason	THREE DIAMOND	✔	272
14 p. 166	Great Wolf Lodge Cincinnati/Mason	THREE DIAMOND		271
15 p. 166	SpringHill Suites by Marriott Cincinnati Northeast/ Mason	THREE DIAMOND	✔	272
16 p. 166	**Hawthorn Suites by Wyndham Cincinnati Northeast/Mason**	APPROVED	✔	271
17 p. 166	Holiday Inn Express Hotel & Suites	THREE DIAMOND		271
18 p. 166	Hilton Garden Inn Cincinnati/Mason	THREE DIAMOND	✔	271
19 p. 166	**Hyatt Place Cincinnati-Northeast**	THREE DIAMOND	✔	271
20 p. 166	**Best Western Mason Inn**	APPROVED	✔	271
21 p. 166	**Cincinnati Marriott Northeast**	THREE DIAMOND	✔	271

MASON (cont'd)

Map Page	Hotels (cont'd)	Designation	Member Savings	Page
22 p. 166	Hampton Inn & Suites Mason-Cincinnati	THREE DIAMOND	✔	271
23 p. 166	Drury Inn & Suites Cincinnati Northeast Mason	THREE DIAMOND		271
24 p. 166	**Comfort Inn Cincinnati Northeast**	APPROVED	✔	271

Map Page	Restaurants	Designation	Cuisine	Price Range	Page
22 p. 166	Woodhouse Kitchen & Bar	THREE DIAMOND	American	$15-$38	272
23 p. 166	The Wildflower Cafe & Coffee House	THREE DIAMOND	American	$12-$38	272
24 p. 166	Pitrelli's Restaurant	APPROVED	Italian	$11-$30	272
25 p. 166	S.W. Clyborne Co.	THREE DIAMOND	American	$13-$34	272
26 p. 166	Rusty Bucket Restaurant and Tavern	APPROVED	American	$6-$21	272
27 p. 166	Grand Oriental Chinese Restaurant	APPROVED	Chinese	$7-$42	272

WEST CHESTER

Map Page	Hotels	Designation	Member Savings	Page
27 p. 166	Quality Inn	APPROVED		308
28 p. 166	Staybridge Suites Cincinnati North	THREE DIAMOND		308
29 p. 166	Courtyard by Marriott-Cincinnati North at Union Centre	THREE DIAMOND	✔	307
30 p. 166	Residence Inn by Marriott Cincinnati North/West Chester	THREE DIAMOND	✔	308
31 p. 166	Cincinnati Marriott North at Union Centre	THREE DIAMOND	✔	307
32 p. 166	**Homewood Suites by Hilton Cincinnati-West Chester**	THREE DIAMOND	✔	308
33 p. 166	Hampton Inn & Suites by Hilton Cincinnati North at Union Centre	THREE DIAMOND	✔	307
34 p. 166	Hilton Garden Inn West Chester	THREE DIAMOND	✔	308
35 p. 166	Holiday Inn Cincinnati North-West Chester	THREE DIAMOND		308

Map Page	Restaurants	Designation	Cuisine	Price Range	Page
30 p. 166	Rusty Bucket Restaurant and Tavern	APPROVED	American	$11-$21	308
31 p. 166	Jag's Steak & Seafood	THREE DIAMOND	Steak Seafood	$29-$75	308
32 p. 166	Dingle House Pub & Grub	APPROVED	American	$9-$22	308
33 p. 166	P.F. Chang's China Bistro	THREE DIAMOND	Chinese	$11-$29	308
34 p. 166	Mitchell's Fish Market	THREE DIAMOND	Seafood	$18-$37 SAVE	308
35 p. 166	Matt the Miller's Tavern	APPROVED	American	$11-$37	308

LOVELAND

Map Page	Hotel	Designation	Member Savings	Page
38 p. 166	**Hilton Garden Inn Cincinnati Northeast**	THREE DIAMOND	✔	267

Map Page	Restaurants	Designation	Cuisine	Price Range	Page
38 p. 166	Tony's Steaks & Seafood	THREE DIAMOND	Steak Seafood	$24-$69	267
39 p. 166	Pizza Tower	APPROVED	Pizza	$7-$18	267

SHARONVILLE

Map Page	Hotels	Designation	Member Savings	Page
41 p. 166	**Sonesta ES Suites Cincinnati Sharonville West**	APPROVED	✔	292
42 p. 166	**Sonesta ES Suites Cincinnati Sharonville East**	THREE DIAMOND	✔	292
43 p. 166	LivInn Hotels	APPROVED		292
44 p. 166	**Hyatt Place Cincinnati/Sharonville Convention Center**	THREE DIAMOND	✔	292
45 p. 166	Hawthorn Suites by Wyndham	APPROVED		292
46 p. 166	Holiday Inn Express Hotel & Suites	APPROVED		292
47 p. 166	**Hilton Garden Inn Cincinnati/Sharonville**	THREE DIAMOND	✔	292

SHARONVILLE (cont'd)

Map Page	Hotels (cont'd)	Designation	Member Savings	Page
48 p. 166	Drury Inn & Suites-Cincinnati Sharonville	⟨♢⟩ THREE DIAMOND		292

Map Page	Restaurant	Designation	Cuisine	Price Range	Page
42 p. 166	Vincenzo's Ristorante Italiano	⟨♢⟩ THREE DIAMOND	Italian	$9-$26	293

FOREST PARK

Map Page	Hotel	Designation	Member Savings	Page
51 p. 166	SpringHill Suites by Marriott Cincinnati North/Forest Park	⟨♢⟩ THREE DIAMOND	✔	254

BLUE ASH

Map Page	Hotels	Designation	Member Savings	Page
54 p. 166	**Hyatt Place Cincinnati/Blue Ash**	⟨♢⟩ THREE DIAMOND	✔	143
55 p. 166	**Sonesta ES Suites Cincinnati Blue Ash**	⟨♢⟩ THREE DIAMOND	✔	143
56 p. 166	The Blu Hotel, an Ascend Hotel Collection Member	⟨♢⟩ THREE DIAMOND		143
57 p. 166	Hilton Garden Inn Cincinnati/Blue Ash	⟨♢⟩ THREE DIAMOND	✔	143
58 p. 166	SpringHill Suites by Marriott	⟨♢⟩ THREE DIAMOND	✔	143
59 p. 166	Comfort Inn	⟨♢⟩ APPROVED		143
60 p. 166	Holiday Inn Express Hotel & Suites	⟨♢⟩ APPROVED		143
61 p. 166	Hawthorn Suites by Wyndham	⟨♢⟩ APPROVED		143
62 p. 166	**Embassy Suites by Hilton Hotel-Cincinnati Northeast**	⟨♢⟩ THREE DIAMOND	✔	143
63 p. 166	**Courtyard by Marriott Cincinnati Blue Ash**	⟨♢⟩ THREE DIAMOND	✔	143
64 p. 166	Wingate by Wyndham Cincinnati Blue Ash	⟨♢⟩ THREE DIAMOND		143

Map Page	Restaurants	Designation	Cuisine	Price Range	Page
45 p. 166	Sammy's Craft Burgers & Beers	⟨♢⟩ APPROVED	Burgers	$8-$14	144
46 p. 166	Firehouse Grill	⟨♢⟩ APPROVED	American	$10-$27	144
47 p. 166	Brown Dog Cafe	⟨♢⟩ THREE DIAMOND	American	$9-$32	144
48 p. 166	Senate	⟨♢⟩ APPROVED	American	$10-$24	144
49 p. 166	Tahona Kitchen & Bar	⟨♢⟩ APPROVED	Mexican	$6-$14	144
50 p. 166	Parker's Blue Ash Tavern	⟨♢⟩ THREE DIAMOND	Steak	$12-$39	144
51 p. 166	Slatt's Pub	⟨♢⟩ APPROVED	American	$9-$24	144

MILFORD

Map Page	Hotel	Designation	Member Savings	Page
67 p. 166	**Homewood Suites by Hilton**	⟨♢⟩ THREE DIAMOND	✔	277

Map Page	Restaurant	Designation	Cuisine	Price Range	Page
54 p. 166	20 Brix	⟨♢⟩ THREE DIAMOND	American	$11-$29	277

KENWOOD

Map Page	Hotels	Designation	Member Savings	Page
70 p. 166	**Best Western Plus Hannaford Inn & Suites**	⟨♢⟩ THREE DIAMOND	✔	262
71 p. 166	Hampton Inn & Suites Cincinnati-Kenwood	⟨♢⟩ THREE DIAMOND	✔	262

Map Page	Restaurants	Designation	Cuisine	Price Range	Page
57 p. 166	Matt the Miller's Tavern	⟨♢⟩ APPROVED	American	$12-$35	262
58 p. 166	Olio Italian	⟨♢⟩ THREE DIAMOND	Italian	$6-$39	262
59 p. 166	Trio	⟨♢⟩ THREE DIAMOND	American	$9-$40	262

NORWOOD

Map Page	Hotels	Designation	Member Savings	Page
74 p. 166	Courtyard by Marriott Cincinnati Midtown/Rookwood	⟨♢⟩ THREE DIAMOND	✔	281
75 p. 166	Residence Inn Cincinnati Midtown/Rookwood	⟨♢⟩ THREE DIAMOND	✔	281

Map Page	Restaurants	Designation	Cuisine	Price Range	Page
62 p. 166	Taste of Belgium Rookwood	APPROVED	Belgian	$13-$24	282
63 p. 166	Seasons 52 Fresh Grill	THREE DIAMOND	American	$10-$33	281
64 p. 166	The Pub at Rookwood Mews	APPROVED	British	$10-$19	281
65 p. 166	P.F. Chang's China Bistro	THREE DIAMOND	Chinese	$8-$25	281
66 p. 166	Betta's Italian Oven	APPROVED	Italian Pizza	$8-$15	281

BATAVIA

Map Page	Hotels	Designation	Member Savings	Page
78 p. 166	**Holiday Inn & Suites Cincinnati Eastgate**	THREE DIAMOND	✔	140
79 p. 166	Fairfield by Marriott Cincinnati Eastgate	THREE DIAMOND	✔	140
80 p. 166	Hampton Inn by Hilton-Cincinnati Eastgate	THREE DIAMOND	✔	140
81 p. 166	Comfort Inn & Suites Eastgate	APPROVED		140

Map Page	Restaurants	Designation	Cuisine	Price Range	Page
69 p. 166	Ban Thai Restaurant	APPROVED	Thai	$7-$17	140
70 p. 166	Highway 55 Burgers	APPROVED	Burgers	$7-$10	140

CHERRY GROVE

Map Page	Hotel	Designation	Member Savings	Page
84 p. 166	**Best Western Clermont**	APPROVED	✔	150

FAIRFIELD

Map Page	Restaurant	Designation	Cuisine	Price Range	Page
19 p. 166	Sabor Peruano	APPROVED	Peruvian	$8-$18	252

DOWNTOWN CINCINNATI

- Restaurants p. 172
- Hotels & Restaurants map & index p. 164

21C MUSEUM HOTEL CINCINNATI   513/578-6600 **1**

FOUR DIAMOND

Boutique Contemporary Hotel

Address: 609 Walnut St 45202 **Location:** Between 6th and 7th sts. **Facility:** Public areas have permanent and rotating exhibits of contemporary art, much of which is self-consciously avant-garde. Rooms have a clean, minimalist luxury décor. Bathrooms have Rookwood tile showers. 156 units. 10 stories, interior corridors. **Parking:** valet only. **Terms:** check-in 4 pm. **Amenities:** safes. **Activities:** recreation programs, bicycles, exercise room, spa. **Guest Services:** valet laundry.

AC HOTEL BY MARRIOTT CINCINNATI AT THE BANKS
513/744-9900 **10**

THREE DIAMOND SAVE Boutique Contemporary Hotel. **Address:** 135 Joe Nuxhall Way 45202

AAA Benefit: Members save 5% or more!

THE CINCINNATIAN HOTEL, CURIO COLLECTION BY HILTON
513/381-3000 **4**

FOUR DIAMOND SAVE Historic Boutique Hotel. **Address:** 601 Vine St 45202

AAA Benefit: Members save up to 15%!

HAMPTON INN & SUITES BY HILTON CINCINNATI DOWNTOWN
513/354-2430 **2**

THREE DIAMOND SAVE Historic Hotel. **Address:** 617 Vine St 45202

AAA Benefit: Members save up to 15%!

HILTON CINCINNATI NETHERLAND PLAZA
513/421-9100 **7**

FOUR DIAMOND

Historic Hotel

 Hilton HOTELS & RESORTS

AAA Benefit: Members save up to 15%!

Address: 35 W 5th St 45202 **Location:** Jct Race St; entrance on Race St. **Facility:** This 1931 classic has been renovated to showcase new guestrooms. The hotel's rare Brazilian rosewood, German silver-nickel fixtures and soaring interior ceiling murals are remarkable French Art-Deco treasures. 561 units. 31 stories, interior corridors. **Parking:** on-site (fee) and valet. **Terms:** check-in 4 pm. **Amenities:** safes. **Dining:** Orchids at Palm Court, see separate listing. **Pool:** heated indoor. **Activities:** hot tub, health club, spa. **Guest Services:** valet laundry, area transportation.

HOMEWOOD SUITES BY HILTON CINCINNATI DOWNTOWN
513/354-2440 **3**

THREE DIAMOND SAVE Historic Extended Stay Hotel. **Address:** 617 Vine St 45202

AAA Benefit: Members save up to 15%!

(See map & index p. 164.)

HYATT REGENCY CINCINNATI   513/579-1234   **8**

THREE DIAMOND

Hotel

AAA Benefit: Members save up to 10%!

Address: 151 W 5th St 45202 **Location:** At Hyatt-Saks Fifth Avenue Center. **Facility:** 491 units. 22 stories, interior corridors. **Parking:** valet only. **Terms:** check-in 4 pm. **Amenities:** safes. **Dining:** 2 restaurants. **Pool:** heated indoor. **Activities:** exercise room, in-room exercise equipment. **Guest Services:** valet laundry, boarding pass kiosk.

RENAISSANCE CINCINNATI DOWNTOWN
   513/333-0000   **9**

FOUR DIAMOND SAVE Historic Hotel. **Address:** 36 E 4th St 45202

AAA Benefit: Members save 5% or more!

RESIDENCE INN BY MARRIOTT CINCINNATI DOWNTOWN/ THE PHELPS   513/651-1234   **5**

THREE DIAMOND SAVE Extended Stay Hotel. **Address:** 506 E Fourth St 45202

AAA Benefit: Members save 5% or more!

THE WESTIN CINCINNATI   513/621-7700   **6**

THREE DIAMOND

Hotel

WESTIN
HOTELS & RESORTS

AAA Benefit: Members save 5% or more!

Address: 21 E 5th St 45202 **Location:** Between Vine and Walnut sts. **Facility:** 456 units. 17 stories, interior corridors. **Parking:** valet only. **Terms:** check-in 4 pm. **Amenities:** safes. **Dining:** McCormick & Schmick's, see separate listing. **Pool:** heated indoor. **Activities:** hot tub, exercise room, in-room exercise equipment, massage. **Guest Services:** valet laundry, boarding pass kiosk.

WHERE TO EAT

BOCA RESTAURANT   513/542-2022   **9**
New American. Fine Dining. **Address:** 114 E 6th St 45202

THE EAGLE OTR   513/802-5007   **2**
APPROVED Southern American. Casual Dining. **Address:** 1342 Vine St 45202

IZZY'S DELICATESSENS
APPROVED Deli. Quick Serve.
LOCATIONS:
Address: 800 Elm St 45202 **Phone:** 513/721-4241
Address: 610 Main St 45202 **Phone:** 513/241-6246

JEFF RUBY'S STEAKHOUSE   513/784-1200   **7**
THREE DIAMOND Steak. Fine Dining. **Address:** 700 Walnut St 45202

MAPLEWOOD KITCHEN AND BAR   513/421-2100   **11**
APPROVED American. Quick Serve. **Address:** 525 Race St 45202

MCCORMICK & SCHMICK'S   513/721-9339   **13**
THREE DIAMOND Seafood. Fine Dining. **Address:** 21 E 5th St 45202

MOERLEIN LAGER HOUSE   513/421-2337   **15**
APPROVED American. Brewpub. **Address:** 115 Joe Nuxhall Way 45202

MONTGOMERY INN, THE BOATHOUSE   513/721-7427
APPROVED American. Casual Dining. **Address:** 925 Riverside Dr 45202

NADA   513/721-6232   **10**
THREE DIAMOND Mexican. Casual Dining. **Address:** 600 Walnut St 45202

NICHOLSON'S TAVERN & PUB   513/564-9111   **8**
APPROVED Scottish. Gastropub. **Address:** 625 Walnut St 45202

NICOLA'S   513/721-6200   **1**
FOUR DIAMOND Italian. Fine Dining. **Address:** 1420 Sycamore St 45202

ORCHIDS AT PALM COURT   513/421-9100   **14**
FIVE DIAMOND American. Fine Dining. **Address:** 35 W 5th St 45202

SCOTTI'S ITALIAN RESTAURANT   513/721-9484   **5**
APPROVED Italian. Casual Dining. **Address:** 919 Vine St 45202

SENATE   513/421-2020   **3**
APPROVED American. Gastropub. **Address:** 1212 Vine St 45202

SKYLINE CHILI
APPROVED American. Quick Serve.
LOCATIONS:
Address: 254 E 4th St 45202 **Phone:** 513/241-4848
Address: 1001 Vine St 45202 **Phone:** 513/721-4715
Address: 643 Vine St 45202 **Phone:** 513/241-2020

TASTE OF BELGIUM: BISTRO ON VINE   513/381-4607   **4**
APPROVED Belgian. Casual Dining. **Address:** 1135 Vine St 45202

VIA VITE   513/721-8483   **12**
THREE DIAMOND Italian. Casual Dining. **Address:** 520 Vine St 45202

WASHINGTON PLATFORM SALOON & RESTAURANT
   513/421-0110   **6**
APPROVED American. Casual Dining. **Address:** 1000 Elm St 45202

CINCINNATI
• Restaurants p. 174
• Hotels & Restaurants map & index p. 166

BEST WESTERN PREMIER MARIEMONT INN
   513/271-2100   **2**

THREE DIAMOND

Historic Hotel

BWP PREMIER
BEST WESTERN

AAA Benefit: Members save up to 15% and earn bonus points!

Address: 6880 Wooster Pike 45227 **Location:** I-71 exit 9, 2.4 mi s on Red Bank Expwy, then 1.9 mi e on US 50 E. **Facility:** This handsome Tudor-style building, constructed in the 1920's, is set in the middle of Mariemont, an upscale Cincinnati suburb. The lobby is adorned with the mounted heads of buffalo, elk and moose. 45 units. 3 stories, interior corridors. **Amenities:** safes. **Activities:** exercise room. **Guest Services:** valet laundry.

(See map & index p. 166.)

GRADUATE CINCINNATI
513/487-3800

 THREE DIAMOND

Hotel

Address: 151 Goodman Dr 45219 **Location:** I-75 exit 3 (Hopple St), 1.9 mi e on Hopple St/Martin Luther King Dr, just n on Eden St, then just w; I-71 exit 3 (Taft Rd), 0.6 mi w, then 0.4 mi n on Jefferson Ave. Next to University of Cincinnati. **Facility:** 206 units, some efficiencies. 8 stories, interior corridors. **Parking:** on-site (fee). **Terms:** check-in 4 pm. **Activities:** exercise room. **Guest Services:** valet and coin laundry, boarding pass kiosk, area transportation.

[SAVE] [🍴] [🍸] CALL [♿] [👪] [BIZ]

[📶] [✕] [🔌] [💻] / SOME UNITS [🐾]

HAMPTON INN & SUITES BY HILTON CINCINNATI/UPTOWN-UNIVERSITY AREA
513/281-2700 [5]

[THREE DIAMOND] [SAVE] Hotel. **Address:** 3024 Short Vine St 45219

AAA Benefit: Members save up to 15%!

HILTON GARDEN INN CINCINNATI MIDTOWN
513/361-9800 [3]

[THREE DIAMOND] [SAVE] Hotel. **Address:** 2145 Dana Ave 45207

AAA Benefit: Members save up to 15%!

SPRINGHILL SUITES BY MARRIOTT CINCINNATI MIDTOWN
513/381-8300 [6]

[THREE DIAMOND]

Hotel

 SPRINGHILL SUITES MARRIOTT

AAA Benefit: Members save 5% or more!

Address: 610 Eden Park Dr 45202 **Location:** I-71 exit 2 (Reading Rd), 0.4 mi n on US 42, then just e. Located in a small office park at base of Mount Adams. **Facility:** 122 units. 5 stories, interior corridors. **Parking:** on-site (fee). **Pool:** heated indoor. **Activities:** exercise room. **Guest Services:** valet and coin laundry.

[HS] [📶] [✕] [📹] [🔌] [🖥] [💻]

THE SUMMIT, A DOLCE HOTEL
513/527-9900 [1]

[THREE DIAMOND]

Contemporary Hotel

Address: 5345 Medpace Way 45227 **Location:** I-71/75 exit 9, just e. **Facility:** 239 units. 9 stories, interior corridors. **Parking:** on-site and valet. **Terms:** check-in 4 pm. **Amenities:** safes. **Activities:** exercise room. **Guest Services:** valet laundry, area transportation. *(See ad this page.)*

[SAVE] [🍴] [👪] [🍸] CALL [♿] [👪]

[📶] [✕] [📹] [🔌] [💻]

/ SOME UNITS [🐾] [HS]

▼ See AAA listing this page ▼

the art of inspiration℠

(See map & index p. 166.)

(See map & index p. 166.)

WHERE TO EAT

ARTHUR'S CAFE   513/871-5543 (7)
APPROVED American. Casual Dining. **Address:** 3516 Edwards Rd 45208

BANGKOK BISTRO   513/871-0707 (6)
APPROVED Thai. Casual Dining. **Address:** 3506 Erie Ave 45208

BONEFISH GRILL   513/321-5222 (4)
THREE DIAMOND Seafood. Fine Dining. **Address:** 2737 Madison Rd 45209

CAMP WASHINGTON CHILI INC   513/541-0061 (10)
APPROVED American. Casual Dining. **Address:** 3005 Colerain Ave 45225

CLOUGH CROSSINGS   513/624-7800 (14)
APPROVED American. Casual Dining. **Address:** 6892 Clough Pike 45244

EL COYOTE   513/232-5757 (16)
APPROVED Tex-Mex. Casual Dining. **Address:** 7404 State Rd 45230

EMBERS   513/984-8090 (1)
THREE DIAMOND Steak Seafood. Fine Dining. **Address:** 8170 Montgomery Rd 45236

GOLD STAR CHILI
APPROVED American. Quick Serve.
LOCATIONS:
Address: 21 E Galbraith Rd 45216 **Phone:** 513/761-8633
Address: 5420 Ridge Ave 45213 **Phone:** 513/631-1990
Address: 4795 Red Bank Expwy 45227 **Phone:** 513/271-0020
Address: 3026 Burnet Ave 45219 **Phone:** 513/751-4929
Address: 9124 Plainfield Rd 45236 **Phone:** 513/891-7432
Address: 7821 Hamilton Ave 45231 **Phone:** 513/522-4376

LE BAR A BOEUF   513/751-2333 (13)
THREE DIAMOND French. Casual Dining. **Address:** 2200 Victory Pkwy 45206

O PIE O   513/274-3238 (11)
APPROVED Desserts Sandwiches. Casual Dining. **Address:** 1527 Madison Rd 45206

THE PRECINCT   513/321-5454 (12)
THREE DIAMOND Steak Seafood. Fine Dining. **Address:** 311 Delta Ave 45202

PRIMAVISTA   513/251-6467 (15)
THREE DIAMOND
Northern Italian Fine Dining $17-$37
AAA Inspector Notes: One cannot avoid being charmed by the view from this restaurant perched atop Price Hill. Drive up here on a summer evening and enjoy the view as the lights of Cincinnati twinkle to life illuminating the valley of the Ohio River. Not a trendy restaurant, this place is simply a purveyor of well-prepared traditional examples of the cuisine. Diners enjoy such classic entrées as risotto, seared lamb loin and shrimp scampi. Be sure to ask about the deliciously fresh seafood special. **Features:** full bar. **Reservations:** suggested. **Address:** 810 Matson Pl 45204 **Location:** Between Price Ave and W 8th St; in Queen's Tower; in Price Hill.
(D)

THE QUARTER BISTRO   513/271-5400 (3)
THREE DIAMOND American. Fine Dining. **Address:** 6904 Wooster Pike 45227

REVOLUTION ROTISSERIE   513/351-4000 (2)
APPROVED Chicken. Casual Dining. **Address:** 6063 Montgomery Rd 45213

SKYLINE CHILI
APPROVED American. Quick Serve.
LOCATIONS:
Address: 8506 Reading Rd 45237 **Phone:** 513/821-1800
Address: 3081 Madison Rd 45209 **Phone:** 513/871-2930
Address: 1705 W Galbraith Rd 45239 **Phone:** 513/729-2200
Address: 10197 Colerain Ave 45251 **Phone:** 513/385-9400
Address: 290 Ludlow Ave 45220 **Phone:** 513/221-2142
Address: 5816 Wooster Pike 45227 **Phone:** 513/271-0611
Address: 85 E Kemper Rd 45246 **Phone:** 513/671-4444
Address: 5137 Delhi Pike 45238 **Phone:** 513/451-7000
Address: 6485 Harrison Ave 45247 **Phone:** 513/598-9798
Address: 7189 Beechmont Ave 45230 **Phone:** 513/231-2064
Address: 5560 Bridgetown Rd 45248 **Phone:** 513/574-4777

TELLERS OF HYDE PARK   513/321-4721 (8)
THREE DIAMOND American. Casual Dining. **Address:** 2710 Erie Ave 45208

WILD GINGER ASIAN BISTRO   513/533-9500 (5)
APPROVED Asian. Casual Dining. **Address:** 3655 Edwards Rd 45208

ZIP'S CAFE   513/871-9876 (9)
APPROVED American. Casual Dining. **Address:** 1036 Delta Ave 45208

Nearby Indiana

BATESVILLE pop. 6,520
• Part of Cincinnati area — see map p. 153

QUALITY INN   812/934-6185
APPROVED Hotel. **Address:** 112 SR 46 E 47006

SURESTAY PLUS HOTEL BY BEST WESTERN BATESVILLE   812/934-6262
APPROVED Hotel. **Address:** 1030 SR 229 N 47006

WHERE TO EAT

ERTEL CELLARS WINERY BISTRO   812/933-1500
THREE DIAMOND American. Fine Dining. **Address:** 3794 E CR 1100 N 47006

LIL' CHARLIE'S RESTAURANT AND BREWERY   812/934-6392
APPROVED American. Brewpub. **Address:** 504 E Pearl St 47006

SKYLINE CHILI   812/934-5554
APPROVED American. Quick Serve. **Address:** 914 SR 229 N 47006

LAWRENCEBURG pop. 5,042, elev. 486'
• Part of Cincinnati area — see map p. 153

Lawrenceburg, founded on a bend in the Ohio River in 1803 by Capt. Samuel Vance, grew quickly after the advent of steamboat shipping. During this era the city's Gamblers' Row was notorious from Pittsburgh to New Orleans. In 1819 Lawrenceburg became the site of the state's first "skyscraper"—The Jessie Hunt House, a three-story brick building at

Walnut and High streets. Due to its location, Lawrenceburg offers many scenic views of the river as well as numerous year-round recreational activities.

Dearborn County Convention and Tourism Bureau: 320 Walnut St., Lawrenceburg, IN 47025. **Phone:** (812) 537-0814 or (800) 322-8198.

COMFORT INN & SUITES   812/539-3600
 **APPROVED** Hotel. **Address:** 1610 Flossie Dr 47025

WHERE TO EAT

SKYLINE CHILI   812/537-4460
APPROVED American. Quick Serve. **Address:** 714 W Eads Pkwy 47025

WHISKY'S FAMILY RESTAURANT   812/537-4239
APPROVED American. Casual Dining. **Address:** 334 Front St 47025

RISING SUN pop. 2,304, elev. 420'
• Part of Cincinnati area — see map p. 153

Rising Sun is the seat of the state's smallest county, Ohio County, 88.43 square miles. The town was named in 1816 for the impressive sunrise over the Kentucky Hills. The first steel-bladed plow was invented here in 1830 at the Clore Plow Co. The 1845 courthouse is the oldest in continuous use in the state.

Rising Sun/Ohio County Convention & Tourism Bureau: 100 S. Walnut St., Rising Sun, IN 47040. **Phone:** (812) 438-4933 or (888) 776-4786.

This ends the Cincinnati section and resumes the alphabetical city listings for Ohio.

CIRCLEVILLE (F-4) pop. 13,314, elev. 702'
• Part of Columbus area — see map p. 205

When you hear someone talking about Circleville, chances are good that the topic of the annual Circleville Pumpkin Show will come up. This celebration of all things related to the pumpkin, which takes place downtown the third Wednesday through Saturday in October, has been held for more than a century. Music, parades, rides, pumpkin sculpting competitions, craft demonstrations and entertainment are part of the festive fall lineup. A highlight is always the exciting weigh-in to see which pumpkin will win the award and see if any records will be broken.

Pickaway County Visitors Bureau: 325 W. Main St., Circleville, OH 43113. **Phone:** (740) 474-3636.

HOLIDAY INN EXPRESS & SUITES   740/420-7711
APPROVED Hotel. **Address:** 23911 US Hwy 23 S 43113

Cleveland

Then & Now

In 1796 surveyor Moses Cleaveland picked his townsite on Lake Erie. By 1832 the Ohio and Erie Canal was completed, and Cleaveland, the northern terminus, had doubled its population. Over the next 10 years it grew by almost 500 percent. It also acquired a trimmer name when *The Cleaveland Gazette and Commercial Register* had to drop a letter from its masthead.

During the 1800s Cleveland was an important stop on the Underground Railroad. The city's port provided a route to freedom across the Canadian border for slaves fleeing the South.

With the canal came Cleveland's first wave of immigrants, the backbone of its labor force. The city transformed from a bustling port to a shipping and industrial giant. The Civil War halted the city's progress, but the subsequent demand for iron spurred new growth.

From 1910-20 Cleveland was the country's second largest center for automobile production. Behind this growth were great industrialists like John D. Rockefeller, the world's first billionaire.

The Cleveland Union Terminal complex with its 52-story Terminal Tower was built in the 1920s. Tower City Center, a three-level mall, now fills the former railroad station. Key Tower on Public Square is Ohio's tallest building at 948 feet tall with 57 stories.

The city is headquarters for more than 20 major corporations—including American Greetings Corp. and The Sherwin-Williams Co.—and many smaller companies. Case Western Reserve and Cleveland State universities as well as The Cleveland Clinic, which administers some of the world's most advanced medical treatments, are other intellectual highlights.

Year-round recreation opportunities include more than 23,000 acres of metropolitan parks districts; surrounding rivers, streams and lakes; and nearby Cuyahoga Valley National Park.

For culture, you can't beat University Circle. This neighborhood's large cluster of cultural goodies includes the Cleveland History Center, the Cleveland Museum of Natural History, and the Cleveland Museum of Art as well as the Cleveland Orchestra, which plays at the exquisite historic Severance Hall.

Visit some of Cleveland's neighborhoods. The Historic Warehouse District offers dining and entertainment with a backdrop of 19th-century architecture. Little Italy is a charming area with places to eat, bakeries and art galleries. The Flats East Bank, a riverfront area once known for heavy industry, is now a

(Continued on p. 178.)

AAA.com/travelguides— more ways to look, book and save

Tower City Center

Destination Cleveland

This map shows cities in the Cleveland vicinity where you will find attractions, hotels and restaurants. Cities are listed alphabetically in this book on the following pages.

Fast Facts

ABOUT THE CITY

POP: 396,815 ■ **ELEV:** 865 ft.

MONEY

SALES TAX: The local sales tax is 8 percent. The city lodging tax is 5.5 percent (less in suburbs).

Cars rented at Cleveland Hopkins International Airport are subject to an 8 percent parking tax, a $6-$25 motor vehicle lessor tax, an 11.1 percent concession fee, a 60-cent per day energy recovery fee, a 15-cent per day license fee and a transportation fee up to $16 per day (transporting cars to airport location costs more than transporting to locations in greater Cleveland).

WHOM TO CALL

EMERGENCY: 911

POLICE (non-emergency): (216) 623-5000

TIME AND TEMPERATURE: (216) 931-1212

HOSPITALS: Cleveland Clinic, (216) 444-2200 ■ St. Vincent Charity Medical Center, (216) 861-6200 ■ University Hospitals Case Medical Center, (216) 844-8447.

VISITOR INFORMATION

Destination Cleveland Convention and Visitors Bureau: 334 Euclid Ave., Cleveland, OH 44114. **Phone:** (216) 875-6680 (visitor center) or (800) 321-1001.

TRANSPORTATION

AIR TRAVEL: Cleveland Hopkins International Airport (CLE) is 13 miles southwest of downtown via I-71. Consult your AAA travel advisor for help with finding cheap airline flights and vacation packages.

Lakefront Lines Cleveland, (216) 267-8282 or (800) 543-9912, provides private van and minibus charter service daily 5 a.m.-11 p.m. Van service is $55 per hour (3-hour minimum), which includes a fuel surcharge and taxes. Minibus charter fares average $65-$85 per hour (3-hour minimum); reservations are required. Taxi fare to downtown averages $30-$50.

Select RTA rapid transit trains provide service to downtown from about daily 4 a.m.-1:15 a.m.

RENTAL CARS: Hertz, which offers discounts to AAA members, has a counter at the airport and at 3663 Park East Dr., Beachwood; phone (216) 831-3836 (Beachwood), (216) 267-8900 (airport) or (800) 654-3080.

 Book and save at AAA.com/hertz

RAIL SERVICE: The Amtrak station is at E. Ninth Street and Cleveland Memorial Shoreway; phone (800) 872-7245.

BUSES: Greyhound Lines Inc., (800) 231-2222, is at 1465 Chester Ave.

TAXIS: Cabs are available at the Public Square taxi stands or they can be ordered by phone. Rates average $2.75 for the first one-eighth mile and 28c for each additional one-eighth mile. The average fee for waiting is $18-$20 an hour. A $1 fuel surcharge also is added to the fare. Companies include Ace Taxi, (216) 361-4700 ■ Americab, (216) 881-1111 ■ and Yellow Cab, (216) 623-1500.

PUBLIC TRANSPORTATION: The Greater Cleveland Regional Transit Authority (RTA) offers bus and train service. Rail service runs from Cleveland Hopkins International Airport to the Tower City Rapid Transit Station on Public Square and continues to the Louis Stokes Station at Windermere in East Cleveland as well as from Tower City Center to points in Shaker Heights. The Waterfront Line transports visitors to popular attractions Mon.-Fri. 6:30 a.m.-midnight; weekends and holidays 9 a.m.-midnight.

There are more than 60 connecting bus routes, including free downtown trolleys operating Mon.-Fri. 7-7 (the C-Line Trolley runs Mon.-Fri. 7 a.m.-11 p.m. and Sat.-Sun. 11-11).

The HealthLine is a Bus Rapid Transit system running along Euclid Avenue and beyond from Public Square to Louis Stokes Station at Windermere. One-way train or bus fare is $2.50; $1.25 (senior citizens and disabled passengers). An all-day pass costs $5.50. Passes can be purchased at fare machines at train stations. For details phone the RTAnswerLine: (216) 621-9500 (Mon.-Fri. 7-6, Sat. 8-4:30) or TTY (216) 781-4271.

(Continued from p. 176.)

mixed-use district with office, dining, entertainment and residential space along with a public park and an extensive riverfront boardwalk.

Jacobs Field (now Progressive Field) and the adjacent Gund Arena (now Rocket Mortgage FieldHouse), homes of the Cleveland Indians and Cleveland Cavaliers, opened in 1994. The Cleveland Browns moved to Baltimore in the late 1990s but returned in 1999 to play at the new state-of-the-art Cleveland Browns Stadium (now FirstEnergy Stadium), reenergizing the city's dedicated fans.

Last but not least, remember that Cleveland rocks! Rock stars of the past and present are immortalized in The Rock and Roll Hall of Fame, which resides in a modern I.M. Pei-designed building on the shore of Lake Erie.

Must Do: AAA Editor's Picks

- If you remember the theme song to "The Drew Carey Show," then you already know that "Cleveland rocks." But see for yourself at the **Rock and Roll Hall of Fame** (751 Erieside Ave.). The massive collection of stage outfits, concert posters, instruments, handwritten lyrics and personal items tells the always interesting and often juicy history of rock and roll. When you need a little break from wandering galleries, have a seat in the theater where a trio of screens continually plays clips and music of each inductee.

- Cleveland rocks in more ways than one, and you don't have to go far to see how. Right next door is the **Great Lakes Science Center** (601 Erieside Ave.), where you can explore hundreds of science exhibits as well as the NASA Glenn Visitor Center, chock full of space history. The center is right on Lake Erie; head outside to tour the **Steamship** *William G. Mather*.

- Visit **The RainForest** at **Cleveland Metroparks Zoo** (3900 Wildlife Way). The re-creation of tropical rain forests is a visual and aural delight with a waterfall and simulated thunderstorms in addition to the 600-plus animals in residence. Once you experience this environment, you'll better understand the importance of saving the world's rain forests, which is the goal of this exhibit.

- If you're a fan of "A Christmas Story" and looking for things to do in Cleveland, you'll have a blast at **A Christmas Story House & Museum** (3159 W. 11th St.). Tour the house, where some scenes were filmed, and check out the movie props and memorabilia.

- Spend some time in **University Circle** (4 miles east of downtown). In addition to medical and education facilities (including the Cleveland Clinic, Case Western Reserve University and the Cleveland Institute of Art), University Circle is a renowned destination for its many cultural sites, including the next four on the list.

- The **Cleveland Museum of Art** (11150 East Blvd.) has just undergone a long renovation and expansion project. Like the rock hall, the art museum's collection is amazing in quantity, quality and diversity. A highlight is the European arms and armor collection.

- Explore the **Cleveland Museum of Natural History** (1 Wade Oval Dr.) galleries for a jam-packed crash course in archeology, astronomy, ecology, geology, human evolution and prehistoric life as well as Ohio's native plants and animals.

- Spend some time relaxing at the **Cleveland Botanical Garden** (11030 East Blvd.), where each season brings its own reason for visiting. Many of the individual gardens, like the Japanese and restorative gardens, are designed with serenity in mind, but one is intended to promote activity: the Hershey Children's Garden, which features a maze and tree house.

- Local history is front and center at **The Cleveland History Center** (10825 East Blvd.). One of the center's highlights is the Crawford Auto Aviation Museum. Temporary exhibits of clothing and textiles are always on view as well.

- Experience the area's beautiful natural scenery and recreation opportunities at one of the 18 reservations making up Cleveland Metroparks.

- Admire the city's architecture and public art either on a self-guiding tour (pick up a brochure at Cleveland Visitors Center, 334 Euclid Ave.) or a guided **Trolley Tours of Cleveland** (2000 Sycamore St.) tour.

- Mingle with Clevelanders at the **West Side Market**'s (1979 W. 25th St.) more than 100 vendor stalls.

- Theater in Cleveland is a pretty big deal. Not counting New York's venues, **PlayhouseSquare** (1501 Euclid Ave.) is the country's largest performing arts center. Plan to spend a night at the theater during your time in the city; it's a great option for those interested in things for couples to do.

Rock and Roll Hall of Fame

Cleveland Botanical Garden

Cleveland 1-day Itinerary

AAA editors suggest these activities for a great short vacation experience.

Morning

- Museums don't open first thing, so start at West Side Market (1979 W. 25th St.) in the Ohio City neighborhood. The building, which opened in 1912, features a vaulted Guastavino tile ceiling and a 137-foot clock tower. More than 100 vendors sell baked goods, produce, meat, seafood, dairy items, flowers and other specialty products.

- The 🧿 **Rock and Roll Hall of Fame** (751 Erieside Ave.) is a must-see. Its massive permanent collection showcases everything you'd want to know about rock and roll, and temporary exhibits enhance the already impressive experience. The story of rock unfolds in creatively themed exhibit areas—highlighting musical giants like Elvis, the Beatles, the Rolling Stones all the way down to one-hit wonders. Memorabilia, films, interactive exhibits and video and audio clips fill the galleries of I.M. Pei's dramatic building on the shore of Lake Erie.

- You could easily spend the whole day here, and why not if you are a big-time music fan? But if you want to see what else the city offers, save the afternoon for something else.

Afternoon

- Head to University Circle, a square mile jam-packed with cultural, educational and health institutions; Wade Oval and Wade Lagoon are beautiful spaces to enjoy the scenic area. You can't go wrong with any of the AAA GEM

attractions: 🧿 **Cleveland Botanical Garden** (11030 East Blvd.), 🧿 **Cleveland Museum of Art** (11150 East Blvd.), 🧿 **Cleveland Museum of Natural History** (1 Wade Oval Dr.) and **The Cleveland History Center** (10825 East Blvd.). Our pick: the art museum. The beautiful 1916 building, home to one of the country's best collections, has recently undergone a major expansion.

- The art spans 6,000 years. Major artists represented among the more than 45,000 works include Mary Cassatt, Claude Monet, Pablo Picasso, Jackson Pollock, Nicholas Poussin, Andy Warhol and a variety of Hudson River School artists. African, Ancient Egyptian, Ancient Near East/Greek/Roman, Chinese, Indian and Southeast Asian, Islamic, Japanese and Korean works of art also are displayed. The medieval collection contains coins, glass, jewelry, manuscripts, metalwork, paintings and sculpture among other objects. The highlight is an extensive arms and armor collection. It features body armor, helmets, crossbows, daggers, knives, swords and shields.

- Have lunch at the museum or head to Little Italy, adjacent to University Circle. The neighborhood offers restaurants, bakeries and art galleries; try **Guarino's** (12309 Mayfield Rd.) for a casual meal.

Evening

- Cleveland has quite the theater scene. PlayhouseSquare, the country's largest performing arts center outside of New York's offerings, features several resident companies, including Cleveland Play House (the country's first regional theater), and also brings in touring productions. Many restaurants are nearby, including **Lola** (2058 E. 4th St.), where the chef/owner is Michael Symon—cookbook author, a Food Network presence and a co-host on "The Chew." Lola is in the East 4th Street district, a good nightlife scene.

- For a more casual outing, head to Ohio City. Bars and breweries offer plentiful nightlife. Tour the **Great Lakes Brewing Co.** (2516 Market Ave.) and then enjoy some of its creations. You'll feel like a Clevelander yourself after sampling the beers with fun, creative names related to all things Cleveland. Another option is McNulty's Bier Markt, serving more than 100 American and Belgian craft beers. Have dinner at the attached **Bar Cento** (1948 25th St.), where the European-inspired menu changes seasonally so the chefs can always use local ingredients. If you're in the mood for a pizza, this is a great place to order one.

- Not ready to call it a night? **Jack Cleveland Casino** (100 Public Sq.) is open 24 hours. You'll be focused on winning big, but take a minute to look around. The building was once the Higbee Co., one of Cleveland's many beautiful—but long gone—department stores.

Arriving
By Car

Cleveland sits in the middle of a "Y" formed by two of the nation's major transcontinental routes: I-90 and I-80. I-90 passes through the heart of the city, bringing traffic along the lakeshore from the east; I-80 channels motorists from the interior through the southern suburbs. From the west, these routes combine over the Ohio Turnpike, with the "Y" beginning at neighboring Elyria.

Both highway systems interchange with important intersecting routes for easy access to the suburbs, and I-90 links conveniently to important city streets. Other supplemental east-west roads are SR 2, US 6 and US 20. These routes primarily serve local traffic, but also follow some of the major city arteries.

Downtown Cleveland is the northern terminus of I-71 and I-77, which bring traffic from the southwest and the south, respectively. I-490, south of the city, provides a connector for I-71 and I-77. SR 176 also channels traffic from the south connecting to I-480 and I-71. Approaching the city, each interchanges frequently with other routes, including I-80 (toll), before joining I-90 near the city's center.

Other routes from the south include SR 8, SR 21 and US 42, which are used chiefly by local traffic. Upon entering Cleveland, these roads constitute some of the principal thoroughfares.

I-271, forming an irregular arc between I-71 and I-90, provides a bypass around Cleveland's east side. I-80 (the Ohio Turnpike), I-480 and I-271 that bypass the city to the east and south, provide connections for I-90 corridor traffic.

Getting Around
Street System

Cleveland's streets are in a grid pattern that centers on Public Square, from which all major avenues radiate. Euclid Avenue is the major business thoroughfare, running from the square through downtown to the eastern suburbs. Ontario Street, running north-south through Public Square, divides the city into east and west. North-south routes are numbered streets, while the majority of east-west thoroughfares are named avenues, roads or boulevards. Right turns on red are permitted unless otherwise posted.

Parking

On-street metered parking is available. Meters operate Monday through Friday from a minimum of 20 minutes to a maximum of 4 hours from 7 a.m. or 9:30 a.m. to 6 p.m. The cost to park at a meter ranges from 50c to $1 per hour. Parking is available in the municipal parking lot on the Memorial Shoreway (SR 2) just east of the 9th Street exit; this affords easy access to the Waterfront Rapid Transit Train serving Tower City Center, The Flats and other Cleveland attractions. Parking lot and garage charges can vary from $2 to $10 daily, and up to $25 for special events. Park and ride lots are at some RTA stations.

The Arcade

Shopping

Tower City Center, 230 W. Huron Rd., is a shopping, dining and entertainment complex surrounding a modernized commuter rail station. Skylights, light and water shows, marble staircases, historic brass storefronts and a glass dome accent the three levels of retail stores and places to eat. **The Arcade,** 401 Euclid Ave., was one of the first indoor malls in the country. This 1890 landmark has been renovated to include a hotel but continues to offer a variety of shops and boutiques. **Galleria at Erieview,** 1301 E. 9th St. at St. Clair St., offers a small collection of shops and galleries.

Those seeking the novel may want to check out the offerings in **The Cop Shop, The Cleveland Police Museum's gift shop at 1300 Ontario St.; the shop is open weekdays 10-4.**

Antique Row, Lorain Avenue from W. 25th to W. 117th streets, and Detroit Avenue from Westwood Avenue to W. Clifton Boulevard, are popular with antiques hunters. The **Little Italy** neighborhood offers shops and galleries along Murray Hill and Mayfield roads.

Some of the Victorian houses in **Ohio City** serve as boutiques and antique shops. On select Saturdays from June through October, the district hosts music and an urban art market in Market Square.

The **West Side Market** at W. 25th Street and Lorain Avenue sells fresh fruit, vegetables, meats, fish, poultry, cheese and ethnic foods Mon. and Wed. 7-4, Fri.-Sat. 7-6 and Sun. 10-4. **Coit Road Farmers Market** is at Coit Avenue and Woodworth Street and offers Ohio produce and products. It is open Sat. year-round 8-1 as well as Wed. 10-1 and 4-7, June-Oct.

Shaker Square, at the junction of Van Aken Boulevard, Shaker Boulevard and E. 130th Street, offers shops, food and entertainment.

Take a trip down memory lane at **b. a. Sweetie Candy Co. Inc.** at 6770 Brookpark Rd. The candy warehouse has a huge inventory, including nostalgic brands.

In the surrounding suburbs are shopping centers and malls offering such department stores as Dillard's, Macy's, Neiman Marcus, Nordstrom and Saks Fifth Avenue as well as many smaller shops. Among the more popular malls are **Beachwood Place,** 26300 Cedar Rd. at Richmond Road in Beachwood; **Great Lakes Mall,** 7850 Mentor Ave. in Mentor; **The Shoppes at Parma,** 7899 W. Ridgewood Dr. in Parma; **Great Northern Mall,** 4954 Great Northern Mall at I-480 in North Olmsted; and **SouthPark Mall,** 500 Southpark Center in Strongsville. The site of the former Westgate Mall in Fairview Park is now the home of **Westgate,** an open-air shopping center at the intersection of W. 210 Street and Center Ridge Road/US 20.

The local vicinity also offers further shopping opportunities to add to your travel plans. **Legacy Village Shopping Center** is in Lyndhurst, 1 mile west of I-271 Cedar Road exit at 25333 Cedar Rd. The village features a main street reminiscent of a 1950s-era small town and includes Crate & Barrel and Restoration Hardware among its many stores and local restaurants. There are more than 80 shops in the outdoor shopping area of **Crocker Park,** a quarter-mile south of I-90 Crocker Road exit in Westlake. At Coventry Road in **Cleveland Heights** between Mayfield and Euclid Heights roads, colorful

shops and boutiques offer offbeat clothing, artworks and crafts.

In Rocky River, **Beachcliff Market Square,** 19300 Detroit Rd., offers upscale retailers and eateries. Also in Rocky River is **Old River,** on Old Detroit and Wooster roads, where shops specialize in gifts, antiques, spa services, gourmet food, wines and specialty clothing.

Big Events

Every season offers a wealth of events and things to do in Cleveland. The **International Exposition Center** (I-X Center) near Cleveland Hopkins International Airport plays host to the **Mid-America Boat Show** in January and then ▽♥**The Great Big Home and Garden Expo** in February.

The **Cleveland Auto Show** is held at the **I-X Center** (late February to early March), and one of Cleveland's most popular traditions, the **St. Patrick's Day parade,** is held March 17. The **Geauga County Maple Festival** in nearby Chardon features crafts, parades, carnival rides, contests and the Sap Run marathon in late April.

In May the **Tremont Greek Fest,** near downtown Cleveland, offers a variety of Mediterranean cuisine and fun things to do with friends.

Parade the Circle Celebration is an art parade that takes place in June in **University Circle,** the heart of the culture area of Cleveland. Also in June, the **Tri-C Jazz Fest showcases local and regional jazz artists** at PlayhouseSquare.

In late June, the **Star-Spangled Spectacular** features performances by the Cleveland Orchestra and a fireworks display. Nearby Cleveland Heights offers music and art during mid-July's **Cain Park Arts Festival.**

In mid-August the **Feast of the Assumption** is held in the **Little Italy** section of Cleveland (also known as Murray Hill). Also in August is the **Cuyahoga County Fair,** one of the largest fairs in the state, at the fairgrounds in nearby Berea. On Labor Day weekend the **Cleveland National Air Show** takes place at **Burke Lakefront Airport.** Throughout the downtown area in late September, **Ingenuity Fest** mixes performing and visual artists with inventive high-tech creations. Little Italy residents and visitors celebrate Columbus Day with the annual **Columbus Day Parade** in October.

The Christmas season is welcomed by **Winterfest,** a holiday lighting program at PlayhouseSquare and fireworks display held the Saturday after Thanksgiving.

Sports & Rec

The more than 23,000 acres of **Cleveland Metroparks** constitute one of the largest concentrations of parkland per capita in the nation. The 100-mile chain of metropolitan parks known as the "Emerald Necklace" is one of the largest park

Crocker Park

districts in the country. The 18 reservations offer opportunities for **biking, boating, fishing, geocaching, golfing, hiking, horseback riding, picnicking, skating, swimming, water sports** and many **winter sports.** The more than 60 miles of all-purpose trails are designed for walking/hiking, running, biking, horseback riding and skating. There are wildlife management areas, waterfowl sanctuaries and seven outdoor education facilities. Some of the reservations fall within the boundaries of **Cuyahoga Valley National Park.** Phone (216) 635-3200.

Biking is a great way to scoot around town whether for recreational enjoyment or as a means to get from one point of interest to another. Bicycles can be rented from **Bike Rack** at 2148 E. 4th St. The facility is open Mon.-Fri. 6:30-6:30. and Sat.-Sun. noon-6, Mar.-Oct.; phone (216) 771-7120.

The **Cleveland Velodrome,** 5033 Broadway Ave., is open Mon.-Fri. 5-8 and Sat.-Sun. 11-6, May-Oct.

Golf enthusiasts can try their skill at any one of the many public courses, including the following Cleveland Metroparks courses: **Big Met,** 4811 Valley Pkwy., (440) 331-1070; **Little Met,** 18599 Old Lorain Rd., (216) 941-9672; **Manakiki,** 35501 Eddy Rd., (440) 942-2500; **Mastick Woods,** 19900 Puritas Rd., (216) 267-5626; **Seneca,** 975 Valley Parkway, (440) 526-0043; **Shawnee Hills,** 18753 Egbert Rd., (440) 232-7184; **Sleepy Hollow,** 9445 Brecksville Rd., (440) 526-4285; and **Washington Golf Learning Center,** 3841 Washington Park Blvd., (216) 641-1864.

Stables offering horseback riding lessons and boarding are at **Rocky River Stables,** (216) 267-2525, and **Brecksville Stables,** (440) 526-6767. **Swimming** can be enjoyed at the sandy Lake Erie beaches, such as the ones found in Cleveland Metroparks Lakefront Reservation (Edgewater Park) and at the Cleveland Metroparks **Huntington Reservation** in Bay Village as well as **Headlands Beach State Park** (see Recreation Areas Chart). Swimming also is available at **Ledge Pool and Recreation Area** in Hinckley.

Fishing and boating are among the popular things to do on **Lake Erie.** Public boat rentals and ramps are at the Cleveland Metroparks **Rocky River and Hinckley reservations,** and fishing piers are at Huntington. Great Lakes Watersports, 1148 Main Ave., offers boat, jet ski and kayak rentals by the hour; phone (216) 771-4386. Trident Marine Corp. offers fishing charters; phone (216) 771-2628. **Wildwood Marina** offers public and private fishing excursions; phone (216) 481-5771. The Cleveland Visitors Center can provide additional fishing charter companies if you're interested in taking a fishing trip; phone (216) 875-6680 or (800) 321-1001.

Skiing, snowboarding and tubing are popular at several nearby sites. Peninsula offers **Boston Mills Ski Resort,** Sagamore Hills has **Brandywine Ski Resort** and **Polar Blast** snow tubing park, and Chesterland has **Alpine Valley.** Several Cleveland

Brandywine Falls in Cuyahoga Valley National Park

Metroparks offer **cross-country skiing** and **sledding.**

The outdoor **Rink at Wade Oval** in University Circle has a polymer surface and is open for **ice-skating** Fri. noon-9, Sat. noon-7, Sun. noon-5, late Nov. to mid-Feb.; closed Jan. 1, Thanksgiving and Christmas. Skate rental is $3; phone (216) 791-3900.

Various recreational opportunities also are found at the Cuyahoga Valley National Park, just southeast of the city (see place listing p. 237 and Recreation Areas Chart).

Because Cleveland is home to several professional sports teams, spectator sports enthusiasts can choose from a variety of activities and fun places to go. At **Progressive Field** (see attraction listing p. 189), Carnegie Avenue between Ontario Avenue and E. 9th Street, the **Cleveland Indians** play **baseball** in the spring, summer and early fall. Guided stadium tours are offered late April through early September; for tour information or game tickets phone (216) 420-4487. The **Rocket Mortgage FieldHouse,** hosts **basketball** and **hockey** October through April with both the NBA's **Cavaliers** and the AHL's **Lake Erie Monsters. Arena football's Cleveland Gladiators** also play at Rocket Mortgage FieldHouse late March to mid-July. For Cavaliers, Lake Erie Monsters or Gladiator tickets phone (216) 420-2200 or (800) 332-2287.

Cleveland Browns football fans head to **FirstEnergy Stadium** at 1085 W. 3rd St. near the North Coast Harbor to watch their team in action; phone (440) 824-3434 or (800) 745-3000.

Thoroughbred racing is held throughout the year at the **Thistledown Racing Club,** 21501

Emery Rd. in North Randall, (216) 662-8600. **Harness races** are featured year-round at **Northfield Park,** 10705 Northfield Rd. in Northfield; phone (330) 467-4101.

Note: Policies vary concerning admittance of children to pari-mutuel betting facilities. Phone for information.

Performing Arts

Those looking for music, theater, opera and other performances will find plenty of options and things to do in Cleveland. The world-renowned **Cleveland Orchestra** performs mid-September through early June in historic **Severance Hall,** opened in 1931, in the University Circle area and at the open-air **Blossom Music Center** in Cuyahoga Falls *(see place listing p. 237)* early July through Labor Day weekend; phone (216) 231-1111 or (800) 686-1141 for tickets. Food is available at both facilities, and the patrons of Blossom Music Center can opt to bring a picnic.

The **Cleveland Chamber Music Society** performs at the Plymouth Church October through May. The **Cleveland Contemporary Players,** performing in the **Music and Communications Building of Cleveland State University,** gives concerts of contemporary music; phone (216) 802-3054 for scheduled programs.

Musical events are presented regularly at various sites across the city, including **The Cleveland Music School Settlement, Rocket Mortgage FieldHouse,** the **Wolstein Center** at Cleveland State University and the civic auditorium at Lakewood High School.

Ohio Theatre

The students and faculty of the **Cleveland Institute of Music** as well as visiting artists perform a variety of musical types—including chamber, orchestra and opera—throughout the year on campus (11021 East Blvd. in University Circle) and at other locations in the city; phone (216) 791-5000 for schedule information.

PlayhouseSquare, on Euclid Avenue between E. 14th and E. 17th streets, is a performing arts destination that began in the 1920s with five theater, vaudeville and movie venues: **Ohio Theatre, State Theatre, Allen Theatre, Connor Palace Theatre** and **Hanna Theatre.** In the 1970s these theaters were saved from demolition by the community. Today the complex boasts nine performing spaces, including the Westfield Insurance Studio Theatre inside the Idea Center at PlayhouseSquare. Among the types of performances offered are Broadway shows, opera, concerts, comedy, family shows and dance programs. PlayhouseSquare is home to resident companies **DANCECleveland, Opera Cleveland, Great Lakes Theater Festival** and **Tri-C.** For ticket information phone (216) 241-6000, or (800) 766-6048 outside the Cleveland area.

PlayhouseSquare recently jazzed up its neighborhood with the outdoor GE Chandelier, which suspends 44 feet above the E. 14th Street and Euclid Avenue intersection. As you can imagine, this 20-foot-tall beauty is a must-see at night.

The **Cleveland Play House** was established in 1915 as America's first permanent regional theater company. The original facility at 8500 Euclid Ave. was built in 1927 and housed two theaters. A 1983 expansion was designed by internationally acclaimed architect Philip Johnson and made it the country's largest regional theater complex. In 2011 the company kicked off the season at a new facility located at PlayhouseSquare's Allen Theatre Complex at 1407 Euclid Ave. The season runs September through May, with productions ranging from the classics to new plays and from comedies to musicals; phone (216) 241-6000.

Also established in 1915 was **Karamu House.** The company offers multicultural performances and programs at 2355 E. 89th St.; phone (216) 795-7070.

The **Gordon Square Arts District** is an emerging arts scene on Cleveland's West Side; it is home to **Cleveland Public Theatre,** (216) 631-2727, at 6415 Detroit Ave. **Near West Theatre,** (216) 961-9750, performs community theater at 6702 Detroit Ave. The 1921 **Capitol Theatre** has been restored and now shows independent, foreign and documentary films on three screens.

Cleveland Shakespeare Festival puts on about a dozen performances of free outdoor plays from mid-June to early August in Cleveland and several surrounding cities; the Cleveland venues include Lincoln Park.

ATTRACTIONS

For a complete list of attractions, visit AAA.com/travelguides/attractions

CLEVELAND BOTANICAL GARDEN is at 11030 East Blvd. in University Circle. Ten acres of beautifully landscaped grounds include the Japanese, herb, theme, natural woodland and rose gardens as well as the popular Hershey Children's Garden. The Eleanor Armstrong Smith Glasshouse is an 18,000-square-foot crystalline conservatory that houses two re-created ecosystems: the Madagascar desert and the butterfly-filled Costa Rican cloud forest.

Stone slab walkways meander through the site, which also features a gardening library, gallery space and seasonal exhibits. Gardening lectures, classes and public programs are offered. **Time:** Allow 2 hours minimum. **Hours:** Tues.-Sat. 10-5, Sun. noon-5 (also Wed. 5-9). **Cost:** $12; $8 (ages 3-12); $7 (ages 60+ on Tues.); free (active military and veterans with ID and immediate family consisting of one adult and two children). **Phone:** (216) 721-1600. ⓉⒾ Ⓟ Cedar-University, 49

CLEVELAND METROPARKS ZOO is at 3900 Wildlife Way. The zoo is home to thousands of mammals, birds, reptiles, amphibians and fish in naturalistic habitats. Giraffes, lions, ostriches and zebras are in the African Savanna; Wolf Wilderness features a pack of Mexican gray wolves and a beaver lodge; and Australian Adventure is home to kangaroos, koalas and wallabies. African Elephant Crossing is a five-acre elephant habitat and education village. In addition to a herd of five elephants the exhibit features meerkats, naked mole rats, an African rock python and an aviary of African birds. The Asian Highlands exhibit gives guests the opportunity to get nose-to-nose with snow leopards and red pandas.

Hours: Mon.-Fri. 10-5, Sat.-Sun. and holidays 10-6, Memorial Day weekend-Labor Day; daily 10-5, rest of year. Last ticket sales 1 hour before closing. **Cost:** (includes The RainForest) $16.25; $14.95 (ages 62+); $12.95 (ages 2-11). **Phone:** (216) 661-6500 or TTY (216) 661-1090. ⓉⒾ Ⓟ

The RainForest is just outside the Cleveland Metroparks Zoo entrance at 3900 Wildlife Way. The RainForest features more than 600 animals and 10,000 plants, trees and shrubs from around the jungles of Africa, Asia and the Americas. The elaborate 2-acre, bi-level re-creation of a tropical habitat includes a 25-foot waterfall and a simulated thunderstorm every 15 minutes.

The depiction of the rain forests of Africa, Asia and the Americas reveals their importance as well as our responsibility to protect them. Exhibits showcase a variety of wildlife, including orangutans, capybaras, giant anteaters, ocelots, fishing cats and sloths. An insectarium and an aviary also are included.

In the zoo, picnicking is permitted and food is available. **Time:** Allow 1 hour minimum. **Hours:** Mon.-Fri. 10-5, Sat.-Sun. 10-6, Memorial Day weekend-Labor Day; daily 10-5, rest of year. Last ticket sales 1 hour before closing. **Cost:** (includes Cleveland Metroparks Zoo) $16.95; $14.95 (ages 62+); $12.95 (ages 2-11). **Phone:** (216) 661-6500 or TTY (216) 661-1090. ⓉⒾ Ⓟ

CLEVELAND MUSEUM OF ART is at 11150 East Blvd. in University Circle. This renowned museum's collection encompasses 6,000 years of history with more than 45,000 works of art. Some of the thousands of artists represented in the more than 40 galleries include Caravaggio, Edgar Degas, El Greco, Childe Hassam, Hans Holbein, Michelangelo, Raphael, Rembrandt, Pierre Auguste Renoir and Benjamin West.

The second floor of the neoclassical 1916 building includes 17th- through 19th-century European art and 18th- and 19th-century American art as well as the Armor Court, a collection of European arms and armor from the 15th- through 18th centuries. The Ancient Egyptian and Ancient Near East, Classical Greek and Roman, Early Christian and Byzantine, Medieval, Sub-Saharan African, prints and drawings collections also are on view in the historical building. The East Wing includes additional European art as well as photography, contemporary art, Cleveland art and American modern art.

The North Wing houses art of the Americas, textiles and Japanese and Korean art. The West Wing features Chinese, Indian and Southeast Asian art. The Ancient Egyptian and Ancient Near East, Classical Greek and Roman, Early Christian and Byzantine, Medieval, Sub-Saharan African, prints and drawings collections also are on view. Ingalls Library has a noncirculating art research collection. The Atrium serves as the centerpiece of the museum with a large courtyard and soaring glass canopy.

Note: Non-flash photography is permitted except for works in special exhibitions, art on loan, and works from 1900 to the present. **Hours:** Museum Tues.-Sun. 10-5 (also Wed. and Fri. 5-9). Library Tues.-Fri. 10-5 (also Wed. 5-7:30 during academic year). Gallery tours depart daily at 1:30 (also Sat.-Sun. at 2:30). **Cost:** Free. Admission may be charged for special exhibitions. **Phone:** (216) 421-7350 or (877) 262-4748. ⒼⓉ ⓉⒾ Ⓟ Cedar-University, 49

CLEVELAND MUSEUM OF NATURAL HISTORY is at 1 Wade Oval Dr. in University Circle. The Shafran Planetarium features more than 5,000 stars, nebulae, galaxies and planets. The Kirtland Hall of Prehistoric Life includes a *Haplocanthosaurus delfsi*, T. rex and triceratops dinosaurs. The Wade Gallery of Gems and Jewels showcases more than 1,500 dazzling objects, including a moon rock.

Lifelike and skeletal reconstructions of "Lucy," whose partial skeleton was discovered in 1974, is displayed; she is one of the oldest known human ancestors. The Ralph Perkins II Wildlife Center and

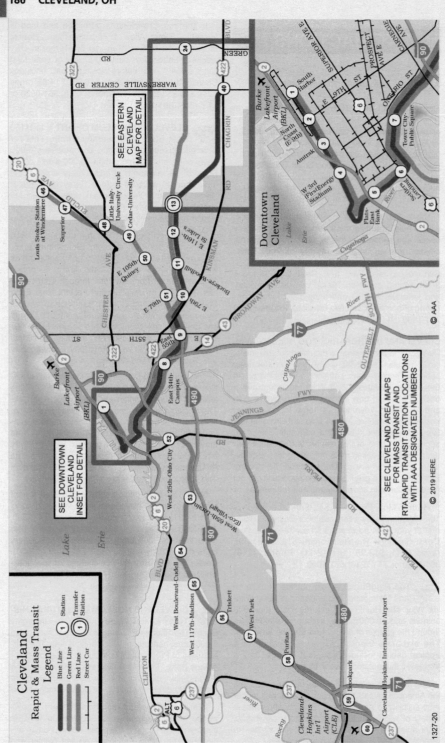

Cleveland
Rapid & Mass Transit
Legend

Blue Line
Green Line
Red Line
Street Car

(1) Station
(1) Transfer Station

SEE DOWNTOWN CLEVELAND INSET FOR DETAIL

SEE EASTERN CLEVELAND MAP FOR DETAIL

Downtown Cleveland

SEE CLEVELAND AREA MAPS FOR MASS TRANSIT AND RTA RAPID TRANSIT STATION LOCATIONS WITH AAA DESIGNATED NUMBERS

© 2019 HERE

© AAA

1327-20

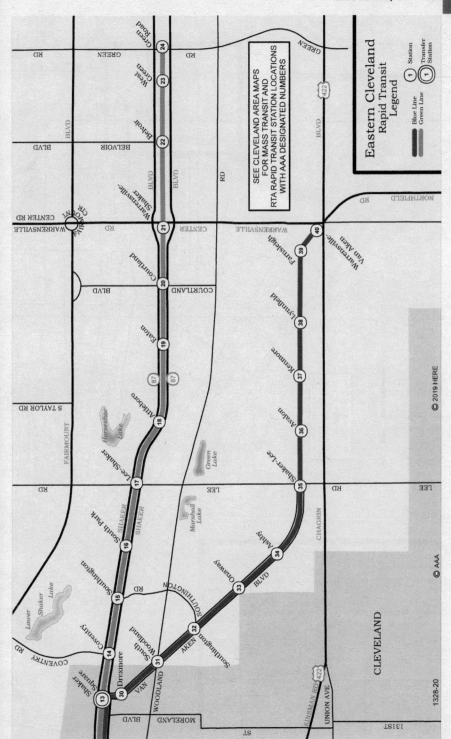

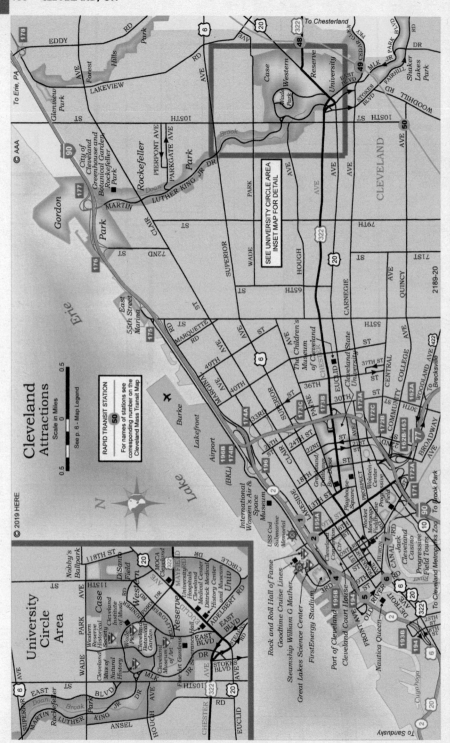

Cleveland Attractions

Scale in Miles

See p. 6 - Map Legend

RAPID TRANSIT STATION

50

For names of stations see corresponding number on the Cleveland Mass Transit Map

SEE UNIVERSITY CIRCLE AREA INSET MAP FOR DETAIL

© 2019 HERE

© AAA

University Circle Area

Rock and Roll Hall of Fame
Goodtime Cruise Lines
Steamship William G Mather
Great Lakes Science Center
Port of Cleveland
Cleveland Court House
Nautica Queen
Rock and Roll Hall of Fame

To Erie, PA
To Chesterland
To Sandusky
To Cleveland Metroparks Zoo
To Brook Park
To Brecksville

Woods Garden—Presented by KeyBank includes flora and fauna indigenous to Ohio, including oak and maple trees, bald eagles, bobcats, owls and river otters plus innovative overhead animal trailways. Other exhibits showcase Ohio archeology, birds, dinosaurs and cultural artifacts from seven continents. An observatory, the hands-on learning Smead Discovery Center and live animal shows also are offered.

The museum is undergoing a major renovation and expansion that is expected to be completed in 2020; the museum intends to stay open throughout the project.

Hours: Museum open Mon.-Sat. 10-5 (also Wed. 5-10), Sun. noon-5. Planetarium shows offered daily. **Cost:** $17; $14 (ages 3-18, ages 60+ and college students with ID). Planetarium $5 extra. **Parking:** $10 for the first 2.5 hours; $1 for each additional 30 minutes, up to the daily maximum of $16. **Phone:** (216) 231-4600, (216) 231-1177 for tickets and planetarium reservations or (800) 317-9155. 🚇 Cedar-University, 49

GREATER CLEVELAND AQUARIUM is at 2000 Sycamore St., in the lower levels of the Powerhouse on the west bank of The Flats. More than 50 exhibits feature themed sections: Ohio Lakes & Rivers, Lakes and Rivers of the World, Rainforest Discovery Zone, Indo-Pacific, Coastal Boardwalk, Tropical Reef, Shark SeaTube (with three species of sharks), Shark-Cam and Imagiquarium Coastal. At the Coastal Touch Pool visitors can pet stingrays and invertebrates. Themed tours and experiences are offered for additional fees. **Time:** Allow 1 hour, 30 minutes minimum. **Hours:** Daily 10-5; last admission 1 hour before closing. **Cost:** $19.95; $17.95 (ages 60+ and military); $13.95 (ages 2-12); free (ages 100+). **Parking:** $3-$6. **Phone:** (216) 862-8803 or (855) 602-3040. GT 🚇 North Coast (E 9th), 2

GREAT LAKES SCIENCE CENTER is at 601 Erieside Ave., between the Rock and Roll Hall of Fame and FirstEnergy Stadium. Through hundreds of interactive exhibits, daily science demonstrations, traveling exhibits and educational programs, the center lets visitors explore aeronautics and space exploration, biomedical technology, renewable energy and the Great Lakes.

The NASA Glenn Visitor Center, which focuses on space exploration and the resulting scientific discoveries, features more than 50 exhibits, including a moon rock and the Apollo command module from its 1973 Skylab 3 mission. The center also incorporates the six-story giant-screen Cleveland Clinic Dome Theater. People can make parachutes, a race car and a rocket in the Cleveland Creates Zone maker space and kids under age 8 can play and learn in the Polymer Funhouse. The Steamship *William G. Mather (see attraction listing)* is on the grounds as well.

Time: Allow 2 hours minimum. **Hours:** Tues.-Sat. 10-5 (also Mon. 10-5, May 1-Labor Day), Sun. noon-5. Closed Easter, Thanksgiving, Christmas and Cleveland Browns regular-season home game

days. **Cost:** $16.95; $14.95 (ages 65+ and students and military with ID); $13.95 (Ohio teachers with ID). Dome Theater only $10.95; $8.95 (ages 65+, students and military with ID, and ages 2-12); free (Ohio teachers with ID). Science center and Dome Theater or Steamship *William G. Mather* $21.95; $19.95 (ages 65+ and students and military with ID); $18.95 (ages 2-12); free (Ohio teachers with ID). Science center, Dome Theater and Steamship *William G. Mather* $24.95; $22.95 (ages 65+ and students and military with ID); $21.95 (ages 2-12); free (Ohio teachers with ID). **Phone:** (216) 694-2000. 🍴 🎡 🚇 North Coast (E 9th), 2

Steamship *William G. Mather* is docked at Great Lakes Science Center at 601 Erieside Ave. The restored 1925 Great Lakes freighter has been preserved as a floating museum ship. Visitors can explore the historic cargo holds, four-story engine room, elegant dining rooms, galley, and the brass and oak pilothouse of this 618-foot vessel. Exhibits and introductory videos focus on the Great Lakes and the history of the Great Lakes shipping industry.

Note: Visitors should wear flat, rubber-soled shoes. Tickets can be purchased on the ship or at Great Lakes Science Center. Parking is available in the Great Lakes Science Center garage. **Time:** Allow 1 hour minimum. **Hours:** Tues.-Sat. 11-5, Sun. noon-5, June-Aug.; Sat. 11-5, Sun. noon-5 in May and Sept.-Oct. Last admission 30 minutes before closing. Phone ahead to confirm schedule. **Cost:** $8.95; $6.95 (ages 65+ and college students and military with ID); $5.95 (ages 5-12). Prices may vary for special events. Combination tickets with Great Lakes Science Center are available. **Phone:** (216) 694-2000. GT 🚇 North Coast (E 9th), 2

PROGRESSIVE FIELD TOURS departs from the Progressive Field Team Shop at 2401 Ontario St. Guided 60-minute tours stop at the indoor batting cages, bullpen, dugout, visitors' clubhouse, press box, club lounge and party suite. The tour also takes visitors to Heritage Park, an area behind center field housing the Indians Hall of Fame and exhibits about the franchise's history. Heritage Park also is open before, during and after home games.

Areas covered on the tour may change based on availability. **Hours:** Tours depart Mon.-Sat. at 10:30, 11:30, 12:30 and 1:30, early May-early Sept. No tours are given when day games are scheduled before 6 p.m., during special events or on holidays. Phone ahead to confirm schedule. **Cost:** $12; $10 (ages 0-14 and 60+). Phone ahead to verify rates. **Phone:** (216) 420-4487. GT 🚇 North Coast (E 9th), 2

ROCK AND ROLL HALL OF FAME is at 751 Erieside Ave. at jct. E. 9th St. The giant 150,000-square-foot space is dedicated to the living legacy of music, from Delta blues, early rock and roll and soul to classic rock, hip-hop and alternative styles. A large collection of images, artifacts and instruments from current performers, Hall of Fame inductees and other legends is imaginatively presented.

Visitors can listen to the songs that shaped rock and roll, a sample of the most popular and influential recordings in the history of the genre. Inside the Hall of Fame gallery, in addition to an exhibit featuring the current class of inductees, visitors will also find The Power of Rock Experience featuring induction performance clips using moving screens, concert lighting and shaking seats. To help achieve its mission to engage, teach and inspire through the power of rock and roll, the museum offers live concert events, community festivals and educational programs.

Time: Allow 3 hours minimum. **Hours:** Daily 10-5:30 (also Wed.-Sat. 5:30-9), July 1-Sept. 1; daily 10-5:30 (also Wed. and Sat. 5:30-9), late May-late June; daily 10-5:30 (also Wed. 5:30-9), rest of year. Museum will close at 5 (June 10) and at 5:30 (July 13 and July 20). **Cost:** $26; $24 (ages 65+, military, first responders and college students with ID); $16 (ages 6-12). **Phone:** (216) 781-7625 or (888) 764-7625. ⛽ 🅿 North Coast (E 9th), 2

WESTERN RESERVE HISTORICAL SO-CIETY, 10825 East Blvd. in University Circle, encompasses The Cleveland History Center—home to the Crawford Auto Aviation Museum and other exhibits as well as the Bingham-Hanna and Hay-McKinney mansions—and The Research Library. **Hours:** The Cleveland History Center open Tues.-Sat. 10-5, Sun. noon-5. The Research Library open Thurs.-Sat. 10-5; closed Jan. 1, July 4, Thanksgiving, Christmas Eve and Christmas. **Cost:** (includes both sites) $10; $9 (ages 62+); $7 (veterans with ID); $5 (ages 3-12). **Parking:** $8-$15. **Phone:** (216) 721-5722. 🅿 Cedar-University, 49

Western Reserve Historical Society

The Cleveland History Center is at 10825 East Blvd., part of the Western Reserve Historical Society in University Circle. The property includes a variety of places to explore the story of Northeast Ohio—the Frederick C. and Kathleen S. Crawford Auto Aviation Museum, the Chisholm Halle Costume Wing, Euclid Beach Park Grand Carousel, Community History & Entrepreneur Galleries, and the historic Bingham-Hanna and Hay-McKinney mansions.

Photography is permitted in most areas. **Hours:** Tues.-Sat. 10-5, Sun. noon-5. Closed major holidays. **Cost:** (includes two carousel rides and The Research Library) $10; $9 (ages 62+); $7 (veterans with ID); $5 (ages 3-12). **Parking:** $8-$15. **Phone:** (216) 721-5722. 🅿 Cedar-University, 49

The Research Library, 10825 East Blvd. at the Western Reserve Historical Society in University Circle, features substantial archives, photographs, published materials and objects relating to the history of life in Cleveland and other northeast Ohio towns. Family history research materials, local newspapers, magazines and government documents also are available. **Hours:** Thurs.-Sat. 10-5. Closed major holidays. **Cost:** (includes The Cleveland History Center) $10; $9 (ages 62+); $5 (ages 3-12). **Parking:** $8-$15. **Phone:** (216) 721-5722. 🅿 Cedar-University, 49

Sightseeing

The Terminal Tower, at 230 W. Huron Rd. and surrounded by Tower City Center, was built 1927-30 and is considered the showpiece of Cleveland's lakefront. The remodeled concourse of this 52-story city landmark contains restaurants, shops, movie theaters and two hotels. The observation deck is open Sat. noon-5 and Sun. noon-4, mid-Apr. to late Dec. Guests can purchase tickets the day of the tour (if available) from the Guest Services desk on the first level.

Boat Tours

GOODTIME CRUISE LINES departs from 825 E. 9th St. Pier at the North Coast Harbor. The 2-hour narrated Lake/River tour takes passengers on a cruise of the Cuyahoga River and the Cleveland lakefront aboard the 1,000-passenger *Goodtime III.* Additional cruises also are offered.

Hours: Narrated Lake/River tour departs Tues.-Sat. at noon and 3, Sun. at 1 and 3:30, June 15-Labor Day; Fri.-Sat. at noon (also Sat. at 3), Sun. at 1 and 3:30, day after Labor Day-late Sept.; limited Sat.-Sun. tours, Memorial Day weekend-June 14. Phone ahead to confirm schedule. **Cost:** $20; $17 (ages 60+); $10 (ages 5-12). **Phone:** (216) 861-5110 or (888) 916-7447. 🄶🅃 🅿 North Coast (E 9th), 2

Industrial Tours

GREAT LAKES BREWING CO. is at 2516 Market Ave. across from the West Side Market; tours begin in the adjacent gift shop. Purportedly the first microbrew in the state, this family-owned company, which opened in 1988 by brothers Patrick and Daniel

Conway, uses all-natural ingredients—some from local vendors. Tours include overviews of production stages and equipment and include the brewhouse, tank farm, bottling and packaging line, beer cooler and quality assurance labs. Samples are offered to visitors who are 21 or older.

Note: The tour includes stairwells; some are steep and narrow. Closed-toe shoes are recommended. **Time:** Allow 1 hour minimum. **Hours:** Guided tours are offered on the hour Fri.-Sat. noon-8; hours vary. Guests should arrive at least 15 minutes prior to tour departure time. A maximum of 15 people is permitted per tour. Closed holidays. **Cost:** $5. Reservations are highly recommended. **Phone:** (216) 771-4404. GT

Trolley and Train Tours

Cuyahoga Valley Scenic Railroad *(see attraction listing p. 260)* offers train excursions through Cuyahoga Valley National Park. Trips include scenic tours of the valley and round-trip travel to Akron destinations.

Walking Tours

Stop by the visitor center at 334 Euclid Avenue for a "Walk Cleveland" brochure. It contains a map with details for a self-guiding tour of Cleveland's architecture, public art and other top things to see.

Self-guiding walking or driving tours are good ways to experience the restoration of Ohio City on Cleveland's west side. A separate municipality that was later annexed, Ohio City is a neighborhood of old Victorian houses, many of which now house boutiques, restaurants and antique shops. Most Saturdays in June, July and August, the district hosts music and an urban art market in Market Square. Many of the neighborhood's restored homes open their doors to the public during the annual "Evening in Ohio City" celebration held the second or third Saturday in May. Brochures about the area are provided by Ohio City Inc., 2525 Market Ave., Suite A, Cleveland, OH 44113; phone (216) 781-3222.

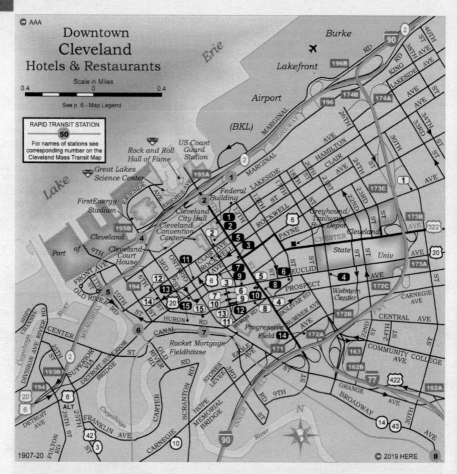

© AAA

Downtown Cleveland
Hotels & Restaurants

Scale in Miles
0.4   0   0.4

See p. 6 - Map Legend

RAPID TRANSIT STATION
50
For names of stations see corresponding number on the Cleveland Mass Transit Map

1907-20

© 2019 HERE   8

Downtown Cleveland

This index helps you "spot" where hotels and restaurants are located on the corresponding detailed maps. Restaurant price range is a combination of lunch and/or dinner. Turn to the listing page for more information and consult display ads for special promotions.

 For more details, rates and reservations: **AAA.com/travelguides/hotels**

DOWNTOWN CLEVELAND

Map Page	Hotels	Designation	Member Savings	Page
1 this page	**DoubleTree by Hilton Hotel Cleveland Downtown-Lakeside**	THREE DIAMOND	✔	200
2 this page	**The Westin Cleveland Downtown Hotel**	THREE DIAMOND	✔	201
3 this page	**Hampton Inn by Hilton Cleveland-Downtown**	THREE DIAMOND	✔	200
4 this page	Comfort Inn Downtown Cleveland	APPROVED		200
5 this page	Drury Plaza Hotel Cleveland Downtown	THREE DIAMOND		200
6 this page	Crowne Plaza Cleveland at Playhouse Square	THREE DIAMOND		200
7 this page	**Hyatt Regency Cleveland at The Arcade**	THREE DIAMOND	✔	201
8 this page	Metropolitan at the 9, Autograph Collection	FOUR DIAMOND	✔	201
9 this page	**Holiday Inn Express-Cleveland Downtown**	THREE DIAMOND	✔	200
10 this page	**Kimpton Schofield Hotel**	THREE DIAMOND	✔	201

DOWNTOWN CLEVELAND (cont'd)

Map Page	Hotels (cont'd)	Designation	Member Savings	Page
⑪ p. 192	**Cleveland Marriott Downtown at Key Tower**	THREE DIAMOND	✔	200
⑫ p. 192	Residence Inn by Marriott Cleveland Downtown	THREE DIAMOND	✔	201
⑬ p. 192	**Renaissance Cleveland Hotel**	THREE DIAMOND	✔	201
⑭ p. 192	Hilton Garden Inn Cleveland Downtown	THREE DIAMOND	✔	200
⑮ p. 192	The Ritz-Carlton, Cleveland	FOUR DIAMOND	✔	201

Map Page	Restaurants	Designation	Cuisine	Price Range	Page
① p. 192	Li Wah	APPROVED	Chinese Dim Sum	$8-$37	201
② p. 192	Urban Farmer	THREE DIAMOND	Steak	$14-$72	202
③ p. 192	1890 at The Arcade	APPROVED	American	$11-$30	201
④ p. 192	Adega	THREE DIAMOND	Mediterranean	$12-$47	201
⑤ p. 192	A Bar and Kitchen	APPROVED	American	$8-$19	201
⑥ p. 192	Pickwick & Frolic	APPROVED	American	$8-$39	201
⑦ p. 192	Greenhouse Tavern	APPROVED	Natural/Organic	$15-$38	201
⑧ p. 192	City Tap	APPROVED	Burgers Wings	$9-$11	201
⑨ p. 192	Society Lounge	THREE DIAMOND	Small Plates	$8-$18	202
⑩ p. 192	Lola	FOUR DIAMOND	American	$12-$41	201
⑪ p. 192	Red, The Steakhouse	THREE DIAMOND	Steak	$14-$85	202
⑫ p. 192	Blue Point Grille	THREE DIAMOND	Seafood	$10-$75	201
⑬ p. 192	Chinato	THREE DIAMOND	Italian	$11-$30	201
⑭ p. 192	Johnny's Downtown	THREE DIAMOND	Northern Italian	$15-$45	201
⑮ p. 192	Hyde Park Prime Steakhouse	THREE DIAMOND	Steak	$12-$45	201

Cleveland and Vicinity
Hotels & Restaurants

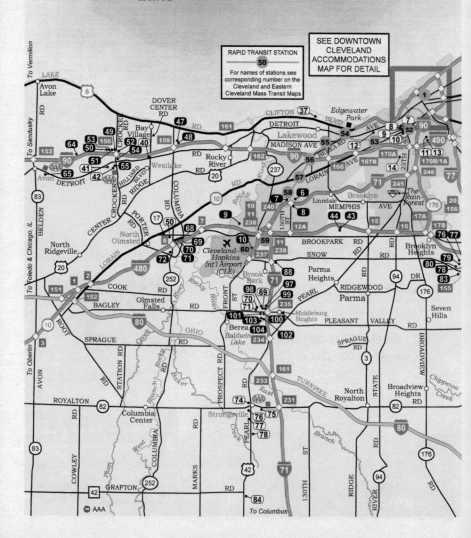

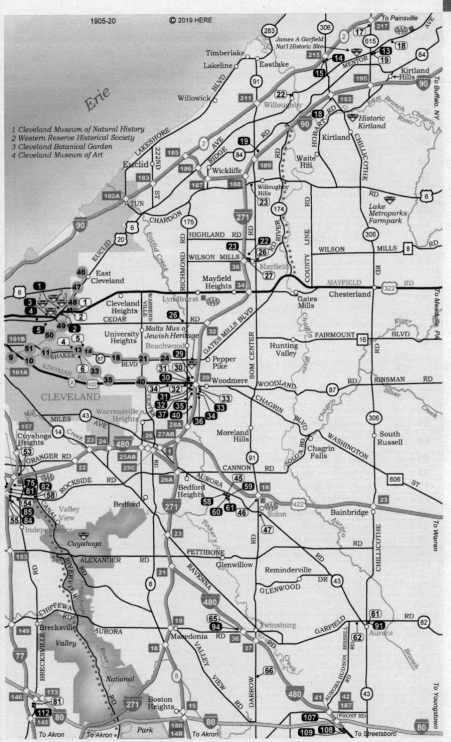

1 Cleveland Museum of Natural History
2 Western Reserve Historical Society
3 Cleveland Botanical Garden
4 Cleveland Museum of Art

✈ **Airport Hotels**				
Map Page	**CLEVELAND HOPKINS INTERNATIONAL AIRPORT** (Maximum driving distance from airport: 4.0 mi)	Designation	Member Savings	Page
88 p. 194	**Best Western Airport Inn & Suites Cleveland, 1.8 mi**	APPROVED	✔	145
8 p. 194	**Cleveland Airport Marriott, 3.8 mi**	THREE DIAMOND	✔	202
6 p. 194	Four Points by Sheraton Cleveland Airport, 3.7 mi	THREE DIAMOND	✔	202
9 p. 194	Hilton Garden Inn Cleveland Airport, 2.8 mi	THREE DIAMOND	✔	202
7 p. 194	La Quinta Inn & Suites-Cleveland Airport North, 3.3 mi	APPROVED		202
10 p. 194	**Sheraton Cleveland Airport Hotel, 0.7 mi**	THREE DIAMOND	✔	203
97 p. 194	Comfort Inn-Cleveland Airport, 3.5 mi	APPROVED		275
101 p. 194	Crowne Plaza Cleveland Airport, 4.0 mi	THREE DIAMOND		275
98 p. 194	Hampton Inn & Suites by Hilton, 3.3 mi	APPROVED	✔	275
100 p. 194	**Red Roof Inn Cleveland-Airport Middleburg Heights, 4.0 mi**	APPROVED	✔	275
99 p. 194	**Sonesta ES Suites Cleveland Airport, 3.5 mi**	THREE DIAMOND	✔	276

Cleveland and Vicinity

This index helps you "spot" where hotels and restaurants are located on the corresponding detailed maps. Restaurant price range is a combination of lunch and/or dinner. Turn to the listing page for more information and consult display ads for special promotions.

 For more details, rates and reservations: AAA.com/travelguides/hotels

CLEVELAND

Map Page	Hotels	Designation	Member Savings	Page
1 p. 194	**Glidden House**	THREE DIAMOND	✔	202
2 p. 194	**Courtyard by Marriott University Circle**	THREE DIAMOND	✔	202
3 p. 194	Residence Inn by Marriott Cleveland University Circle/Medical Center	THREE DIAMOND	✔	202
4 p. 194	**Holiday Inn Cleveland Clinic**	THREE DIAMOND	✔	202
5 p. 194	**InterContinental Hotel Cleveland**	FOUR DIAMOND	✔	202
6 p. 194	Four Points by Sheraton Cleveland Airport	THREE DIAMOND	✔	202
7 p. 194	La Quinta Inn & Suites-Cleveland Airport North	APPROVED		202
8 p. 194	**Cleveland Airport Marriott**	THREE DIAMOND	✔	202
9 p. 194	Hilton Garden Inn Cleveland Airport	THREE DIAMOND	✔	202
10 p. 194	**Sheraton Cleveland Airport Hotel**	THREE DIAMOND	✔	203

Map Page	Restaurants	Designation	Cuisine	Price Range	Page
1 p. 194	Guarino's	APPROVED	Italian	$9-$22	203
2 p. 194	Presti's Bakery	APPROVED	Breads/Pastries	$5-$8	203
4 p. 194	Academy Tavern	APPROVED	Comfort Food	$6-$18	203
5 p. 194	Zanzibar Soul Fusion	APPROVED	Soul Food	$14-$22	203
6 p. 194	fire food & drink	THREE DIAMOND	American	$17-$40	203
7 p. 194	Bar Cento	THREE DIAMOND	Continental	$7-$28	203
8 p. 194	Great Lakes Brewing Co.	APPROVED	American	$10-$18	203
9 p. 194	Flying Fig	THREE DIAMOND	Continental	$16-$28	203
10 p. 194	Crop Bistro & Bar	THREE DIAMOND	American	$11-$49	203
11 p. 194	Fahrenheit	THREE DIAMOND	New American	$14-$35	203
12 p. 194	Luxe Kitchen & Lounge	THREE DIAMOND	Mediterranean	$15-$26	203
13 p. 194	Lucky's Cafe	APPROVED	American	$6-$15	203
14 p. 194	Johnny's Bar	THREE DIAMOND	Northern Italian	$19-$47	203

MENTOR

Map Page	Hotels	Designation	Member Savings	Page
13 p. 194	**Best Western Plus Lawnfield Inn & Suites**	💎 THREE DIAMOND	✔	274
14 p. 194	Holiday Inn Cleveland Northeast-Mentor	💎 THREE DIAMOND		274
15 p. 194	Super 8	💎 APPROVED		274

Map Page	Restaurants	Designation	Cuisine	Price Range	Page
17 p. 194	El Rodeo Mexican Restaurant	💎 APPROVED	Mexican	$5-$16	274
18 p. 194	Molinari's	💎 THREE DIAMOND	American	$9-$42	274
19 p. 194	Skye Bistro	💎 THREE DIAMOND	American	$9-$25	274

WILLOUGHBY

Map Page	Hotels	Designation	Member Savings	Page
18 p. 194	**Red Roof Inn Cleveland Mentor-Willoughby**	💎 APPROVED	✔	310
19 p. 194	Courtyard by Marriott	💎 THREE DIAMOND	✔	310

Map Page	Restaurants	Designation	Cuisine	Price Range	Page
22 p. 194	The Wild Goose	💎 APPROVED	American	$6-$14	310
23 p. 194	Firehouse Grille & Pub	💎 APPROVED	American	$9-$17	310

MAYFIELD

Map Page	Hotels	Designation	Member Savings	Page
22 p. 194	Hilton Garden Inn Cleveland East/Mayfield Village	💎 THREE DIAMOND	✔	273
23 p. 194	Holiday Inn Cleveland-Mayfield	💎 THREE DIAMOND		273

Map Page	Restaurants	Designation	Cuisine	Price Range	Page
26 p. 194	Pizza Roma	💎 APPROVED	Pizza	$7-$18	273
27 p. 194	Austin's Smokin' Steakhouse	💎 APPROVED	American	$10-$35	273

LYNDHURST

Map Page	Hotel	Designation	Member Savings	Page
26 p. 194	**Hyatt Place Cleveland/Lyndhurst/Legacy Village**	💎 THREE DIAMOND	✔	267

BEACHWOOD

Map Page	Hotels	Designation	Member Savings	Page
29 p. 194	Homewood Suites by Hilton	💎 THREE DIAMOND	✔	141
30 p. 194	Home2 Suites by Hilton	💎 THREE DIAMOND	✔	141
31 p. 194	**Residence Inn by Marriott Cleveland-Beachwood**	💎 THREE DIAMOND	✔	141
32 p. 194	DoubleTree by Hilton Hotel-Cleveland East/Beachwood	💎 THREE DIAMOND	✔	141
33 p. 194	Courtyard by Marriott Cleveland Beachwood	💎 THREE DIAMOND	✔	141
34 p. 194	**Fairfield Inn & Suites by Marriott**	💎 APPROVED	✔	141
35 p. 194	**Embassy Suites by Hilton Cleveland - Beachwood**	💎 THREE DIAMOND	✔	141
36 p. 194	Hampton Inn & Suites by Hilton Cleveland-Beachwood	💎 THREE DIAMOND	✔	141
37 p. 194	Aloft Cleveland Beachwood	💎 THREE DIAMOND	✔	141

Map Page	Restaurants	Designation	Cuisine	Price Range	Page
30 p. 194	Moxie The Restaurant	💎 THREE DIAMOND	American	$12-$29	141
31 p. 194	Red, The Steakhouse	💎 THREE DIAMOND	Steak	$29-$48	141
32 p. 194	**Ristorante Giovanni's**	💎 THREE DIAMOND	Northern Italian	$15-$70	141
33 p. 194	Choolaah Indian BBQ	💎 APPROVED	Indian	$7-$11	141
34 p. 194	Shuhei	💎 THREE DIAMOND	Japanese Sushi	$7-$30	141

WARRENSVILLE HEIGHTS

Map Page	Hotel	Designation	Member Savings	Page
40 p. 194	Cleveland Marriott East	💎 THREE DIAMOND	✔	306

BROOKLYN

Map Page	Hotels	Designation	Member Savings	Page
43 p. 194	Extended Stay America Cleveland-Brooklyn	💎 APPROVED		145

BROOKLYN (cont'd)

Map Page	Hotels (cont'd)	Designation	Member Savings	Page
44 p. 194	**Hampton Inn-Cleveland Airport/Tiedeman Rd**	◈ THREE DIAMOND	✔	145

WESTLAKE

Map Page	Hotels	Designation	Member Savings	Page
47 p. 194	TownePlace Suites by Marriott Cleveland Westlake	◈ THREE DIAMOND	✔	309
48 p. 194	Courtyard by Marriott Cleveland Westlake	◈ THREE DIAMOND	✔	309
49 p. 194	DoubleTree by Hilton Cleveland/Westlake	◈ THREE DIAMOND	✔	309
50 p. 194	Holiday Inn Express & Suites Westlake	◈ THREE DIAMOND		309
51 p. 194	Sonesta ES Suites Cleveland Westlake	◈ APPROVED		309
52 p. 194	**Red Roof Inn Cleveland-Westlake**	◈ APPROVED	✔	309
53 p. 194	Extended Stay America Cleveland-Westlake	◈ APPROVED		309
54 p. 194	Hampton Inn By Hilton Cleveland-Westlake	◈ APPROVED	✔	309
55 p. 194	**Hyatt Place Cleveland Westlake Crocker Park**	◈ THREE DIAMOND	✔	309

Map Page	Restaurants	Designation	Cuisine	Price Range	Page
40 p. 194	Sangria Tapas & Bar	◈ THREE DIAMOND	Spanish Small Plates	$9-$45	309
41 p. 194	Cabin Club	◈ THREE DIAMOND	Steak Seafood	$15-$49	309
42 p. 194	Burntwood Tavern	◈ APPROVED	American	$12-$22	309

SOLON

Map Page	Hotels	Designation	Member Savings	Page
58 p. 194	SpringHill Suites by Marriott Cleveland Solon	◈ THREE DIAMOND	✔	293
59 p. 194	Hampton Inn by Hilton	◈ THREE DIAMOND	✔	293
60 p. 194	TownePlace Suites by Marriott Cleveland-Solon	◈ THREE DIAMOND	✔	293
61 p. 194	Homewood Suites by Hilton Cleveland-Solon	◈ THREE DIAMOND	✔	293

Map Page	Restaurants	Designation	Cuisine	Price Range	Page
45 p. 194	Señorita Bonitas	◈ APPROVED	Mexican	$6-$15	293
46 p. 194	Rose Italian Kitchen	◈ APPROVED	Italian	$12-$24	293
47 p. 194	Chicago Deli & Grill	◈ APPROVED	American	$6-$17	293

AVON

Map Page	Hotels	Designation	Member Savings	Page
64 p. 194	Residence Inn by Marriott Cleveland/Avon at the Emerald Event Center	◈ THREE DIAMOND	✔	139
65 p. 194	Cambria Hotel & Suites Cleveland/Avon	◈ THREE DIAMOND		139

NORTH OLMSTED

Map Page	Hotels	Designation	Member Savings	Page
68 p. 194	Hampton Inn North Olmstead Cleveland Airport	◈ THREE DIAMOND	✔	281
69 p. 194	Candlewood Suites Cleveland/North Olmsted	◈ THREE DIAMOND		280
70 p. 194	Extended Stay America-North Olmsted	◈ APPROVED		281
71 p. 194	Courtyard by Marriott-Airport North	◈ THREE DIAMOND	✔	280
72 p. 194	**Aloft Cleveland Airport**	◈ THREE DIAMOND	✔	280

Map Page	Restaurant	Designation	Cuisine	Price Range	Page
50 p. 194	The Rail	◈ APPROVED	Burgers	$7-$12	281

INDEPENDENCE

Map Page	Hotels	Designation	Member Savings	Page
75 p. 194	**Embassy Suites by Hilton Hotel/Cleveland-Rockside**	◈ THREE DIAMOND	✔	260
76 p. 194	Courtyard by Marriott	◈ THREE DIAMOND		260
77 p. 194	**Hyatt Place Cleveland/Independence**	◈ THREE DIAMOND	✔	261
78 p. 194	Hampton Inn & Suites by Hilton	◈ THREE DIAMOND	✔	260
79 p. 194	**Residence Inn by Marriott Cleveland Independence**	◈ THREE DIAMOND	✔	261
80 p. 194	**Home2 Suites by Hilton Independence**	◈ THREE DIAMOND	✔	261

INDEPENDENCE (cont'd)

Map Page	Hotels (cont'd)	Designation	Member Savings	Page
81 p. 194	SpringHill Suites by Marriott Cleveland Independence	THREE DIAMOND	✔	261
82 p. 194	Holiday Inn-Independence/Cleveland South	THREE DIAMOND		260
83 p. 194	Crowne Plaza Cleveland South Independence	THREE DIAMOND		260
84 p. 194	DoubleTree by Hilton Hotel Cleveland-Independence	THREE DIAMOND	✔	260
85 p. 194	Comfort Inn	APPROVED		260

Map Page	Restaurants	Designation	Cuisine	Price Range	Page
53 p. 194	Harry's Steakhouse	APPROVED	Steak	$14-$35	261
54 p. 194	Slyman's Tavern	APPROVED	Sandwiches	$4-$17	261
55 p. 194	Delmonico's	THREE DIAMOND	Steak	$12-$55	261

BROOK PARK

Map Page	Hotel	Designation	Member Savings	Page
88 p. 194	**Best Western Airport Inn & Suites Cleveland**	APPROVED	✔	145

AURORA

Map Page	Hotel	Designation	Member Savings	Page
91 p. 194	Aurora Inn Hotel and Event Center	THREE DIAMOND		139

Map Page	Restaurants	Designation	Cuisine	Price Range	Page
61 p. 194	The Cutting Board	APPROVED	American	$8-$33	139
62 p. 194	Cafe Toscano	APPROVED	Italian	$9-$40	139

TWINSBURG

Map Page	Hotel	Designation	Member Savings	Page
94 p. 194	Hilton Garden Inn Cleveland/Twinsburg	THREE DIAMOND	✔	304

Map Page	Restaurants	Designation	Cuisine	Price Range	Page
65 p. 194	**Blue Canyon Kitchen & Tavern**	THREE DIAMOND	American	$13-$33	304
66 p. 194	D'Angelo's	THREE DIAMOND	Italian	$10-$25	304

MIDDLEBURG HEIGHTS

Map Page	Hotels	Designation	Member Savings	Page
97 p. 194	Comfort Inn-Cleveland Airport	APPROVED		275
98 p. 194	Hampton Inn & Suites by Hilton	APPROVED	✔	275
99 p. 194	**Sonesta ES Suites Cleveland Airport**	THREE DIAMOND	✔	276
100 p. 194	**Red Roof Inn Cleveland-Airport Middleburg Heights**	APPROVED	✔	275
101 p. 194	Crowne Plaza Cleveland Airport	THREE DIAMOND		275
102 p. 194	TownePlace Suites by Marriott Cleveland Airport	APPROVED	✔	276
103 p. 194	Courtyard by Marriott Cleveland Airport South	THREE DIAMOND	✔	275
104 p. 194	Home2 Suites by Hilton	THREE DIAMOND	✔	275

Map Page	Restaurants	Designation	Cuisine	Price Range	Page
69 p. 194	Blue Jade Restaurant	APPROVED	Asian	$6-$17	276
70 p. 194	Two Bucks Food & Spirit	APPROVED	American	$6-$10	276
71 p. 194	Brew Garden	APPROVED	American	$10-$17	276

STREETSBORO

Map Page	Hotels	Designation	Member Savings	Page
107 p. 194	Fairfield Inn & Suites by Marriott	APPROVED	✔	296
108 p. 194	TownePlace Suites by Marriott	APPROVED	✔	296
109 p. 194	Hampton Inn & Suites by Hilton	THREE DIAMOND	✔	296

RICHFIELD

Map Page	Hotel	Designation	Member Savings	Page
112 p. 194	**Hampton Inn by Hilton**	THREE DIAMOND	✔	288

Map Page	Restaurant	Designation	Cuisine	Price Range	Page
⟨81⟩ p. 194	Cozumel Restaurant and Cantina	◈ APPROVED	Mexican	$7-$18	288

LAKEWOOD

Map Page	Restaurant	Designation	Cuisine	Price Range	Page
⟨37⟩ p. 194	Pier W	◈ THREE DIAMOND	Seafood	$13-$46	263

VALLEY VIEW

Map Page	Restaurant	Designation	Cuisine	Price Range	Page
⟨58⟩ p. 194	Lockkeepers	◈ THREE DIAMOND	Italian	$15-$45	304

STRONGSVILLE

Map Page	Restaurants	Designation	Cuisine	Price Range	Page
⟨74⟩ p. 194	Don's Pomeroy House	◈ THREE DIAMOND	American	$14-$40	296
⟨75⟩ p. 194	The Rail	◈ APPROVED	Burgers	$7-$13	296
⟨76⟩ p. 194	La Kabob Lebanese Grill	◈ APPROVED	Lebanese	$6-$9	296
⟨77⟩ p. 194	Sakura Sushi House	◈ APPROVED	Japanese	$6-$24	296
⟨78⟩ p. 194	Italian Village	◈ APPROVED	Italian	$8-$24	296

BRUNSWICK

Map Page	Restaurant	Designation	Cuisine	Price Range	Page
⟨84⟩ p. 194	Cozumel	◈ APPROVED	Mexican	$7-$18	145

DOWNTOWN CLEVELAND
• Hotels & Restaurants map & index p. 192

CLEVELAND MARRIOTT DOWNTOWN AT KEY TOWER
216/696-9200 ⓫

◈ THREE DIAMOND
Hotel

AAA Benefit: Members save 5% or more!

Address: 1360 W Mall Dr 44114 **Location:** Northeast corner of Public Square. 🚇 North Coast (E 9th), 2. **Facility:** 400 units. 25 stories, interior corridors. **Parking:** on-site (fee) and valet. **Terms:** check-in 4 pm. **Amenities:** safes. **Dining:** 2 restaurants. **Activities:** health club, spa. **Guest Services:** valet laundry.

COMFORT INN DOWNTOWN CLEVELAND
216/861-0001 ❹

◈ APPROVED Hotel. **Address:** 1800 Euclid Ave 44115

CROWNE PLAZA CLEVELAND AT PLAYHOUSE SQUARE
216/615-7500 ❻

◈ THREE DIAMOND Hotel. **Address:** 1260 Euclid Ave 44115

DOUBLETREE BY HILTON HOTEL CLEVELAND DOWNTOWN-LAKESIDE
216/241-5100 ❶

◈ THREE DIAMOND
Hotel

DOUBLETREE

AAA Benefit: Members save up to 15%!

Address: 1111 Lakeside Ave E 44114 **Location:** Jct E 12th St. 🚇 North Coast (E 9th), 2. **Facility:** 379 units. 18 stories, interior corridors. **Parking:** on-site (fee). **Amenities:** safes. **Pool:** heated indoor. **Activities:** hot tub, exercise room. **Guest Services:** valet and coin laundry, area transportation.

DRURY PLAZA HOTEL CLEVELAND DOWNTOWN
216/357-3100 ❺

◈ THREE DIAMOND Historic Hotel. **Address:** 1380 E 6th St 44114

HAMPTON INN BY HILTON CLEVELAND-DOWNTOWN
216/241-6600 ❸

◈ THREE DIAMOND
Hotel

Hampton

AAA Benefit: Members save up to 15%!

Address: 1460 E 9th St 44114 **Location:** Jct Superior Ave. 🚇 North Coast (E 9th), 2. **Facility:** 194 units. 14 stories, interior corridors. **Parking:** valet only. **Activities:** exercise room. **Guest Services:** valet laundry. **Featured Amenity:** full hot breakfast.

HILTON GARDEN INN CLEVELAND DOWNTOWN
216/658-6400 ⓮

◈ THREE DIAMOND ⟨SAVE⟩ Hotel. **Address:** 1100 Carnegie Ave 44115

AAA Benefit: Members save up to 15%!

HOLIDAY INN EXPRESS-CLEVELAND DOWNTOWN
216/443-1000 ❾

◈ THREE DIAMOND
Historic Hotel

Address: 629 Euclid Ave 44114 **Location:** Jct E 9th St. 🚇 North Coast (E 9th), 2. **Facility:** Housed in an 1895 bank and office building, this hotel features spacious guest rooms with unusual features, like vintage hardwood floors and high ceilings, coupled with modern décor and amenities. 141 units. 16 stories, interior corridors. **Parking:** valet only. **Activities:** game room, exercise room. **Guest Services:** valet laundry.

(See map & index p. 192.)

HYATT REGENCY CLEVELAND AT THE ARCADE
216/575-1234 **7**

 THREE DIAMOND

Historic Hotel

HYATT REGENCY

AAA Benefit: Members save up to 10%!

Address: 420 Superior Ave E 44114 **Location:** Just e of Public Square. North Coast (E 9th), 2. **Facility:** Built in 1890, this hotel's four-story atrium is a Victorian marvel of architecture, with scrolling iron railings, mosaic tile floors and a massive glass ceiling. 293 units. 9 stories, interior corridors. **Parking:** valet only. **Amenities:** safes. **Dining:** 1890 at The Arcade, see separate listing. **Activities:** exercise room, spa. **Guest Services:** valet laundry.

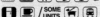

KIMPTON SCHOFIELD HOTEL
216/357-3250 **10**

THREE DIAMOND

Boutique Contemporary Hotel

Address: 2000 E 9th St 44115 **Location:** Jct Euclid Ave. North Coast (E 9th), 2. **Facility:** This beautifully restored, 1902 landmark building features whimsical artwork and clever designs. 122 units, some three bedrooms. 7 stories, interior corridors. **Parking:** valet only. **Amenities:** safes. **Activities:** bicycles, exercise room. **Guest Services:** valet laundry.

METROPOLITAN AT THE 9, AUTOGRAPH COLLECTION
216/239-1200 **8**

FOUR DIAMOND Boutique Contemporary Hotel. **Address:** 2017 E 9th St 44115

AAA Benefit: Members save 5% or more!

RENAISSANCE CLEVELAND HOTEL
216/696-5600 **13**

THREE DIAMOND

Historic Hotel

R RENAISSANCE HOTELS

AAA Benefit: Members save 5% or more!

Address: 24 Public Square 44113 **Location:** At Superior Ave and W 3rd St. Connected to shopping complex. North Coast (E 9th), 2. **Facility:** Built in 1918, this landmark hotel displays the grandeur of yesteryear in its ornate lobby, which features glamorous crystal chandeliers, a domed ceiling, gold-painted trim and marble accents. 491 units. 15 stories, interior corridors. **Terms:** check-in 4 pm. **Amenities:** safes. **Activities:** exercise room. **Guest Services:** valet laundry, boarding pass kiosk.

RESIDENCE INN BY MARRIOTT CLEVELAND DOWNTOWN
216/443-9043 **12**

THREE DIAMOND Historic Extended Stay Hotel. **Address:** 527 Prospect Ave E 44115

AAA Benefit: Members save 5% or more!

THE RITZ-CARLTON, CLEVELAND
216/623-1300 **15**

FOUR DIAMOND Hotel. **Address:** 1515 W 3rd St 44113

AAA Benefit: Unequaled service at special member savings!

THE WESTIN CLEVELAND DOWNTOWN HOTEL
216/771-7700 **2**

THREE DIAMOND

Hotel

WESTIN HOTELS & RESORTS

AAA Benefit: Members save 5% or more!

Address: 777 St. Clair Ave NE 44114 **Location:** Jct E 6th St. North Coast (E 9th), 2. **Facility:** 484 units. 23 stories, interior corridors. **Parking:** valet only. **Amenities:** safes. **Dining:** Urban Farmer, see separate listing. **Activities:** health club. **Guest Services:** valet laundry.

WHERE TO EAT

1890 AT THE ARCADE 216/776-4576 **3**
APPROVED American. Casual Dining. **Address:** 420 Superior Ave E 44114

A BAR AND KITCHEN 216/644-8954 **5**
APPROVED American. Gastropub. **Address:** 850 Euclid Ave 44114

ADEGA 216/505-9332 **4**
THREE DIAMOND Mediterranean. Fine Dining. **Address:** 2017 E 9th St 44115

BLUE POINT GRILLE 216/875-7827 **12**
THREE DIAMOND Seafood. Fine Dining. **Address:** 700 W St. Clair Ave 44113

CHINATO 216/298-9080 **13**
THREE DIAMOND Italian. Fine Dining. **Address:** 2079 E 4th St 44115

CITY TAP 216/696-2337 **8**
APPROVED Burgers Wings. Quick Serve. **Address:** 748 Prospect Ave E 44115

GREENHOUSE TAVERN 216/443-0511 **7**
APPROVED Natural/Organic. Casual Dining. **Address:** 2038 E 4th St 44115

HYDE PARK PRIME STEAKHOUSE 216/344-2444 **15**
THREE DIAMOND Steak. Fine Dining. **Address:** 123 W Prospect Ave 44115

JOHNNY'S DOWNTOWN 216/623-0055 **14**
THREE DIAMOND Northern Italian. Fine Dining. **Address:** 1406 W 6th St 44113

LI WAH 216/696-6556 **1**
APPROVED Chinese Dim Sum. Casual Dining. **Address:** 2999 Payne Ave 44114

LOLA 216/621-5652 **10**
FOUR DIAMOND American. Fine Dining. **Address:** 2058 E 4th St 44115

PICKWICK & FROLIC 216/241-7425 **6**
APPROVED American. Casual Dining. **Address:** 2035 E 4th St 44115

(See map & index p. 192.)

RED, THE STEAKHOUSE   216/664-0941   ⑪
THREE DIAMOND Steak. Fine Dining. **Address:** 417 Prospect Ave 44115

SOCIETY LOUNGE   216/781-9050   ⑨
THREE DIAMOND Small Plates. Casual Dining. **Address:** 2063 E 4th St 44115

URBAN FARMER   216/771-7707   ②
THREE DIAMOND Steak. Casual Dining. **Address:** 1325 E 6th St 44114

WINKING LIZARD TAVERN   216/589-0313
APPROVED American. Casual Dining. **Address:** 811 Huron Rd 44115

CLEVELAND
• Hotels & Restaurants map & index p. 194

CLEVELAND AIRPORT MARRIOTT   216/252-5333   ⑧
THREE DIAMOND
Hotel

AAA Benefit: Members save 5% or more!

Address: 4277 W 150th St 44135 **Location:** I-71 exit 240, just s. **Facility:** 372 units. 4-9 stories, interior corridors. **Parking:** on-site (fee). **Amenities:** safes. **Pool:** heated indoor. **Activities:** hot tub, exercise room. **Guest Services:** valet and coin laundry, boarding pass kiosk, area transportation.

COURTYARD BY MARRIOTT UNIVERSITY CIRCLE
    216/791-5678   ②
THREE DIAMOND
Hotel

COURTYARD **AAA Benefit:** Members save 5% or more!

Address: 2021 Cornell Rd 44106 **Location:** Jct US 322 (Mayfield Rd), just w on Euclid Ave, then just s. Located in the University Circle area. Cedar-University, 49. **Facility:** 153 units, some cottages. 8 stories, interior corridors. **Parking:** valet only. **Pool:** heated indoor. **Activities:** exercise room. **Guest Services:** valet and coin laundry, area transportation.

FOUR POINTS BY SHERATON CLEVELAND AIRPORT
    216/252-7700   ⑥
THREE DIAMOND SAVE Hotel. **Address:** 4181 W 150th St 44135

AAA Benefit: Members save 5% or more!

GLIDDEN HOUSE   216/231-8900   ①
THREE DIAMOND
Historic Hotel

Address: 1901 Ford Dr 44106 **Location:** Jct US 322 (Mayfield Rd), just e on Euclid Ave, then just n. Located in University Circle. Cedar-University, 49. **Facility:** The lobby, breakfast area and suites of the charming hotel are housed in a historic mansion built in 1910. Additional rooms are located in a modern annex, featuring soft bedding and plush easy chairs. 60 units. 3 stories, interior corridors. **Parking:** on-site (fee). **Terms:** check-in 4 pm, age restrictions may apply. **Guest Services:** valet laundry.
Featured Amenity: breakfast buffet.

HILTON GARDEN INN CLEVELAND AIRPORT
    216/898-1898   ⑨
THREE DIAMOND SAVE Hotel. **Address:** 4900 Emerald Ct SW 44135

AAA Benefit: Members save up to 15%!

HOLIDAY INN CLEVELAND CLINIC   216/707-4200   ④
THREE DIAMOND
Hotel

Address: 8650 Euclid Ave 44106 **Location:** Jct E 86th St. **Facility:** 276 units. 9 stories, interior corridors. **Parking:** valet only. **Amenities:** safes. **Pool:** heated indoor. **Activities:** sauna, exercise room, in-room exercise equipment. **Guest Services:** valet and coin laundry, area transportation.

INTERCONTINENTAL HOTEL CLEVELAND
    216/707-4100   ⑤
FOUR DIAMOND
Hotel

Address: 9801 Carnegie Ave 44106 **Location:** I-90 exit 172C, 2.8 mi e. Adjacent to Cleveland Clinic Main Campus. Cedar-University, 49. **Facility:** Guest rooms are spacious with a sedate, white and taupe décor, comfortable bedding and a large desk; most have oversize windows that let in lots of light. 294 units, some two bedrooms. 15 stories, interior corridors. **Parking:** valet only. **Amenities:** safes. **Dining:** 2 restaurants. **Activities:** sauna, health club, massage. **Guest Services:** valet laundry, area transportation.

LA QUINTA INN & SUITES-CLEVELAND AIRPORT NORTH
    216/251-8500   ⑦
APPROVED Hotel. **Address:** 4222 W 150th St 44135

RESIDENCE INN BY MARRIOTT CLEVELAND UNIVERSITY CIRCLE/MEDICAL CENTER   216/249-9090   ③
THREE DIAMOND SAVE Extended Stay Hotel. **Address:** 1914 E 101st St 44106

AAA Benefit: Members save 5% or more!

(See map & index p. 194.)

SHERATON CLEVELAND AIRPORT HOTEL
216/267-1500 **10**

THREE DIAMOND
Hotel

SHERATON

AAA Benefit: Members save 5% or more!

Address: 5300 Riverside Dr 44135 **Location:** I-71 exit 237, just s of I-480 on SR 237, follow signs. Located on airport grounds. **Facility:** 243 units. 9 stories, interior corridors. **Parking:** on-site (fee). **Pool:** heated indoor. **Activities:** hot tub, exercise room. **Guest Services:** valet laundry, boarding pass kiosk, area transportation.

SAVE 🚶 🍽 🛗 🍸 CALL ♿ 🏊 ✚ BIZ 📶 ✕ 🖨

WHERE TO EAT

ACADEMY TAVERN 216/229-1171 **4**
APPROVED Comfort Food. Casual Dining. **Address:** 12800 Larchmere Blvd 44120

BAR CENTO 216/274-1010 **7**
THREE DIAMOND Continental. Casual Dining. **Address:** 1948 25th St 44113

CROP BISTRO & BAR 216/696-2767 **10**
THREE DIAMOND American. Casual Dining. **Address:** 2537 Lorain Ave 44113

FAHRENHEIT 216/781-8858 **11**
THREE DIAMOND New American. Casual Dining. **Address:** 2417 Professor Ave 44113

FIRE FOOD & DRINK 216/921-3473 **6**
THREE DIAMOND American. Casual Dining. **Address:** 13220 Shaker Square 44120

FLYING FIG 216/241-4243 **9**
THREE DIAMOND Continental. Casual Dining. **Address:** 2523 Market St 44113

GREAT LAKES BREWING CO. 216/771-4404 **8**
APPROVED American. Gastropub. **Address:** 2516 Market Ave 44113

GUARINO'S 216/231-3100 **1**
APPROVED Italian. Casual Dining. **Address:** 12309 Mayfield Rd 44106

JOHNNY'S BAR 216/281-0055 **14**
THREE DIAMOND Northern Italian. Fine Dining. **Address:** 3164 Fulton Rd 44109

LUCKY'S CAFE 216/622-7773 **13**
APPROVED American. Casual Dining. **Address:** 777 Starkweather Ave 44113

LUXE KITCHEN & LOUNGE 216/920-0600 **12**
THREE DIAMOND Mediterranean. Casual Dining. **Address:** 6605 Detroit Ave 44102

PRESTI'S BAKERY 216/421-3060 **2**
APPROVED Breads/Pastries. Quick Serve. **Address:** 12101 Mayfield Rd 44106

YOURS TRULY RESTAURANT 216/751-8646
APPROVED American. Casual Dining. **Address:** 13228 Shaker Square 44120

ZANZIBAR SOUL FUSION 216/752-1035 **5**
APPROVED Soul Food. Casual Dining. **Address:** 13225 Shaker Square 44120

COLUMBIANA pop. 6,384

BEST WESTERN PLUS DUTCH HAUS INN AND SUITES
330/482-5050

THREE DIAMOND
Hotel

Best Western PLUS

AAA Benefit: Members save up to 15% and earn bonus points!

Address: 150 E SR 14 44408 **Location:** Jct SR 14 and 164, just e. **Facility:** 52 units, some efficiencies. 3 stories, interior corridors. **Pool:** heated indoor. **Activities:** hot tub, exercise room. **Guest Services:** valet and coin laundry. **Featured Amenity:** breakfast buffet.

SAVE 🍽 CALL ♿ 🚶 ✚ BIZ 📶 ✕ 🖨 / SOME UNITS

Columbus

Then & Now

Author James Thurber said of his birthplace, "Columbus is a town in which almost anything is likely to happen and in which almost everything has."

Yet Columbus is a city that almost wasn't. When Ohio gained statehood in 1803, it hadn't yet chosen a permanent capital. Political maneuvering almost landed the state government in Zanesville and Chillicothe. In 1812, however, the residents of Franklinton, a county seat in the heart of Ohio along the Scioto River, tempted the state with 1,200 acres of land and a commitment to spend $50,000 to construct a capitol building and a penitentiary. Within a matter of days the general assembly accepted the offer, and Columbus was born on the opposite bank of the river.

The Civil War initiated a wave of unprecedented growth; the population soared and manufacturing and government became the city's primary industries.

The opening in 1873 of Ohio Agriculture and Mechanical College, later renamed The Ohio State University, spawned a new outlook for the city. Education was thrust to the forefront, and the intellectual atmosphere helped contribute to the forerunner of the computer, the development of the xerography process and numerous advancements in the medical treatment of the physically impaired.

AAA.com/travelguides—
more ways to look, book and save

Today the phrase "state of the art" is synonymous with Columbus, which ranks with Silicon Valley as a center for scientific and technological information. Ohio's capital built its solid reputation over several decades; it was one of the first cities in the country to offer citywide cable television and introduced such technology as the 24-hour banking machine, interactive cable television and the electronic newspaper. Thousands of high-tech companies, including Battelle Memorial Institute, Mettler-Toledo International and Vertiv, now call Columbus home.

Besides its well-deserved reputation in the high-tech world, the city houses the headquarters of several Fortune 1000 companies, including Aflac, Big Lots, Express, L Brands and Nationwide Insurance. Columbus also is known for retail banking, insurance and real estate, and has emerged as a leading convention city.

Modern-day Columbus continually earns top accolades from highly regarded sources. In 2013 Forbes magazine ranked Columbus as a Top Place for Business and in 2011 as one of the Top 15 Most Affordable Cities to Live;

Columbus skyline

(Continued on p. 206.)

Destination Columbus

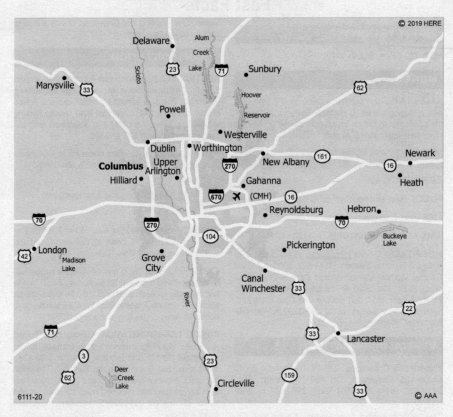

© 2019 HERE

6111-20

© AAA

This map shows cities in the Columbus vicinity where you will find attractions, hotels and restaurants. Cities are listed alphabetically in this book on the following pages.

Fast Facts

ABOUT THE CITY

POP: 787,033 ▪ **ELEV:** 777 ft.

MONEY

SALES TAX: Columbus has a sales tax of 7.5 percent and a lodging tax of 10 percent. There is an 11 percent concession fee on rental cars picked up at Port Columbus International Airport.

WHOM TO CALL

EMERGENCY: 911

POLICE (non-emergency): (614) 645-4545

FIRE (non-emergency): (614) 221-3132

TIME AND TEMPERATURE: (614) 281-8211

HOSPITALS: Doctors Hospital, (614) 544-1000 ▪ Grant Medical Center, (614) 566-9000 ▪ Mount Carmel Medical Center (Mount Carmel West Hospital), (614) 234-5000 ▪ The Ohio State University Hospital East, (614) 257-3000 ▪ The Ohio State University Medical Center, (614) 293-8300 ▪ Riverside Methodist Hospital, (614) 566-5000.

VISITOR INFORMATION

Experience Columbus: 277 W. Nationwide Blvd., Suite 125, Columbus, OH 43215. **Phone:** (614) 221-6623, (614) 221-2489, (866) 397-2657 or (800) 354-2657.

The Nationwide Blvd. headquarters is open Mon.-Fri. 8-5. A walk-in visitor information office also is in Easton Town Center, off I-270 exit 33. The walk-in center is open Mon.-Sat. 10-9, Sun. noon-6; closed Easter, Thanksgiving and Christmas. Phone ahead to confirm schedule.

TRANSPORTATION

AIR TRAVEL: Port Columbus International Airport (CMH), 7 miles east of downtown inside the beltway off Stelzer Road, is served by major carriers. A free shuttle bus runs to the terminal from remote parking areas. Taxi service is offered to downtown, with average fares between $25 and $28.

RENTAL CARS: Hertz offers discounts to AAA members; phone (614) 239-1084 or (800) 654-3080.

 Book and save at **AAA.com/hertz**

BUSES: Greyhound Lines Inc., (614) 228-2266 or (800) 231-2222, 111 E. Town St. between S. 3rd and S. 4th streets, serves Columbus.

TAXIS: Yellow Cab, (614) 444-4444, is the largest cab company. Fixed fares are $3 base rate, $4.50 for the first mile, 45c for each additional 2/9 mile and $2.25 for each mile outside Franklin County. A $3 surcharge is added for fares originating at the airport.

PUBLIC TRANSPORTATION: Central Ohio Transit Authority (COTA) provides bus transportation throughout the city and suburbs Mon.-Fri. 5:30 a.m.- 11:45 p.m., Sat. 6 a.m.-10 p.m., Sun. 8-7. The basic fare is $2, express fare is $2.75 and transfers are free. Multiday passes and reduced rates for children and senior citizens are available. Passengers must have exact change.

For details about routes and timetables, contact the COTA Pass Sales Office, 33 N. High St.; phone (614) 228-1776.

(Continued from p. 204.)
CIO Magazine named it one of the Top 7 Cities for Finding IT Jobs; and Bloomberg Businessweek awarded it the title of Economically Strongest Metro.

The state of the city's visual arts deserves equally high praise. Ohio's capital offers an assortment of art-centered attractions, including the Billy Ireland Cartoon Library & Museum and the Columbus Museum of Art. The Franklin Park Conservatory and Botanical Gardens cleverly displays thousands of otherworldly glass pieces by artist Dale Chihuly in artfully presented gardens. And the Topiary Park in Old Deaf School Park interprets the 1884 oil painting "A Sunday Afternoon on the Island of La Grande Jatte" by Georges Seurat with larger-than-life topiary bushes snipped into the shapes of Parisians at leisure near the Seine River.

In addition, colorful murals clothe many of the city's brick walls. A majority of these are in the thriving SoHo-like Short North Arts District, a once-blighted area now filled with independently owned boutiques, many local places to eat and pubs that owes its present-day popularity to citywide revitalization projects begun in the 1980s.

The same efforts resulted in the urban renewal of downtown's Arena District, transformed from its former neglected state to an area brimming with restaurants, shops and nightspots as well as Nationwide Arena, home to the NHL's Columbus Blue Jackets.

The city's proud residents have lovingly preserved a host of 19th-century homes in Victorian Village and German Village. More examples of Columbus's exquisite architecture include the Greek Revival Ohio Statehouse along with an array of churches, office buildings and homes in Art Deco, Gothic, Italianate and Queen Anne styles.

Must Do: AAA Editor's Picks

- Hear the Victory Bell ring at a football game at The Ohio State University. Weighing 2,420 pounds, the bell sounds at **Ohio Stadium** (411 Woody Hayes Dr.) after every Buckeye win. Get into the spirit of things by donning scarlet and gray, OSU's official school colors.

- Visit the "Umbrella Girl" in **German Village** (588 S. 3rd St.), one of the city's oldest neighborhoods. In the 1950s, this bronze statue mysteriously disappeared from Schiller Park. The village dedicated a new version of the young girl, garbed in traditional Bavarian dress and carrying an umbrella, in 1996.

- Taste such Mediterranean staples as tabbouleh and baklava, inhale pungent spices, bite into a juicy locally-grown tomato and snap up some snapdragons at the **North Market** (59 Spruce St.), one of the area's best places to eat. This public farmers market on Spruce Street is the last of its kind in central Ohio.

- Take a tour of a tropical rain forest, the Himalayan Mountains or an arid desert at ▽ **Franklin Park Conservatory and Botanical Gardens** (1777 E. Broad St.), which also features the Palm House, a 12,500-square-foot glass structure built in the style of the Glass Palace at Chicago's World Fair and Columbian Exposition in 1893.

- While in German Village, get some sweets for you and your sweetie pie at **Pistacia Vera** (541 S. Third St.), where glass cases are filled with delicate creations like melt-in-your-mouth macarons and cookies, tantalizing tarts and tortes, and buttery croissants and brioche.

- Lift a car all by yourself at ▽ **COSI Columbus** (333 W. Broad St.), a science center boasting a mix of education and fun. At COSI's outdoor Big Science Park, the Big Giant Lever exhibit lets you raise a 2,437-pound automobile. Or ride a unicycle on a tightrope several stories high in the center's atrium – yes, you *can* do it!

- Coo at koalas at the ▽ **Columbus Zoo and Aquarium** (4850 W. Powell Rd.), one of the few U.S. zoos permanently housing the marsupials. Like the kangaroo, the koala carries its newborn, which is only about the size of a jelly bean, in a pouch. You can also go on a walkabout with gallivanting kangaroos, ogle polar bears swimming in icy waters and giggle at manatees and penguins cavorting in the aquarium.

- Watch a newsreel from the 1920s while exploring the 271,000-square-foot ▽ **Ohio History Center** (800 E. 17th Ave.). The expansive collection includes animal and plant specimens (including the extinct ivory-billed woodpecker), prehistoric Native American art, Civil War artifacts and classic cars. A gigantic mastodon skeleton greets visitors at the entrance.

- Unearth a few gems in the **Short North Arts District.** This urban neighborhood on North High Street embraces an eclectic array of art galleries, restaurants, antique shops, coffee bars and hip boutiques selling everything from Indonesian baskets and Native American jewelry to vintage clothing and designer fashions.

    - Dip a spoon into a cup of **Graeter's Ice Cream** (2555 Bethel Rd.). Heralded as the best ice cream around, the creamy dessert is a lasting tradition in the Midwest. Try Graeter's best seller, Black Raspberry Chip, or Oprah Winfrey's personal favorite, Butter Pecan. Another sweet favorite is **Jeni's Splendid Ice Creams** (714 N. High St.). Flavors include salty caramel and Riesling poached pear sorbet as well as such seasonal offerings as sweet corn and black raspberries.

    - Pose among the figures sculpted from shrubbery at **The Topiary Park** (480 E. Town St.) in Old Deaf School Park; it's one of many fun things to do with friends in Columbus. You'll feel like you're actually inside the painting "A Sunday Afternoon on the Island of La Grande Jatte" by post-impressionist artist Georges Seurat. The park's beautiful landscaping lends itself nicely to a relaxing picnic and some Frisbee-tossing.

Franklin Park Conservatory and Botanical Gardens

Columbus 1-day Itinerary

AAA editors suggest these activities for a great short vacation experience. Those staying in the area for a longer visit can access a 3-day itinerary at AAA.com/TravelGuides.

Morning

- One of the country's top-rated zoos, **Columbus Zoo and Aquarium** (4850 W. Powell Rd.), in nearby Powell is a must-see. It's preferable to spend a day here, but even a few hours will give you a good sampling of the zoo's top exhibits. Arrive early as there's a lot to see. If time only allows an abbreviated tour, don't miss the kangaroos; dozens of these bouncy marsupials hop about freely on the grass or lounge under trees in a fenced-in area. A roped-off path is all that separates you from the roos. Be sure to also see the polar bear and the koala; for the rest of your tour, choose your favorites from a cornucopia of wild beasts, birds, and reptiles, including moose, gorillas, bison, a variety of wild cats, African lions, Asian elephants, Arctic foxes, sharks, manatees, penguins and flamingos.

Afternoon

- Head back to the Short North Arts District for lunch and stimulate your taste buds with Asian fusion dishes at **Lemongrass Fusion Bistro** (641 N High St.) (think sushi, lemongrass soup and pad thai).

- While away the afternoon with a stroll on **North High Street.** Wander in and out of independently owned shops in this bohemian district; you'll find merchandise ranging from affordable antiques to trendy and expensive designer denim.

- The **North Market** (59 Spruce St.) is a mostly-indoor farmers market that will delight foodies. Marked by a huge neon sign, the bustling market holds local vendors hawking everything from farm-fresh produce to spices to bakery treats.

- If time allows, drive over to **German Village** (588 S. 3rd St.) for a little taste of old Europe. The charming brick homes and shops complete with flower-filled window boxes are a visual treat; just watch your step as you tread along the village's equally charming yet uneven cobblestone sidewalks. Stop in at **Juergens German Bakery & Restaurant** (525 S. 4th St.) for some freshly baked apple strudel or pumpernickel bread, and wend your way through 32 rooms at block-long **The Book Loft** (631 S. 3rd St.), a literature-lover's delight.

Evening

- Time for dinner? **Martini Modern Italian** (445 N. High St.) wins points for its ambience alone, with red and white modern décor, white leather chairs and massive sparkling chandeliers, but its menu earns it a gold star. Albeit pricey, the restaurant offers a palate-pleasing range of pasta, chicken veal and seafood entrées as well as martinis in offbeat flavors.

Columbus Zoo and Aquarium

- If you're near the German Village, try **Schmidt's Restaurant und Sausage Haus** (240 E. Kossuth St.), with German favorites like Wiener schnitzel, bratwurst, potato pancakes and Schmidt's signature jumbo cream puffs. On weekends, the high-energy oompah duo Squeezin' n' Wheezin' performs.

- For a more casual evening, grab a brew and a hot dog while cheering on the National Hockey League's Columbus Blue Jackets at **Nationwide Arena** (200 W. Nationwide Blvd.). If minor league baseball is your thing, watch the Columbus Clippers, Triple-A National Champions in 2010 and 2011, play at **Huntington Park Stadium** (330 Huntington Park Ln.).

- Time for dessert? If you've supped at one of the fine restaurants of the Short North, walk off your recently consumed calories and make room for the frozen treats at **Jeni's Splendid Ice Creams** (714 N. High St.). It's open till 11 p.m. daily, and the menu features such out-of-the-ordinary flavors like wildberry lavender, beet cake with black walnuts, and coriander raspberry.

- For the incurable chocoholic, stop in at **Le Chocoholique** (601 N. High St.) open until 10 or 11 on most nights. A bakery case holds a massive collection of exquisitely decorated chocolates that look like miniature works of art. The flavors are equally artful and include Velvet Elvis (peanut butter, banana and bacon-flavored), chipotle cherry and limoncello espresso. Or have a Picasso-esque slice of cake with a cappuccino; it's all served by chic, well-mannered college girls. Take a window seat to watch the locals stroll by.

Top Picks for Kids

Under 13

- View more than 10,000 animals, from beasts that roam the African savanna to animals that traverse the Arctic plains, at the **Columbus Zoo and Aquarium** (4850 Powell Rd.) in nearby Powell, one of many fun things to do with kids here. Have a close encounter with land and sea animals by enjoying animal rides, shows and a tide pool touch tank.

- If the kids are craving a cold treat, take them to **Jeni's Splendid Ice Creams** (714 N. High St.) at the **North Market** (59 Spruce St.). While you browse for fresh-picked produce, they can choose from a variety of flavors that change with the seasons. Local bakers, butchers, chocolatiers, farmers, fishmongers and florists sell their wares at the indoor market Tues.-Sat. 9-7 and Sun.-Mon. 10-5.

- Even if your little ones aren't familiar with Georges Seurat's pointillism masterpiece "A Sunday Afternoon on the Island of La Grande Jatte" that inspired **The Topiary Park** (480 E. Town St.), they will certainly think the many topiaries representing the figures from the painting are pretty cool. Ducks—always popular with kids—hang out by the water. This a great picnic locale.

- At the **Ohio State Fair**, held from late July through early August at **Ohio Expo Center** (717 E. 17th Ave.), kids will be amazed after touching exotic animals at the free petting zoo and riding with their parents on Kiddieland rides. See agriculture and creative arts exhibits, witness livestock competitions, ride a few of the more than 70 thrilling midway rides and work up an appetite for some of the hundreds of fair foods, including 30 types of food on a stick.

Teens

- Teens will be thrilled zipping around town on a Segway tour while learning about many of the city's popular sites. Guides at **SegAway Tours of Columbus** (400 N. High St.) provide instructional/practice sessions before leading a guided tour.

- **Easton Town Center** (160 Easton Station) is an open-air shopping mall with nearly 200 dining, shopping and entertainment venues, including a 30-screen AMC & IMAX theater. After shopping at favorites like American Eagle, Hollister and PacSun, nosh on a burger and fries at **Flip Side** (3945 Easton Station.).

- Have a couple hours? Try one of the several zipline experiences offered at **ZipZone Canopy Tours** (7925 N. High St.). You'll soar above 20 acres of central Ohio's forests.

- **Graeter's Ice Cream** (2555 Bethel Rd.) boasts that it has the world's best ice cream; fussy foodies and persnickety teens will agree. The craft ice cream and gelato will tempt your taste buds. This dense ice cream is created in spinning French Pot freezers.

- Can't wait for St. Patrick's Day? Teens can don green garb and head to Dublin for the **Dublin Irish Festival** (5200 Emerald Pkwy.) held in August; it offers more than 20 activities, games and inflatables as well as Highland sports competitions and energetic Celtic dancing and music. Fun contests include the most freckles, greenest eyes and reddest hair.

All Ages

- Demonstrations, exhibits, movies, a planetarium and live shows at **COSI Columbus** (333 W. Broad St.) teach science concepts and take the mystery out of technological advancements. Build a bridge, control waves in a tank, dissect computers, lift a car using a lever, maneuver a rover on a Mars-like landscape and split a laser beam. Daredevils can ride a unicycle on a wire suspended 17 feet above ground.

- **German Village** (588 S. 3rd St.) has enough small-town charm to captivate the entire family. Take a self-guiding tour past parks, residences, restaurants and shops along the red-brick paved, tree-lined streets and you might glimpse fossils in the limestone stoops and foundations. Dine on hearty German fare at **Schmidt's Restaurant und Sausage Haus** (240 E. Kossuth St.) followed by French pastries at **Pistacia Vera** (541 S. Third St.).

COSI Columbus

Arriving
By Car

The intersection of two interstate highways and a number of lesser routes makes Columbus accessible from all directions. The primary east-west highway is I-70, which spans about two-thirds of the nation and connects such cities as Baltimore, Md., Wheeling, W.Va. and Indianapolis, Ind.; I-70 passes through downtown Columbus, with convenient interchanges at major streets.

Closely paralleling the freeway is old US 40, which serves local traffic and provides a link to other downtown avenues. US 62 approaches Columbus from the northeast and southwest to bring the city a steady flow of in-state traffic, as does SR 16, combining with US 40 coming in from the northeastern suburbs.

Mainly an intrastate interstate, I-71 links Cleveland to the north and Cincinnati to the south, passing through Columbus and continuing southward to Louisville.

Running north-south through the city is US 23, which collects traffic from northern Ohio and Michigan as well as from southern Ohio, Kentucky and West Virginia. US 33, leading directly downtown, connects towns northwest and southeast of Columbus.

I-270 is a circumferential freeway that swings in a wide path around Columbus and, with interchanges with all major highways, provides a bypass of the city. I-670 combines with I-70 and I-71 to form a tight rectangle around downtown Columbus, offering the usual convenient interchanges.

North Market

Getting Around
Street System

Despite Columbus' growth to big-city status, driving in and around the city is not as hectic as in many metropolitan areas. Driving from one end of downtown to the opposite end averages 25 minutes, and few suburban commutes take more than 45 minutes at non-peak traffic hours. Right turns on red are permitted unless otherwise posted.

Streets are organized on a grid system, with addresses beginning at 1 at the corner of Broad and High streets in the center of downtown and increasing as routes go out of the city. Numbered streets, running north-south, are divided by Broad Street; numbered avenues, running east-west, are divided by High Street.

Parking

Parking lots and garages are plentiful downtown, with rates ranging from $2 to $10 Monday through Friday and generally decreasing on the weekends. Higher rates may apply during special events. On-street metered parking, costing 50c to $1 per hour, can be found along most downtown streets; parking is restricted to 3 hours or less at most meters. Park and Ride lots are at many suburban shopping centers. Credit and debit cards can be used at many of the lots and at parking meters.

Shopping

Columbus is a natural for discovering bargains and hard-to-find items. If you like the time-saving convenience of shopping at malls, choose from these: **Easton Town Center,** off I-270 exit 33 at Easton Way; **The Mall at Tuttle Crossing,** off I-270 and Tuttle Crossing Blvd. (in Dublin); and **Polaris Fashion Place,** off I-71 and Polaris Parkway.

The sprawling Easton Town Center, off I-270 exit 33 at Easton Way, is a shopper's delight. Set up as an old-fashioned open-air village market, the upscale center has more than 200 retailers and restaurants, including Banana Republic, Barnes & Noble, Bose, Burberry, Chico's, Coach, The Container Store, Crate & Barrel, Gap, H & M, Macy's and Nordstrom. Quaint, British-style red phone booths and fountains sprinkled throughout the center add panache to this already chic center. Five free parking garages allow for plentiful parking.

If you'd rather ferret out more unique merchandise, explore the city's shopping districts and specialty shops. Local bakers, butchers, chocolatiers, fishmongers, florists, farmers and ice cream makers sell their wares at the **North Market,** 59 Spruce St. On Saturdays during growing season (May-October), more than 20 farmers set up shop. Saturdays also feature live music, and festivals are held throughout the year. In operation since 1876, the indoor market is open Tues.-Sat. 9-7 and Sun.-Mon. 10-5.

Step into the brick-fronted shops in the restored 19th-century **German Village,** south of I-70/I-7 on 3rd Street, where shopkeepers will give you a warm "Wilkommen" as you sort through their delightful collections of books, home decor and even baked goods. Wandering through the 32 rooms of books in the labyrinthine **The Book Loft,** 631 S. 3rd St., might make you feel like a mouse in a maze. Instead of finding cheese, though, you'll find countless numbers of books, many with a discounted price. Be forewarned: Some staircases are narrow and you may have to step aside to let another customer pass.

The relaxing scent of French lavender bath products infuses the air on the first floor of **Caterina Ltd., European Housewares, Art & Gifts,** 571 S. 3rd St., where armoires and tables are stacked with vibrantly colored Italian ceramics, Polish pottery, and French and German linens; the shop also showcases local artists in galleries on the second and third floors. Pick up a crusty loaf of pumpernickel or some flaky Old-World-style apple strudel made from generations-old family recipes at **Juergen's German Bakery and Restaurant,** 525 S. 4th St., where you can also snap up hard-to-find imported European foods. **Pistacia Vera,** 541 S. 3rd St., is a modern French patisserie; try melt-in-your-mouth pastel macarons in flavors like lavender honey and black raspberry hibiscus, flourless passion fruit Chambord and chocolate bombe tortes, and pastries such as pain au chocolat and orange brioche.

The **Short North Arts District,** along N. High Street from Poplar Street to Smith Place, offers boutiques, antique shops, restaurants and eclectic art galleries behind restored 1930s facades. **Posh Pets Boutique,** 743 N. High St. treats pet lovers to irresistible items like pearl-studded kitty collars, dog T-shirts with cute sayings like "favorite grandchild," fruit-shaped crocheted toys and The Ohio State University pet beds and hooded sweatshirts.

Tigertree, 787 N. High St., deals in trendsetting apparel for 20- and 30-something women and men by Fred Perry and Ben Sherman as well as newer labels like Dear Creatures and Ace & Jig. Sweet floral dresses and cute tops for the gals, and plaid shirts and casual pants for the guys are mixed in with pendants, backpacks, vases and pillows. **Rowe Boutique,** 718 N. High St., carries a well-edited collection of contemporary fashions by lines such as Lauren Moffatt and Foley & Corinna, curated by former PR director Maren Roth, who earned her stripes in New York City handling accounts for fashion designers.

One man's trash is another's treasure at **Rag-O-Rama,** 3301 N. High St., a consignment shop where you can also find patent leather go-go boots, candy-colored Afro wigs and a sea of racks filled with gently used vintage and modern clothes, most contributed by college students. Among some recent findings: Paige Denim jeans, an Odile top and Chloe sunglasses.

It's practically a rule that college towns have to have a used record store, and Columbus is no different. **Used Kids Records,** 2500 Summit St., fills the bill with a collection ranging from Nat King Cole to Florence + the Machine. Vinyl geeks can excavate for quasi-buried treasure to stock their collection, quite cheaply in fact; most used records and

The Book Loft

CDs sell for under $10. Used Kids' well-informed clerks are not the pretentious music snobs you might expect and will gladly help you in your search for hard-to-find discs. The go-to shops for avid Buckeye boosters are **College Traditions,** 286 W. Lane Ave., and **Conrads College Gifts,** 316 W. Lane Ave., which carry everything from sweatshirts to dog collars to football-shaped soap dishes with The Ohio State University logo.

Behold beautiful objects from decades and centuries past at Columbus-area antique malls. Try **Eclectiques Antique Mall,** 3265 N. High St.; **Grandview Mercantile,** 873 N. High St., in the Short North District; **Greater Columbus Antique Mall,** 1045 S. High St., and **Heritage Square Antique Mall,** 1865 Brice Rd.

Nightlife

You might think that Columbus would be hard-pressed to satisfy the entertainment needs of its diverse populace of college students, entrepreneurs and suit-and-tie business types, but guess again. Whether you're a mellowed-out jazz aficionado, a fist-pumping rock fan or you just want to dance until you drop, you'll find a night spot in Columbus that suits your fancy.

Sometimes the best place to experience a city's music scene and feel its flavor is a local "dive" bar. You can hear live jazz almost every night of the week at the saloon-like **Ruby Tuesday** (not affiliated with the national chain restaurant), 1978 Summit St. This long-lived local haunt has been open since 1973 and yes, it was named after that song. Phone (614) 291-8313.

Dick's Den, 2417 N. High St., also fits right in to the "dive" category and is a favorite with the college crowd since it's on The Ohio State University campus. Rough-hewn wood and an old jukebox mark the décor of this fairly nondescript hangout. It's not a rock and roll bar as you might expect of the usual college juke joint; instead, blues, soul and jazz bands play Wednesday through Monday and there are bluegrass jams on Tuesday. Phone (614) 268-9573. Also on the OSU campus is the **Wexner Center for the Arts,** High Street and 15th Avenue, where you can catch underground acts like indie songstress St. Vincent, or enjoy screenings of alternative and foreign films; phone (614) 292-3535.

The **Short North Arts District** has its fair share of evening entertainment and is easy to spot, especially at night, with colorfully lit high arches that stretch over North High Street from one side to the other, luring lounge lizards and barflies like moths to a flame.

If it's cold outside, baby, **Barrel,** 1120 N. High St., has just the thing to warm you up. Have the barkeep mix you a hot toddy from its more than 80 varieties of whiskey, or, if the weather calls for something on the rocks, go for an Old-Fashioned or a Rusty Nail (just like Dad used to drink). This whiskey bar and restaurant is located in a building that was a speakeasy and brothel more than 100 years ago, which adds to its mystique. Phone (614) 564-9058.

Restaurant by day, nightclub by night (and they make a darn good hamburger), **Skully's Music & Diner,** 1151 N. High St., hosts one of the most popular theme nights in town: Thursday's Ladies' 80s. A large, 1950's-style sign grabs your attention

Wexner Center for the Arts

outside; inside, leopard print and the color red highlight the décor. Crowds of revelers gather on the large dance floor to groove to alternative, indie and reggae bands; phone (614) 291-8856.

Going downtown? The Arena District has a small but diverse mix of entertainment choices. Conveniently, three of them reside within just a few steps of each other. **The Basement,** 391 Neil Ave., is the place to go to see the coolest underground acts, both locally and nationally known (at least to those "in the know"), including acts like Fall Out Boy and The Whigs. The dark, intimate space comes complete with thrift-store sofas and graffiti-covered walls. **EXPRESS LIVE!** (formerly LC Pavilion), 405 Neil Ave., is a concert venue where bands that are too famous to play at the Basement perform. Arctic Monkeys, Buddy Guy, Indigo Girls, Insane Clown Posse and The Killers are just a few current acts that have played here. The walls at **A & R Music Bar,** 391 Neil Ave., are plastered with 30 years' worth of concert posters and photos of well-known performers. Live bands don't play here, but it's a popular pre- or post-game gathering spot convenient to nearby Huntington Park or Nationwide Arena, as well as a perfect place to stop in for a cocktail after a concert at EXPRESS LIVE!, right next door. Phone (614) 461-5483 for all three Neil Avenue venues.

For something completely different, make your way to **The Big Bang Dueling Piano Bar,** 401 N. Front St. Despite its name, it's not just a couple of pianists having a faceoff. The show, which mixes music and comedy (and alcohol if you so choose), almost always requires audience participation, so be prepared to take part in a sing-along or even go on stage, all in the name of a good time. Phone (614) 233-9999.

R Bar Arena, 413 N. Front St. is not your usual sports bar. Yes, it has pool tables, sports memorabilia everywhere you look, beer-drinking sports fans and flat-screen TVs, but take a closer look. This bar is devoted to the sport of ice hockey and the memorabilia (jerseys, hockey sticks, pucks, framed autographs) are covered with the logo of the Columbus Blue Jackets, who play at Nationwide Arena. R Bar is within walking distance of the arena, so it's a natural gathering spot for hockey fans. Phone (614) 221-4950.

Big Events

The **Ohio State University Jazz Festival** in March features college and high school bands. Origami, kite-making, cultural displays, martial arts performances, cooking demonstrations and an open market selling exotic Asian goods are on tap at the **Asian Festival,** held Memorial Day weekend in Franklin Park.

The Memorial Tournament in late May and early June epitomizes the rich history and traditions of golf. Started in 1976 by Columbus native Jack Nicklaus, the PGA Tour event takes place at Muirfield Village Golf Club in nearby **Dublin.** A portion of the proceeds benefits Ohio charities.

In June the **Columbus Arts Festival** features music, dance and theater performances, arts, crafts and food. On the last Sunday in June a walking tour of the renovated homes of **German Village** is offered in the ⊗ **Haus und Garten Tour.** Festivities include gardening demonstrations and a watercolor competition. The city celebrates our nation's independence with **Red, White and Boom** in July.

If there's one don't-miss festival in town, it's the Columbus ⊗ **Jazz and Rib Fest** in July. Some 400,000 people bring their bibs to this event, which boasts performances by premier jazz artists and local bands—plus 50 tons of barbecued ribs. After sampling the award-winning food, relax to mellow tunes.

In late July to early August, Columbus is the home of the ⊗ **Ohio State Fair,** probably the biggest shindig in the state and one of the largest fairs in the nation. Held at the **Ohio Expo Center** off I-71 between 11th and 17th avenues, the 12-day event, which is attended by more than 800,000, has livestock displays, exhibits, midway rides, entertainment and food. The fair has been held since 1850.

Early August's **Festival Latino** attracts growing crowds with Latin American music and food as well as educational workshops and cultural performances. Traditional and modern music and dance are highlights of the 3-day ⊗ **Dublin Irish Festival** in August. Cultural draws include Irish storytelling and English Civil War reenactments. Also in August, Reynoldsburg residents celebrate the birth of the commercially sold tomato at the **Reynoldsburg Tomato Festival.**

In September private residences are opened during the **Short North Tour of Homes & Gardens.** In mid-September is ⊗ **Country Living Fair;** inspired by the popular magazine, it features more than 150 booths filled with antiques and handcrafted goods, seminars, music and food. Polka bands, bratwurst, beer and thousands of people combine at the **Ohio Expo Center** in September to give Columbus one of its grandest celebrations: ⊗ **Columbus Oktoberfest.** The month closes out with entertainment, food and music at the **Columbus International Festival** at Franklin Park Adventure Center.

The **Columbus Italian Festival** takes place Columbus Day weekend and revolves around **St. John the Baptist Catholic Church.** The convening of the **All American Quarter Horse Congress** also in October, brings one of the world's largest quarter horse shows to the city. It attracts more than 650,000 people to the Ohio Expo Center and includes horse-judging contests and educational lectures.

Stand on the sidelines to cheer thousands of runners in the **Columbus Marathon** in October. Ranked as one of the top U.S. marathons, the course is mostly flat with a clover-leaf design, looping through downtown and the surrounding suburbs.

In mid-October, head to Circleville for the ⊗ **Circleville Pumpkin Show,** which hosts fall exhibits and activities centered around pumpkins.

Wildlights, held mid-November through New Year's in Powell, includes musical performances, animal exhibits at the **Columbus Zoo and Aquarium,** an ice-skating rink and a display of holiday lights. The year ends with **First Night Columbus,** a community-wide event featuring dancing, music and fun in downtown.

Sports & Rec

Columbus does not lack sports enthusiasts. **The Ohio State University football** commands the attention of the city on autumn Saturdays; tailgate parties, Buckeye banners and 100,000 fervent fans color horseshoe-shaped **Ohio Stadium** scarlet and gray with excitement. Ohio State also fields competitive **basketball** and **ice hockey** teams. For information contact the OSU ticket office in the Jerome Schottenstein Center at 555 Borror Dr.; phone (614) 292-2624 or (800) 462-8257.

The **Columbus Blue Jackets,** (614) 246-7825, play NHL **hockey** at the **Nationwide Arena** at 200 W. Nationwide Blvd. Two hours before each match, 250 $10 tickets are released to the public at the box office.

The **Columbus Crew,** (614) 447-2739, plays major league **soccer** at the **MAPFRE Stadium** at the Ohio State Expo Center. The **Ohio Machine** plays major league lacrosse at **Panther Stadium** at Ohio Dominican University.

Baseball is also a popular spectator sport in Columbus. The **Columbus Clippers,** the Cleveland Indians Triple A minor league affiliate, is part of the International League. Games are held downtown at **Huntington Park;** phone (614) 462-5250 or (614) 462-2757 for ticket information.

Horse racing fans have a variety of tracks and styles from which to choose. Harness racing is held May to mid-September at **Eldorado Scioto Downs,** (614) 295-4700, 6000 S. High St. The biggest pacing event of the year, the **Little Brown Jug,** is held the third Thursday after Labor Day at the **Delaware County Fairgrounds.**

Note: Policies vary concerning admittance of children to pari-mutuel betting facilities. Phone for information.

For racing fans who demand more horsepower, **stock car racing** is held Saturday nights at 7 p.m. during the summer at the **Columbus Motor Speedway,** (614) 491-1047, at 1845 Williams Rd. **Drag racing** excitement revs engines May through October at **National Trail Raceway,** 2650 National Rd. S.W. in nearby Hebron; phone (740) 928-5706.

Columbus offers an abundance of public golf courses, including **Blacklick Woods,** (614) 861-3193, 7309 E. Livingston Ave. in Reynoldsburg; **Raymond Memorial,** (614) 645-3276, 3860 Trabue Rd.; and **Thorn Apple Country Club,** (614) 878-7703, 1051 Alton Darby Creek Rd. in Galloway.

The Memorial Tournament, a 4-day professional golf competition, is held at the end of May or early

June at **Muirfield Village,** a course in Dublin designed by Columbus native Jack Nicklaus; phone (614) 889-6712.

Columbus operates an extensive park system with miles of trails for **bicyclists** and **joggers.** One of the most scenic routes takes bicyclists 8 miles along the Olentangy River. Columbus hosts the Columbus Marathon in October and other long-distance running events throughout the year.

The **Scioto Mile,** running along the riverfront between the Arena District and the Whittier Peninsula, offers more than 145 acres of park space. Visitors can walk along the promenade for great views. There also are fountains, gardens, swings and benches.

Tennis courts are abundant in Columbus, with more than 140 run by the city and numerous others at local colleges and high schools. Phone Columbus' Department of Recreation and Parks at (614) 645-3300 for details.

Despite its moderate climate, Columbus is within about an hour's drive of several popular **skiing** areas. **Snow Trails,** (419) 774-9818, is 60 miles northeast near Mansfield and is considered to be Ohio's first ski area. **Mad River Mountain,** (937) 599-1015, or (800) 231-7669 outside Ohio, about 40 miles northwest in Zanesfield, is a large resort with night skiing. *See individual place listings.*

Performing Arts

The **Columbus Association for the Performing Arts,** (614) 469-1045, brings to the area productions that include well-known musical performers and plays. Professional theater and Broadway shows visit area stages on a regular basis; **PNC Broadway in Columbus** performs at the **Ohio Theatre** and **Palace Theatre;** phone (800) 294-1892.

Jazz is prevalent in Columbus, with the **Jazz Arts Group's Columbus Jazz Orchestra** playing the familiar Big Band sounds of Count Basie, Louis Armstrong and Woody Herman; phone (614) 294-5200. The 17-piece big band plays a subscription series at the **Southern Theatre,** 21 E. Main St.; phone (614) 469-0939 for tickets. The **ProMusica Chamber Orchestra** also offers concert series at the Southern Theatre; phone (614) 464-0066. Aspiring musicians comprise **The Ohio State University Jazz Ensemble,** which performs on campus.

The **Columbus Symphony Orchestra** plays a regular 9-month concert season in the opulent Ohio Theatre, directly across from the Ohio Statehouse *(see attraction listing p. 217).* The venue is decorated with plaster ceilings, brocaded paneling, gold leaf trim and a chandelier in the grand foyer; phone (614) 469-0939. The symphony also presents pops and chamber music concerts as well as youth concerts. Popular in the summer is Picnic with the Pops, an outdoor concert at the Columbus Commons downtown.

Opera Columbus presents several major opera productions throughout the year; phone (614) 461-8101 for information or (614) 469-0939 for tickets. **BalletMet,** (614) 229-4848, produces classical and contemporary works.

Community groups also provide a full schedule. **Gallery Players** at the **Jewish Community Center** offers productions, including musicals; phone (614) 231-2731 for tickets. **Contemporary American Theater Company (CATCo)** performs in the **Riffe Center,** 77 S. High St.; phone (614) 469-0939 for tickets. Grove City's **Little Theatre Off Broadway** performs comedies, dramas and musicals; phone (614) 875-3919. **Short North Stage** performs in the 1920 **Garden Theater,** 1187 N. High St.; phone (614) 725-4042. **Available Light Theatre** is at 77 S. High St.; phone (614) 558-7408.

Shadowbox Live, 503 S. Front St., presents a schedule of performances blending seemingly unrelated forms of entertainment like sketch comedy, live rock and roll and new media; phone (614) 416-7625.

ATTRACTIONS

 For a complete list of attractions, visit AAA.com/travelguides/attractions

BILLY IRELAND CARTOON LIBRARY & MUSEUM is at 1813 N. High St. in Sullivant Hall on The Ohio State University campus. The museum features changing exhibits of artwork and artifacts related to the field of comics and cartoons, and the library contains newspapers, comic strips, cartoons, books and serials. **Time:** Allow 1 hour minimum. **Hours:** Museum Tues.-Sun. 1-5. Library Mon.-Fri. 9-5 (also Sun. 1-5, during fall and spring semesters). Closed Jan. 1, Martin Luther King Jr. Day, Memorial Day, July 3, Veterans Day, Thanksgiving, day after Thanksgiving, Christmas Eve, Christmas and during new exhibit installations. Phone ahead to confirm schedule. **Cost:** Free. **Phone:** (614) 292-0538.

COLUMBUS MUSEUM OF ART, 480 E. Broad St., houses art that speaks to diverse interests and styles. The collection includes late 19th- and early 20th-century American and European modern art. The museum also features extraordinary photography and regional collections, where local artists George Bellows, Elijah Pierce and Aminah Brenda Lynn Robinson are represented. In addition, you will see contemporary art, folk art and glass. The new Margaret M. Walter Wing presents traveling exhibitions, and the Patricia M. Jurgensen Sculpture Garden is on the grounds.

Hours: Tues.-Sun. 10-5 (also Thurs. 5-9). Guided 40-minute tours depart Sun. at 1, Thurs. at 6:30 and Fri. at noon. Closed Jan. 1, Martin Luther King Jr. Day, Presidents Day, Memorial Day, July 4, Labor Day, Columbus Day, Thanksgiving and Christmas. **Cost:** $14; $8 (ages 60+ and college students with ID); $5 (ages 6-17); free (Sun.). Fees may be charged for special exhibitions. **Phone:** (614) 221-6801. GT ⅠⅠ

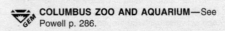 **COLUMBUS ZOO AND AQUARIUM**—See Powell p. 286.

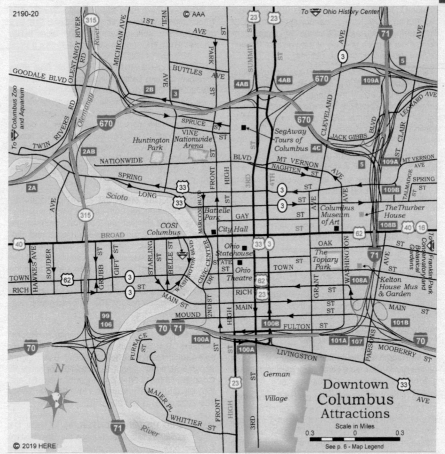

2190-20

© AAA

To Ohio History Center

Downtown
Columbus
Attractions

Scale in Miles
0.3   0   0.3

See p. 6 - Map Legend

© 2019 HERE

COSI COLUMBUS is off I-70W exit 100B, or I-70E exit 97, following signs to 333 W. Broad St. The dynamic hands-on science center features more than 300 interactive exhibits, and live shows are presented throughout the themed exhibition areas. Exhibits are designed to teach science to all age levels through play. Some of the science concepts covered include the ocean, outer space, energy, engineering and health.

Daring types will want to ride the high-wire unicycle several stories aboveground across the atrium, a gravity-defying feat that provides a thrill for all visitors. Future doctors may unravel the mysteries of the human body in the Life exhibit, which covers such subjects as exercise, diseases and bones. At Labs in Life, visitors may see researchers using state-of-the-art diagnostic equipment to conduct various studies.

In the Progress exhibit, stroll down the same street as it appeared in 1898 and then in 1962 and see how everyday life changed drastically due to technological advancements. In 1898, exhibits include farm implements, telegraph equipment and a horse-drawn buggy. In 1962, faux storefronts display toys and drugstore products; behind another window, a deejay plays vinyl records at a radio station; and a gas station highlights a gleaming vintage automobile.

Submerse yourself into the world of underwater technology such as sonar and submarines in the Ocean exhibit. Little ones can enter a submersible for a glimpse of underwater life. Explore the concepts of water flow and water bells, and control waves in a tank filled with 1,000 pounds of H20. In the Space exhibit, aspiring astronauts may control a robot on Mars using a robotic rover, pilot a space capsule and learn about gravity and the laws of motion.

In the Gadgets Café, future engineers and scientists can discover the inner workings of machinery through dissecting computers and CD drives, or try their hand at splitting a laser beam or building a bridge. At Big Science Park, kids will feel like superheroes as they lift a car using a lever or move a 2.5-ton granite sphere. There also is a special area for babies up to youngsters in first grade.

Movies are shown on a digital screen in the National Geographic Giant Screen Theater. Live shows include Chemistry LIVE!, Gadgets LIVE!, rat basketball and an electrostatic generator show. The COSI Planetarium features state-of-the-art digital technology that offers a glimpse of the universe through several different experience options.

Courtesy strollers and wheelchairs are available. **Time:** Allow 2 hours minimum. **Hours:** Wed.-Sun. 10-5 (also last Fri. of the month 5-9). Planetarium schedule varies by show. Hours are extended during school spring, summer and winter breaks; phone to confirm schedules. Closed Easter, July 1, Thanksgiving and Christmas.

Cost: (includes exhibits and live shows) $25; $20 (ages 2-12). National Geographic movie ticket only $8. Movie and planetarium show $5 each. **Parking:** $6-$15. **Phone:** (614) 228-2674, (888) 819-2674 or TTY (614) 228-1445. 🍴

FRANKLIN PARK CONSERVATORY AND BOTANICAL GARDENS is in Franklin Park at 1777 E. Broad St. The site includes the John F. Wolfe Palm House, built in 1895 and designed in the style of the Glass Palace at Chicago's World Fair and Columbian Exposition in 1893. Several modern glasshouses are interconnected. Visitors can view more than 400 plant varieties as they travel through simulated habitats of the world, including a tropical rain forest, the Himalayan Mountains, an arid desert and a Pacific Island water garden.

The conservatory also has a bonsai collection, a bride's garden, a 4-acre community garden campus, a 1-mile walking loop and sculptures.

The John F. Wolfe Palm House holds more than 40 species of palms (some are endangered species) and tropical flowers. Light artist James Turrell has dressed up the Palm House with his permanent installation of 7,000 LED bulbs that glow through a changing program each evening from sunset until dawn. Visitors can watch the free show from the Grand Mallway, a large outdoor botanical garden to the west of the Palm House.

Multiple installations from the conservatory's signature collection of Dale Chihuly glass artwork are on long-term display; it's reputedly the only botanical garden in the world to own such a large collection—about 3,000 pieces—by the artist. His glassworks are creatively placed in unexpected places throughout the gardens. Some pieces, tall and spear-shaped in brilliant reds, purples and greens, are interspersed in the foliage and look like they sprouted from the ground.

During the Blooms & Butterflies exhibition, held early March to mid-September, visitors can observe as newly hatched butterflies are released daily, adding splashes of color to the emerald foliage of the Pacific Island Water Garden. The conservatory's holiday exhibition, Merry & Bright, is held from mid-November through early January. Orchids are displayed from mid-January to early March. Glassblowing demonstrations are offered April through December.

Courtesy wheelchairs are available. **Time:** Allow 1 hour minimum. **Hours:** Daily 10-5. **Cost:** $18; $15 (ages 60+ and students with ID); $11 (ages 3-12). **Phone:** (614) 715-8000 or (800) 214-7275. 🍴

JACK NICKLAUS MUSEUM is on The Ohio State University campus between Ackerman Rd. and Lane Ave. at 2355 Olentangy River Rd. The facility includes three theaters, vintage media footage and memorabilia tracing the life and career of the Columbus-born golfer. Among the more than 2,000 pieces on display are his six Masters trophies. Artifacts detail the history of golf from the 1400s to the present. **Time:** Allow 1 hour minimum. **Hours:** Tues.-Sat. 9-5. Closed major holidays. **Cost:** $10; $5 (students with ID); free (ages 0-6). **Phone:** (614) 247-5959.

KELTON HOUSE MUSEUM & GARDEN, 586 E. Town St., is a restored 19th-century brick house that reflects Greek Revival and Italianate architectural styles. Most of the furnishings are original and offer insight into the prominent upper-class family who lived here. The house also was a station on the Underground Railroad where escaped slaves from the South were sheltered on their journeys to Canada; an exhibit in the basement offers details about this part of the house's history. The Victorian garden features statuary.

Time: Allow 1 hour, 15 minutes minimum. **Hours:** Mon.-Fri. 10-4, Sat.-Sun. 1-4. Last audio tour available 1 hour, 15 minutes before closing. Guided tours depart Sun. on the hour 1-3. Closed major holidays. **Cost:** $6; $5 (ages 56+); $4 (students ages 18+ with ID); $3 (students grades K-12) . **Phone:** (614) 464-2022 or (614) 464-2045. GT

OHIO HISTORY CENTER, off I-71 exit 111 at 800 E. 17th Ave., houses the Ohio History Connection's administrative offices, the state history museum, a historical research library and the state archives. Exhibits at the 271,000-square-foot museum include items related to Ohio's archeological, agricultural, industrial, social and natural history. Galleries feature the state's plants, animals, geology, geography and climate plus a history timeline stretching from the Ice Age through modern times. Touring exhibits also are featured.

Open since 1970, the center is designed in the mid-20th-century-modern Brutalist style and resembles a huge, concrete box floating in the air. As visitors enter the museum, a massive, life-size skeleton of the Conway mastodon welcomes them.

A large portion of the museum chronicles Ohio's role in wars in which the United States took part, from the War of 1812 through World War II, with an emphasis on the Civil War. Displays contain weapons, medical equipment, and uniforms and civilian clothing worn by men, women and children. Restored but well-worn Civil War battle flags are paired with narratives written by soldiers who survived the war. This 15,000-square-foot gallery also provides details about Ohio's progress in agriculture and industry with a collection of more than 5,000 artifacts, including newsreels from the 1920s and vintage 20th-century automobiles.

Ohio's Ancient Past delves into the history of the First Ohioans through displays of arrowheads, pottery, beads and animal effigy pipes. Visitors are invited to handle some of the pieces used regularly by the Native Americans.

Kids can fire up their imaginations through the museum's hands-on activities, such as using computers to learn about Ohio's natural history. A replica of a log cabin with a pioneer kitchen allows children to play dress-up with pioneer clothes and make yarn on a spinning wheel.

Ohio's natural history is preserved through a display of mounted animals which includes such specimens as a bear, wolf, cougar, bison, ivory-billed woodpecker and the world's last documented passenger pigeon. Other exhibits devoted to natural history explore Ohio's plant life, geology, geography and climate.

Time: Allow 1 hour, 30 minutes minimum. **Hours:** Museum open Wed.-Sun. 10-5. Library open Wed.-Sat. 10-5. Closed major holidays. Phone ahead to confirm schedule. **Cost:** $12; $10 (ages 60+ and college students with ID); $6 (ages 4-12). Rates may vary; phone ahead. **Phone:** (614) 297-2300 for the museum or (800) 686-6124.

OHIO STATEHOUSE is at Broad and High sts. at 1 Capitol Square; tours depart from the Map Room on the ground floor. Considered to be one of the best examples of Greek Revival architecture in the United States, the 1861 building contains historical documents, portraits and other works commemorating Ohio's noted governors and U.S. presidents. A stained-glass Great Seal of Ohio is in the center of the rotunda dome.

The Ohio Statehouse Museum on the ground floor features a variety of interactive exhibits related to state government and history. The Ohio Holocaust and Liberators Memorial stands on the grounds. **Hours:** Statehouse open Mon.-Fri. 8-5, Sat.-Sun. 11-5. Guided 45- to 60-minute tours depart Mon.-Fri. on the hour 10-3, Sat.-Sun. noon-3. Closed major holidays. **Cost:** Free. **Phone:** (614) 752-9777 or (888) 644-6123. GT

ZOOMBEZI BAY—see Powell p. 287.

Sightseeing

An excellent vantage point from which to view the city is the 40th-floor observation deck of the Rhodes State Office Tower. The building, Columbus' tallest structure, also can be toured. Phone (614) 466-7361 for more information.

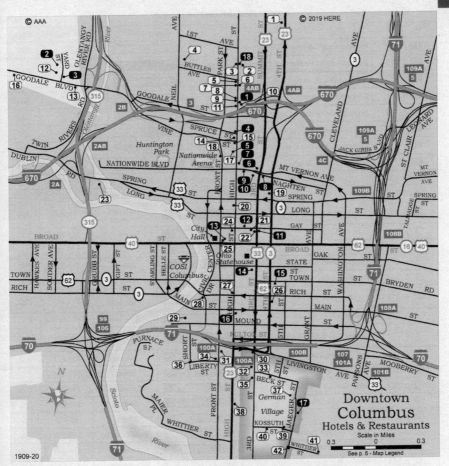

Downtown Columbus

This index helps you "spot" where hotels and restaurants are located on the corresponding detailed maps. Restaurant price range is a combination of lunch and/or dinner. Turn to the listing page for more information and consult display ads for special promotions.

 For more details, rates and reservations: AAA.com/travelguides/hotels

DOWNTOWN COLUMBUS

Map Page	Hotels	Designation	Member Savings	Page
1 this page	Le Meridien Columbus, The Joseph	◈ FOUR DIAMOND	✔	229
2 this page	**Hyatt Place Columbus/OSU**	◈ THREE DIAMOND	✔	229
3 this page	**Courtyard by Marriott Grandview Yard**	◈ THREE DIAMOND	✔	228
4 this page	**Hampton Inn & Suites by Hilton Downtown**	◈ THREE DIAMOND	✔	228
5 this page	Hilton Columbus Downtown	◈ FOUR DIAMOND	✔	228
6 this page	Drury Inn & Suites-Columbus Convention Center	◈ THREE DIAMOND		228
7 this page	**Hyatt Regency Columbus**	◈ THREE DIAMOND	✔	229
8 this page	**Red Roof PLUS+ Columbus Downtown-Convention Center**	◈ APPROVED	✔	229
9 this page	Crowne Plaza Columbus Downtown	◈ THREE DIAMOND		228
10 this page	Canopy Columbus Downtown Short North	◈ THREE DIAMOND	✔	228

DOWNTOWN COLUMBUS (cont'd)

Map Page	Hotels (cont'd)	Designation	Member Savings	Page
⑪ p. 219	Renaissance Columbus Downtown Hotel	THREE DIAMOND	✔	229
⑫ p. 219	Residence Inn by Marriott Downtown	THREE DIAMOND	✔	229
⑬ p. 219	Hotel LeVeque, Autograph Collection	FOUR DIAMOND	✔	229
⑭ p. 219	Sheraton Columbus at Capitol Square	THREE DIAMOND	✔	229
⑮ p. 219	Holiday Inn Columbus Downtown Capitol Square	APPROVED		229
⑯ p. 219	The Westin Great Southern Columbus	THREE DIAMOND	✔	230
⑰ p. 219	German Village Guest House	THREE DIAMOND		228
⑱ p. 219	Moxy Columbus Short North	THREE DIAMOND	✔	229

Map Page	Restaurants	Designation	Cuisine	Price Range	Page
① p. 219	Cosecha Cochina	APPROVED	Mexican	$4-$20	230
② p. 219	The Eagle Food & Beer Hall	APPROVED	Southern American	$7-$20	230
③ p. 219	Hubbard Grille	APPROVED	American	$18-$38	230
④ p. 219	Basi Italia	THREE DIAMOND	Italian	$13-$26	230
⑤ p. 219	Forno Kitchen & Bar	APPROVED	Italian	$14-$29	230
⑥ p. 219	Harvey & Ed's	APPROVED	Jewish Deli	$9-$31	230
⑦ p. 219	Del Mar SoCal Kitchen	THREE DIAMOND	Southern California	$16-$37	230
⑧ p. 219	The Pearl	THREE DIAMOND	American	$11-$39	230
⑨ p. 219	Lemongrass Fusion Bistro	APPROVED	Asian Fusion Sushi	$9-$32	230
⑩ p. 219	The Guild House	THREE DIAMOND	American	$14-$37	230
⑪ p. 219	Marcella's Short North	APPROVED	Italian	$12-$24	230
⑫ p. 219	Eddie George's Grille 27	APPROVED	American	$11-$29	230
⑬ p. 219	Hofbrauhaus Columbus	APPROVED	German	$10-$27	230
⑭ p. 219	Bareburger	APPROVED	Burgers	$8-$13	230
⑮ p. 219	Martini Modern Italian	THREE DIAMOND	Regional Italian	$19-$49	230
⑯ p. 219	High Bank Distillery	APPROVED	American	$14-$38	230
⑰ p. 219	Gallerie Bar & Bistro	THREE DIAMOND	New American	$11-$30	230
⑱ p. 219	Gordon Biersch Brewery Restaurant	THREE DIAMOND	American	$9-$22	230
⑲ p. 219	Wolf's Ridge Brewing	APPROVED	American	$14-$100	231
⑳ p. 219	Elevator Brewery & Draught Haus	APPROVED	American	$9-$33	230
㉑ p. 219	Due Amici	THREE DIAMOND	Italian	$13-$34	230
㉒ p. 219	Mitchell's Steakhouse	THREE DIAMOND	Steak	$14-$52	230
㉓ p. 219	The Boat House	THREE DIAMOND	American	$13-$26	230
㉔ p. 219	Veritas	THREE DIAMOND	Small Plates	$12-$29	231
㉕ p. 219	The Keep Kitchen and Liquor Bar	THREE DIAMOND	French	$10-$36	230
㉖ p. 219	Dirty Frank's Hot Dog Palace	APPROVED	Hot Dogs	$3-$7	230
㉗ p. 219	The Goat at LC RiverSouth	APPROVED	American	$11-$30	230
㉘ p. 219	Milestone 229	THREE DIAMOND	American	$11-$36	230
㉙ p. 219	M at Miranova	FOUR DIAMOND	American	$29-$62	230
㉚ p. 219	Katzinger's Delicatessen	APPROVED	Jewish Deli	$12-$17	230
㉛ p. 219	Basil Thai Restaurant	APPROVED	Thai	$8-$19	230
㉜ p. 219	Pistacia Vera	APPROVED	Breads/Pastries	$7-$13	231
㉝ p. 219	Lindey's	THREE DIAMOND	American	$11-$38	230
㉞ p. 219	Rockmill Tavern	THREE DIAMOND	American	$10-$36	231

Map Page	Restaurants (cont'd)	Designation	Cuisine	Price Range	Page
㉟ p. 219	G. Michael's Bistro	THREE DIAMOND	Regional American	$22-$44	230
㊱ p. 219	Matt and Tony's Wood-Fired Grill	APPROVED	American	$10-$32	230
㊲ p. 219	The Sycamore	THREE DIAMOND	American	$20-$31	231
㊳ p. 219	Ambrose & Eve	THREE DIAMOND	American	$10-$25	230
㊴ p. 219	Schmidt's Restaurant und Sausage Haus	APPROVED	German	$10-$23	231
㊵ p. 219	Old Mohawk Restaurant	APPROVED	American	$5-$14	230
㊶ p. 219	Skillet, Rustic Urban Food	APPROVED	American	$10-$23	231
㊷ p. 219	Barcelona	THREE DIAMOND	Spanish	$6-$35	230

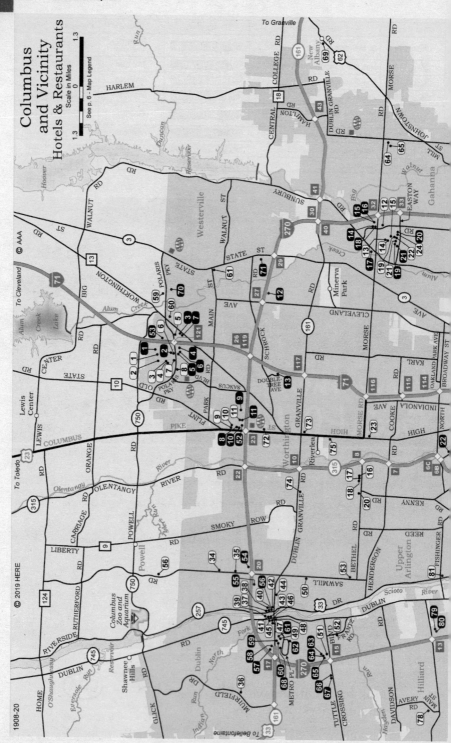

Columbus
and Vicinity
Hotels & Restaurants

See p. 6 - Map Legend

Scale in Miles
0

© AAA

© 2019 HERE

1908-20

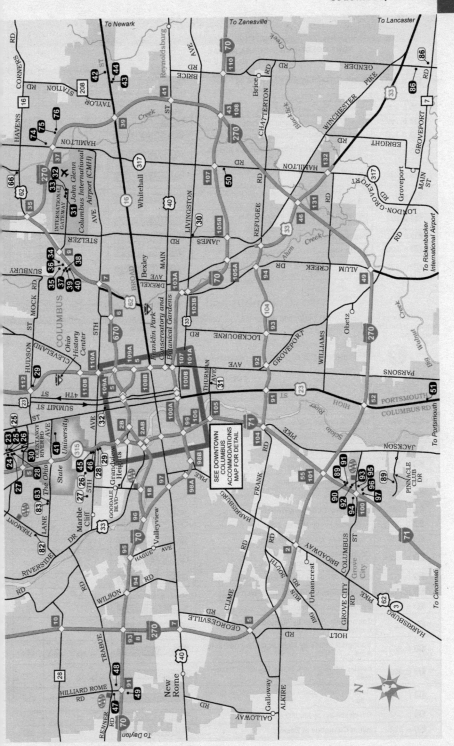

✈ Airport Hotels

Map Page	**PORT COLUMBUS INTERNATIONAL** (Maximum driving distance from airport: 3.5 mi)	Designation	Member Savings	Page
36 p. 222	**Best Western Port Columbus, 2.9 mi**	🔷 APPROVED	✔	231
40 p. 222	Columbus Airport Marriott, 2.9 mi	🔷 THREE DIAMOND	✔	231
35 p. 222	Comfort Suites Columbus Airport, 3.0 mi	🔷 THREE DIAMOND		231
37 p. 222	Country Inn & Suites Columbus Airport, 3.0 mi	🔷 APPROVED		231
38 p. 222	Courtyard by Marriott-Columbus Airport, 2.8 mi	🔷 THREE DIAMOND	✔	231
39 p. 222	**Embassy Suites by Hilton Columbus Airport, 2.6 mi**	🔷 THREE DIAMOND	✔	232
32 p. 222	Fairfield Inn & Suites by Marriott Columbus Airport, 0.4 mi	🔷 THREE DIAMOND	✔	232
34 p. 222	Four Points by Sheraton Columbus Ohio Airport, 2.8 mi	🔷 THREE DIAMOND	✔	232
33 p. 222	**Hampton Inn by Hilton at Columbus International Airport, 0.5 mi**	🔷 THREE DIAMOND	✔	233
31 p. 222	**Hilton Garden Inn Columbus Airport, 0.6 mi**	🔷 THREE DIAMOND	✔	233
75 p. 222	Candlewood Suites Columbus Airport, 3.4 mi	🔷 APPROVED		255
76 p. 222	TownePlace Suites by Marriott Columbus Airport, 3.5 mi	🔷 APPROVED	✔	255

Columbus and Vicinity

This index helps you "spot" where hotels and restaurants are located on the corresponding detailed maps. Restaurant price range is a combination of lunch and/or dinner. Turn to the listing page for more information and consult display ads for special promotions.

 For more details, rates and reservations: AAA.com/travelguides/hotels

COLUMBUS

Map Page	Hotels	Designation	Member Savings	Page
1 p. 222	Cambria Hotel & Suites Columbus/Polaris	🔷 THREE DIAMOND		231
2 p. 222	Hilton Columbus/Polaris	🔷 FOUR DIAMOND	✔	233
3 p. 222	Hampton Inn & Suites by Hilton Columbus-Polaris	🔷 THREE DIAMOND	✔	232
4 p. 222	Comfort Inn Polaris	🔷 APPROVED		231
5 p. 222	Hilton Garden Inn Columbus/Polaris	🔷 THREE DIAMOND	✔	233
6 p. 222	Candlewood Suites Polaris	🔷 APPROVED		231
7 p. 222	Fairfield Inn & Suites by Marriott Columbus Polaris	🔷 THREE DIAMOND	✔	232
8 p. 222	**Hyatt Place Columbus/Worthington**	🔷 THREE DIAMOND	✔	234
9 p. 222	Residence Inn by Marriott Columbus-Worthington	🔷 THREE DIAMOND	✔	234
10 p. 222	Courtyard by Marriott Worthington	🔷 THREE DIAMOND	✔	231
11 p. 222	**DoubleTree by Hilton Hotel Columbus-Worthington**	🔷 THREE DIAMOND	✔	232
12 p. 222	Embassy Suites by Hilton Hotel-Columbus	🔷 THREE DIAMOND	✔	232
13 p. 222	**Crowne Plaza Columbus North-Worthington**	🔷 THREE DIAMOND	✔	231
14 p. 222	Extended Stay America-Columbus-Easton	🔷 APPROVED		232
15 p. 222	**TownePlace Suites by Marriott Columbus Easton Area**	🔷 THREE DIAMOND	✔	234
16 p. 222	**SpringHill Suites by Marriott Columbus Easton Area**	🔷 THREE DIAMOND	✔	234
17 p. 222	Holiday Inn Express & Suites Columbus Easton Area	🔷 THREE DIAMOND		233
18 p. 222	Hampton Inn & Suites by Hilton Columbus Easton Area	🔷 THREE DIAMOND	✔	232
19 p. 222	Residence Inn by Marriott Easton	🔷 THREE DIAMOND	✔	234
20 p. 222	**Hilton Columbus at Easton**	🔷 FOUR DIAMOND	✔	233

COLUMBUS (cont'd)

Map Page	Hotels (cont'd)	Designation	Member Savings	Page
21 p. 222	Courtyard by Marriott Columbus-Easton	THREE DIAMOND	✔	231
22 p. 222	Hilton Garden Inn Columbus-University Area	THREE DIAMOND	✔	233
23 p. 222	**Hampton Inn & Suites by Hilton Columbus/University Area**	THREE DIAMOND	✔	232
24 p. 222	Staybridge Suites Columbus University Area	THREE DIAMOND		234
25 p. 222	**Marriott Columbus University Area**	THREE DIAMOND	✔	234
26 p. 222	**Residence Inn Columbus University Area**	THREE DIAMOND	✔	234
27 p. 222	Holiday Inn Express & Suites OSU	THREE DIAMOND		233
28 p. 222	Fairfield Inn & Suites by Marriott OSU	THREE DIAMOND	✔	232
29 p. 222	**Holiday Inn Express Ohio Expo Center**	THREE DIAMOND	✔	233
30 p. 222	**Red Roof PLUS+ Columbus-The Ohio State University**	APPROVED	✔	234
31 p. 222	Hilton Garden Inn Columbus Airport	THREE DIAMOND	✔	233
32 p. 222	Fairfield Inn & Suites by Marriott Columbus Airport	THREE DIAMOND	✔	232
33 p. 222	**Hampton Inn by Hilton at Columbus International Airport**	THREE DIAMOND	✔	233
34 p. 222	Four Points by Sheraton Columbus Ohio Airport	THREE DIAMOND	✔	232
35 p. 222	Comfort Suites Columbus Airport	THREE DIAMOND		231
36 p. 222	**Best Western Port Columbus**	APPROVED	✔	231
37 p. 222	Country Inn & Suites Columbus Airport	APPROVED		231
38 p. 222	Courtyard by Marriott-Columbus Airport	THREE DIAMOND	✔	231
39 p. 222	**Embassy Suites by Hilton Columbus Airport**	THREE DIAMOND	✔	232
40 p. 222	Columbus Airport Marriott	THREE DIAMOND	✔	231
41 p. 222	The Blackwell Inn & Pfahl Conference Center	THREE DIAMOND		231
42 p. 222	**Comfort Suites East Broad at 270**	THREE DIAMOND	✔	231
43 p. 222	Holiday Inn Express & Suites Columbus Airport East	THREE DIAMOND		233
44 p. 222	Home2 Suites by Hilton Columbus Airport East Broad	THREE DIAMOND	✔	233
45 p. 222	**The Varsity Inn**	APPROVED	✔	235
46 p. 222	**SpringHill Suites by Marriott Columbus OSU**	THREE DIAMOND	✔	234
47 p. 222	Hawthorn Suites by Wyndham	APPROVED		233
48 p. 222	Hampton Inn by Hilton Columbus West	THREE DIAMOND	✔	233
49 p. 222	**Best Western Suites**	APPROVED	✔	231
50 p. 222	Hampton Inn by Hilton Columbus I-70 East/Hamilton Road	THREE DIAMOND	✔	233
51 p. 222	Hampton Inn & Suites Columbus Scioto Downs	THREE DIAMOND	✔	233
52 p. 222	Holiday Inn Express Hotel & Suites Columbus-Worthington	THREE DIAMOND		233
53 p. 222	Drury Inn and Suites Columbus Polaris	THREE DIAMOND		232

Map Page	Restaurants	Designation	Cuisine	Price Range	Page
1 p. 222	Chile Verde Cafe: Polaris	APPROVED	Southwestern	$7-$16	235
2 p. 222	Matt the Miller's Tavern	APPROVED	American	$13-$36	235
3 p. 222	Molly Woo's Asian Bistro	THREE DIAMOND	Asian	$11-$21	235
4 p. 222	Brio Tuscan Grille	THREE DIAMOND	Regional Italian	$13-$32	235
5 p. 222	Polaris Grill	THREE DIAMOND	American	$13-$30	235
6 p. 222	Eddie Merlot's	THREE DIAMOND	Steak	$30-$99	235
7 p. 222	Mitchell's Steakhouse	THREE DIAMOND	Steak	$24-$62	235
8 p. 222	Marcella's Italian Kitchen Polaris	APPROVED	Italian	$11-$30	235

Map Page	Restaurants (cont'd)	Designation	Cuisine	Price Range	Page
⑨ p. 222	J. Gilbert's Wood Fired Steaks & Seafood	THREE DIAMOND	Steak Seafood	$19-$59	235
⑩ p. 222	J. Alexander's Redlands Grill	THREE DIAMOND	American	$10-$35	235
⑪ p. 222	Lotus Grill	APPROVED	Chinese	$6-$7	235
⑫ p. 222	Melt Bar and Grilled	APPROVED	Sandwiches	$6-$16	235
⑬ p. 222	Cafe Istanbul	THREE DIAMOND	Turkish	$12-$29	235
⑭ p. 222	McCormick & Schmick's	THREE DIAMOND	Seafood	$13-$49	235
⑮ p. 222	Rusty Bucket Restaurant and Tavern	APPROVED	American	$11-$20	235
⑯ p. 222	Bamboo Café	APPROVED	Thai	$9-$18	235
⑰ p. 222	Min-Ga Korean Restaurant	APPROVED	Korean	$11-$30	235
⑱ p. 222	Hoggy's	APPROVED	Barbecue	$10-$18	235
⑲ p. 222	Mitchell's Ocean Club	THREE DIAMOND	Seafood Steak	$26-$49	235
⑳ p. 222	**The Refectory Restaurant & Wine Shop**	FOUR DIAMOND	French	$21-$51	235
㉑ p. 222	Flip Side	APPROVED	Burgers	$8-$19	235
㉒ p. 222	Brio Tuscan Grille	THREE DIAMOND	Regional Italian	$11-$30	235
㉓ p. 222	Mozart's Restaurant, Bakery and Piano Cafe	APPROVED	Austrian Breads/ Pastries	$7-$16	235
㉔ p. 222	P.F. Chang's China Bistro	THREE DIAMOND	Chinese	$9-$25	235
㉕ p. 222	Harvest Clintonville	APPROVED	Pizza	$12-$19	235
㉖ p. 222	Watershed Kitchen & Bar	THREE DIAMOND	New American	$18-$35	236
㉗ p. 222	Bonifacio	APPROVED	Philippine	$8-$14	235
㉘ p. 222	Cap City Fine Diner & Bar	APPROVED	Comfort Food	$11-$30	235
㉙ p. 222	Columbus Fish Market	THREE DIAMOND	Seafood	$9-$32	235
㉚ p. 222	Tat Ristorante di Famiglia	APPROVED	Southern Italian	$9-$25	236
㉛ p. 222	The Thurman Cafe	APPROVED	Burgers Pizza	$8-$22	236
㉜ p. 222	Fireproof Short North	THREE DIAMOND	Small Plates	$7-$124	235

DUBLIN

Map Page	Hotels	Designation	Member Savings	Page
❺❹ p. 222	**Fairfield by Marriott North Columbus/Dublin**	THREE DIAMOND	✔	249
❺❺ p. 222	Hampton Inn by Hilton Columbus-Dublin	APPROVED	✔	249
❺❻ p. 222	**AC Hotel Columbus Dublin**	THREE DIAMOND	✔	248
❺❼ p. 222	**Courtyard by Marriott-Dublin**	THREE DIAMOND	✔	248
❺❽ p. 222	**Red Roof PLUS+ Columbus/Dublin**	APPROVED	✔	249
❺❾ p. 222	**Home2 Suites by Hilton Columbus Dublin**	THREE DIAMOND	✔	249
❻⓿ p. 222	Embassy Suites by Hilton Columbus-Dublin	THREE DIAMOND	✔	249
❻❶ p. 222	Residence Inn by Marriott Columbus Dublin	THREE DIAMOND	✔	249
❻❷ p. 222	**Sonesta ES Suites Dublin**	THREE DIAMOND	✔	249
❻❸ p. 222	Columbus Marriott Northwest	THREE DIAMOND	✔	248
❻❹ p. 222	Drury Inn & Suites-Columbus Northwest	APPROVED		248
❻❺ p. 222	**Hyatt Place Columbus/Dublin**	THREE DIAMOND	✔	249
❻❻ p. 222	Holiday Inn Express Dublin	THREE DIAMOND		249
❻❼ p. 222	Extended Stay America (Columbus/Tuttle)	APPROVED		249
❻❽ p. 222	Hilton Garden Inn Columbus/Dublin	THREE DIAMOND	✔	249

Map Page	Restaurants	Designation	Cuisine	Price Range	Page
㉞ p. 222	Siam Orchid	APPROVED	Thai	$8-$15	250
㉟ p. 222	Anna's Restaurant	APPROVED	Greek	$7-$19	249
㊱ p. 222	Napa Kitchen & Bar	APPROVED	American	$12-$32	250
㊲ p. 222	Hen Quarter	THREE DIAMOND	Southern	$14-$42	250

Map Page	Restaurants (cont'd)	Designation	Cuisine	Price Range	Page
㊳ p. 222	Fukuryu Ramen Dublin	APPROVED	Japanese	$9-$13	250
㊴ p. 222	The Avenue Steak Tavern	THREE DIAMOND	Steak	$14-$50	249
㊵ p. 222	Cap City Fine Diner and Bar	APPROVED	Comfort Food	$11-$30	249
㊶ p. 222	Oscar's of Dublin	THREE DIAMOND	American	$10-$31	250
㊷ p. 222	Vaso	THREE DIAMOND	Spanish Small Plates	$9-$18	250
㊸ p. 222	Brazenhead Irish Pub	APPROVED	American	$9-$14	249
㊹ p. 222	La Scala Italian Bistro	THREE DIAMOND	Italian	$9-$44	250
㊺ p. 222	Tucci's	THREE DIAMOND	American	$9-$62	250
㊻ p. 222	Mezzo	THREE DIAMOND	Italian	$16-$37	250
㊼ p. 222	J. Liu of Dublin	THREE DIAMOND	New American	$11-$42	250
㊽ p. 222	Dublin Village Tavern	APPROVED	American	$10-$16	250
㊾ p. 222	Hyde Park Prime Steakhouse	THREE DIAMOND	Steak	$31-$60	250
㊿ p. 222	Moretti's Cafe	APPROVED	Italian	$12-$28	250
51 p. 222	P.F. Chang's China Bistro	THREE DIAMOND	Chinese	$11-$29	250
52 p. 222	The Rail	APPROVED	Burgers	$7-$29	250
53 p. 222	Chile Verde Cafe	APPROVED	Southwestern	$6-$16	249

WESTERVILLE

Map Page	Hotels	Designation	Member Savings	Page
70 p. 222	**Renaissance Columbus Westerville-Polaris Hotel**	THREE DIAMOND	✔	308
71 p. 222	Aloft Columbus Westerville	THREE DIAMOND	✔	308

Map Page	Restaurants	Designation	Cuisine	Price Range	Page
59 p. 222	Q2 Bistro	APPROVED	Chinese	$7-$17	309
60 p. 222	101 Beer Kitchen	APPROVED	American	$10-$25	309
61 p. 222	The Old Bag of Nails Pub	APPROVED	American	$10-$22	309

GAHANNA

Map Page	Hotels	Designation	Member Savings	Page
75 p. 222	Candlewood Suites Columbus Airport	APPROVED		255
76 p. 222	TownePlace Suites by Marriott Columbus Airport	APPROVED	✔	255

Map Page	Restaurants	Designation	Cuisine	Price Range	Page
64 p. 222	Asian Gourmet & Sushi Bar	APPROVED	Asian Sushi	$9-$20	255
65 p. 222	Cap City Fine Diner & Bar	APPROVED	Comfort Food	$8-$30	255
66 p. 222	The Old Bag of Nails Pub	APPROVED	American	$10-$23	255

HILLIARD

Map Page	Hotels	Designation	Member Savings	Page
79 p. 222	**Best Western Hilliard Inn & Suites**	THREE DIAMOND	✔	258
80 p. 222	Homewood Suites by Hilton-Columbus Hilliard	THREE DIAMOND	✔	258

Map Page	Restaurant	Designation	Cuisine	Price Range	Page
78 p. 222	Otie's Tavern & Grill	APPROVED	American	$5-$15	258

UPPER ARLINGTON

Map Page	Hotel	Designation	Member Savings	Page
83 p. 222	Homewood Suites by Hilton Columbus/OSU	THREE DIAMOND	✔	304

Map Page	Restaurants	Designation	Cuisine	Price Range	Page
81 p. 222	Figlio Upper Arlington	APPROVED	Pizza	$14-$23	304
82 p. 222	Moretti's of Arlington	THREE DIAMOND	Italian	$10-$25	304
83 p. 222	Hudson 29 Kitchen + Drink	THREE DIAMOND	American	$12-$42	304

CANAL WINCHESTER

Map Page	Hotel	Designation	Member Savings	Page
86 p. 222	**Best Western Canal Winchester Inn-Columbus South East**	APPROVED	✔	147

Map Page	Restaurant	Designation	Cuisine	Price Range	Page
86 p. 222	Brewdog Dogtap	APPROVED	American	$10-$16	147

GROVE CITY

Map Page	Hotels	Designation	Member Savings	Page
89 p. 222	Hilton Garden Inn Columbus/Grove City	THREE DIAMOND	✔	257
90 p. 222	Holiday Inn Express Hotel & Suites	APPROVED		257
91 p. 222	La Quinta Inn Grove City	THREE DIAMOND		257
92 p. 222	Hampton Inn by Hilton Columbus South	APPROVED	✔	257
93 p. 222	Best Western Executive Inn	APPROVED	✔	256
94 p. 222	Travelodge Grove City	APPROVED	✔	257
95 p. 222	Drury Inn & Suites-Columbus South	THREE DIAMOND		256
96 p. 222	Courtyard by Marriott Columbus/Grove City	THREE DIAMOND	✔	256
97 p. 222	Fairfield Inn & Suites by Marriott Columbus Grove City	THREE DIAMOND	✔	257

Map Page	Restaurant	Designation	Cuisine	Price Range	Page
89 p. 222	Cimi's Bistro at Pinnacle	THREE DIAMOND	American	$10-$32	257

POWELL

Map Page	Restaurant	Designation	Cuisine	Price Range	Page
56 p. 222	Vittoria Ristorante & Bar	THREE DIAMOND	Italian	$17-$52	287

NEW ALBANY

Map Page	Restaurant	Designation	Cuisine	Price Range	Page
69 p. 222	Hudson 29 Kitchen & Drink	THREE DIAMOND	American	$14-$42	278

WORTHINGTON

Map Page	Restaurants	Designation	Cuisine	Price Range	Page
72 p. 222	J. Liu Restaurant & Bar	THREE DIAMOND	American	$10-$29	313
73 p. 222	The Whitney House	THREE DIAMOND	American	$12-$27	313
74 p. 222	Cameron's American Bistro	THREE DIAMOND	American	$19-$42	313
75 p. 222	Natalie's Coal-Fired Pizza	APPROVED	Pizza	$12-$16	313

DOWNTOWN COLUMBUS

- **Restaurants p. 230**
- **Hotels & Restaurants map & index p. 219**

CANOPY COLUMBUS DOWNTOWN SHORT NORTH
614/223-1400 **10**
THREE DIAMOND SAVE Boutique Contemporary Hotel. **Address:** 77 E Nationwide Blvd 43215

AAA Benefit: Members save up to 15%!

COURTYARD BY MARRIOTT GRANDVIEW YARD
614/453-4420 **3**
THREE DIAMOND
Hotel

COURTYARD **AAA Benefit:** Members save 5% or more!

Address: 780 Yard St 43212 **Location:** SR 315 exit Goodale Blvd, just w. **Facility:** 135 units. 4 stories, interior corridors. **Pool:** heated indoor. **Activities:** exercise room. **Guest Services:** valet and coin laundry, boarding pass kiosk, area transportation.

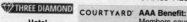

CROWNE PLAZA COLUMBUS DOWNTOWN
614/461-4100 **9**
THREE DIAMOND Hotel. **Address:** 33 E Nationwide Blvd 43215

DRURY INN & SUITES-COLUMBUS CONVENTION CENTER
614/221-7008 **6**
THREE DIAMOND Hotel. **Address:** 88 E Nationwide Blvd 43215

GERMAN VILLAGE GUEST HOUSE
614/437-9712 **17**
THREE DIAMOND Contemporary Bed & Breakfast. **Address:** 748 Jaeger St 43206

HAMPTON INN & SUITES BY HILTON DOWNTOWN
614/559-2000 **4**
THREE DIAMOND
Hotel

AAA Benefit: Members save up to 15%!

Address: 501 N High St 43215 **Location:** Corner of N High and Spruce sts, just n. **Facility:** 179 units. 7 stories, interior corridors. **Parking:** valet only. **Terms:** check-in 4 pm. **Pool:** heated indoor. **Activities:** exercise room. **Guest Services:** valet laundry. **Featured Amenity:** breakfast buffet.

HILTON COLUMBUS DOWNTOWN
614/384-8600 **5**
FOUR DIAMOND SAVE
Contemporary Hotel. **Address:** 401 N High St 43215

AAA Benefit: Members save up to 15%!

(See map & index p. 219.)

HOLIDAY INN COLUMBUS DOWNTOWN CAPITOL SQUARE
614/221-3281 **15**
⬥ APPROVED   Hotel. **Address:** 175 E Town St 43215

HOTEL LEVEQUE, AUTOGRAPH COLLECTION
614/224-9500 **13**

⬥ FOUR DIAMOND

Historic Boutique Hotel

AUTOGRAPH COLLECTION HOTELS **AAA Benefit:** Members save 5% or more!

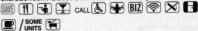

Address: 50 W Broad St 43215 **Location:** Jct Front St. **Facility:** Built in 1924, this soaring Art Deco tower is a monument to the exuberant spirit of America in the Roaring Twenties. Lovingly restored, it now combines historical features with modern conveniences. 149 units. 45 stories, interior corridors. **Parking:** valet only. **Terms:** check-in 4 pm. **Amenities:** safes. **Dining:** The Keep Kitchen and Liquor Bar, see separate listing. **Activities:** exercise room. **Guest Services:** valet laundry.

HYATT PLACE COLUMBUS/OSU   614/280-1234 **2**

⬥ THREE DIAMOND

Hotel

HYATT PLACE **AAA Benefit:** Members save up to 10%!

Address: 795 Yard St 43212 **Location:** US 315 exit Goodale Blvd, just w. **Facility:** 126 units. 6 stories, interior corridors. **Pool:** heated indoor. **Activities:** exercise room. **Guest Services:** valet laundry, area transportation. **Featured Amenity:** full hot breakfast.

HYATT REGENCY COLUMBUS   614/463-1234 **7**

⬥ THREE DIAMOND

Hotel

HYATT REGENCY **AAA Benefit:** Members save up to 10%!

Address: 350 N High St 43215 **Location:** 0.3 mi n on US 23. Located at Columbus Convention Center and Nationwide Arena. **Facility:** 633 units. 20 stories, interior corridors. **Parking:** on-site (fee) and valet. **Amenities:** video games, safes. **Activities:** exercise room. **Guest Services:** valet laundry, boarding pass kiosk.

LE MERIDIEN COLUMBUS, THE JOSEPH   614/227-0100 **1**
⬥ FOUR DIAMOND 🅢 Boutique
Contemporary Hotel. **Address:** 620 N High St 43215

AAA Benefit: Members save 5% or more!

MOXY COLUMBUS SHORT NORTH   614/412-7664 **18**
⬥ THREE DIAMOND 🅢 Boutique
Contemporary Hotel. **Address:** 810 N High St 43215

AAA Benefit: Members save 5% or more!

RED ROOF PLUS+ COLUMBUS
DOWNTOWN-CONVENTION CENTER
614/224-6539 **8**

⬥ APPROVED
Hotel

Address: 111 E Nationwide Blvd 43215 **Location:** Jct 3rd St. **Facility:** 149 units. 7 stories, interior corridors. **Parking:** on-site (fee). **Amenities:** safes. **Guest Services:** valet and coin laundry.

RENAISSANCE COLUMBUS DOWNTOWN HOTEL
614/228-5050 **11**

⬥ THREE DIAMOND

Hotel

R RENAISSANCE HOTELS **AAA Benefit:** Members save 5% or more!

Address: 50 N 3rd St 43215 **Location:** Corner of 3rd and Gay sts. **Facility:** 408 units. 22 stories, interior corridors. **Parking:** valet only. **Terms:** check-in 4 pm. **Amenities:** safes. **Pool:** heated outdoor. **Activities:** sauna, hot tub, exercise room. **Guest Services:** valet and coin laundry, boarding pass kiosk.

RESIDENCE INN BY MARRIOTT DOWNTOWN
614/222-2610 **12**

⬥ THREE DIAMOND

Historic Extended Stay Hotel

Residence INN. **AAA Benefit:** Members save 5% or more!

Address: 36 E Gay St 43215 **Location:** Between High and S 3rd sts. **Facility:** The hotel, set in a former bank building built in 1927, has a massive lobby with marble floor and soaring coffered ceiling. The lobby also has a bourbon bar. The breakfast bar is inside the old vault. 126 units, some two bedrooms, efficiencies and kitchens. 15 stories, interior corridors. **Parking:** valet only. **Terms:** check-in 4 pm. **Activities:** exercise room. **Guest Services:** valet and coin laundry. **Featured Amenity:** breakfast buffet.

SHERATON COLUMBUS AT CAPITOL SQUARE
614/365-4500 **14**

⬥ THREE DIAMOND

Hotel

SHERATON **AAA Benefit:** Members save 5% or more!

Address: 75 E State St 43215 **Location:** Corner of State and 3rd sts. Next to the State Capitol. **Facility:** 403 units. 22 stories, interior corridors. **Parking:** valet only. **Terms:** check-in 4 pm. **Amenities:** safes. **Activities:** exercise room. **Guest Services:** valet laundry, area transportation.

(See map & index p. 219.)

THE WESTIN GREAT SOUTHERN COLUMBUS
614/228-3800 (16)
▼ THREE DIAMOND [SAVE] Classic
Historic Hotel. **Address:** 310 S High St
43215

AAA Benefit:
Members save 5%
or more!

WHERE TO EAT

AMBROSE & EVE　　　614/725-2080 (38)
▼ THREE DIAMOND American. Casual Dining. **Address:** 716
S High St 43206

BARCELONA　　　614/443-3699 (42)
▼ THREE DIAMOND Spanish. Fine Dining. **Address:** 263 E
Whittier St 43206

BAREBURGER　　　614/706-4790 (14)
▼ APPROVED Burgers. Casual Dining. **Address:** 463 N
High St 43215

BASI ITALIA　　　614/294-7383 (4)
▼ THREE DIAMOND Italian. Casual Dining. **Address:** 811
Highland St 43215

BASIL THAI RESTAURANT　　　614/525-0049 (31)
▼ APPROVED Thai. Casual Dining. **Address:** 460 S
Front St 43215

THE BOAT HOUSE　　　614/469-0000 (23)
▼ THREE DIAMOND American. Casual Dining. **Address:** 679
W Spring St 43215

COSECHA COCHINA　　　614/369-1129 (1)
▼ APPROVED Mexican. Casual Dining. **Address:** 987 N
4th St 43201

DEL MAR SOCAL KITCHEN　　　614/300-9500 (7)
▼ THREE DIAMOND Southern California. Casual Dining.
Address: 705 N High St 43215

DIRTY FRANK'S HOT DOG PALACE　　　614/824-4673 (26)
▼ APPROVED Hot Dogs. Quick Serve. **Address:** 248 S
4th St 43215

DUE AMICI　　　614/224-9373 (21)
▼ THREE DIAMOND Italian. Casual Dining. **Address:** 67 E
Gay St 43215

THE EAGLE FOOD & BEER HALL　　　614/745-3397 (2)
▼ APPROVED Southern American. Casual Dining.
Address: 790 N High St 43215

EDDIE GEORGE'S GRILLE 27　　　614/421-2727 (12)
▼ APPROVED American. Sports Bar. **Address:** 775 Yard
St 43212

ELEVATOR BREWERY & DRAUGHT HAUS
614/228-0500 (20)
▼ APPROVED American. Brewpub. **Address:** 161 N
High St 43215

FORNO KITCHEN & BAR　　　614/469-0053 (5)
▼ APPROVED Italian. Casual Dining. **Address:** 721 N
High St 43201

GALLERIE BAR & BISTRO　　　614/484-5287 (17)
▼ THREE DIAMOND New American. Fine Dining. **Address:**
401 N High St 43215

G. MICHAEL'S BISTRO　　　614/464-0575 (35)
▼ THREE DIAMOND Regional American. Fine Dining.
Address: 595 S 3rd St 43215

THE GOAT AT LC RIVERSOUTH　　　614/779-0830 (27)
▼ APPROVED American. Casual Dining. **Address:** 219
S High St 43215

GORDON BIERSCH BREWERY RESTAURANT
614/246-2900 (18)
▼ THREE DIAMOND American. Casual Dining. **Address:** 401
N Front St 43215

THE GUILD HOUSE　　　614/280-9780 (10)
▼ THREE DIAMOND American. Fine Dining. **Address:** 624 N
High St 43215

HARVEY & ED'S　　　614/641-4040 (6)
▼ APPROVED Jewish Deli. Casual Dining. **Address:**
698 N High St 43215

HIGH BANK DISTILLERY　　　614/826-5347 (16)
▼ APPROVED American. Casual Dining. **Address:** 1051
Goodale Blvd 43212

HOFBRAUHAUS COLUMBUS　　　614/294-2437 (13)
▼ APPROVED German. Brewpub. **Address:** 800
Goodale Blvd 43212

HUBBARD GRILLE　　　614/291-5000 (3)
▼ APPROVED American. Casual Dining. **Address:** 793
N High St 43215

KATZINGER'S DELICATESSEN　　　614/228-3354 (30)
▼ APPROVED Jewish Deli. Quick Serve. **Address:** 475
S 3rd St 43215

THE KEEP KITCHEN AND LIQUOR BAR　　　614/745-0322 (25)
▼ THREE DIAMOND French. Gastropub. **Address:** 50 W
Broad St 43215

LEMONGRASS FUSION BISTRO　　　614/224-1414 (9)
▼ APPROVED Asian Fusion Sushi. Casual Dining.
Address: 641 N High St, Suite 103 43215

LINDEY'S　　　614/228-4343 (33)
▼ THREE DIAMOND American. Fine Dining. **Address:** 169 E
Beck St 43206

MARCELLA'S SHORT NORTH　　　614/223-2100 (11)
▼ APPROVED Italian. Casual Dining. **Address:** 615 N
High St 43215

MARTINI MODERN ITALIAN　　　614/224-8259 (15)
▼ THREE DIAMOND Regional Italian. Casual Dining. **Address:**
445 N High St 43215

M AT MIRANOVA　　　614/629-0000 (29)
▼ FOUR DIAMOND American. Fine Dining. **Address:** 2
Miranova Pl, Suite 100 43215

MATT AND TONY'S WOOD-FIRED GRILL　　　614/732-5098 (36)
▼ APPROVED American. Casual Dining. **Address:** 525
Short St 43215

MILESTONE 229　　　614/427-0276 (28)
▼ THREE DIAMOND American. Casual Dining. **Address:** 229
Civic Center Dr 43215

MITCHELL'S STEAKHOUSE　　　614/621-2333 (22)
▼ THREE DIAMOND Steak. Fine Dining. **Address:** 45 N 3rd St
43215

OLD MOHAWK RESTAURANT　　　614/444-7204 (40)
▼ APPROVED American. Casual Dining. **Address:** 819
Mohawk St 43206

THE PEARL　　　614/227-0151 (8)
▼ THREE DIAMOND American. Gastropub. **Address:** 641 N
High St 43215

(See map & index p. 219.)

PISTACIA VERA 614/220-9070 **32**
 APPROVED Breads/Pastries. Quick Serve. **Address:** 541 S Third St 43215

ROCKMILL TAVERN 614/732-4364 **34**
THREE DIAMOND American. Gastropub. **Address:** 503 S Front St 43215

SCHMIDT'S RESTAURANT UND SAUSAGE HAUS
614/444-6808 **39**
APPROVED German. Casual Dining. **Address:** 240 E Kossuth St 43206

SKILLET, RUSTIC URBAN FOOD 614/443-2266 **41**
APPROVED American. Casual Dining. **Address:** 410 E Whittier St 43206

THE SPAGHETTI WAREHOUSE 614/464-0143
APPROVED Italian. Casual Dining. **Address:** 397 W Broad St 43215

THE SYCAMORE 614/754-1460 **37**
THREE DIAMOND American. Gastropub. **Address:** 262 E Sycamore St 43206

VERITAS 614/745-3864 **24**
THREE DIAMOND Small Plates. Fine Dining. **Address:** 11 W Gay St 43215

WOLF'S RIDGE BREWING 614/429-3936 **19**
APPROVED American. Brewpub. **Address:** 215 N 4th St 43215

COLUMBUS
- **Restaurants p. 235**
- **Hotels & Restaurants map & index p. 222**

BEST WESTERN PORT COLUMBUS 614/337-8400 **36**
APPROVED
Hotel

 Best Western. **AAA Benefit:** Members save up to 15% and earn bonus points!

 Address: 1450 Airpointe Dr 43219 **Location:** I-670 exit 9 (Johnstown Rd) eastbound; exit 9 (Cassady Ave) westbound, just n. **Facility:** 87 units. 3 stories, interior corridors. **Amenities:** safes. **Pool:** heated indoor. **Activities:** exercise room. **Guest Services:** coin laundry, area transportation. **Featured Amenity:** breakfast buffet.

BEST WESTERN SUITES 614/870-2378 **49**
APPROVED
Hotel

Best Western. **AAA Benefit:** Members save up to 15% and earn bonus points!

Address: 1133 Evans Way Ct 43228 **Location:** I-70 exit 91 eastbound; exit 91A westbound, just sw. **Facility:** 66 units. 2 stories, interior corridors. **Parking:** winter plug-ins. **Pool:** heated indoor. **Activities:** hot tub, exercise room. **Guest Services:** valet and coin laundry. **Featured Amenity:** full hot breakfast.

THE BLACKWELL INN & PFAHL CONFERENCE CENTER
614/247-4000 **41**
THREE DIAMOND Hotel. **Address:** 2110 Tuttle Park Pl 43210

CAMBRIA HOTEL & SUITES COLUMBUS/POLARIS
614/841-9100 **1**
THREE DIAMOND Hotel. **Address:** 9100 Lyra Dr 43240

CANDLEWOOD SUITES POLARIS 614/436-6600 **6**
APPROVED Extended Stay Hotel. **Address:** 8515 Lyra Dr 43240

COLUMBUS AIRPORT MARRIOTT 614/475-7551 **40**
THREE DIAMOND SAVE Hotel. **Address:** 1375 N Cassady Ave 43219
AAA Benefit: Members save 5% or more!

COMFORT INN POLARIS 614/791-9700 **4**
APPROVED Hotel. **Address:** 8400 Lyra Dr 43240

COMFORT SUITES COLUMBUS AIRPORT
614/532-1570 **35**
THREE DIAMOND Hotel. **Address:** 1521 N Cassady Ave 43219

COMFORT SUITES EAST BROAD AT 270
614/604-6400 **42**
THREE DIAMOND
Hotel

 Address: 70 Chris Perry Ln 43213 **Location:** I-270 exit 39, 1 mi e on E Broad St. **Facility:** 85 units, some kitchens. 4 stories, interior corridors. **Parking:** winter plug-ins. **Terms:** check-in 4 pm. **Pool:** heated indoor. **Activities:** hot tub, exercise room. **Guest Services:** valet and coin laundry. **Featured Amenity:** continental breakfast.

COUNTRY INN & SUITES COLUMBUS AIRPORT
614/478-2900 **37**
APPROVED Hotel. **Address:** 2900 Airport Dr 43219

COURTYARD BY MARRIOTT-COLUMBUS AIRPORT
614/475-8530 **38**
THREE DIAMOND SAVE Hotel. **Address:** 2901 Airport Dr 43219
AAA Benefit: Members save 5% or more!

COURTYARD BY MARRIOTT COLUMBUS-EASTON
614/416-8000 **21**
THREE DIAMOND SAVE Hotel. **Address:** 3900 Morse Crossing 43219
AAA Benefit: Members save 5% or more!

COURTYARD BY MARRIOTT WORTHINGTON
614/436-7070 **10**
THREE DIAMOND SAVE Hotel. **Address:** 7411 Vantage Dr 43235
AAA Benefit: Members save 5% or more!

CROWNE PLAZA COLUMBUS NORTH-WORTHINGTON
614/885-1885 **13**
THREE DIAMOND
Hotel

 Address: 6500 Doubletree Ave 43229 **Location:** I-71 exit 117, 0.3 mi w on SR 161, 0.8 mi n on Busch Blvd, then 0.3 mi e on Kingsmill Pkwy. **Facility:** 300 units. 9 stories, interior corridors. **Parking:** winter plug-ins. **Terms:** check-in 4 pm. **Pool:** heated outdoor, heated indoor. **Activities:** hot tub, exercise room. **Guest Services:** valet and coin laundry, area transportation.

(See map & index p. 222.)

DOUBLETREE BY HILTON HOTEL COLUMBUS-WORTHINGTON
614/885-3334 **11**

THREE DIAMOND
Hotel

AAA Benefit: Members save up to 15%!

Address: 175 Hutchinson Ave 43235 **Location:** I-270 exit 23, just n on US 23, just e on Dimension Dr, then just s on High Cross Blvd. Next to a theater. **Facility:** 306 units. 6 stories, interior corridors. **Terms:** check-in 4 pm. **Amenities:** safes. **Pool:** heated indoor. **Activities:** hot tub, exercise room. **Guest Services:** valet and coin laundry, boarding pass kiosk.

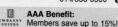

DRURY INN AND SUITES COLUMBUS POLARIS
614/854-0216 **53**

THREE DIAMOND Hotel. **Address:** 8805 Orion Pl 43240

EMBASSY SUITES BY HILTON COLUMBUS AIRPORT
614/536-0500 **39**

THREE DIAMOND
Hotel

AAA Benefit: Members save up to 15%!

Address: 2886 Airport Dr 43219 **Location:** I-670 exit 9 (Johnstown Rd) eastbound; exit 9 (Cassady Ave) westbound. **Facility:** 198 units. 7 stories, interior corridors. **Terms:** check-in 4 pm. **Amenities:** safes. **Pool:** heated indoor. **Activities:** hot tub, exercise room. **Guest Services:** valet and coin laundry, boarding pass kiosk, luggage security pick-up, area transportation.
Featured Amenity: full hot breakfast.

EMBASSY SUITES BY HILTON HOTEL-COLUMBUS
614/890-8600 **12**

THREE DIAMOND Hotel. **Address:** 2700 Corporate Exchange Dr 43231

AAA Benefit: Members save up to 15%!

EXTENDED STAY AMERICA-COLUMBUS-EASTON
614/428-6022 **14**

APPROVED Extended Stay Hotel. **Address:** 4200 Stelzer Rd 43230

FAIRFIELD INN & SUITES BY MARRIOTT COLUMBUS AIRPORT
614/237-2100 **32**

THREE DIAMOND **SAVE** Hotel. **Address:** 4300 International Gateway 43219

AAA Benefit: Members save 5% or more!

FAIRFIELD INN & SUITES BY MARRIOTT COLUMBUS POLARIS
614/568-0770 **7**

THREE DIAMOND **SAVE** Hotel. **Address:** 9000 Worthington Rd 43240

AAA Benefit: Members save 5% or more!

FAIRFIELD INN & SUITES BY MARRIOTT OSU
614/267-1111 **28**

THREE DIAMOND **SAVE** Hotel. **Address:** 3031 Olentangy River Rd 43202

AAA Benefit: Members save 5% or more!

FOUR POINTS BY SHERATON COLUMBUS OHIO AIRPORT
614/475-8383 **34**

THREE DIAMOND **SAVE** Hotel. **Address:** 3030 Plaza Properties Blvd 43219

AAA Benefit: Members save 5% or more!

HAMPTON INN & SUITES BY HILTON COLUMBUS EASTON AREA
614/473-9911 **18**

THREE DIAMOND **SAVE** Hotel. **Address:** 4150 Stelzer Rd 43230

AAA Benefit: Members save up to 15%!

HAMPTON INN & SUITES BY HILTON COLUMBUS-POLARIS
614/885-8400 **3**

THREE DIAMOND **SAVE** Hotel. **Address:** 8411 Pulsar Pl 43240

AAA Benefit: Members save up to 15%!

HAMPTON INN & SUITES BY HILTON COLUMBUS/ UNIVERSITY AREA
614/268-8700 **23**

THREE DIAMOND
Hotel

AAA Benefit: Members save up to 15%!

Address: 3160 Olentangy River Rd 43202 **Location:** Waterfront. SR 315 exit N Broadway St, 0.3 mi s. **Facility:** 152 units. 7 stories, interior corridors. **Parking:** winter plug-ins. **Amenities:** safes. **Pool:** heated indoor. **Activities:** exercise room. **Guest Services:** valet laundry, area transportation.

(See map & index p. 222.)

HAMPTON INN & SUITES COLUMBUS SCIOTO DOWNS
614/491-3800 **51**

 THREE DIAMOND SAVE Hotel. **Address:** 5950 S High St 43125

AAA Benefit: Members save up to 15%!

HAMPTON INN BY HILTON AT COLUMBUS INTERNATIONAL AIRPORT 614/235-0717 **33**

 THREE DIAMOND
Hotel

AAA Benefit: Members save up to 15%!

Address: 4280 International Gateway 43219 **Location:** At John Glenn Columbus International Airport. **Facility:** 129 units. 4 stories, interior corridors. **Terms:** check-in 4 pm. **Pool:** heated outdoor. **Activities:** exercise room. **Guest Services:** valet laundry, area transportation.

 SAVE ✈ ⓘ CALL ♿ 🏊 👪
BIZ 📶 ✕ 🅿 💻

HAMPTON INN BY HILTON COLUMBUS I-70 EAST/HAMILTON ROAD 614/552-2400 **50**

THREE DIAMOND SAVE Hotel. **Address:** 2093 S Hamilton Rd 43232

AAA Benefit: Members save up to 15%!

HAMPTON INN BY HILTON COLUMBUS WEST
614/851-5599 **48**

THREE DIAMOND SAVE Hotel. **Address:** 5625 Trabue Rd 43228

AAA Benefit: Members save up to 15%!

HAWTHORN SUITES BY WYNDHAM 614/853-6199 **47**

APPROVED Extended Stay Hotel. **Address:** 5505 Keim Cir 43228

HILTON COLUMBUS AT EASTON 614/414-5000 **20**

FOUR DIAMOND
Hotel

Hilton
HOTELS & RESORTS

AAA Benefit: Members save up to 15%!

Address: 3900 Chagrin Dr 43219 **Location:** I-270 exit 33, 0.5 mi w. **Facility:** Located near the Easton Town Center shopping mall, this red-brick, Georgian-style building has public areas adorned with bright, modern décor. Guest rooms have a comparably contemporary style. 345 units. 7 stories, interior corridors. **Parking:** on-site (fee) and valet. **Terms:** check-in 4 pm. **Amenities:** safes. **Pool:** heated indoor. **Activities:** hot tub, exercise room, massage. **Guest Services:** valet laundry, boarding pass kiosk, area transportation.

SAVE 🍴 ✈ ⓘ 🛎 CALL ♿ 🏊 👪 BIZ
📶 ✕ 🅿 💻 / SOME UNITS 🐾 HS

HILTON COLUMBUS/POLARIS 614/885-1600 **2**

FOUR DIAMOND SAVE Hotel. **Address:** 8700 Lyra Dr 43240

AAA Benefit: Members save up to 15%!

ⓘ **For complete hotel, dining and attraction listings: AAA.com/travelguides**

HILTON GARDEN INN COLUMBUS AIRPORT
614/231-2869 **31**

 THREE DIAMOND
Hotel

Hilton Garden Inn

AAA Benefit: Members save up to 15%!

Address: 4265 Sawyer Rd 43219 **Location:** I-670 exit 9, 1.8 mi e; at Port Columbus International Airport. **Facility:** 156 units. 3 stories, interior corridors. **Pool:** heated indoor. **Activities:** exercise room. **Guest Services:** valet and coin laundry, area transportation.

SAVE ✈ ⓘ ✈ CALL ♿ ✈
👪 BIZ 📶 ✕ 🅿 🖥 💻

HILTON GARDEN INN COLUMBUS/POLARIS
614/846-8884 **5**

THREE DIAMOND SAVE Hotel. **Address:** 8535 Lyra Dr 43240

AAA Benefit: Members save up to 15%!

HILTON GARDEN INN COLUMBUS-UNIVERSITY AREA
614/263-7200 **22**

THREE DIAMOND
Hotel

Hilton Garden Inn

AAA Benefit: Members save up to 15%!

Address: 3232 Olentangy River Rd 43202 **Location:** SR 315 exit Olentangy River Rd, just s. Near The Ohio State University campus. **Facility:** 158 units. 4 stories, interior corridors. **Pool:** heated indoor. **Activities:** exercise room. **Guest Services:** valet and coin laundry, area transportation.

SAVE 🍴 ✈ CALL ♿ 🏊 👪
BIZ 📶 ✕ 🅿 🖥 💻

HOLIDAY INN EXPRESS & SUITES COLUMBUS AIRPORT EAST 614/322-8000 **43**

THREE DIAMOND Hotel. **Address:** 6305 E Broad St 43213

HOLIDAY INN EXPRESS & SUITES COLUMBUS EASTON AREA 614/476-1100 **17**

THREE DIAMOND Hotel. **Address:** 4899 Sunbury Rd 43230

HOLIDAY INN EXPRESS & SUITES OSU 614/447-1212 **27**

THREE DIAMOND Hotel. **Address:** 3045 Olentangy River Rd 43202

HOLIDAY INN EXPRESS HOTEL & SUITES COLUMBUS-WORTHINGTON 614/977-0520 **52**

THREE DIAMOND Hotel. **Address:** 55 Hutchinson Ave 43235

HOLIDAY INN EXPRESS OHIO EXPO CENTER
614/263-7725 **29**

 THREE DIAMOND
Hotel

Address: 701 E Hudson St 43211 **Location:** I-71 exit 112, just e. **Facility:** 71 units. 4 stories, interior corridors. **Amenities:** safes. **Pool:** heated indoor. **Activities:** exercise room. **Guest Services:** valet and coin laundry. **Featured Amenity:** full hot breakfast.

SAVE ⓘ CALL ♿ 🏊 👪 BIZ
📶 ✕ 🅿 🖥 💻
/ SOME UNITS 🐾

HOME2 SUITES BY HILTON COLUMBUS AIRPORT EAST BROAD 614/604-9113 **44**

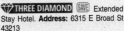 **THREE DIAMOND** SAVE Extended Stay Hotel. **Address:** 6315 E Broad St 43213

AAA Benefit: Members save up to 15%!

(See map & index p. 222.)

HYATT PLACE COLUMBUS/WORTHINGTON
614-846-4355 **8**

THREE DIAMOND
Hotel

HYATT PLACE **AAA Benefit:** Members save up to 10%!

Address: 7490 Vantage Dr 43235 **Location:** I-270 exit 23, 0.4 mi n on US 23, just e on Dimension Dr, then just s. **Facility:** 124 units. 6 stories, interior corridors. **Pool:** heated outdoor. **Activities:** exercise room. **Guest Services:** valet laundry. **Featured Amenity:** full hot breakfast.

/ SOME UNITS

MARRIOTT COLUMBUS UNIVERSITY AREA
614-447-9777 **25**

THREE DIAMOND
Hotel

MARRIOTT **AAA Benefit:** Members save 5% or more!

Address: 3100 Olentangy River Rd 43202 **Location:** SR 315 exit 5, 0.4 mi n. **Facility:** 240 units. 5 stories, interior corridors. **Bath:** shower only. **Amenities:** safes. **Pool:** heated indoor. **Activities:** exercise room. **Guest Services:** valet and coin laundry, area transportation.

RED ROOF PLUS+ COLUMBUS-THE OHIO STATE UNIVERSITY
614-267-9941 **30**

APPROVED
Hotel

Address: 441 Ackerman Rd 43202 **Location:** SR 315 exit Ackerman Rd, 0.6 mi e. **Facility:** 113 units. 3 stories, exterior corridors. **Amenities:** safes.

/ SOME UNITS

RESIDENCE INN BY MARRIOTT COLUMBUS-WORTHINGTON
614-885-0799 **9**

THREE DIAMOND SAVE Extended Stay Hotel. **Address:** 7300 Huntington Park Dr 43235

AAA Benefit: Members save 5% or more!

RESIDENCE INN BY MARRIOTT EASTON 614-414-1000 **19**

THREE DIAMOND SAVE Extended Stay Hotel. **Address:** 3999 Easton Loop W 43219

AAA Benefit: Members save 5% or more!

 Rest assured:
AAA.com/travelguides/hotels

RESIDENCE INN COLUMBUS UNIVERSITY AREA
614-261-7994 **26**

THREE DIAMOND
Extended Stay Hotel

Residence INN **AAA Benefit:** Members save 5% or more!

Address: 3100 Olentangy River Rd 43202 **Location:** SR 315 exit 5, 0.4 mi n. **Facility:** 114 units, some two bedrooms, efficiencies and kitchens. 8 stories, interior corridors. **Bath:** shower only. **Amenities:** safes. **Pool:** heated indoor. **Activities:** exercise room. **Guest Services:** valet and coin laundry, area transportation.

SPRINGHILL SUITES BY MARRIOTT COLUMBUS EASTON AREA
614-471-3500 **16**

THREE DIAMOND
Hotel

SPRINGHILL SUITES MARRIOTT **AAA Benefit:** Members save 5% or more!

Address: 4048 Morse Rd 43230 **Location:** I-270 exit 32, 0.3 mi n. **Facility:** 122 units. 4 stories, interior corridors. **Pool:** heated indoor. **Activities:** exercise room. **Guest Services:** valet and coin laundry, area transportation. **Featured Amenity:** breakfast buffet.

SPRINGHILL SUITES BY MARRIOTT COLUMBUS OSU
614-297-9912 **46**

THREE DIAMOND
Hotel

SPRINGHILL SUITES MARRIOTT **AAA Benefit:** Members save 5% or more!

Address: 1421 Olentangy River Rd 43212 **Location:** SR 315 exit King Ave southbound; exit Lane Ave northbound, 1 mi s. **Facility:** 136 units. 4 stories, interior corridors. **Pool:** heated indoor. **Activities:** exercise room. **Guest Services:** valet and coin laundry, area transportation. **Featured Amenity:** breakfast buffet.

STAYBRIDGE SUITES COLUMBUS UNIVERSITY AREA
614-262-6900 **24**

THREE DIAMOND Extended Stay Contemporary Hotel. **Address:** 3121 Olentangy River Rd 43202

TOWNEPLACE SUITES BY MARRIOTT COLUMBUS EASTON AREA
614-471-6300 **15**

THREE DIAMOND
Extended Stay Hotel

TOWNEPLACE SUITES MARRIOTT **AAA Benefit:** Members save 5% or more!

Address: 4048 Morse Rd 43230 **Location:** I-270 exit 32, 0.3 mi w. **Facility:** 140 units, some efficiencies and kitchens. 4 stories, interior corridors. **Pool:** heated indoor. **Activities:** exercise room. **Guest Services:** valet and coin laundry, area transportation. **Featured Amenity:** breakfast buffet.

/ SOME UNITS

(See map & index p. 222.)

THE VARSITY INN   614/291-2983   **45**

APPROVED

Motel

Address: 1445 Olentangy River Rd 43212 **Location:** SR 315 exit King Ave southbound; exit Lane Ave northbound, 1 mi s. Next to railroad tracks. **Facility:** 119 units. 2 stories (no elevator), exterior corridors. **Terms:** check-in 4 pm. **Pool:** heated outdoor.

  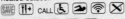

WHERE TO EAT

BAMBOO CAFÉ   614/326-1950   **16**
APPROVED   Thai. Casual Dining. **Address:** 774 Bethel Rd 43214

BONIFACIO   614/914-8115   **27**
APPROVED   Philippine. Casual Dining. **Address:** 1577 King Ave 43212

BRIO TUSCAN GRILLE
THREE DIAMOND   Regional Italian. Casual Dining.
LOCATIONS:
Address: 3993 Easton Station 43219 **Phone:** 614/416-4745   **22**
Address: 1500 Polaris Pkwy, Suite 200 43240
Phone: 614/410-0310   **4**

CAFE ISTANBUL   614/473-9144   **13**
THREE DIAMOND   Turkish. Casual Dining. **Address:** 3983 Worth Ave 43219

CANTINA LAREDO   614/781-1139
APPROVED   Mexican. Casual Dining. **Address:** 8791 Lyra Dr 43240

CAP CITY FINE DINER & BAR   614/291-3663   **28**
APPROVED   Comfort Food. Casual Dining. **Address:** 1299 Olentangy River Rd 43212

CHILE VERDE CAFE: POLARIS   614/846-8773   **1**
APPROVED   Southwestern. Casual Dining. **Address:** 1522 Gemini Pl 43240

CITY BARBEQUE   614/755-8890
APPROVED   Barbecue. Quick Serve. **Address:** 5979 E Main St 43213

COLUMBUS FISH MARKET   614/291-3474   **29**
THREE DIAMOND   Seafood. Casual Dining. **Address:** 1245 Olentangy River Rd 43212

EDDIE MERLOT'S   614/433-7307   **6**
THREE DIAMOND   Steak. Fine Dining. **Address:** 1570 Polaris Pkwy 43240

FIREPROOF SHORT NORTH   614/706-4425   **32**
THREE DIAMOND   Small Plates. Fine Dining. **Address:** 1026 N High St 43215

FLIP SIDE   614/472-3547   **21**
APPROVED   Burgers. Casual Dining. **Address:** 3945 Easton Station 43219

HARVEST CLINTONVILLE   614/947-7133   **25**
APPROVED   Pizza. Casual Dining. **Address:** 2885 N High St 43202

HOGGY'S   614/442-1800   **18**
APPROVED   Barbecue. Quick Serve. **Address:** 830 Bethel Rd 43214

J. ALEXANDER'S REDLANDS GRILL   614/847-1166   **10**
THREE DIAMOND   American. Casual Dining. **Address:** 7550 Vantage Dr 43235

J. GILBERT'S WOOD FIRED STEAKS & SEAFOOD
614/840-9090   **9**
THREE DIAMOND   Steak Seafood. Fine Dining. **Address:** 1 E Campus View Blvd 43235

LOTUS GRILL   614/781-8883   **11**
APPROVED   Chinese. Quick Serve. **Address:** 150 Hutchinson Ave 43235

MARCELLA'S ITALIAN KITCHEN POLARIS   614/844-6500   **8**
APPROVED   Italian. Casual Dining. **Address:** 1319 Polaris Pkwy 43240

MATT THE MILLER'S TAVERN   614/841-4430   **2**
APPROVED   American. Gastropub. **Address:** 1436 Gemini Pl 43240

MCCORMICK & SCHMICK'S   614/476-3663   **14**
THREE DIAMOND   Seafood. Fine Dining. **Address:** 3965 New Bond St 43219

MELT BAR AND GRILLED   614/934-6020   **12**
APPROVED   Sandwiches. Casual Dining. **Address:** 4206 Worth Ave 43219

MIN-GA KOREAN RESTAURANT   614/457-7331   **17**
APPROVED   Korean. Casual Dining. **Address:** 800 Bethel Rd 43214

MITCHELL'S OCEAN CLUB   614/416-2582   **19**
THREE DIAMOND   Seafood Steak. Fine Dining. **Address:** 4002 Easton Station 43219

MITCHELL'S STEAKHOUSE   614/888-2467   **7**
THREE DIAMOND   Steak. Fine Dining. **Address:** 1408 Polaris Pkwy 43240

MOLLY WOO'S ASIAN BISTRO   614/985-9667   **3**
THREE DIAMOND   Asian. Casual Dining. **Address:** 1500 Polaris Pkwy 43240

MOZART'S RESTAURANT, BAKERY AND PIANO CAFE
614/268-3687   **23**
APPROVED   Austrian Breads/Pastries. Casual Dining. **Address:** 4784 N High St 43214

P.F. CHANG'S CHINA BISTRO   614/416-4100   **24**
THREE DIAMOND   Chinese. Casual Dining. **Address:** 4040 Townsfair Way 43219

POLARIS GRILL   614/431-5598   **5**
THREE DIAMOND   American. Casual Dining. **Address:** 1835 Polaris Pkwy 43240

THE REFECTORY RESTAURANT & WINE SHOP
614/451-9774   **20**

FOUR DIAMOND

French
Fine Dining
$21-$51

AAA Inspector Notes: This restaurant, located in a historic remodeled church and school, features a ceiling of exposed original walnut log beams. The chef de cuisine offers a seasonally revised menu that balances selections of fresh seafood, veal, game and poultry with an emphasis on local, sustainably produced meats and produce. An extensive wine list is oriented toward French and California vintages but also is well balanced with choices from other regions. Special desserts include crème brûlée and pear tarte. **Features:** full bar, patio dining, happy hour. **Reservations:** suggested. **Address:** 1092 Bethel Rd 43220 **Location:** SR 315 exit 8, 0.8 mi w.   **D**

RUSTY BUCKET RESTAURANT AND TAVERN
614/342-2063   **15**
APPROVED   American. Casual Dining. **Address:** 4062 Gramercy St 43219

(See map & index p. 222.)

SKYLINE CHILI

▼▼ **APPROVED** American. Quick Serve.

LOCATIONS:
Address: 1790 Hilliard-Rome Rd 43026 **Phone:** 614/529-1548
Address: 8550 Orion Pl 43240 **Phone:** 614/781-6370
Address: 7026 E Broad St 43213 **Phone:** 614/751-8312
Address: 3720 S High St 43207 **Phone:** 614/409-9275
Address: 6111 Busch Blvd 43229 **Phone:** 614/848-3855

TAT RISTORANTE DI FAMIGLIA   614/236-1392 ③⓪
▼▼ **APPROVED** Southern Italian. Casual Dining.
Address: 1210 S James Rd 43227

THE THURMAN CAFE   614/443-1570 ③①
▼▼ **APPROVED** Burgers Pizza. Casual Dining. **Address:**
183 Thurman Ave 43206

WATERSHED KITCHEN & BAR   614/357-1936 ②⑥
▼▼ **THREE DIAMOND** New American. Casual Dining. **Address:**
1145 Chesapeake Ave 43212

CONNEAUT (A-9) pop. 12,841, elev. 650'

The first survey party of the Western Reserve Region reached Conneaut Harbor on July 4, 1796. As settlers arrived, the town adopted the name the Native Americans had given to the nearby river, Conneaut. The word is believed to have come from the Seneca Indians, but there have been several translations and it remains a name of disputed meaning. The body of water is now known as Conneaut Creek State Wild And Scenic River and is a good location for steelhead trout fishing.

The development of industry along Lake Erie's harbor made the town a busy port, with shipments running into millions of tons annually. Visitors can look down and watch the dock activities from the viewing area on Day Street, near Harbor Street.

To see the more recreational side of the lake as well as a good view of the lighthouse, follow Broad Street north to the Conneaut Port Authority. You can drive around the marina and stroll along the walkways; there is ample parking. Boat ramps are open daily May through October. Fishing right off the public dock might yield perch and walleye catches, and ice fishing is possible during winter. Nature trails and a bird observatory have been added to the sandbar that has developed.

Another good spot for lake and lighthouse viewing is nearby Conneaut Township Park, at the junction of Lake Road (SR 531) and Grove Street—both from the bluffs and on the public beach. Stairs lead from the bluff area down to the beach, which is about a half-mile long. There are no lifeguards; use extreme caution in the water due to known undertows. Other park amenities include picnic tables; grills; exercise walkways; boardwalks providing access to the water's edge; and various sports fields and courts, including two boccie courts. Each Thursday night during summer (6-9 p.m., generally the third week in May through September) an antique car show is held here. The number of cars varies, but occasionally it has reached upwards of 100. The park is also the site of the annual ▼▼ D-Day Conneaut, usually held in mid- or late August. History buffs meet to re-create the Allied troops' June 6, 1944, amphibious landing during World War II in Normandy, France.

Other amenities include summer cottages and a golf course as well as covered bridges on Creek, Middle and State roads. The Conneaut Area Historical Society features local history displays and is open Fri.-Sun. noon to 5 from Memorial Day through Labor Day. Just across the railroad tracks is the Conneaut Historical Railroad Museum.

The Conneaut Arts Center—just above the harbor at 1025 Buffalo St.—offers monthly art exhibits and special events throughout the year, including free concerts on the lawn Wednesday evenings in July. Lake Erie can be seen in the distance. The building was originally known as Kilpi Hall, built in 1899 as a Finnish meeting hall; phone (440) 593-5888.

Conneaut Area Chamber of Commerce: 235 Main St., Conneaut, OH 44030. **Phone:** (440) 593-2402.

DAYS INN OF CONNEAUT   440/593-6000
▼▼ **APPROVED** Motel. **Address:** 600 Days Blvd 44030

COSHOCTON (E-6) pop. 11,216, elev. 790'

Coshocton County Convention and Visitors Bureau: 432 N. Whitewoman St., Coshocton, OH 43812. **Phone:** (740) 622-4877 or (800) 338-4724.

▼GEM▼ **SAVE** **ROSCOE VILLAGE** is at 600 N. Whitewoman St. The restored 1830s Ohio & Erie Canal town has living-history buildings, a museum, restaurants and quaint shops. The Living History Tour features costumed interpreters. Adjacent to the property are the mile-long foot and bicycle Towpath trail and Lake Park, a recreational complex. Horse-drawn canal boat rides are offered at the Canal Boat Landing.

The visitor center includes a lock model and a gristmill model as well as dioramas depicting the construction of the canal. The center's theater shows the 15-minute "Ditches of Destiny" video. Annual festivals and special events are held throughout the year.

Hours: Visitor center open Mon.-Sat. 10-4, Sun. noon-5, Apr.-Dec. Ticket office open Mon.-Sat. 10-4, Sun. noon-5, Apr.-Dec.; daily noon-4, rest of year. Living History Tours depart 10-4, Memorial Day-Labor Day; at 1, Apr. 1-day before Memorial Day and day after Labor Day-Dec. 31. Phone ahead to confirm schedule. **Cost:** Living History Tour $10.95; $9.95 (ages 60+); $4.95 (students ages 6-18). Exhibit hall $4; $3 (students with ID). Canal boat ride $8; $7 (ages 60+); $6 (students with ID). **Phone:** (740) 622-7644 or (800) 877-1830. GT 🍽 ⊠

Johnson-Humrickhouse Museum is at 300 N. Whitewoman St. at Roscoe Village. Displays contain Native American, European and Asian art as well as changing exhibits. Basketry, pottery, prehistoric tools, lacquerware, Samurai swords, weaponry, early American tools and firearms, Coshocton advertising art and the controversial Newark Holy Stones also are included. **Hours:** Daily noon-5, Memorial Day-Labor Day; Tues.-Sun. noon-4, day after Labor Day-Dec. 31 and Mar. 1-day before Memorial Day; Fri.-Sun. noon-4, rest of year. **Cost:** $4; $3 (students with ID); $11 (family, two adults and children ages 0-18). **Phone:** (740) 622-8710.

Monticello III is .5 mi. n. of Roscoe Village on SR 83. Visitors are taken on 40-minute horse-drawn canal boat rides. **Hours:** Trips depart on the hour Tues.-Sun. 1-3 (also Sat.-Sun. 3-4), Memorial Day weekend-Labor Day weekend; Sat.-Sun. 1-4, Labor Day to mid-Oct. Phone ahead to confirm schedule. **Cost:** $8; $7 (senior citizens); $6 (ages 5-12). **Phone:** (740) 622-7528. GT

COSHOCTON VILLAGE INN & SUITES 740/622-9455
APPROVED Hotel. **Address:** 115 N Water St 43812

WHERE TO EAT

THE WAREHOUSE STEAK & STEIN 740/622-4001
APPROVED Steak. Casual Dining. **Address:** 400 N Whitewoman St 43812

CUMBERLAND (F-7) pop. 367, elev. 857'

GEM **THE WILDS** entrance is s. off SR 146 between Chandlersville and Cumberland at 14000 International Rd. Situated on nearly 10,000 acres, this wildlife conservation center provides habitat for rare and endangered species from around the world. Interpretive guides offer narrated safari rides through the open range; they describe the animals and the conservation work the staff is performing here. Animal sightings often include camels, cheetahs, giraffes and rhinos as well as a variety of indigenous species like trumpeter swans and bison.

The grounds include a bird-watching station and a walking trail through a 10-acre butterfly habitat. Sunset safari rides, zipline tours, horseback riding and fishing safaris also are available by reservation.

Time: Allow 2 hours, 30 minutes minimum. **Hours:** Daily 10-4, May-Sept.; Sat.-Sun. 10-4, in Oct. Last tour begins at closing. Phone ahead to confirm tour schedules. **Cost:** Safari Transport Ride $20; $19 (senior citizens); $15 (ages 4-12); free (military with ID). Open-Air Safari $30; free (military with ID). Wildside Tour $125. Zipline Safari $84. Horseback Safari $30. Sunset Safari $75. Sunset Horseback Safari $75. Sunset Wildside Tour $150. Phone ahead to confirm rates. Reservations are required for some tours and recommended for others. **Parking:** $6. **Phone:** (740) 638-5030. GT

CUYAHOGA FALLS (D-11) pop. 49,652, elev. 870'

Blossom Music Center, within the boundaries of Cuyahoga Valley National Park *(see place attraction listing this page)*, is at 1145 W. Steels Corner Rd. and is the summer home of the Cleveland Orchestra. In July Blossom Music Center hosts GEM A Salute to America, featuring orchestral concerts of patriotic music, cannons and fireworks. The pavilion, in an 800-acre woodland, has perfect acoustics and unobstructed views. It seats more than 6,000 people under cover and an additional 13,500 on the lawns. Performers range from symphony orchestras to rock groups. Concerts take place May through September; phone (330) 920-8040. For Cleveland Orchestra information phone the Severance Hall ticket office at (216) 231-1111 or (800) 686-1141.

Blossom Music Center is also home to Porthouse Theatre, which is affiliated with Kent State University. Professional summer theater takes place within the 500-seat outdoor covered pavilion; phone (330) 672-3884.

ECONOMY INN 330/929-8200
APPROVED Motel. **Address:** 1070 Graham Rd 44224

SHERATON SUITES AKRON-CUYAHOGA FALLS 330/929-3000

THREE DIAMOND **Hotel**

SHERATON **AAA Benefit:** Members save 5% or more!

Address: 1989 Front St 44221 **Location:** Waterfront. SR 8 exit Broad Blvd, just w. **Facility:** 209 units, some two bedrooms and efficiencies. 5 stories, interior corridors. **Amenities:** safes. **Pool:** heated indoor. **Activities:** sauna, hot tub, exercise room, massage. **Guest Services:** valet and coin laundry.

SAVE CALL BIZ

/ SOME UNITS

WHERE TO EAT

MANDARIN HOUSE 330/929-8157
APPROVED Chinese. Casual Dining. **Address:** 3201 State Rd 44223

ON TAP GRILLE & BAR 330/922-0464
APPROVED American. Casual Dining. **Address:** 3263 State Rd 44223

RETRO DOG 330/928-3500
APPROVED American. Quick Serve. **Address:** 350 E Steels Corners Rd 44224

GEM CUYAHOGA VALLEY NATIONAL PARK (C-11)

Between Cleveland and Akron, Cuyahoga Valley National Park encompasses 33,000 acres of valley along a 22-mile section of the Cuyahoga River. The area is characterized by a river flood plain, streams, creeks, forested valleys and upland plateaus. It offers picnicking, hiking, bicycle trails, horse trails, winter sports, ranger-guided programs and an excursion railroad. Special events are held throughout the year.

The reconstructed Ohio & Erie Canal Towpath Trail runs the length of the park and parallels remnants of the Ohio & Erie Canal and the twisting Cuyahoga River. Many historical structures, canal locks and wayside exhibits highlighting the history of the Cuyahoga Valley can be seen along the trail.

The 65-foot Brandywine Falls, on Brandywine Road in Sagamore Hills, is set amid red maple trees and is one of many spectacular natural features in the park. This popular site has a boardwalk leading into the waterfall's gorge, allowing for close-up looks. Tinkers Creek Gorge and the Ritchie Ledges are additional natural features where there are overlooks for sightseeing. A beautiful man-made structure can be found in the Everett Road Covered Bridge in Peninsula. This 1980s reconstruction of the late 19th-century one that used to occupy the site is about a half-mile west of Riverview Road.

Beaver Marsh, on Riverview Road in Cuyahoga Falls, is a good destination for wildlife viewing. You can park at Ira Trailhead and walk the Towpath Trail north to the boardwalk, where you might see beavers, otters, birds, frogs, muskrats and turtles.

The national park has one main visitor center and one canal-themed attraction *(see attraction listings)*. The Boston Store Visitor Center is at 1550 Boston Mills Rd., east of Riverview Road, in Peninsula. It offers a comprehensive overview of the national park and offers park planning. The Canal Exploration Center is in the northern tip of the park at 7104 Canal Rd. at jct. Hillside Road in Valley View. It features interactive and in-depth exhibits focused on canal history.

The Winter Sports Center, located within Kendall Lake Shelter on Truxell/Kendall Park Rd. between Akron Cleveland and Akron Peninsula roads in Peninsula, offers ski and snowshoe instruction programs and cross-country ski and snowshoe rentals on a first-come, first-served basis (weather permitting). Boston Mills Ski Resort in Peninsula as well as Brandywine Ski Resort and Polar Blast snow tubing park in Sagamore Hills offer additional winter fun. Special events, including lectures and concerts, are held at Happy Days Lodge, 1 mile west of SR 8 at 500 W. Streetsboro Rd. (SR 303) in Peninsula.

The park and Towpath Trail are open daily 24 hours except for Brandywine Falls, the Ledges, the Octagon shelter, Kendall Lake, the Kendall Hill area on Quick Road and the Happy Days south parking area, which are open dawn-dusk. Hours vary at Kendall Lake Winter Sports Center; phone ahead. Flooding after heavy rains may cause some sections of the park to close. Some areas may be closed part of the year to protect nesting bald eagles. Phone Boston Store Visitor Center at (330) 657-2752 to confirm hours of operations for park facilities.

ADMISSION to the park is free.

PETS must be restricted at all times, either in vehicles or by leash (no longer than 6 feet), and are not allowed in public buildings or on the train. Pet owners must clean up and dispose of pet waste and should not leave pets unattended in vehicles. Service animals are permitted in all areas of the park.

ADDRESS inquiries to the Superintendent, Cuyahoga Valley National Park, 15610 Vaughn Rd., Brecksville, OH 44141; phone (330) 657-2752 for information. *See Recreation Areas Chart.*

BOSTON STORE VISITOR CENTER is just e. of Riverview Rd. at 1550 Boston Mills Rd. in Peninsula. The circa 1836 Boston Store is the main visitor center for Cuyahoga Valley National Park. Interactive canal boatbuilding exhibits occupy the space that once served as a warehouse, a post office and the Boston Land and Manufacturing Company Store. The building features canal maps, tools, photographs, building diagrams and a cross-section of a canal boat made by a Hale Farm woodworker. **Hours:** Daily 8-6, May-Aug.; 9:30-5, rest of year. **Cost:** Free. **Phone:** (330) 657-2752.

CANAL EXPLORATION CENTER is 1.5 mi. s. of Rockside Rd. at 7104 Canal Rd. at jct. Hillside Rd. in Valley View. Once used as a tavern, a general store and a residence, it now is a newly revised center offering exhibits, some of which are interactive, about the Ohio & Erie Canal. The exhibits connect topics relating to progress in the canal era that are relevant today: immigration, transportation and a free market economy. The general store sells a selection of goods reminiscent of the canal era.

Hours: Daily 10-4:30, June-Aug.; Wed.-Sun. 10-4:30, Sept.-Oct.; Wed.-Sun. 10-4, in May; Sat.-Sun. 10-4:30, rest of year. Phone ahead to confirm schedule. **Cost:** Free. **Phone:** (216) 524-1497.

CUYAHOGA VALLEY SCENIC RAILROAD—see Independence p. 260.

HALE FARM AND VILLAGE—see Bath p. 140.

DAYTON (F-2) pop. 141,527, elev. 740'

Dayton is at the confluence of three rivers and two creeks that drain the upper portion of the rich Miami Valley. The site was first surveyed in November 1795, and the following spring three small groups of settlers named the new settlement in honor of Gen. Jonathan Dayton. Today Dayton is home to more than 830 high-technology companies.

Many original buildings still stand in one of the city's first communities, now known as the Oregon Historic District. This 12-block area is bordered by E. 5th Street, Wayne Avenue, US 35 and S. Patterson Boulevard.

Dayton was the home of the Wright brothers. Both are buried at Woodland Cemetery and Arboretum, 118 Woodland Ave.

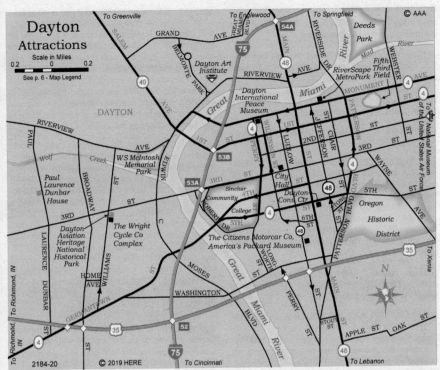

Dayton
Attractions
Scale in Miles
0.2   0   0.2
See p. 6 - Map Legend

© AAA

(See map & index p. 242.)

Wright-Patterson Air Force Base *(see Dayton Aviation Heritage National Historical Park attraction listings)*, contiguous to Dayton and Fairborn, is headquarters of the Air Force Material Command, the acquisition, procurement, maintenance, transportation and supply agency for the U.S. Air Force. It also is the home of the Air Force Institute of Technology, the service's graduate school for engineers.

Courthouse Square, at 3rd and Main streets, is the center of downtown and the site of many events such as concerts and impromptu entertainment. At 130 Riverside Dr. is the Ohio Korean War Memorial and Veterans Walkway.

Dayton is the home of 17,000-student Wright State University as well as the University of Dayton. The Cincinnati Reds' Class A minor league team, the Dayton Dragons, play at Fifth Third Field.

Downtown Dayton features RiverScape MetroPark, an attractively landscaped park with gardens and reflecting pools. A host of activities such as free summer concerts, fitness programs, community festivals and family walks take place in the park. Bicycles and kayaks can be rented as well. In winter visitors can skate on an outdoor ice-skating rink, enjoy festive light displays and partake in other family activities.

Additional opportunities in the area include bicycling and hiking on the more than 330 paved miles of Miami Valley Bikeways. For information about local parks contact Five Rivers MetroParks at (937) 275-7275. *See Recreation Areas Chart for more details about RiverScape and other Dayton parks.*

Dayton and Montgomery County Convention and Visitors Bureau: 1 Chamber Plaza, Suite A, Dayton, OH 45402-2400. **Phone:** (937) 226-8211 or (800) 221-8235.

The visitor center is in the Dayton Convention Center at jct. 5th and Main sts.

Shopping: At the intersection of E. Second and Webster streets is the National City 2nd Street Market, which operates out of an early 20th-century building that once was a railroad freight warehouse. Vendors sell a large variety of items, including baked goods, produce, meat, flowers and handmade and imported goods. The market is open Thurs.-Fri. 11-3 and Sat. 8-3; closed Jan. 1, Thanksgiving and Christmas.

BOONSHOFT MUSEUM OF DISCOVERY is off I-75 exit 57B, w. on Wagner Ford Rd., .2 mi. n. on N. Dixie Dr., .5 mi. w. on E. Siebenthaler Ave. then .7 mi. s. to 2600 DeWeese Pkwy., following signs. Permanent and changing interactive exhibits as well as science shows explore the processes of the natural world and of physical science. Inspiring curiosity and wonder are hands-on labs and fiery demonstrations in Science Central and dynamic images of the Earth and space in Science on a Sphere and the Hall of the Universe. Search the

(See map & index p. 242.)

stars in the Caryl D. Philips Space Theater and meet live animals in the Discovery Zoo.

Time: Allow 2 hours minimum. **Hours:** Mon.-Sat. 9-5, Sun. noon-5. Closed Jan. 1, Easter, Thanksgiving, Christmas Eve, Christmas and Dec. 31. Phone for planetarium schedule. **Cost:** Museum (includes planetarium) $14.50; $12.50 (ages 60+); $11.50 (ages 3-17). **Phone:** (937) 275-7431.

CARRIAGE HILL METROPARK—see Huber Heights p. 259.

[SAVE] **THE CITIZENS MOTORCAR CO., AMERICA'S PACKARD MUSEUM** is at 420 S. Ludlow St. The museum is housed in the original Packard dealership building built for Dayton in 1917. Approximately 50 Packard automobiles dating 1903-58 are displayed. Other exhibits include Packard marine and aircraft engines, items from the Detroit Packard factory, and dealership and salesmen memorabilia.

Time: Allow 1 hour minimum. **Hours:** Daily noon-5. **Cost:** $6; $5 (ages 65+); free (students ages 0-18 with ID). **Phone:** (937) 226-1710.

[GEM] **DAYTON ART INSTITUTE** is at 456 Belmonte Park N. African, American, Ancient, Asian, European, Native American, Oceanic and Pre-Columbian art galleries as well as a glass gallery are housed in a 1930 Italian Renaissance building. Works include paintings, prints, drawings and photography; the collection also features furniture and decorative art. Several outdoor sculptures are on the grounds. The Experiencenter, a participatory family center, presents thematic shows and exhibits.

Temporary exhibits and special events are held throughout the year. **Time:** Allow 2 hours minimum. **Hours:** Wed.-Sat. 11-5, (also Thurs. 5-8), Sun. noon-5. Guided tours are available by reservation. **Cost:** $8; $5 (ages 60+ and active military with ID); free (ages 0-17 and students with ID). **Phone:** (937) 223-4278. [GT] [restaurant]

DAYTON AVIATION HERITAGE NATIONAL HISTORICAL PARK contains five geographically separate sites. The park was established to honor Wilbur and Orville Wright and Paul Laurence Dunbar. The five sites to visit are Carillon Historical Park, Huffman Prairie Flying Field and Interpretive Center at Wright-Patterson Air Force Base (also the site of the Wright Brothers Memorial), Paul Laurence Dunbar House, and The Wright Cycle Co. Complex (see attraction listings). Tours of Hawthorn Hill, home to Orville Wright for nearly 35 years, are available by appointment.

Hours: Schedules vary per site. **Cost:** Carillon Historical Park $10; $9 (ages 60+); $7 (ages 3-17). Hawthorn Hill $12. Other sites free. **Phone:** (937) 225-7705, (937) 425-0008, or (937) 293-2841 for Hawthorn Hill appointments. [GT]

[GEM] [SAVE] **Carillon Historical Park,** at 1000 Carillon Blvd., is part of the Dayton Aviation Heritage National Historical Park. The 30 structures on the 65-acre campus relate America's development over the past 2 centuries, with emphasis on the contributions made by Dayton's heritage of creativity and invention in transportation. A presentation features animatronic figures representing the Wright brothers, Charles Kettering and two other Dayton industrialists sharing the story of how Dayton changed the world.

The John W. Berry, Sr. Wright Brothers National Museum displays the original 1905 *Wright Flyer III,* the first practical airplane. Other displays include a 1930s print shop, vintage bicycles, antique automobiles and a 1903 Barney & Smith parlor car. The attraction is also home to the Deeds Carillon, a carousel, a restored canal lock and a 1796 log tavern, purportedly the oldest building in Dayton. **Time:** Allow 2 hours minimum. **Hours:** Mon.-Sat. 9:30-5, Sun. noon-5. Carillon concerts are held select Sun. at 3, Mar.-Dec. Open until 9 p.m. during holiday lights and programming. Closed Jan. 1, Thanksgiving, Christmas Eve, Christmas and Dec. 31. **Cost:** $10; $9 (ages 60+); $7 (ages 3-17). **Phone:** (937) 293-2841. [restaurant] [picnic]

Huffman Prairie Flying Field and Interpretive Center is 5 mi. n. on SR 4 to SR 444, then e. on Kauffman Rd. to 2380 Memorial Rd., adjacent to Gate 16B on Wright-Patterson Air Force Base. The flying field, part of the Dayton Aviation Heritage National Historical Park, was used by the Wright brothers for test flying and crafting their airplanes and piloting skills. Tests were conducted in 1904-05, and in 1910 the brothers established a school of flight on the site. The Interpretive Center contains exhibits about the Air Force Base and the brothers' perfection of flight.

Adjacent to the interpretive center is the Wright Brothers Memorial, erected in 1940. The 27-acre site overlooks Huffman Prairie Flying Field. **Time:** Allow 30 minutes minimum. **Hours:** Interpretive Center open daily 9-5, Mar.-Oct.; Wed.-Sun. 9-5, rest of year. Closed Jan. 1, Air Force Marathon Day, Thanksgiving and Christmas. **Cost:** Free. **Phone:** (937) 425-0008.

Paul Laurence Dunbar House is at 219 N. Paul Laurence Dunbar St. and is part of the Dayton Aviation Heritage National Historical Park. The restored former home of the poet, novelist and civil rights advocate contains many of his personal belongings dating from the late 19th- and early 20th centuries.

Time: Allow 1 hour minimum. **Hours:** Fri.-Sun. 10-4. Closed major holidays. Phone ahead to confirm schedule. **Cost:** Free. **Phone:** (937) 224-7061 or (937) 225-7705. [GT]

The Wright Cycle Co. Complex is at 16 S. Williams St. and is part of the Dayton Aviation Heritage National Historical Park. The complex consists of The

(See map & index p. 242.)

Wright Cycle Co. building and the Wright-Dunbar Interpretive Center. At the original bicycle shop, their fourth of five shops in the area, exhibits provide information about the Wright Brothers' business, while the interpretive center details the history of bicycles and the Wright brothers' invention of the airplane. **Time:** Allow 1 hour minimum. **Hours:** Daily 9-5, early Mar.-early Nov.; Wed.-Sun. 9-5, rest of year. Phone ahead to confirm schedule. **Cost:** Free. **Phone:** (937) 225-7705.

NATIONAL MUSEUM OF THE UNITED STATES AIR FORCE is off Springfield Pike at Wright Field on Wright-Patterson Air Force Base. Said to be the oldest and largest military aviation museum in the world, it features more than 400 aerospace vehicles and missiles along with thousands of personal artifacts, photographs and documents. The museum showcases the early days of military flight to today's war on terrorism.

The collection includes the B-29 Bockscar that dropped the atomic bomb on Nagasaki, Japan, during World War II; Air Force One used by all presidents from Kennedy through Clinton; a B-2 stealth bomber; and NASA's first Crew Compartment Trainer, which aided in astronaut training. Visitors will find out how astronauts trained for their missions and get a detailed look at what their living quarters were like aboard the shuttle. Movies are shown in a digital 3-D theater, and special events are held throughout the year.

Time: Allow 4 hours minimum. **Hours:** Museum open daily 9-5. Tours of the Early Years and World War II galleries depart at 10 and 1:30. Tours of the Korea, Southeast Asia and Cold War galleries depart at 11:30. Tours of the Space, Research & Development, Presidential and Global Reach galleries depart at noon and 3. Behind the Scenes Tours depart Fri. at 12:15; reservations are required. Digital movies offered daily; phone for schedule. **Cost:** Museum free. Theater $8; $7 (ages 60+ and military with ID); $6 (ages 3-12 and students with ID). **Phone:** (937) 255-3286, or (937) 253-4629 for the theater. GT ▯

Let Your Voice Be Heard

- If a AAA listed establishment doesn't meet your expectations, tell us so we can help.

- Recommend a favorite hotel, restaurant or attraction you'd like AAA to inspect.

Visit us at **AAA.com/MemberFeedback**

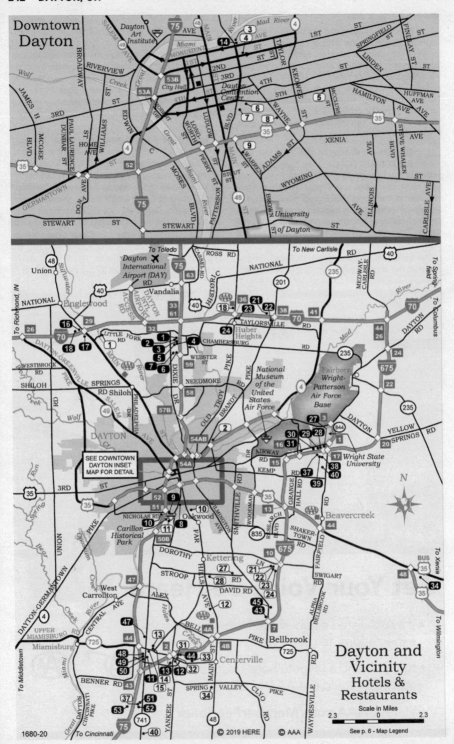

Downtown Dayton

Dayton and Vicinity
Hotels & Restaurants

Scale in Miles
2.3   0   2.3

See p. 6 - Map Legend

1680-20

© 2019 HERE   © AAA

Dayton and Vicinity

This index helps you "spot" where hotels and restaurants are located on the corresponding detailed maps. Restaurant price range is a combination of lunch and/or dinner. Turn to the listing page for more information and consult display ads for special promotions.

 For more details, rates and reservations: AAA.com/travelguides/hotels

DAYTON

Map Page	Hotels	Designation	Member Savings	Page
1 p. 242	Comfort Inn & Suites Dayton North	APPROVED		245
2 p. 242	TownePlace Suites by Marriott Dayton North	APPROVED	✔	246
3 p. 242	Courtyard by Marriott Dayton North	THREE DIAMOND	✔	245
4 p. 242	Hampton Inn & Suites Dayton/Vandalia	THREE DIAMOND	✔	245
5 p. 242	Residence Inn by Marriott Dayton Vandalia	THREE DIAMOND	✔	246
6 p. 242	Drury Inn & Suites-Dayton North	THREE DIAMOND		245
7 p. 242	Home2 Suites By Hilton Dayton Vandalia	THREE DIAMOND	✔	245
8 p. 242	**The Marriott at the University of Dayton**	THREE DIAMOND	✔	246
9 p. 242	**Courtyard by Marriott-University of Dayton**	THREE DIAMOND	✔	245
10 p. 242	Holiday Inn Express & Suites Dayton SW - University Area	THREE DIAMOND		245
11 p. 242	Hampton Inn by Hilton Dayton Mall	THREE DIAMOND	✔	245
12 p. 242	Fairfield Inn & Suites by Marriott Dayton South	APPROVED	✔	245
13 p. 242	**Country Inn & Suites by Radisson Dayton South**	APPROVED	✔	245
14 p. 242	Fairfield Inn & Suites by Marriott	THREE DIAMOND	✔	245

Map Page	Restaurants	Designation	Cuisine	Price Range	Page
1 p. 242	Buckhorn Tavern	APPROVED	Comfort Food	$7-$28	246
2 p. 242	Amber Rose	APPROVED	Eastern European	$10-$23	246
3 p. 242	Basil's on Market	APPROVED	American	$12-$26	246
4 p. 242	Lock 27 Brewing	APPROVED	American	$10-$16	246
5 p. 242	Fifth Street Brewpub	APPROVED	Sandwiches	$9-$13	246
6 p. 242	Thai 9 Restaurant	APPROVED	Thai	$8-$25	246
7 p. 242	**Jay's Restaurant**	THREE DIAMOND	Seafood	$20-$55	246
8 p. 242	Wheat Penny Oven & Bar	APPROVED	Pizza	$13-$33	246
9 p. 242	Coco's Bistro	THREE DIAMOND	American	$12-$38	246
10 p. 242	The Pine Club	APPROVED	Steak	$20-$43	246
11 p. 242	Carillon Brewing Company	APPROVED	American	$9-$17	246
12 p. 242	The Meadowlark Restaurant	THREE DIAMOND	American	$11-$34	246
13 p. 242	Amar India Restaurant	APPROVED	Northern Indian	$10-$17	246
14 p. 242	P.F. Chang's China Bistro	THREE DIAMOND	Chinese	$10-$29	246
15 p. 242	Rusty Bucket Corner Tavern	APPROVED	American	$10-$23	246

ENGLEWOOD

Map Page	Hotels	Designation	Member Savings	Page
16 p. 242	**Best Western Plus Dayton Northwest**	APPROVED	✔	251
17 p. 242	Comfort Inn & Suites-Englewood	APPROVED		251
18 p. 242	Hampton Inn & Suites by Hilton Dayton Airport	APPROVED	✔	251

HUBER HEIGHTS

Map Page	Hotels	Designation	Member Savings	Page
21 p. 242	Tru by Hilton Huber Heights/Dayton	APPROVED	✔	259
22 p. 242	Comfort Inn Dayton	APPROVED		259
23 p. 242	Holiday Inn Express Hotel & Suites	APPROVED		259
24 p. 242	Hampton Inn by Hilton Huber Heights	THREE DIAMOND	✔	259

Map Page	Restaurant	Designation	Cuisine	Price Range	Page
18 p. 242	El Toro Mexican Restaurant	APPROVED	Mexican	$9-$18	260

FAIRBORN

Map Page	Hotels	Designation	Member Savings	Page
27 p. 242	Hampton Inn by Hilton	◈ APPROVED	✔	252
28 p. 242	Homewood Suites by Hilton Dayton-Fairborn	◈ THREE DIAMOND	✔	252
29 p. 242	**Holiday Inn Dayton/Fairborn**	◈ THREE DIAMOND	✔	252
30 p. 242	La Quinta Inn & Suites Fairborn-Wright Patterson	◈ APPROVED		252
31 p. 242	Country Inn & Suites by Radisson, Fairborn South	◈ THREE DIAMOND		251

XENIA

Map Page	Hotel	Designation	Member Savings	Page
34 p. 242	Hampton Inn & Suites by Hilton Xenia/Dayton	◈ THREE DIAMOND	✔	313

BEAVERCREEK

Map Page	Hotels	Designation	Member Savings	Page
37 p. 242	Hilton Garden Inn Dayton/Beavercreek	◈ THREE DIAMOND	✔	142
38 p. 242	Courtyard by Marriott Beavercreek	◈ THREE DIAMOND	✔	142
39 p. 242	Residence Inn by Marriott Beavercreek	◈ THREE DIAMOND	✔	142
40 p. 242	SpringHill Suites by Marriott Dayton Beavercreek	◈ THREE DIAMOND	✔	142

Map Page	Restaurants	Designation	Cuisine	Price Range	Page
21 p. 242	The Pub at Beavercreek	◈ APPROVED	British	$10-$19	142
22 p. 242	Pies & Pints	◈ APPROVED	Pizza	$10-$26	142
23 p. 242	Pasha Grill	◈ THREE DIAMOND	Turkish	$10-$31	142
24 p. 242	Ace Asian Cafe	◈ APPROVED	Asian	$12-$33	142

CENTERVILLE

Map Page	Hotels	Designation	Member Savings	Page
43 p. 242	Holiday Inn Express & Suites Dayton/Centerville	◈ APPROVED		150
44 p. 242	Holiday Inn Express & Suites Dayton/South I-675	◈ THREE DIAMOND		150
45 p. 242	Home2 Suites by Hilton Dayton-Centerville	◈ THREE DIAMOND	✔	150

Map Page	Restaurants	Designation	Cuisine	Price Range	Page
31 p. 242	Chappy's Social House	◈ APPROVED	Comfort Food	$9-$25	150
32 p. 242	J. Alexander's Redlands Grill	◈ THREE DIAMOND	American	$14-$35	150
33 p. 242	The Paragon Supper Club	◈ APPROVED	Steak Seafood	$24-$44	150
34 p. 242	The Famous Restaurant	◈ APPROVED	Comfort Food	$8-$13	150

MIAMISBURG

Map Page	Hotels	Designation	Member Savings	Page
47 p. 242	SpringHill Suites by Marriott Dayton South/Miamisburg	◈ THREE DIAMOND	✔	275
48 p. 242	**Courtyard by Marriott Dayton South/Mall** *(See ad p. 245.)*	◈ THREE DIAMOND	✔	275
49 p. 242	Homewood Suites by Hilton-Dayton South	◈ THREE DIAMOND	✔	275
50 p. 242	**DoubleTree Suites by Hilton Dayton-Miamisburg**	◈ THREE DIAMOND	✔	275
51 p. 242	Staybridge Suites Miamisburg	◈ THREE DIAMOND		275
52 p. 242	Hilton Garden Inn Dayton South/Austin Landing	◈ THREE DIAMOND	✔	275
53 p. 242	Home2 Suites By Hilton Dayton South	◈ THREE DIAMOND	✔	275

Map Page	Restaurant	Designation	Cuisine	Price Range	Page
37 p. 242	Ele Bistro & Wine Bar	◈ APPROVED	American	$9-$24	275

KETTERING

Map Page	Restaurants	Designation	Cuisine	Price Range	Page
27 p. 242	Mamma DiSalvo's Italian Ristorante	◈ APPROVED	Italian	$8-$30	262
28 p. 242	Figlio	◈ APPROVED	Pizza	$13-$21	262

SPRINGBORO

Map Page	Restaurant	Designation	Cuisine	Price Range	Page
40 p. 242	China Cottage	◈ APPROVED	Chinese	$7-$28	293

(See map & index p. 242.)

COMFORT INN & SUITES DAYTON NORTH
937/890-1221 **1**
◆ APPROVED Hotel. **Address:** 3661 Maxton Rd 45414

COUNTRY INN & SUITES BY RADISSON DAYTON SOUTH 937/425-7400 **13**

◆ APPROVED
Hotel

Address: 8277 Yankee St 45458 **Location:** I-675 exit 2 northbound, just e on SR 725, then just s; exit 2 southbound, 0.5 mi e. **Facility:** 80 units. 3 stories, interior corridors. **Pool:** heated indoor. **Activities:** sauna, exercise room. **Guest Services:** valet and coin laundry. **Featured Amenity: continental breakfast.**

SAVE [†] CALL [&] [≈] [†] [BIZ]
[≈] [×] [🍴] [📷] [▭]

COURTYARD BY MARRIOTT DAYTON NORTH
937/890-6112 **3**
◆ THREE DIAMOND SAVE Hotel. **Address:** 7087 Miller Ln 45414

AAA Benefit:
Members save 5% or more!

COURTYARD BY MARRIOTT-UNIVERSITY OF DAYTON
937/220-9060 **9**

◆ THREE DIAMOND
Hotel

COURTYARD' **AAA Benefit:**
Members save 5% or more!

Address: 2006 S Edwin C Moses Blvd 45417 **Location:** Waterfront. I-75 exit 51, just e. Near the University of Dayton campus. **Facility:** 101 units. 4 stories, interior corridors. **Pool:** heated indoor. **Activities:** hot tub, bicycles, exercise room. **Guest Services:** valet and coin laundry, boarding pass kiosk.

SAVE [Y] CALL [&] [≈] [†] [BIZ]
[HS] [≈] [×] [🍴] [▭]

/ SOME UNITS [📷]

DRURY INN & SUITES-DAYTON NORTH 937/454-5200 **6**
◆ THREE DIAMOND Hotel. **Address:** 6616 Miller Ln 45414

FAIRFIELD INN & SUITES BY MARRIOTT 937/331-9330 **14**
◆ THREE DIAMOND SAVE Hotel. **Address:** 305 E Monument Ave 45402

AAA Benefit:
Members save 5% or more!

FAIRFIELD INN & SUITES BY MARRIOTT DAYTON SOUTH
937/428-7736 **12**
◆ APPROVED SAVE Hotel. **Address:** 8035 Washington Village Dr 45458

AAA Benefit:
Members save 5% or more!

HAMPTON INN & SUITES DAYTON/VANDALIA
937/387-0598 **4**
◆ THREE DIAMOND SAVE Hotel. **Address:** 7043 Miller Ln 45414

AAA Benefit:
Members save up to 15%!

HAMPTON INN BY HILTON DAYTON MALL
937/439-1800 **11**
◆ THREE DIAMOND SAVE Hotel. **Address:** 8960 Mall Ring Rd 45459

AAA Benefit:
Members save up to 15%!

HOLIDAY INN EXPRESS & SUITES DAYTON SW - UNIVERSITY AREA 937/250-6400 **10**
◆ THREE DIAMOND Hotel. **Address:** 2140 S Edwin C Moses Blvd 45417

HOME2 SUITES BY HILTON DAYTON VANDALIA
937/949-6200 **7**
◆ THREE DIAMOND SAVE Extended Stay Contemporary Hotel. **Address:** 6615 Town Center Dr 45414

AAA Benefit:
Members save up to 15%!

▼ See AAA listing p. 275 ▼

(See map & index p. 242.)

THE MARRIOTT AT THE UNIVERSITY OF DAYTON
937/223-1000 8

THREE DIAMOND
Hotel

AAA Benefit: Members save 5% or more!

Address: 1414 S Patterson Blvd 45409 **Location:** Waterfront. I-75 exit 51, 0.8 mi s on Edwin C Moses Blvd, just e on Stewart St, then just s. **Facility:** 399 units. 6 stories, interior corridors. **Pool:** heated outdoor, heated indoor. **Activities:** hot tub, exercise room. **Guest Services:** complimentary and valet laundry, boarding pass kiosk, area transportation.

RESIDENCE INN BY MARRIOTT DAYTON VANDALIA
937/890-2244 5

THREE DIAMOND Extended Stay Hotel. **Address:** 7227 York Center Dr 45414

AAA Benefit: Members save 5% or more!

TOWNEPLACE SUITES BY MARRIOTT DAYTON NORTH
937/898-5700 2

APPROVED Extended Stay Hotel. **Address:** 3642 Maxton Rd 45414

AAA Benefit: Members save 5% or more!

WHERE TO EAT

AMAR INDIA RESTAURANT   937/439-9005 13
APPROVED Northern Indian. Casual Dining. **Address:** 2751 Miamisburg-Centerville Rd 45459

AMBER ROSE   937/228-2511 2
APPROVED Eastern European. Casual Dining. **Address:** 1400 Valley St 45404

BASIL'S ON MARKET   937/818-4390 3
APPROVED American. Casual Dining. **Address:** 312 N Patterson Blvd 45402

BUCKHORN TAVERN   937/890-3261 1
APPROVED Comfort Food. Casual Dining. **Address:** 8800 Meeker Rd 45414

CARILLON BREWING COMPANY   937/293-2841 11
APPROVED American. Brewpub. **Address:** 1000 Carillon Blvd 45409

COCO'S BISTRO   937/228-2626 9
THREE DIAMOND American. Fine Dining. **Address:** 250 Warren St 45402

FIFTH STREET BREWPUB   937/443-0919 5
APPROVED Sandwiches. Brewpub. **Address:** 1600 E Fifth St 45403

JAY'S RESTAURANT   937/222-2892 7
THREE DIAMOND

Seafood
Casual Dining
$20-$55

AAA Inspector Notes: *Historic.* Located in a restored 1852 gristmill, this place has a cozy 19th-century atmosphere. The dining room is framed by redbrick walls and massive wooden ceiling beams. The lounge has a 32-foot ornately carved mahogany bar salvaged from a Victorian era tavern. There are daily specials based on market availability. Fried oysters and oysters on the half shell are available. A fine conclusion to dinner here is the bourbon pecan pie. **Features:** full bar, happy hour. **Reservations:** suggested. **Address:** 225 E 6th St 45402 **Location:** In Historic Oregon District. D

LOCK 27 BREWING   937/433-2739 4
APPROVED American. Brewpub. **Address:** 329 E First St 45402

THE MEADOWLARK RESTAURANT   937/434-4750 12
THREE DIAMOND American. Casual Dining. **Address:** 5531 Far Hills Ave 45429

P.F. CHANG'S CHINA BISTRO   937/428-6085 14
THREE DIAMOND Chinese. Casual Dining. **Address:** 2626 Miamisburg-Centerville Rd 45459

THE PINE CLUB   937/228-5371 10
APPROVED Steak. Casual Dining. **Address:** 1926 Brown St 45409

RUSTY BUCKET CORNER TAVERN   937/436-2426 15
APPROVED American. Casual Dining. **Address:** 2812 Miamisburg-Centerville Rd 45459

SKYLINE CHILI   937/898-9970
APPROVED American. Quick Serve. **Address:** 6910 Miller Ln 45414

THAI 9 RESTAURANT   937/222-3227 6
APPROVED Thai. Casual Dining. **Address:** 11 Brown St 45402

WHEAT PENNY OVEN & BAR   937/496-5268 8
APPROVED Pizza. Casual Dining. **Address:** 515 Wayne Ave 45410

DEFIANCE (B-2) pop. 16,494, elev. 710'

Gen. Anthony Wayne chose a location in the Maumee Valley for Fort Defiance, which he built in 1794. The site of the fort is marked by plaques and stones in the Defiance city park. Old earthworks are visible. Other marked historic sites in Defiance include Fort Winchester, built in 1812 by Gen. William Henry Harrison; the 1650 French Mission in Kingsbury Park; the 1811-28 Johnny Appleseed Nursery; and the birthplace of Ottawa Indian Chief Pontiac.

Defiance Development and Visitors Bureau: 325 Clinton St., Defiance, OH 43512. **Phone:** (419) 782-0739.

Shopping: Northtowne Mall, at 1500 N. Clinton St., features JCPenney and Marshalls.

HAMPTON INN BY HILTON DEFIANCE   419/784-1515
THREE DIAMOND Hotel. **Address:** 1037 Hotel Dr 43512

AAA Benefit: Members save up to 15%!

HOLIDAY INN EXPRESS & SUITES DEFIANCE   419/784-0782
THREE DIAMOND Hotel. **Address:** 1148 Hotel Dr 43512

WHERE TO EAT

SWEETWATER CHOPHOUSE   419/785-4434
APPROVED American. Casual Dining. **Address:** 211 Carpenter Rd 43512

DELAWARE (E-4) pop. 34,753, elev. 869'
• Part of Columbus area — see map p. 205

Founded in 1808, Delaware is the birthplace of President Rutherford B. Hayes. Born in 1822, he served as governor of Ohio three times and was a member of the House of Representatives before being elected president in 1877.

Delaware County Convention and Visitors Bureau: 34 S. Sandusky St., Delaware, OH 43015. **Phone:** (740) 368-4748 or (888) 335-6446.

Self-guiding tours: Brochures describing notable downtown structures are available from the visitors bureau and the Delaware County Historical Society, 157 E. William St.; phone (740) 369-3831.

BAYMONT INN & SUITES DELAWARE   740/363-3510

| ▽ APPROVED | **Address:** 1720 Columbus Pike 43015 |
| Hotel | **Location:** I-270 exit 23, 11 mi n on US 23. Located in a busy commercial area. **Facility:** 71 units. 2 stories (no elevator), interior corridors. **Parking:** winter plug-ins. **Amenities:** safes. **Pool:** heated indoor. **Activities:** hot tub, exercise room. **Guest Services:** coin laundry. **Featured Amenity: continental breakfast.** |

SAVE ❘↑ CALL ⬇ 🏊 ♿ BIZ
🛜 ✕ 🔋 🖥 🖨
/SOME UNITS 🐾 HS

PACER INN & SUITES MOTEL   740/362-0050
▽ APPROVED   Motel. **Address:** 259 S Sandusky St 43015

WHERE TO EAT

BUN'S RESTAURANT   740/363-2867
▽ APPROVED   American. Casual Dining. **Address:** 14 W Winter St 43015

THE OLD BAG OF NAILS PUB   740/368-8083
▽ APPROVED   American. Casual Dining. **Address:** 66 N Sandusky St 43015

DENNISON (E-7) pop. 2,655, elev. 908'

DENNISON RAILROAD DEPOT MUSEUM is at 400 Center St. This 1873 railroad depot was a popular stop for servicemen during World War II who nicknamed it "Dreamsville" because of the exemplary service they received. Volunteers and the Salvation Army gave free food and comfort to more than 1.5 million soldiers passing through the depot.

Five railroad cars are on the grounds, including a World War II hospital car. Railroad memorabilia, uniforms, photographs and World War II relics are displayed. A theater presents a film about the depot's role from 1941-45, and an interactive children's railroad car is available.

Time: Allow 1 hour minimum. **Hours:** Tues.-Fri. 10-5, Sat. 11-4, Sun. 11-3. Closed major holidays. **Cost:** $8; $6 (senior citizens and students); $4 (ages 7-17). **Phone:** (740) 922-6776. GT ❘↑

DOVER (D-7) pop. 12,826, elev. 875'

THE ERNEST WARTHER MUSEUM & GARDENS, .5 mi. e. of I-77 exit 83 at 331 Karl Ave., showcases 64 ebony, ivory and walnut train carvings created by "world master carver" Ernest "Mooney" Warther. A highlight is the Tree of Pliers—more than 500 interconnecting pairs of working pliers carved out of a solid piece of walnut. Also included are carvings depicting Abraham Lincoln's life and death and an arrowhead collection.

Visitors can stroll through Mrs. Warther's Swiss-style gardens in the 8-acre park surrounding the original home. Her button collection, numbering more than 73,000 pieces, is also displayed. **Time:** Allow 1 hour, 30 minutes minimum. **Hours:** Daily 9-5. Last tour begins 1 hour before closing. **Cost:** $15; $13.50 (ages 65+); $7 (ages 12-17); $5 (ages 4-11). **Phone:** (330) 505-6003. GT

COMFORT INN   330/364-8881
▽ APPROVED   Hotel. **Address:** 2024 SR 39 NW 44622

COUNTRY INN & SUITES BY RADISSON   330/365-9388
▽ THREE DIAMOND   Hotel. **Address:** 1120 Gateway Pl 44622

DUBLIN (E-4) pop. 41,751, elev. 830'
• Hotels p. 248 • Restaurants p. 249
• Hotels & Restaurants map & index p. 222
• Part of Columbus area — see map p. 205

The bonny city of Dublin was originally settled by a German family in 1801, who were assisted in surveying the town by Irishman John Shields. To show their appreciation, they allowed Shields to name the area. In accepting, he said: "If I have the honor conferred upon me to name your village, with the brightness of the morn, and the beaming of the sun on the hills and dales surrounding this beautiful valley, it would give me great pleasure to name your new town after my birthplace, Dublin, Ireland."

The settlement began to flourish in 1833, when the National Road reached Columbus and canals were completed. However, when the Columbus, Piqua and Indiana Railroad bypassed Dublin its heydays ended and it became just a trade center for the nearby farmers. Prosperity once more came in 1970 when the I-70 bypass, I-270, linked Dublin with Columbus, and the transformation from a village of 861 residents into a city began.

Today, low limestone fences form a border between emerald-green lawns and local roads in this quaint Columbus suburb. Historic Dublin, on North and South High Street and South Riverview Street roughly between Bridge Street and Waterford Drive/Short Street, contains examples of 19th-century architecture on a streetscape as well-scrubbed as a Hollywood movie set. Fronted by

(See map & index p. 222.)

brick sidewalks, the same 19th-century buildings now house lovely shops, galleries, pubs and cafés. Have the barkeep pour you an Irish whiskey or choose from a list of more than 60 imports, crafts and microbrews at Brazenhead Irish Pub, 56 N. High St.; the pub is named after Ireland's oldest pub, established in 1198, and its owners have faithfully created a near-perfect Irish pub experience, down to the drawing room fireplace and the bar itself. At Ha'Penny Bridge Imports, 75 S. High St., experience shopping in Ireland without the expensive airfare and peruse the historic home's collection of Galway Irish crystal, fine jewelry, wool sweaters, and other fine imported goods from the motherland.

Have fun outdoors courtesy of the city's 1,500 acres of parkland and the town's proximity to the Scioto River. Ninety-six miles of bike trails connect 56 parks that feature hardwood forests and wetlands. Area parks feature playgrounds, basketball and tennis courts, and fishing ponds. Check out the fishing pier and pond, sensory garden and restored log cabin at the M.L. Red Trabue Nature Reserve, 6500 Post Rd. Test your disc-tossing skills at a 9-hole disc golf course across from Balgriffin Park, 5715 Norn St. Phone (614) 410-4400 for further park information.

Dublin's parks also are home to outdoor art installations. A 12-foot-tall sculpture of Wyandot Native American "Chief Leatherlips," made of stacks of native limestone, resides at Scioto Park; in the whimsical "Field of Corn (with Osage Orange Trees)," 109 gigantic ears of corn stand at attention in Sam and Eulalia Frantz Park.

Although their ancestry may not be entirely Irish, Dublin townspeople embrace the folklore of its namesake city. That includes hosting several Celtic-themed events each year. The 3-day ⚑ Dublin Irish Festival is held in late July or early August at Coffman Park and has drawn more than 100,000 guests. The celebration showcases Irish culture with an assortment of entertainment and activities, including Irish storytelling, sporting events, musical performances, professional genealogy services and craft workshops; even the town's fire hydrants are painted green.

Do the jig, do a jog at the annual St. Patrick's Day Parade in mid-March. The event features an Irish breakfast, a 5K run through town and a 90-minute parade with Irish dancers and marching bands playing traditional Irish music. The Blarney Bash, featuring live music, food trucks, beer and Irish dancers, begins immediately after the parade and continues into the evening. Venues throughout town also celebrate the day with Irish step dancing, classic Irish cuisine, music by bagpipe and drum corps, activities for wee ones and a pot of gold relay.

The Abbey Theater of Dublin, located in the Dublin Community Recreation Center, 5600 Post Rd., presents children's theater and holiday programs such as "A Christmas Carol." Phone (614) 410-4550 for schedules.

Native Dubliner and pro golfer Jack Nicklaus created The Memorial Tournament, an annual stop on the PGA tour held in late May or early June at the Nicklaus-designed course at Muirfield Village Golf Club. Tickets are available for practice rounds; phone (614) 889-6712.

Dublin Convention & Visitors Bureau: 9 S. High St., Dublin, OH 43017. **Phone:** (614) 792-7666 or (800) 245-8387.

Self-guiding tours: A map and brochure detailing a tour of Historic Dublin is available from the convention and visitors bureau.

Shopping: The 120 establishments in The Mall at Tuttle Crossing, southeast corner of I-270 and Tuttle Crossing Boulevard, are anchored by JCPenney, Macy's and Sears.

AC HOTEL COLUMBUS DUBLIN   614/798-8652   **56**

◆◆◆ THREE DIAMOND

Boutique Contemporary Hotel

 AAA Benefit: Members save 5% or more!

Address: 6540 Riverside Dr 43017 **Location:** I-270 exit 17, 1.5 mi e on SR 161; in Bridge Park District. Located in new urban district of shops and apartments. **Facility:** This hotel is located in a newly developed urban area with a splendid view of the Scioto River. Guest rooms have a European-style décor scheme with abstract art, smart TVs and glass showers. 150 units. 8 stories, interior corridors. **Bath:** shower only. **Amenities:** safes. **Dining:** Vaso, see separate listing. **Activities:** exercise room. **Guest Services:** valet and coin laundry.

[SAVE] 🍴 ⊕ 🍸 CALL 🔁 ⊕ BIZ 🛜 ✕ ⊟ 🔲

COLUMBUS MARRIOTT NORTHWEST   614/791-1000   **63**

◆◆◆ THREE DIAMOND [SAVE] Hotel. **Address:** 5605 Blazer Pkwy 43017

AAA Benefit: Members save 5% or more!

COURTYARD BY MARRIOTT-DUBLIN
614/764-9393   **57**

◆◆◆ THREE DIAMOND

Hotel

COURTYARD **AAA Benefit:** Members save 5% or more!

Address: 5175 Post Rd 43017 **Location:** I-270 exit 17A, just ne. **Facility:** 147 units. 2-3 stories, interior corridors. **Pool:** heated indoor. **Activities:** exercise room. **Guest Services:** valet and coin laundry, boarding pass kiosk.

[SAVE] [ECO] 🍸 CALL 🔁 ⊇ ⊕ BIZ 🛜 ✕ ⊟ 🔲

/ SOME UNITS 🔲

DRURY INN & SUITES-COLUMBUS NORTHWEST
614/798-8802   **64**

◆ APPROVED   Hotel. **Address:** 6170 Parkcenter Cir 43017

(See map & index p. 222.)

EMBASSY SUITES BY HILTON COLUMBUS-DUBLIN
614/790-9000   **60**

THREE DIAMOND SAVE Hotel. **Address:** 5100 Upper Metro Pl 43017

AAA Benefit: Members save up to 15%!

EXTENDED STAY AMERICA (COLUMBUS/TUTTLE)
614/760-0245   **67**

APPROVED Extended Stay Hotel. **Address:** 5530 Tuttle Crossing Blvd 43016

FAIRFIELD BY MARRIOTT NORTH COLUMBUS/DUBLIN
614/389-3036   **54**

THREE DIAMOND Fairfield
Hotel

AAA Benefit: Members save 5% or more!

Address: 7150 Sawmill Rd 43235 **Location:** I-270 exit 20, just n. Located in a suburban, commercial area. **Facility:** 83 units. 4 stories, interior corridors. **Pool:** heated indoor. **Activities:** exercise room. **Guest Services:** valet and coin laundry.

SAVE ↑↓ CALL ♿ 🔁 ⛄ BIZ
🛜 ✕ 🍴 📷 💻

HAMPTON INN BY HILTON COLUMBUS-DUBLIN
614/889-0573   **55**

APPROVED SAVE Hotel. **Address:** 3920 Tuller Rd 43017

AAA Benefit: Members save up to 15%!

HILTON GARDEN INN COLUMBUS/DUBLIN
614/766-9900   **68**

THREE DIAMOND SAVE Hotel. **Address:** 500 Metro Pl N 43017

AAA Benefit: Members save up to 15%!

HOLIDAY INN EXPRESS DUBLIN
614/793-5500   **66**

THREE DIAMOND Hotel. **Address:** 5500 Tuttle Crossing Blvd 43016

HOME2 SUITES BY HILTON COLUMBUS DUBLIN
614/889-7540   **59**

THREE DIAMOND
Extended Stay Hotel

HOME2 SUITES BY HILTON

AAA Benefit: Members save up to 15%!

Address: 5000 Upper Metro Pl 43017 **Location:** I-270 exit 17A, 0.5 mi e to Frantz Rd, then just s. **Facility:** 126 units. 4 stories, interior corridors. **Bath:** shower only. **Pool:** heated indoor. **Activities:** exercise room. **Guest Services:** valet and coin laundry.

SAVE ↑↓ CALL ♿ 🔁 ⛄ BIZ
HS 🛜 ✕ 🍴 📷 💻
/ SOME UNITS 🐾

🔗 For complete hotel, dining and attraction listings:
AAA.com/travelguides

HYATT PLACE COLUMBUS/DUBLIN   614/799-1913   **65**

THREE DIAMOND
Hotel

HYATT PLACE

AAA Benefit: Members save up to 10%!

Address: 6161 Parkcenter Cir 43017 **Location:** I-270 exit 15 (Tuttle Crossing Blvd), just e on Tuttle Pkwy, then just n on Blazer Pkwy. **Facility:** 123 units. 6 stories, interior corridors. **Pool:** heated outdoor. **Activities:** exercise room. **Guest Services:** valet laundry, area transportation. **Featured Amenity: full hot breakfast.**

SAVE ↑↓ 📺 CALL ♿ 🔁 🏊 ✈
BIZ 🛜 ✕ 📹 🍴 💻 / SOME UNITS 🐾 HS

RED ROOF PLUS+ COLUMBUS/DUBLIN
614/764-3993   **58**

APPROVED
Motel

Address: 5125 Post Rd 43017 **Location:** I-270 exit 17A, just ne. **Facility:** 106 units. 2 stories (no elevator), exterior corridors. **Amenities:** safes. **Guest Services:** coin laundry.

SAVE ↑↓ CALL ♿ 🛜 ✕ 🍴
📷 💻 / SOME UNITS 🐾

RESIDENCE INN BY MARRIOTT COLUMBUS DUBLIN
614/389-6600   **61**

THREE DIAMOND SAVE Extended Stay Hotel. **Address:** 6364 Frantz Rd 43017

AAA Benefit: Members save 5% or more!

SONESTA ES SUITES DUBLIN   614/791-0403   **62**

THREE DIAMOND
Extended Stay Hotel

Address: 435 Metro Pl S 43017 **Location:** I-270 exit 17A, 0.5 mi e on SR 161, 0.5 mi s on Frantz Rd, then just w. **Facility:** 106 kitchen units, some two bedrooms. 2 stories (no elevator), interior/exterior corridors. **Amenities:** safes. **Pool:** heated outdoor. **Activities:** exercise room. **Guest Services:** valet and coin laundry, area transportation. **Featured Amenity: breakfast buffet.**

SAVE ↑↓ CALL ♿ 🔁 ✈
BIZ 🛜 ✕ 🍴 📷 💻
/ SOME UNITS 🐾

WHERE TO EAT

ANNA'S RESTAURANT   614/799-2207   **35**
APPROVED Greek. Casual Dining. **Address:** 7370 Sawmill Center 43235

THE AVENUE STEAK TAVERN   614/591-9000   **39**
THREE DIAMOND Steak. Casual Dining. **Address:** 94 N High St 43017

BRAZENHEAD IRISH PUB   614/792-3738   **43**
APPROVED American. Casual Dining. **Address:** 56 N High St 43017

CAP CITY FINE DINER AND BAR   614/889-7865   **40**
APPROVED Comfort Food. Casual Dining. **Address:** 6644 Riverside Dr 43017

CHILE VERDE CAFE   614/442-6630   **53**
APPROVED Southwestern. Casual Dining. **Address:** 4852 Sawmill Rd 43235

(See map & index p. 222.)

DUBLIN VILLAGE TAVERN   614/766-6250   (48)
APPROVED American. Casual Dining. **Address:** 27 S High St 43017

FUKURYU RAMEN DUBLIN   614/553-7392   (38)
APPROVED Japanese. Quick Serve. **Address:** 4540 Bridge Park Ave 43017

HEN QUARTER   614/905-1666   (37)
THREE DIAMOND Southern. Casual Dining. **Address:** 6628 Riverside Dr 43017

HYDE PARK PRIME STEAKHOUSE   614/717-2828   (49)
THREE DIAMOND Steak. Fine Dining. **Address:** 6360 Frantz Rd 43017

J. LIU OF DUBLIN   614/718-1818   (47)
THREE DIAMOND New American. Casual Dining. **Address:** 50 W Bridge St 43017

LA SCALA ITALIAN BISTRO   614/889-9431   (44)
THREE DIAMOND Italian. Casual Dining. **Address:** 4199 W Dublin-Granville Rd 43017

MEZZO   614/889-6100   (46)
THREE DIAMOND Italian. Casual Dining. **Address:** 12 W Bridge St 43017

MORETTI'S CAFE   614/717-0400   (50)
APPROVED Italian. Casual Dining. **Address:** 5849 Sawmill Rd 43017

NAPA KITCHEN & BAR   614/726-9799   (36)
APPROVED American. Gastropub. **Address:** 7148 Muirfield Dr 43017

OSCAR'S OF DUBLIN   614/792-3424   (41)
THREE DIAMOND American. Casual Dining. **Address:** 84 N High St 43017

P.F. CHANG'S CHINA BISTRO   614/726-0070   (51)
THREE DIAMOND Chinese. Fine Dining. **Address:** 6135 Parkcenter Cir 43017

THE RAIL   614/725-3200   (52)
APPROVED Burgers. Casual Dining. **Address:** 5839 Frantz Rd 43016

SIAM ORCHID   614/792-1112   (34)
APPROVED Thai. Casual Dining. **Address:** 7654 Sawmill Rd 43016

TUCCI'S   614/792-3466   (45)
THREE DIAMOND American. Casual Dining. **Address:** 35 N High St 43017

VASO   614/698-2525   (42)
THREE DIAMOND Spanish Small Plates. Fine Dining. **Address:** 6540 Riverside Dr 43017

EAST LIVERPOOL (D-9) pop. 11,195, elev. 686'

Founded in 1798 on the banks of the Ohio River, East Liverpool was once a leading producer of pottery. Surrounded by an area rich in natural clays and coal, the city manufactured about half the nation's pottery until the industry declined in the early 1930s. The city's downtown sits along the route of the Old Lincoln Highway and is near the first survey line for the Northwest Territory.

Hall China Co., on the eastern edge of town on SR 39, offers guided tours by advanced reservation

explaining the making of chinaware from raw clay to the finished product; phone (330) 385-2900.

MUSEUM OF CERAMICS is at 400 E. Fifth St. in the renovated 1909 post office building. The Beaux Arts structure features decorated domed ceilings, antique glass pendant lamps, and marble and terrazzo floors. Exhibits trace the rise and decline of the ceramics industry in East Liverpool 1840-1930 and its effects on the town and its people. Since the late 19th century, area potteries in the town have been producing more than half of the nation's ceramic products.

The ceramics collection spans three centuries. The collection features WPA-era paintings and a large display of Victorian Lotus Ware porcelain, which won the gold medal at the 1893 Columbian Exposition in Chicago. A 10-minute video introduces the history of East Liverpool and the pottery industry. Life-size dioramas include a jigger shop, kiln and a decorating shop while photographs, charts and maps trace local history. Also displayed are an 1850s two-person potter's wheel, murals and paintings from the 1930s and early 1940s, six rare 1900s Craven Art Pottery objects, a 1930s Fiesta Ware tray with Art Deco handle and a 1940s Hall China Donut Teapot.

Guided tours are available with advance notice, depending on staff availability. **Hours:** Tues.-Sat. 9:30-3:30, Apr.-Dec. The site is subject to closure during extreme weather. Closed major holidays. Phone ahead to confirm schedule. **Cost:** $6; $3 (students); free (ages 0-5 and active military with ID and their dependents). Reservations are required for guided tours. **Phone:** (330) 386-6001 or (800) 600-7180. (GT)

HOT DOG SHOPPE   330/386-6688
APPROVED Hot Dogs. Quick Serve. **Address:** 320 Market St 43920

ELYRIA (B-6) pop. 54,533, elev. 733'

The 1835 Monteith Hall, now home to the Elyria Woman's Club, was built by Rev. John Monteith, an abolitionist who used his home as a station on the Underground Railroad. The basement led to the Black River via a tunnel, and fugitive slaves stayed in the house until safe passage to Lorain and then to Canada could be arranged. The tunnel no longer exists as it was filled in to avoid an impending collapse. Phone (440) 322-0524.

Numerous parks and recreational centers are scattered throughout the community, notably the 195-acre Cascade Park near downtown, with its two 40-foot waterfalls in addition to picnic and playground facilities. Lorain Community College's Stocker Arts Center brings artists and traveling Broadway shows; phone (440) 366-4040, or (800) 995-5222 ext. 4040 for ticket information.

The 1867 City Hall faces historic Ely Square, which is home to the Elyria Veterans' Memorial and the Civil War Memorial as well as a fountain, gazebo, picnic tables and benches. The fountain is not the original, but one has been on this site since 1851; it operates mid-May to mid-October. During summer there are live music performances and festivals, and it is decorated with a lovely light display during the holiday season.

A library (open by appointment only) at the Lorain County History Center, 284 Washington Ave., offers genealogical information; phone (440) 322-3341.

Author Sherwood Anderson, born in nearby Camden in 1876, lived in Elyria for several years in the early 20th century and supported his family by making and selling roofing products. One of his well-known works is "Winesburg, Ohio." Nearby Lorain was the 1931 birthplace and childhood home of author and Nobel Laureate Toni Morrison.

BEST WESTERN INN   440/324-5050

APPROVED
Hotel

Best Western

AAA Benefit: Members save up to 15% and earn bonus points!

Address: 636 W Griswold Rd 44035 **Location:** I-80 exit 145A, just n on SR 57, then just w; I-90 exit 145, just s on SR 57, then just w. **Facility:** 57 units. 2 stories, interior corridors. **Amenities:** safes. **Pool:** heated indoor. **Activities:** exercise room. **Featured Amenity:** full hot breakfast.

COUNTRY INN & SUITES BY RADISSON   440/324-0099
APPROVED Hotel. **Address:** 645 Griswold Rd 44035

COURTYARD BY MARRIOTT CLEVELAND ELYRIA
440/284-3000
THREE DIAMOND Hotel. **Address:** 1755 Travelers Ln 44035

AAA Benefit: Members save 5% or more!

HAMPTON INN & SUITES BY HILTON   440/324-7755
THREE DIAMOND Hotel. **Address:** 1795 Lorain Blvd 44036

AAA Benefit: Members save up to 15%!

WHERE TO EAT

RUBIN'S DELI & RESTAURANT   440/324-3666
APPROVED Sandwiches. Casual Dining. **Address:** 616 Leona St 44035

ENGLEWOOD (F-11) pop. 13,465, elev. 915'
• Hotels & Restaurants map & index p. 242

AULLWOOD GARDEN METROPARK, 955 Aullwood Rd. next to Englewood MetroPark, encompasses 31 acres and is the former home of John and Marie Aull. Marie was one of the Dayton region's most beloved environmentalists and naturalists. There are native plants as well as plants they acquired from their many travels abroad. The site

features a creek, forest, planted prairie and nature trails. A highlight is a 600-year-old twin sycamore.

Pets are not permitted. **Time:** Allow 1 hour minimum. **Hours:** Daily 8 a.m.-10 p.m., Apr.-Oct.; 8-8, rest of year. **Cost:** Free. **Phone:** (937) 275-7275.

BEST WESTERN PLUS DAYTON NORTHWEST
937/832-2222 **16**

APPROVED
Hotel

 Best Western PLUS

AAA Benefit: Members save up to 15% and earn bonus points!

Address: 20 Rockridge Rd 45322 **Location:** I-70 exit 29, just n. **Facility:** 127 units. 4 stories, interior corridors. **Activities:** exercise room. **Guest Services:** valet and coin laundry.

COMFORT INN & SUITES-ENGLEWOOD   937/836-9400 **17**
APPROVED Hotel. **Address:** 9305 N Main St 45415

HAMPTON INN & SUITES BY HILTON DAYTON AIRPORT
937/832-3333 **18**
APPROVED Hotel. **Address:** 180 Rockridge Rd 45322

AAA Benefit: Members save up to 15%!

WHERE TO EAT

SKYLINE CHILI   937/832-3222
APPROVED American. Quick Serve. **Address:** 1321 S Main St 45322

FAIRBORN pop. 32,352, elev. 837'
• Restaurants p. 252
• Hotels & Restaurants map & index p. 242

Fairborn Area Chamber of Commerce: 12 N. Central Ave., Fairborn, OH 45324. **Phone:** (937) 878-3191.

Shopping: For an old-time shopping experience try Foy's Halloween and Variety Store at 18-20 E. Main St. The variety store has been open since the 1920s and maintains its original ambience. The Halloween store and the costume store at 10 W. Main St. are more recent, and from late September through All Hallows' Eve are joined by other temporary establishments such as the Haunted Museum and the Glow in the Dark Shop to form the Halloween Mini Mall; look for appropriate decorations on some of the stores downtown. Phone (937) 878-0671 or (800) 642-9686.

HUFFMAN PRAIRIE FLYING FIELD AND INTERPRETIVE CENTER—see Dayton p. 240.

NATIONAL MUSEUM OF THE UNITED STATES AIR FORCE—see Dayton p. 241.

COUNTRY INN & SUITES BY RADISSON, FAIRBORN SOUTH
937/429-2222 **31**
THREE DIAMOND Hotel. **Address:** 3971 Colonel Glenn Hwy 45324

(See map & index p. 242.)

HAMPTON INN BY HILTON 937/429-5505 ㉗
APPROVED [SAVE] Hotel. **Ad-dress:** 2550 Paramount Pl 45324
AAA Benefit: Members save up to 15%!

HOLIDAY INN DAYTON/FAIRBORN 937/426-7800 ㉙
THREE DIAMOND
Hotel

Address: 2800 Presidential Dr 45324 **Location:** I-675 exit 17 (N Fairfield Rd), just w. **Facility:** 203 units. 6 stories, interior corridors. **Pool:** heated indoor. **Activities:** exercise room. **Guest Services:** valet and coin laundry.

HOMEWOOD SUITES BY HILTON DAYTON-FAIRBORN
937/429-0600 ㉘
THREE DIAMOND [SAVE] Extended Stay Hotel. **Address:** 2750 Presidential Dr 45324
AAA Benefit: Members save up to 15%!

LA QUINTA INN & SUITES FAIRBORN-WRIGHT PATTERSON
937/490-2000 ㉚
APPROVED Hotel. **Address:** 2540 University Blvd 45324

WHERE TO EAT

SKYLINE CHILI 937/879-7125
APPROVED American. Quick Serve. **Address:** 1223 Dayton-Yellow Springs Rd 45324

FAIRFIELD pop. 42,510
• Hotels & Restaurants map & index p. 166
• Part of Cincinnati area — see map p. 153

GOLD STAR CHILI
APPROVED American. Quick Serve.
LOCATIONS:
Address: 470 Nilles Rd 45014 **Phone:** 513/858-3400
Address: 6755 Dixie Hwy 45014 **Phone:** 513/860-0444

SABOR PERUANO 513/860-0349 ⑲
APPROVED Peruvian. Casual Dining. **Address:** 7245 Dixie Hwy 45014

SKYLINE CHILI 513/829-8777
APPROVED American. Quick Serve. **Address:** 1190 Hicks Blvd 45014

FAIRLAWN (D-11) pop. 7,437, elev. 1,007'

A suburb of Akron, Fairlawn is home to several parks. Fort Island/Griffiths Park on Trunko Road features a boardwalk where you can enjoy the views of the wetlands that may include ducks, turtles and a variety of birds. Summit Mall, 3265 W. Market St.; has Dillard's and Macy's as anchors and nearly 100 other stores, including Ann Taylor, Banana Republic, Coach, Eddie Bauer, Hollister, J. Crew, Journeys and Swarovski.

BEST WESTERN PLUS WEST AKRON INN & SUITES
330/670-0888
APPROVED
Hotel

AAA Benefit: Members save up to 15% and earn bonus points!

Address: 160 Montrose West Ave 44321 **Location:** I-77 exit 137B, 0.3 mi w on SR 18, then 0.5 mi s. **Facility:** 51 units. 4 stories, interior corridors. **Pool:** heated indoor. **Activities:** hot tub, exercise room. **Guest Services:** valet and coin laundry. **Featured Amenity:** full hot breakfast.

/ SOME UNITS

COURTYARD BY MARRIOTT-AKRON FAIRLAWN
330/668-9090
THREE DIAMOND [SAVE] Hotel. **Ad-dress:** 100 Springside Dr 44333
AAA Benefit: Members save 5% or more!

DOUBLETREE BY HILTON HOTEL AKRON-FAIRLAWN
330/869-9000
THREE DIAMOND
Hotel
DOUBLETREE
BY HILTON
AAA Benefit: Members save up to 15%!

Address: 3150 W Market St 44333 **Location:** I-77 exit 137A, 2 mi e on SR 18. **Facility:** 92 units. 3 stories, interior corridors. **Terms:** check-in 4 pm. **Amenities:** safes. **Pool:** heated indoor. **Activities:** exercise room. **Guest Services:** valet laundry.
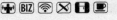

EXTENDED STAY AMERICA-AKRON-COPLEY 330/666-3177
APPROVED Extended Stay Hotel. **Address:** 170 Montrose West Ave 44321

EXTENDED STAY AMERICA AKRON EAST 330/668-9818
APPROVED Extended Stay Hotel. **Address:** 185 Montrose West Ave 44321

FAIRFIELD INN & SUITES BY MARRIOTT AKRON/FAIRLAWN
330/665-0641
THREE DIAMOND
Hotel
Fairfield
AAA Benefit: Members save 5% or more!

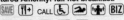
Address: 208 Springside Dr 44333 **Location:** I-77 exit 137A, just e, then n. **Facility:** 98 units. 4 stories, interior corridors. **Pool:** heated indoor. **Activities:** hot tub, exercise room. **Guest Services:** valet and coin laundry. **Featured Amenity:** full hot breakfast.

HAMPTON INN-AKRON/FAIRLAWN 330/666-7361
THREE DIAMOND [SAVE] Hotel. **Ad-dress:** 80 Springside Dr 44333
AAA Benefit: Members save up to 15%!

HILTON AKRON/FAIRLAWN
330/867-5000

WHERE THREE DIAMOND

Hotel

AAA Benefit:
Members save up to 15%!

Address: 3180 W Market St 44333 **Location:** I-77 exit 137A, 2 mi e on SR 18. Located in business district. **Facility:** 203 units, some efficiencies and kitchens. 4 stories, interior corridors. **Terms:** check-in 4 pm. **Amenities:** safes. **Dining:** Beau's Grille, see separate listing. **Pool:** outdoor, heated indoor. **Activities:** sauna, hot tub, steamroom, exercise room, massage. **Guest Services:** valet and coin laundry.

 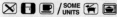 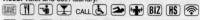

HOLIDAY INN-AKRON WEST FAIRLAWN
330/666-4131

WHERE THREE DIAMOND Hotel. **Address:** 4073 Medina Rd 44333

HOMEWOOD SUITES BY HILTON AKRON/FAIRLAWN
330/664-6000

WHERE THREE DIAMOND SAVE Extended Stay Hotel. **Address:** 210 Springside Dr 44333

AAA Benefit:
Members save up to 15%!

RADISSON HOTEL AKRON/FAIRLAWN
330/666-9300

WHERE THREE DIAMOND Hotel. **Address:** 200 Montrose West Ave 44321

RESIDENCE INN BY MARRIOTT AKRON/FAIRLAWN
330/664-7800

WHERE THREE DIAMOND SAVE Extended Stay Hotel. **Address:** 4080 Embassy Pkwy 44333

AAA Benefit:
Members save 5% or more!

WHERE TO EAT

BEAU'S GRILLE
330/867-5218

WHERE THREE DIAMOND

American Fine Dining

$9-$37

AAA Inspector Notes: The menu displays an adventurous spirit and range, with nearly 20 appetizers and a varied entrée selection. Chef Beau Schmidt excels in creating his chicken sausage with Creole mustard sauce appetizer. Other entrées include the grilled American sea bass with lobster mashed potatoes, chive velouté and grilled asparagus; and the 8-ounce filet served with creamed spinach, Pontalba potatoes topped with cornmeal-dusted fried oysters and sauce béarnaise. **Features:** full bar, patio dining, happy hour. **Reservations:** suggested. **Address:** 3180 W Market St 44333 **Location:** I-77 exit 137A, 2 mi e on SR 18; in Hilton Akron/Fairlawn.

B L D

FLEMING'S PRIME STEAKHOUSE & WINE BAR
330/670-5200

WHERE THREE DIAMOND Steak. Fine Dining. **Address:** 4000 Medina Rd 44333

HOOLEY HOUSE SPORTS PUB AND GRILLE
234/466-0060

WHERE APPROVED American. Sports Bar. **Address:** 145 Montrose Ave W 44321

MUSTARD SEED CAFE
330/666-7333

WHERE APPROVED Natural/Organic. Casual Dining. **Address:** 3885 W Market St 44321

THE RAIL
330/864-7245

WHERE APPROVED Burgers. Casual Dining. **Address:** 3265 W Market St 44333

SKYWAY DRIVE-IN
330/836-2806

WHERE APPROVED Burgers. Quick Serve. **Address:** 2781 W Market St 44333

TRES POTRILLOS
330/668-9779

WHERE APPROVED Mexican. Casual Dining. **Address:** 115 Montrose West Ave 44321

FINDLAY (C-3) pop. 41,202, elev. 774'
• Restaurants p. 254

In the mid-1960s, Findlay resident John B. Cooke began a project to request that all citizens and business owners fly an American flag on Flag Day, June 14. This popular show of patriotism resulted in a 1974 Congressional Designation that declared Findlay "Flag City USA."

The University of Findlay was established in 1882. At its Center for Equine and Pre-Veterinary Studies, 14700 US 68, students and instructors ride and train horses. Guided tours by appointment and summer horse shows are offered; phone (800) 472-9502.

Findlay-Hancock County Convention and Visitors Bureau: 123 E. Main Cross St., Findlay, OH 45840. **Phone:** (419) 422-3315 or (800) 424-3315.

Shopping: Findlay has a variety of antique shops, boutiques and gift shops. Jeffrey's Antique Gallery, I-75 exit 161, features more than 250 antiques dealers.

HANCOCK HISTORICAL MUSEUM is at 422 W. Sandusky St. The restored two-story 1881 Hull-Flater House is furnished in period. Artifacts from different eras—including furniture, toys, games and textiles—are displayed. The Exhibit Center focuses on local history, the barn addition houses transportation and agricultural displays, and the Crawford Log House is a restored mid-19th century log home. The Energy and Transportation History Annex includes two Grant cars and exhibits pertaining to the history of area gas and oil manufacturing and hometown producer, Marathon Petroleum.

Time: Allow 1 hour minimum. **Hours:** Wed.-Fri. 10-4, Sun. 1-4. **Cost:** $5; $3 (ages 55+); $2 (ages 0-18); $12 (family). **Phone:** (419) 423-4433. GT

BAYMONT INN & SUITES BY WYNDHAM FINDLAY
419/420-1776

WHERE APPROVED Hotel. **Address:** 941 Interstate Dr 45840

COMFORT SUITES FINDLAY NORTH
419/420-1212

WHERE APPROVED Hotel. **Address:** 3700 Speedway Dr 45840

COUNTRY INN & SUITES BY RADISSON FINDLAY
419/422-4200

WHERE APPROVED Hotel. **Address:** 903 Interstate Dr 45840

DRURY INN & SUITES FINDLAY
419/422-9700

WHERE THREE DIAMOND Hotel. **Address:** 820 Trenton Ave 45840

EXTENDED STAY AMERICA FINDLAY-TIFFIN AVE
419/425-9696

WHERE APPROVED Extended Stay Hotel. **Address:** 2355 Tiffin Ave 45840

FAIRFIELD INN & SUITES BY MARRIOTT FINDLAY
419/424-9940

APPROVED [SAVE] Hotel. **Address:** 2000 Tiffin Ave 45839

AAA Benefit: Members save 5% or more!

HAMPTON INN FINDLAY
419/422-5252

THREE DIAMOND [SAVE] Hotel. **Address:** 921 Interstate Dr 45840

AAA Benefit: Members save up to 15%!

HANCOCK HOTEL
419/423-0631

FOUR DIAMOND

Hotel

Address: 631 S Main St 45840 **Location:** Just s. **Facility:** The spacious lobby has upscale décor including a fireplace, leather chairs and landscape art. Rooms have cherry furniture and soft bed linens. Bathrooms have marble counter tops and glass showers. 99 units. 5 stories, interior corridors. **Parking:** valet only. **Amenities:** safes. **Dining:** Mancy's Steakhouse at the Hancock Hotel, see separate listing. **Activities:** bicycles, exercise room. **Guest Services:** valet laundry, area transportation.

[SAVE] [icons]

HILTON GARDEN INN FINDLAY
567/250-2525

THREE DIAMOND [SAVE] Hotel. **Address:** 1050 Interstate Dr W 45840

AAA Benefit: Members save up to 15%!

QUALITY INN
419/423-4303

APPROVED Motel. **Address:** 1020 Interstate Ct 45840

TOWNEPLACE SUITES BY MARRIOTT FINDLAY
419/425-9545

APPROVED [SAVE] Extended Stay Hotel. **Address:** 2501 Tiffin Ave 45840

AAA Benefit: Members save 5% or more!

WHERE TO EAT

BISTRO ON MAIN
419/425-4900

THREE DIAMOND Italian. Casual Dining. **Address:** 407 S Main St 45840

FINDLAY BREWING
419/419-2739

APPROVED American. Brewpub. **Address:** 213 E Crawford St 45840

LOGAN'S IRISH PUB
419/420-3602

APPROVED Irish. Casual Dining. **Address:** 414 S Main St 45840

MANCY'S STEAKHOUSE AT THE HANCOCK HOTEL
419/423-0631

THREE DIAMOND Steak. Fine Dining. **Address:** 631 S Main St 45840

RANCHO FIESTA RESTAURANT
419/424-9363

APPROVED Mexican. Casual Dining. **Address:** 1739 Tiffin Ave 45840

ROSSILLI'S
419/423-5050

APPROVED Italian. Casual Dining. **Address:** 217 S Main St 45840

STEVE'S DAKOTA GRILL
419/420-9394

APPROVED Steak. Casual Dining. **Address:** 1600 Broad St 45840

TAVERN AT THE INN RESTAURANT AND LOUNGE
419/422-5682

APPROVED American. Casual Dining. **Address:** 200 E Main Cross St 45840

TONY'S RESTAURANT & PUB
419/424-3100

APPROVED American. Casual Dining. **Address:** 10280 US 224 W 45840

FOREST PARK pop. 18,720
• Hotels & Restaurants map & index p. 166
• Part of Cincinnati area — see map p. 153

SPRINGHILL SUITES BY MARRIOTT CINCINNATI NORTH/ FOREST PARK
513/825-9035 [51]

THREE DIAMOND [SAVE] Hotel. **Address:** 12001 Chase Plaza Dr 45240

AAA Benefit: Members save 5% or more!

WHERE TO EAT

IZZY'S DELICATESSENS
513/825-3888

APPROVED Deli. Quick Serve. **Address:** 1198 Smiley Ave 45240

SKYLINE CHILI
513/851-3929

APPROVED American. Quick Serve. **Address:** 1180 Kemper Meadow Dr 45240

FOSTORIA (C-3) pop. 13,441, elev. 780'

Fostoria was created when the two small villages of Risdon and Rome were unified in 1854. The new town was named in honor of C.W. Foster, a prominent pioneer whose son Charles later became governor of Ohio and secretary of the U.S. Treasury.

During the late 19th- and early 20th centuries, Fostoria was the home of several glass manufacturing plants. Although their furnaces are now cold, the local glass companies and the craftsmanship for which they were known are remembered at Glass Heritage Gallery at 109 N. Main St.; phone (419) 435-5077.

BEST WESTERN FOSTORIA INN & SUITES
419/436-3600

APPROVED

Hotel

 Best Western

AAA Benefit: Members save up to 15% and earn bonus points!

Address: 1690 N County Line Rd 44830 **Location:** SR 12, 2 mi n on SR 23. **Facility:** 52 units. 2 stories (no elevator), interior corridors. **Amenities:** safes. **Pool:** heated indoor. **Activities:** hot tub. **Featured Amenity:** full hot breakfast.

[SAVE] CALL [icons]

FREMONT (B-4) pop. 16,734, elev. 613'

Fremont is on the site of 1813 Fort Stephenson, where 21-year-old Maj. George Croghan and 150 American soldiers repelled an attack by 400 British soldiers and 300 Native Americans.

Rodger Young Park, on the Sandusky State Scenic River, is dedicated to the World War II hero and to all Sandusky County servicemen and women.

Fremont/Sandusky County Convention and Visitors Bureau: 712 North St., Suite 102, Fremont, OH 43420. **Phone:** (419) 332-4470 or (800) 255-8070.

RUTHERFORD B. HAYES LIBRARY AND MUSEUMS is at 1337 Hayes Ave. on the 25-acre grounds of Spiegel Grove. This is the former estate of 19th U.S. President Rutherford B. Hayes and First Lady Lucy Webb Hayes. The site includes the couple's recently restored 31-room mansion, the first official presidential library, a museum, paved walking trails and President Hayes' tomb. The iron gates at the entrances to the site were at the White House during the Hayes administration.

The collections include family mementos and the public and private papers and books of the president and his family as well as local history items and genealogical material. **Hours:** Museum and mansion Tues.-Sat. 9-5 (also Mon., Apr.-Dec.), Sun. and holidays noon-5. Library Tues.-Sat. 9-5 (also Mon., Apr.-Dec.); closed holidays. All facilities closed Jan. 1, Easter, Thanksgiving and Christmas. Phone ahead to confirm schedule. **Cost:** Museum only $13. Combination ticket to museum and mansion $20; $18 (ages 65+ and military with ID); $10 (ages 13-18); $5 (ages 6-12). Library free. Rates may vary; phone ahead. **Phone:** (419) 332-2081 or (800) 998-7737.

COMFORT INN & SUITES   419/355-9300
APPROVED Hotel. **Address:** 840 Sean Dr 43420

HAMPTON INN & SUITES BY HILTON FREMONT
419/332-7650
THREE DIAMOND
Hotel

AAA Benefit: Members save up to 15%!

Address: 540 E CR 89 43420 **Location:** I-80/90 exit 91, just s. **Facility:** 82 units. 3 stories, interior corridors. **Pool:** heated indoor. **Activities:** exercise room. **Guest Services:** valet and coin laundry. **Featured Amenity: breakfast buffet.**

SAVE CALL 🛌 ♿ 🚐 🛗 BIZ 📶
✕ 🛏 🖨 💻

HOLIDAY INN EXPRESS & SUITES NORTH FREMONT
419/332-7700
THREE DIAMOND Hotel. **Address:** 1501 Hospitality Ct 43420

WHERE TO EAT

THE 818 CLUB RESTAURANT   419/334-9122
APPROVED American. Casual Dining. **Address:** 818 Croghan St 43420

EL RANCHO   419/334-3475
APPROVED Mexican. Casual Dining. **Address:** 2100 W State St 43420

JIMMY G'S BARBEQUE   567/201-2920
APPROVED Barbecue. Quick Serve. **Address:** 1321 W State St 43420

GAHANNA pop. 33,248
• **Hotels & Restaurants map & index p. 222**
• **Part of Columbus area — see map p. 205**

CANDLEWOOD SUITES COLUMBUS AIRPORT
614/863-4033 **75**
APPROVED Extended Stay Hotel. **Address:** 590 Taylor Rd 43230

TOWNEPLACE SUITES BY MARRIOTT COLUMBUS AIRPORT
614/861-1400 **76**
APPROVED SAVE Extended Stay Hotel. **Address:** 695 Taylor Rd 43230
AAA Benefit: Members save 5% or more!

WHERE TO EAT

ASIAN GOURMET & SUSHI BAR   614/471-8871 **64**
APPROVED Asian Sushi. Casual Dining. **Address:** 1325 Stoneridge Ln 43230

CAP CITY FINE DINER & BAR   614/478-9999 **65**
APPROVED Comfort Food. Casual Dining. **Address:** 1301 Stone Ridge Dr 43230

CITY BARBEQUE   614/416-8890
APPROVED Barbecue. Quick Serve. **Address:** 108 S Stygler Rd 43230

THE HICKORY HOUSE   614/428-7427
APPROVED American. Casual Dining. **Address:** 550 Officenter Pl 43230

THE OLD BAG OF NAILS PUB   614/337-9430 **66**
APPROVED American. Casual Dining. **Address:** 63 Mill St 43230

SKYLINE CHILI   614/337-9870
APPROVED American. Quick Serve. **Address:** 1350 Stone Ridge Dr 43230

GALLIPOLIS (H-6) pop. 3,641, elev. 561'
• **Restaurants p. 256**

The second permanent settlement in the Northwest Territory, Gallipolis (gal-a-po-LEES), meaning "the city of the Gauls," was founded in 1790 by French Royalists who were fleeing the French Revolution.

The city park overlooking the Ohio River is the original settlement of the "French 500"; it was known then as Le Place. The town's heritage is evident in the old houses surrounding the park.

Fortification Hill, in Mound Hill Cemetery, offers a view of Gallipolis and the Ohio River Valley to the hills of West Virginia. French Art Colony, 530 1st Ave., is a multicultural arts center housed in an 1855 Greek Revival house; phone (740) 446-3834.

Gallia County Convention and Visitors Bureau: 441 Second Ave., Gallipolis, OH 45631. **Phone:** (740) 446-6882 or (800) 765-6482.

HAMPTON INN GALLIPOLIS   740/446-8000
THREE DIAMOND SAVE Hotel. **Address:** 444 SR 7 S 45631
AAA Benefit: Members save up to 15%!

SUPER 8   740/446-8080
APPROVED Motel. **Address:** 321 Upper River Rd 45631

WILLIAM ANN MOTEL   740/446-3373

Motel

Address: 918 2nd Ave 45631 **Location:** 1.6 mi n on SR 7. **Facility:** 50 units. 1-2 stories (no elevator), exterior corridors.

EL TORIL MEXICAN RESTAURANT   740/446-1375

Mexican. Casual Dining. **Address:** 2145 Eastern Ave 45631

TUSCANY ITALIAN RESTAURANT   740/446-7800

Italian. Casual Dining. **Address:** 1308 Eastern Ave 45631

GENEVA-ON-THE-LAKE (A-8) pop. 1,288, elev. 600'

This family resort town on Lake Erie has been attracting crowds since 1869 when a public picnic grounds opened. The site gradually grew to include a carousel, campgrounds and then primitive cottages and a dance hall. Visitors still flock to this lakefront town for family fun and outdoor recreation. During the summer The Strip, a 1-mile stretch of Lake Road (SR 531), features arcades, batting cages, miniature golf courses, a merry-go-round, waterslides and a variety of other amusements. There is an 18-hole golf course as well as opportunities for boating, fishing and swimming on Lake Erie. Nearby Geneva State Park *(see Recreation Areas Chart)* offers abundant recreational opportunities as well, including a beach. A free concert series is offered Tuesday evenings at Geneva Township Park mid-June through late August. Shoppers also can enjoy a flea market at the Geneva-on-the-Lake Visitor Information Center Sat. 9-5, Memorial Day-Labor Day.

Geneva-on-the-Lake Visitor Information Center: 5536 Lake Rd., Geneva-on-the-Lake, OH 44041-9786. **Phone:** (440) 466-8600 or (800) 862-9948.

THE LODGE & CONFERENCE CENTER AT GENEVA-ON-THE-LAKE   440/466-7100

Resort Hotel

Address: 4888 N Broadway (SR 534) 44041 **Location:** Waterfront. I-90 exit 218, 6.1 mi n. **Facility:** On the shores of Lake Erie, this lodge features stylish rooms with comfortable bedding. Many have water views, some have a balcony or small patio, and others have an electric fireplace. 134 units, some cottages. 4 stories, interior corridors. **Terms:** check-in 4 pm. **Dining:** Horizons, see separate listing. **Pool:** heated outdoor, heated indoor. **Activities:** hot tub, self-propelled boats, cross country skiing, bicycles, playground, game room, lawn sports, picnic facilities, trails, exercise room. **Guest Services:** coin laundry. **Featured Amenity:** full hot breakfast.

HORIZONS   440/466-7100

American. Casual Dining. **Address:** 4888 N Broadway (SR 534) 44041

GREEN

CAMBRIA HOTEL & SUITES AKRON-CANTON AIRPORT   330/899-1990

Hotel. **Address:** 1787 Thorn Dr 44685

MENCHES BROS   330/896-2288

Burgers. Casual Dining. **Address:** 3700 Massillon Rd 44685

GREENVILLE (E-1) pop. 13,227, elev. 1,030'

Greenville was the site of Fort Greenville, built in 1793 by Gen. Anthony Wayne and named for Gen. Nathanael Greene. After his victory at Fallen Timbers, Wayne signed a treaty at the fort with several tribes, which opened up the Northwest Territory for settlement. The fort was later burned and abandoned, but the site is marked by the Fort Greenville Treaty Memorial in front of the City Building. The Greenville Treaty scene is etched on a stone at the corner of Elm and West Main streets.

Darke County Visitors Bureau: 421 S. Broadway, Greenville, OH 45331. **Phone:** (937) 548-5158 or (800) 504-2995.

BISTRO OFF BROADWAY   937/316-5000

American. Casual Dining. **Address:** 117 E Fifth St 45331

GROVE CITY pop. 35,575, elev. 851'
- Hotels & Restaurants map & index p. 222
- Part of Columbus area — see map p. 205

BEST WESTERN EXECUTIVE INN   614/875-7770   93

Motel

Best Western. **AAA Benefit:** Members save up to 15% and earn bonus points!

Address: 4026 Jackpot Rd 43123 **Location:** I-71 exit 100, just e. **Facility:** 50 units. 2 stories (no elevator), exterior corridors. **Parking:** winter plug-ins. **Pool:** outdoor. **Activities:** exercise room. **Guest Services:** coin laundry. **Featured Amenity:** continental breakfast.

COURTYARD BY MARRIOTT COLUMBUS/GROVE CITY   614/782-8292   96

Hotel. **Address:** 1668 Buckeye Pl 43123

AAA Benefit: Members save 5% or more!

DRURY INN & SUITES-COLUMBUS SOUTH   614/875-7000   95

Hotel. **Address:** 4109 Parkway Centre Dr 43123

(See map & index p. 222.)

FAIRFIELD INN & SUITES BY MARRIOTT COLUMBUS GROVE CITY 614/808-8200 **97**

THREE DIAMOND SAVE Hotel. **Address:** 1722 Buckeye Pl 43123

AAA Benefit: Members save 5% or more!

HAMPTON INN BY HILTON COLUMBUS SOUTH 614/539-1177 **92**

APPROVED SAVE Hotel. **Address:** 4017 Jackpot Rd 43123

AAA Benefit: Members save up to 15%!

HILTON GARDEN INN COLUMBUS/GROVE CITY 614/539-8944 **89**

THREE DIAMOND SAVE Hotel. **Address:** 3928 Jackpot Rd 43123

AAA Benefit: Members save up to 15%!

HOLIDAY INN EXPRESS HOTEL & SUITES 614/801-9000 **90**

APPROVED Hotel. **Address:** 3951 Jackpot Rd 43123

LA QUINTA INN GROVE CITY 614/539-6200 **91**

THREE DIAMOND Hotel. **Address:** 3962 Jackpot Rd 43123

TRAVELODGE GROVE CITY 614/991-5301 **94**

APPROVED

Motel

Address: 4029 Marlane Dr 43123 **Location:** I-71 exit 100, just w. **Facility:** 43 units. 2 stories (no elevator), exterior corridors. **Parking:** winter plug-ins.

SAVE 🍴 HS 📶 🛗 🖥 📺

WHERE TO EAT

CIMI'S BISTRO AT PINNACLE 614/539-0397 **89**

THREE DIAMOND American. Casual Dining. **Address:** 1500 Pinnacle Club Dr 43123

LA FIESTA MARIACHI 614/539-4540

APPROVED Mexican. Casual Dining. **Address:** 1998 Stringtown Rd 43123

HAMILTON (G-1) pop. 62,477, elev. 593'
• Hotels & Restaurants map & index p. 166
• Part of Cincinnati area — see map p. 153

Founded as Fort Hamilton in 1791, Hamilton became a prosperous industrial community due to immigrant labor and canals. In the late 1820s a wharf basin was dug, linking the town to the Miami and Erie Canal. At the same time an influx of German and Irish immigrants provided the labor for new enterprises.

Heavy industry expanded when Hamilton Hydraulic was completed in 1852. In addition to industry, the Hamilton region enjoys the agricultural yields of the fertile Great Miami River Valley. Hamilton's historic houses and commercial buildings, which show a variety of architectural styles, are concentrated in three districts: Rossville, Dayton Lane and German Village.

On Monument Avenue, the Soldiers, Sailors and Pioneers Monument is topped by a 17-foot brass figure of a Civil War private. The monument contains a library with the names of all Ohioans who served in the Civil War and World War I as well as exhibits containing military weapons, uniforms and medals; phone (513) 867-5823.

In mid- or late January, ❄ IceFest brings in ice sculptors from around the world for this exciting competition held downtown.

Hamilton Welcome Center: 1 High St., Hamilton, OH 45011. **Phone:** (513) 844-8080.

Self-guiding tours: Brochures describing walking tours of three historic districts are available from the welcome center.

COURTYARD BY MARRIOTT HAMILTON
513/896-6200 **9**

THREE DIAMOND

Hotel

COURTYARD **AAA Benefit:** Members save 5% or more!

Address: 1 Riverfront Plaza 45011 **Location:** Waterfront. Just off High St. Located in historic district. **Facility:** 120 units. 6 stories, interior corridors. **Pool:** heated indoor. **Activities:** exercise room. **Guest Services:** valet and coin laundry.

SAVE 🍴 🛗 📺 CALL 🛗 🏊
🐾 BIZ HS 📶 ✕ 🖥 📺
/SOME UNITS 📺

WHERE TO EAT

GOLD STAR CHILI 513/863-8956

APPROVED American. Quick Serve. **Address:** 1246 Main St 45013

SKYLINE CHILI

APPROVED American. Quick Serve.

LOCATIONS:
Address: 1496 S Erie Blvd 45011 **Phone:** 513/737-3330
Address: 8386 W Princeton-Glendale Rd 45069 **Phone:** 513/874-4211

HARRISON pop. 9,897
• Restaurants p. 258
• Part of Cincinnati area — see map p. 153

BEST WESTERN PLUS WHITEWATER INN
513/845-4970

THREE DIAMOND

Hotel

Best Western PLUS **AAA Benefit:** Members save up to 15% and earn bonus points!

Address: 391 Comfort Dr 45030 **Location:** I-74 exit 1, just n on New Haven Rd, then just e on Biggs Blvd. **Facility:** 57 units. 3 stories, interior corridors. **Parking:** winter plug-ins. **Pool:** heated indoor. **Activities:** exercise room. **Guest Services:** valet and coin laundry. **Featured Amenity:** continental breakfast.

SAVE 🍴 CALL 🛗 🏊 🐾 BIZ
📶 ✕ 🖥 📺 📺

/SOME UNITS 🐾

HOLIDAY INN EXPRESS HOTEL & SUITES 513/367-1111

THREE DIAMOND Hotel. **Address:** 10906 New Haven Rd 45030

WHERE TO EAT

SKYLINE CHILI   513/367-0614
APPROVED American. Quick Serve. **Address:** 10429 Harrison Ave 45030

HEATH (E-5) pop. 10,310, elev. 860'
• Part of Columbus area — see map p. 205

Greater Licking County Convention and Visitors Bureau: 455 Hebron Rd., Heath, OH 43056. **Phone:** (740) 345-8224.

NEWARK EARTHWORKS is comprised of three sites: Great Circle is 1 mi. s.w. of SR 16 at 455 Hebron Rd. (SR 79); Wright Earthworks can be viewed from James Street, near jct. SR 79 and Grant St. in nearby Newark; and Octagon Earthworks is at jct. N. 33rd St. and Parkview Rd. in Newark. The memorial preserves a portion of the Newark Earthworks, a system of prehistoric mounds used for astronomical, ceremonial and social purposes; they are believed to be the largest such mounds ever built.

Great Circle is 1,200 feet in diameter with grass-covered earthen walls ranging from 8 to 14 feet in height. In the center are four lower connected mounds. On the grounds is a museum/visitor center, which includes an exhibit and a 15-minute video about the site.

Time: Allow 30 minutes minimum. **Hours:** Great Circle, Octagon and Wright grounds open daily dawn-dusk. Great Circle museum open Mon.-Fri. 8:30-5 (also Sat. 10-4, Sun. noon-4, Memorial Day-Labor Day). Closed major holidays. Phone ahead to confirm schedule. **Cost:** Free. **Phone:** (740) 345-8224 or (800) 589-8224. ⌆

HAMPTON INN BY HILTON HEATH-NEWARK   740/788-8991
THREE DIAMOND [SAVE] Hotel. **Ad-** **dress:** 1008 Hebron Rd 43056

AAA Benefit: Members save up to 15%!

WHERE TO EAT

SHADE ON 30TH STREET   740/788-9287
APPROVED Sandwiches Pizza. Sports Bar. **Address:** 850 S 30th St 43056

TOKYO JAPANESE STEAKHOUSE   740/281-0909
APPROVED Japanese. Casual Dining. **Address:** 789 Hebron Rd 43056

HEBRON pop. 2,336
• Part of Columbus area — see map p. 205

BEST WESTERN LAKEWOOD INN   740/928-1800
APPROVED
Hotel

Best Western.
AAA Benefit: Members save up to 15% and earn bonus points!

Address: 122 Arrowhead Blvd 43025 **Location:** I-70 exit 129, 1 mi n on SR 79. **Facility:** 70 units. 2 stories (no elevator), interior corridors. **Amenities:** safes. **Pool:** heated indoor. **Activities:** hot tub, exercise room. **Guest Services:** coin laundry. **Featured Amenity:** full hot breakfast.

[SAVE] CALL 🐾 ⊞ [BIZ] 📶
✕ 🅷 📷 🖥 / SOME UNITS [HS]

HILLIARD pop. 28,435
• Hotels & Restaurants map & index p. 222
• Part of Columbus area — see map p. 205

BEST WESTERN HILLIARD INN & SUITES
                                         614/529-8118 (79)
THREE DIAMOND
Hotel

Best Western.
AAA Benefit: Members save up to 15% and earn bonus points!

Address: 3831 Park Mill Run Dr 43026 **Location:** I-270 exit 13 southbound; exit 13A northbound, 0.4 mi e on Fishinger Blvd. **Facility:** 60 units. 3 stories, interior corridors. **Pool:** heated indoor. **Activities:** limited exercise equipment. **Guest Services:** valet and coin laundry. **Featured Amenity:** full hot breakfast.

[SAVE] 🍴 CALL 🐾 ⊞ 📶 ✕
🅷 📷 🖥

HOMEWOOD SUITES BY HILTON-COLUMBUS HILLIARD
                                         614/529-4100 (80)
THREE DIAMOND [SAVE] Extended Stay Hotel. **Address:** 3841 Park Mill Run Dr 43026

AAA Benefit: Members save up to 15%!

WHERE TO EAT

OTIE'S TAVERN & GRILL   614/876-1548 (78)
APPROVED American. Casual Dining. **Address:** 5344 Center St 43026

SKYLINE CHILI   614/777-8922
APPROVED American. Quick Serve. **Address:** 3693 Fishinger Blvd 43026

HILLSBORO pop. 6,605, elev. 1,132'

GOLD STAR CHILI — 937/393-4422
 APPROVED American. Quick Serve. **Address:** 585 Harry Sauner Rd 45133

HOLLAND pop. 1,764
• Hotels & Restaurants map & index p. 299

COURTYARD BY MARRIOTT TOLEDO AIRPORT HOLLAND — 419/866-1001 **20**

THREE DIAMOND Hotel

COURTYARD **AAA Benefit:** Members save 5% or more!

Address: 1435 E Mall Dr 43528 **Location:** I-475 exit 8, 0.5 mi w on SR 2. **Facility:** 149 units. 3 stories, interior corridors. **Pool:** heated indoor. **Activities:** exercise room. **Guest Services:** valet and coin laundry, boarding pass kiosk. *(See ad p. 302.)*

EXTENDED STAY AMERICA TOLEDO-HOLLAND — 419/861-1133 **19**
APPROVED Extended Stay Hotel. **Address:** 6155 W Trust Dr 43528

HOPEWELL CULTURE NATIONAL HISTORICAL PARK (G-4)

The park preserves six earthwork complexes concentrated in the Scioto River valley: High Bank Works, Hopeton Earthworks, Hopewell Mound Group, Mound City Group, Seip Earthworks and Spruce Hill Earthworks.

The Mound City Group is about 3 miles north of Chillicothe on SR 104. This 120-acre tract with a 13-acre earth wall enclosure preserves at least 23 prehistoric burial mounds that lie within a low embankment. Native Americans of the Hopewell Culture, who inhabited the area about 2,000 years ago, were noted for their artistry and their practice of building enormous geometric earthworks as ceremonial sites. These artisans fashioned ornaments from materials foreign to Ohio.

The Mound City Group visitor center contains exhibits and public facilities, including an auditorium with a 21-minute orientation film and recorded description about the history of the site. Marked trails and trailside exhibits also can be found. Pets must remain on a leash.

Seip Earthworks, about 2 mi. e. of Bainbridge on US 50. is a 10-acre site containing the great central mound (240 ft. long, 160 ft. wide and 30 ft. high) of a group of geometric earthworks built by the Hopewell Indians for ceremonial purposes. A trail and wayside exhibits help visitors understand the park.

Allow 1 hour minimum. The Hopewell Mound Group, Mound City Group and Seip Earthworks are open daily dawn-dusk. High Bank and Hopeton earthworks are only open during special events. Mound City Group visitor center open daily 8:30-5 (also 5-6,

Memorial Day-Labor Day); closed Jan. 1, Thanksgiving and Christmas. Free. Phone (740) 774-1126.

HUBBARD pop. 7,874

BEST WESTERN PENN-OHIO INN & SUITES — 330/534-5100

THREE DIAMOND Hotel Best Western. **AAA Benefit:** Members save up to 15% and earn bonus points!

 Address: 6828 Commerce Dr 44425 **Location:** I-80 exit 234B, just n. **Facility:** 63 units. 3 stories, interior corridors. **Pool:** heated indoor. **Activities:** hot tub, exercise room. **Guest Services:** coin laundry.

JULIA'S BED & BREAKFAST — 330/534-1342
THREE DIAMOND Historic Bed & Breakfast. **Address:** 6219 W Liberty St 44425

TRAVELODGE HUBBARD — 330/534-8191
APPROVED Hotel. **Address:** 2375 N Main St 44425

HUBER HEIGHTS (F-12) pop. 38,101, elev. 970'
• Hotels & Restaurants map & index p. 242

CARRIAGE HILL METROPARK is off I-70 exit 38, 1 mi. n. on SR 201, then .5 mi. e. on E. Shull Rd. Farm life in the 1880s is showcased here with historical buildings, a blacksmith shop, a country store, farm animals and interactive displays in the visitor center. There also are scenic woodlands, meadows, a lake and a pond, providing opportunities for fishing, hiking, horseback riding and cross-country skiing. *See Recreation Areas Chart.*

Time: Allow 1 hour minimum. **Hours:** Visitor center and farm open Tues.-Sat. 10-5, Sun. noon-5. Farm grounds open daily 8 a.m.-10 p.m., Apr.-Oct.; daily 8-8 rest of year. **Cost:** Donations. **Phone:** (937) 274-3120.

COMFORT INN DAYTON — 937/237-7477 **22**
APPROVED Hotel. **Address:** 7907 Brandt Pike 45424

HAMPTON INN BY HILTON HUBER HEIGHTS — 937/233-4300 **24**
THREE DIAMOND Hotel. **Address:** 5588 Merily Way 45424 **AAA Benefit:** Members save up to 15%!

HOLIDAY INN EXPRESS HOTEL & SUITES — 937/235-2000 **23**
APPROVED Hotel. **Address:** 5612 Merily Way 45424

TRU BY HILTON HUBER HEIGHTS/DAYTON — 937/660-9001 **21**
APPROVED Contemporary Hotel. **Address:** 7000 Executive Blvd 45424 Members save up to 15%!

(See map & index p. 242.)

WHERE TO EAT

EL TORO MEXICAN RESTAURANT   937/235-6244   (18)
APPROVED   Mexican. Casual Dining. **Address:** 8321 Old Troy Pike 45424

GOLD STAR CHILI   937/233-1450
APPROVED   American. Quick Serve. **Address:** 3034 Harshman Rd 45424

SKYLINE CHILI   937/233-6005
APPROVED   American. Quick Serve. **Address:** 7603 Old Troy Pike 45424

HURON (B-5) pop. 7,149, elev. 584'

The Huron Playhouse began in 1949 and continues its summer theater today. Performances are held June-July at McCormick School, 325 Ohio St.; phone (419) 433-4744.

Old Woman Creek National Estuarine Research Reserve is a freshwater estuary on Lake Erie. The 573-acre site protects a variety of habitats, including marshes, swamps, a forest and a barrier beach and is home to a variety of fish and waterfowl. The reserve offers more than 2 miles of pedestrian trails, an observation deck, nature programs and nature exhibits. The trails and beach are open daily dawn-dusk, and the visitor center is open Tues.-Fri. 9-4 year-round and also weekends 1-5, Apr.-Sept.

JAMES H. MCBRIDE ARBORETUM is just s. of jct. SR 2 and Rye Beach Rd., on the campus of Fire-lands College of Bowling Green State University, at One University Dr. The arboretum encompasses nearly 50 acres. At the center is Parker Lake, which features an arched bridge. The lake is home to fish and aquatic plants and wildlife, including migrating birds. Tree species include bald cypresses, dogwoods, evergreens, maples, oaks, pines and spruces. There also are more than 52 varieties of crab apple trees. The Parker Lake Pathway is about a 10-minute walk and the Woodland Trail takes about 20 minutes.

Some of the walking trails are shaded from mature trees, but most of the trails are in open sunlight. Pets are not permitted. **Time:** Allow 30 minutes minimum. **Hours:** Daily 8 a.m.-dusk. **Cost:** Free. **Phone:** (419) 625-7783.

MOTEL 6 HURON   419/433-7829
APPROVED   Motel. **Address:** 601 Rye Beach Rd 44839

WHERE TO EAT

I-5'S BAR AND GRILL   419/433-2726
APPROVED   American. Casual Dining. **Address:** 356 N Main St 44839

LEMMY'S EATERY   419/433-5501
APPROVED   American. Casual Dining. **Address:** 2027 Cleveland Rd W 44839

INDEPENDENCE (C-10) pop. 7,133, elev. 855'
- Hotels & Restaurants map & index p. 194
- Part of Cleveland area — see map p. 177

CUYAHOGA VALLEY SCENIC RAILROAD main departure location is off I-77 exit 155 (Rockside Rd.), 1.2 mi. e. on Rockside Rd., 1 blk. n. on Canal Rd., then w. to 7900 Old Rockside Rd., following signs. Trains also depart from other stations in the local vicinity. The train runs through the heart of Cuyahoga Valley National Park. Passengers can take sightseeing tours or excursions to regional attractions aboard vintage railroad coaches built 1939-55. Themed trips also are offered.

Hours: The National Park Scenic excursion runs seasonally. Departures begin at 9 a.m. out of Rockside Station. Boarding stations are at Rockside Station, Peninsula Station and Akron Northside Station. Departure times vary seasonally. Wed.-Sun., June-Oct.; Fri.-Sun., Apr.-May; Sat. -Sun., Jan.-Mar. and Nov. 1-10. Phone for schedules of special events. **Cost:** $15; $10 (ages 3-12). Reservations are recommended. **Phone:** (330) 439-5708 or (800) 468-4070. GT TI

COMFORT INN   216/328-7777   (85)
APPROVED   Hotel. **Address:** 6191 Quarry Ln 44131

COURTYARD BY MARRIOTT   216/901-9988   (76)
THREE DIAMOND SAVE Hotel. **Address:** 5051 W Creek Rd 44131

AAA Benefit: Members save 5% or more!

CROWNE PLAZA CLEVELAND SOUTH INDEPENDENCE
216/524-0700   (83)
THREE DIAMOND Hotel. **Address:** 5300 Rockside Rd 44131

DOUBLETREE BY HILTON HOTEL CLEVELAND-INDEPENDENCE   216/447-1300   (84)
THREE DIAMOND SAVE Hotel. **Address:** 6200 Quarry Ln 44131

AAA Benefit: Members save up to 15%!

EMBASSY SUITES BY HILTON HOTEL/CLEVELAND-ROCKSIDE   216/986-9900   (75)
THREE DIAMOND
Hotel

AAA Benefit: Members save up to 15%!

Address: 5800 Rockside Woods Blvd 44131 **Location:** I-77 exit 155 (Rockside Rd), just e, then 0.4 mi n. **Facility:** 271 units. 8 stories, interior corridors. **Parking:** on-site (fee). **Terms:** check-in 4 pm. **Pool:** heated indoor. **Activities:** exercise room. **Guest Services:** valet and coin laundry, area transportation. **Featured Amenity:** full hot breakfast.

SAVE CALL

HAMPTON INN & SUITES BY HILTON   216/520-2020   (78)
THREE DIAMOND SAVE Hotel. **Address:** 6020 Jefferson Dr 44131

AAA Benefit: Members save up to 15%!

HOLIDAY INN-INDEPENDENCE/CLEVELAND SOUTH
216/524-8050   (82)
THREE DIAMOND Hotel. **Address:** 6001 Rockside Rd 44131

(See map & index p. 194.)

HOME2 SUITES BY HILTON INDEPENDENCE
216/264-4272

THREE DIAMOND

Extended Stay Contemporary Hotel

AAA Benefit: Members save up to 15%!

Address: 6200 Patriots Way 44131 **Location:** I-77 exit 155 (Rockside Rd), just w, just n on W Creek Rd, then just w. **Facility:** 105 units. 4 stories, interior corridors. **Pool:** heated indoor. **Activities:** exercise room. **Guest Services:** valet and coin laundry. **Featured Amenity:** continental breakfast.

 CALL BIZ

/SOME UNITS

HYATT PLACE CLEVELAND/INDEPENDENCE
216/328-1060 **77**

THREE DIAMOND

Hotel

HYATT PLACE·

AAA Benefit: Members save up to 10%!

Address: 6025 Jefferson Dr 44131 **Location:** I-77 exit 155 (Rockside Rd), just w, just n on W Creek Dr, then just e. **Facility:** 127 units. 6 stories, interior corridors. **Pool:** heated indoor. **Activities:** exercise room. **Guest Services:** valet and coin laundry, area transportation. **Featured Amenity:** full hot breakfast.

SAVE  CALL BIZ

/SOME UNITS HS

RESIDENCE INN BY MARRIOTT CLEVELAND INDEPENDENCE
216/520-1450 **79**

THREE DIAMOND

Extended Stay Hotel

Residence INN. **AAA Benefit:** Members save 5% or more!

Address: 5101 W Creek Rd 44131 **Location:** I-77 exit 155 (Rockside Rd), just w, then just n. **Facility:** 118 units, some two bedrooms, efficiencies and kitchens. 2 stories (no elevator), interior/exterior corridors. **Pool:** heated outdoor. **Activities:** hot tub, exercise room. **Guest Services:** valet and coin laundry.

SAVE CALL BIZ

/SOME UNITS

SPRINGHILL SUITES BY MARRIOTT CLEVELAND INDEPENDENCE
216/264-4190 **81**

THREE DIAMOND SAVE Hotel. **Address:** 6060 Rockside Pl 44131

AAA Benefit: Members save 5% or more!

WHERE TO EAT

ALADDIN'S EATERY   216/642-7550
APPROVED Lebanese. Casual Dining. **Address:** 6901 Rockside Rd 44131

DELMONICO'S   216/573-1991 **55**
THREE DIAMOND Steak. Fine Dining. **Address:** 6001 Quarry Ln 44131

HARRY'S STEAKHOUSE   216/524-5300 **53**
APPROVED Steak. Casual Dining. **Address:** 5664 Brecksville Rd 44131

SHULA'S 2   216/901-7852
APPROVED Steak. Casual Dining. **Address:** 6200 Quarry Ln 44131

SLYMAN'S TAVERN   216/642-0062 **54**
APPROVED Sandwiches. Casual Dining. **Address:** 6901 Rockside Rd 44131

IRONTON pop. 11,129, elev. 540'

MELINI CUCINA ITALIAN RESTAURANT   740/534-5988
APPROVED Italian. Casual Dining. **Address:** 124 2nd St 45638

JACKSON (H-5) pop. 6,397, elev. 689'

Jackson was settled by accident in the early 1800s when a group of Welsh immigrants traveling down the Ohio River were stranded in Gallipolis after its boats were stolen. Making the best of the situation, the six families decided to stay.

Copies of a pamphlet describing Welsh communities in America brought more Welsh settlers to the area. Many of the men took jobs working on the Gallipolis/Chillicothe road and at the many coal mines and iron furnaces in Jackson County. The region's once-great iron industry has since diversified into aluminum, wood and plastic products, and food processing.

Lake Katharine State Nature Preserve offers 6 miles of trails. Scenery includes sandstone cliffs and many spring wildflowers.

Jackson Area Chamber of Commerce: 234 Broadway St., Jackson, OH 45640. **Phone:** (740) 286-2722.

DAKOTA'S ROADHOUSE   740/288-7427
APPROVED Steak. Casual Dining. **Address:** 451 McCarty Ln 45640

JEFFERSONVILLE pop. 1,203

FAIRFIELD INN & SUITES BY MARRIOTT   740/948-9305
THREE DIAMOND SAVE Hotel. **Address:** 11349 Allen Rd NW 43128

AAA Benefit: Members save 5% or more!

WHERE TO EAT

WERNER'S SMOKEHOUSE   740/948-2989
APPROVED Barbecue. Casual Dining. **Address:** 11396 Allen Rd 43128

KENT (D-11) pop. 28,904, elev. 965'

Established in 1910 as Kent Normal School, a teacher-training facility, Kent State University has earned many national and international distinctions, including recognition by The Carnegie Foundation for the Advancement of Teaching for its optimal blending of teaching and research. The combined enrollment on its eight campuses is more than 42,000. Of interest on the nearly 28,000-student Kent campus are the planetarium, art galleries, gardens, the Liquid Crystal Institute and the Kent State University Museum *(see attraction listing)*.

The Kent State University campus is also home to the May 4th Site, Memorial and Visitors Center, which commemorate the events of May 4, 1970, when four students were killed and nine wounded by the Ohio National Guard troops during a protest against the Vietnam War. The memorial sits on a sloped, wooded area at the northern corner of Taylor Hall overlooking the University Commons. Every spring the bloom of the 58,175 daffodils planted at the site symbolizes the nation's losses in Vietnam. For the 40th anniversary of the events, seven trail markers with descriptions, maps and pictures were installed so visitors can walk part of the campus and learn about what occurred that day. To further enhance their self-guiding walking tour, visitors can call (330) 672-6294 to hear audio narration on their cellphone by civil rights activist and NAACP Chairman Emeritus Julian Bond.

KENT STATE UNIVERSITY MUSEUM is in Rockwell Hall at 515 Hilltop Dr. at jct. E. Main and S. Lincoln sts. This 1927 Beaux-Arts building was the college's first library. Focusing on fashion and decorative arts, the museum houses one of the nation's largest and finest collections of 18th-through 21st-century American and European gowns and traditional dress. Also featured are historic women's periodicals, international textiles, decorative arts, collectible glass and paintings. Eight galleries feature changing exhibitions from a permanent collection of nearly 40,000 pieces.

Guided tours are available by reservation. **Time:** Allow 1 hour minimum. **Hours:** Tues.-Sat. 10-5 (also Thurs. 5-8), Sun. noon-4. Closed major holidays. **Cost:** $6; $5 (ages 55+); $4 (ages 7-18); free to all (Sun.). **Phone:** (330) 672-3450. GT

HAMPTON INN BY HILTON   330/673-8555
APPROVED SAVE Hotel. **Ad-**
dress: 4406 SR 43 44240   **AAA Benefit:**
                                     Members save up to
                                     15%!

HOLIDAY INN EXPRESS HOTEL & SUITES   330/673-9200
THREE DIAMOND Hotel. **Address:** 1215 Sanctuary View Dr 44240

KENT STATE UNIVERSITY HOTEL & CONFERENCE CENTER
                                        330/346-0100
THREE DIAMOND Boutique Contemporary Hotel. **Address:** 215 S Depeyster St 44240

ERIE STREET KITCHEN   330/593-5928
APPROVED Southern. Quick Serve. **Address:** 163 W Erie St 44240

LAZIZA   330/677-7000
THREE DIAMOND Mediterranean. Casual Dining. **Address:** 195 E Erie St 44240

MIKE'S PLACE   330/673-6501
APPROVED American. Casual Dining. **Address:** 1700 S Water St 44240

TRENO'S RISTORANTE   330/676-5139
THREE DIAMOND Italian. Casual Dining. **Address:** 152 Franklin Ave 44240

KENWOOD pop. 6,981
• Hotels & Restaurants map & index p. 166
• Part of Cincinnati area — see map p. 153

BEST WESTERN PLUS HANNAFORD INN & SUITES
                                        513/936-0525 **70**

THREE DIAMOND   Best   **AAA Benefit:**
Hotel   BW Western Members save up to
                      PLUS.   15% and earn bonus
                                points!

Address: 5900 E Galbraith Rd 45236 **Location:** I-71 exit 12, 0.5 mi e, then 0.3 mi n. **Facility:** 79 units, some efficiencies. 4 stories, interior corridors. **Pool:** outdoor. **Activities:** exercise room. **Guest Services:** valet and coin laundry. **Featured Amenity:** breakfast buffet.

SAVE [] [] [] [] BIZ HS [wifi]
X [] [] []

HAMPTON INN & SUITES CINCINNATI-KENWOOD
                                        513/794-0700 **71**
THREE DIAMOND SAVE Hotel. **Ad-**   **AAA Benefit:**
dress: 2000 Ronald Reagan Dr 45236   Members save up to
                                          15%!

MATT THE MILLER'S TAVERN   513/914-4903 **57**
APPROVED American. Casual Dining. **Address:** 5901 E Galbraith Rd 45236

OLIO ITALIAN   513/792-2000 **58**
THREE DIAMOND Italian. Fine Dining. **Address:** 5901 E Galbraith Rd 45236

SKYLINE CHILI   513/791-7902
APPROVED American. Quick Serve. **Address:** 7707 Montgomery Rd 45236

TRIO   513/984-1905 **59**
THREE DIAMOND American. Casual Dining. **Address:** 7565 Kenwood Rd 45236

KETTERING pop. 56,163
• Hotels & Restaurants map & index p. 242

FIGLIO   937/534-0494 **28**
APPROVED Pizza. Casual Dining. **Address:** 424 E Stroop Rd 45429

MAMMA DISALVO'S ITALIAN RISTORANTE
                                        937/299-5831 **27**
APPROVED Italian. Casual Dining. **Address:** 1375 E Stroop Rd 45429

(See map & index p. 242.)

SKYLINE CHILI   937/299-9061
APPROVED   American. Quick Serve. **Address:** 2724 Wilmington Pike 45419

KIRTLAND (B-11) pop. 6,866, elev. 667'

The first permanent settler came to this area in 1811, and the township was formed in 1822. In 1831 the settlement expanded when Mormon leader Joseph Smith and many of his followers arrived; Smith wrote much of the doctrine of the Church of Latter Day Saints while he lived here. Nearly 3,000 people lived in Kirtland by the time the Mormons moved westward in 1838.

Today this historic village is known for its amenities, both man-made and natural. Lakeland Community College occupies 400 rolling, wooded acres. Chapin Forest Reservation's 390 acres offer an opportunity to picnic or hike.

HISTORIC KIRTLAND is at jct. SR 306 and SR 615 (Chillicothe Rd.) The village interprets the history of Kirtland and the Mormon Church in America. In the 1830s Joseph Smith Jr., leader and first president of the Mormon Church, established church headquarters at Kirtland. Meticulously restored structures—such as Newel K. and Elizabeth Ann Whitney Home, Johnson Inn, the 1826 Newel K. Whitney Store, an ashery, a sawmill, a schoolhouse—and two farms convey the history of the community.

Time: Allow 2 hours minimum. **Hours:** Mon.-Sat. 9-9, Sun. 1-9. **Cost:** Free. **Phone:** (440) 256-9805. GT

Kirtland Temple is at 9020 Chillicothe Rd. near Historic Kirtland; tours begin at the nearby visitor center at 7809 Joseph St. Kirtland once was home to some of the 19th century's most successful community builders. Under the leadership of Joseph Smith Jr., followers built this temple 1833-36. In 1838 it was the center of community life for more than 2,000 believers; within a year, only 100 members remained. Guided 1-hour tours begin with an audiovisual presentation.

The 12,000-square-foot Kirtland Temple Visitor Center features interactive museum exhibits and video. **Time:** Allow 1 hour minimum. **Hours:** Mon.-Sat. 9-5, Sun. 1-5, May-Oct.; Wed.-Sat. 10-4, Sun. 1-4, Mar.-Apr. and in Nov.; Wed.-Sun. 1-4, in Dec. Last tour begins 30 minutes before closing. **Cost:** $7; free (ages 0-3). **Phone:** (440) 256-1830. GT

LAKE METROPARKS FARMPARK is 4.5 mi. s. of I-90 on SR 306 to SR 6, then 1 mi. e. at 8800 Euclid Chardon Rd. This 235-acre park is a science and educational center dedicated to explaining how farmers raise food, fiber and other agricultural products that sustain and enhance human life. Visitors can milk a cow, take a wagon ride, watch border collies skillfully herding, meet more than 50 breeds of farm animals and on weekends watch an ice cream production demonstration.

Visitors can explore plant life in The Great Tomato Works and Hydroponics exhibits, established orchards, vineyards, themed gardens and field crops areas. Renewable energy sources such as wind and solar power are explored and explained. Seasonal activities include maple sugaring and cider pressing. A corn maze is open mid-August to early October. Vintage Ohio Wine Festival takes place in early August.

Time: Allow 2 hours minimum. **Hours:** Tues.-Sun. 9-5. A list of the daily activities and demonstrations is provided upon arrival. **Cost:** $8; $7 (ages 60+); $6 (ages 2-11); free (active military with ID). Separate admission charged for special events. **Phone:** (440) 256-2122 or (800) 366-3276. ⛔ ⛱

LAKE METROPARKS PENITENTIARY GLEN NATURE CENTER is at 8668 Kirtland-Chardon Rd. The center is on 424 acres and is part of the early 20th-century estate of Sam and Blanche Halle. A deep gorge divides the park, which features fields, forests and wetlands, a butterfly garden, wildlife center, live animal displays and a nature center with interactive exhibits and art shows. More than 7 miles of paved and gravel trails with scenic overlooks and a bridle trail can be explored. A miniature steam-powered train provides rides to the rim of the gorge a few times each month on Sundays April through December.

Snowshoe rentals are available. **Time:** Allow 1 hour minimum. **Hours:** Trails and garden open daily 6 a.m.-11 p.m. Nature and wildlife centers open daily 9-5. **Cost:** Free. **Phone:** (440) 256-1404. ⛱

LAKEWOOD pop. 52,131
• **Hotels & Restaurants map & index p. 194**
• **Part of Cleveland area — see map p. 177**

ALADDIN'S EATERY   216/521-4005
APPROVED   Lebanese. Casual Dining. **Address:** 14536 Detroit Ave 44107

PIER W   216/228-2250 37
THREE DIAMOND Seafood. Casual Dining. **Address:** 12700 Lake Ave at Winton Pl 44107

WINKING LIZARD TAVERN   216/226-6693
APPROVED   American. Casual Dining. **Address:** 14018 Detroit Ave 44107

LANCASTER (F-5) pop. 38,780, elev. 898'
• **Hotels p. 264** • **Restaurants p. 264**
• **Part of Columbus area — see map p. 205**

Settled in 1800 and designated as the county seat by 1806, Lancaster grew even faster after 1836, when the Lancaster Lateral Canal was connected with the Ohio and Erie Canal. With the coming of the railroads in the 1850s and the discovery of natural gas in 1887, the town became one of Ohio's manufacturing and distribution centers, a status it retains.

Native son Gen. William Tecumseh Sherman is honored with a statue at the intersection of Main and Broad streets on Zane Square.

Preserving the city's heritage are the early 19th-century houses on Square 13, which is bounded by N. High, Broad, Main and Wheeling streets.

Fairfield County Visitors and Convention Bureau: 205 W. Main St., Lancaster, OH 43130. **Phone:** (740) 654-5929 or (800) 626-1296.

DECORATIVE ARTS CENTER OF OHIO is e. of jct. US 33 and US 22 at 145 E. Main St. in the Reese-Peters House. Built in 1835, the two-story mansion has been renovated to reflect its original Greek Revival grandeur, which is evident from the high-quality wood and plaster work, marble mantels and custom-woven carpeting on the main floor. The second floor is unfurnished and used entirely to display artwork; there are three exhibitions per year. **Time:** Allow 1 hour minimum. **Hours:** Tues.-Fri. 10-4, Sat.-Sun. 1-4. Closed major holidays. **Cost:** Free. **Phone:** (740) 681-1423.

THE GEORGIAN is at 105 E. Wheeling St. at jct. Broad St. The 1832 Federal-style house features superb architecture, period furnishings and fine early cabinets. **Time:** Allow 1 hour minimum. **Hours:** Guided 45-minute tours depart as needed Tues.-Sun. 1-4, Apr.-Dec.; by appointment rest of year. Last tour begins 45 minutes before closing. Closed major holidays. **Cost:** $6; $4 (ages 65+); $2 (ages 6-18). Combination ticket with The Sherman House Museum $10; $6 (ages 65+); $3 (ages 6-18). **Phone:** (740) 654-9923. [GT]

THE SHERMAN HOUSE MUSEUM is at 137 E. Main St. The structure was the birthplace and early home of brothers William T. Sherman, Civil War general, and Sen. John Sherman, author of the Sherman Anti-Trust Act. Sherman family mementos, Civil War artifacts and other antiques are displayed in this 1811 house.

Time: Allow 1 hour minimum. **Hours:** Guided 1-hour tours depart as needed Tues.-Sun. noon-4, Apr.-Dec. Last tour begins 1 hour before closing. **Cost:** $6; $4 (ages 65+); $2 (ages 6-18). Combination ticket with The Georgian $10; $6 (ages 65+); $3 (ages 6-18). **Phone:** (740) 687-5891 or (740) 654-9923. [GT]

BAYMONT INN & SUITES-LANCASTER   740/654-8413
[W] **APPROVED** Hotel. **Address:** 1721 River Valley Cir N 43130

HAMPTON INN BY HILTON LANCASTER   740/654-2999
[W] **APPROVED** [SAVE] Hotel. **Address:** 2041 Schorrway Dr 43130

AAA Benefit: Members save up to 15%!

WHERE TO EAT

DOWNTOWN BISTRO   740/785-9900
[W] **APPROVED** American. Casual Dining. **Address:** 123 N Broad St 43130

FOUR REASONS BAKERY & DELI   740/654-2253
[W] **APPROVED** Breads/Pastries. Quick Serve. **Address:** 135 W Main St 43130

LEBANON (H-12) pop. 20,033, elev. 696'
• Part of Cincinnati area — see map p. 153

Old houses and buildings, including the 1803 Golden Lamb Inn, give Lebanon a Colonial atmosphere that is unusual in the Midwest. Many of the city's historic structures are within an area bounded by Orchard Avenue and West, Silver, Pleasant and High streets; most are private residences and are closed to the public.

Shopping: Downtown Lebanon offers more than 50 antiques and specialty shops.

THE GOLDEN LAMB RESTAURANT   513/932-5065
[W] **THREE DIAMOND** American. Casual Dining. **Address:** 27 S Broadway St 45036

GOLD STAR CHILI   513/932-4642
[W] **APPROVED** American. Quick Serve. **Address:** 10 Dave Ave 45036

SKYLINE CHILI   513/932-4334
[W] **APPROVED** American. Quick Serve. **Address:** 718 E Main St 45036

LIMA (D-2) pop. 38,771, elev. 860'

Lima (LYE-ma) gained national attention in 1933 when members of John Dillinger's gang murdered the town sheriff. The shooting precipitated a nationwide manhunt that led to the gangster's death in Chicago.

Lincoln Park, at the intersection of Shawnee and E. Elm streets, offers picnic facilities and a display of the last steam locomotive built at Lima Locomotive Works and an 1895 country railroad station.

The Veterans Memorial Freedom Flag Monument, 1191 Buckeye Rd., is the largest free-standing permanent flag in the United States. Each tower is made of red, white and blue granite "bricks" engraved to honor our nation's veterans.

Lima/Allen County Convention & Visitors Bureau: 144 S. Main St., Suite 101, Lima, OH 45801. **Phone:** (419) 222-6075 or (888) 222-6075.

Shopping: Lima Mall (Lima Center), off I-75 exit 125 on SR 309W at 2400 Elida Rd., features JC-Penney and Macy's.

THE MACDONELL HOUSE is at 632 W. Market St. The lavishly decorated Victorian mansion has period furnishings. A trophy room contains big game and smaller animals and birds. **Time:** Allow 30 minutes minimum. **Hours:** Tues.-Fri. 1-5, Sat.-Sun. 1-4, Mar.-Dec. Closed major holidays. **Cost:** $3; free (ages 0-8). **Phone:** (419) 222-9426.

COUNTRY INN & SUITES BY RADISSON LIMA   419/999-9992
 APPROVED   Hotel. **Address:** 804 S Leonard Ave 45404

COURTYARD BY MARRIOTT LIMA OHIO   419/222-9000
 THREE DIAMOND
Hotel

 **COURTYARD** **AAA Benefit:** Members save 5% or more!

 Address: 936 Greely Chapel Rd 45804 **Location:** I-75 exit 125A southbound; exit 125 northbound. **Facility:** 99 units. 4 stories, interior corridors. **Pool:** heated indoor. **Activities:** exercise room. **Guest Services:** valet and coin laundry.

FAIRFIELD INN & SUITES BY MARRIOTT LIMA   419/224-8496
APPROVED SAVE Hotel. **Address:** 2179 Elida Rd 45805

AAA Benefit: Members save 5% or more!

HAMPTON INN BY HILTON   419/225-8300
THREE DIAMOND SAVE Hotel. **Address:** 1933 Roschman Ave 45804

AAA Benefit: Members save up to 15%!

HOLIDAY INN & SUITES LIMA   419/879-4000
THREE DIAMOND
Hotel

 Address: 803 S Leonard Ave 45804 **Location:** I-75 exit 125, just w. **Facility:** 116 units. 4 stories, interior corridors. **Parking:** on-site (fee), winter plug-ins. **Pool:** heated indoor. **Activities:** hot tub, exercise room. **Guest Services:** valet and coin laundry. *(See ad this page.)*

HOWARD JOHNSON LIMA   419/222-0004
 APPROVED
Hotel

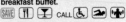 **Address:** 1920 Roschman Ave 45804 **Location:** I-75 exit 125, just e. **Facility:** 150 units. 4 stories, interior corridors. **Pool:** heated indoor. **Activities:** sauna, game room, exercise room. **Guest Services:** valet laundry. **Featured Amenity:** breakfast buffet.

WINGATE BY WYNDHAM LIMA DOWNTOWN   419/228-7000
APPROVED   Hotel. **Address:** 175 W Market St 45801

WHERE TO EAT

KEWPEE   419/227-9791
APPROVED   Burgers. Quick Serve. **Address:** 2111 Allentown Rd 45805

LOCK SIXTEEN STEAKHOUSE   419/229-5625
APPROVED   Steak. Casual Dining. **Address:** 706 N Cable Rd 45805

THE MET   419/999-9463
APPROVED   American. Gastropub. **Address:** 306 N Main St 45801

MILANO CAFE   419/331-2220
APPROVED   Italian. Casual Dining. **Address:** 2383 Elida Rd 45805

OLD CITY PRIME   419/227-7463
THREE DIAMOND   Steak. Fine Dining. **Address:** 215 S Main St 45801

SKYLINE CHILI   419/991-1990
APPROVED   American. Quick Serve. **Address:** 1990 Harding Hwy 45804

▼ *See AAA listing this page* ▼

LOGAN (G-5) pop. 7,152, elev. 741'

Logan is the county seat of Hocking County, which is known for its scenic natural attributes. Clay pottery was one of the area's first industries. Rolling hills, craggy cliffs, caves and cascading waterfalls pepper the area, providing ample opportunities for hiking, canoeing and horseback riding. The day-use Lake Logan State Park (see Recreation Areas Chart) is 4 miles west of Logan off SR 664; catches include bluegill, crappie, bass, muskie, catfish, northern pike and saugeye.

Hocking Hills Tourism Association: 13178 SR 664S, Logan, OH 43138. **Phone:** (740) 385-9706 or (800) 462-5464.

COLUMBUS WASHBOARD CO. is at 14 Gallagher Ave. Much of the original machinery at the factory—which has been in continuous operation since 1895—is still used to create a variety of washboards, including those made of glass, stainless steel, corkboard, mirror and slate. A museum area showcases the company's history.

Time: Allow 1 hour minimum. **Hours:** Museum open Mon.-Fri. 9-4, Sat. 11-2, May-Oct.; Mon.-Fri. 9-3, rest of year. Guided tours by appointment. Closed major holidays. **Cost:** Museum free. Tour $4; $3 (ages 60+); $2 (ages 12-18); free (active military with ID). **Phone:** (740) 380-3828. GT

HOCKING HILLS STATE PARK is in Hocking State Forest, 10 mi. s.w. of US 33 at 19852 SR 664 S. This 2,356-acre area boasts cliffs, a river, waterfalls and hemlock-shaded gorges. About 110 kinds of birds are known to nest in the park—50 species spend the winter, and others are migratory.

Rock formations include cross-bedding and honeycomb weathering. The park's caves attracted indigenous people; evidence of the ancient Adena culture dates from more than 7,000 years ago. Native American tribes visited or lived here during the 1700s, including the Delaware, Shawnee and Wyandot. They called the river Hockhocking because of its gourd-shaped valley.

More than 25 miles of trails wind through the park's gorges and ridges. A swimming pool is open Memorial Day through Labor Day. See Recreation Areas Chart. **Hours:** Daily dawn-dusk. **Cost:** Park free. A fee is charged for pool use. **Phone:** (740) 385-6842, or (866) 644-6727 for camping reservations. 🅰 🍴 ⊠ 🎣 🍴

Ash Cave is 15 mi. s. of Logan and 5 mi. e. of South Bloomingville on SR 56, within Hocking Hills State Park; the park office is at 19852 SR 664 S. A semicircular recess, the cave is 700 feet long and 90 feet high. A stream falls from the cave's roof into a splash pool. The quarter-mile trail leading to the cave is wheelchair and stroller accessible. **Hours:** Daily dawn-dusk. **Cost:** Free. **Phone:** (740) 385-6842.

Cantwell Cliffs are 12 mi. w. of Logan and 5 mi. s.w. of Rockbridge on SR 374, within Hocking Hills

State Park; the park office is at 19852 SR 664 S. The area consists of 386 acres of impressive cliffs and a deeply cut, rugged glen. **Hours:** Daily dawn-dusk. **Cost:** Free. **Phone:** (740) 385-6842.

Cedar Falls is 13 mi. s. of Logan and 2 mi. n. of Ash Cave on SR 374, within Hocking Hills State Park; the park office is at 19852 SR 664 S. The area includes 50 acres. A path leads from Old Man's Cave up the gorge of Clear Creek. Cedar Falls is found at the head of the gorge; just below it is a saltpeter cave. A 3-mile trail connects with Old Man's Cave. **Hours:** Daily dawn-dusk. **Cost:** Free. **Phone:** (740) 385-6842.

Conkles Hollow Nature Preserve is 14 mi. s.w. of Logan and 4 mi. n. of South Bloomingville on SR 374, within Hocking Hills State Park; the park office is at 19852 SR 664 S. This rugged 87-acre area contains 200-foot cliffs studded with waterfalls and a deep gorge. The area is explored by a gorge trail accessible for wheelchairs and strollers or a strenuous rim trail that offers sweeping vistas. **Hours:** Daily dawn-dusk. **Cost:** Free. **Phone:** (740) 385-6842.

Old Man's Cave is 12 mi. s.w. of Logan within Hocking Hills State Park, behind the park office at 19852 SR 664 S. The 417-acre area features 2 miles of a heavily wooded, winding ravine, picturesque waterfalls, two recessed caves and interesting rock formations. A visitor center offers displays. Rose Lake, accessible by a half-mile walk, is stocked with trout annually; a fishing license is required. **Note:** Visitors are advised to arrive early on weekends since parking is often limited. **Hours:** Daily dawn-dusk. **Cost:** Free. **Phone:** (740) 385-6842.

Rock House is 12 mi. w. of Logan on SR 374, within Hocking Hills State Park; the park office is at 19852 SR 664 S. The unusual rock shelter in the face of a perpendicular cliff served as a dwelling for Native Americans and as a hideout for frontier outlaws. **Hours:** Daily dawn-dusk. **Cost:** Free. **Phone:** (740) 385-6842.

THE INN & SPA AT CEDAR FALLS	740/380-7489
▽▽ THREE DIAMOND Country Inn. **Address:** 21190 SR 374 43138	

WHERE TO EAT

JACK'S STEAK HOUSE	740/385-9909
▽ APPROVED Steak. Casual Dining. **Address:** 35770 Hocking Dr 43138	

THE OLDE DUTCH RESTAURANT	740/385-1000
▽ APPROVED Comfort Food. Casual Dining. **Address:** 12791 SR 664 S 43138	

LONDON pop. 9,904
• Part of Columbus area — see map p. 205

LOS MARIACHIS MEXICAN RESTAURANT	740/845-1388
▽ APPROVED Mexican. Casual Dining. **Address:** 289 Lafayette St 43140	

LOUDONVILLE (D-6) pop. 2,641, elev. 971'

Loudonville was the birthplace of Charles F. Kettering, an engineer whose invention of the electric starter was an important milestone in the development of the modern automobile. Because of the many picturesque streams and rivers in the area, Loudonville is called the "Official Canoe Capital of Ohio."

Mohican Visitors Bureau: 544 N. Union St., Loudonville, OH 44842. **Phone:** (419) 994-2519.

LANDOLL'S MOHICAN CASTLE   419/994-3427
THREE DIAMOND Country Inn. **Address:** 561 TWP Rd 3352 44842

WHERE TO EAT

MOHICAN COUNTRY MARKET   419/994-1414
APPROVED Deli. Quick Serve. **Address:** 1014 S Market St 44842

LOVELAND (H-11) pop. 12,081, elev. 584'
• **Hotels & Restaurants map & index p. 166**
• **Part of Cincinnati area — see map p. 153**

The Little Miami Scenic Trail, an approximately 78-mile paved trail that averages 66 feet wide and runs between Cincinnati and Springfield, passes through Loveland. The park/trail is a converted, abandoned railroad right-of-way that offers opportunities for bicycling, in-line skating, hiking, backpacking, cross-country skiing, horseback riding and canoeing the Little Miami National and State Scenic River. *See Recreation Areas Chart (Little Miami State Park).*

LOVELAND CASTLE (CHATEAU LAROCHE) is .5 mi. w. on Loveland Ave., 1 mi. n. on Rich Rd., .5 mi. e. on Mulberry St. (which becomes Shore Rd.), then s. to 12025 Shore Rd. Harry D. Andrews, who utilized stones from nearby Little Miami River, built the 17-room medieval-style castle over a 51-year span.

The whimsical building features masonry techniques used in German, French and English castles. Included are a great hall, banquet hall, German game room, armory, bedroom, chapel, dungeon and gardens. **Time:** Allow 1 hour minimum. **Hours:** Daily 11-5, Apr.-Sept.; Sat.-Sun. 11-5, rest of year (weather permitting). **Cost:** $5; $3 (ages 0-12). Prices vary for special events. **Phone:** (513) 683-4686.

HILTON GARDEN INN CINCINNATI NORTHEAST
                                                           513/576-6999 38
THREE DIAMOND   **AAA Benefit:**
Hotel   Members save up to 15%!

Address: 6288 Tri-Ridge Blvd 45140 **Location:** I-275 exit 54, just w. **Facility:** 84 units. 3 stories, interior corridors. **Pool:** heated indoor. **Activities:** exercise room. **Guest Services:** valet and coin laundry.

 / SOME UNITS

WHERE TO EAT

PIZZA TOWER   513/683-8400 39
APPROVED Pizza. Casual Dining. **Address:** 6405 Branch Hill-Guinea Pike Dr 45140

TONY'S STEAKS & SEAFOOD   513/677-1993 38
THREE DIAMOND Steak Seafood. Fine Dining. **Address:** 12110 Montgomery Rd 45249

LYNDHURST pop. 14,001
• **Hotels & Restaurants map & index p. 194**
• **Part of Cleveland area — see map p. 177**

HYATT PLACE CLEVELAND/LYNDHURST/LEGACY VILLAGE   216/382-3350 26
THREE DIAMOND   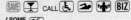 **AAA Benefit:**
Hotel   HYATT PLACE   Members save up to 10%!

Address: 24665 Cedar Rd 44124 **Location:** I-271 exit 32, 1.2 mi w on Cedar Rd, just n on Richmond Rd, then just w; in Legacy Village. **Facility:** 135 units. 6 stories, interior corridors. **Amenities:** safes. **Pool:** heated indoor. **Activities:** exercise room. **Guest Services:** valet and coin laundry, area transportation. **Featured Amenity:** breakfast buffet.

WHERE TO EAT

BROWN DERBY ROADHOUSE   440/720-1173
APPROVED Steak Seafood. Casual Dining. **Address:** 5370 Mayfield Rd 44124

MANSFIELD (D-5) pop. 47,821, elev. 1,152'
• **Hotels p. 268** • **Restaurants p. 268**

Mansfield was laid out in 1808 under the direction of Surveyor General of the United States Jared Mansfield. As the surrounding lands were cleared and cultivated in the 1820s, Mansfield became a center of trade and commerce. In the late 1840s and 1850s the arrivals of the railroads and telegraph drew the first industries, such as the Ohio Brass Co. and Aultman and Taylor, makers of threshing machines.

Pulitzer Prize-winning author Louis Bromfield is a native of Mansfield. John Sherman, brother of Gen. William T. Sherman and author of the Sherman Anti-Trust Act, practiced law here for a time. Mansfield also has fostered artists. Displays of their works, including acrylic paintings, watercolors, photographs, quilts and weavings, can be seen at the Mansfield Art Center, 700 Marion Ave; phone (419) 756-1700.

Destination Mansfield — Richland County: 124 N. Main St., Mansfield, OH 44902. **Phone:** (419) 525-1300 or (800) 642-8282.

Self-guiding tours: The convention and visitors bureau offers brochures detailing a driving tour of local film sites used in the 1994 movie "The Shawshank Redemption." Among the locations are the 1896 Ohio State Reformatory, Oak Tree and Central Park.

Shopping: Richland Mall, 1 mile south of US 30 at W. Fourth Street and Lexington-Springmill Road, features JCPenney, Macy's and Sears.

BIBLEWALK is .5 mi. n. of US 30 via SR 545 at 500 Tingley Ave. This wax museum brings the Bible to life with five different tours, each with an accompanying non-denominational audio-visual presentation. The Life of Christ and the Miracles of the Old Testament each last 60 minutes. The Museum of Christian Martyrs, the Heart of the Reformation and Amazing Grace: The Journeys of Paul each last 30 minutes. Also displayed are collections of rare Bibles, American votive folk art and wood carvings and three animated scenes. Walk of the Parables features large-scale paintings representing Christ's parables. A Christian art gallery and a dinner theater also are available.

Time: Allow 1 hour minimum. **Hours:** Mon.-Sat. 9-5, Sun. 3-7, Apr.-Oct.; Mon.-Sat. 10-4, rest of year. Dinner theater available Sat. by reservation. **Cost:** Life of Christ or Miracles of the Old Testament $6; $5.75 (ages 55+); $4.75 (ages 6-18). Museum of Christian Martyrs, Heart of the Reformation or Amazing Grace $5.25; $5 (ages 55+); $4 (ages 6-18). All five $26.75; $25.50 (ages 55+); $20.50 (ages 6-18). **Phone:** (419) 524-0139 or (800) 222-0139. [GT]

KINGWOOD CENTER GARDENS is off I-71 exit US 30, w. to Trimble Rd., then s. to entrance at 50 N. Trimble Rd. The public garden covers 47 acres and contains landscaped gardens, trails that meander through woodland settings and two ponds that harbor waterfowl. Greenhouses are filled with distinctive plant displays. Kingwood Hall is a 1926 26-room French Provincial-style mansion.

Kingwood is known for its spring show, which includes massive bulb displays, spring flowering trees and a general explosion of flowers. Summer annual displays along with a wide range of blooming trees, shrubs and perennials are highlights in the setting of a former estate garden. Pets are not permitted. **Time:** Allow 1 hour minimum for the center and 30 minutes minimum for Kingwood Hall.

Hours: Gardens open daily 9-7, Apr.-Oct. Greenhouse open daily 9-6, Apr.-Oct. Kingwood Hall self-guiding tours Mon.-Fri. 10-2, guided tours depart Sat. at 11, Sun. at 2, early May-late Sept.; closed most major holidays. Phone to verify schedule and for holiday tour schedule late Nov.-Dec. 30. **Cost:** Kingwood Center Gardens $5; free (ages 0-12). Kingwood Hall self-guiding tour free. **Phone:** (419) 522-0211. [GT]

RICHLAND CARROUSEL PARK is at 75 N. Main St. The downtown historic district houses a hand-carved carousel with 30 horse figures and 22 other animal figures. The figures were created by Carousel Works, a Mansfield company, for the 1991 opening of the park. The carousel's top panels feature scenes of local attractions, both historic and current. A Stinson Band Organ provides music.

Hours: Mon.-Sat. 10-5, Sun. 11-5 (also Fri. 5-8), Memorial Day-Labor Day; daily 11-5 (also first Fri. of the month 5-8), rest of year. Closed the first week of Jan., Easter, July 4, Thanksgiving and Christmas. **Cost:** Rides $1. **Phone:** (419) 522-4223. [YI] [A]

BEST WESTERN RICHLAND INN-MANSFIELD
419/756-6670

APPROVED
Hotel

Best Western.

AAA Benefit: Members save up to 15% and earn bonus points!

Address: 180 E Hanley Rd 44903 **Location:** I-71 exit 169, jct SR 13. **Facility:** 57 units. 2 stories (no elevator), interior corridors. **Amenities:** safes. **Pool:** heated indoor. **Activities:** hot tub, exercise room. **Guest Services:** coin laundry. **Featured Amenity:** full hot breakfast.

HOLIDAY INN HOTEL & SUITES MANSFIELD   419/525-6000
APPROVED   Hotel. **Address:** 116 Park Ave W 44902

LA QUINTA INN & SUITES BY WYNDHAM MANSFIELD
419/774-0005
APPROVED   Hotel. **Address:** 120 Stander Ave 44903

WHERE TO EAT

OAK PARK TAVERN   419/589-2637
APPROVED   American. Casual Dining. **Address:** 2919 Park Ave E 44903

RANCHO FIESTA RESTAURANT   419/774-1744
APPROVED   Mexican. Casual Dining. **Address:** 1360 S Trimble Rd 44907

THE SKYWAY EAST   419/589-9929
APPROVED   American. Fine Dining. **Address:** 2461 Emma Ln 44903

STEVE'S DAKOTA GRILL   419/529-9064
APPROVED   Steak. Casual Dining. **Address:** 3101 Park Ave W 44906

MARIETTA (G-7) pop. 14,085, elev. 618'

Forty-eight pioneers led by Rufus Putnam arrived in Marietta during April 1788. They platted the future community, built a land office, erected a fort and chose the name Marietta in honor of Queen Marie Antoinette, in recognition of the aid rendered to the Colonies by France during the American Revolution.

In Muskingum Park is the Memorial to the Start Westward, a stone sculpture created by Mount Rushmore sculptor Gutzon Borglum to commemorate the opening of the Northwest Territory and the 150th anniversary of the Northwest Ordinance of 1787.

Marietta also serves as the southern terminus for the Covered Bridge Scenic Byway that runs through Wayne National Forest (see place listing p. 307).

Marietta/Washington County Convention and Visitors Bureau: 241 Front St., Suite 7, Marietta, OH 45750. **Phone:** (740) 373-5178 or (888) 861-7684.

Self-guiding tours: A map and brochure detailing a tour of scenic and historic points is available from the convention and visitors bureau.

CAMPUS MARTIUS MUSEUM is at Second St. and Washington St./SR 7, 1 blk. e. of the Ohio River Museum. Early settlers of Marietta built the fortification to protect the settlement from Native American attacks known as Campus Martius, Latin for "Field of Mars," the military camp where the legions of ancient Rome trained. Exhibits re-create the founding and early development of Marietta as the first organized American settlement in the Northwest Territory. Exhibits and artifacts focusing on Appalachian migration into Ohio 1850-1970 are included. The museum encloses the Rufus Putnam House, home to the settlement's leader, and the only surviving dwelling of the original settlement.

Hours: Mon. and Wed.-Sat. 9:30-5, Sun. (and major holidays) noon-5. Phone ahead to confirm schedule. **Cost:** $7; $4 (students with ID). Combination ticket with Ohio River Museum and the *W.P. Snyder Jr.* $10; $5 (students with ID). **Phone:** (740) 373-3750 or (800) 860-0145.

Ohio River Museum and the *W.P. Snyder Jr.* are at Washington, Front and St. Clair sts., 1 blk. w. of the Campus Martius Museum. The museum displays steamboat-era items, including scale models of late 19th-century riverboats, paintings, photographs and steam whistles. The theater presents a 10-minute film about the history of transportation on the Ohio and Muskingum rivers. The *W.P. Snyder Jr.*, moored alongside the museum, is the last steam-powered, stern-wheeled towboat of its type in America; guided tours are available.

Hours: Mon. and Wed.-Sat. 9:30-5, Sun. (also Memorial Day, July 4 and Labor Day) noon-5, Apr. 1-Labor Day; Sat. 9:30-5, Sun. noon-5, first weekend after Labor Day-Oct. 31. Last tour of the towboat begins 1 hour before closing. Towboat tours also are available by appointment, rest of year. Phone ahead to confirm schedule. **Cost:** $7; $4 (students with ID). Combination ticket with Campus Martius Museum $10; $5 (students with ID). **Phone:** (740) 373-3750 or (800) 860-0145. GT

BAYMONT INN & SUITES   740/374-9660
THREE DIAMOND Hotel. **Address:** 701 Pike St 45750

COMFORT SUITES MARIETTA   740/376-1600
THREE DIAMOND Hotel. **Address:** 202 Cherry Tree Ln 45750

FAIRFIELD INN & SUITES BY MARRIOTT MARIETTA
          740/374-3000
THREE DIAMOND SAVE Hotel. **Address:** 200 Cherry Tree Ln 45750

| **AAA Benefit:** Members save 5% or more! |

HAMPTON INN BY HILTON MARIETTA   740/373-5353
THREE DIAMOND SAVE Hotel. **Address:** 508 Pike St 45750

| **AAA Benefit:** Members save up to 15%! |

THE LAFAYETTE HOTEL   740/373-5522
APPROVED Historic Hotel. **Address:** 101 Front St 45750

MICROTEL INN & SUITES BY WYNDHAM MARIETTA
          740/373-7373
APPROVED Hotel. **Address:** 506 Pike St 45750

WHERE TO EAT

AUSTYN'S   740/374-8188
THREE DIAMOND International. Casual Dining. **Address:** 130 Front St 45750

THE BUCKLEY HOUSE RESTAURANT   740/374-4400
THREE DIAMOND American. Fine Dining. **Address:** 332 Front St 45750

THE GALLEY   740/374-8278
APPROVED American. Casual Dining. **Address:** 203 2nd St 45750

THE GUN ROOM   740/373-5522
APPROVED American. Casual Dining. **Address:** 101 Front St 45750

SPAGNA'S   740/376-9245
APPROVED Italian. Casual Dining. **Address:** 301 Gilman Ave 45750

MARION (D-4) pop. 36,837, elev. 923'
• Hotels p. 270 • Restaurants p. 270

In 1821 the combination of a steady diet of salt pork and a lack of water caused Jacob Foos to dig into a few feet of moist dirt. Discovering an abundant spring, he named the site Jacob's Well, and the area grew to become the county seat. The town was renamed in honor of Revolutionary War general Francis Marion, the "Swamp Fox."

Marion's economy, once based on the manufacture of the steam shovel and road roller, now depends on such agricultural goods as dairy products and popping corn. The Marion Popcorn Festival, held the first weekend after Labor Day, celebrates the area's beloved snack.

Architect John Eberson's Marion Palace Theatre, 276 W. Center St., opened in 1928 and remains a focal point of the city. This atmospheric theater features seats and a stage curtain in vibrant reds, and the rest of the interior—complete with a night sky overhead—looks like a European courtyard. The event schedule consists of local theater and touring productions along with movies and musical acts. Guided theater tours are available by appointment; phone (740) 383-2101.

Marion Area Convention and Visitors Bureau: 1713 Marion-Mt. Gilead Rd., Suite 110, Marion, OH 43302. **Phone:** (740) 389-9770 or (800) 371-6688.

THE WARREN G. HARDING HOME AND MEMORIAL is at 380 Mount Vernon Ave., 4 mi. w. of SR 23 on SR 95. It was from this house that Warren G. Harding conducted his "front porch" campaign in the 1920 presidential election. Visitors can see a portion of the more than 5,000 original objects in the Harding Collections, including White House items, clothing and furniture. From gaslight fixtures to original furnishings, the home was first restored in 1965 and will be restored to its 1920 appearance by 2020.

In the back of the house the former campaign press building, a catalog kit home, contains a museum chronicling the Harding life and campaign and the construction of the Harding Memorial presidential gravesite. CLOSURE INFORMATION: The Warren G. Harding Home is currently closed for major renovations; reopening is expected in spring 2020. **Time:** Allow 1 hour, 30 minutes minimum. **Hours:** Wed.-Sun. noon-5, first Sat. in May-first Sun. in Nov.; by appointment rest of year. Closed Labor Day. Phone ahead to confirm schedule. **Cost:** $7; $6 (ages 60+); $4 (ages 12-17); $3 (ages 6-11). **Phone:** (740) 387-9630 or (800) 600-6894. GT

Harding Memorial is on Delaware Ave. (SR 423) at Vernon Heights Blvd., about 1 mi. s. of The Warren G. Harding Home and Memorial. The circular, pillared monument is made of white Georgian marble. It contains the graves of President and Mrs. Warren G. Harding. **Hours:** Daily dawn-dusk. **Cost:** Free. **Phone:** (740) 387-9630 or (800) 600-6894.

BEST WESTERN PLUS UNIVERSITY INN   740/389-1998

APPROVED   Hotel

Best Western PLUS.

AAA Benefit: Members save up to 15% and earn bonus points!

Address: 2117 Marion-Mt. Gilead Rd 43302 **Location:** Jct US 23 and SR 95, just e. **Facility:** 60 units. 3 stories, interior corridors. **Amenities:** safes. **Pool:** heated indoor. **Activities:** exercise room. **Guest Services:** valet and coin laundry.

COMFORT INN BY CHOICE HOTELS   740/389-5552
APPROVED   Hotel. **Address:** 256 Jamesway Dr 43302

COUNTRY INN & SUITES BY RADISSON   740/386-5451
APPROVED   Hotel. **Address:** 2091 Marion-Mt. Gilead Rd 43302

QUALITY INN   740/389-6636
APPROVED   Hotel. **Address:** 227 Jamesway Dr 43302

WHERE TO EAT

HOUSE OF HUNAN   740/387-0032
APPROVED   Chinese. Casual Dining. **Address:** 1583 Marion-Waldo Rd 43302

THE WAREHOUSE   740/387-8124
APPROVED   Italian. Casual Dining. **Address:** 320 W Center St 43302

MARTINS FERRY (E-9) pop. 6,915, elev. 660'

The Betty Zane Memorial at the entrance of Walnut Grove Cemetery at the end of Fourth Street honors the Revolutionary War heroine for her bravery during the siege of Fort Henry in 1782. Pulitzer Prize winning poet James Wright was born in Martins Ferry in 1927, and Pro Football Hall of Fame member Lou "The Toe" Groza entered the world here in 1924.

MARYSVILLE pop. 22,094
- Part of Columbus area — see map p. 205

COMFORT SUITES MARYSVILLE COLUMBUS-NORTHWEST
937/672-9600
THREE DIAMOND Hotel. **Address:** 1081 Lydia Dr 43040
HOLIDAY INN EXPRESS & SUITES MARYSVILLE
937/738-7710
APPROVED Hotel. **Address:** 411 Allenby Dr 43040

MASON (H-11) pop. 30,712, elev. 810'
- Restaurants p. 272
- Hotels & Restaurants map & index p. 166
- Part of Cincinnati area — see map p. 153

Warren County Convention & Visitors Bureau: 5412 Courseview Dr., Suite 220, Mason, OH 45040. **Phone:** (513) 204-1900 or (800) 791-4386.

Shopping: Deerfield Towne Center has nearly three dozen stores—including Dick's Sporting Goods, Gymboree, Lane Bryant, Talbots and White House/Black Market—in an open-air market.

SAVE **THE BEACH WATERPARK** is off I-71 exit 25A at 2590 Waterpark Dr. The 35-acre park offers slides, inner-tube rides, children's water play areas, a water coaster, a wave pool, a spa pool, a zipline, sand volleyball courts and more. Entertainment offerings include an arcade as well as live music and dive-in movies, where movies appropriate for children are shown. During winter months the park has snow tubing available.

Note: Some rides and activities may not be suitable to visitors with certain health conditions, and height restrictions apply to inner tube and body flume rides; check with the park for further details. Changing rooms, showers and locker rentals are available. Food and drink may not be brought into the park, but a picnic area is on the east side of the parking lot.

Hours: Park generally open daily 10-8, Memorial Day weekend-early Aug. (weather permitting). Also open some Sat.-Sun. in mid-May and early Aug. to mid-Sept.; phone for hours. Dive-in movies are shown on select Sat. after sunset. Phone to confirm schedules, including dates and times for snow tubing. **Cost:** All-day pass $28.99; $23.99 (children under 48 inches tall); $22.99 (military with ID); $19.99 (ages 60+); free (ages 0-3). Admission after 3 p.m. $17.99. Phone to confirm prices. **Parking:** $8. **Phone:** (513) 398-7946.

KINGS ISLAND is at 6300 Kings Island Dr. This family entertainment park offers more than 100 rides, shows and attractions, including more

(See map & index p. 166.)

than a dozen thrill rides. Banshee is the world's longest steel inverted coaster and features seven inversions and hits 68 mph. Diamondback is the tallest and fastest roller coaster in the park. It reaches speeds of more than 80 mph and has 10 vertical drops; the first one is 215 feet. Other thrills are provided by The Beast, the world's longest wooden roller coaster; the 26-story free-fall gyro ride Drop Tower; and the face-to-face inverted Invertigo. Boo Blasters on Boo Hill is an interactive dark ride experience.

Planet Snoopy, a children's area, features 18 Peanuts-themed rides, shows and attractions. Soak City Waterpark, the park's 33-acre water playground, offers more than 50 water activities, with 30 waterslides, tropical lagoons, rushing rivers, waterfalls and two wave pools. An array of live stage shows rounds out the fun.

Time: Allow a full day. **Hours:** Park opens daily at 10 a.m., Memorial Day-late Aug.; Sat.-Sun. at 10, early Apr.-late May and late Aug.-Labor Day. Open select Fri.-Sun. after Labor Day, depending on private party schedule. Phone for Halloween Haunt hours. Closing times vary. Soak City Waterpark opens daily at 11, late May-late Aug.; closing times vary. Phone ahead to confirm schedule. **Cost:** (includes Soak City Waterpark) $72; $44 (ages 62+ and children under 48 inches tall). Reduced admission is available after 4 p.m. Prices vary throughout the season; phone ahead to confirm. **Parking:** $20. **Phone:** (513) 754-5700.

BEST WESTERN MASON INN
513/336-7911

APPROVED
Hotel

Best Western. **AAA Benefit:** Members save up to 15% and earn bonus points!

Address: 9665 Mason-Montgomery Rd 45040 **Location:** I-71 exit 19, just w. **Facility:** 92 units. 3 stories, interior corridors. **Parking:** winter plug-ins. **Pool:** heated indoor. **Activities:** hot tub, exercise room. **Guest Services:** valet and coin laundry. **Featured Amenity:** continental breakfast.

CINCINNATI MARRIOTT NORTHEAST
513/459-9800

THREE DIAMOND
Hotel

AAA Benefit: Members save 5% or more!

Address: 9664 Mason-Montgomery Rd 45040 **Location:** I-71 exit 19, just w. **Facility:** 306 units. 6 stories, interior corridors. **Terms:** check-in 4 pm. **Amenities:** safes. **Pool:** heated outdoor, heated indoor. **Activities:** exercise room. **Guest Services:** valet and coin laundry, boarding pass kiosk.

COMFORT INN CINCINNATI NORTHEAST
513/683-9700   24

APPROVED
Hotel
Address: 9011 Fields-Ertel Rd 45249 **Location:** I-71 exit 19, just e. **Facility:** 106 units. 3 stories, interior corridors. **Parking:** winter plug-ins. **Pool:** outdoor. **Activities:** exercise room. **Guest Services:** valet and coin laundry. **Featured Amenity:** full hot breakfast.

COMFORT SUITES-MASON-KINGS ISLAND
513/336-9000   12

THREE DIAMOND Hotel. **Address:** 5457 Kings Center Dr 45040

DRURY INN & SUITES CINCINNATI NORTHEAST MASON
513/336-0108   23

THREE DIAMOND Hotel. **Address:** 9956 Escort Dr 45040

GREAT WOLF LODGE CINCINNATI/MASON
513/459-8885   14

THREE DIAMOND Resort Hotel. **Address:** 2501 Great Wolf Dr 45040

HAMPTON INN & SUITES MASON-CINCINNATI
513/492-8585   22

THREE DIAMOND Hotel. **Address:** 5232 Bardes Rd 45040
AAA Benefit: Members save up to 15%!

HAWTHORN SUITES BY WYNDHAM CINCINNATI NORTHEAST/MASON
513/774-0610   16

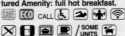
APPROVED
Extended Stay Hotel
Address: 9369 Waterstone Blvd 45249 **Location:** I-71 exit 19, just e on Mason-Montgomery Rd, then 0.9 mi n on Fields-Ertel and Union Cemetery rds. **Facility:** 94 kitchen units, some two bedrooms. 3 stories, interior corridors. **Pool:** heated outdoor. **Activities:** exercise room. **Guest Services:** valet and coin laundry, area transportation. **Featured Amenity:** full hot breakfast.

HILTON GARDEN INN CINCINNATI/MASON
513/204-6000   18

THREE DIAMOND Hotel. **Address:** 5200 Natorp Blvd 45040
AAA Benefit: Members save up to 15%!

HOLIDAY INN EXPRESS HOTEL & SUITES
513/387-6000   17

THREE DIAMOND Hotel. **Address:** 5100 Natorp Blvd 45040

HYATT PLACE CINCINNATI-NORTHEAST
513/754-0003   19

THREE DIAMOND
Hotel

HYATT PLACE
AAA Benefit: Members save up to 10%!

Address: 5070 Natorp Blvd 45040 **Location:** I-71 exit 19, 0.5 mi w. **Facility:** 127 units. 6 stories, interior corridors. **Pool:** heated indoor. **Activities:** exercise room. **Guest Services:** valet laundry. **Featured Amenity:** full hot breakfast.

(See map & index p. 166.)

**RESIDENCE INN BY MARRIOTT CINCINNATI NORTHEAST/
MASON** 513/972-8500 **13**
THREE DIAMOND SAVE Extended
Stay Hotel. **Address:** 2511 Kings Center
Ct 45040

AAA Benefit:
Members save 5%
or more!

**SPRINGHILL SUITES BY MARRIOTT CINCINNATI
NORTHEAST/MASON** 513/683-7797 **15**
THREE DIAMOND SAVE Hotel. **Ad-
dress:** 9365 Waterstone Blvd 45249

AAA Benefit:
Members save 5%
or more!

WHERE TO EAT

GOLD STAR CHILI 513/770-4305
APPROVED American. Quick Serve. **Address:** 8150
Arbor Square Dr 45040

GRAND ORIENTAL CHINESE RESTAURANT
513/677-3388 **27**
APPROVED Chinese. Casual Dining. **Address:** 4800
Field Ertel Rd 45249

PITRELLI'S RESTAURANT 513/770-0122 **24**
APPROVED Italian. Casual Dining. **Address:** 404
Second Ave 45040

RUSTY BUCKET RESTAURANT AND TAVERN
513/339-0150 **26**
APPROVED American. Casual Dining. **Address:**
15035 Deerfield Blvd 45040

SKYLINE CHILI
APPROVED American. Quick Serve.
LOCATIONS:
Address: 5214 Bardes Rd 45040 **Phone:** 513/398-4986
Address: 2711 Water Park Dr 45040 **Phone:** 513/336-7009

S.W. CLYBORNE CO. 513/204-7922 **25**
THREE DIAMOND American. Casual Dining. **Address:** 5948
Snider Rd 45040

THE WILDFLOWER CAFE & COFFEE HOUSE
513/492-7514 **23**
THREE DIAMOND American. Casual Dining. **Address:** 207
E Main St 45040

WOODHOUSE KITCHEN & BAR 513/466-8170 **22**
THREE DIAMOND American. Casual Dining. **Address:** 2629
Water Park Dr 45040

MASSILLON (E-11) pop. 32,149, elev. 975'

Named for Bishop Jean-Baptiste Massillon, a
clergyman and writer at the French court of Louis
XIV, Massillon came into being in the 19th century
when five villages joined together. The city prospered during the Ohio & Erie Canal era, thrived as a
site of steam engine manufacturing in the latter half
of the 1800s and continued to grow as a center of
steel production through the first half of the 1900s.

Massillon's heritage is most visible in the 19th-
century architecture of its downtown area and brick-
paved Fourth Street historic district between Lincoln
Way and Cherry Road. One of the most notable

buildings in this area is the three-story Five Oaks
house at 210 Fourth St. This Romanesque-Gothic
structure was designed in the early 1890s by noted
architect Charles Schweinfurth, designer of many of
the mansions on Cleveland's Millionaires' Row. St.
Mary Church, an impressive Gothic-style stone
church at 206 Cherry Rd N.E., was begun in 1876
and dedicated in 1892.

Artist Eric Grohe's three downtown murals depict
vibrant and colorful scenes. The "Ohio & Erie
Canal" at 39 Lincoln Way West portrays the days
when the canal ran through the town, and "A Century of Heroes" captures high school football glory at
50 Lincoln Way East. Grohe created a scene perfect
for storytelling with his "55 Diamond Court" mural at
32 E. Erie Street South; the painting portrays a brick
building with lots of windows and lively occupants.

One of Massillon's historic houses, Spring Hill, off
Wales Rd. N.E. at 1401 Springhill Ln. N.E., was built
about 1821 and was a stop on the Underground
Railroad. The grounds of the restored house have
herb and flower gardens, a smokehouse, springhouse and other outbuildings; phone (330)
833-6749 for tour information.

**Massillon WestStark Area Chamber of Com-
merce:** 137 Lincoln Way E., Massillon, OH 44646.
Phone: (330) 833-3146.

HAMPTON INN BY HILTON-CANTON/MASSILLON
330/834-1144
APPROVED SAVE Hotel. **Address:** 44 First St SW 44647

AAA Benefit:
Members save up to
15%!

WHERE TO EAT

KOZMO'S GRILLE 330/832-8807
APPROVED American. Casual Dining. **Address:** 37
First St SW 44647

MAUMEE (B-3) pop. 14,286, elev. 638'
• Hotels & Restaurants map & index p. 299

During the late 18th century much of Ohio's Native American population was concentrated along
the Maumee River, a vital link to the British army
post in Detroit, Mich. Repeated Native American
raids delayed settlement of the area until 1794,
when American forces led by Gen. Anthony Wayne
won the decisive Battle of Fallen Timbers.

The War of 1812 permanently secured the area
for the United States, and Maumee was founded in
1817 by William Oliver, a former scout and officer at
nearby Fort Meigs *(see attraction listing p. 284)*. A
blockhouse and stockade of the fort can be seen
from the old canal towpath. By the mid-1800s the
Miami and Erie Canal had made Maumee a center
of trade and commerce. The locks that connected
the Maumee River and the canal can be seen in
Side Cut Metropark; (419) 407-9700.

(See map & index p. 299.)

BEST WESTERN TOLEDO SOUTH MAUMEE
419/865-9400 **43**

APPROVED
Hotel

Best Western.

AAA Benefit: Members save up to 15% and earn bonus points!

Address: 6425 Kit Ln 43537 **Location:** I-475 exit 6, just sw. **Facility:** 83 units. 3 stories, interior corridors. **Pool:** heated indoor. **Activities:** exercise room. **Guest Services:** valet laundry. **Featured Amenity:** breakfast buffet.

SAVE 🍴 🏊 👥 BIZ 📶 ✕
🛗 🖨 ☕

COMFORT INN & SUITES MAUMEE-TOLEDO (I80-90)
419/897-5555 **35**
APPROVED Hotel. **Address:** 1702 Tollgate Dr 43537

COUNTRY INN & SUITES BY RADISSON, TOLEDO
419/893-8576 **39**
APPROVED Hotel. **Address:** 541 W Dussel Dr 43537

COURTYARD BY MARRIOTT-TOLEDO/MAUMEE
419/897-2255 **38**
THREE DIAMOND SAVE Hotel. **Address:** 415 W Dussel Dr 43537

AAA Benefit: Members save 5% or more!

EXTENDED STAY AMERICA-TOLEDO-MAUMEE
419/891-1211 **42**
APPROVED Extended Stay Hotel. **Address:** 542 W Dussel Dr 43537

FAIRFIELD INN & SUITES BY MARRIOTT TOLEDO MAUMEE
419/897-0865 **41**
APPROVED SAVE Hotel. **Address:** 521 W Dussel Dr 43537

AAA Benefit: Members save 5% or more!

HAMPTON INN TOLEDO SOUTH/MAUMEE
419/893-1004 **37**
THREE DIAMOND SAVE Hotel. **Address:** 1409 Reynolds Rd 43537

AAA Benefit: Members save up to 15%!

HOME2 SUITES BY HILTON MAUMEE TOLEDO
419/887-9062 **36**
THREE DIAMOND SAVE Extended Stay Contemporary Hotel. **Address:** 1701 Tollgate Rd 43537

AAA Benefit: Members save up to 15%!

HOMEWOOD SUITES BY HILTON TOLEDO/MAUMEE
419/897-0980 **40**
THREE DIAMOND SAVE Extended Stay Hotel. **Address:** 1410 Arrowhead Rd 43537

AAA Benefit: Members save up to 15%!

RESIDENCE INN BY MARRIOTT TOLEDO MAUMEE
419/891-2233 **45**
THREE DIAMOND SAVE Extended Stay Hotel. **Address:** 1370 Arrowhead Dr 43537

AAA Benefit: Members save 5% or more!

SUPER 8 BY WYNDHAM MAUMEE/TOLEDO AREA
419/897-3800 **44**

APPROVED
Hotel

Address: 1390 Arrowhead Rd 43537 **Location:** I-475 exit 6, just e. Located in a business park. **Facility:** 64 units. 2 stories (no elevator), interior corridors. **Activities:** exercise room. **Guest Services:** valet and coin laundry. **Featured Amenity:** continental breakfast.

SAVE 🍴 👥 BIZ HS 📶 ✕
🛗 🖨 ☕

WHERE TO EAT

BANGKOK KITCHEN 419/897-7777 **34**
APPROVED Thai. Casual Dining. **Address:** 582 Dussel Dr 43537

BARR'S PUBLIC HOUSE 419/866-8466 **36**
APPROVED American. Gastropub. **Address:** 3365 Briarfield Blvd 43537

MANCY'S BLUEWATER GRILLE 419/724-2583 **33**
THREE DIAMOND Seafood. Casual Dining. **Address:** 461 W Dussel Dr 43537

SAM'S DINER 419/897-0284 **35**
APPROVED American. Casual Dining. **Address:** 578 W Dussel Dr 43537

MAYFIELD pop. 3,460
- Hotels & Restaurants map & index p. 194
- Part of Cleveland area — see map p. 177

HILTON GARDEN INN CLEVELAND EAST/MAYFIELD VILLAGE
440/646-1777 **22**
THREE DIAMOND SAVE Hotel. **Address:** 700 Beta Dr 44143

AAA Benefit: Members save up to 15%!

HOLIDAY INN CLEVELAND-MAYFIELD 440/461-9200 **23**
THREE DIAMOND Hotel. **Address:** 780 Beta Dr 44143

WHERE TO EAT

AUSTIN'S SMOKIN' STEAKHOUSE 440/442-4340 **27**
APPROVED American. Casual Dining. **Address:** 6535 Wilson Mills Rd 44143

PIZZA ROMA 440/684-1984 **26**
APPROVED Pizza. Quick Serve. **Address:** 785 Som Center Rd 44143

YOURS TRULY RESTAURANT 440/461-0000
APPROVED American. Casual Dining. **Address:** 6675 Wilson Mills Rd 44124

MEDINA pop. 26,678, elev. 1,089'
- Restaurants p. 274
- Part of Cleveland area — see map p. 177

FAIRFIELD INN & SUITES BY MARRIOTT 330/722-1722
THREE DIAMOND SAVE Hotel. **Address:** 3125 Eastpointe Dr 44256

AAA Benefit: Members save 5% or more!

HAMPTON INN BY HILTON   330/721-8955
THREE DIAMOND [SAVE] Hotel. **Address:** 3073 Eastpointe Dr 44256

AAA Benefit: Members save up to 15%!

HOLIDAY INN EXPRESS & SUITES MEDINA   330/722-6006
THREE DIAMOND Hotel. **Address:** 5185 Gateway Dr 44256

QUALITY INN & SUITES   330/723-4994
APPROVED Hotel. **Address:** 2850 Medina Rd 44256

WHERE TO EAT

FIESTA JALAPENOS   330/723-9896
APPROVED Mexican. Casual Dining. **Address:** 4136 Pearl Rd 44256

ON TAP GRILLE & BAR   330/725-1972
APPROVED American. Sports Bar. **Address:** 2736 Medina Rd 44256

TWIISTED BURGERS & SUSHI   330/661-0606
APPROVED Burgers Sushi. Casual Dining. **Address:** 985 Boardman Alley 44256

YOURS TRULY RESTAURANT   330/722-5800
APPROVED American. Casual Dining. **Address:** 3725 Medina Rd 44256

MENTOR (A-11) pop. 47,159, elev. 651'
• Hotels & Restaurants map & index p. 194

Shopping: Great Lakes Mall, 7850 Mentor Ave., features Dillard's, JCPenney and Macy's as well as nearly 90 additional stores.

JAMES A. GARFIELD NATIONAL HISTORIC SITE is 2 mi. e. of I-90 on US 20 at 8095 Mentor Ave. A 45-minute guided tour takes visitors through the home of the 20th president. The memorial library, added by Lucretia Garfield after her husband's death, and Garfield's private study as well as many original furnishings and memorabilia belonging to the family, who remained in the house until the 1930s, can be seen. A fireproof vault is a highlight of the tour. Outbuildings include the campaign office, a barn and a windmill.

The 1893 carriage house has been repurposed and is now a visitor center with exhibits about Garfield's life, covering his childhood on the Western Reserve; education; service during the Civil War to the Union army and in the House of Representatives; presidential election; and his assassination, funeral and memorial. An 18-minute biographical film is shown throughout the day.

Special themed tours are given regularly and include a 2-hour behind-the-scenes tour that includes the basement, attic and outbuildings and a 90-minute tour focusing on Garfield's Civil War service. The Behind the Ropes tour offers further access into some of the rooms in the house. Dozens of special events are held throughout the year.

Hours: Daily 10-5, May-Oct.; Fri.-Sun. 10-5, rest of year. Tour departure times vary; last tour begins 45 minutes before closing. Behind-the-scenes tour offered the first Sat. of the month. Behind the Ropes tour offered the second Sat. of the month. Phone for departure times. **Cost:** $10; free (ages 0-15). Themed tours $15; ages 0-15 are not permitted. Reservations are required for themed tours. **Phone:** (440) 255-8722. [GT] [↺]

BEST WESTERN PLUS LAWNFIELD INN & SUITES
    440/205-7378   **13**

THREE DIAMOND
Hotel

Best Western PLUS

AAA Benefit: Members save up to 15% and earn bonus points!

Address: 8434 Mentor Ave 44060 **Location:** I-90 exit 195, 1.5 mi n on SR 615, then just e on US 20. **Facility:** 49 units. 3 stories, interior corridors. **Amenities:** safes. **Dining:** Skye Bistro, see separate listing. **Pool:** heated outdoor. **Activities:** exercise room. **Guest Services:** valet laundry. **Featured Amenity:** breakfast buffet.

[SAVE] [||] [▽] CALL [♿] [⊸] [⊹]
[BIZ] [⊚] [✕] [⊟] [▣] / SOME UNITS [⚘] [▦]

HAMPTON INN & SUITES   440/358-1441
THREE DIAMOND [SAVE] Hotel. **Address:** 5675 Emerald Ct 44060

AAA Benefit: Members save up to 15%!

HOLIDAY INN CLEVELAND NORTHEAST-MENTOR
    440/951-7333   **14**
THREE DIAMOND Hotel. **Address:** 7701 Reynolds Rd 44060

RESIDENCE INN BY MARRIOTT   440/392-0800
THREE DIAMOND [SAVE] Extended Stay Hotel. **Address:** 5660 Emerald Ct 44060

AAA Benefit: Members save 5% or more!

SUPER 8   440/951-8558   **15**
APPROVED Motel. **Address:** 7325 Palisades Pkwy 44060

WHERE TO EAT

EL RODEO MEXICAN RESTAURANT   440/205-8740   **17**
APPROVED Mexican. Casual Dining. **Address:** 6900 Center St 44060

MOLINARI'S   440/974-2750   **18**
THREE DIAMOND American. Fine Dining. **Address:** 8900 Mentor Ave 44060

SKYE BISTRO   440/974-3572   **19**
THREE DIAMOND American. Casual Dining. **Address:** 8434 Mentor Ave 44060

YOURS TRULY RESTAURANT   440/954-9393
APPROVED American. Casual Dining. **Address:** 7280 Center St 44060

MIAMISBURG (G-11) pop. 20,181, elev. 704'
• Hotels & Restaurants map & index p. 242

WRIGHT "B" FLYER INC. is at 10550 Springboro Pike at the Dayton Wright Brothers Airport. This is a look-alike of the 1911 Wright "B" Flyer, the first mass-produced airplane in the world. The hangar is

(See map & index p. 242.)

a museum about the Wright brothers and has a Model B simulator. The plane offers rides for those who have donated at the honorary aviator level. **Hours:** Tues., Thurs. and Sat. 9-2:30 and by appointment. Closed major holidays. **Cost:** Museum free. **Phone:** (937) 885-2327.

COURTYARD BY MARRIOTT DAYTON SOUTH/MALL
937/433-3131 **48**

THREE DIAMOND
Hotel

COURTYARD **AAA Benefit:** Members save 5% or more!

Address: 100 Prestige Pl 45342 **Location:** I-75 exit 44, just e on SR 725, just s on Prestige Plaza Dr, then just se. Located in Prestige Plaza Complex. **Facility:** 146 units. 3 stories, interior corridors. **Parking:** on-site (fee). **Pool:** heated indoor. **Activities:** hot tub, exercise room. **Guest Services:** valet and coin laundry, boarding pass kiosk. *(See ad p. 245.)*

DOUBLETREE SUITES BY HILTON DAYTON-MIAMISBURG
937/436-2400 **50**

THREE DIAMOND
Hotel

DOUBLETREE **AAA Benefit:** Members save up to 15%!

Address: 300 Prestige Pl 45342 **Location:** I-75 exit 44, just e on SR 725, just s on Prestige Plaza Dr, then just se. Located in Prestige Plaza Complex. **Facility:** 137 units. 3 stories, interior corridors. **Amenities:** safes. **Pool:** heated outdoor. **Activities:** exercise room. **Guest Services:** valet and coin laundry.

HILTON GARDEN INN DAYTON SOUTH/AUSTIN LANDING
937/247-5850 **52**

THREE DIAMOND SAVE Hotel. **Address:** 12000 Innovation Dr 45342

AAA Benefit: Members save up to 15%!

HOME2 SUITES BY HILTON DAYTON SOUTH
937/530-8450 **53**

THREE DIAMOND SAVE Extended Stay Hotel. **Address:** 200 Austin West Blvd 45342

AAA Benefit: Members save up to 15%!

HOMEWOOD SUITES BY HILTON-DAYTON SOUTH
937/432-0000 **49**

THREE DIAMOND SAVE Extended Stay Hotel. **Address:** 3100 Contemporary Ln 45342

AAA Benefit: Members save up to 15%!

SPRINGHILL SUITES BY MARRIOTT DAYTON SOUTH/MIAMISBURG
937/432-9277 **47**

THREE DIAMOND SAVE Hotel. **Address:** 417 N Springboro Pike 45449

AAA Benefit: Members save 5% or more!

STAYBRIDGE SUITES MIAMISBURG 937/535-2222 **51**
THREE DIAMOND Extended Stay Hotel. **Address:** 10110 Landing Way 45342

WHERE TO EAT

ELE BISTRO & WINE BAR 937/384-2253 **37**
APPROVED American. Casual Dining. **Address:** 3680 Rigby Rd 45342

MIDDLEBURG HEIGHTS (C-10) pop. 15,946, elev. 853'
• Restaurants p. 276
• Hotels & Restaurants map & index p. 194
• Part of Cleveland area — see map p. 177

This Cleveland suburb is less than 10 miles from Cleveland Hopkins International Airport, I-80 (Ohio Turnpike) and I-480. I-71 runs right through the town.

COMFORT INN-CLEVELAND AIRPORT 440/234-3131 **97**
APPROVED Hotel. **Address:** 17550 Rosbough Blvd 44130

COURTYARD BY MARRIOTT CLEVELAND AIRPORT SOUTH
440/243-8785 **103**
THREE DIAMOND SAVE Hotel. **Address:** 7345 Engle Rd 44130

AAA Benefit: Members save 5% or more!

CROWNE PLAZA CLEVELAND AIRPORT 440/243-4040 **101**
THREE DIAMOND Hotel. **Address:** 7230 Engle Rd 44130

HAMPTON INN & SUITES BY HILTON 440/234-0206 **98**
APPROVED SAVE Hotel. **Address:** 7074 Engle Rd 44130

AAA Benefit: Members save up to 15%!

HOME2 SUITES BY HILTON 440/403-9793 **104**
THREE DIAMOND SAVE Extended Stay Contemporary Hotel. **Address:** 7355 Engle Rd 44130

AAA Benefit: Members save up to 15%!

RED ROOF INN CLEVELAND-AIRPORT MIDDLEBURG HEIGHTS
440/243-2441 **100**
APPROVED
Hotel

Address: 17555 Bagley Rd 44130 **Location:** I-71 exit 235, just w. **Facility:** 116 units. 3 stories, interior/exterior corridors. **Amenities:** safes.

(See map & index p. 194.)

SONESTA ES SUITES CLEVELAND AIRPORT
440/234-6688 **99**

THREE DIAMOND
Extended Stay Hotel

Address: 17525 Rosbough Dr 44130 **Location:** I-71 exit 235, just w on Bagley Rd, then just n on Engle Rd. **Facility:** 158 units, some two bedrooms, efficiencies and kitchens. 2-3 stories (no elevator), interior/exterior corridors. **Pool:** heated outdoor. **Activities:** hot tub, exercise room. **Guest Services:** valet and coin laundry, area transportation. **Featured Amenity:** breakfast buffet.

SAVE ✈ ⓘ CALL ⑤ ➔ ⓦ
BIZ 🛜 ✕ 🖥 🖼 ▣
/SOME UNITS 🐾 HS

TOWNEPLACE SUITES BY MARRIOTT CLEVELAND AIRPORT
440/816-9300 **102**

APPROVED SAVE Extended
Stay Hotel. **Address:** 7325 Engle Rd 44130

AAA Benefit:
Members save 5% or more!

WHERE TO EAT

BLUE JADE RESTAURANT 440/234-1668 **69**
APPROVED Asian. Casual Dining. **Address:** 7080B Engle Rd 44130

BREW GARDEN 440/234-1001 **71**
APPROVED American. Casual Dining. **Address:** 18590 Bagley Rd 44130

BROWN DERBY 440/826-9900
APPROVED Steak Seafood. Casual Dining. **Address:** 18332 Bagley Rd 44130

TWO BUCKS FOOD & SPIRIT 440/234-8344 **70**
APPROVED American. Sports Bar. **Address:** 18336 Bagley Rd 44130

MIDDLETOWN pop. 48,694
• Part of Cincinnati area — see map p. 153

DRURY INN & SUITES MIDDLETOWN FRANKLIN
513/425-6650
THREE DIAMOND Hotel. **Address:** 3320 Village Dr 45005

FAIRFIELD BY MARRIOTT 513/424-5444
APPROVED SAVE Hotel. **Address:** 6750 Roosevelt Pkwy 45044

AAA Benefit:
Members save 5% or more!

HAMPTON INN BY HILTON 513/422-6880
THREE DIAMOND SAVE Hotel. **Address:** 2880 Towne Blvd 45044

AAA Benefit:
Members save up to 15%!

WHERE TO EAT

FRICKER'S 513/420-9464
APPROVED American. Casual Dining. **Address:** 4810 Roosevelt Blvd 45005

MILAN (B-5) pop. 1,367, elev. 602'

Founded in the early 1800s on a bluff overlooking the Huron River, Milan overcame its landlocked handicap by building a canal to the river, which flows into Lake Erie. By the early 1840s, with the canal newly completed, Milan was booming as one of the largest wheat-shipping centers in the country.

The prosperity lasted until the town refused right-of-way to the Lake Shore and Michigan Southern Railroad. The railroad went through Norwalk instead, and Milan's commerce abruptly declined. To add to the city's problems, deforestation caused the river to diminish and become unnavigable. By the 1870s the canal was abandoned, and Milan entered an era of light industry and farming.

EDISON BIRTHPLACE MUSEUM is at 9 N. Edison Dr. This is the house where inventor Thomas A. Edison, born in 1847, spent his first 7 years. Guided 45- to 60-minute tours of the well-preserved house are available.

Time: Allow 1 hour minimum. **Hours:** Tours available Tues.-Sat. 10-5, Sun. 1-5, June-Aug.; Tues.-Sun. 1-5, Apr.-May and Sept.-Oct.; Fri.-Sun. 1-5, Feb.-Mar. and Nov.-Dec. Last tour begins 30 minutes before closing. Closed Easter, July 4, Labor Day weekend, Thanksgiving and Christmas. **Cost:** $9; $8 (ages 60+); $5 (ages 5-17); $25 (family). **Phone:** (419) 499-2135. **GT**

MILAN HISTORICAL MUSEUM is at 10 N. Edison Dr. The seven-building campus features art, historical exhibits and a glass collection. Family activities are held throughout the year. **Time:** Allow 1 hour minimum. **Hours:** Tues.-Sat. 10-5, Sun. 1-5, June-Aug.; Fri.-Sun. 1-5, Feb.-May and Sept.-Dec.; other times by appointment. **Cost:** $9; $8 (ages 60+); $5 (ages 6-17); $25 (family, two adults and three children). **Phone:** (419) 499-2968.

Edna Roe Newton Memorial Building is at 12 Edison Dr. next to the Milan Historical Museum. Exhibits include items Edna and Bert Newton collected as they traveled throughout the world. Antiques, artwork and needlework are displayed. **Hours:** Tues.-Sat. 10-5, Sun. 1-5, June-Aug.; Fri.-Sun. 1-5, Feb.-May and Sept.-Dec. Closed Easter, July 4 and Labor Day weekend. **Cost:** Free. **Phone:** (419) 499-2968.

COUNTRY INN & SUITES BY RADISSON SANDUSKY SOUTH
419/499-4911
APPROVED Hotel. **Address:** 11600 US 250/Milan Rd 44846

MOTEL 6 SANDUSKY-MILAN 419/499-8001
APPROVED Motel. **Address:** 11406 US 250/Milan Rd 44846

QUALITY INN MILAN-SANDUSKY 419/499-4681
APPROVED Hotel. **Address:** 11020 US 250/Milan Rd 44846

RED ROOF INN SANDUSKY-MILAN 419/499-4347
APPROVED Hotel. **Address:** 11303 US 250 Milan Rd 44846

MILFORD (I-11) pop. 6,709, elev. 548'
- Hotels & Restaurants map & index p. 166
- Part of Cincinnati area — see map p. 153

Promont House Museum, 906 Main St., is a three-story Italianate house set on spacious wooded grounds. The house was built 1865-67 for a wealthy businessman, and through the years several other families took up residency, including Ohio's 43rd governor, John Pattison. The house currently reflects the Victorian era. Visitors can get a nice view of the area from the third-story tower. The site is open weekends 1-4, March through December; phone (513) 248-0324 to confirm schedule.

Among the town's annual events are Buskerfest in the fall and Hometown Holidays during Thanksgiving weekend.

Milford Miami Township Chamber of Commerce: 745 Center St., #302, Milford, OH 45150. **Phone:** (513) 831-2411.

Shopping: Milford's historic district offers several antique and specialty shops.

HOMEWOOD SUITES BY HILTON   513/248-4663 **67**
 THREE DIAMOND
Extended Stay Hotel

 HOMEWOOD SUITES BY HILTON **AAA Benefit:** Members save up to 15%!

Address: 600 Chamber Dr 45150 **Location:** I-275 exit 59 southbound; exit 59A northbound, 0.5 mi w on Milford Pkwy, then 0.5 mi s. **Facility:** 76 efficiencies. 4 stories, interior corridors. **Pool:** heated indoor. **Activities:** exercise room. **Guest Services:** valet and coin laundry.

WHERE TO EAT

20 BRIX   513/831-2749 **54**
 THREE DIAMOND American. Casual Dining. **Address:** 101 Main St 45150

MILLERSBURG (D-6) pop. 3,025, elev. 892'

The "old town" of Millersburg was laid out by Adam Johnson and Charles Miller in November 1815. In April 1824, a plat was filed for the present "new town" of Millersburg, which contained 194 lots. The town is in a rural section of Amish Country.

Holmes County Chamber of Commerce and Tourism Bureau: 6 W. Jackson St., Millersburg, OH 44654. **Phone:** (330) 674-3975.

COMFORT INN MILLERSBURG   330/674-7400
THREE DIAMOND Hotel. **Address:** 1102 Glen Dr 44654

FIELDS OF HOME LODGE AND CABINS   330/674-7152
APPROVED Bed & Breakfast. **Address:** 7278 CR 201 44654

HOLIDAY INN EXPRESS   234/301-9005
THREE DIAMOND Hotel. **Address:** 1005 S Washington St 44654

WHERE TO EAT

TARRAGON AT THE INN AT HONEY RUN   330/674-0011
THREE DIAMOND American. Fine Dining. **Address:** 6920 CR 203 44654

THE TAVERN AT HOTEL MILLERSBURG   330/674-1457
APPROVED American. Casual Dining. **Address:** 35 W Jackson St 44654

MONROE pop. 12,442
- Part of Cincinnati area — see map p. 153

BEST WESTERN MONROE INN   513/539-4400
APPROVED
Hotel

 Best Western. **AAA Benefit:** Members save up to 15% and earn bonus points!

Address: 40 New Garver Rd 45050 **Location:** I-75 exit 29, just w. **Facility:** 49 units. 2 stories, interior corridors. **Pool:** heated outdoor. **Activities:** exercise room. **Guest Services:** valet and coin laundry.

MOUNT GILEAD pop. 3,660

BEST WESTERN EXECUTIVE INN   419/768-2378
APPROVED
Hotel

 Best Western. **AAA Benefit:** Members save up to 15% and earn bonus points!

Address: 3991 County Rd 172 43338 **Location:** I-71 exit 151, just e on SR 95. Located in a rural area. **Facility:** 33 units. 2 stories (no elevator), interior corridors. **Parking:** winter plug-ins. **Pool:** outdoor. **Guest Services:** coin laundry. **Featured Amenity:** full hot breakfast.

MOUNT VERNON pop. 16,990

HOLIDAY INN EXPRESS MT. VERNON   740/392-1900
APPROVED Hotel. **Address:** 11555 Upper Gilchrist Rd 43050

WHERE TO EAT

THE ALCOVE   740/392-3076
THREE DIAMOND American. Casual Dining. **Address:** 116 S Main St 43050

FIESTA MEXICANA   740/397-6325
APPROVED Mexican. Casual Dining. **Address:** 308 W High St 43050

JAKE'S RESTAURANT   740/397-1418
APPROVED American. Casual Dining. **Address:** 996 Coshocton Rd 43050

NELSONVILLE (G-6) pop. 5,392, elev. 681'

HOCKING VALLEY SCENIC RAILWAY depot is at US 33 and Hocking Pkwy. A 14-mile round-trip to Haydenville and a 22-mile round-trip to Logan are offered. Both include a 30-minute stop at Robbins Crossing, a small 1840s log village with reenactors, Memorial Day weekend through October. Special themed excursions also are offered.

There are picnic tables at the train depot. **Time:** Allow 2 hours minimum. **Hours:** Departures Sat.-Sun. at noon to Haydenville and at 2:30 to Logan, Memorial Day weekend-Oct. 31 (also to Logan at 1:30 Memorial Day and Labor Day). Phone for fall foliage and other special themed tours schedules.

Cost: Logan fare $17; $15 (ages 60+); $12 (ages 3-12). Haydenville fare $13; $11 (ages 60+); $10 (ages 3-12). Santa Train $17; $15 (ages 60+); $13 (ages 3-12). Phone for other trip fares. Reservations are recommended for fall foliage and all other themed trips. **Phone:** (740) 753-9531 Sat.-Sun. 10-4 or (740) 249-1452. GT ⊼

NEW ALBANY
- **Hotels & Restaurants map & index p. 222**
- **Part of Columbus area — see map p. 205**

COURTYARD BY MARRIOTT-NEW ALBANY	614/855-1505
THREE DIAMOND SAVE Hotel. **Address:** 5211 Forest Dr 43054	**AAA Benefit:** Members save 5% or more!

HAMPTON INN & SUITES BY HILTON	614/855-8335
THREE DIAMOND SAVE Hotel. **Address:** 5220 Forest Dr 43054	**AAA Benefit:** Members save up to 15%!

HOME2 SUITES BY HILTON NEW ALBANY	614/305-4257
THREE DIAMOND SAVE Extended Stay Contemporary Hotel. **Address:** 5095 Forest Dr 43054	**AAA Benefit:** Members save up to 15%!

WHERE TO EAT

HUDSON 29 KITCHEN & DRINK	614/859-2900 69
THREE DIAMOND American. Casual Dining. **Address:** 260 Market St 43054	

NEWARK (E-5) pop. 47,573, elev. 822'
- **Part of Columbus area — see map p. 205**

The site of several large prehistoric Native American mounds, Newark was founded in 1802 by a New Jersey man who named the new plot after his hometown. Like its namesake, Newark became a busy center of trade and industry, especially after the completion of the Ohio & Erie Canal in 1832 and the arrival of railroads in the 1850s.

A monument commemorating the canal's groundbreaking ceremony, presided over by New York governor DeWitt Clinton on July 4, 1825, is 3 miles south on SR 79. Also of interest is Cranberry Island on nearby Buckeye Lake in Buckeye Lake State Park *(see Recreation Areas Chart)*. The island is a sphagnum bog that was formed at the end of the ice age; it contains various species of plants, including alder bush, sundew and poison sumac. Due to the island's fragile state, though, access is by guided tour only; phone (740) 929-1998.

Not to be missed by vaudeville, film and architecture buffs is the Midland Theatre, an opulent 1928 movie palace that reopened in 2002 following an 8-year, $8.5 million renovation and restoration. Marble columns, a gilded proscenium arch, and an alabaster chandelier suspended from an ornate medallion grace the interior of the Spanish motif, 1,200-seat structure at 36 N. Park Pl. Guided tours sometimes are available on a walk-in basis or by appointment. For a schedule of live and film offerings or for tour information phone (740) 345-5483.

The former Longaberger National Headquarters at 1500 E. Main St., a seven-story replica of a Longaberger market basket, will surely catch your eye.

THE DAWES ARBORETUM is 5 mi. s. on SR 13 to 7770 Jacksontown Rd. The nearly 2,000-acre arboretum has plant collections, gardens and natural areas. Twelve miles of hiking trails and a 4-mile automobile route are on the grounds. The Daweswood House Museum is furnished with 19th- and 20th-century antiques and family memorabilia.

Time: Allow 1 hour minimum. **Hours:** Daily 7 a.m.-dusk. Visitor center open Mon.-Sat. 8-5, Sun. and holidays 10-5. Guided tours of Daweswood House Museum depart Fri.-Sun. at noon and 2, May-Oct.; Sat.-Sun. at noon and 2, Mar.-Apr. Phone ahead to confirm schedule. **Cost:** Arboretum free. Daweswood House Museum $2; $1 (ages 0-12). **Phone:** (740) 323-2355 or (800) 443-2937. GT 🏕

NEWARK EARTHWORKS—see Heath p. 258.

COURTYARD BY MARRIOTT-NEWARK/GRANVILLE	740/344-1800
◆ **APPROVED** Hotel	COURTYARD **AAA Benefit:** Members save 5% or more!

Address: 500 Highland Blvd 43055 **Location:** SR 16 exit Church St and Country Club Dr, just se. **Facility:** 84 units. 3 stories, interior corridors. **Pool:** heated indoor. **Activities:** exercise room. **Guest Services:** valet and coin laundry, boarding pass kiosk.
SAVE 🍴 🍸 CALL 🛗 🐾 ♿ BIZ HS 📶 ✉ 🔌 📺 / SOME UNITS 🍳

DOUBLETREE BY HILTON NEWARK, OHIO	740/322-6455
THREE DIAMOND SAVE Hotel. **Address:** 50 N 2nd St 43055	**AAA Benefit:** Members save up to 15%!

RED OAK PUB   740/366-5999
APPROVED   American. Casual Dining. **Address:** 250 Goosepond Rd 43055

NEWCOMERSTOWN pop. 3,822

HAMPTON INN BY HILTON   740/498-9800
APPROVED SAVE Hotel. **Ad-dress:** 200 Morris Crossing 43832

> **AAA Benefit:** Members save up to 15%!

NEW PHILADELPHIA (D-7) pop. 17,288, elev. 878'

New Philadelphia was founded in the early 1800s by Moravian missionaries and Swiss-German immigrants who were undaunted by the hard times faced by their brethren in previous unsuccessful settlements. Surviving Native American raids and the Revolutionary War, the village soon saw economic growth and prosperity.

A light industrial center, New Philadelphia also is a popular vacation spot. Recreational opportunities are abundant on the 16,000 acres of lakes in the Muskingum Watershed Conservancy District *(see Recreation Areas Chart).*

Tuscarawas County Convention and Visitors Bureau: 124 E. High Ave., New Philadelphia, OH 44663. **Phone:** (330) 602-2420 or (800) 527-3387.

SCHOENBRUNN VILLAGE is on SR 259 at 1984 E. High Ave., 4 mi. e. of I-77 exit 81. Founded by David Zeisberger in 1772 as a Moravian mission to the Delaware Indians, Schoenbrunn was the first missionary settlement in Ohio. The town grew to include more than 60 log buildings. Its 300 settlers drew up Ohio's first civil code and built the first church and schoolhouse. British and Native American hostilities caused the abandonment of Schoenbrunn in 1777.

The village has 16 reconstructed log buildings, an original mission cemetery and planted fields. **Hours:** Tues.-Sat. 9:30-5, Sun. noon-5, Memorial Day-Labor Day; Sat. 9:30-5, Sun. noon-5, day after Labor Day-Oct. 31. Phone ahead to confirm schedule. **Cost:** $7; $5 (ages 65+); $4 (ages 6-17). Rates may vary; phone ahead. **Phone:** (740) 922-6776 or (800) 752-2711.

"TRUMPET IN THE LAND" is performed in the Trumpet in the Land Amphitheatre, off I-77 exit 81. This outdoor historical drama recounts the efforts of Moravian missionary David Zeisberger as he brought Christianity to the Delaware Indians during the late 1700s. Performances feature horses, fire dances and pyrotechnics.

Inquire about weather policies, rain checks and additional productions. **Hours:** Performances Mon.-Tues. and Thurs.-Sat. at 8:30 p.m., mid-June to late Aug. **Cost:** $20; $18 (ages 13-17 and 60+); $10

(ages 3-12). Reduced rates on Tues. Reservations are recommended. **Phone:** (330) 339-1132.

BEST WESTERN DUTCH VALLEY INN   330/339-6500
APPROVED
Hotel

> **AAA Benefit:** Members save up to 15% and earn bonus points!

Address: 161 Bluebell Dr SW 44663 **Location:** I-77 exit 81, 0.7 mi e. **Facility:** 66 units. 2 stories, interior corridors. **Pool:** heated indoor. **Activities:** exercise room. **Guest Services:** valet and coin laundry.

HAMPTON INN BY HILTON   330/339-7000
APPROVED SAVE Hotel. **Ad-dress:** 1299 W High Ave 44663

> **AAA Benefit:** Members save up to 15%!

HOLIDAY INN EXPRESS & SUITES   330/339-7731
THREE DIAMOND Hotel. **Address:** 145 Bluebell Dr SW 44663

SCHOENBRUNN INN   330/339-4334
APPROVED Hotel. **Address:** 1186 W High Ave 44663

EL SAN JOSE   330/308-8928
APPROVED Mexican. Casual Dining. **Address:** 1240 W High Ave 44663

GAVINS   330/343-2490
APPROVED American. Casual Dining. **Address:** 110 S Broadway 44663

HOG HEAVEN OPEN FLAME BBQ   330/308-8040
APPROVED Barbecue. Casual Dining. **Address:** 1290 W High Ave 44663

NILES (C-8) pop. 19,266, elev. 882'
• Hotels p. 280

Founded in 1806 by James Heaton, the settlement was originally named Heaton Furnace and soon after was changed to Nilestown. Heaton is credited with manufacturing the first bar iron in Ohio in 1809; by 1880 Niles had become one of the leading iron manufacturers in the state due to local industrialists. The era of steel and automobile manufacturing brought continued prosperity to the area through the mid-1900s.

The town was the 1842 birthplace of William McKinley, the nation's 25th president.

Mahoning Valley Scrappers, a New York-Penn Class A affiliate team of the Cleveland Indians, play at Eastwood Field.

Shopping: At US 422 and SR 46, the Eastwood Mall Shopping and Entertainment Complex features more than 200 stores and eateries; anchors include Dillard's, JCPenney, Macy's and Sears.

NATIONAL MCKINLEY BIRTHPLACE MEMORIAL is at 40 N. Main St. The 1915-17 Classical Greek structure is made of Georgian marble to honor William McKinley, who served as the nation's 25th president 1897-1901. An ornate museum contains McKinley memorabilia, a collection of J. Massey-Rhind bronze busts from the late 19th- and early 20th centuries, an auditorium and library. The McKinley Birthplace Home and Research Center, at 40 S. Main St., is a reconstruction of the president's birthplace home and is furnished in period.

Time: Allow 30 minutes minimum. **Hours:** Library open Mon.-Thurs. 9-8, Fri.-Sat. 9-5. Museum open Mon.-Wed. 9-5, Thurs. 9-3; last tour begins 30 minutes before closing. Phone for McKinley Birthplace Home and Research Center schedule. Closed major holidays. **Cost:** Free. **Phone:** (330) 652-1704, ext. 203. GT

HAMPTON INN & SUITES NILES/WARREN   330/652-1277
THREE DIAMOND SAVE Hotel. **Address:** 5581 Youngstown Warren Rd 44446

AAA Benefit: Members save up to 15%!

RESIDENCE INN BY MARRIOTT YOUNGSTOWN/WARREN-NILES   330/505-3655
THREE DIAMOND SAVE Extended Stay Hotel. **Address:** 5555 Youngstown-Warren Rd 44446

AAA Benefit: Members save 5% or more!

NORTH CANTON (E-11) pop. 17,488, elev. 1,158'

FANNIE MAY & HARRY LONDON CHOCOLATE FACTORY is just n. of I-77 exit 113 at 5353 Lauby Rd. The factory produces more than 500 varieties of chocolate and gourmet candies. Tours provide insight into the candy making process and history of the company.

Time: Allow 1 hour minimum. **Hours:** Tours (maximum 60 people) are offered Mon.-Thurs. on the hour 10-4. Closed major holidays. Phone ahead to confirm schedule. **Cost:** Free. Reservations are recommended. **Phone:** (330) 494-0833, or (800) 321-0444, ext. 119 for tour reservations. GT

MAPS AIR MUSEUM is at 2260 International Pkwy., at the Akron-Canton Airport. This museum of the Military Aviation Preservation Society uses vintage aircraft and artifacts to relate the history of military aviation. Visitors can sit in the cockpit of an MiG 17. The Ohio Society of Military History Museum, which features a collection of congressional medals, photographs, clothing and other items from the Civil War through Operation Desert Storm, also is included. **Time:** Allow 1 hour minimum. **Hours:** Tues.-Sat. 9-4:30, Sun. 11:30-4. Closed major holidays. **Cost:** $10; $9 (ages 60+); $6 (ages 6-12). Rates may vary; phone ahead. **Phone:** (330) 896-6332.

EMBASSY SUITES BY HILTON-AKRON CANTON AIRPORT   330/305-0500
THREE DIAMOND SAVE Hotel. **Address:** 7883 Freedom Ave NW 44720

AAA Benefit: Members save up to 15%!

HILTON GARDEN INN AKRON-CANTON AIRPORT   330/966-4907
THREE DIAMOND SAVE Hotel. **Address:** 5251 Landmark Blvd 44720

AAA Benefit: Members save up to 15%!

MICROTEL INN & SUITES BY WYNDHAM NORTH CANTON   330/966-7551
APPROVED Hotel. **Address:** 7046 Sunset Strip Ave 44720

WHERE TO EAT

91 WOOD FIRED OVEN   330/498-9191
THREE DIAMOND American. Casual Dining. **Address:** 1983 E Maple St 44720

EADIE'S FISH HOUSE GRILL & PUB   330/494-4000
APPROVED Seafood. Casual Dining. **Address:** 6616 Wise Ave NW 44720

MAIN STREET GRILLE   330/497-1117
THREE DIAMOND American. Casual Dining. **Address:** 123 S Main St 44720

MAMA GUZZARDI'S ITALIAN RESTAURANT   330/499-1247
APPROVED Italian. Casual Dining. **Address:** 1107 N Main St 44720

TABLE SIX KITCHEN + BAR   330/305-1666
APPROVED New American. Gastropub. **Address:** 6113 Whipple Ave NW 44720

THE TWISTED OLIVE ITALIAN AMERICAN KITCHEN   330/899-0550
THREE DIAMOND Italian. Fine Dining. **Address:** 5430 Massillon Rd 44720

WALTHER'S TWIN TAVERN   234/714-9533
APPROVED Comfort Food. Casual Dining. **Address:** 440 Applegrove Rd 44720

NORTH OLMSTED pop. 32,718
• Hotels & Restaurants map & index p. 194
• Part of Cleveland area — see map p. 177

ALOFT CLEVELAND AIRPORT   440/772-4300   72
THREE DIAMOND
Contemporary Hotel

AAA Benefit: Members save 5% or more!

Address: 5550 Great Northern Blvd 44070 **Location:** I-480 exit 6B westbound, exit 6 eastbound, just s on SR 252. **Facility:** 137 units. 4 stories, interior corridors. *Bath:* shower only. **Amenities:** safes. **Pool:** heated indoor. **Activities:** exercise room. **Guest Services:** complimentary and valet laundry, area transportation.

CANDLEWOOD SUITES CLEVELAND/NORTH OLMSTED   440/716-0584   69
THREE DIAMOND Extended Stay Hotel. **Address:** 24741 Country Club Blvd 44070

COURTYARD BY MARRIOTT-AIRPORT NORTH   440/716-9977   71
THREE DIAMOND SAVE Hotel. **Address:** 24901 Country Club Blvd 44070

AAA Benefit: Members save 5% or more!

(See map & index p. 194.)

EXTENDED STAY AMERICA-NORTH OLMSTED
440/777-8585 **70**

◆ **APPROVED** Extended Stay Hotel. **Address:** 24851 Country Club Blvd 44070

HAMPTON INN NORTH OLMSTEAD CLEVELAND AIRPORT
440/617-6306 **68**

THREE DIAMOND SAVE Hotel. **Address:** 24601 Country Club Blvd 44070

AAA Benefit: Members save up to 15%!

WHERE TO EAT

THE RAIL
440/979-1979 **50**

◆ **APPROVED** Burgers. Gastropub. **Address:** 400 Great Northern Mall 44070

NORWALK (C-5) pop. 17,012, elev. 713'

During the Western Reserve era, settlers came to the Norwalk area from parts of New England ravaged by British raids. Because the land was deeded as compensation for Revolutionary War fire destruction, it was called the "Firelands." The West Main Historic District showcases some of the Classic Revival houses built by the original settlers.

Summit Motorsports Park on SR 18 hosts more than 60 drag racing events April through October. Phone (419) 668-5555 for event and ticket information.

Huron County Visitors Bureau: 10 W. Main St., Norwalk, OH 44857. **Phone:** (419) 668-4155 or (877) 668-4155.

BEST WESTERN NORWALK
419/663-3501

◆ **APPROVED**
Hotel

BW Best Western.
AAA Benefit: Members save up to 15% and earn bonus points!

Address: 351 Milan Ave 44857 **Location:** 3.5 mi n on US 250; 4.5 mi s of I-80/90 (Ohio Tpke). **Facility:** 58 units. 2 stories, interior corridors. **Pool:** heated indoor. **Activities:** hot tub, exercise room. **Guest Services:** coin laundry. **Featured Amenity: full hot breakfast.**
SAVE CALL 🔊 ♿ 🛄 🐾 ➕ BIZ 📶 ✕ 🔌 🖥️ 🖨️

GEORGIAN MANOR INN-B & B
419/663-8132

FOUR DIAMOND
Historic Bed & Breakfast

Address: 123 W Main St 44857 **Location:** Jct SR 61 and US 250, just w. Located in historic district. **Facility:** This lovely 1906 Georgian Revival home offers manicured grounds and Edwardian-era décor, including in the spacious public areas. Book the Lady Anne room with a large balcony that overlooks the garden. 4 units. 2 stories (no elevator), interior corridors. **Terms:** age restrictions may apply. **Featured Amenity: full hot breakfast.**
SAVE 📶 ✕ 🐾 🚭

THE VICTORIAN LADY
419/660-9860

THREE DIAMOND Historic Bed & Breakfast. **Address:** 175 W Main St 44857

WHERE TO EAT

BERRY'S RESTAURANT
419/668-2394

◆ **APPROVED** American. Casual Dining. **Address:** 15 W Main St 44857

CASA FIESTA
419/660-8085

◆ **APPROVED** Mexican. Casual Dining. **Address:** 344 Milan Ave 44857

SIDELINES SPORTS BAR & EATERY
567/743-9392

◆ **APPROVED** American. Sports Bar. **Address:** 230 Milan Ave 44857

NORWICH (F-7) pop. 102, elev. 968'

GEM **NATIONAL ROAD-ZANE GREY MUSEUM** is off I-70 exit 164 at 8850 E. Pike. The museum traces the development of the country's first "highway"—the National Road from Cumberland, Md., to Vandalia, Ill. Exhibits, including a 136-foot miniature diorama, depict the history of both the road and vehicle technology. The museum features an original Conestoga wagon and harnesses as well as art pottery and decorative tile produced by local potteries. Objects belonging to Western novelist Zane Grey and copies of his manuscripts also are displayed.

Time: Allow 1 hour minimum. **Hours:** Wed.-Sat. 10-4, Sun. 1-4, May-Oct. **Cost:** $7; $6 (ages 55+ and active military with ID); $3 (students). Combination ticket with John & Annie Glenn Historic Site $12; $10 (ages 55+); $5 (students). Rates may vary; phone ahead. **Phone:** (740) 826-3305 or (800) 752-2602.

NORWOOD pop. 19,207

- **Hotels & Restaurants map & index p. 166**
- **Part of Cincinnati area — see map p. 153**

COURTYARD BY MARRIOTT CINCINNATI MIDTOWN/ROOKWOOD
513/672-7100 **74**

THREE DIAMOND SAVE Hotel. **Address:** 3813 Edwards Rd 45209

AAA Benefit: Members save 5% or more!

RESIDENCE INN CINCINNATI MIDTOWN/ROOKWOOD
513/873-2400 **75**

THREE DIAMOND SAVE Extended Stay Hotel. **Address:** 3815 Edwards Rd 45209

AAA Benefit: Members save 5% or more!

WHERE TO EAT

BETTA'S ITALIAN OVEN
513/631-6836 **66**

◆ **APPROVED** Italian Pizza. Casual Dining. **Address:** 3764 Montgomery Rd 45212

P.F. CHANG'S CHINA BISTRO
513/531-4567 **65**

THREE DIAMOND Chinese. Fine Dining. **Address:** 2633 Edmondson Rd 45209

THE PUB AT ROOKWOOD MEWS
513/841-2748 **64**

◆ **APPROVED** British. Gastropub. **Address:** 2692 Madison Rd 45208

SEASONS 52 FRESH GRILL
513/631-5252 **63**

THREE DIAMOND American. Casual Dining. **Address:** 3819 Edwards Rd 45209

(See map & index p. 166.)

TASTE OF BELGIUM ROOKWOOD   513/396-5800 (62)
APPROVED Belgian. Casual Dining. **Address:** 3825 Edwards Rd 45209

OAK HARBOR (B-4) pop. 2,759, elev. 590'

OTTAWA NATIONAL WILDLIFE REFUGE is 6.6 mi. n. on SR 19 then 3 mi. w. to 14000 W. SR 2. This nearly 5,500-acre site (some of which is closed to the public) is on Lake Erie and offers several walking/hiking trails ranging from .5 to 4.5 miles. One is an accessible wooden boardwalk and the others are covered in gravel; all are mostly flat and level. From the trails visitors can see spectacular views of marsh, meadow, scrub/shrub and wetland areas as well as an estuary.

This is a great bird-watching locale, and the site is also home to coyotes, white-tailed deer, squirrels and other wildlife. A 3-story visitor center features interactive exhibits about local birds and wildlife in the refuge, and the third-floor observation deck is stocked with binoculars. Bird checklists are available. Limited hunting opportunities are available; contact the visitor center for details.

Time: Allow 1 hour minimum. **Hours:** Trails daily dawn-dusk. Visitor center daily 9-4; closed Jan. 1, Martin Luther King Jr. Day, Presidents' Day, Columbus Day, Veterans Day, Thanksgiving, Christmas Eve and Christmas. **Cost:** Free. **Phone:** (419) 898-0014.

OBERLIN (B-6) pop. 8,286, elev. 855'

Co-founded with Oberlin College, the town of Oberlin was established as a colony pledged to "plainest living and highest thinking." The town and college were hotbeds of abolitionist sentiment and a major stop on the Underground Railroad; Oberlin has been called "The town that started the Civil War."

Charles M. Hall, an 1885 Oberlin College graduate, discovered the electrolytic process of producing aluminum the following year in his Oberlin woodshed workshop as he was working with his sister Julia. Frenchman Paul Louis Toussaint Héroult independently discovered the same process in Europe a few months later. Hall later co-founded the Aluminum Company of America, Alcoa.

Oberlin Business Partnership: 23 E. College St., Oberlin, OH 44074. **Phone:** (440) 774-6262.

THE HOTEL AT OBERLIN   440/775-7001
THREE DIAMOND Contemporary Hotel. **Address:** 10 E College St 44074

WHERE TO EAT

THE MANDARIN   440/774-4500
APPROVED Mandarin. Casual Dining. **Address:** 82 S Main St 44074

ONTARIO pop. 6,225

FAIRFIELD INN & SUITES BY MARRIOTT ONTARIO/MANSFIELD   419/747-2200
APPROVED (SAVE) Hotel. **Address:** 1065 N Lexington-Springmill Rd 44906
AAA Benefit: Members save 5% or more!

HAMPTON INN BY HILTON   419/747-5353
THREE DIAMOND (SAVE) Hotel. **Address:** 1051 N Lexington-Springmill Rd 44906
AAA Benefit: Members save up to 15%!

WHERE TO EAT

EL CAMPESTRE   419/529-5330
APPROVED Mexican. Casual Dining. **Address:** 1971 W 4th St 44862

OREGON pop. 20,291
• Hotels & Restaurants map & index p. 299

HAMPTON INN TOLEDO/OREGON   419/724-3333 (14)
THREE DIAMOND (SAVE) Hotel. **Address:** 2931 Navarre Ave 43616
AAA Benefit: Members save up to 15%!

HOLIDAY INN EXPRESS TOLEDO-OREGON   419/691-8800 (16)
THREE DIAMOND Hotel. **Address:** 3154 Navarre Ave 43616

TOWNEPLACE SUITES BY MARRIOTT TOLEDO OREGON   419/724-0044 (15)
THREE DIAMOND (SAVE) Extended Stay Hotel. **Address:** 2851 Navarre Ave 43616
AAA Benefit: Members save 5% or more!

WHERE TO EAT

OSAKA SUSHI AND HIBACHI   419/697-2669 (23)
APPROVED Japanese. Casual Dining. **Address:** 3150 Navarre Ave 43616

OXFORD (G-10) pop. 21,371, elev. 918'
• Part of Cincinnati area — see map p. 153

A college town with many beautiful and architecturally significant older houses and buildings, Oxford derives much of its charm from the attractive campus of 17,720-student Miami University, founded in 1809. Paul Brown, Weeb Ewbank, Woody Hayes, Ara Parseghian, Bo Schembechler and other gridiron notables are a part of Miami's football history. Points of interest include outdoor sculpture, formal gardens, Kumler Chapel on the Western Campus, and University Art Museum (see attraction listing). Guided tours of the campus are available through the Admissions Office; phone (513) 529-2531. Miami University information is available by phoning (513) 529-1809.

Other features of the town include red brick streets, a variety of locally owned shops, the 1870 Black Covered Bridge, Pioneer Farm & House Museum, golf and disc golf courses, Hueston Woods and hiking trails. Public ice-skating is offered at the

Goggin Ice Center at 610 S. Oak St. Oxford's historic houses include the 1838 Lewis Place, traditional home of the Miami University presidents; the 1837 Simpson House, a guesthouse; the "Coffee Mill House"; and the home of Lorenzo Lorrain Langstroth, inventor of the revolutionary movable comb beehive.

Hueston Woods State Park, 5 miles north on SR 732, offers a variety of recreational opportunities, including hiking, biking and sailing; there also is a nature center; phone (513) 523-6347. *See Recreation Areas Chart.*

Oxford Visitors & Convention Bureau: 14 W. Park Pl., Suite C, Oxford, OH 45056. **Phone:** (513) 523-8687.

Self-guiding tours: The Oxford Visitors & Convention Bureau offers brochures for self-guiding walking tours of the historic uptown area and the Miami University campus; both focus on the areas' historical buildings.

MIAMI UNIVERSITY ART MUSEUM is at 801 S. Patterson Ave. Five galleries present changing exhibits ranging from national loan shows to the museum's permanent collection of contemporary, historical, decorative and ethnographical art. **Time:** Allow 1 hour minimum. **Hours:** Tues.-Fri. 10-5, Sat. noon-5. Closed major holidays and during installations. Phone ahead to confirm schedule. **Cost:** Free. **Phone:** (513) 529-2232.

BEST WESTERN SYCAMORE INN   513/523-0000

APPROVED   Hotel

Best Western. **AAA Benefit:** Members save up to 15% and earn bonus points!

Address: 6 E Sycamore St 45056 **Location:** 0.5 mi n on SR 732. **Facility:** 61 units. 2 stories (no elevator), interior corridors. **Parking:** winter plug-ins. **Pool:** heated indoor. **Activities:** hot tub, exercise room.

THE ELMS HOTEL   513/524-2002
APPROVED   Hotel. **Address:** 75 S Main St 45056

HAMPTON INN BY HILTON OXFORD-MIAMI UNIVERSITY AREA   513/524-2012
THREE DIAMOND SAVE Hotel. **Address:** 375 S College Ave 45056

AAA Benefit: Members save up to 15%!

WHERE TO EAT

DIM SUM YUAN   513/344-7611
APPROVED   Chinese Dim Sum. Casual Dining. **Address:** 313 S College St 45056

MIA   513/523-1541
THREE DIAMOND Italian. Fine Dining. **Address:** 77 S Main St 45056

SKYLINE CHILI   513/523-3330
APPROVED   American. Quick Serve. **Address:** 1 E High St 45056

STEINKELLER   513/524-2437
APPROVED   German. Casual Dining. **Address:** 15 E High St 45056

PAINESVILLE (A-12) pop. 19,563, elev. 676'

LAKE COUNTY HISTORY CENTER, 415 Riverside Dr., is housed in an 1876 Italianate building that once served as the county's infirmary and poor house. The building now features exhibit galleries and a research library. Rotating exhibits include various objects from the 30,000-piece collection. A Civil War wing includes clothing and weapons as well as displays about medicine and the Underground Railroad. The superintendent's original private quarters showcase Victorian lifestyle through period furnishings and clothing, and a formal parlor includes a collection of "Magical Musical Machines," 1900s music boxes.

Behind the center is the Living History Village; visitors can view the exteriors of an 1813 log cabin, a one-room school, a blacksmith shop and a general store. **Hours:** Center open Tues.-Sat. 10-2. Library open Tues.-Fri. by appointment. **Cost:** Center $3; free (ages 0-11). Library $7; free (students). **Phone:** (440) 639-2945.

STEELE MANSION INN & GATHERING HUB   440/639-7948
FOUR DIAMOND Historic Boutique Hotel. **Address:** 348 Mentor Ave 44077

WHERE TO EAT

REDHAWK GRILLE   440/354-4040
APPROVED   American. Casual Dining. **Address:** 7481 Auburn Rd 44077

PEEBLES (H-3) pop. 1,782, elev. 827'

SERPENT MOUND is n. on SR 41, then 4 mi. n.w. on SR 73. One of the finest remaining prehistoric Native American effigy mounds, this immense earthwork's sinuous curves lie on the crest of a ridge paralleling Ohio Brush Creek. The archeological feature is nearly a quarter-mile long and is 5 feet high. The head of the serpent is aligned to the summer solstice sunset. A museum features exhibits about the earthwork and the local geology of an ancient cryptic explosion.

Hours: Park open daily dawn-dusk. Museum open Mon.-Thurs. 10-4, Apr.-Oct. (also Fri.-Sun. 9-5, in May, and Fri.-Sun 9-6, June-Oct.); Sat.-Sun. 10-4, Nov.-Dec. **Cost:** $8 (per private vehicle). **Phone:** (937) 587-2796 or (800) 752-2757.

PENINSULA (C-11) pop. 565, elev. 755'

The Cuyahoga Valley National Park *(see place attraction listing p. 237)* Boston Store Visitor Center is in Peninsula.

PERRYSBURG pop. 20,623, elev. 628'
• Hotels & Restaurants map & index p. 299

CANDLEWOOD SUITES PERRYSBURG   419/872-6161   **30**
APPROVED Extended Stay Hotel. **Address:** 27350 Lake Vue Dr 43551

HILTON GARDEN INN TOLEDO/PERRYSBURG
419/873-0700   **32**
THREE DIAMOND SAVE Hotel. **Address:** 6165 Levis Commons Blvd 43551

| **AAA Benefit:** Members save up to 15%! |

HOME2 SUITES BY HILTON PERRYSBURG LEVIS COMMONS TOLEDO   419/931-8900   **31**
THREE DIAMOND SAVE Extended Stay Hotel. **Address:** 5995 Levis Commons Blvd 43551

| **AAA Benefit:** Members save up to 15%! |

LA QUINTA INN BY WYNDHAM TOLEDO PERRYSBURG
419/872-0000   **29**
APPROVED Hotel. **Address:** 1154 Professional Dr 43551

WHERE TO EAT

BAI DU   419/874-7077   **27**
APPROVED Chinese. Casual Dining. **Address:** 580 Craig Dr 43551

POCO PIATTI   419/931-0281   **29**
THREE DIAMOND Mediterranean Small Plates. Casual Dining. **Address:** 3155 Chappel Dr 43551

SOCIAL GASTROPUB   419/931-9936   **28**
APPROVED American. Gastropub. **Address:** 25818 Dixie Hwy 43551

SWIG RESTAURANT   419/873-6224   **26**
APPROVED American. Casual Dining. **Address:** 219 Louisiana Ave 43551

TEA TREE ASIAN BISTRO   419/874-8828   **30**
THREE DIAMOND Asian. Casual Dining. **Address:** 4100 Chappel Dr 43551

PERRY'S VICTORY AND INTERNATIONAL PEACE MEMORIAL (A-5)

Perry's Victory and International Peace Memorial is reached during summer by automobile and passenger ferry from Catawba and Port Clinton and by plane from Port Clinton. The memorial, at Put-in-Bay (see place listing p. 287) on South Bass Island in Lake Erie, commemorates the Battle of Lake Erie and the ensuing years of peace between the United States, Britain and Canada.

During the War of 1812 Master Commandant Oliver Hazard Perry commanded the American fleet, consisting of the *Lawrence*, the *Niagara* and seven smaller vessels assembled on the British-controlled lake. On Sept. 10, 1813, he met and defeated the British fleet and forced Robert Heriott Barclay's flagship and five other vessels to surrender. Perry then sent his famous message to Gen. William Henry Harrison: "We have met the enemy and they are

ours." This victory made possible both the recapture of Detroit and Gen. Harrison's invasion of Canada.

The memorial is 352 feet high and 45 feet in diameter at its base. Built of pink granite from Milford, Mass., the memorial has an observation deck at 317 feet. The visitor center shows a movie and has exhibits about the Battle of Lake Erie and the building of the monument.

Allow 30 minutes minimum. Visitor center and memorial open daily 10-6, late May to mid-Sept.; daily 10-5, mid-Sept. to early Oct.; Fri.-Mon. 10-5, early Oct.-late Oct. Park rangers provide interpretive talks Mon.-Thurs. on the hour 11-5. Visitor center free. Memorial $5; free (ages 0-15 with adult). Phone (419) 285-2184.

PICKERINGTON (F-5) pop. 18,291, elev. 842'
• Part of Columbus area — see map p. 205

The town was established shortly after 1811 when Abraham and Ann Pickering built a home and trading post. In 1815 it was finally given a name, Jacksonville, commemorating Andrew Jackson's defeat of British forces in the battle of New Orleans during the War of 1812; citizens changed the name to Pickerington in 1827. The 1,608 acres of Pickerington Ponds Wetlands Wildlife Refuge feature observation areas with waterfowl, shorebirds and raptors.

Pickerington Area Chamber of Commerce: 107 W. Columbus St., Pickerington, OH 43147. **Phone:** (614) 837-1958.

BEST WESTERN EXECUTIVE SUITES-COLUMBUS EAST   614/860-9804
APPROVED
Hotel

| **AAA Benefit:** Members save up to 15% and earn bonus points! |

Address: 1899 Winderly Ln 43147 **Location:** I-70 exit 112; eastbound; exit 112A, just sw. **Facility:** 68 units. 3 stories, interior corridors. **Parking:** winter plug-ins. **Pool:** heated indoor. **Activities:** exercise room. **Guest Services:** valet laundry. **Featured Amenity:** full hot breakfast.

HAMPTON INN BY HILTON COLUMBUS EAST
614/864-8383
APPROVED
Hotel

| **AAA Benefit:** Members save up to 15%! |

Address: 1890 Winderly Ln 43147 **Location:** I-70 exit 112 westbound; exit 112A eastbound, just sw. **Facility:** 76 units. 3 stories, interior corridors. **Pool:** heated indoor. **Activities:** limited exercise equipment. **Guest Services:** valet laundry. **Featured Amenity:** full hot breakfast.

WHERE TO EAT

LA FOGATA GRILL 614/864-9154
APPROVED Mexican. Casual Dining. **Address:** 1849 Winderly Ln 43147

SKYLINE CHILI 614/856-9515
APPROVED American. Quick Serve. **Address:** 1530 Cross Creeks Blvd 43147

PIQUA (E-2) pop. 20,522, elev. 884'

Three Native American villages once existed near the present city. In 1747 the Miami tribe built Pickawillany; shortly thereafter an English trading post, Fort Pickawillany, was established, but it was destroyed in 1752 by the French and their Native American allies. In 1780 the Shawnee tribe took possession of this territory. At the end of the century European-American settlers arrived, formally laying out a village in 1807.

The 1891 Fort Piqua Plaza, on the downtown public square at 116 W. High St., is a stone and brick Richardsonian Romanesque building that was once a hotel. The exterior features more than 100 carvings of faces, animals, plants, dragons and other creatures. Former visitors include Harry Houdini, Teddy Roosevelt and John Philip Sousa. It now houses the Piqua Public Library; phone (937) 773-6753.

Remnants of the Miami and Erie Canal, which reached the area in 1837, are visible from Lock Nine Riverfront Park.

Self-guiding tours: Self-guiding walking and driving maps and brochures detailing the historic district—including a brochure about Fort Piqua Plaza's art, architecture and historical artifacts—are available from the library.

Shopping: Miami Valley Centre Mall, at I-75 and US 36, features Dunham's Sports, JCPenney and Sears. Downtown Piqua has antique and specialty shops.

JOHNSTON FARM & INDIAN AGENCY is off I-75 exit 83, 1 mi. w. on CR 25A, 2.5 mi. n. on SR 66, then .2 mi. e. to 9845 N. Hardin Rd. This 1815 two-story brick house on a 250-acre farmstead is furnished as it was in 1829 when John Johnston and his family lived there. A museum features displays about the Eastern Woodland Indians who inhabited the area; Pickawillany, the first large English trading post in Ohio; and the canal era in Ohio. Costumed interpreters lead house tours and demonstrate pioneer crafts, and a mule-drawn canal boat ride takes visitors through a restored portion of the Miami-Erie Canal.

Time: Allow 2 hours minimum. **Hours:** Thurs.-Fri. 10-5, June-Aug.; by appointment Mon.-Fri. 9-2, Apr.-May and Sept.-Oct. Boat rides offered at 12:30, 2:30 and 4. Phone ahead to confirm schedule. **Cost:** (includes canal boat ride) $9; $8 (ages 65+ and military with ID); $4 (ages 6-12). Rates may vary; phone ahead. **Phone:** (937) 773-2522 or (800) 752-2619. GT

COMFORT INN MIAMI VALLEY CENTRE MALL
937/778-8100

APPROVED
Hotel

Address: 987 E Ash St, Suite 171 45356 **Location:** I-75 exit 82, just w. **Facility:** 101 units. 5 stories, interior corridors. **Parking:** winter plug-ins. **Pool:** heated indoor. **Activities:** exercise room. **Guest Services:** valet laundry. **Featured Amenity:** full hot breakfast.

POLAND pop. 2,555

BEST WESTERN PLUS BOARDMAN INN & SUITES
330/629-6900

THREE DIAMOND
Hotel

AAA Benefit: Members save up to 15% and earn bonus points!

Address: 7400 Tiffany S 44514 **Location:** I-680 exit 11, just w. **Facility:** 67 units, some efficiencies. 3 stories, interior corridors. **Pool:** heated indoor. **Activities:** hot tub, exercise room. **Guest Services:** valet and coin laundry.

FAIRFIELD INN & SUITES BY MARRIOTT YOUNGSTOWN BOARDMAN/POLAND
330/726-5979
APPROVED SAVE Hotel. **Address:** 7397 Tiffany S 44514

AAA Benefit: Members save 5% or more!

HAMPTON INN BY HILTON-YOUNGSTOWN
330/758-5191
THREE DIAMOND SAVE Hotel. **Address:** 7395 Tiffany S 44514

AAA Benefit: Members save up to 15%!

WHERE TO EAT

MICHAEL ALBERINI'S RESTAURANT AND WINE SHOP
330/965-2524
THREE DIAMOND Italian. Fine Dining. **Address:** 1140 Boardman-Poland Rd 44514

NICOLINNI'S 330/259-3343
APPROVED Italian. Casual Dining. **Address:** 1247 Boardman-Poland Rd 44514

SPRINGFIELD GRILLE 330/726-0895
THREE DIAMOND Steak. Casual Dining. **Address:** 7413 Tiffany S 44514

PORT CLINTON (B-4) pop. 6,056, elev. 592'
• Hotels p. 286 • Restaurants p. 286

Port Clinton, the self-styled "Walleye Capital of the World," celebrates New Year's Eve with the outdoor Walleye Madness at Midnight, culminating at midnight with fireworks and the descent of a 20-foot, 600-pound fiberglass walleye. The festivities begin late in the afternoon with activities for kids, street vendors and music. Exotic culinary treats such as Walleye Cinnamon Chips and Walleye White wine are available.

Great Lakes Popcorn Co. at 60 N. Madison St., with its red and white striped awning and music playing from outdoor speakers, makes and sells more than 30 flavors of popcorn. Stop in for a sample or to buy a bag or tin to take home.

Lake Erie Shores & Islands Welcome Center— West: 770 S.E. Catawba Rd., Port Clinton, OH 43452. **Phone:** (419) 734-4386 or (800) 441-1271.

AFRICAN SAFARI WILDLIFE PARK is off SR 53, then just e. on SR 163 to 267 S. Lightner Rd. The 100-acre preserve is home to many species of animals roaming free in a natural habitat. Visitors feed the animals from their cars; one free cup of food is provided. Animal programs and a walk-through area also are offered. During the summer season and on select weekends in May and September, animal rides are given and pig races are presented.

Time: Allow 1 hour minimum. **Hours:** Daily 9-7, Memorial Day weekend-Labor Day; 10-5, late Feb.-Thurs. before Memorial Day and day after Labor Day-early Dec. (select Sat.-Sun. 9-6 in May and Sept.; phone to verify). Last car admitted 1 hour before closing. **Cost:** Memorial Day weekend-Labor Day and select Sat.-Sun. in May and Sept. $23.95; $15.95 (ages 4-6). Rest of season $17.95; $11.95 (ages 4-6). **Phone:** (419) 732-3606. [image icons]

GRIFFING FLYING SERVICE is in the Erie-Ottawa International Airport at 3255 E. State Rd. The company offers 20-minute airborne sightseeing tours. Air transportation to the islands and other destinations also is available. **Hours:** Daily 8-5:30 (weather permitting). **Cost:** Sightseeing tours start at $45. Round-trip fare starts at $93.50. Reservations are required. **Phone:** (419) 734-5400. [GT]

BEST WESTERN PORT CLINTON   419/734-2274

▼▼ APPROVED

Hotel

[Best Western logo] Best Western.

AAA Benefit: Members save up to 15% and earn bonus points!

Address: 1734 E Perry St 43452 **Location:** Waterfront. 1.7 mi e on SR 163, w of jct SR 2. **Facility:** 41 units. 2 stories (no elevator), interior/exterior corridors. **Amenities:** safes. **Pool:** outdoor. **Activities:** in-room exercise equipment. **Guest Services:** coin laundry.

[SAVE] [icons] CALL [icons] [BIZ] [icons]
[icons]
/ SOME UNITS [icons] [HS]

COUNTRY INN & SUITES BY RADISSON   419/732-2434
▼▼THREE DIAMOND Hotel. **Address:** 3760 E State Rd 43452

HOLIDAY INN EXPRESS HOTEL & SUITES-PORT CLINTON/ CATAWBA ISLAND   419/732-7322
▼▼THREE DIAMOND Hotel. **Address:** 50 NE Catawba Rd 43452

QUALITY INN   419/732-2929
▼▼ APPROVED Hotel. **Address:** 1723 E Perry St 43452

DIANNA'S DELI & RESTAURANT   419/732-2200
▼▼ APPROVED American. Casual Dining. **Address:** 2853 E Harbor Rd 43452

MON AMI RESTAURANT   419/797-4445
▼▼THREE DIAMOND American. Casual Dining. **Address:** 3845 E Wine Cellar Rd 43452

NAGOYA JAPANESE STEAKHOUSE AND SUSHI
419/734-6400
▼▼ APPROVED Japanese. Sushi. Casual Dining. **Address:** 3975 E Harbor Rd 43452

THE ORCHARD RESTAURANT & BAR   419/797-7324
▼▼THREE DIAMOND American. Casual Dining. **Address:** 3266 NE Catawba Rd 43452

PORTSMOUTH (H-4) pop. 20,226, elev. 532'

At the confluence of the Ohio and Scioto rivers, Portsmouth was a manufacturing center where steel and clay products were made for more than 100 years. The Ohio & Erie Canal that once ran from Cleveland to Portsmouth impacted the development of the area, but the great flood of 1913 terminated canal use in this region. Many of the city's 19th-century buildings are restored, including structures in the Boneyfiddle District.

Portsmouth was the boyhood home of motion picture and television cowboy star Roy Rogers, who was born in Cincinnati in 1911 but lived here most of his first 17 years, and of baseball great Branch Rickey, who broke the major league baseball color barrier in 1947 when he signed Jackie Robinson to play for the Brooklyn Dodgers. Both men are depicted in the 2,000-foot-long Portsmouth Floodwall Murals along Front Street on the Ohio River; the 50-plus scenes chronicle more than 2,000 years of Portsmouth and Scioto County history.

Shawnee State Park, which occupies former Shawnee hunting grounds, lies west; phone (740) 858-6621. *See Recreation Areas Chart.*

Portsmouth - Scioto County Visitors Bureau: 342 2nd St., Portsmouth, OH 45662. **Phone:** (740) 353-1116.

Shopping: Antique shops are found in Boneyfiddle Historic District.

FRED'S PIZZA EXPRESS   740/353-1218
▼▼ APPROVED Pizza. Casual Dining. **Address:** 1920 11th St 45662

POWELL (E-4) pop. 11,500, elev. 922'

• Hotels & Restaurants map & index p. 222
• Part of Columbus area — see map p. 205

[GEM logo] **COLUMBUS ZOO AND AQUARIUM** is off I-270 Sawmill Rd. exit, following signs to jct. Riverside Dr. and Powell Rd. The zoo, which opened in 1927, has six regions totaling nearly 140 acres of gardens and natural habitats. Stroll on paths, many though wooded areas, to travel among

(See map & index p. 222.)

the zoo's regions: Congo Expedition, Heart of Africa, Asia Quest, Australia and the Islands, North America and Shores, and Jungle Jack's Landing. More than 10,000 animals representing more than 600 species call the zoo home.

Enjoy a walking safari through the forests of Africa and see bonobos (pygmy chimpanzees), colobus monkeys, gorillas (including Colo, the first gorilla born in human care), a leopard, mandrills, okapi and red river hogs. The new 43-acre Heart of Africa exhibit offers a variety of animals, including cheetahs, lions, gazelles and wildebeests; visitors also have the opportunity to ride a camel and feed giraffes. In Asia Quest, exotic animals—Asian elephants, giant fruit bats, red pandas, pheasants and Amur tigers—roam their habitats.

In the Australia and the Islands region, check out the Kangaroo Walk-about, where you can get surprisingly close to these Aussies. Only a roped path separates onlookers from the kangaroos, who hop around on a grassy lawn and recline under trees. A bird sanctuary, koalas, komodo dragons, nocturnal animals, orangutans and otters complete this group.

In the section devoted to North American creatures, polar bears swim and play in a 167,000-gallon pool or recline on rocks above water, soaking in the sun at Polar Frontier. North America also is home to brown bears, black bears, bison, eagles, Arctic foxes, Mexican wolves, moose, otters, trumpeter swans, cougars and wolverines as well as a songbird aviary.

Manatees occupy a 250,000-gallon home in the Shores region, which also houses alligators, Humboldt penguins, the Discovery Reef aquarium, a touch pool and a reptile house.

Rides include a 1914 carousel, train and pony rides and a boat ride through the Islands of Southeast Asia; there also are two playgrounds and a marine-themed play space. Jungle Jack's Landing is home to 13 amusement park rides, including a 1,250-foot log flume with two drops, a roller coaster and a whirligig. You also can touch docile cownose and Southern stingrays in the 18,000-gallon saltwater pool at Stingray Bay.

Hours: Daily 9-7, June-Aug. (with special hours for the Zoofari event); 9-5, Mar.-May and in Sept.; 10-5, Oct.-Dec.; 10-4, rest of year (also Sun.-Thurs. 5-9, Fri.-Sat. 5-10, Nov.-Dec. for Wildlights event). Carousel and train rides open daily 10-close. **Cost:** $21.99; $16.99 (ages 3-9 and 60+). Franklin County residents $16.99; $11.99 (ages 3-9 and 60+). Combination 2-day ticket with Zoombezi Bay $48.99; $36.99 (ages 3-9). Combination 2-day ticket with Zoombezi Bay (Franklin County residents) $43.99; $31.99 (ages 3-9). Half-off admission is offered for ages 60+ Tues. Pony ride $5. Carousel $2. Train $2. Stingray Bay $3. Zoo-It-All wristband (admission to zoo not included) $14.99. Ride wristband (admission to zoo not included) $9.99. Phone to verify rates. **Parking:** $10. **Phone:** (614) 645-3550 or (800) 666-5397. [Ⅱ]

Columbus Zoo and Aquarium

Zoombezi Bay is at 4850 Powell Rd. at the Columbus Zoo and Aquarium. The park features 19 water attractions including a wave pool, a children's splash pool, an action river, an adults-only river and Baboon Lagoon—a multilevel play structure with 90 interactive aquatic controls, waterslides and a 1,000-gallon tipping water bucket, and Otter Banks — a new aquatic adventure area that includes two waterslides with a surprise drop at the end, a challenging aquacourse and an activity pool complete with cascading waterfalls and water basketball.

Hours: Open daily at 10:30, Memorial Day weekend-Labor Day; closing hours vary by season. **Cost:** $34.99; $26.99 (ages 3-9 and 60+). Combination 2-day ticket with Columbus Zoo and Aquarium $48.99; $36.99 (ages 3-9 and 60+). Combination 2-day ticket with Columbus Zoo and Aquarium (Franklin County residents) $43.99; $31.99 (ages 3-9 and 60+). **Parking:** $10. **Phone:** (614) 724-3600 or (800) 666-5397.

CITY BARBEQUE   614/224-8224
▼ **APPROVED** Barbecue. Quick Serve. **Address:** 3758 W Powell Rd 43065

VITTORIA RISTORANTE & BAR   614/791-8100 [56]
▼**THREE DIAMOND** Italian. Fine Dining. **Address:** 10241 Sawmill Pkwy 43065

PUT-IN-BAY (B-5) pop. 138, elev. 568'
• Restaurants p. 288

You won't find an abundance of cars at this popular summer resort destination. Although vehicles are permitted on South Bass Island, parking is very limited. The alternative is to rent a bicycle or golf cart once you arrive. The main visitation season runs April through October; if you prefer fewer crowds, consider visiting Sunday through Thursday. Two ferries provide transportation from the mainland. Jet Express Ferry, (800) 245-1538, carries passengers from Port Clinton and Sandusky to the island May through October. Miller Boat Line, (419) 285-2421 or (800) 500-2421, transports passengers and automobiles late March through November from Catawba Island. In addition to its extensive access to Lake Erie, the island's other claim to fame is Perry's Victory and International Peace Memorial *(see place listing p. 284)*, just outside the village.

Lake Erie affords great recreational opportunities like boating, kayaking, parasailing, sailing and jet skiing; there are multiple places to rent watercraft. Put-In-Bay has two public beaches, both of which offer nice scenery; a sandy beach is at the end of Delaware Avenue and a pebble beach is in South Bass Island State Park. A boat ramp is located downtown next to the Jet Express Ferry dock. You can fish at South Bass Island and Oak Point state parks; picnicking is permitted at both. South Bass Island State Park also offers camping facilities, boat rentals and a launch ramp, and if you look closely at some of the limestone bedrock in the park, you may be able to see some glacial striations, small grooves created from rocks in the glaciers that once covered the area. If you plan to fish with children while you're here, you may want to go to the Aquatic Visitors Center on SR 357. The facility offers free bait and fishing gear for those under age 16.

There are many other activities to occupy your time. Watch the lake and Delaware Avenue activity from DeRivera Park, a grassy area with picnic tables, benches, a fountain and a playground. The area is a good locale for bird-watching, particularly May 1-20 and in September during migrations. Stroll the downtown streets and do some boutique and souvenir shopping. Pop into the Carriage House gift shop, 150 Delaware Ave., to buy tickets to ride Kimberly's Carousel, a 1917 Allen Herschel creation from North Tonawanda, N.Y., that usually runs mid-June through Labor Day. Several dozen special events are held during the main tourist season. A regularly held event is an antique car parade passing through downtown each Sunday afternoon—a big treat for classic and historic car fans.

Put-in-Bay Chamber of Commerce & Visitors Bureau: 148 Delaware Ave., Put-in-Bay, OH 43456. **Phone:** (419) 285-2832.

PUT-IN-BAY TOUR TRAIN boards at the depot at 154 Delaware Ave. One-hour narrated guided tours traverse South Bass Island. The tours allow passengers to disembark at several different areas and reboard without cost. **Hours:** Tours depart daily every 30 minutes 10:15-5:15, Memorial Day weekend-Labor Day weekend; Sat.-Sun. every hour 10:15-5:15, third Sun. in Sept.-fourth Sun. in Oct. Phone

ahead to confirm schedule. **Cost:** $10; $5 (ages 6-12). Phone ahead to confirm prices. **Phone:** (419) 285-4855. GT

HOOLIGANS IRISH PUB   419/285-8000
▼▼▼ APPROVED   Irish. Gastropub. **Address:** 421 Catawba Ave 43456

REYNOLDSBURG pop. 35,893
• Part of Columbus area — see map p. 205

FAIRFIELD INN & SUITES BY MARRIOTT COLUMBUS EAST
                                        614/864-4555
▼▼▼ APPROVED SAVE Hotel. **Ad-**   **AAA Benefit:**
dress: 2826 Taylor Rd Ext 43068   Members save 5%
                                        or more!

HOLIDAY INN EXPRESS & SUITES COLUMBUS EAST
                                        614/861-8888
▼▼▼ APPROVED   Hotel. **Address:** 2806 Taylor Rd Ext 43068

WHERE TO EAT

THE HICKORY HOUSE   614/861-5962
▼▼▼ APPROVED   American. Casual Dining. **Address:** 7051
E Main St 43068

RICHFIELD pop. 3,648
• Hotels & Restaurants map & index p. 194
• Part of Cleveland area — see map p. 177

HAMPTON INN BY HILTON   330/659-6662 112
▼▼▼ THREE DIAMOND   **AAA Benefit:**
     Hotel   Members save up to
                                   15%!

Address: 4860 Brecksville Rd 44286
Location: I-80 exit 173, just s; I-77 southbound exit 146, 0.5 mi s; northbound exit 145, 0.5 mi n. **Facility:** 64 units. 3 stories, interior corridors. **Pool:** heated indoor. **Activities:** exercise room. **Guest Services:** valet and coin laundry.

SAVE ¶↑ CALL & ◢ ⊞ BIZ
⊚ ⊠ ⋮ ⊟ ⊡

WHERE TO EAT

COZUMEL RESTAURANT AND CANTINA 234/400-0401 81
▼▼▼ APPROVED   Mexican. Casual Dining. **Address:** 4880
Brecksville Rd 44286

ROSSFORD pop. 6,293
• Hotels & Restaurants map & index p. 299

COUNTRY INN & SUITES BY RADISSON, TOLEDO
SOUTH   419/872-9900 23
▼▼▼ APPROVED   **Address:** 9790 Clark Dr 43460 **Loca-**
     Hotel   **tion:** I-75 exit 195A, just e. **Facility:** 80 units. 3 stories, interior corridors. **Pool:** heated indoor. **Activities:** hot tub, exercise room. **Guest Services:** valet and coin laundry. **Featured Amenity:** breakfast buffet.

SAVE CALL &   BIZ HS
 ⊚ ⊠ ⋮ ⊟ ⊡
/ SOME
  UNITS 🛏

(See map & index p. 299.)

COURTYARD BY MARRIOTT TOLEDO PERRYSBURG/ROSSFORD   419/872-5636   **24**

 THREE DIAMOND SAVE Hotel. **Address:** 9789 Clark Dr 43460

AAA Benefit: Members save 5% or more!

HAMPTON INN & SUITES TOLEDO-PERRYSBURG   419/662-8800   **25**

 **THREE DIAMOND**

Hotel

Hampton

AAA Benefit: Members save up to 15%!

Address: 9753 Clark Dr 43460 **Location:** I-75 exit 195A, just e. **Facility:** 98 units. 4 stories, interior corridors. **Pool:** heated indoor. **Activities:** exercise room. **Guest Services:** valet and coin laundry.

SAVE CALL (access) (dumbbell) (cross) BIZ HS
(wifi) (X) (fridge) (laptop) / SOME UNITS (no-smoking) (microwave)

STAYBRIDGE SUITES TOLEDO-ROSSFORD-PERRYSBURG   419/872-3700   **26**

 THREE DIAMOND Extended Stay Hotel. **Address:** 9749 Clark Dr 43460

ST. CLAIRSVILLE (E-8) pop. 5,184, elev. 1,266'

St. Clairsville is about 2 hours south of Akron. The downtown historic district features a mix of houses and retail and office buildings from the 1800s and early 1900s. The charm of Main Street is enhanced with lovely hanging flower baskets.

AMERICAS BEST VALUE INN ST. CLAIRSVILLE/WHEELING   740/695-5038

 APPROVED

Motel

Address: 51260 National Rd 43950 **Location:** I-70 exit 218, 0.5 mi ne on US 40. **Facility:** 104 units, some efficiencies. 1 story, exterior corridors. **Parking:** winter plug-ins. **Pool:** outdoor. **Guest Services:** coin laundry. **Featured Amenity: continental breakfast.**

SAVE (fork) CALL (access) (dumbbell) HS (wifi)
(fridge) (laptop) / SOME UNITS (no-smoking) (microwave)

BEST WESTERN ST. CLAIRSVILLE INN & SUITES   740/699-0010

 APPROVED

Hotel

BW **Best Western.**

AAA Benefit: Members save up to 15% and earn bonus points!

Address: 51654 National Rd E 43950 **Location:** I-70 exit 218, 0.5 mi ne on US 40. **Facility:** 65 units. 3 stories, interior corridors. **Pool:** heated indoor. **Activities:** exercise room. **Guest Services:** valet and coin laundry.

SAVE (fork) CALL (access) (dumbbell) (cross) BIZ
(wifi) (X) (fridge) (laptop) (microwave)

CANDLEWOOD SUITES ST. CLAIRSVILLE   740/695-9200

 THREE DIAMOND Extended Stay Contemporary Hotel. **Address:** 67689 Mall Ring Rd 43950

COMFORT INN   740/296-5549

 THREE DIAMOND Hotel. **Address:** 52509 National Rd 43950

FAIRFIELD INN & SUITES BY MARRIOTT WHEELING-ST. CLAIRSVILLE   740/699-4980

 APPROVED SAVE Hotel. **Address:** 67731 Mall Rd 43950

AAA Benefit: Members save 5% or more!

HAWTHORN SUITES BY WYNDHAM   740/650-2035

 THREE DIAMOND Hotel. **Address:** 51110 National Rd E 43950

MICROTEL INN & SUITES BY WYNDHAM   740/338-4500

 APPROVED Hotel. **Address:** 51128 National Rd E 43950

RED ROOF INN ST CLAIRSVILLE-WHEELING WEST   740/695-4057

 APPROVED

Motel

Address: 68301 Red Roof Ln 43950 **Location:** I-70 exit 218, just n. Located near Ohio Valley Mall. **Facility:** 108 units. 2 stories (no elevator), exterior corridors. **Amenities:** safes.

SAVE CALL (access) (wifi) (X) (cross) (fridge)
(laptop) / SOME UNITS (no-smoking) (microwave)

RESIDENCE INN BY MARRIOTT WHEELING-ST. CLAIRSVILLE, OH   740/695-9320

 THREE DIAMOND SAVE Extended Stay Contemporary Hotel. **Address:** 50694 Ohio Valley Pl 43950

AAA Benefit: Members save 5% or more!

WINGATE BY WYNDHAM ST. CLAIRSVILLE/WHEELING   740/695-3961

 THREE DIAMOND Hotel. **Address:** 51130 National Rd E 43950

WHERE TO EAT

EAT'N PARK   740/695-5507

 APPROVED American. Casual Dining. **Address:** 50620 Valley Centre Blvd 43950

MEHLMAN CAFETERIA   740/695-1000

 APPROVED American. Buffet Style. **Address:** 51800 National Rd 43950

TLAQUEPAQUE MEXICAN GRILL & RESTAURANT   740/695-2560

 APPROVED Mexican. Casual Dining. **Address:** 50601 Valley Plaza Dr 43950

UNDO'S WEST   740/695-8888

 APPROVED Italian. Casual Dining. **Address:** 51130 National Rd E 43950

WEST TEXAS ROADHOUSE   740/695-6611

 APPROVED

Steak
Casual Dining
$9-$24

AAA Inspector Notes: Near the Ohio Valley Mall, this restaurant plays with its Western theme with animal skins along the unfinished wooden walls and country music playing in the background. Don't fill up on the peanuts that will be brought to your table as the menu has a number of hearty dishes, including steaks, tender ribs, burgers and chicken entrées. Freshly baked bread, spicy Texas chili and homemade desserts round out the menu. **Features:** full bar. **Address:** 50880 National Rd 43950 **Location:** I-70 exit 218, just n. [L] [D]

SANDUSKY (B-5) pop. 25,793, elev. 597'

Although Sandusky was explored by Robert La-Salle in 1679 and visited by English trader George Croghan in 1760, it was not until 1816 that the town was settled. Its location on Sandusky Bay, a natural harbor on Lake Erie formed by the Cedar Point and Marblehead peninsulas, quickly made it a major center of shipping and industry. It is one of the largest coal-shipping ports on the Great Lakes.

Sandusky still has time for relaxation; its lakeside resorts, abundant fishing opportunities and access to Lake Erie's islands make it a popular summer vacation spot.

Lake Erie Shores & Islands Welcome Center—East: 216 E. Water St., Sandusky, OH 44870. **Phone:** (419) 625-2984 or (800) 255-3743.

Shopping: Off the Ohio Turnpike exit 118 on US 250 is Sandusky Mall; department stores include JCPenney and T.J. Maxx.

CASTAWAY BAY, 2001 Cleveland Rd., is an indoor water park with a Caribbean theme featuring waterslides, a giant tree house with a variety of children's activities, a wave pool with 3-foot-high waves, a toddler tide pool and adults-only hot tubs. Lounge chairs are scattered throughout the park.

Lockers are available. **Time:** Allow 2 hours minimum. **Hours:** Daily 9 a.m.-10 p.m., June-Aug. Schedule varies in the off-season; phone ahead to confirm. **Cost:** $29; free (ages 0-2); $15 (after 5 p.m.). Phone ahead to verify rates. **Phone:** (419) 627-2500. ⊓

CEDAR POINT is off US 6, 10 mi. n. of Ohio Tpke. exit 118 at 1 Cedar Point Dr. This 364-acre amusement/theme park and resort opened in 1870. Cedar Point offers more than 150 rides, shows and attractions, including 17 roller coasters and more than a dozen thrill rides. Valravn reaches 75 mph and includes a 90-degree drop. Other coasters include Steel Vengeance, a hybrid of steel and wood; Rougarou, a floorless coaster; the 420-foot-tall, 120 mph Top Thrill Dragster; the 310-foot-tall Millennium Force; the six-inversion Raptor; Magnum XL-200, the first roller coaster to break the 200-foot barrier; and GateKeeper, a winged coaster. Two water rides offer refreshing thrills. SlingShot is a two-person experience that launches participants 360 feet in the air. Other thrill rides include Ocean Motion (a ship that swings back and forth), Scrambler, Power Tower and WindSeeker.

If all those sound a bit intense, fear not. Most of the park's rides cater to families and young children. Pipe Scream takes riders back and forth several times across a 300-foot track, twisting and turning as it maneuvers across the hills. On Lake Erie Eagles riders fly in individual eagle cars and can control how mild or wild to make their flight. There are also carousels, three kids' areas, the Cedar Point & Lake Erie Railroad and an array of other classic amusement park rides.

Cedar Point also presents a variety of live shows, including the high-energy nighttime show Luminosity and several shows starring PEANUTS characters like Snoopy, Lucy and Charlie Brown. Other offerings are pioneer crafts, a marina and a sandy beach on the shore of Lake Erie. The Forbidden Frontier on Adventure Island offers an interactive adventure using both brain and brute power.

HalloWeekends is an annual fall favorite that offers daytime events like a parade and The Great Pumpkin Fest as well as the nighttime Haunt. Select rides are open Friday nights and all non-water rides are usually open on Saturdays and Sundays.

Hours: Cedar Point opens daily at 10 (closing times are between 8 p.m. and midnight), mid-May through Labor Day; open Fri. 6 p.m.-midnight, Sat.-Sun. all day for HalloWeekends (park opens at 11 and closes between 8 p.m. and midnight), mid-Sept. to late Oct. Phone ahead to confirm schedule.

Cost: $74; $46 (ages 62+ and under 48 inches tall in shoes); free (ages 0-2). Reduced admission is available after 4 p.m. Multiday combination tickets with Cedar Point Shores are available. Fast Lane wristbands may be purchased to help minimize wait times at certain rides. Phone ahead to verify all rates. **Parking:** $20. **Phone:** (419) 627-2350. ⊓

Cedar Point Shores is at the n.e. corner of Cedar Point amusement park off US 6, 10 mi. n. of Ohio Tpke. exit 118, at 1 Cedar Point Dr. A variety of additions to this 18-acre water park include the six-story Point Plummet four-person drop as well as Portside Plunge, which features two five-story tube slides. Also new is Lakeslide Landing and Lemmy's Lagoon, a family-play area with 12 waterslides for kids, geysers, water toys and a lounge area for parents. Existing attractions have undergone makeovers as well.

Hours: Opens daily at 11 (closing times between 6 and 8 p.m.), Memorial Day weekend-Labor Day. Phone ahead to confirm schedule. **Cost:** $39.99; $25 (ages 62+ and under 48 inches tall in bare feet); free (ages 0-2). Multiday combination tickets with Cedar Point are available. Phone ahead to verify all rates. **Parking:** $20. **Phone:** (419) 627-2350. ⊓

COOKE-DORN HOUSE is at 1415 Columbus Ave. This three-story 1844 house was built by Eleutheros Cooke, Sandusky's first lawyer and a politician. By 1878 Cooke and his wife, Martha, had died and the house was moved to its current location; since then, it has changed ownership several times. The furnishings, mostly from the 1950s, are in mint condition and reflect the wealth of the Dorn family, the last residents of the house. The first two floors are open to the public. A garden and greenhouse also are featured.

Time: Allow 30 minutes minimum. **Hours:** Tues.-Fri. noon-3, Sat. 10-1, Apr.-Dec.; by appointment rest of year. Closed major holidays. Phone ahead to confirm schedule. **Cost:** Free. **Phone:** (419) 627-0640 or (877) 734-1386. GT

FOLLETT HOUSE MUSEUM is 2 blks. s. of US 6 at 404 Wayne St. The 1834 Greek Revival stone mansion was built by prominent businessman Oran Follett, who fought against slavery and helped establish the Republican Party. Items displayed reflect Erie County history from its earliest times to the present, including a collection of Civil War items from the Confederate officers' prison on Johnson's Island.

Guided tours are available by appointment. **Time:** Allow 1 hour minimum. **Hours:** Wed. and Fri. noon-4, Sat. 10-1, June-Aug.; Sat. noon-4, Apr.-May and Sept.-Dec. Phone for holiday closures. **Cost:** Free. **Phone:** (419) 627-9608, or (419) 625-3834 (Sandusky Library) to schedule a guided tour. GT

GHOSTLY MANOR THRILL CENTER is 2.2 mi. n. of SR 2 at 3319 Milan Rd. This family entertainment spot features Ghostly Manor Haunted House, a 4-D movie theater, bounce houses, a play area and a roller skating rink. Wizard's Journey is an indoor 3-D miniature golf course. **Hours:** Opens daily at noon; closing times vary.

Cost: Thrill Pass $25 (includes haunted house, 4-D theater, roller skating and miniature golf). Junior Thrill Pass $22 (includes 4-D theater, roller skating, bounce houses, play area and miniature golf). Jump Climb & Skate Pass $11 (includes roller skating, bounce houses and play area). Ghostly Manor Haunted House $11. Wizard's Journey $7. Bounce houses (includes play area) $7. Play area $3. Roller skating $5 plus $2 rental (roller skates, Rollerblades or scooter). 4-D Movie: $7 (one); $12 (two); $16 (three); $20 (four); $24 (five). **Phone:** (419) 626-4467. ▮▮

MARITIME MUSEUM OF SANDUSKY is at 125 Meigs St. across from Battery Park. Local maritime history is revealed through exhibits about a variety of topics, including boatbuilding, commercial fishing and shipping, ice harvesting, navigation, recreational boating and shipwrecks. A 15-minute film about the area's 19th- and 20th-century history is shown in a small theater. Interactive exhibits provide additional detailed information about maritime stories. Several restored boats are on the grounds. Also offered is an exhibit where children can build model boats. Changing exhibits are presented as well.

Time: Allow 1 hour minimum. **Hours:** Tues.-Sat. 10-4, Sun. noon-4, June-Aug.; Fri.-Sat. 10-4, Sun. noon-4, rest of year. Closed major holidays. **Cost:** $7; $6 (ages 0-11 and 62+); $18 (family). **Phone:** (419) 624-0274.

MERRY-GO-ROUND MUSEUM is at 301 Jackson St. at W. Washington St. The museum features a working merry-go-round, exhibits, photographs and carving demonstrations as well as animals and chariots from carousels. **Time:** Allow 1 hour minimum. **Hours:** Mon.-Sat. 10-4, Sun. noon-4, Memorial Day-Labor Day; Wed.-Sat. 11-4, Sun. noon-4, Mar. 1-day before Memorial Day and day after Labor Day-Dec. 31; Sat. 11-4, Sun. noon-4, in Feb. Last tour begins 1

hour, 15 minutes before closing. **Cost:** $6; $5 (ages 60+); $4 (ages 4-14). **Phone:** (419) 626-6111. GT

BEST WESTERN PLUS SANDUSKY HOTEL & SUITES
419/627-9595

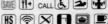

THREE DIAMOND Hotel

AAA Benefit: Members save up to 15% and earn bonus points!

Address: 6011 Milan Rd 44870 **Location:** Jct SR 2, just se on US 250. **Facility:** 89 units, some two bedrooms. 4 stories, interior corridors. **Amenities:** safes. **Pool:** heated indoor. **Activities:** game room, exercise room. **Guest Services:** valet and coin laundry. **Featured Amenity:** continental breakfast.

CEDAR STABLES INN   419/626-6761
fyi Boutique Hotel. Under major renovation, call for details. **Last Designation:** Three Diamond. **Address:** 1935 E Cleveland Rd 44870

COMFORT INN SANDUSKY   419/621-0200
APPROVED Hotel. **Address:** 5909 Milan Rd 44870

FAIRFIELD INN & SUITES BY MARRIOTT   419/621-9500
THREE DIAMOND SAVE Hotel. **Address:** 6220 Milan Rd 44870

AAA Benefit: Members save 5% or more!

GREAT WOLF LODGE   419/609-6000
THREE DIAMOND Resort Hotel. **Address:** 4600 Milan Rd 44870

HAMPTON INN BY HILTON SANDUSKY CENTRAL
419/609-9000
APPROVED SAVE Hotel. **Address:** 6100 Milan Rd 44870

AAA Benefit: Members save up to 15%!

HOLIDAY INN EXPRESS & SUITES   419/624-1515
THREE DIAMOND Hotel. **Address:** 1515 Cedar Point Dr 44870

LA QUINTA INN SANDUSKY-CEDAR POINT   419/626-6766
APPROVED Motel. **Address:** 3304 Milan Rd 44870

SOUTH SHORE INN   419/626-4436
APPROVED Motel. **Address:** 2047 Cleveland Rd 44870

WHERE TO EAT

THE BRICK OVEN BISTRO   419/624-1400
APPROVED Pizza. Casual Dining. **Address:** 1012 Cleveland Rd 44870

CHET & MATT'S   419/626-6000
APPROVED Pizza. Casual Dining. **Address:** 1013 E Strub Rd 44870

CRUSH WINE BAR   419/502-9463
THREE DIAMOND Small Plates. Casual Dining. **Address:** 145 Columbus Ave 44870

DANNY BOY'S ITALIAN EATERY   419/621-1000
APPROVED Italian Pizza. Casual Dining. **Address:** 6207 Milan Rd 44870

MANNY'S SPORTS TAVERN 419/626-9517
▼ APPROVED American. Sports Bar. **Address:** 6201 Milan Rd 44870

MEKONG AUTHENTIC VIETNAMESE CUISINE 419/502-9476
▼ APPROVED Vietnamese. Casual Dining. **Address:** 3321 Milan Rd 44870

RED GABLES MESQUITE GRILL 419/625-0036
▼ APPROVED Steak. Casual Dining. **Address:** 2350 Cleveland Rd 44870

SAMURAI 419/609-6888
▼ APPROVED Japanese. Casual Dining. **Address:** 5500 Milan Rd 44870

THE THIRSTY PONY 419/626-6761
▼ APPROVED American. Sports Bar. **Address:** 1935 Cleveland Rd 44870

ZINC BRASSERIE 419/502-9462
▼ THREE DIAMOND French. Casual Dining. **Address:** 215 E Water St 44870

SEVILLE pop. 2,296

QUALITY INN & SUITES 330/769-4949
▼ APPROVED Hotel. **Address:** 4949 Park Ave W 44273

SUPER 8-SEVILLE 330/769-8880
▼ APPROVED Hotel. **Address:** 6116 Speedway Dr 44273

WHERE TO EAT

AMERICAN HERITAGE RESTAURANT 330/769-9900
▼ APPROVED American. Casual Dining. **Address:** 31 W Main St 44273

SHARONVILLE (H-11) pop. 13,560, elev. 587'
- Hotels & Restaurants map & index p. 166
- Part of Cincinnati area — see map p. 153

HERITAGE VILLAGE MUSEUM is 1 mi. s. of I-275 exit 46 on US 42 in Sharon Woods Park. The village consists of restored 19th-century buildings moved from other areas of southwest Ohio. A medical office has Civil War medical and pharmaceutical equipment. The 1804 Kemper Log House contains period furnishings. Greek Revival, rural Federal and Carpenter Gothic architecture is represented.

Outbuildings include an early 1800s barn with agricultural tools, a corncrib, icehouse and smokehouse. **Time:** Allow 2 hours minimum. **Hours:** Wed.-Sat. 10-5, Sun. 1-5, May-Sept.; Wed.-Fri. 10-4, rest of year. Guided tours depart Wed.-Sat. at 10:30, 12:45 and 3, Sun. at 1:30 and 3:30, May-Sept. Building interiors are only accessible during guided tours. **Cost:** Guided tour $5; $3 (ages 5-11). Self-guiding tour $3; $1 (ages 5-11). Prices may vary during special events. **Phone:** (513) 563-9484. GT

DRURY INN & SUITES-CINCINNATI SHARONVILLE
513/771-5601 48
▼ THREE DIAMOND Hotel. **Address:** 2265 E Sharon Rd 45241

HAWTHORN SUITES BY WYNDHAM 513/354-1000 45
▼ APPROVED Extended Stay Hotel. **Address:** 11180 Dowlin Dr 45241

HILTON GARDEN INN CINCINNATI/SHARONVILLE
513/772-2837 47
▼ THREE DIAMOND
Hotel

Hilton Garden Inn **AAA Benefit:** Members save up to 15%!

Address: 11149 Dowlin Dr 45241 **Location:** I-75 exit 15, just e. **Facility:** 90 units. 3 stories, interior corridors. **Pool:** heated indoor. **Activities:** exercise room. **Guest Services:** valet and coin laundry.
SAVE 🍴 CALL ♿ 🏊 ✚ BIZ
HS 🛜 ✕ 🛗 🛗 🖥

HOLIDAY INN EXPRESS HOTEL & SUITES
513/771-9080 46
▼ APPROVED Hotel. **Address:** 11160 Dowlin Dr 45241

HYATT PLACE CINCINNATI/SHARONVILLE CONVENTION CENTER 513/771-1718 44
▼ THREE DIAMOND
Hotel

HYATT PLACE **AAA Benefit:** Members save up to 10%!

Address: 11345 Chester Rd 45246 **Location:** I-75 exit 15, just w on Sharon Rd, then 0.5 mi n. **Facility:** 125 units. 5 stories, interior corridors. **Amenities:** safes. **Pool:** heated indoor. **Activities:** exercise room. **Guest Services:** valet and coin laundry. **Featured Amenity:** breakfast buffet.
SAVE 🍷 CALL ♿ 🏊 ✚ BIZ
🛜 ✕ 🛗 🖥 / SOME UNITS 🐾

LIVINN HOTELS 513/772-7877 43
▼ APPROVED Hotel. **Address:** 11385 Chester Rd 45246

SONESTA ES SUITES CINCINNATI SHARONVILLE EAST
513/772-8888 42
▼ THREE DIAMOND
Extended Stay
Hotel

Address: 2670 E Kemper Rd 45241 **Location:** I-275 exit 44, just s. **Facility:** 112 units, some efficiencies. 3 stories, interior corridors. **Pool:** outdoor. **Activities:** hot tub, exercise room. **Guest Services:** valet and coin laundry. **Featured Amenity:** breakfast buffet.
SAVE CALL ♿ 🏊 ✚ BIZ 🛜
✕ 🛗 🛗 🖥 / SOME UNITS 🐾

SONESTA ES SUITES CINCINNATI SHARONVILLE WEST
513/771-2525 41
▼ APPROVED
Extended Stay
Hotel

Address: 11689 Chester Rd 45246 **Location:** I-75 exit 15, just w on Sharon Rd, then 1 mi n. **Facility:** 144 units, some two bedrooms, efficiencies and kitchens. 2 stories (no elevator), exterior corridors. **Pool:** heated outdoor. **Activities:** exercise room. **Guest Services:** valet and coin laundry. **Featured Amenity:** breakfast buffet.
SAVE CALL ♿ 🏊 ✚ BIZ 🛜
✕ 🛗 🛗 🖥 / SOME UNITS 🐾

(See map & index p. 166.)

WHERE TO EAT

VINCENZO'S RISTORANTE ITALIANO   513/771-0022 (42)
THREE DIAMOND Italian. Casual Dining. **Address:** 11525 Chester Rd 45246

SHEFFIELD VILLAGE

HOMEWOOD SUITES BY HILTON   440/695-0735
THREE DIAMOND SAVE Extended Stay Hotel. **Address:** 4930 Transportation Dr 44054

AAA Benefit: Members save up to 15%!

WHERE TO EAT

QUAKER STEAK & LUBE   440/934-9464
APPROVED American. Sports Bar. **Address:** 4900 Transportation Dr 44054

SIDNEY (E-2) pop. 21,229, elev. 1,003'

Named for poet and British Parliament member Sir Philip Sidney, the town was established on donated land. The 192 acres of Tawawa Civic Park, off I-75 exit 92 and east on SR 47, contain a covered bridge, bike trails, sports fields and picnic areas.

Sidney Visitors Bureau: 101 S. Ohio Ave., Floor 2, Sidney, OH 45365. **Phone:** (937) 492-9122 or (866) 892-9122.

GREATSTONE CASTLE   937/498-4728
THREE DIAMOND Historic Bed & Breakfast. **Address:** 429 N Ohio Ave 45365

HAMPTON INN BY HILTON SIDNEY   937/498-8888
APPROVED SAVE Hotel. **Address:** 1600 Hampton Ct 45365

AAA Benefit: Members save up to 15%!

WHERE TO EAT

CAZADORES MEXICAN RESTAURANT   937/492-9883
APPROVED Mexican. Casual Dining. **Address:** 2200 W Michigan Ave 45365

SOLON pop. 23,348
• Hotels & Restaurants map & index p. 194
• Part of Cleveland area — see map p. 177

HAMPTON INN BY HILTON   440/542-0400 (59)
THREE DIAMOND SAVE Hotel. **Address:** 6035 Enterprise Pkwy 44139

AAA Benefit: Members save up to 15%!

HOMEWOOD SUITES BY HILTON CLEVELAND-SOLON   440/519-9500 (61)
THREE DIAMOND SAVE Extended Stay Hotel. **Address:** 6085 Enterprise Pkwy 44139

AAA Benefit: Members save up to 15%!

SPRINGHILL SUITES BY MARRIOTT CLEVELAND SOLON   440/248-9600 (58)
THREE DIAMOND SAVE Hotel. **Address:** 30100 Aurora Rd 44139

AAA Benefit: Members save 5% or more!

TOWNEPLACE SUITES BY MARRIOTT CLEVELAND-SOLON   440/394-1270 (60)
THREE DIAMOND SAVE Extended Stay Hotel. **Address:** 6040 Enterprise Pkwy 44139

AAA Benefit: Members save 5% or more!

WHERE TO EAT

CHICAGO DELI & GRILL   440/248-8018 (47)
APPROVED American. Casual Dining. **Address:** 34390 Aurora Rd 44139

ROSE ITALIAN KITCHEN   440/600-7900 (46)
APPROVED Italian. Casual Dining. **Address:** 6140 Som Center Rd 44139

SEÑORITA BONITAS   440/498-1067 (45)
APPROVED Mexican. Casual Dining. **Address:** 6000 Enterprise Pkwy 44139

SPRINGBORO pop. 17,409
• Hotels & Restaurants map & index p. 242
• Part of Cincinnati area — see map p. 153

HAMPTON INN & SUITES BY HILTON-DAYTON SOUTH
937/743-2121

THREE DIAMOND
Hotel

AAA Benefit: Members save up to 15%!

Address: 25 Greenwood Ln 45066 **Location:** I-75 exit 38, just e. **Facility:** 99 units. 3 stories, interior corridors. **Pool:** heated indoor. **Activities:** exercise room. **Guest Services:** valet and coin laundry. **Featured Amenity:** breakfast buffet.

SAVE 📶 CALL 🛗 🅿️ 🛗 BIZ
📶 ✕ 🗄️ 📠 💻
/ SOME UNITS HS

WHERE TO EAT

CHINA COTTAGE   937/748-8866 (40)
APPROVED Chinese. Casual Dining. **Address:** 784 N Main St 45066

SPRINGFIELD (F-3) pop. 60,608, elev. 984'
• Hotels p. 294 • Restaurants p. 294

Springfield was settled about 1800 by a group of Kentuckians, including the frontiersman and Native American scout Simon Kenton. Kenton's wife named the town for the numerous springs found there. In 1802 a water-powered flour mill was built nearby on a gorge in what is now Clifton, where visitors can take a self-guiding tour of the mill and explore a country store.

After the road came through in 1838 it became known as the "town at the end of the National Pike."

Now US 40, the pike connected Springfield with industrial cities as far east as Cumberland, Md., and opened new markets for the city's harvests. Agricultural machinery firms set up shops, and slowly Springfield's complexion changed from rural to industrial. Its industries have diversified, producing turbines, engines and piano plates. Wittenberg University and its 2,000 students add a college-town flavor to this bustling city.

Greater Springfield Convention and Visitors Bureau: 20 S. Limestone St., Suite 100, Springfield, OH 45502. **Phone:** (937) 325-7621 or (800) 803-1553.

WESTCOTT HOUSE, 85 S. Greenmount Ave. (visitor center entrance), was designed for the prominent Westcott family by Frank Lloyd Wright in 1906 and construction was completed in 1908. In the 1940s the home was altered into an apartment building, completely changing the original design. In 2005 a five-year restoration was completed, and the house once again reflects Wright's design. The house is Wright's only use of Prairie Style architecture in Ohio. One-hour tours begin with a brief video about the house's history and restoration.

Note: To protect the house's floors, guests should wear flat shoes. **Hours:** Guided tours depart on the hour Tues.-Sat. 11-4, Sun. 1-4, May-Oct.; Tues.-Fri. at 11, 1 and 3, Sat. on the hour 11-4, Sun. on the hour 1-4, rest of year. Last tour begins at closing. **Cost:** $18; $15 (ages 6-18, ages 65+ and college students with ID). Reservations are recommended. **Phone:** (937) 327-9291.

COMFORT SUITES SPRINGFIELD 937/322-0707
 Hotel

Address: 121 Raydo Cir 45506 **Location:** I-70 exit 54, just n. **Facility:** 78 units. 4 stories, interior corridors. **Pool:** heated indoor. **Activities:** exercise room. **Guest Services:** coin laundry. **Featured Amenity:** full hot breakfast.

COURTYARD BY MARRIOTT SPRINGFIELD DOWNTOWN 937/322-3600
 Hotel
'COURTYARD' **AAA Benefit:** Members save 5% or more!

Address: 100 S Fountain Ave 45502 **Location:** I-70 exit 54, 2 mi n on SR 72 (Limestone St), just w on Main St, then just s; downtown. Located close to railroad tracks. **Facility:** 120 units. 6 stories, interior corridors. **Dining:** Mela Urban Bistro, see separate listing. **Pool:** heated indoor. **Activities:** exercise room. **Guest Services:** valet and coin laundry.

 / SOME UNITS

FAIRFIELD INN & SUITES BY MARRIOTT SPRINGFIELD 937/323-9554
 THREE DIAMOND [SAVE] Hotel. **Address:** 1870 W 1st St 45504
AAA Benefit: Members save 5% or more!

HAMPTON INN BY HILTON SPRINGFIELD 937/325-8480
THREE DIAMOND Hotel
 Hampton
AAA Benefit: Members save up to 15%!

 Address: 101 W Leffel Ln 45506 **Location:** I-70 exit 54, just n, then w. **Facility:** 100 units. 4 stories, interior corridors. **Pool:** heated indoor. **Activities:** exercise room. **Guest Services:** valet laundry. **Featured Amenity:** breakfast buffet.

WHERE TO EAT

EL TORO MEXICAN RESTAURANT 937/325-7898
APPROVED Mexican. Casual Dining. **Address:** 2100 S Limestone St 45505

MELA URBAN BISTRO 937/471-9009
THREE DIAMOND American. Casual Dining. **Address:** 100 S Fountain Ave 45502

RUDY'S SMOKEHOUSE 937/324-0884
APPROVED Barbecue. Quick Serve. **Address:** 2222 S Limestone St 45505

STELLA BLUE BISTRO 937/717-0478
THREE DIAMOND American. Casual Dining. **Address:** 20 N Fountain Ave 45502

STEUBENVILLE (E-9) pop. 18,659, elev. 719'

At S. 3rd and Adams streets, adjacent to Historic Fort Steuben, is the First Federal Land Office of the United States; it was built in 1801 and served as a 19th-century home office. A new roof and floor have been constructed, but the building's logs are original.

As part of Steubenville's City of Murals project, the exteriors of 23 buildings in downtown Steubenville and Hollywood Plaza are painted with large murals depicting historical scenes relating to the city, including one of Steubenville native Dean Martin. Tour maps are available at the visitor center.

The town is home to the Catholic Franciscan University of Steubenville and its nearly 2,500 students.

Steubenville's Hometown Celebration, held in June, features a variety of events, including the Grecian Food Festival, Ohio Valley Frontier Days and Dean Martin celebrations.

Steubenville/Jefferson County Visitor Center: 120 S. Third St., Steubenville, OH 43952. **Phone:** (740) 283-4935 or (866) 301-1787.

HISTORIC FORT STEUBEN is at 120 S. Third St. This reconstructed 1787 fort provides a taste of military life on the frontier in 18th-century Ohio. Visitors can view displays in the exhibition hall and tour the enlisted men's quarters, the officers' quarters, commissary, guardhouse and hospital as well as the artificer's and quartermaster's shops and an archaeology dig. In addition, the visitor center offers information for travelers. Adjacent to the site is the First Federal Land Office as well as Fort Steuben Park, which includes the Veterans Memorial Fountain. Concerts are held at the Louis Berkman Amphitheater.

Time: Allow 1 hour minimum. **Hours:** Fort and visitor center open Mon.-Sat. 10-4, Sun. 11-4, May-Oct. Visitor center open Mon.-Fri. 10-4; closed major holidays and Christmas-Jan. 1. Guided tours of the First Federal Land Office Building are available by appointment. **Cost:** Fort $9; $8 (ages 60+); $6 (ages 6-12). **Phone:** (740) 283-1787 or (866) 301-1787.

BEST WESTERN PLUS INN AT FRANCISCAN SQUARE
740/282-0901

| THREE DIAMOND | | |
| Hotel | Best Western PLUS | **AAA Benefit:** Members save up to 15% and earn bonus points! |

Address: 200 Franciscan Square Blvd 43952 **Location:** Jct US 22 and SR 7, 1 mi sw. **Facility:** 113 units. 4 stories, interior corridors. **Amenities:** safes. **Pool:** heated indoor. **Activities:** exercise room. **Guest Services:** valet and coin laundry.

HAMPTON INN   740/282-9800
THREE DIAMOND [SAVE] Hotel. **Address:** 820 University Blvd 43952

AAA Benefit: Members save up to 15%!

MICROTEL INN & SUITES BY WYNDHAM STEUBENVILLE
740/282-1800
APPROVED Hotel. **Address:** 875 University Blvd 43952

SUPER 8-STEUBENVILLE
740/282-4565
APPROVED
Motel

Address: 1505 University Blvd 43952 **Location:** Jct US 22 and SR 7, 1 mi sw. **Facility:** 63 units. 3 stories (no elevator), interior corridors. **Featured Amenity:** continental breakfast.

NAPLES STEAK & SPAGHETTI HOUSE   740/283-3405
APPROVED Italian. Casual Dining. **Address:** 329 North St 43952

SESAME GRILL   740/282-6688
APPROVED Chinese. Casual Dining. **Address:** 805 University Blvd 43952

SUMO SUSHI & HIBACHI   740/346-4188
APPROVED Japanese. Casual Dining. **Address:** 4170 Sunset Blvd 43952

YORGO'S GYROS - POTATOES   740/282-9663
APPROVED Greek. Quick Serve. **Address:** 127 N 4th St 43952

STOW pop. 34,837

COURTYARD BY MARRIOTT AKRON STOW   330/945-9722
THREE DIAMOND [SAVE] Hotel. **Address:** 4047 Bridgewater Pkwy 44224

AAA Benefit: Members save 5% or more!

FAIRFIELD BY MARRIOTT AKRON STOW   330/940-1450
THREE DIAMOND [SAVE] Hotel. **Address:** 4170 Steels Pointe 44224

AAA Benefit: Members save 5% or more!

HAMPTON INN BY HILTON STOW   330/945-4160
THREE DIAMOND [SAVE] Hotel. **Address:** 4331 Lakepointe Corporate Dr 44224

AAA Benefit: Members save up to 15%!

HOME2 SUITES BY HILTON AKRON STOW   330/835-6400
THREE DIAMOND [SAVE] Extended Stay Contemporary Hotel. **Address:** 4097 Bridgewater Pkwy 44224

AAA Benefit: Members save up to 15%!

CEEDO'S EATERY   330/940-2424
APPROVED Mediterranean. Quick Serve. **Address:** 4147 Bridgewater Pkwy 44224

ON TAP GRILLE & BAR   330/686-5359
APPROVED American. Casual Dining. **Address:** 4396 Kent Rd 44224

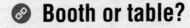

STRASBURG pop. 2,608

RAMADA BY WYNDHAM DOVER/STRASBURG 330/878-1400

APPROVED Hotel

Address: 509 S Wooster Ave 44680 **Location:** I-77 exit 87, 0.4 mi w on US 250 and SR 21. **Facility:** 57 units. 3 stories, interior corridors. **Parking:** winter plug-ins. **Pool:** heated indoor. **Activities:** hot tub, exercise room. **Guest Services:** valet and coin laundry. **Featured Amenity:** continental breakfast.

SAVE CALL BIZ / SOME UNITS

WHERE TO EAT

SHY CELLARS 330/878-4163
THREE DIAMOND American. Casual Dining. **Address:** 9185 US 250 NW 44680

STREETSBORO pop. 16,028

• Hotels & Restaurants map & index p. 194

FAIRFIELD INN & SUITES BY MARRIOTT 330/422-1166 107
APPROVED SAVE Hotel. **Address:** 9783 SR 14 44241

AAA Benefit: Members save 5% or more!

HAMPTON INN & SUITES BY HILTON 330/422-0500 109
THREE DIAMOND SAVE Hotel. **Address:** 800 Mondial Pkwy 44241

AAA Benefit: Members save up to 15%!

HOLIDAY INN EXPRESS & SUITES 330/422-1888
APPROVED Hotel. **Address:** 9459 SR 14 44241

TOWNEPLACE SUITES BY MARRIOTT 330/422-1855 108
APPROVED SAVE Extended Stay Hotel. **Address:** 795 Mondial Pkwy 44241

AAA Benefit: Members save 5% or more!

WHERE TO EAT

EL CAMPESINO 330/626-9777
APPROVED Mexican. Casual Dining. **Address:** 9169 SR 14 44241

GIRVES BROWN DERBY 330/626-2171
APPROVED Steak Seafood. Casual Dining. **Address:** 9230 SR 14 44241

STRONGSVILLE pop. 44,750

• Hotels & Restaurants map & index p. 194
• Part of Cleveland area — see map p. 177

DON'S POMEROY HOUSE 440/572-1111 74
THREE DIAMOND American. Fine Dining. **Address:** 13664 Pearl Rd 44136

ITALIAN VILLAGE 440/572-1414 78
APPROVED Italian. Casual Dining. **Address:** 16605 Pearl Rd 44136

LA KABOB LEBANESE GRILL 440/846-5100 76
APPROVED Lebanese. Quick Serve. **Address:** 14228 Pearl Rd 44136

THE RAIL 440/783-1275 75
APPROVED Burgers. Casual Dining. **Address:** 17885 Southpark Cir 44136

SAKURA SUSHI HOUSE 440/268-9668 77
APPROVED Japanese. Casual Dining. **Address:** 15040 Pearl Rd 44136

SUNBURY (E-4) pop. 4,389, elev. 971'

• Part of Columbus area — see map p. 205

Shopping: SAVE Tanger Outlets is at 400 S. Wilson Rd.

SYLVANIA pop. 18,965

• Hotels & Restaurants map & index p. 299

WINGATE BY WYNDHAM SYLVANIA/TOLEDO 419/517-2000 11
THREE DIAMOND Hotel. **Address:** 5480 S Main St 43560

WHERE TO EAT

CIAO 419/882-2334 19
THREE DIAMOND Italian. Casual Dining. **Address:** 6064 Monroe St 43560

SHORTY'S TRUE AMERICAN ROADHOUSE 419/841-9505 20
APPROVED American. Casual Dining. **Address:** 5111 Monroe St 43623

TIFFIN (C-4) pop. 17,963, elev. 760'

The meticulously restored 1928 Ritz Theatre, 30 S. Washington St., is the venue for live performances and motion pictures on many weekends. During the week, guided tours reveal design delights such as garden murals, intricate stenciling and plasterwork, and a 1,200-pound crystal chandelier; advance reservations are required for the tour. Phone the box office at (419) 448-8544.

Destination Seneca County: 19 W. Market St., Suite C, Tiffin, OH 44883. **Phone:** (567) 220-6387.

HOLIDAY INN EXPRESS TIFFIN 419/443-5100
THREE DIAMOND Hotel. **Address:** 78 Shaffer Park Dr 44883

TIPP CITY (F-2) pop. 9,689, elev. 830'

Tipp City was named for presidential candidate William Henry Harrison's campaign slogan, "Tippecanoe and Tyler too." The 19th-century downtown of this town along the Miami-Erie Canal draws antiques shoppers and those looking for crafts objects. The restored 1839 Tipp Roller Mill and Theater at 225 E. Main St. offers entertainment the second and fourth Thursday of the month at 7, June through the second Thursday in December; phone (937) 667-3696.

HOLIDAY INN EXPRESS DAYTON NORTH 937/667-5161
THREE DIAMOND Hotel. **Address:** 1100 W Main St 45371

LA QUINTA INN BY WYNDHAM DAYTON NORTH-TIPP CITY
937/667-1574

▼▼ **APPROVED**   Hotel. **Address:** 19 Weller Dr 45371

TOLEDO (B-3) pop. 287,208, elev. 572'
• Hotels p. 302 • Restaurants p. 302
• **Hotels & Restaurants map & index p. 299**

A great industrial center, Toledo is one of the world's busiest freshwater ports, ranking third on the Great Lakes. The city's importance as a port stems from its location at the mouth of the Maumee River, the largest river flowing into the lakes. Its natural harbor has 35 miles of frontage. Pipelines for crude oil and gas terminate in Toledo, which is a major refining center. The city also is a large producer of glass.

Toledo occupies the site of old Fort Industry, which was built in 1794 and stood near the present Summit and Monroe streets. Fallen Timbers Monument, off SR 24 on Jerome Road, commemorates Gen. Anthony Wayne's 1794 defeat of the Native Americans, ending the bloody conflicts between the colonists and Native Americans.

As a result of his victory the Native Americans relinquished their rights to the Firelands *(see Norwalk p. 281)*, which comprised most of the Native American lands remaining in the vicinity. A consequence of the Toledo War of 1835, a vociferous boundary dispute with Michigan, gave Toledo to Ohio and granted Michigan its northern peninsula in compensation.

The Erie and Kalamazoo Railroad, completed in 1836, was the first American railroad built west of the Alleghenies. Toledo is now one of the nation's largest rail centers.

Toledo provides opportunities for outdoor recreation at its numerous public Metroparks of the Toledo Area. Promenade Park, a peaceful, landscaped setting along the Maumee River, is a favorite spot for viewing freighters and towboats. Oak Openings Preserve and Pearson Metropark are popular spots for watching wildlife, especially migrating birds.

A large collection of Victorian, Edwardian and Arts and Crafts homes in the Old West End provides a glimpse of architectural styles popular with wealthy industrialists in the late 19th- and early 20th centuries.

Notable among institutions of higher learning in the city is the 21,500-student University of Toledo, established in 1872. Guided tours of the campus, at 2801 W. Bancroft St., are available by appointment; phone (419) 530-8888 or (800) 586-5336. The university's Ritter Planetarium and the Brooks Observatory offer weekend shows throughout the year Fri. starting at 7:30 p.m. (8:30, May-Aug.) and Sat. at 1 during the academic year; phone (419) 530-2650 or (419) 530-4037.

Destination Toledo Convention and Visitors Bureau: 401 Jefferson Ave., Toledo, OH 43604. **Phone:** (419) 321-6404 or (800) 243-4667.

Self-guiding tours: Brochures and maps of a walking or driving tour of Old West End are available from the convention and visitors bureau. "Discover Downtown Toledo," a guidebook with a walking tour highlighting the history and architecture of Toledo, is available for $5 at the Urban Affairs Center at the University of Toledo or at the Toledo Lucas County Public Library; for information phone (419) 530-3591 or (419) 259-5233.

Shopping: Franklin Park Mall, 5001 Monroe St., includes Dillard's, JCPenney and Macy's.

FORT MEIGS—see Perrysburg p. 284.

▼▼ **IMAGINATION STATION** is at jct. Summit and Adams sts. on the riverfront at 1 Discovery Way; parking is at Adams and Superior sts. The science learning center features interactive exhibits focused on health sciences, alternative energy and energy efficiency as well as magnetism, air compression and perception. Visitors can ride a bike suspended 18 feet in the air on the High Wire Cycle, become a human yo-yo on the BOYO and run on the Wheel of Fire.

Time: Allow 1 hour minimum. **Hours:** Tues.-Sat. and some Mon. holidays 10-5, Sun. noon-5. **Cost:** $13; $12 (ages 65+); $11 (ages 3-12). **Phone:** (419) 244-2674. 🔟

TOLEDO BOTANICAL GARDEN is at 5403 Elmer Dr. The garden encompasses 60 acres and includes roses, herbs, wildflowers, azaleas and rhododendrons as well as woodlands, hosta, vegetable and extensive perennial gardens. Also on the grounds are a re-created pioneer homestead and artists' guilds. In June the annual Crosby Festival of Arts features more than 215 artists. **Time:** Allow 1 hour minimum. **Hours:** Daily dawn-dusk. **Cost:** Free. Admission may be charged during special events. **Phone:** (419) 536-5566.

▼▼ **THE TOLEDO MUSEUM OF ART** is at 2445 Monroe St., 1 blk. e. of I-75. This Grecian-style marble structure contains works tracing the history of art from ancient Egypt to the present. Among its more than 30,000 works of art are paintings and sculptures by such artists as Alexander Calder, Edgar Degas, El Greco, Paul Gauguin, Hans Holbein, Anselm Kiefer, Henri Matisse, Joan Miró, Claude Monet, Pablo Picasso, Rembrandt, Pierre-Auguste Renoir, Peter Paul Rubens and Vincent van Gogh as well as African and Asian works.

Also featured are books, manuscripts, prints, sculpture, medieval ivories, glass items, decorative arts objects and tapestries. A glass collection chronicles the history of glass over the course of 3,500 years. **Time:** Allow 2 hours minimum. **Hours:** Tues.-Wed. 10-4, Thurs.-Fri. 10-9, Sat. 10-5, Sun. noon-5. **Cost:** Free. Special exhibitions or events may require purchased tickets. **Parking:** $5. **Phone:** (419) 255-8000 or TTY (800) 644-6862.

▼▼ **TOLEDO ZOO,** 4 mi. s.w. on SR 25, is home to more than 9,000 animals representing more than 700 species of mammals, birds, fish and reptiles. Tembo Trail features elephants, rhinos,

(See map & index p. 299.)

camels and meerkats along with the Hippoquarium, which offers an underwater view of a hippopotamus family. Arctic Encounter offers close-up views of polar bears and seals. At Penguin Beach you can watch the black-and-white cuties' above- and below-water antics. Flamingo Key is home to flamingos and other waterfowl, and Primate Forest houses white-cheeked gibbons, swamp monkeys, ring-tailed lemurs and more. Also featured throughout the zoo are cheetahs, Amur tigers, great apes and Asian sloth bears as well as Amazing Amphibians, an aviary and pheasantry, a reptile house, gardens, a train and two carousels.

The Aquarium area is home to rays and sharks as well as other aquatic life. Nature's Neighborhood features play activities to help children learn about nature; birds, fish, goats, guinea pigs and insects are housed here. In warmer weather visitors can experience *Africa!*, home to giraffes, zebras, ostriches and more. Behind-the-scenes tours of the zoo are available. **Hours:** Opens daily at 10; closing times vary. *Africa!* is usually open May-Oct. Phone ahead to confirm schedule. **Cost:** $21; $18 (ages 2-11 and 60+). Reservations and an additional fee are required for behind-the-scenes tours. **Parking:** $8; $16 (oversize vehicles). **Phone:** (419) 385-4040 or (419) 385-5721. GT ⓣ

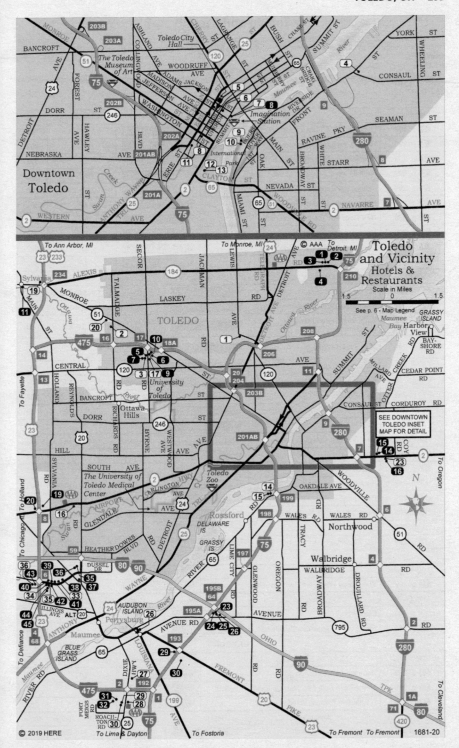

Toledo and Vicinity

This index helps you "spot" where hotels and restaurants are located on the corresponding detailed maps. Restaurant price range is a combination of lunch and/or dinner. Turn to the listing page for more information and consult display ads for special promotions.

 For more details, rates and reservations: AAA.com/travelguides/hotels

TOLEDO

Map Page	Hotels	Designation	Member Savings	Page
1 p. 299	Hampton Inn & Suites Toledo-North	◈ THREE DIAMOND	✔	302
2 p. 299	Holiday Inn Express Toledo North	◈ THREE DIAMOND		302
3 p. 299	Courtyard by Marriott Toledo North	◈ THREE DIAMOND	✔	302
4 p. 299	Fairfield Inn & Suites by Marriott Toledo North	◈ THREE DIAMOND	✔	302
5 p. 299	Holiday Inn Express & Suites Toledo West	◈ THREE DIAMOND		302
6 p. 299	Hampton Inn & Suites Toledo/Westgate	◈ THREE DIAMOND	✔	302
7 p. 299	**Red Roof Inn Toledo University**	◈ APPROVED	✔	302
8 p. 299	**Renaissance Toledo Downtown Hotel**	◈ FOUR DIAMOND	✔	302
9 p. 299	Courtyard by Marriott Toledo West	◈ THREE DIAMOND	✔	302
10 p. 299	Residence Inn by Marriott Toledo West	◈ THREE DIAMOND	✔	302

Map Page	Restaurants	Designation	Cuisine	Price Range	Page
① p. 299	Mancy's Steakhouse	◈ THREE DIAMOND	Steak	$10-$66	303
② p. 299	J. Alexander's Restaurant	◈ THREE DIAMOND	American	$14-$36	303
③ p. 299	ZaZa Wood-Fired Pizza & Mediterranean Cuisine	◈ APPROVED	Mediterranean Pizza	$6-$20	303
④ p. 299	Tony Packo's Cafe	◈ APPROVED	Hungarian Hot Dogs	$4-$40	303
⑤ p. 299	Fowl and Fodder	◈ APPROVED	American	$8-$13	303
⑥ p. 299	Georgio's Cafe International	◈ APPROVED	Mediterranean	$12-$40	303
⑦ p. 299	Brim House	◈ THREE DIAMOND	New American	$10-$38	302
⑧ p. 299	Pizza Papalis	◈ APPROVED	Pizza	$10-$25	303
⑨ p. 299	Zia's	◈ APPROVED	Southern Italian	$13-$30	303
⑩ p. 299	Real Seafood Company Toledo	◈ THREE DIAMOND	Seafood	$12-$50	303
⑪ p. 299	Grumpy's	◈ APPROVED	Deli	$5-$13	303
⑫ p. 299	The Café	◈ APPROVED	International	$7-$12	303
⑬ p. 299	Rockwell's	◈ THREE DIAMOND	Steak	$21-$48	303
⑭ p. 299	Epic Buffet	◈ APPROVED	American	$16-$40	303
⑮ p. 299	Final Cut Steak & Seafood	◈ THREE DIAMOND	Steak Seafood	$38-$66	303
⑯ p. 299	La Scola	◈ THREE DIAMOND	Italian	$12-$33	303
⑰ p. 299	QQ Kitchen	◈ APPROVED	Asian	$10-$17	303

SYLVANIA

Map Page	Hotel	Designation	Member Savings	Page
11 p. 299	Wingate by Wyndham Sylvania/Toledo	◈ THREE DIAMOND		296

Map Page	Restaurants	Designation	Cuisine	Price Range	Page
⑲ p. 299	Ciao	◈ THREE DIAMOND	Italian	$13-$32	296
⑳ p. 299	Shorty's True American Roadhouse	◈ APPROVED	American	$9-$27	296

OREGON

Map Page	Hotels	Designation	Member Savings	Page
14 p. 299	Hampton Inn Toledo/Oregon	◈ THREE DIAMOND	✔	282
15 p. 299	TownePlace Suites by Marriott Toledo Oregon	◈ THREE DIAMOND	✔	282
16 p. 299	Holiday Inn Express Toledo-Oregon	◈ THREE DIAMOND		282

Map Page	Restaurant	Designation	Cuisine	Price Range	Page
㉓ p. 299	Osaka Sushi and Hibachi	◈ APPROVED	Japanese	$10-$30	282

HOLLAND

Map Page	Hotels	Designation	Member Savings	Page
19 p. 299	Extended Stay America Toledo-Holland	APPROVED		259
20 p. 299	**Courtyard by Marriott Toledo Airport Holland** (See ad p. 302.)	THREE DIAMOND	✔	259

ROSSFORD

Map Page	Hotels	Designation	Member Savings	Page
23 p. 299	**Country Inn & Suites by Radisson, Toledo South**	APPROVED	✔	288
24 p. 299	Courtyard by Marriott Toledo Perrysburg/Rossford	THREE DIAMOND	✔	289
25 p. 299	**Hampton Inn & Suites Toledo-Perrysburg**	THREE DIAMOND	✔	289
26 p. 299	Staybridge Suites Toledo-Rossford-Perrysburg	THREE DIAMOND		289

PERRYSBURG

Map Page	Hotels	Designation	Member Savings	Page
29 p. 299	La Quinta Inn by Wyndham Toledo Perrysburg	APPROVED		284
30 p. 299	Candlewood Suites Perrysburg	APPROVED		284
31 p. 299	Home2 Suites by Hilton Perrysburg Levis Commons Toledo	THREE DIAMOND	✔	284
32 p. 299	Hilton Garden Inn Toledo/Perrysburg	THREE DIAMOND	✔	284

Map Page	Restaurants	Designation	Cuisine	Price Range	Page
26 p. 299	Swig Restaurant	APPROVED	American	$4-$16	284
27 p. 299	Bai Du	APPROVED	Chinese	$7-$17	284
28 p. 299	Social Gastropub	APPROVED	American	$11-$18	284
29 p. 299	Poco Piatti	THREE DIAMOND	Mediterranean Small Plates	$10-$24	284
30 p. 299	Tea Tree Asian Bistro	THREE DIAMOND	Asian	$12-$27	284

MAUMEE

Map Page	Hotels	Designation	Member Savings	Page
35 p. 299	Comfort Inn & Suites Maumee-Toledo (I80-90)	APPROVED		273
36 p. 299	Home2 Suites by Hilton Maumee Toledo	THREE DIAMOND	✔	273
37 p. 299	Hampton Inn Toledo South/Maumee	THREE DIAMOND	✔	273
38 p. 299	Courtyard by Marriott-Toledo/Maumee	THREE DIAMOND	✔	273
39 p. 299	Country Inn & Suites by Radisson, Toledo	APPROVED		273
40 p. 299	Homewood Suites by Hilton Toledo/Maumee	THREE DIAMOND	✔	273
41 p. 299	Fairfield Inn & Suites by Marriott Toledo Maumee	APPROVED	✔	273
42 p. 299	Extended Stay America-Toledo-Maumee	APPROVED		273
43 p. 299	**Best Western Toledo South Maumee**	APPROVED	✔	273
44 p. 299	**Super 8 by Wyndham Maumee/Toledo Area**	APPROVED	✔	273
45 p. 299	Residence Inn by Marriott Toledo Maumee	THREE DIAMOND	✔	273

Map Page	Restaurants	Designation	Cuisine	Price Range	Page
33 p. 299	Mancy's Bluewater Grille	THREE DIAMOND	Seafood	$10-$45	273
34 p. 299	Bangkok Kitchen	APPROVED	Thai	$9-$30	273
35 p. 299	Sam's Diner	APPROVED	American	$3-$15	273
36 p. 299	Barr's Public House	APPROVED	American	$10-$18	273

Turn dreams into plans using
AAA travel planning tools: AAA.com/maps

(See map & index p. 299.)

COURTYARD BY MARRIOTT TOLEDO NORTH

419/392-9637 **3**

THREE DIAMOND SAVE Hotel. **Address:** 5875 Hagman Rd 43612

AAA Benefit:
Members save 5%
or more!

COURTYARD BY MARRIOTT TOLEDO WEST

419/724-0444 **9**

THREE DIAMOND SAVE Hotel. **Address:** 3536 Secor Rd 43606

AAA Benefit:
Members save 5%
or more!

FAIRFIELD INN & SUITES BY MARRIOTT TOLEDO NORTH

419/725-0050 **4**

THREE DIAMOND SAVE Hotel. **Address:** 5685 Benore Rd 43612

AAA Benefit:
Members save 5%
or more!

HAMPTON INN & SUITES TOLEDO-NORTH

419/727-8725 **1**

THREE DIAMOND SAVE Hotel. **Address:** 5865 Hagman Rd 43612

AAA Benefit:
Members save up to
15%!

HAMPTON INN & SUITES TOLEDO/WESTGATE

419/214-5555 **6**

THREE DIAMOND SAVE Hotel. **Address:** 3434 Secor Rd 43606

AAA Benefit:
Members save up to
15%!

HOLIDAY INN EXPRESS & SUITES TOLEDO WEST

419/214-4700 **5**

THREE DIAMOND Hotel. **Address:** 3440 Secor Rd 43606

HOLIDAY INN EXPRESS TOLEDO NORTH

419/574-0292 **2**

THREE DIAMOND Hotel. **Address:** 5855 Hagman Rd 43612

RED ROOF INN TOLEDO UNIVERSITY

419/536-0118 **7**

◆ **APPROVED**
Motel

Address: 3530 Executive Pkwy 43606
Location: I-475 exit 17, 0.5 mi s on Secor Rd, then just e. **Facility:** 117 units. 3 stories, exterior corridors. **Amenities:** safes.

SAVE 🛏 🛜 ✕ 🎥
/SOME UNITS 🐾 🎁 🛢 🖨 🖥

RENAISSANCE TOLEDO DOWNTOWN HOTEL

419/244-2444 **8**

FOUR DIAMOND
Hotel

R
RENAISSANCE
HOTELS

AAA Benefit:
Members save 5%
or more!

Address: 444 N Summit St 43604 **Location:** Waterfront. Downtown. **Facility:** Featuring Toledo-focused design elements, this property boasts chic public spaces and a rooftop cocktail bar. Guest rooms are contemporary with custom furniture and plush bedding. 241 units. 13 stories, interior corridors. **Parking:** valet only. **Amenities:** safes. **Activities:** bicycles, exercise room. **Guest Services:** valet laundry.

SAVE 🛏 🛗 🍽 CALL 🛢 ⚕ BIZ 🛜 ✕ 🎁
🖥 /SOME UNITS 🐾

RESIDENCE INN BY MARRIOTT TOLEDO WEST

419/724-2555 **10**

THREE DIAMOND SAVE Extended Stay Hotel. **Address:** 3554 Secor Rd 43606

AAA Benefit:
Members save 5%
or more!

WHERE TO EAT

BRIM HOUSE

419/243-7664 **7**

THREE DIAMOND New American. Casual Dining. **Address:** 444 N Summit St 43604

▼ See AAA listing p. 259 ▼

(See map & index p. 299.)

THE CAFÉ   419/243-1302   (12)
W APPROVED International. Casual Dining. **Address:** 27 Broadway St 43604

CITY BARBEQUE   419/517-7777
W APPROVED Barbecue. Quick Serve. **Address:** 7402 W Central Ave 43617

EPIC BUFFET   419/661-5200   (14)
W APPROVED American. Buffet Style. **Address:** 1968 Miami St 43605

FINAL CUT STEAK & SEAFOOD   419/661-5381   (15)
W THREE DIAMOND Steak Seafood. Fine Dining. **Address:** 777 Hollywood Blvd 43605

FOWL AND FODDER   419/690-2490
W APPROVED Natural/Organic. Casual Dining. **Address:** 7408 Central Ave 43617

FOWL AND FODDER   419/214-1588   (5)
W APPROVED American. Casual Dining. **Address:** 614 Adams St 43604

GEORGIO'S CAFE INTERNATIONAL   419/242-2424   (6)
W APPROVED Mediterranean. Casual Dining. **Address:** 426 N Superior St 43604

GRUMPY'S   419/241-6728   (11)
W APPROVED Deli. Casual Dining. **Address:** 34 S Huron St 43604

J. ALEXANDER'S RESTAURANT   419/474-8620   (2)
W THREE DIAMOND American. Casual Dining. **Address:** 4315 Talmadge Rd 43623

LA SCOLA   419/381-2100   (16)
W THREE DIAMOND Italian. Casual Dining. **Address:** 5375 Airport Hwy 43615

MANCY'S STEAKHOUSE   419/476-4154   (1)
W THREE DIAMOND Steak. Casual Dining. **Address:** 953 Phillips Ave 43612

PIZZA PAPALIS   419/244-7722   (8)
W APPROVED Pizza. Casual Dining. **Address:** 519 Monroe St 43604

QQ KITCHEN   419/720-8703   (17)
W APPROVED Asian. Casual Dining. **Address:** 3324 Secor Rd #4 43606

REAL SEAFOOD COMPANY TOLEDO   419/697-5427   (10)
W THREE DIAMOND Seafood. Casual Dining. **Address:** 22 Main St 43605

ROCKWELL'S   419/243-1302   (13)
W THREE DIAMOND Steak. Fine Dining. **Address:** 27 Broadway St 43604

TONY PACKO'S CAFE   419/691-6054   (4)
W APPROVED Hungarian Hot Dogs. Quick Serve. **Address:** 1902 Front St 43605

ZAZA WOOD-FIRED PIZZA & MEDITERRANEAN CUISINE   419/531-2400   (3)
W APPROVED Mediterranean Pizza. Quick Serve. **Address:** 3550 Executive Pkwy 43606

ZIA'S   419/697-4559   (9)
W APPROVED Southern Italian. Casual Dining. **Address:** 20 Main St 43605

TROY (E-2) pop. 25,058, elev. 836'
• Restaurants p. 304

   The Eldean Covered Bridge, 2 miles north at the junction of CR 25A and Eldean Road, is a long-type truss bridge. Built in 1860, the 223-foot bridge crosses the Great Miami River. Also noteworthy is Troy's public square at Main Street and SR 55. The restored Miami County Courthouse, with its frescoes and five cast-iron domes, is particularly impressive.

Miami County Visitors and Convention Bureau: 405 S.W. Public Square, Suite 272, Troy, OH 45373. **Phone:** (800) 348-8993.

BRUKNER NATURE CENTER is off I-75 exit 73, 3 mi. s.w. on SR 55, then 3 mi. w. to 5995 Horseshoe Bend Rd. This 165-acre nature preserve offers 6 miles of hiking trails, a pine forest and prairie. The interpretive center features a treetop-level bird-viewing room. The 1804 Iddings log house is open for viewing. Rehabilitated but permanently impaired animals, including a coyote and a bald eagle, can be seen. Frequently scheduled events include live creature features, night hikes and stargazing.

   Pets are not permitted. **Time:** Allow 4 hours minimum. **Hours:** Center open Mon.-Sat. 9-5, Sun. 12:30-5. Trails open daily dawn-dusk. Buildings closed major holidays. **Cost:** Mon.-Sat. $2.50; Sun. free; $10 (family of 4 or more). **Phone:** (937) 698-6493 for program information.

WACO AIR MUSEUM, 1865 S. CR 25A, preserves the history of the Waco Aircraft Co., which was the leading U.S. manufacturer of civil airplanes in the 1920s and early 1930s. During World War II the company specialized in glider production for the military. The museum features restored aircraft (including a World War II glider display), a library and aviation exhibits. A flight simulator is on-site as well.

   Photography is permitted. **Time:** Allow 1 hour minimum. **Hours:** Mon.-Fri. 9-1:30, Sat.-Sun. noon-5. Closed major holidays. **Cost:** $6; $5 (military with ID); $3 (ages 7-17). **Phone:** (937) 335-9226. **GT**

COMFORT SUITES   937/339-2525
W THREE DIAMOND Hotel. **Address:** 1800 Towne Park Dr 45373

FAIRFIELD BY MARRIOTT   937/332-1446
W APPROVED **SAVE** Hotel. **Address:** 83 Troy Town Dr 45373

> **AAA Benefit:** Members save 5% or more!

HAMPTON INN BY HILTON   937/339-7801
W THREE DIAMOND **SAVE** Hotel. **Address:** 45 Troy Town Dr 45373

> **AAA Benefit:** Members save up to 15%!

RESIDENCE INN BY MARRIOTT 937/440-9303
▼▼THREE DIAMOND ⟨SAVE⟩ Extended Stay Hotel. **Address:** 87 Troy Town Dr 45373

AAA Benefit: Members save 5% or more!

WHERE TO EAT

SAKAI JAPANESE BISTRO 937/440-1302
▼▼ APPROVED Japanese. Casual Dining. **Address:** 2303 W Main St 45373

SKYLINE CHILI 937/335-7005
▼▼ APPROVED American. Quick Serve. **Address:** 1775 W Main St 45373

TWINSBURG (C-11) pop. 18,795, elev. 1,004'
• Hotels & Restaurants map & index p. 194
• Part of Cleveland area — see map p. 177

Settled in 1817, Twinsburg was originally called Millsville. In 1819 two identical twin merchants from Connecticut, Moses and Aaron Wilcox, gave land for a public square and funded a school in exchange for the town naming rights. Settling in Twinsburg in 1823, they married sisters, were life-long business partners, had the same number of children, died within hours of one another and are buried together.

Today Twinsburg, one of the fastest growing communities in the state, is the site of the area's largest annual gathering of twins. Twinsburg residents and nearly 35,000 visitors see double the first full weekend in August during the Twins Days Festival. Highlights of this gathering of twins, triplets and quadruplets from around the world include a parade, arts and crafts, live entertainment, fireworks display, Twins Contest talent show and a golf tournament. Phone (330) 425-3652.

Shopping: A weekly fresh farmers market is held at 2695 Creekside Commons Thurs. 3-6:30, early June-early Oct.

HILTON GARDEN INN CLEVELAND/TWINSBURG
330/405-4488 ⟨94⟩
▼▼THREE DIAMOND ⟨SAVE⟩ Hotel. **Address:** 8971 Wilcox Dr 44087

AAA Benefit: Members save up to 15%!

WHERE TO EAT

BLUE CANYON KITCHEN & TAVERN
330/486-2583 ⟨65⟩
▼▼THREE DIAMOND

American Casual Dining $13-$33

AAA Inspector Notes: Western lodge-style décor with pine logs and beams can be found in this tavern. Guests can sit in any of several dining areas, including one with window views of the valley, at counters near the open kitchen and on the patio when the weather is nice. The bar has Wild West stools trimmed in faux game fur. Menu selections are creative and innovative. **Features:** full bar, patio dining, senior menu, Sunday brunch, happy hour. **Reservations:** suggested. **Address:** 8960 Wilcox Dr 44087 **Location:** I-480 exit 36, just w on SR 82. ⟨D⟩ CALL ♿

D'ANGELO'S 330/963-0603 ⟨66⟩
▼▼THREE DIAMOND Italian. Casual Dining. **Address:** 7995 Darrow Rd 44087

UPPER ARLINGTON pop. 33,771
• Hotels & Restaurants map & index p. 222
• Part of Columbus area — see map p. 205

HOMEWOOD SUITES BY HILTON COLUMBUS/OSU
614/488-1500 ⟨83⟩
▼▼THREE DIAMOND ⟨SAVE⟩ Extended Stay Hotel. **Address:** 1576 W Lane Ave 43221

AAA Benefit: Members save up to 15%!

WHERE TO EAT

CITY BARBEQUE 614/538-8890
▼▼ APPROVED Barbecue. Quick Serve. **Address:** 2111 W Henderson Rd 43220

FIGLIO UPPER ARLINGTON 614/459-6575 ⟨81⟩
▼▼ APPROVED Pizza. Casual Dining. **Address:** 3712 Riverside Dr 43221

HUDSON 29 KITCHEN + DRINK 614/487-0622 ⟨83⟩
▼▼THREE DIAMOND American. Casual Dining. **Address:** 1600 W Lane Ave 43221

MORETTI'S OF ARLINGTON 614/486-2333 ⟨82⟩
▼▼THREE DIAMOND Italian. Casual Dining. **Address:** 2124 Tremont Center 43221

UPPER SANDUSKY (C-4) pop. 6,596, elev. 850'

Established in 1843, Upper Sandusky overlooks the Sandusky State Scenic River, whose name comes from a Native American word meaning "water within pools." This site was headquarters for the Wyandot Indians, who controlled the area that is now Ohio.

Swartz Bridge, southeast of town on CR 130, and Parker Bridge, northeast of town on CR 40, are covered bridges found within the area.

Wyandot County Visitors Bureau: 108 E. Wyandot Ave., Upper Sandusky, OH 43351-1430. **Phone:** (419) 294-3556.

QUALITY INN 419/294-3891
▼▼ APPROVED Hotel. **Address:** 105 Comfort Dr 43351

WHERE TO EAT

THE STEER BARN 419/294-3860
▼▼ APPROVED Steak. Casual Dining. **Address:** 1144 E Wyandot Ave 43351

VALLEY VIEW pop. 2,034
• Hotels & Restaurants map & index p. 194
• Part of Cleveland area — see map p. 177

LOCKKEEPERS 216/524-9404 ⟨58⟩
▼▼THREE DIAMOND Italian. Fine Dining. **Address:** 8001 Rockside Rd 44125

VAN WERT pop. 10,846

COMFORT INN 419/232-6040
APPROVED Hotel. **Address:** 840 N Washington St 45891

HOLIDAY INN EXPRESS & SUITES VAN WERT 419/238-2600
THREE DIAMOND Hotel. **Address:** 140 N Valam Dr 45891

VIENNA (B-9) pop. 650, elev. 1,150'

Vienna is home to the Youngstown Air Reserve Station, which is headquarters for the Air Force's 910th Airlift Wing.

WAGON TRAILS ANIMAL PARK is at 907 Youngstown-Kingsville Rd. In this 62-acre park visitors can feed more than 300 exotic animals from six continents, including bison, water buffalo, deer, elk, zebras, camels and ostriches. Two-mile narrated safari rides afford the opportunity to get close to the animals. A petting zoo and aviary also are on the grounds.

Time: Allow 1 hour, 30 minutes minimum. **Hours:** Wed.-Mon. 10-3:30, June 1-Labor Day; Fri. 10-2, Sat.-Sun. 10-3:30, day after Labor Day-late Oct.; Sat.-Sun. 10-3:30, in May. Safari rides depart throughout the day with the last departure 15 minutes before closing, June-Aug.; safari rides depart at 10:45 11:45 and 12:45, Sept.-Oct. Phone ahead to confirm schedule. **Cost:** $16.95; $13.95 (ages 2-12). Cash only. **Phone:** (330) 539-4494.

WALNUT CREEK pop. 878

CARLISLE INN OF WALNUT CREEK 330/893-3636
THREE DIAMOND Hotel. **Address:** 4949 SR 515 44687

THE INN AT WALNUT CREEK 330/893-3599
APPROVED Motel. **Address:** 4869 Olde Pump St 44687

OAK RIDGE INN 330/893-3811
THREE DIAMOND Bed & Breakfast. **Address:** 4845 Milo Dr 44687

THE WALLHOUSE HOTEL, AN ASCEND HOTEL COLLECTION MEMBER 330/852-6105
THREE DIAMOND **Address:** 2870 Cove Ln 44687 **Location:** Jct US 403 and SR 39. **Facility:** 62 units, some two bedrooms. 6 stories, interior corridors. *Bath:* shower only. **Parking:** winter plug-ins. **Pool:** heated indoor. **Activities:** hot tub, exercise room. **Guest Services:** complimentary laundry. **Featured Amenity:** breakfast buffet.
Contemporary Hotel

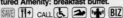

WHERE TO EAT

DER DUTCHMAN RESTAURANT 330/893-2981
APPROVED Comfort Food. Casual Dining. **Address:** 4967 Walnut St 44687

WAPAKONETA (D-2) pop. 9,867, elev. 898'

Neil Armstrong (1930-2012), who on July 20, 1969, became the first person to walk on the moon, was born in Wapakoneta.

 ARMSTRONG AIR & SPACE MUSEUM is just w. off I-75 exit 111 at 500 Apollo Dr. Exhibits follow the history of flight from the dreams of science fiction to the reality of space exploration. On view are full-size airplanes, a moon rock and the Gemini VIII capsule in which Neil Armstrong completed the first spacecraft docking in orbit. Several motion picture presentations are shown.

The dome-shaped Astro Theater features a documentary about America in space. The Infinity Room, an 18-foot square lined with mirrors, offers the illusion of walking in space. **Time:** Allow 2 hours minimum. **Hours:** Mon.-Sat. 9:30-5, Sun. 11-5, Apr.-Sept.; Tues.-Sat. 9:30-5, Sun. 11-5, rest of year. Phone ahead to confirm schedule. **Cost:** $8; $7 (ages 60+); $4 (ages 6-12). Rates may vary; phone ahead. **Phone:** (419) 738-8811 or (800) 860-0142.

BEST WESTERN WAPAKONETA INN 419/738-2050
APPROVED
Hotel
Best Western. **AAA Benefit:** Members save up to 15% and earn bonus points!

Address: 1008 Lunar Dr 45895 **Location:** I-75 exit 111, just w. **Facility:** 54 units. 2 stories, interior corridors. **Parking:** winter plug-ins. **Amenities:** safes. **Pool:** heated indoor. **Activities:** exercise room.

WARREN (C-8) pop. 41,557, elev. 894'
• Hotels p. 306 • Restaurants p. 306

Settled in 1799, Warren was named after the territorial surveyor Moses Warren. The site of early iron and coal production, the city served as the first capital of the historic Connecticut Western Reserve. Trumbull County, including Warren, played a significant role in the Underground Railroad.

Local industrialists William Doud and James Ward Packard established the Packard Electric Co. in 1890. The first Packard automobile was built in Warren. The success of the Packard brought prosperity to the town, as evidenced by the unusual architectural styles of the grand homes along "Millionaires Row" on Mahoning Avenue. Warren was the first U.S. city to light its streets with incandescent bulbs.

You can visit two historic houses downtown. The John Stark Edwards House Museum, 303 Monroe St. N.W., dates to 1807 and is open the first Sun. of the month 2-5 and other times by appointment. It showcases some of the former residents' belongings; phone (330) 394-4653 to confirm tour schedule. The Upton House, 380 Mahoning Ave. N.W., was built in

1840 by Gen. Simon Perkins and was later inhabited by Harriet Taylor Upton, a prominent suffragist. In fact, the house even served as temporary headquarters of the National American Woman Suffrage Association. The home is open for tours by appointment; phone (330) 395-1840. Across the street is The Women's Park, which features a stone bridge and brick walkways inscribed with dedications to women who have inspired others.

Northwest on US 422 next to the McDonald's at 2487 Parkman Rd. is the former site of the Warren Airways Airport from which Neil Armstrong, at the age of 6, took his first flight; 33 years later he became the first human to walk on the moon. Commemorating both firsts is the Neil Armstrong "First Flight" Lunar Memorial, a half-scale replica of the *Apollo 11* Lunar Module set on a concrete slab cratered to resemble the moon's surface, and a 1/16-scale model rocket replicating the Gemini V mission.

The W.D. Packard Music Hall, built in 1955, is used for concerts, lectures and other programs. The 43-mile Western Reserve Greenway trail runs between Ashtabula and Warren. The trail offers opportunities for biking, hiking and horseback riding.

Trumbull County Tourism Bureau: 321 Mahoning Ave. N.W., Warren, OH 44483. **Phone:** (330) 675-3081 or (866) 360-1552.

NATIONAL PACKARD MUSEUM is 1.5 mi. s. of SRs 5 and 82 at 1899 Mahoning Ave. Displays detail the history of the Packard family, as well as the Packard Motor Car Co. and the Packard Electric Co., from their beginnings in Warren in 1890 to the present. The museum houses the largest collection of Packard family and business memorabilia and also features a Packard automobile collection dating 1900-56.

Time: Allow 1 hour minimum. **Hours:** Tues.-Sat. noon-5, Sun. 1-5. Closed Jan. 1, Easter, July 4, Thanksgiving, Christmas Eve, Christmas and Dec. 31. **Cost:** $8; $5 (ages 7-12 and 65+). **Phone:** (330) 394-1899.

BEST WESTERN PARK HOTEL   330/393-1200

 THREE DIAMOND

Hotel   Best Western.   **AAA Benefit:** Members save up to 15% and earn bonus points!

Address: 136 N Park Ave 44481 **Location:** East side of Courthouse Square; downtown. **Facility:** 54 units. 46 stories, interior corridors. **Parking:** on-site (fee). **Activities:** exercise room. **Guest Services:** coin laundry. **Featured Amenity:** full hot breakfast.

SAVE 🍴 🍸 CALL 📶 ♿ BIZ
HS 📶 ✕ 🔌 🖥 💻

FAIRFIELD BY MARRIOTT-WARREN/NILES   330/544-5774
APPROVED SAVE Hotel. **Address:** 1860 Niles-Cortland Rd 44484   **AAA Benefit:** Members save 5% or more!

HOLIDAY INN EXPRESS HOTEL & SUITES   330/544-8807
THREE DIAMOND Hotel. **Address:** 135 Highland Terrace Blvd 44484

WHERE TO EAT

CAFE 422   330/369-2422
APPROVED   Italian. Casual Dining. **Address:** 4422 Youngstown Rd SE 44484

THE CHOPHOUSE   330/856-2121
THREE DIAMOND   Steak. Casual Dining. **Address:** 9519 E Market St 44484

LEO'S RISTORANTE   330/856-5291
APPROVED   Italian. Casual Dining. **Address:** 7042 E Market St 44446

SALVATORE'S ITALIAN GRILL   330/609-7777
APPROVED   Italian. Casual Dining. **Address:** 8720 E Market St 44484

WARRENSVILLE HEIGHTS pop. 13,542
• Hotels & Restaurants map & index p. 194
• Part of Cleveland area — see map p. 177

CLEVELAND MARRIOTT EAST   216/378-9191 40
THREE DIAMOND SAVE Hotel. **Address:** 26300 Harvard Rd 44122   **AAA Benefit:** Members save 5% or more!

WASHINGTON COURT HOUSE (G-3)
pop. 14,192, elev. 973'

The town was originally named Washington, and the affix "Court House" was added in the late 1820s to distinguish the town from four other Washingtons in Ohio.

The Fayette County Court House contains murals by Archibald M. Willard, who created the painting "Spirit of '76."

Fayette County Chamber of Commerce: 101 E. East St., Washington Court House, OH 43160. **Phone:** (740) 335-0761.

Shopping: There are several antique shops, craft stores and boutiques in the downtown business district.

HOLIDAY INN EXPRESS WASHINGTON COURT HOUSE JEFFERSONVILLE SOUTHWEST   740/335-9310
THREE DIAMOND Hotel. **Address:** 101 Courthouse Pkwy 43160

WHERE TO EAT

HONG KONG BUFFET   740/636-8888
APPROVED   Chinese. Buffet Style. **Address:** 1142 Columbus Ave 43160

STREETSIDE 62 LOCAL BISTRO   740/335-6262
APPROVED   American. Casual Dining. **Address:** 2007 Columbus Ave 43160

WAYNE NATIONAL FOREST (F-6)

Elevations in the forest range from 630 ft. on the Ohio River near Newport to 1,320 ft. on the Narrows River on a ridge near Sardis. Refer to AAA maps for additional information.

In the southeastern portion of the state is Wayne National Forest, named in honor of Revolutionary War hero Gen. Anthony Wayne. The forest encompasses three general areas totaling 244,000 acres. More than 300 miles of hiking, mountain biking, horse and off-highway vehicle trails wind through the forest; the trails are open mid-April to mid-December. Redbuds and dogwoods bloom in spring, and the fall foliage is stunning. Starting in Marietta and ending in Woodsfield, the Covered Bridge Scenic Byway stretches 35 miles and leads travelers to 10 interpretive stops, including a historical mill site, covered bridges, a painted barn advertising Mail Pouch Tobacco, a historic inn, a homestead and an oil well.

Flowing through the forest's Marietta unit, the Little Muskingum River offers opportunities for canoeing and kayaking as well as fishing. Lake Vesuvius Recreation Area, north of Ironton off SR 93, includes a lake, campground and a 19th-century furnace left from Ohio's iron industry. Primitive camping is available throughout the forest and both the Athens and Ironton units have developed campgrounds; a small fee is charged. Hunting is permitted in season.

The forest is free and open all year. For maps and information contact the Supervisor's Office/Athens District, (740) 753-0101, at 13700 US 33, Nelsonville, OH 45764; Ironton District, (740) 534-6500, at 6518 SR 93, Pedro, OH 45659; or the Marietta District, (740) 373-9055, 27515 SR 7, Marietta, OH 45750. *See Recreation Areas Chart.*

WELLINGTON (C-6) pop. 4,802, elev. 855'

Established in 1818, Wellington did not achieve its potential until 1850 when the railroad arrived. A station on the Underground Railroad, the town was the site of the Oberlin/Wellington Slave Rescue of 1858. By 1880 the town was known as the "Cheese Capital of the United States," with more than 40 cheese factories in the area.

Wellington was the 1855-75 home of Archibald M. Willard, painter of the classic "Spirit of '76." A copy of the artwork, along with many Willard originals, hangs in the town library at 101 Willard Memorial Square and in the Spirit of '76 Museum at 201 N. Main St.; phone (440) 647-2120 and (440) 647-4367, respectively. Another notable native was Myron T. Herrick, governor of Ohio 1904-06 and ambassador to France, 1912-14 and 1921-29.

There are many opportunities to enjoy outdoor activities such as hiking, mountain biking, fishing, camping, kayaking, disc golf and paddleboating at Wellington Reservation and Findley State Park. *See Recreation Areas Chart.*

WEST CHESTER (H-11) elev. 653'

- **Restaurants p. 308**
- **Hotels & Restaurants map & index p. 166**
- **Part of Cincinnati area — see map p. 153**

Butler County Visitors Bureau: 8756 Union Centre Blvd., West Chester, OH 45069. **Phone:** (888) 462-2282.

SAVE **ENTERTAINMENT JUNCTION** is off I-75 exit 22, just e. on Tylersville Rd., just s. on Kingsgate Rd., then just w. to 7379 Squire Ct. Train Journey, billed as the world's largest indoor train display, has 25,000 square feet of G-scale model trains (1/24 the size of real trains) that travel along more than 2 miles of track through detailed displays representing different eras in railroad history. There even is an 11-foot waterfall. The American Railroading Museum includes railroad artifacts, trivia kiosks and a video theater. At Imagination Junction, kids can play at an indoor 5,000-square-foot railroad-themed play area. From Memorial Day through Labor Day, children can ride a hand-cranked locomotive around a 300-foot track, and the Narrow Gauge Kid's Train is in operation on 1,000 feet of track, weather permitting.

The second main attraction of the complex is the A-Maze-N FunHouse, where visitors can attempt to make their way through a tilt room, mirror maze, claustrophobia hallway, black light walk-through and the Ames Room (distorted to create optical illusions). Special events include Christmas at the Junction, Jack O'Lantern Junction and Thomas the Tank Engine month. A behind-the-scenes tour also is available.

Hours: Mon.-Sat. 10-6, Sun. noon-6. Phone for seasonal activity/display and behind-the-scenes tour schedules. **Cost:** Train Journey $13.95; $11.95 (ages 65+); $9.95 (ages 3-12). Funhouse $9.95; free (ages 0-2). Combination tickets are available. **Phone:** (513) 898-8000 or (877) 898-4656. GT

CINCINNATI MARRIOTT NORTH AT UNION CENTRE
513/874-7335 **31**
THREE DIAMOND SAVE Hotel. **Address:** 6189 Muhlhauser Rd 45069
AAA Benefit: Members save 5% or more!

COURTYARD BY MARRIOTT-CINCINNATI NORTH AT UNION CENTRE
513/341-4140 **29**
THREE DIAMOND SAVE Hotel. **Address:** 6250 Muhlhauser Rd 45069
AAA Benefit: Members save 5% or more!

HAMPTON INN & SUITES BY HILTON CINCINNATI NORTH AT UNION CENTRE
513/341-2040 **33**
THREE DIAMOND SAVE Hotel. **Address:** 9266 Schulze Dr 45069
AAA Benefit: Members save up to 15%!

🔗 **For complete hotel, dining and attraction listings: AAA.com/travelguides**

(See map & index p. 166.)

HILTON GARDEN INN WEST CHESTER   513/860-3170 **34**
THREE DIAMOND SAVE Hotel. **Address: 9306 Schulze Dr 45069**

AAA Benefit:
Members save up to 15%!

HOLIDAY INN CINCINNATI NORTH-WEST CHESTER
513/874-2744 **35**
THREE DIAMOND Hotel. **Address:** 5800 Muhlhauser Rd 45069

HOMEWOOD SUITES BY HILTON CINCINNATI-WEST CHESTER   513/805-4400 **32**
THREE DIAMOND

Extended Stay Hotel

HOMEWOOD **AAA Benefit:**
SUITES Members save up
BY HILTON to 15%!

Address: 9226 Schulze Dr 45069 **Location:** I-75 exit 19, just w on Union Centre Blvd, just s on Muhlhauser Rd, then just e. **Facility:** 112 efficiencies. 5 stories, interior corridors. **Pool:** heated indoor. **Activities:** exercise room. **Guest Services:** valet and coin laundry. **Featured Amenity:** breakfast buffet.

SAVE ♦ CALL ♿ ⛱ ♿ BIZ
HS 🛜 ✕ 🖥 🖥 🖥

QUALITY INN   513/755-3900 **27**
APPROVED Hotel. **Address:** 8567 Cincinnati-Dayton Rd 45069

RESIDENCE INN BY MARRIOTT CINCINNATI NORTH/WEST CHESTER   513/341-4040 **30**
THREE DIAMOND SAVE Extended Stay Hotel. **Address:** 6240 Muhlhauser Rd 45069

AAA Benefit:
Members save 5% or more!

STAYBRIDGE SUITES CINCINNATI NORTH
513/874-1900 **28**
THREE DIAMOND Extended Stay Hotel. **Address:** 8955 Lakota Dr W 45069

WHERE TO EAT

CITY BARBEQUE   513/755-0518
APPROVED Barbecue. Quick Serve. **Address:** 7706 Voice of America Centre Dr 45069

DINGLE HOUSE PUB & GRUB   513/874-7468 **32**
APPROVED American. Casual Dining. **Address:** 9102 West Chester Towne Center Dr 45069

JAG'S STEAK & SEAFOOD   513/860-5353 **31**
THREE DIAMOND Steak Seafood. Fine Dining. **Address:** 5980 West Chester Rd 45069

MATT THE MILLER'S TAVERN   513/298-4050 **35**
APPROVED American. Casual Dining. **Address:** 9558 Civic Centre Blvd 45069

MITCHELL'S FISH MARKET   513/779-5292 **34**
THREE DIAMOND SAVE Seafood. Casual Dining. **Address:** 9456 Waterfront Dr 45069

P.F. CHANG'S CHINA BISTRO   513/779-5555 **33**
THREE DIAMOND Chinese. Fine Dining. **Address:** 9435 Civic Centre Blvd 45069

RUSTY BUCKET RESTAURANT AND TAVERN
513/463-2600 **30**
APPROVED American. Casual Dining. **Address:** 7524 Bales St 45069

SKYLINE CHILI
APPROVED American. Quick Serve.
LOCATIONS:
Address: 6098 West Chester Rd 45069 **Phone:** 513/860-5300
Address: 7132 Cincinnati-Dayton Rd, Suite 100 45069
Phone: 513/777-7555

WESTERVILLE (E-4) pop. 36,120, elev. 874'

- **Hotels & Restaurants map & index p. 222**
- **Part of Columbus area — see map p. 205**

Westerville, incorporated in 1858, became known as the "dry capital of the world" when the Anti-Saloon League settled here in 1909 and led the successful campaign for the 18th amendment prohibiting alcohol. The Westerville Public Library houses the Anti-Saloon League Museum, which contains printed materials used in the fight against alcohol, including posters, fliers and booklets, as well as the John R. Kasich Congressional Collection papers and memorabilia; phone (614) 882-7277 or (800) 816-0662.

Nearby is the nationally known Temperance Row Historic District where the anti-liquor leaders lived. The Hanby House at 160 W. Main St. is the restored and furnished pre-Civil War home of Benjamin Hanby, author and composer of "Darling Nelly Gray" and "Up on the House Top." The house is open weekends 1-4 May through September and other times by appointment; phone (614) 891-6289 or (800) 600-6843 to confirm schedule.

Westerville Visitors and Convention Bureau: 20 W. Main St., Westerville, OH 43081. **Phone:** (614) 794-0401.

INNISWOOD METRO GARDENS is off I-270 exit 29, .4 mi. n. to Schrock Rd., then 1.5 mi. e. to 940 S. Hempstead Rd. The 123-acre gardens feature mixed perennial and shrub borders, annual display beds, an herb garden, a children's garden, a rose garden, a rock garden with waterfalls and nicely landscaped grounds. Paved walking paths and a boardwalk trail pass through a hardwood forest. **Time:** Allow 1 hour, 30 minutes minimum. **Hours:** Daily 7 a.m.-dusk. **Cost:** Free. **Phone:** (614) 895-6216.

ALOFT COLUMBUS WESTERVILLE   614/899-6560 **71**
THREE DIAMOND SAVE
Contemporary Hotel. **Address:** 32 Heatherdown Dr 43081

AAA Benefit:
Members save 5% or more!

RENAISSANCE COLUMBUS WESTERVILLE-POLARIS HOTEL   614/882-6800 **70**
THREE DIAMOND

Contemporary Hotel

R
RENAISSANCE°
HOTELS

AAA Benefit:
Members save 5% or more!

Address: 409 Altair Pkwy 43082 **Location:** I-71 exit 121, 1.3 mi e on Polaris Pkwy. **Facility:** 222 units. 8 stories, interior corridors. **Terms:** check-in 4 pm. **Amenities:** safes. **Pool:** heated indoor. **Activities:** lawn sports, exercise room. **Guest Services:** valet laundry.

SAVE ♦ ♿ ♿ CALL ♿ ⛱
♿ BIZ 🛜 ✕ 🖥 🖥

(See map & index p. 222.)

WHERE TO EAT

101 BEER KITCHEN   614/776-4775 (60)
APPROVED   American. Gastropub. **Address:** 817 Polaris Pkwy 43082

CITY BARBEQUE   614/823-8890
APPROVED   Barbecue. Quick Serve. **Address:** 600 S State St 43081

THE OLD BAG OF NAILS PUB   614/794-6900 (61)
APPROVED   American. Casual Dining. **Address:** 24 N State St 43081

Q2 BISTRO   614/898-1988 (59)
APPROVED   Chinese. Casual Dining. **Address:** 472 Polaris Pkwy 43082

SKYLINE CHILI   614/890-8400
APPROVED   American. Quick Serve. **Address:** 117 Westerville Plaza 43081

WESTLAKE (B-9) pop. 32,729, elev. 709'
- **Hotels & Restaurants map & index p. 194**
- **Part of Cleveland area — see map p. 177**

The pond at Clague Park, 1400 Clague Rd., is a nice place to relax and watch the adorable goings-on of the ducks. I-90 runs through this Cleveland suburb, making city life available in just about a 15-mile drive.

COURTYARD BY MARRIOTT CLEVELAND WESTLAKE
                                              440/871-3756 (48)
THREE DIAMOND SAVE Hotel. **Address:** 25050 Sperry Dr 44145

AAA Benefit: Members save 5% or more!

DOUBLETREE BY HILTON CLEVELAND/WESTLAKE
                                              440/871-6000 (49)
THREE DIAMOND SAVE Hotel. **Address:** 1100 Crocker Rd 44145

AAA Benefit: Members save up to 15%!

EXTENDED STAY AMERICA CLEVELAND-WESTLAKE
                                              440/899-4160 (53)
APPROVED   Extended Stay Hotel. **Address:** 30360 Clemens Rd 44145

HAMPTON INN BY HILTON CLEVELAND-WESTLAKE
                                              440/892-0333 (54)
APPROVED SAVE Hotel. **Address:** 29690 Detroit Rd 44145

AAA Benefit: Members save up to 15%!

HOLIDAY INN EXPRESS & SUITES WESTLAKE
                                              440/808-0500 (50)
THREE DIAMOND Hotel. **Address:** 30500 Clemens Rd 44145

HYATT PLACE CLEVELAND WESTLAKE CROCKER PARK   440/871-3100 (55)
THREE DIAMOND   Hotel

HYATT PLACE

AAA Benefit: Members save up to 10%!

Address: 2020 Crocker Rd 44145 **Location:** I-90 exit 156, 0.7 mi s. Located in Crocker Park shopping complex. **Facility:** 110 units. 6 stories, interior corridors. **Pool:** heated indoor. **Activities:** exercise room. **Guest Services:** valet laundry. **Featured Amenity: breakfast buffet.**

RED ROOF INN CLEVELAND-WESTLAKE
                                              440/892-7920 (52)
APPROVED   Motel

Address: 29595 Clemens Rd 44145 **Location:** I-90 exit 156, just n. **Facility:** 98 units. 2 stories (no elevator), exterior corridors. **Amenities:** safes.

SONESTA ES SUITES CLEVELAND WESTLAKE
                                              440/892-2254 (51)
APPROVED   Extended Stay Hotel. **Address:** 30100 Clemens Rd 44145

TOWNEPLACE SUITES BY MARRIOTT CLEVELAND WESTLAKE   440/892-4275 (47)
THREE DIAMOND SAVE Extended Stay Hotel. **Address:** 25052 Sperry Dr 44145

AAA Benefit: Members save 5% or more!

WHERE TO EAT

BURNTWOOD TAVERN   440/455-1732 (42)
APPROVED   American. Casual Dining. **Address:** 12 Main St 44145

CABIN CLUB   440/899-7111 (41)
THREE DIAMOND Steak Seafood. Casual Dining. **Address:** 30651 Detroit Rd 44145

SANGRIA TAPAS & BAR   440/617-6476 (40)
THREE DIAMOND Spanish Small Plates. Casual Dining. **Address:** 27200 Detroit Rd 44145

Find AAA Inspected & Approved
campgrounds at AAA.com/campgrounds

WEST LIBERTY (E-3) pop. 1,805, elev. 1,009'

OHIO CAVERNS is 4 mi. s.e. on SR 245. Discovered in 1897, the caves maintain a constant temperature of 54 degrees F. Vividly colored walls contrast with pure white stalactites and stalagmites. The guided 1-mile Natural Wonder Tour, which lasts 50-55 minutes, takes visitors through the caverns along electrically lighted passageways. On the .75-mile Historic Tour visitors take a shuttle bus to the original entrance where the cavern was first discovered and then are shown the parts of the cavern that were toured 1897-1925; the tour lasts about 45 minutes.

The Limestone Tour is a 25-minute handicap-accessible, quarter-mile tour featuring the first part of the Natural Wonder tour. Above the site is a 35-acre park with a playground and opportunities for gem mining.

Photography is permitted but video cameras are not allowed in the caverns. **Time:** Allow 1 hour minimum. **Hours:** Natural Wonder and Historic tours are given as needed daily 9-5, May-Sept.; 10-4, rest of year. Limestone Tour offered by appointment, May-Sept. **Cost:** Natural Wonder and Historic tours $19; $10 (ages 5-12). Limestone tour $12; $9 (ages 5-12). **Phone:** (937) 465-4017. GT 🎫

THE PIATT CASTLES are 1 and 2 mi. e. on SR 245. Self-guiding tours let visitors explore the 1871 limestone Mac-A-Cheek Castle and acquaint them with the lives of several generations of former occupants. Mac-O-Chee Castle was begun in the 1860s as a modest Gothic retreat and was remodeled in 1881 with a Flemish-inspired limestone addition. It contains mostly American furnishings with a few European pieces. Mac-O-Chee was the home of Donn Piatt, a well-known publisher and author, and his wife, Ella, an artist.

Time: Allow 1 hour minimum. **Hours:** Both castles open daily 11-5, Memorial Day-Labor Day; Sat.-Sun. 11-4, mid-Apr. through day before Memorial Day and day after Labor Day-Nov. 1. Last tour begins at closing. **Cost:** (per castle) $15; $13 (ages 65+); $9 (ages 5-15). Combination ticket for both castles $25; $20 (ages 65+); $15 (ages 5-15). **Phone:** (937) 465-2821.

WHEELERSBURG pop. 6,437

COMFORT INN 740/574-1046
⬥ **APPROVED** **Address:** 8226 Ohio River Rd 45694 **Location:** US 52 exit Wheelersburg. Located in a commercial area. **Facility:** 52 units. 2 stories, interior corridors. **Pool:** heated indoor. **Guest Services:** valet and coin laundry. **Featured Amenity: full hot breakfast.**
Hotel

FRED'S RESTAURANT 740/574-2507
⬥ **APPROVED** American. Casual Dining. **Address:** 8228 Ohio River Rd 45694

WILBERFORCE (F-2) pop. 2,271, elev. 1,007'

In 1856 the Methodist Episcopal Church purchased a tract of land in southwest Ohio for the purpose of opening a college, then known as Ohio African University, for escaped and freed slaves. This college, the first African-American university in the country, is now Wilberforce University, named after the 18th-century British abolitionist William Wilberforce.

THE NATIONAL AFRO-AMERICAN MUSEUM & CULTURAL CENTER is off US 42 at 1350 Brush Row Rd. The museum educates the public about African-American history and culture from African origins to the present through the collection, preservation and interpretation of material evidence. Changing exhibits, artifacts and manuscripts are included.

Time: Allow 1 hour, 30 minutes minimum. **Hours:** Mon.-Fri. and Martin Luther King Jr. Day 8-4, Sat. 9-4. Guided tours are available with 2-week notice. Closed major holidays. Phone ahead to confirm schedule. **Cost:** $6; $5 (ages 60+); $3 (ages 6-18 and college students with ID). Rates may vary; phone ahead. **Phone:** (937) 376-4944 or (800) 752-2603, ext. 114. GT

WILLOUGHBY pop. 22,268, elev. 659'
• **Hotels & Restaurants map & index p. 194**
• **Part of Cleveland area — see map p. 177**

COURTYARD BY MARRIOTT 440/530-1100 🆗
⬥ **THREE DIAMOND** SAVE Hotel. **Address:** 35103 Maplegrove Rd 44094
AAA Benefit:
Members save 5% or more!

RED ROOF INN CLEVELAND MENTOR-WILLOUGHBY 440/946-9872 🔞
⬥ **APPROVED** **Address:** 4166 SR 306 44094 **Location:** I-90 exit 193, just s. **Facility:** 108 units. 2 stories (no elevator), exterior corridors. **Amenities:** safes.
Motel
SAVE CALL 🐾 🛜 ✕ / SOME UNITS 🐾 🔇 🍽 💻

FIREHOUSE GRILLE & PUB 440/943-4983 ㉓
⬥ **APPROVED** American. Casual Dining. **Address:** 2768 Stark Dr 44094

THE WILD GOOSE 440/951-6644 ㉒
⬥ **APPROVED** American. Gastropub. **Address:** 4144 Erie St 44094

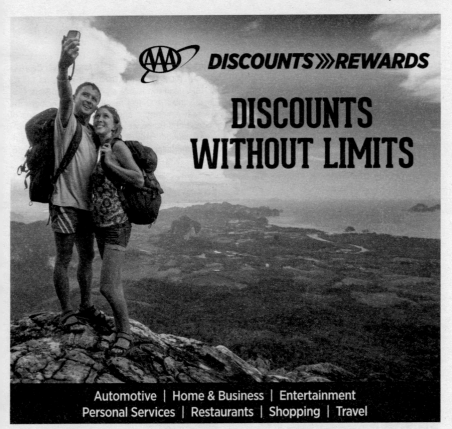

WILMINGTON (G-3) pop. 12,520, elev. 1,017'
• Part of Cincinnati area — see map p. 153

The Clinton County Courthouse was completed in 1919 and restored in 1999. This aesthetically pleasing and imposing three-story limestone structure is a fine example of Second Renaissance Revival architecture. Among the interior architectural details are marble columns, faux marble walls, ornamental plasterwork, ceiling decorations, a 36-foot diameter dome with 128-panels with rosettes and ornate bronze light fixtures. This working courthouse is open Mon.-Fri. 8-4. For more information phone (937) 382-2103.

Clinton County Convention & Visitor's Bureau: 13 N. South St., Wilmington, OH 45177. **Phone:** (937) 382-1965 or (877) 428-4748.

HAMPTON INN & SUITES BY HILTON WILMINGTON
937/382-4400

THREE DIAMOND **SAVE** Hotel. **Address:** 201 Holiday Dr 45177

AAA Benefit:
Members save up to 15%!

HOLIDAY INN EXPRESS 937/382-5858
THREE DIAMOND Hotel. **Address:** 155 Holiday Dr 45177

HOLIDAY INN WILMINGTON & ROBERTS CONFERENCE CENTRE 937/283-3200
THREE DIAMOND Hotel. **Address:** 123 Gano Rd 45177

WHERE TO EAT

THE MEDITERRANEAN RESTAURANT & CAFE 937/382-6300
APPROVED Italian. Casual Dining. **Address:** 53 E Main St 45177

WOOSTER (E-9) pop. 26,119, elev. 912'

During the War of 1812, an Army headquarters and a land office were established in Wooster. These drew permanent settlers, including the young German immigrant August Imgard, who local historians claim introduced Christmas trees to America in 1847.

The Ohio Light Opera, the residential professional company of The College of Wooster, performs operetta and lyric theater mid-June to mid-August at Freedlander Theatre at 329 E. University St.; phone (330) 263-2345 for tickets. The college is a private liberal arts school with about 2,000 students.

Alice Noble Ice Arena, at 851 Oldman Rd. on the Wooster High School campus, offers public skating times. The arena also is home to the Wooster Oilers hockey team. The arena hosts a variety of activities, so phone for public skating schedule; (330) 345-8686.

Wayne County Convention and Visitors Bureau: 428 W. Liberty St., Wooster, OH 44691. **Phone:** (330) 264-1800 or (800) 362-6474.

Shopping: Downtown Wooster is a vibrant shopping area featuring many upscale shops. Gallery in the Vault, 105 E. Liberty St., offers art and gift items in an old bank building where shoppers can go inside the vault. Stock up on laundry, kitchen, home organization and cleaning goods at the Everything Rubbermaid retail store at 115 S. Market St, right off the town square.

OHIO AGRICULTURAL RESEARCH AND DEVELOPMENT CENTER (OARDC) is 1 mi. s. on SR 83 at 1680 Madison Ave. Part of The Ohio State University, this 2,100-acre research center includes the Secrest Arboretum and the Garden of Roses of Legend and Romance. **Time:** Allow 1 hour, 30 minutes minimum. **Hours:** Grounds open daily dawn-dusk. Phone for guided tour information. **Cost:** Free. **Phone:** (330) 263-3700. GT

BEST WESTERN WOOSTER HOTEL AND CONFERENCE CENTER 330/264-7750
THREE DIAMOND
Hotel

AAA Benefit: Members save up to 15% and earn bonus points!

Address: 243 E Liberty St 44691 **Location:** Just e of Town Square. **Facility:** 100 units. 3 stories, interior corridors. **Pool:** outdoor. **Activities:** exercise room. **Guest Services:** valet and coin laundry. **Featured Amenity: breakfast buffet.**

COMFORT SUITES WOOSTER 855/772-2577
THREE DIAMOND
Hotel

Address: 965 Dover Rd 44691 **Location:** 2.5 mi s on SR 83 from US 30. **Facility:** 80 units. 4 stories, interior corridors. **Parking:** winter plug-ins. **Pool:** heated indoor. **Activities:** exercise room. **Guest Services:** coin laundry. **Featured Amenity: full hot breakfast.**

HAMPTON INN BY HILTON 330/345-4424
THREE DIAMOND **SAVE** Hotel. **Address:** 4253 Burbank Rd 44691

AAA Benefit:
Members save up to 15%!

HILTON GARDEN INN 330/202-7701
THREE DIAMOND **SAVE** Hotel. **Address:** 959 Dover Rd 44691

AAA Benefit:
Members save up to 15%!

ST. PAUL HOTEL WOOSTER 330/601-1900
THREE DIAMOND
Boutique Hotel

Address: 203 S Market St 44691 **Location:** US 30 exit Madison Ave, 0.7 mi nw on SR 302. **Facility:** Nestled in the center of a small city with numerous restaurants and shops, this stylish hotel is a fine place for a relaxing weekend. Rooms juxtapose black walnut furniture with sassy orange chairs. 16 units. 3 stories, interior corridors. *Bath:* shower only. **Activities:** exercise room. **Guest Services:** valet laundry. **Featured Amenity: continental breakfast.**

WHERE TO EAT

BASIL ASIAN BISTRO   330/601-0885
APPROVED Asian. Casual Dining. **Address:** 145 W Liberty St 44691

BROKEN ROCKS CAFE & BAKERY   330/263-2949
THREE DIAMOND American. Casual Dining. **Address:** 123 E Liberty St 44691

CW BURGERSTEINS   330/264-6263
APPROVED American. Casual Dining. **Address:** 359 W Liberty St 44691

FARMER BOY FAMILY RESTAURANT   330/345-7799
APPROVED Comfort Food. Casual Dining. **Address:** 2558 Cleveland Rd 44691

JAKE'S RESTAURANT   330/345-5523
APPROVED American. Casual Dining. **Address:** 6655 E Lincoln Way 44691

OLDE JAOL STEAKHOUSE   330/262-3333
THREE DIAMOND Steak. Fine Dining. **Address:** 215 N Walnut St 44691

TJ'S RESTAURANT   330/264-6263
APPROVED American. Casual Dining. **Address:** 359 W Liberty St 44691

WORTHINGTON pop. 13,575
- **Hotels & Restaurants map & index p. 222**
- **Part of Columbus area — see map p. 205**

CAMERON'S AMERICAN BISTRO   614/885-3663 **74**
THREE DIAMOND American. Casual Dining. **Address:** 2185 W Dublin-Granville Rd 43085

J. LIU RESTAURANT & BAR   614/888-1818 **72**
THREE DIAMOND American. Casual Dining. **Address:** 6880 N High St 43085

NATALIE'S COAL-FIRED PIZZA   614/436-2625 **75**
APPROVED Pizza. Casual Dining. **Address:** 5601 N High St 43085

THE WHITNEY HOUSE   614/396-7846 **73**
THREE DIAMOND American. Casual Dining. **Address:** 666 High St 43085

XENIA pop. 25,719, elev. 910'
- **Hotels & Restaurants map & index p. 242**

HAMPTON INN & SUITES BY HILTON XENIA/DAYTON
                                 937/347-1029 **34**
THREE DIAMOND SAVE Hotel. **Address:** 194 S Progress Dr 45385

AAA Benefit: Members save up to 15%!

YOUNGSTOWN (C-9) pop. 66,982, elev. 856'
- **Hotels p. 314**

Youngstown was named after John Young, a surveyor who purchased 15,600 acres of land in 1797. The town's development was slow until 1803, when iron ore was discovered and the first blast furnace was established in the area. The opening of the Pennsylvania and Ohio Canal increased both the population and industrialization of the area during the 1820s. In 1862 the first coal mine was opened, and the first steel plant, the Union Iron and Steel

Co., was built in 1892. Most early settlers came from Pennsylvania, New York and New England; however, the growing industrial economy soon attracted European emigrants.

Youngstown State University, with an enrollment of nearly 15,000 undergraduate and graduate students, was established in 1908.

Mahoning County Convention & Visitors Bureau: 21 W. Boardman St., Youngstown, OH 44503. **Phone:** (330) 740-2130 or (800) 447-8201.

Shopping: Along the US 224 corridor is Southern Park Mall—anchored by Dillard's, JCPenney and Macy's—and Boardman Plaza, one of the country's first strip malls.

THE BUTLER INSTITUTE OF AMERICAN ART is at 524 Wick Ave. The museum was founded in 1919 by Youngstown industrialist Joseph G. Butler Jr. The collection focuses on American art from the Colonial period to the present, including a wing dedicated to digital art. Highlights include works by Mary Cassatt, John Copley, Thomas Eakins, Winslow Homer, Georgia O'Keeffe, Frederic Remington, Norman Rockwell, Charles Sheeler, Robert Vonnoh, Andy Warhol and Benjamin West.

The Trumbull branch (about 12 miles north in Howland Township) showcases works by international artists as well as contemporary sculptors and painters. **Time:** Allow 1 hour minimum. **Hours:** Wed.-Sat. 11-4, Sun. noon-4. Closed most major holidays. **Cost:** Free. **Phone:** (330) 743-1107. **11**

MILL CREEK PARK is s. of Mahoning Ave. off Glenwood Ave. The 2,882-acre park contains a 6-mile-long gorge, 15 miles of foot trails, 20 miles of drives, a pond and three lakes. Opportunities for biking, boating, cross-country skiing, fishing, golf, hiking, sledding and tennis are available. The largest of the lakes is 60-acre Lake Newport, which also includes 40 acres of wetlands that can be explored on the interpretive boardwalk along the Albert E. Davies Wetland Trail.

Four viewing platforms on the 1913 Parapet Bridge afford pleasant views of the area. Fellows Riverside Gardens, Ford Nature Center and Lanterman's Mill also are on the grounds. *See Recreation Areas Chart.* **Hours:** Daily dawn-dusk. **Cost:** Free. **Phone:** (330) 702-3000.

Fellows Riverside Gardens is s. off Mahoning Ave. at 123 McKinley Ave. at the north end of Mill Creek Park. The 12-acre garden encompasses a formal rose garden, perennials, shrubs, trees and seasonal displays of some 40,000 tulips in the spring and flowering annuals in the summer. Two overlooks provide views of the park and city. The architecturally interesting D.D. and Velma Davis Education & Visitor Center features the John C. Melnick Mill Creek Park Museum and the Andrew and Carol Weller Gallery and an observation tower and also provides maps and other visitor information. **Time:**

Allow 1 hour minimum. **Hours:** Grounds daily dawn-dusk. Visitor center Tues.-Sun. 10-5; closed Jan. 1, Thanksgiving and Christmas. **Cost:** Free. **Phone:** (330) 740-7116. (ℹ️)

Ford Nature Center is at 840 Old Furnace Rd. and is part of Mill Creek Park. This former residence built of stone now houses a naturalist staff and a variety of displays. Three rooms feature native plants and animals as well as hands-on exhibits. Wildlife gardens, walking trails and areas for bird-watching are included. Nature programs and hikes also are offered. **Hours:** Tues.-Sat. 10-5, Sun. noon-5. Phone for holiday closures. **Cost:** Free. **Phone:** (330) 740-7107.

Lanterman's Mill is at 1001 Canfield Rd. and is part of Mill Creek Park. The restored 1846 water-powered gristmill has been completely renovated and still operates. The grounds also include hiking trails, one of which is a boardwalk; a covered bridge; and an observation deck for viewing Lanterman Falls. **Time:** Allow 30 minutes minimum. **Hours:** Tues.-Sun. 10-5, May-Oct.; Sat.-Sun. noon-4, in Apr. and Nov. **Cost:** $2; $1 (Mahoning County residents); 75c (ages 6-18 and 60+). **Phone:** (330) 740-7115.

YOUNGSTOWN HISTORICAL CENTER OF IN-DUSTRY & LABOR is at 151 W. Wood St. Exhibits chronicle the impact of the iron and steel industries upon Mahoning Valley communities. The museum's permanent exhibit explores labor, immigration and urban history using videos, photographs, reconstructed scenes and historic objects. Items displayed range from workers' tools and clothing to "last heats," the final batches of steel produced at a mill before it closes.

Time: Allow 1 hour minimum. **Hours:** Center open Wed.-Fri. 10-4, Sat. noon-4. Archives/library open Wed.-Fri. noon-4 (also Thurs. 4-7 during YSU spring and fall semesters) and first and third Sat. of each month noon-4. Closed major holidays. Phone ahead to confirm schedule. **Cost:** Center $7; $5 (senior citizens); $3 (students with ID); free (ages 0-5). Archives/library free. Rates may vary; phone ahead. **Phone:** (330) 941-1314 or (800) 262-6137.

ZANESVILLE (F-6) pop. 25,487, elev. 699'

Settled in 1799, Zanesville was once considered the pottery capital of the United States; its surrounding areas still support a number of pottery factories. Zanesville was the birthplace of such notables as the architect of New York's 1913 Woolworth Building, Cass Gilbert, in 1859, and novelists Charles D. Stewart in 1868 and Zane Grey in 1872.

The Y-Bridge, which carries US 40 over the junction of the Muskingum and Licking rivers, is shaped like the letter Y; the design is uncommon in the United States. Since the early 1800s, the bridge has been rebuilt several times. US 40 is the contemporary name for the first federal road, the National Road, authorized by Congress in 1806 to extend from Cumberland, Md., to the Ohio River.

Zanesville is at the junction of two scenic highways. US 22 runs southwest to Lancaster, and a scenic portion of I-70 runs east to Bridgeport, then through West Virginia and into Pennsylvania.

Lorena Sternwheeler is moored at Zane's Landing Park. This riverboat offers 1-hour sightseeing, lunch and twilight cruises as well as 2-hour dinner cruises on the Muskingum River. Tours are offered select dates early June to late October; phone (740) 455-8282.

Zanesville-Muskingum County Convention and Visitors Bureau: 205 N. Fifth St., Zanesville, OH 43701. **Phone:** (740) 455-8282 or (800) 743-2303.

Self-guiding tours: Brochures and maps are available from the visitor bureau. "The Muskingum County's Official Visitors Guide" is a comprehensive 48-page guide. Two walking maps detail the town's architecture and history and its artist colony. The brochure "America's First Main Street: National Road East" explains a driving tour of stops and shops along the Historic National Road Scenic Byway; "A Guide to Pottery" details a driving tour of the pottery outlets and stores and museums in the area; "Your Guide to Muskingum County Antique Dealers" relates a driving tour.

Shopping: Colony Square Mall, 3575 N. Maple Ave., features Dunham's Sports, JCPenney and T.J. Maxx. Freight Shops, at Third and Market streets, offers shops in the restored 1917 New York Central Railroad Depot.

ALAN COTTRILL SCULPTURE MUSEUM & STUDIO is at 110 S. 6th St. An accomplished sculptor, Alan Cottrill works mainly in bronze. His entire body of work is represented, including smaller pieces and photographs and narratives of his nationwide monuments. Visitors may tour the studio and wax and mold rooms, where artists and artisans are at work, and learn about the creation of a sculpture from idea to finished work.

A second-floor gallery features more than 400 bronze sculptures, dozens of which are on a monumental scale. **Time:** Allow 45 minutes minimum. **Hours:** Mon.-Sat. 9-5. Closed major holidays. **Cost:** $2. **Phone:** (740) 453-9822.

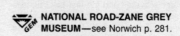 **NATIONAL ROAD-ZANE GREY MUSEUM**—see Norwich p. 281.

ZANESVILLE MUSEUM OF ART is 3.2 mi. n. via Maple Ave. at 620 Military Rd. The museum features

Ohio art pottery and glass as well as a diverse collection of traditional and contemporary art and fine craft from America, Africa, Asia and Europe. The museum has paintings, drawings, photographs, sculpture, prints and ceramics. Varied temporary exhibitions are presented throughout the year, and an art library is on the premises.

Paintings by old masters and decorative arts adorn a room that was once part of a 17th-century house in London, England. The paneling and carved fireplace enclosure create a fitting environment for the 15th- to mid-19th-century English, Flemish, Dutch, French and American paintings, sculpture and porcelain as well as the 18th- and 19th-century furnishings.

Time: Allow 1 hour minimum. **Hours:** Wed.-Sat. 10-5 (also Thurs. 5-7:30). Closed major holidays. **Cost:** $6; $4 (ages 10-18 and 60+). **Phone:** (740) 452-0741.

BEST WESTERN B. R. GUEST
740/453-6300

 APPROVED

Hotel

Best Western **AAA Benefit:** Members save up to 15% and earn bonus points!

Address: 4929 East Pike 43701 **Location:** I-70 exit 160, just s. **Facility:** 75 units. 3 stories, interior corridors. **Parking:** winter plug-ins. **Amenities:** safes. **Pool:** heated indoor. **Activities:** exercise room. **Guest Services:** coin laundry. **Featured Amenity:** full hot breakfast.

SAVE 📶 CALL 🛗 🏊 ♿ BIZ 🛜 💻 /SOME UNITS 🐾 🧳 🔲

HAMPTON INN BY HILTON
740/453-6511

THREE DIAMOND SAVE Hotel. **Address:** 1009 Spring St 43701

AAA Benefit: Members save up to 15%!

HOLIDAY INN EXPRESS & SUITES
740/297-4751

THREE DIAMOND Hotel. **Address:** 1101 Spring St 43701

QUALITY INN & SUITES
740/454-4144

 APPROVED

Hotel

Address: 500 Monroe St 43701 **Location:** I-70 exit 155, just e on Elberon Ave to light, then just n on Underwood St. **Facility:** 93 units. 2-3 stories, interior corridors. **Parking:** winter plug-ins. **Amenities:** safes. **Pool:** heated indoor. **Activities:** hot tub, exercise room. **Guest Services:** valet and coin laundry. **Featured Amenity:** full hot breakfast.

SAVE 📶 CALL 🛗 🏊 🧳 🛜 ❌ 🔲 🔳 💻 /SOME UNITS 🐾 HS

WHERE TO EAT

GIACOMO'S BREAD & MORE 740/452-7323

 APPROVED Breads/Pastries. Quick Serve. **Address:** 2236 Maple Ave 43701

MARK PI'S CHINA GATE 740/453-6655

 APPROVED Chinese. Casual Dining. **Address:** 2502 Maple Ave 43701

MUDDY MISER'S RESTAURANT 740/588-9210

APPROVED American. Casual Dining. **Address:** 112 Muskingum Ave 43701

OLDE FALLS INN 740/452-2300

APPROVED American. Casual Dining. **Address:** 3452 Newark Rd 43701

OLD MARKET HOUSE INN 740/454-2555

APPROVED American. Casual Dining. **Address:** 424 Market St 43701

ZOAR (D-7) pop. 169, elev. 883'

ZOAR VILLAGE is on SR 212, 3 mi. s.e. of I-77 exit 93 to 198 Main St. The village, founded in 1817 by German immigrants who acquired several thousand acres along the Tuscarawas River, is in the center of what was once the Zoar community. Their practically self-sustaining community prospered until it was dissolved in 1898, when village industries failed to keep pace with those of the rest of the country.

Visitors can tour restored buildings include Number One House, the home of leader Joseph Bimeler; a bakery; tin shop; wagon shed; general store; kitchen; dairy; blacksmith shop; and garden house. The community garden is geometrically patterned to symbolize the New Jerusalem.

Hours: Guided tours Wed.-Sat. 11-4, June-Sept.; other times by reservation. Zoar Store and Visitors Center open Wed.-Sat. 10-5, Sun. noon-5, Apr.-Dec.; Fri.-Sat. 10-5, Sun. noon-5, in Mar. Closed major holidays. Phone ahead to confirm schedule. **Cost:** $8; $4 (ages 5-17). **Phone:** (330) 874-3011 or (800) 262-6195. GT

New River Gorge National River

West Virginia

The Mountain State has endured a troubled history of Civil War battles, mountaineer feuds and coal mining labor disputes. But thanks to abundant highland beauty, the state has left its past difficulties far behind to become a playground for skiers, white-water rafters, hikers and anyone else who loves the outdoors.

This is not to say that West Virginians have forgotten their heritage. Descendants of self-reliant pioneers still craft objects that were once necessities of frontier life. And carefully restored sites like Harpers Ferry, Blennerhassett Island and Wheeling's Independence Hall show how seriously the locals take their history.

"Mountaineers Are Always Free"

Aptly named, the Mountain State is indeed the most mountainous east of the Mississippi. Blanketed with trees and cut through by swift-flowing streams, the chain of craggy peaks—part of the ancient Appalachians—

Spruce Knob-Seneca Rocks National Recreation Area

stretches along West Virginia's entire eastern border. This may once have been the capital of coal country, but today the most used natural resources are above ground.

West Virginia's ski slopes are considered some of the best east of the Rockies; names like Timberline, Canaan Valley and Snowshoe come to mind. An ever-growing number of white-water rafters challenge the rapids of the New, Gauley and Cheat rivers.

The thrill of these sports is intensified by the scenery. One sight to behold is the 1,000-foot-deep canyons of the New River Gorge National River, most dazzlingly viewed from the bridge perched above its raging waters. And although no one rafts down the plummeting streams of Blackwater, Hill Creek and Holly River falls, their beauty still draws tourists from all over.

Perhaps the greatest natural assets are stunning mountain vistas like those at Spruce Knob, the highest point in West Virginia. This peak is in Spruce Knob-Seneca Rocks National Recreation Area, one of the most popular rock climbing areas in the East.

Scenic Railways and Fall Foliage

Part of a once-extensive railway network for transporting lumber, the Cass Scenic Railroad carries passengers to a viewing area just below lofty Bald Knob for breathtaking views of the surrounding countryside. In fall, the landscape blazes with color as untold millions of leaves change hue. Similarly, West Virginia's many picturesque covered bridges were originally built for practical reasons but are now the focus of the pleasantly impractical endeavor of sightseeing.

Other man-made attractions also are worth seeking out. Victorian historic districts in Parkersburg, Wheeling and Charleston, the state capital, evoke the coal boom era. You'll also want to see the capitol building and its impressive 293-foot-tall golden dome.

The state's dramatic scenery continues underground thanks to the many caves scattered throughout the highlands. In Greenbrier Valley, Lost World Caverns features huge subterranean rooms and waterfalls up to 235 feet below the surface. And even if you can't tell the difference between a stalagmite and a stalactite you'll still enjoy Smoke Hole Caverns west of Petersburg and Seneca Caverns near Riverton, which have both.

Today bathers in search of therapeutic balm still flock to White Sulphur Springs and Berkeley Springs. The warm, mineral-laden waters bubbling up from these depths were discovered by American colonists more than 200 years ago.

Recreation

If white-water rafting floats your boat, remember these names: Gauley, Cheat and New. The big three of West Virginia rafting rivers enjoy a world-wide reputation for superior white water. The Gauley River has 100 major rapids on a 25-mile course. Exciting boulder-strewn rapids also characterize the Cheat River, but because there are no dams controlling its flow, suitable water levels are limited to spring. The Lower New has swirling Class IV and V rapids, while the Upper New features calmer water.

Another thrilling way to enjoy the outdoors here is skiing. The renowned Snowshoe ski area on top of Cheat Mountain features a network of 60 slopes and trails including Cupp Run, with its 1,500-foot vertical drop lasting more than 1.5 miles. On the northern edge of Monongahela National Forest, Canaan Valley Resort State Park has 39 interconnecting slopes running the gamut from beginner to expert. Timberline Four Seasons Resort features Salamander Run, the longest ski trail south of New England.

Cliffs at New River Gorge near Fayetteville challenge even expert rock climbers. Those who are unafraid of heights will be amply rewarded after a climb up the sandstone tower of Seneca Rocks; a stunning panorama of North Fork River and its environs awaits.

Avid anglers won't have any trouble finding a spot to cast a lure in West Virginia. Places such as Laura Anderson Lake are stocked with trout and are open for fishing year-round. Middle Island Creek, which is more river than creek, teems with largemouth bass and channel catfish. Catches to brag about at Stonewall Jackson Lake are bass, crappie and walleye.

The state has more than 300 miles of rails-to-trails paths offering a range of scenic treks. One standout is North Bend Rail Trail, which ascends to the Wolf Summit terminus of the old rail line. Stretching 72 miles between Parkersburg and Wolf Summit, it passes over numerous bridges and through tunnels. Another favorite is scenic Greenbrier River Trail, a narrow strip of state park that passes through two tunnels and follows alongside the river for part of its length.

Hikers can wander along paths that meander past hemlock groves, red spruce woods, moors, bogs and waterfalls in Monongahela National Forest. Trails connect several scenic locales at Camp Creek State Park south of Beckley. Savor the rugged landscape from the 24-mile trail through Smoke Hole Canyon, offering views of both the canyon and North Fork Valley.

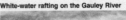

White-water rafting on the Gauley River

Historic Timeline

1669	Colonial governor William Berkeley sends an expedition to the West Virginia region.
1726	The first permanent settler, Morgan Morgan, moves to Bunker Hill in Berkeley County.
1742	Coal is discovered in Kanawha County.
1782	The last battle of the Revolutionary War is fought at Fort Henry in Wheeling.
1859	John Brown and a small band of abolitionists raid the federal arsenal at Harpers Ferry.
1863	President Lincoln declares West Virginia the 35th state.
1892	Pearl S. Buck is born in Hillsboro; she receives the Nobel Prize in Literature in 1938.
1920	The "Matewan Massacre" leads to widespread clashes between unionizing miners, coal operators, police and federal troops.
1972	The Buffalo Creek mining dam collapses, killing 118 people and leaving thousands homeless.
2000	Peace talks between Israel and Syria are held in Shepherdstown.
2010	An explosion in the Upper Big Branch coal mine about 30 miles south of Charleston leaves 29 workers dead.

What To Pack

Temperature Averages Maximum/Minimum	JANUARY	FEBRUARY	MARCH	APRIL	MAY	JUNE	JULY	AUGUST	SEPTEMBER	OCTOBER	NOVEMBER	DECEMBER
Charleston	45/28	47/28	55/34	66/44	76/53	82/61	85/64	83/63	79/57	68/46	55/36	46/29
Charles Town	39/20	43/22	52/30	64/39	73/48	82/57	86/62	84/59	78/52	66/39	55/32	44/24
Huntington	47/28	49/29	57/34	69/44	79/53	86/62	88/66	88/65	82/58	71/46	58/36	48/30
Morgantown	39/22	43/24	53/32	64/40	73/50	80/59	83/64	82/62	76/56	65/44	54/35	44/27
Parkersburg	43/26	47/27	53/33	65/43	75/53	83/62	86/65	85/64	79/57	68/46	54/35	44/28
Wheeling	38/21	42/23	51/31	63/39	73/50	82/59	85/64	84/63	77/56	66/43.	54/35	42/27

From the records of The Weather Channel Interactive, Inc.

Good Facts To Know

ABOUT THE STATE

POPULATION: 1,819,777.

AREA: 24,230 square miles; ranks 45th.

CAPITAL: Charleston.

HIGHEST POINT: 4,861 ft., Spruce Knob.

LOWEST POINT: 240 ft., Potomac River at Harpers Ferry.

TIME ZONE(S): Eastern. DST.

GAMBLING

MINIMUM AGE FOR GAMBLING: 21.

REGULATIONS

TEEN DRIVING LAWS: The minimum age for an unrestricted driver's license is 17. No passengers under age 20 (family exempted) for first 6 months; no more than one passenger under age 20 (family exempted) for the second 6 months. Driving from 10 p.m. to 5 a.m. is prohibited for drivers under 17. Phone (304) 558-3900 for more information about West Virginia's driver's license regulations.

SEAT BELT/CHILD RESTRAINT LAWS: Seat belts are required for driver and front-seat passengers ages 18 and over. Children ages 8-18 and at least 57 inches tall must be in a child restraint or seat belt; child restraints are required for children under age 8 and under 57 inches tall. AAA recommends seat belts/child restraints for driver and all passengers.

CELLPHONE RESTRICTIONS: Drivers under age 18 with an instruction permit or intermediate license may not operate a cellphone while driving. All drivers are prohibited from texting or using a handheld cellphone while driving.

HELMETS FOR MOTORCYCLISTS: Required for all riders.

RADAR DETECTORS: Permitted.

MOVE OVER LAW: Driver is required to vacate the lane nearest stopped police, fire and rescue vehicles using flashing signals, if safe to do so, or slow to no more than 15 mph on a non-divided highway or 25 mph on a divided highway. The law also applies to recovery vehicles, including tow trucks.

FIREARMS LAWS: Vary by state/county. Contact the West Virginia Office of the Attorney General, 1900 Kanawha Blvd. E., Building 1, Room E-26, Charleston, WV 25305; phone (304) 558-2021 or (800) 368-8808.

HOLIDAYS

HOLIDAYS: Jan. 1 ▪ Martin Luther King Jr. Day, Jan. (3rd Mon.) ▪ Washington's Birthday/Presidents Day, Feb. (3rd Mon.) ▪ Primary Election Day, May (2nd Tues. in an election year) ▪ Memorial Day, May (last Mon.) ▪ West Virginia Day, June 20 ▪ July 4 ▪ Labor Day, Sept. (1st Mon.) ▪ Columbus Day, Oct. (2nd Mon.) ▪ Election Day, Nov. (1st Tues. in an election year) ▪ Veterans Day, Nov. 11 ▪ Thanksgiving ▪ day after Thanksgiving ▪ Christmas, Dec. 25.

MONEY

TAXES: West Virginia's statewide sales tax is 6 percent. Cities and counties may levy extra local sales and use taxes and lodging taxes of up to 7 percent.

VISITOR INFORMATION

INFORMATION CENTERS: State welcome centers are on US 340 at Harpers Ferry ▪ on I-64 westbound at White Sulphur Springs and eastbound at Huntington ▪ on I-77 north- or southbound at Princeton (exit 9), northbound at Milepost 18 near Princeton, northbound near Mahan, southbound at Beckley and north- or southbound at Williamstown ▪ on I-70 westbound near the Pennsylvania state line, close to Valley Grove ▪ on I-79 southbound north of Morgantown ▪ on I-81 northbound 2 miles north of the Virginia state line near Ridgeway and southbound 1 mile south of the Maryland state line near Falling Waters ▪ and on I-68 westbound in Bruceton Mills. Except major holidays, most are open daily 9-5, November through April, and 8-6, in summer ▪ otherwise varies.

FURTHER INFORMATION FOR VISITORS:
West Virginia Division of Tourism
Bldg. 3, Suite 100, State Capitol Complex
1900 Kanawha Blvd. E.
Charleston, WV 25305
(304) 558-2200
(800) 225-5982

NATIONAL FOREST INFORMATION:
West Virginia Division of Forestry
7 Players Club Dr.
Charleston, WV 25311
(304) 558-2788

FISHING AND HUNTING REGULATIONS:
West Virginia Division of Natural Resources
324 Fourth Ave.
Building 74
South Charleston, WV 25303
(304) 558-2758
(304) 558-2754

RECREATION INFORMATION:
West Virginia Division of Tourism
Bldg. 3, Suite 100, State Capitol Complex
1900 Kanawha Blvd. E.
Charleston, WV 25305
(304) 558-2200
(800) 225-5982

West Virginia Annual Events

Please call ahead to confirm event details.

 Visit **AAA.com/travelguides/events** to find
AAA-listed events for every day of the year

WINTER

Dec. - Captain Flagg's US Quartermaster
City: Prospects of Peace / Harpers
Ferry / 304-535-6881
- Appalachian Coal Town Christmas
and Light Festival / Beckley
304-256-1747
- Feast of the Seven Fishes / Fairmont
304-366-0468
Jan. - West Virginia's Martin Luther King
Day Celebration / Charleston
304-558-0162
- West Virginia Hunting and Fishing
Show / Charleston / 304-345-1500
- Shanghai Parade / Lewisburg
304-645-2080
Feb. - International Water Tasting / Berkeley
Springs / 304-258-2210

SPRING

Mar. - Homegrown Music and Arts Festival
Snowshoe / 304-572-1000
- Snowy Luau Festival at Timberline
Davis / 800-766-9464
Apr. - Spring Mountain Festival
Parkersburg / 304-257-2722
- Uniquely West Virginia / Berkeley
Springs / 800-447-8797
- Ramps & Rails Festival / Elkins
877-686-7245
May - Strawberry Festival / Buckhannon
304-472-9036
- Vandalia Gathering / Charleston
304-558-0220

SUMMER

June - Mid-Ohio Valley Multicultural Festival
Parkersburg / 304-424-3457, ext. 139
- Fostoria Glass Society Show & Sale
Moundsville / 304-845-9188
July - The Contemporary American Theater
Festival / Shepherdstown
304-876-3473
- Upper Ohio Valley Italian Heritage
Festival / Wheeling / 304-233-1090
Aug. - Appalachian Festival / Beckley
304-252-7328
- West Virginia State Honey Festival
Parkersburg / 304-295-6941
- State Fair of West Virginia
Lewisburg / 304-645-1090

FALL

Sept. - Leaf Peepers Festival / Davis
304-259-5315
Oct. - Mountain State Forest Festival
Elkins / 304-636-1824
- Oglebayfest / Wheeling
304-243-4000
- Apple Butter Festival / Berkeley
Springs / 304-258-9147
Nov. - Festival of Lights / Wheeling
304-243-4132
- Guyandotte Civil War Days: Thunder
in the Village / Huntington
304-617-6719
- West Virginia Arts and Crafts
Christmas Spectacular / Morgantown
724-863-4577

West Virginia State Capitol, Charleston

Harpers Ferry National Historical Park

Blennerhassett Island Historical State Park, Parkersburg

Charleston

Covered bridge in Lewisburg

Index: Great Experience for Members

AAA editor's picks of exceptional note

West Virginia State
Capitol

Blackwater Falls State
Park

Harpers Ferry
National Historical
Park

Blennerhassett Island
Historical State Park

See Orientation map on p. 328 for corresponding grid coordinates, if applicable.
*Indicates the GEM is temporarily closed.

West Virginia
Atlas Section

WEST VIRGINIA

West Virginia

3

1:1,330,560
Scale in Miles

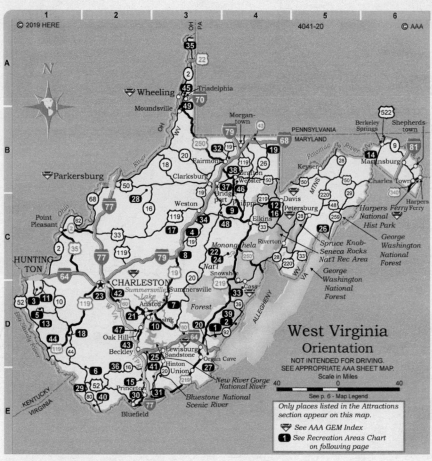

West Virginia
Orientation
NOT INTENDED FOR DRIVING.
SEE APPROPRIATE AAA SHEET MAP.
Scale in Miles

See p. 6 - Map Legend

Only places listed in the Attractions
section appear on this map.

See AAA GEM Index
See Recreation Areas Chart
on following page

Recreation Areas Chart

The map location numerals in column 2 show an
area's location on the preceding map.

Find thousands of places to camp
at AAA.com/campgrounds

	MAP LOCATION	CAMPING	PICNICKING	HIKING TRAILS	BOATING	BOAT RAMP	BOAT RENTAL	FISHING	SWIMMING	PET FRIENDLY	BICYCLE TRAILS	WINTER SPORTS	VISITOR CENTER	LODGE/CABINS	FOOD SERVICE
NATIONAL FORESTS (See place listings.)															
Monongahela (C-3) 920,000 acres in eastern West Virginia. Cross-country skiing, horseback riding, hunting, mountain biking, rock climbing, snowmobiling.		•	•	•	•	•	•	•	•	•	•	•	•	•	•
Blue Bend (D-3) 4 mi. w. of Alvon off SR 92 in Monongahela National Forest. Playground.	❶	•	•	•				•	•	•			•		
Lake Sherwood (D-4) 11 mi. n.e. of Neola on SR 14 in Monongahela National Forest.	❷	•	•	•	•	•	•	•	•	•			•		
NATIONAL RECREATION AREAS (See place listings.)															
Spruce Knob-Seneca Rocks (C-5) Eastern West Virginia. Cross-country skiing, hunting.		•	•	•	•			•	•	•			•	•	
NATIONAL RIVERS															
Bluestone National Scenic River (E-3) 4,300 acres on SR 20 s. of Hinton in Bluestone State Park. Hunting; guided hikes (seasonal).			•	•	•			•					•	•	

Recreation Areas Chart

The map location numerals in column 2 show an area's location on the preceding map.

🔗 Find thousands of places to camp at AAA.com/campgrounds

	MAP LOCATION	CAMPING	PICNICKING	HIKING TRAILS	BOATING	BOAT RAMP	BOAT RENTAL	FISHING	SWIMMING	PET FRIENDLY	BICYCLE TRAILS	WINTER SPORTS	VISITOR CENTER	LODGE/CABINS	FOOD SERVICE
New River Gorge (E-3) 70,000 acres between Fayetteville and Hinton. White-water rafting.		•	•	•	•			•	•	•	•		•		
ARMY CORPS OF ENGINEERS															
Beech Fork Lake (D-1) 720 acres about 15 mi. s.e. of Huntington on SR 152.	③	•	•	•	•	•	•	•	•	•			•		•
Burnsville Lake (C-3) 970 acres just off I-79 Burnsville exit. Water skiing.	④	•	•	•	•	•	•	•	•	•			•		
East Lynn Lake (D-1) 1,005 acres 12 mi. s.e. of Wayne on SR 37. Hunting, water skiing.	⑤	•	•	•	•	•	•	•	•	•			•		•
R.D. Bailey Lake (E-2) 630 acres 30 mi. e. of Logan. Hunting, water skiing.	⑥	•	•	•	•	•	•	•	•	•			•		
Summersville Lake (D-3) 2,790 acres 7 mi. s. of Summersville off US 19 on SR 129. Scuba diving, water skiing; marina.	⑦	•	•	•	•	•	•	•	•	•			•	•	•
Sutton Lake (C-3) 1,440 acres 5 mi. n.e. of Sutton off I-79, exit 62. Horseback riding, hunting, water skiing; marina.	⑧	•	•	•	•	•	•	•	•	•			•		•
STATE															
Audra (C-4) 355 acres 10 mi. w. of Belington off CR 11. Kayaking; playground.	⑨	•	•	•				•	•	•					
Babcock (D-3) 4,127 acres 4 mi. n.w. of Clifftop on SR 41. Nature programs. Scenic. Boating (no motors); gristmill, horse rental, swimming pool.	⑩	•	•	•	•			•	•	•		•	•	•	•
Beech Fork (D-1) 3,144 acres 12 mi. s.e. of Huntington on SR 152. Game room, playground, swimming pool.	⑪	•	•	•	•	•	•	•	•	•			•	•	•
Blackwater Falls (C-4) 1,688 acres about .25 mile s.w. of Davis off SR 32 via signs. Nature programs and nature center. Scenic. Cross-country skiing, horse rental, sledding, tennis, sport courts.	⑫	•	•	•				•	•	•		•	•	•	•
Cabwaylingo (D-1) 8,123 acres 5 mi. s.e. of Dunlow off SR 152. Hunting; swimming pool.	⑬	•	•					•	•	•					
Cacapon Resort (B-6) 6,115 acres 10 mi. s. of Berkeley Springs on US 522. Golf (18 holes); trap shooting; beach, horse rental, nature center, playground, sports courts.	⑭		•	•	•	•	•	•	•	•			•	•	•
Camp Creek (E-2) 5,300 acres 3 mi. n.w. of Camp Creek. Playground.	⑮	•	•	•				•		•	•				
Canaan Valley Resort (C-4) 6,015 acres 10 mi. s. of Davis on SR 32. Nature programs. Cross-country and downhill skiing, geocaching, golf (18 holes); tennis; bicycle rental, paintball field, summer chairlift and tube rides, swimming pool.	⑯	•						•	•			•	•	•	•
Cedar Creek (C-3) 2,588 acres 8 mi. s. of Glenville off US 33. Miniature golf, paddleboats, playground, sports courts, swimming pool.	⑰	•	•	•	•	•	•								
Chief Logan (D-1) 4,068 acres 3 mi. n. of Logan off SR 10. Horseback riding; amphitheater, miniature golf, museum, sports courts, swimming pool, waterslide.	⑱	•	•	•				•	•					•	•
Coopers Rock (B-4) 12,713 acres 8 mi. w. of Bruceton Mills on I-68. Hunting; playground.	⑲	•	•	•				•							•
Greenbrier (D-3) 5,130 acres 4 mi. s.w. of White Sulphur Springs via US 60 and Harts Run Rd. Archery range, Disc golf, hunting, nature programs, rifle range, swimming pool.	⑳	•	•						•	•	•		•		
Hawks Nest (D-2) 276 acres 1.75 mi. w. on US 60 in Ansted. Historic. Scenic. Golf (9 holes); aerial tramway, boat tour, swimming pool.	㉑		•	•	•	•	•	•	•				•	•	•
Holly River (C-3) 8,101 acres 2 mi. n. of Hacker Valley off SR 20. Sports courts, swimming pool.	㉒	•	•	•				•	•					•	•
Kanawha (D-2) 9,302 acres 7 mi. s. of Charleston on Kanawha Forest Dr. Cross-country skiing, hunting, mountain biking; horse rental, playground, shooting range, swimming pool.	㉓	•	•					•	•	•	•				
Kumbrabow (C-3) 9,474 acres 5 mi. w. of Elkwater off US 219. Hunting.	㉔	•	•	•				•		•			•		

Recreation Areas Chart

The map location numerals in column 2 show an area's location on the preceding map.

Find thousands of places to camp at AAA.com/campgrounds

	MAP LOCATION	CAMPING	PICNICKING	HIKING TRAILS	BOATING	BOAT RAMP	BOAT RENTAL	FISHING	SWIMMING	PET FRIENDLY	BICYCLE TRAILS	WINTER SPORTS	VISITOR CENTER	LODGE/CABINS	FOOD SERVICE
Little Beaver (D-3) 562 acres 10 mi. s.e. of Beckley on I-64 to SR 9, following signs. Geocaching; playgrounds.	25	•	•	•	•		•	•			•				
Lost River (C-5) 3,712 acres 4 mi. w. of Mathias on SR 259 and CR 12, following signs. Historic. Horseback riding; archery range, games room, swimming pool.	26	•	•	•				•	•	•	•			•	
Moncove Lake (D-3) 896 acres 6 mi. n. of SR 3 on SR 8 near Gap Mills. Bird-watching, hunting; swimming pool.	27	•	•	•	•	•		•	•						
North Bend (C-2) 2,400 acres 2 mi. e. of Cairo off SR 31. Nature programs. Horseback riding, tennis; bicycle rental, fishing pier, swimming pool.	28	•	•	•	•	•		•	•	•	•			•	
Panther (E-1) 7,810 acres 3 mi. s. of Panther, following signs. Hunting; swimming pool.	29	•	•	•				•	•	•					
Pinnacle Rock (E-2) 396 acres 5 mi. s.e. of Bramwell on US 52. Scenic. Playground.	30		•	•				•		•	•		•		
Pipestem Resort (E-3) 4,050 acres on SR 20. Nature programs. Scenic. Cross-country skiing, golf (18 holes), sledding, tennis; aerial tram, amphitheater, disc golf, fling golf, foot golf, horse and paddleboat rental, miniature golf, swimming pool.	31	•	•	•	•		•	•	•	•	•	•	•	•	•
Prickett's Fort (B-3) 188 acres about 2.5 mi. w. off I-79 exit 139 n. of Fairmont. Amphitheater.	32		•	•				•		•	•		•		
Seneca (D-4) 11,684 acres 4 mi. s.w. of Dunmore off SR 28. Hunting.	33	•	•	•	•	•		•	•		•			•	
Stonewall Resort (C-3) more than 2,000 acres 3 mi. e. of I-79 near Weston. Geocaching, golf (18 holes); boat and Segway tours, swimming pool.	34	•	•	•	•	•	•	•	•	•	•		•	•	•
Tomlinson Run (A-3) 1,398 acres 2 mi. n. of New Manchester off SR 8. Boat docks, camping gear and tent rental, disc golf (18 holes), miniature golf, swimming pool.	35	•	•	•	•	•	•	•	•	•	•				
Twin Falls Resort (D-2) 3,776 acres 8 mi. n.e. of Pineville. Nature programs. Golf (18 holes), tennis; amphitheater, swimming pool.	36	•	•	•				•	•	•	•		•	•	•
Tygart Lake (B-4) 2,134 acres 2 mi. s. of Grafton on CR 44 along e. bank of Tygart River Reservoir. Canoeing, kayaking, scuba diving, water skiing.	37	•	•	•	•	•	•	•	•	•				•	•
Valley Falls (B-4) 1,145 acres 9 mi. s. of Fairmont off I-79 exit 137 on SR 310. Historic. Playground, waterfalls.	38		•	•				•		•	•				
Watoga (D-4) 10,100 acres 10 mi. s. of Huntersville (turn at park sign on SR 39, then 10 mi. s.). Nature programs. Swimming pool.	39	•	•	•	•		•	•	•	•			•	•	
OTHER															
Berwind Lake Wildlife Management Area (E-2) 18,000 acres 17 mi. s. of Welch off SR 16. Hunting.	40	•	•	•	•	•		•	•	•					
Bluestone (D-3) 2,155 acres 4 mi. s. of Hinton on SR 20. Water skiing; marina, swimming pool.	41	•	•	•	•	•		•	•				•	•	
Coonskin Park (D-2) 850 acres 5 mi. n. of Charleston on SR 114. Golf (18 holes), miniature golf, tennis; amphitheater, paddle-boats, playground, soccer stadium, swimming pool.	42		•	•	•		•	•	•	•				•	•
Lake Stephens (D-2) 2,300 acres 9 mi. w. of Beckley on SR 3. Horseback riding; beach.	43	•	•	•	•	•	•	•	•	•				•	
Laurel Lake (D-1) 12,851 acres 7 mi. n.e. of Lenore off SR 65. Hunting; playgrounds, swimming pool.	44		•	•	•	•		•	•	•					
Oglebay Resort (A-3) 1,650 acres in Wheeling 5 mi. n.e. on SR 88. Gardens, horse rental, museums, zoo.	45		•	•				•	•	•	•	•	•	•	•
Pleasant Creek (B-4) 3,030 acres 6 mi. n. of Philippi off US 119/250. Hunting; shooting range.	46	•			•	•		•							
Plum Orchard Lake (D-2) 3,201 acres e. off I-77 exit 54 or 60 on CR 23 between Mount Hope and Oak Hill. Hunting; rifle range.	47	•	•		•	•		•							
Pringle Tree (C-4) 4.5 acres 2 mi. n. of Buckhannon off US 119 and SR 20. Historic. Playground.	48		•		•	•		•		•					

Recreation Areas Chart

The map location numerals in column 2 show an area's location on the preceding map.

 Find thousands of places to camp at **AAA.com/campgrounds**

	MAP LOCATION	CAMPING	PICNICKING	HIKING TRAILS	BOATING	BOAT RAMP	BOAT RENTAL	FISHING	SWIMMING	PET FRIENDLY	BICYCLE TRAILS	WINTER SPORTS	VISITOR CENTER	LODGE/CABINS	FOOD SERVICE
Wheeling Park (A-3) 406 acres in Wheeling 4 mi. e. on US 40 at 1801 National Rd. Golf (nine holes), ice skating, tennis; amphitheater, miniature golf (18 holes), playground, swimming pool, waterslide.	**49**	•		•					•	•			•	•	

Love the Great Outdoors?

iStockphoto.com_pixelfit

When getting away means getting off the beaten path, visit **AAA.com/campgrounds** or **AAA.com/maps** for:

⚠ Thousands of places to camp across the U.S. and Canada

⚠ Complete mapping and travel information to plan your adventure

Look for locations with the trusted mark of approval.

Inspected & Approved

ANSTED (D-2) pop. 1,404, elev. 1,312'

Ansted, originally settled by Baptists in 1790, was named New Haven by a group of New England Spiritualists who came to the town in 1830. The following year it was renamed after British scientist David T. Ansted, who had interested English investors in building coal-mining operations. On a knoll overlooking the town, Westlake Cemetery contains the grave of Julia Jackson Woodson, Gen. Thomas "Stonewall" Jackson's mother.

The Ansted Culture and Heritage Museum, 19940 Midland Tr., features exhibits about the Midland Trail, the area's Native Americans, pioneers, the Civil War and the region's African-American and industrial history; phone (304) 658-5901.

CONTENTMENT COMPLEX is .75 mi. n.w. on US 60 to 19295 Midland Tr. Confederate Colonel George Imboden's antebellum home, built in 1830, has been restored. A museum and one-room country schoolhouse are on the grounds. **Hours:** Wed.-Sat. 10-4, June-Aug. Phone ahead to confirm schedule. **Cost:** $6; $3 (ages 0-12). **Phone:** (304) 658-4448.

HAWKS NEST STATE PARK is 1.75 mi. w. on US 60 to 49 Hawks Nest Park Rd. The 276-acre park is named for a sweeping lookout point above the New River. A nature center, open daily Memorial Day through Labor Day, has hands-on displays. Hiking trails of varying lengths and intensity, including the Hawks Nest Rail Trail, lead to scenic views and overlooks. *See Recreation Areas Chart.* **Hours:** Daily 6 a.m.-10 p.m., Memorial Day-Labor Day; Sat.-Sun. 6 a.m.-10 p.m., day after Labor Day-late Oct. **Cost:** Free. **Phone:** (304) 658-5212 or (800) 225-5982.

Hawks Nest Aerial Tramway, 1.75 mi. w. on US 60 to Hawks Nest State Park, runs from the park lodge to the marina. The aerial tram descends 446 feet to the bottom of the New River Gorge. **Hours:** The tramway operates Mon.-Tues. and Thurs.-Fri. 11-4:45, Sat.-Sun. 11-6:45, Memorial Day-Labor Day and in Oct.; Sat.-Sun. 11-6:45, May 1-day before Memorial Day and day after Labor Day-Sept. 30. **Cost:** Round-trip fare $5; $4 (ages 5-16 and 60+); $2.50 (ages 5-12). **Phone:** (304) 658-5212 or (800) 225-5982.

NEW RIVER JETBOATS departs from the dock in Hawks Nest State Park at 49 Hawks Nest Park Rd.; passengers must take the Hawks Nest Aerial Tramway *(see attraction listing this page)* from the park lodge to reach the dock. A 6-mile, 30-minute round-trip takes passengers upstream to the New River Gorge Bridge on the *Miss M. Rocks,* providing scenic views of the New River Valley and opportunities to see wildlife.

Hours: Mon.-Tues. and Thurs.-Fri. 11-4, Sat.-Sun. 11-6, Memorial Day-Labor Day and in Oct.; Sat.-Sun. 11-6, May 1-day before Memorial Day and day after Labor Day-Sept. 30. **Cost:** Fare (including tram) $29; $27 (ages 60+); $14 (ages 5-16). **Phone:** (304) 640-0924 or (304) 469-2525.

HAWKS NEST LODGE   304/658-5212
◆ **APPROVED**   Motel. **Address:** 49 Hawks Nest Park Rd 25812

WHERE TO EAT

TUDOR'S BISCUIT WORLD   304/658-5235
◆ **APPROVED**   American. Casual Dining. **Address:** 126 W Main St 25812

BARBOURSVILLE pop. 3,964

BEST WESTERN HUNTINGTON MALL INN
304/736-9772

APPROVED
Motel

Best Western

AAA Benefit: Members save up to 15% and earn bonus points!

Address: 3441 US 60 E 25504 **Location:** I-64 exit 20A eastbound; exit 20 westbound, 0.3 mi s. **Facility:** 127 units. 2 stories (no elevator), interior corridors. **Pool:** outdoor. **Activities:** exercise room. **Guest Services:** coin laundry. **Featured Amenity: full hot breakfast.**

SAVE 📶 🏊 🐾 BIZ HS 🛜
📠 🖨 💲 / SOME UNITS 🐾

COMFORT INN BY CHOICE HOTELS
304/733-2122
THREE DIAMOND Hotel. **Address:** 249 Mall Rd 25504

DELTA HOTELS HUNTINGTON MALL
304/733-3338
THREE DIAMOND SAVE Hotel. **Address:** 3551 Rt 60 E 25504

AAA Benefit: Members save 5% or more!

HAMPTON INN HUNTINGTON/BARBOURSVILLE
304/733-5300
THREE DIAMOND SAVE Hotel. **Address:** 1 Cracker Barrel Dr 25504

AAA Benefit: Members save up to 15%!

WHERE TO EAT

OSCAR'S BREAKFAST, BURGERS & BREWS
304/948-6916
APPROVED American. Casual Dining. **Address:** 6007 US 60 25504

TORTILLA FACTORY MEXICAN RESTAURANT
304/948-7518
APPROVED Mexican. Casual Dining. **Address:** 3419 US 60 25504

BECKLEY (D-2) pop. 17,614, elev. 2,300'
• Restaurants p. 334

Beckley is the center of southern West Virginia's smokeless coal region. The bituminous coal mined in this area is a higher grade of coal that produces less smoke when burned.

Beckley is the northern anchor of the 187-mile Coal Heritage Trail which winds its way past company stores, miners' houses, railroad yards, coal tipples and 500 small company towns on its way south to Bluefield; follow SR 16 southwest to US 52, which heads south and east to Bluefield, the end of the trail. Mile markers along the way indicate points of interest; phone (304) 465-3720 or (855) 982-2625. Another scenic drive runs south along US 19 in Bluestone Canyon.

Visit Southern West Virginia: 1408 Harper Rd., Beckley, WV 25801. **Phone:** (304) 252-2244 or (800) 847-4898.

Shopping: Crossroads Mall, at SR 16 and US 19 in north Beckley, houses such stores as Belk and JCPenney.

BECKLEY EXHIBITION COAL MINE is at 513 Ewart Ave. adjacent to New River Park. Veteran miners lead 35-minute underground tours of a vintage coal mine, providing visitors an opportunity to see how a turn-of-the-20th-century mine operated. A coal mining museum and coal camp homes, schools, a miner's shanty and churches provide a glimpse into life in a typical coal camp. Bring a jacket, as the mine is a constant 58 F.

Time: Allow 1 hour, 30 minutes minimum. **Hours:** Daily 10-6, Apr. 1-Nov. 1. Last admission 30 minutes before closing. **Cost:** (includes Youth Museum of Southern West Virginia & Mountain Homestead) $20; $15 (ages 55+); $14 (military with ID or in uniform); $12 (ages 4-17). Grounds only $10. Museum only $5. **Phone:** (304) 256-1747. 🎟

BAYMONT INN & SUITES
304/255-9091

APPROVED
Hotel

Address: 134 Harper Park Dr 25801 **Location:** I-64/77 exit 44, just w on SR 3. **Facility:** 55 units. 3 stories, interior corridors. **Pool:** outdoor. **Guest Services:** valet laundry. **Featured Amenity: continental breakfast.**

SAVE 📶 🏊 BIZ 🛜 ✕ 📠
🖨 💲

COMFORT INN
304/255-5291
APPROVED Motel. **Address:** 300 Harper Park Dr 25801

COUNTRY INN & SUITES BY RADISSON
304/252-5100
THREE DIAMOND Hotel. **Address:** 2120 Harper Rd 25801

COURTYARD BY MARRIOTT
304/252-9800
THREE DIAMOND SAVE Hotel. **Address:** 124 Hylton Ln 25801

AAA Benefit: Members save 5% or more!

ECONO LODGE
304/255-2161
APPROVED Motel. **Address:** 1909 Harper Rd 25801

FAIRFIELD INN & SUITES BY MARRIOTT
304/252-8661
THREE DIAMOND SAVE Hotel. **Address:** 125 Hylton Ln 25801

AAA Benefit: Members save 5% or more!

HAMPTON INN
304/252-2121
THREE DIAMOND SAVE Hotel. **Address:** 110 Harper Park Dr 25801

AAA Benefit: Members save up to 15%!

HOLIDAY INN & SUITES
304/252-2250
THREE DIAMOND Hotel. **Address:** 114 Dry Hill Rd 25801

MICROTEL INN & SUITES BY WYNDHAM BECKLEY EAST
304/255-2200
APPROVED Hotel. **Address:** 1001 S Eisenhower Dr 25801

QUALITY INN OF BECKLEY   304/255-1511

▼▼ **THREE DIAMOND**
Hotel. **Address:** 1924 Harper Rd 25801
(See ad this page.)

RODEWAY INN   304/461-1000
▼▼ APPROVED   Motel. **Address:** 1909B Harper Rd 25801

TRAVELODGE   304/252-0671
▼▼ APPROVED   Motel. **Address:** 1939 Harper Rd 25801

WHERE TO EAT

THE CHAR   304/253-1760

▼▼ THREE DIAMOND **AAA Inspector Notes:** Family-owned
American   and -operated since 1965, this spot is
Fine Dining   known for quality steaks, seafood and
$16-$38   Italian specialties. The restaurant boasts
                    brascioli—a beef fillet with bread crumbs
                    and cheese—as its specialty. The at-
mosphere, enhanced by soothing background music and service
are great. **Features:** full bar. **Address:** 100 Char Dr 25801 **Location:** I-64/77 exit 44, 0.3 mi w on SR 3, then 0.5 mi n on Dry
Hill Rd. **Parking:** on-site and valet. D

LITTLE SICILY   304/255-4976
▼▼ APPROVED   Italian. Casual Dining. **Address:** 3144
Robert C. Byrd Dr 25801

MICKEY'S PIZZA   304/253-3278
▼▼ APPROVED   Pizza. Quick Serve. **Address:** 2813
Harper Rd 25801

PASQUALE MIRA'S ITALIAN RESTAURANT
                                          304/255-5253
▼▼ THREE DIAMOND **AAA Inspector Notes:** Excellent spe-
Italian   cialties, including veal and seafood
Casual Dining   dishes, are offered in two dining
$9-$28   rooms—one casual and one more
                    formal—and on the patio. Family-owned
                    since 1960, the restaurant prepares fare
with a welcome homemade flavor. **Features:** full bar. **Address:**
224 Harper Park Dr 25801 **Location:** I-64/77 exit 44, just w, then
0.3 mi s. L D

PONCHO & LEFTY'S   304/237-1600
▼▼ APPROVED   Mexican. Quick Serve. **Address:** 1318
Harper Rd 25801

YOUNG CHOW'S   304/253-2469
▼▼ APPROVED   Chinese. Casual Dining. **Address:** 219
Pikeview Dr 25801

BERKELEY SPRINGS (B-6) elev. 612'

The Berkeley Springs, famous for their supposed
curative properties, were a haven for Native Americans long before Europeans discovered their
soothing waters. A thriving community had been established by the time George Washington arrived in
1748 to survey the area for its owner, Lord Thomas
Fairfax. In 1776, Washington assisted in estab-
lishing the town as a health resort under the name
of Bath, which remains its official name.

More than a dozen members of the Colonial elite
were among original lot owners—George and
Martha Washington bought property in the area. The
springs continue to flow from five main sources at
the rate of 1,000-1,500 gallons per minute; the water
maintains a uniform temperature of 74 F.

Though known for its spas, Berkeley Springs is
also gaining notice as an arts community. The town
is home to a growing number of art and craft galleries and shows. Ten miles south, Cacapon Resort
State Park *(see Recreation Areas Chart)* offers an
18-hole golf course, a lodge, a lake beach, a trap
shooting range, a nature center and trails to the top
of Cacapon Mountain; phone (304) 258-1022 or
(800) 225-5982.

**Berkeley Springs-Morgan County Chamber of
Commerce:** 127 Fairfax St., Berkeley Springs, WV
25411. **Phone:** (304) 258-3738.

▼ See AAA listing this page ▼

SURESTAY PLUS HOTEL BY BEST WESTERN BERKELEY
SPRINGS 304/258-9400
APPROVED Motel. **Address:** 1776 Valley Rd 25411

WHERE TO EAT

MARIA'S GARDEN & INN 304/258-2021
APPROVED Italian. Casual Dining. **Address:** 42
Independence St 25411

MORGAN'S ON MAIN 304/258-5999
APPROVED American. Casual Dining. **Address:** 174
N Washington St 25411

BLUEFIELD (E-2) pop. 10,447, elev. 2,560'

Founded in 1889 as the regional headquarters of
the Norfolk & Western Railway, remnants of the
natural-gravity switching yards remain in Bluefield.
Named for the many chicory flowers growing wild
along the hillsides, the town attracted many industries in addition to the railroad, such as coal mining.

South of town, the border between the two Vir-
ginias is on the crest of East River Mountain. Some
of the best views can be found at the East River
Mountain Scenic Overlook (1780 Stadium Dr.);
phone (304) 327-2448. A sister city, Bluefield, Va.,
lies to the southwest.

The West Virginia city's original municipal
building, built in 1924, now houses The Bluefield
Performing Arts Center, an active center for visual
and performing arts that hosts regular concerts at
Bluefield High School, Bluefield College and
Harman Chapel; phone (304) 325-9117.

The Granada Theater, featuring 1920s Spanish-
Moorish design, was one of several theaters built in
the early 20th century when Bluefield was a popular
railroad stopover and known as "Little New York."
(The city received a nod in the 1934 film, "Red
Dust," when the character, played by Jean Harlow,
revealed she had lived in Bluefield.) **Note:** The 1928
theater is closed for renovations; it will feature live
performances as well as classic and indie movies;
phone Bluefield Preservation Society at (304)
589-0239 for updates.

Bluefield is the southern anchor of the 187-mile
Coal Heritage Trail which winds its way past company stores, miners' houses, railroad yards, coal
tipples and 500 small company towns on its way
north to Beckley; phone (304) 465-3720 or (855)
982-2625. Follow US 52 northwest to SR 16, which
meanders north and east to Beckley; mile markers
along the way indicate points of interest.

Baseball comes to Bluefield in mid-June when the
minor league Bluefield Blue Jays, part of the Appalachian League, play ball at Bowen Field in City
Park; phone (304) 324-1326.

Mercer County Convention and Visitors Bureau:
621 Commerce St., Bluefield, WV 24701. **Phone:**
(304) 325-8438 or (800) 221-3206.

Self-guiding tours: Examples of historic Victorian
architecture can be seen on a walking tour of downtown Bluefield. Brochures are available at the convention and visitors bureau and chamber of
commerce offices on Bland Street.

Shopping: Mercer Mall, 261 Mercer Mall Rd. at US
460 and SR 25, has more than 40 services and
stores, including Belk and JCPenney. There are a
number of antiques shops and art galleries on Bluefield Avenue and Mercer Street.

BLUEFIELD INN 304/323-2200
THREE DIAMOND Historic Bed & Breakfast. **Address:** 2109
Jefferson St 24701

WHERE TO EAT

TUDOR'S BISCUIT WORLD 304/589-3383
APPROVED American. Casual Dining. **Address:** SR
52 24701

BRIDGEPORT (B-3) pop. 8,149, elev. 1,020'
• Restaurants p. 336

An ultimate example of recycling is on display in the
community, about two hours north of Charleston,
where a former coal mine has been transformed into a
prestigious golf course. The Pete Dye Golf Club, a
250-acre-course in the beautiful Appalachian Mountains, opened in 1993 to critical acclaim. Visitors come
to the area via I-79 or US 50, and those not interested
in hitting the links often make a stop at Meadowbrook
Mall, a 100-store regional shopping complex that
serves much of north-central West Virginia.

BEST WESTERN PLUS BRIDGEPORT INN 304/842-5411

Hotel

AAA Benefit:
Members save up to
15% and earn bonus
points!

Address: 100 Lodgeville Rd 26330 **Location:** I-79 exit 119, just e on US 50.
Located in a busy commercial area. **Facility:** 164 units. 2 stories, interior corridors. **Pool:** outdoor. **Activities:** exercise
room. **Guest Services:** valet and coin
laundry.

COMFORT SUITES BRIDGEPORT-CLARKSBURG
304/933-3390
THREE DIAMOND Hotel. **Address:** 285 White Oaks Blvd
26330

COURTYARD BY MARRIOTT   304/842-0444

▼▼ THREE DIAMOND [SAVE] Hotel. **Address:** 30 Shaner Dr 26330

| **AAA Benefit:** Members save 5% or more! |

DAYS INN & SUITES BRIDGEPORT-CLARKSBURG
304/842-7371

◆ APPROVED Hotel. **Address:** 112 Tolley St 26330

HAWTHORN SUITES BY WYNDHAM   304/848-8700

▼▼ THREE DIAMOND Hotel. **Address:** 75 Southview Dr 26330

MICROTEL INN & SUITES BY WYNDHAM BRIDGEPORT
304/808-2000

▼▼ APPROVED Hotel. **Address:** 201 Conference Center Way 26330

SLEEP INN   304/842-1919

▼▼ APPROVED Motel. **Address:** 115 Tolley Dr 26330

SPRINGHILL SUITES BY MARRIOTT   304/842-5200

▼▼ THREE DIAMOND [SAVE] Hotel. **Address:** 97 Platinum Dr 26330

| **AAA Benefit:** Members save 5% or more! |

TOWNEPLACE SUITES BY MARRIOTT-BRIDGEPORT
CLARKSBURG   304/842-3600

▼▼ THREE DIAMOND [SAVE] Extended Stay Hotel. **Address:** 101 Platinum Dr 26330

| **AAA Benefit:** Members save 5% or more! |

WINGATE BY WYNDHAM   304/808-1000

▼▼ THREE DIAMOND Hotel. **Address:** 350 Conference Center Way 26330

WHERE TO EAT

EL RINCON   304/842-4636

▼▼ APPROVED Mexican. Casual Dining. **Address:** 112 Thompson Dr 26330

MIA MARGHERITA   304/808-6400

▼▼ APPROVED Italian. Casual Dining. **Address:** 139 Conference Center Way 26330

OLIVERIO'S RISTORANTE   304/842-7388

▼▼ THREE DIAMOND Italian. Fine Dining. **Address:** 507 E Main St 26330

PROVENCE MARKET CAFE   304/848-0911

▼▼ THREE DIAMOND Southern French. Casual Dining. **Address:** 603 S Virginia Ave 26330

BUCKHANNON pop. 5,639

THE BICENTENNIAL INN   304/472-5000

▼▼ APPROVED Hotel. **Address:** 90 E Main St 26201

HAMPTON INN   304/473-0900

▼▼ THREE DIAMOND [SAVE] Hotel. **Address:** 1 Commerce Blvd 26201

| **AAA Benefit:** Members save up to 15%! |

MICROTEL INN & SUITES BY WYNDHAM, BUCKHANNON
304/460-2525

▼▼ APPROVED Hotel. **Address:** 2 Northridge Dr 26201

CASS (D-4) pop. 52, elev. 2,437'

Once a large lumbering community, Cass retains the history of its greatness at the beginning of the 20th century. The Cass Country Store is in the former West Virginia Pulp and Paper General Store, purported to have been the largest company store in the world.

CASS SCENIC RAILROAD STATE PARK departs from the downtown depot at 242 Main St. Passenger trains make several runs with the old steam Shay and Heisler locomotives that once hauled logging trains up the steep slopes of Cheat Mountain.

The rail excursions, which offer scenic mountain vistas, include an 8-mile, 2-hour round-trip to Whittaker Station and a 22-mile, 4.5-hour round-trip excursion to the top of Bald Knob. Other trips, including dinner trains, caboose rides and overnight packages with train rides to Old Spruce and Elkins also are available. Trips are preceded by a free show that includes a diorama and audiovisual orientation film that relate the town's lumbering history.

The Cass Historical Museum houses a collection of photographs and relics pertaining to the logging industry, including one of the largest band saws in the world. The Cass Showcase is a historic diorama depicting the Cass Railroad in its lumbering days and includes a reproduction of the town during the lumber boom at the beginning of the 19th century.

Note: Layered clothing is recommended on rail excursions due to cooler temperatures at higher elevations. **Hours:** Tues.-Sun. and holidays, Memorial Day weekend-late Oct. Departs Cass Depot 11 and 1:30; departs Bald Knob 11:45. Schedule may vary; phone ahead. **Cost:** Whittaker fare $41; $39 (ages 65+); $31 (ages 4-11). Bald Knob fare, including boxed lunch $61; $59 (ages 65+); $51 (ages 4-11). An additional $5 person is charged Sat. in fall. Reservations are recommended. **Phone:** (304) 456-4300, (866) 460-7265 or (800) 225-5982.

CHAPMANVILLE pop. 1,256

BEST WESTERN LOGAN INN   304/831-2345

▼▼ THREE DIAMOND Hotel

 **Best Western.** | **AAA Benefit:** Members save up to 15% and earn bonus points!

Address: 47 Central Ave 25508 **Location:** Just s on US 119. **Facility:** 60 units. 3 stories, interior corridors. **Pool:** heated indoor. **Activities:** exercise room. **Guest Services:** coin laundry. **Featured Amenity:** continental breakfast.

CHARLESTON (D-2) pop. 51,400, elev. 601'
• Restaurants p. 338

Capital of the state, Charleston was founded in 1794. From 1788-95, Daniel Boone lived across the river. He served in the Virginia Assembly in 1791. Remains of a Native American burial ground are in South Charleston at MacCorkle Avenue and D Street.

Serving as a regional cultural center, Clay Center for the Arts & Sciences of West Virginia houses a performance hall and a black box theater as well as museums, a planetarium and outdoor sculptures. Off I-64 exit 100 (Leon Sullivan Way) to 1 Clay Sq., the center is home to the West Virginia Symphony Orchestra; phone (304) 561-3570.

The Midland Trail National Scenic Highway/US 60 travels from Charleston to White Sulphur Springs through pastoral scenery and past the rugged New River Gorge.

Appalachian music, ethnic and traditional foods, West Virginia arts and crafts, dancing, storytelling and contests are part of the Vandalia Gathering, held on the Capitol Complex grounds and in the Cultural Center on Memorial Day weekend. Vandalia, proposed as the 14th colony during the late 1760s, had many backers, including Benjamin Franklin; the new colony's boundaries would have encompassed most of present-day West Virginia, in addition to much of what is now Kentucky. However, because of the strained relations between the fledgling American colonies and Great Britain, the plan never came to fruition.

For racing fans, Mardi Gras Casino & Resort, 12 miles west of Charleston off I-64 exit 47, offers greyhound racing. The glass-enclosed facility has more than 4,000 seats and a clubhouse; phone (304) 776-1000 or (800) 224-9683.

Note: Policies concerning admittance of children to pari-mutuel betting facilities vary. Phone for information.

Charleston Convention and Visitors Bureau: 800 Smith St., Charleston, WV 25301. **Phone:** (304) 344-5075 or (800) 733-5469.

Shopping: Charleston Town Center, downtown between Quarrier and Lee streets, has more than 130 stores including JCPenney, Macy's and numerous specialty shops. Capitol Street, the main street of Old Charleston, offers shops and restaurants housed in 19th-century buildings.

Open daily year-round, the Capitol Market at 800 Smith St. offers both indoor and outdoor shopping; phone (304) 344-1905. The restored former Kanawha and Michigan Railway Depot now houses specialty shops and eateries, and an outdoors farmers market provides fresh local produce as well as flowers, shrubs and trees.

CLAY CENTER'S AVAMPATO DISCOVERY MUSEUM, downtown at 300 Leon Sullivan Way, has interactive science exhibits, an art gallery and a theater with a planetarium and large-format films. Science galleries include Milton Gardner's Earth City, which explores the forces that shaped the state; Health Royale, a gallery about health and wellness; Kidspace, a fanciful area for children under 5; Mylan Explore-Atory, hosting changing hands-on science exhibits and STEAMworks, a changing exhibit gallery. The art museum's primary focus is on 19th- and 20th-century paintings.

Time: Allow 1 hour, 30 minutes minimum. **Hours:** Tues.-Sat. 10-5, Sun. noon-5. Planetarium shows and films are offered several times daily. Closed major holidays. **Cost:** (includes museum, planetarium and film) $17.50; $15 (ages 3-18, ages 65+ and students with ID). Museum and film $13.50; $11.50 (ages 3-18, ages 65+ and students with ID). Museum and planetarium $11.50; $9.50 (ages 3-18, ages 65+ and students with ID). Film only $7. Planetarium only $7. Museum only $9; $7.50 (ages 3-18, ages 65+ and students with ID). **Parking:** $3; $5 (during special events). **Phone:** (304) 561-3500, or (304) 561-3570 for ticket information. (TI)

THE CULTURE CENTER is in the West Virginia State Capitol Complex at 1900 Kanawha Blvd. E. The center houses a 500-seat theater, reference library, the state archives and art exhibits. **Hours:** Tues.-Sat. 9-5. Last admission 45 minutes before closing. Archive library Mon.-Sat. 9-5 (also Thurs. 5-8). Reference library Mon.-Fri. 8:30-5. **Cost:** Free. **Phone:** (304) 558-0220 or TTY (304) 558-3562.

West Virginia State Museum West Virginia State Capitol Complex, on the lower level of The Culture Center at 1900 Kanawha Blvd. E.

The museum traces the state's history from prehistoric times to today, with exhibits featuring local culture, art, paleontology, archaeology and geology. **Hours:** Tues.-Sat. 9-5. Last admission 45 minutes before closing. **Cost:** Free. **Phone:** (304) 558-0220.

WEST VIRGINIA STATE CAPITOL is on Kanawha Blvd. E., facing the Kanawha River. This masterpiece of architect Cass Gilbert was completed in 1932. The outstanding feature is the rotunda's dome, 180 feet above the main floor. From its center hangs a 2-ton rock crystal chandelier, 8 feet in diameter. The second-floor ceiling is decorated with a panel design showing leaves of West Virginia's native trees.

The building's office wings house the state administrative departments, including the Supreme Court and Law Library. The governor's mansion is next door. **Hours:** Capitol open Mon.-Fri. 8-5:30, Sat. 9-5:30, Sun. and holidays noon-5:30. Capitol tours are given Mon.-Fri. 9-3. Tours of the governor's mansion is available by appointment Mon.-Fri. 9-3; reservations are required. **Cost:** Free. **Phone:** (304) 558-4839. (GT) (TI)

BUDGET HOST INN   304/925-2592

 APPROVED

Motel

Address: 3313 Kanawha Blvd E 25306 **Location:** I-64/77 exit 96, just w. **Facility:** 26 units. 1 story, exterior corridors.

(SAVE) (TI+) (wifi) / SOME UNITS (handicap)

CHARLESTON MARRIOTT TOWN CENTER HOTEL
304/345-6500

 THREE DIAMOND
Hotel

 AAA Benefit: Members save 5% or more!

 Address: 200 Lee St E 25301 **Location:** I-64 exit 58C; downtown. Opposite Charleston Civic Center. **Facility:** 352 units. 16 stories, interior corridors. **Parking:** on-site (fee). **Terms:** check-in 4 pm. **Pool:** heated indoor. **Activities:** sauna, exercise room. **Guest Services:** coin laundry.

/ SOME UNITS

CHARLESTON RESIDENCE INN BY MARRIOTT   304/345-4200

THREE DIAMOND [SAVE] Extended Stay Hotel. **Address:** 200 Hotel Cir 25311

AAA Benefit: Members save 5% or more!

COUNTRY INN & SUITES BY RADISSON   304/925-4300

THREE DIAMOND Hotel. **Address:** 105 Alex Ln 25304

DAYS INN CHARLESTON EAST
304/925-1010

APPROVED
Motel

Address: 6400 MacCorkle Ave SE 25304 **Location:** I-77 exit 95, just s on SR 61. **Facility:** 139 units. 3 stories, interior corridors. **Pool:** outdoor. **Activities:** exercise room. **Guest Services:** coin laundry.

EMBASSY SUITES BY HILTON CHARLESTON   304/347-8700

THREE DIAMOND [SAVE] Hotel. **Address:** 300 Court St 25301

AAA Benefit: Members save up to 15%!

FOUR POINTS BY SHERATON CHARLESTON
304/344-4092

THREE DIAMOND
Hotel

FOUR POINTS BY SHERATON **AAA Benefit:** Members save 5% or more!

 Address: 600 Kanawha Blvd E 25301 **Location:** I-64 exit 58B eastbound; exit 58C westbound, Virginia St to corner of Laidley St and Kanawha Blvd; I-64/77 exit 97, 4.5 mi w on US 60 (Kanawha Blvd); downtown. **Facility:** 176 units. 12 stories, interior corridors. **Parking:** on-site (fee). **Amenities:** safes. **Pool:** heated indoor. **Activities:** exercise room. **Guest Services:** valet laundry, area transportation.

 **Get the scoop from AAA inspectors:**

 **AAA.com/travelguides/restaurants**

HAMPTON INN SOUTHRIDGE
304/746-4646

THREE DIAMOND
Hotel

Hampton by Hilton **AAA Benefit:** Members save up to 15%!

 Address: 1 Preferred Pl 25309 **Location:** I-64 exit 58A, 4 mi s on US 119. Adjacent to a shopping center. **Facility:** 139 units. 6 stories, interior corridors. **Amenities:** video games, safes. **Pool:** heated indoor. **Activities:** hot tub, exercise room. **Guest Services:** valet and coin laundry, area transportation. **Featured Amenity: full hot breakfast.**

HOLIDAY INN EXPRESS CHARLESTON CIVIC CENTER
304/345-0600

THREE DIAMOND
Hotel

Address: 100 Civic Center Dr 25301 **Location:** I-64 exit 58B eastbound; exit 58C westbound, just s; downtown. **Facility:** 196 units. 6 stories, interior corridors. **Amenities:** video games. **Activities:** exercise room. **Guest Services:** valet and coin laundry, area transportation. **Featured Amenity: full hot breakfast.**

/ SOME UNITS

HOLIDAY INN EXPRESS CHARLESTON-KANAWHA CITY
304/925-1171

THREE DIAMOND Hotel. **Address:** 107 Alex Ln 25304

KNIGHTS INN-CHARLESTON EAST
304/925-0451

APPROVED
Motel

Address: 6401 MacCorkle Ave SE 25304 **Location:** I-77 exit 95, just s on SR 61. **Facility:** 78 units, some kitchens. 1 story, exterior corridors. **Pool:** outdoor. **Guest Services:** coin laundry. **Featured Amenity: continental breakfast.**

/ SOME UNITS

SLEEP INN
304/345-5111

APPROVED Hotel. **Address:** 2772 Pennsylvania Ave 25302

WHERE TO EAT

BLUEGRASS KITCHEN   304/346-2871
APPROVED American. Casual Dining. **Address:** 1600 Washington St E 25311

BRIDGE ROAD BISTRO   304/720-3500
APPROVED American. Casual Dining. **Address:** 915 Bridge Rd 25314

THE CHOP HOUSE   304/344-3954
APPROVED Steak Seafood. Casual Dining. **Address:** 1003 Charleston Town Center 25389

COZUMEL MEXICAN RESTAURANT   304/342-0113
APPROVED Mexican. Casual Dining. **Address:** 1120 Fledderjohn Rd 25314

DEM 2 BROTHERS AND A GRILL BBQ   304/550-4431
APPROVED American. Quick Serve. **Address:** 423 Virginia St W 25302

FAZIO'S   304/344-3071
THREE DIAMOND Italian. Casual Dining. **Address:** 1008 Bullitt St 25301

GRAZIANO'S PIZZA   304/342-8554
APPROVED Italian. Quick Serve. **Address:** 243 Capital St 25301

HARDING'S FAMILY RESTAURANT   304/344-5044
APPROVED American. Casual Dining. **Address:** 2772 Pennsylvania Ave 25302

LA CARRETA   304/925-4590
APPROVED Mexican. Casual Dining. **Address:** 5790 MacCorkle Ave SE 25304

LOLA'S   304/343-5652
APPROVED Pizza. Casual Dining. **Address:** 1038 Bridge Rd 25314

PIES AND PINTS PIZZERIA   304/342-7437
APPROVED Pizza Sandwiches. Casual Dining. **Address:** 222 Capital St 25301

RECOVERY SPORTS GRILL   681/205-8395
APPROVED American. Sports Bar. **Address:** 600 Virginia St E 25301

SOHO'S   304/720-7646
THREE DIAMOND Italian. Casual Dining. **Address:** 800 Smith St 25301

TIDEWATER GRILL   304/345-2620
APPROVED American. Casual Dining. **Address:** 1060 Charleston Town Center 25389

TRICKY FISH   304/344-3474
APPROVED Hot Dogs. Quick Serve. **Address:** 1611 Washington St E 25311

TUDOR'S BISCUIT WORLD
APPROVED American. Casual Dining.
LOCATIONS:
Address: 5403 MacCorkle Ave SW 25304 **Phone:** 304/768-0782
Address: 10501 MacCorkle Ave 25315 **Phone:** 304/949-2088

CHARLES TOWN (B-6) pop. 5,259, elev. 513'

Charles Town was named for George Washington's brother, who laid out the town in 1786. Streets bear the names of Washington's family members. After his raid on Harpers Ferry, John Brown was tried and hanged for treason in Charles Town.

Automobile races take place at Summit Point Motorsports Park, 201 Motorsports Park Cir. in Summit Point, March through October; phone (304) 725-8444. Thoroughbred horse racing has drawn crowds since 1786. Charles Town Races, 1 mile east on US 340, is open all year; phone (304) 725-7001 or (800) 795-7001.

Note: Policies concerning admittance of children to pari-mutuel betting facilities vary. Phone for information.

Charles Town marks the West Virginia terminus of the scenic portion of SR 9, which runs eastward into Virginia. From Charles Town it is 6 miles to the Virginia border.

Jefferson County Chamber of Commerce: 201 E. Washington St., Charles Town, WV 25414. **Phone:** (304) 725-2055 or (800) 624-0577.

JEFFERSON COUNTY MUSEUM is at 200 E. Washington St. in the lower level of the Charles Town Library. Displays include memorabilia of the Washington family and John Brown, Jefferson County historical relics and many Civil War items. **Hours:** Tues.-Sat. 11-4, mid-Mar. to mid-Dec. Closed major holidays. **Cost:** $4; free (ages 0-18). Cash or check only. **Phone:** (304) 725-8628.

HAMPTON INN & SUITES CHARLES TOWN   304/725-2200
THREE DIAMOND [SAVE] Hotel. **Address:** 157 Pimlico Dr 25414

> **AAA Benefit:**
> Members save up to 15%!

THE INN AT CHARLES TOWN   304/885-5800
THREE DIAMOND Hotel. **Address:** 100 Hollywood Dr 25414

WHERE TO EAT

HILLBROOK INN   304/725-4223
THREE DIAMOND American. Fine Dining. **Address:** 4490 Summit Point Rd 25414

MI DEGOLLADO MEXICAN RESTAURANT   304/725-0333
APPROVED Mexican. Casual Dining. **Address:** 92 Somerset Blvd 25414

CLARKSBURG (B-3) pop. 16,578, elev. 1,034'
• Hotels p. 340 • Restaurants p. 340

From 1861 until the first battle of Bull Run, Clarksburg was the headquarters for Gen. George B. McClellan. It also served as a Union supply depot throughout the war. Gen. William E. Jones' Confederate cavalry passed through in 1863 on the raid that destroyed military points on the B & O Railroad.

Clarksburg was the birthplace in 1824 of Gen. Thomas J. "Stonewall" Jackson, hero of the Confederacy. The site is marked by a bronze plate at 326-328 W. Main St. An equestrian statue of Jackson is on the northeast corner of the Court House Plaza. The military leader spent most of his boyhood 20 miles south at Jackson's Mill.

More than 100,000 visitors come to Clarksburg over Labor Day weekend to join in the merriment of the West Virginia Italian Heritage Festival. The 3-day street festival features name entertainment, traditional Italian foods, a pasta cook-off, a children's area, a parade and a bocce tournament.

Greater Clarksburg Convention & Visitors Bureau: 215 S. Third St., Suite 101. **Phone:** (304) 622-2157 or (877) 622-2157.

Shopping: Meadowbrook Mall, off I-79 exit 121 at Bridgeport, has JCPenney among its stores.

HILTON GARDEN INN CLARKSBURG/BRIDGEPORT
304/326-9200
THREE DIAMOND SAVE Hotel. **Address:** 606 Emily Dr 26301

AAA Benefit: Members save up to 15%!

WHERE TO EAT

MINARD'S SPAGHETTI INN   304/623-1711
APPROVED Italian. Casual Dining. **Address:** 813 E Pike St 26301

DANIELS pop. 1,881

THE RESORT AT GLADE SPRINGS   304/763-2000
THREE DIAMOND Resort Hotel. **Address:** 255 Resort Dr 25832

WHERE TO EAT

GLADE'S GRILL & BAR   304/763-3033
THREE DIAMOND American. Fine Dining. **Address:** 255 Resort Dr 25832

DAVIS (C-4) pop. 660, elev. 3,200'

Incorporated in 1885, Davis was born of the lumber boom. Today the area is a mecca for mountain bikers and rafters. Ten miles south, Canaan Valley Resort State Park *(see Recreation Areas Chart)* is an all-year resort and conference center. Downhill and cross-country skiing are popular in winter; golf on an 18-hole championship course, hiking, tennis and swimming prevail during the summer. Deer often cross the golf course early and late in the day. Other privately operated resorts and camping facilities also are available in the Canaan (ka-NAIN) valley.

Of historical significance is the Fairfax Stone, 7 miles north of town off US 219, which marked the western boundary of Lord Fairfax's lands. Under the terms of the grant issued by the king of England, Lord Fairfax owned all the lands between the Potomac and the Rappahannock rivers, and this marker served as the base point for the boundary between Maryland and Virginia (now West Virginia).

Tucker County Convention and Visitors Bureau: 410 William Ave., Davis, WV 26260. **Phone:** (304) 259-5315 or (800) 782-2775.

BLACKWATER FALLS STATE PARK is at 1584 Blackwater Lodge Rd. The scenic Blackwater Falls are 57 feet high, and the gorge below is more than 525 feet deep. An observation point is on the gorge's rim; stairways descend to the foot of the falls. A nature center is open Memorial Day to Labor Day. Recreational activities include cross-country skiing, paddleboating, hiking, picnicking, swimming, tennis, bicycling, sledding, volleyball and nature programs *(see Recreation Areas Chart)*. Campgrounds are available last week in April through October 31; cabins and lodge facilities are available all year.

Hours: Park open daily 6 a.m.-10 p.m. Waterfall accessible 6 a.m.-dusk. **Cost:** Free. **Phone:** (304) 259-5216 or (800) 225-5982.

BLACK BEAR RESORT   304/866-4391
THREE DIAMOND Cabin. **Address:** 247 Lodge Dr 26260

CANAAN VALLEY RESORT STATE PARK   304/866-4121
THREE DIAMOND Resort Hotel. **Address:** 230 Main Lodge Rd 26260

WHERE TO EAT

HELLBENDER BURRITOS   304/259-5557
APPROVED Mexican. Casual Dining. **Address:** 457 William Ave 26260

EDRAY

MARLINTON MOTOR INN   304/799-4711
APPROVED
Motel
Address: 21507 Seneca Tr N 24954 **Location:** Center. **Facility:** 69 units. 2 stories (no elevator), exterior corridors. **Pool:** outdoor. **Activities:** hot tub.

/ SOME UNITS

ELKINS (C-4) pop. 7,094, elev. 1,940'

Elkins, on the Tygart Valley River in the Potomac Highlands, is in a region that contains many of West Virginia's highest mountains. Named for Stephen B. Elkins, secretary of war and U.S. senator 1895-1911, the city was a center for railroad, timber and coal operations. The mountains provide a variety of recreational opportunities, including the Mountain State Forest Festival, held each fall. Ski areas are nearby in the Monongahela National Forest *(see place listing p. 347)*, which maintains its headquarters in Elkins.

Elkins is at the crossroads of three scenic highways. From Fairmont to the north, the scenic section of US 250 passes through, running south to Huttonsville. US 219 runs south jointly with US 250 to Huttonsville and then continues on to White Sulphur Springs. US 33 crosses them in Elkins, following the Tygart River into town before heading east into some of the region's most spectacular scenery. The Stuart Memorial Drive, which passes Stuart Recreation Area and 4,020-foot Bickles Knob, runs between Elkins and Alpena.

Elkins-Randolph County Chamber of Commerce: 10 Eleventh St., Elkins, WV 26241. **Phone:** (304) 636-2717.

CHEAT MOUNTAIN SALAMANDER departs from the depot at 315 Railroad Ave. A 9-hour, 128-mile round-trip train ride takes passengers through the rugged, scenic Cheat Mountains. The tracks run through spruce forests and an "S" curve tunnel, passing rock walls along Shavers Fork River. There are layovers at Cheat Bridge and High Falls of the Cheat and Spruce. Lunch is included.

Time: Allow 9 hours minimum. **Hours:** Departures 9:15 a.m. Tues.-Sun., mid-Sept. to mid-Oct. (also Oct. 27); Thurs.-Sun., June to mid-Sept. (except July 16); Sat.-Sun. in May. Phone ahead to confirm schedule. **Cost:** Fare $81; $79 (ages 65+); $71 (ages 4-11). An additional $5 per person is charged Sat. in fall. Reservations are required. **Phone:** (304) 636-9477 or (877) 686-7245.

NEW TYGART FLYER departs from the depot at 315 Railroad Ave. A 4-hour, 46-mile round-trip takes passengers by train along the Shavers Fork River through an "S" curve tunnel, across a bridge over the Cheat River, and to an 18-foot-high waterfall. Lunch is included. A 1922-era parlor car, featuring seating in cushioned armchairs and refreshments, is available. Other excursions also are offered.

Time: Allow 4 hours minimum. **Hours:** All departures at 11 Tues.-Sun., mid-Sept. to mid-Oct.; Thurs.-Sun., June to mid-Sept. and Oct. 27-30; Sat.-Sun. in May; Sat., Apr. 2-23. Phone ahead to confirm schedule. **Cost:** Coach buffet-class fare $61; $59 (ages 65+); $51 (ages 4-11). Parlor car (ages 12+ only) $76. An additional $5 is charged Sat. in fall. Reservations are recommended. **Phone:** (304) 636-9479 or (877) 686-7245. 🍴

HAMPTON INN BY HILTON ELKINS   304/630-7500
▼▼ **THREE DIAMOND** ⟨SAVE⟩ Hotel. **Ad-**   **AAA Benefit:**
dress: 480 Plantation Dr 26241   Members save up to
                                                         15%!

WHERE TO EAT

C. J. MAGGIE'S   304/636-1730
▼▼ **APPROVED**   American. Casual Dining. **Address:** 309 Davis St 26241

FAIRMONT (B-4) pop. 18,704, elev. 884'

Fairmont occupies the steep hills surrounding the Monongahela River, which divides the town into east and west sections. Originally two towns, Palatine and Middletown, Fairmont was incorporated in 1843. Ferries shuttled people and supplies across the river until 1852, when a suspension bridge unified the town.

During the 1850s railroad access encouraged the development of coal mines in the area. While coal continues to be a source of employment, today the town is on a high-tech corridor with a NASA software facility and a software consortium. Other Fairmont products include mine machinery and aluminum.

Fifteen miles south off SR 310, Valley Falls State Park (see Recreation Areas Chart) features a series of waterfalls generated by the Tygart Valley River.

The park's 1,145 acres are popular with anglers, picnickers and hikers; phone (304) 367-2719 or (800) 225-5982. Fairmont is the northern end of the scenic section of US 250, which runs 73 miles to Huttonsville and continues as US 219 to Lewisburg.

AMERICAN MOUNTAIN THEATER is at 22 Pinch Gut Hollow Rd. This family-friendly music and comedy show features a mix of musical styles including country, gospel, bluegrass, pop and patriotic music. **Time:** Allow 2 hours minimum. **Hours:** Performances Mon.-Sat. at 7:30, in Oct.; Wed.-Sat. at 7:30 p.m., June-Sept.; Thurs.-Sat. at 7:30, in May; Fri.-Sat. at 7:30, in Apr. Closed major holidays. Phone ahead to confirm schedule. **Cost:** $25; $23 (ages 55+); $15 (ages 0-11). Reservations are recommended. **Phone:** (304) 630-3040 or (800) 943-3670. 🍴

PRICKETT'S FORT STATE PARK, about 2.5 mi. w. off I-79 exit 139 at 106 Overfort Ln., contains a reconstructed log fort similar to one built in 1774 to protect settlers from Native American attacks. The museum captures West Virginia's 18th-century lifestyle through costumed interpreters and craft demonstrations.

The visitor center offers exhibits about the Monongahela Valley's history and has bike rentals for riding the park's trails. The park has a nature trail and a hiking trail that follows a converted rail bed to Fairmont and Morgantown. A 400-seat amphitheater hosts summer concerts and performances. See Recreation Areas Chart.

Time: Allow 2 hours minimum. **Hours:** Mon.-Sat. 10-4:30, Sun. noon-4:30, mid-Apr. to Labor Day; Wed.-Sat. 10-4:30, Sun. noon-4:30, Labor Day-Oct.31. Last admission half hour before closing. **Cost:** Park free. Historical attractions $8; $6 (ages 60+); $4 (ages 6-12). **Phone:** (304) 363-3030. ✕ 🐕 🏕

FAIRFIELD INN & SUITES BY MARRIOTT   304/367-9150
▼▼ **THREE DIAMOND** ⟨SAVE⟩ Hotel. **Ad-**   **AAA Benefit:**
dress: 27 Southland Dr 26554   Members save 5%
                                                         or more!

MICROTEL INN & SUITES BY WYNDHAM, FAIRMONT
                                                   304/363-3100
▼▼ **APPROVED**   Hotel. **Address:** 20 Southland Dr 26554

QUALITY INN   304/367-1370
▼▼ **APPROVED**   Hotel. **Address:** 1185 Airport Rd 26554

SUPER 8   304/363-1488
▼▼ **APPROVED**   Motel. **Address:** 2208 Pleasant Valley Rd 26554

WHERE TO EAT

DJ'S 50'S & 60'S DINER   304/366-8110
▼▼ **APPROVED**   American. Casual Dining. **Address:** 1181 Airport Rd 26554

MURIALE'S RESTAURANT   304/363-3190
 APPROVED   Southern   Italian.   Casual   Dining.
Address: 1742 Fairmont Ave Ext 26554

POKY DOT   304/366-3271
APPROVED   American. Casual Dining. **Address:** 1111
Fairmont Ave 26554

SAY-BOY RESTAURANT   304/366-7252
APPROVED   American. Casual Dining. **Address:** 1228
Country Club Rd 26554

GLENVILLE pop. 1,537

THE GLENVILLE INN   304/462-5511
THREE DIAMOND   **Address:** 61 Development Dr 26351
Hotel   **Location:** 1.5 mi e on SR 5. **Facility:** 57
units. 3 stories, interior corridors. **Terms:**
check-in 4 pm. **Activities:** sauna, exercise room. **Guest Services:** coin
laundry. **Featured Amenity: continental breakfast.**

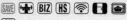

GRAFTON (B-4) pop. 5,164, elev. 1,002'

While still a part of Virginia, Grafton was incorporated in 1856. The town was a key point in the
Civil War because of its location on the B&O Railroad. At the beginning of the war, Confederate
Colonel George A. Porterfield and a small contin-
gent established a base in Grafton. Bailey Brown,
who during the Battle of Philippi became the first
Union soldier killed by Confederate forces, is buried
in Grafton National Cemetery at 431 Walnut St.

THE INTERNATIONAL MOTHER'S DAY SHRINE
is at 11 E. Main St. Andrews Methodist Episcopal
Church was the site of the first observance of Mother's Day, May 10, 1908. **Hours:** Mon.-Fri. 10-4:30,
mid-Apr. through Oct. 31. Phone ahead to confirm
schedule. **Cost:** Donations. **Phone:** (304) 265-1589.

TYGART RIVER DAM AND LAKE is 2 mi. s., following signs from US 50 or US 119. The dam was
built to control floods on the Monongahela River and
reduce the crest of the Ohio River during flood times.
The dam is 207 feet thick at the base, 1,921 feet long
and 230 feet high. The reservoir, which covers 1,750
acres and has a 32-mile shoreline, provides opportunities for fishing and hiking. *See Recreation Areas
Chart.* **Note:** Photo ID is required for tours. Foreign
nationals must reserve 30 days prior to tour date.
Hours: Daily 24 hours, mid-Apr. through Dec. 31.
Dam tours depart Fri. at 1, June-Aug.; check-in 15
minutes before departure. **Cost:** Free. Reservations
are required for dam tours. **Phone:** (304) 265-5953,
or (304) 265-1760 for dam tours.

HARPERS FERRY (B-6) pop. 286, elev. 282'

The town of Harpers Ferry is at the confluence of
the Potomac and Shenandoah rivers, separating
Maryland, Virginia and West Virginia. The federal arsenal and armory built in 1796 manufactured many

of the muskets and rifles used in the War of 1812
and the Civil War. These buildings were the targets
of abolitionist John Brown's notorious raid.

On the night of Oct. 16, 1859, Brown, accompanied by 18 members of his 21-man "army," surprised and captured the armory and arsenal. His
intent was to incite the slaves to insurrection and
arm them from the government stores. After consid-
erable bloodshed, the raiders were captured by U.S.
Marines under Col. Robert E. Lee. Brown and six of
his followers were tried for treason, convicted and
hanged at Charles Town.

During the Civil War, Harpers Ferry was regarded
by the Union command as a key to the safety of
Washington, D.C. In 1861 the small federal garrison
abandoned the town before a force of Virginians, but
destroyed the arsenal before leaving. It was never
rebuilt. The following year Gen. Thomas "Stonewall"
Jackson captured the federal garrison after a terrific
bombardment, taking 12,500 Union soldiers as pris-
oners before moving on to join Lee at Antietam.

The Appalachian Trail passes nearby, and the
Shenandoah and Potomac rivers offer opportunities
for fishing, canoeing and rafting.

Jefferson County Convention & Visitors Bureau:
37 Washington Ct., Harpers Ferry, WV 25425.
Phone: (304) 535-2627 or (866) 435-5698.

CLARION INN HARPERS FERRY-CHARLES TOWN
                                            304/535-6302
APPROVED   Hotel. **Address:** 4328 William L Wilson
Frwy 25425

QUALITY INN   304/535-6391
APPROVED   Motel. **Address:** 25 Union St 25425

HARPERS FERRY NATIONAL HISTORICAL PARK (C-6)

Harpers Ferry National Historical Park is on US
340 at the scenic confluence of the Shenandoah
and Potomac rivers. The 3,823-acre park is comprised of several areas: the Lower Town, Maryland
Heights, Loudoun Heights, Bolivar Heights, Cavalier
Heights, Short Hill, Virginius Island, Murphy Farm
and School House Ridge North and South. Maps
and guides are available at the park visitor center on
Cavalier Heights, about 1 mile west of the Shenandoah River bridge.

Congress authorized a national monument here
in 1944, and the area was declared a National Historical Park in 1963. Shuttle buses connect the
visitor center with the Lower Town, the site where
George Washington persuaded the federal government to construct a national armory and arsenal and
where John Brown led his famous raid in 1859.

Park exhibits and museums in more than two
dozen restored 19th-century buildings, including
John Brown's fort, John Brown Museum, the Provost
Marshal office, Civil War Museum, Industry Museum

and Restoration Museum, reflect the diverse historical events that shaped the region: the first successful application of interchangeable manufacture; the arrival of the first successful American railroad; John Brown's attack on slavery; the largest surrender of Federal troops during the Civil War; and the education of former slaves at Storer College, one of the earliest integrated schools in the United States.

John Brown's Fort, on Arsenal Square, was the scene of Brown's capture. The 1848 brick armory firehouse was dismantled and moved to Chicago after the Civil War; the building was later moved to the Murphy Farm then Storer College campus before being restored to a site 150 feet east of its original location. The granite John Brown Monument marks the original site of the firehouse where Brown and his men made their stand.

The 1782 Harper House is the oldest surviving structure in Harpers Ferry. The lower level of this home exhibits an armory worker's apartment.

Guided tours are available throughout the summer. Hiking trails lead to Maryland Heights, 1,448 feet above the rivers, where remnants of Civil War fortifications and campsites are visible. A walking tour of Virginius Island on the banks of the Shenandoah River reveals the ruins of a once-thriving industrial community. The foundries, mills and factories that survived the war were leveled by record floods in 1870 and 1889.

The park and visitor center are open daily 9-5; closed Jan. 1, Thanksgiving and Christmas. Admission (valid for 3 days) is $10 per private vehicle carrying up to 7 passengers; $5 for individuals (ages 16+) arriving by foot or bicycle. Credit cards are only accepted at Cavalier Heights entrance. Phone (304) 535-6029.

HICO pop. 272, elev. 2,056'

COUNTRY ROAD CABINS   304/658-5267
THREE DIAMOND Cabin. **Address:** 1508 Sunday Rd 25854

HINTON (D-3) pop. 2,676, elev. 1,372'

Hinton, a historic railroad town on the New River, was once the main terminal for the Chesapeake & Ohio Railway. Ten miles north via SR 26 (River Road) is Sandstone Falls, a noted spot among anglers for catfish and bass. West on SR 20, the New River Gorge National River's Sandstone Visitor Center features interactive exhibits; phone (304) 466-0417.

Memorabilia and exhibits at the Veterans Memorial Museum, 419 Ballengee St., highlight every major conflict and era. The collection includes General Douglas MacArthur's footlocker, a vintage 151A2 jeep and a rare Nazi dagger.

Bluestone Dam, 1 mile south via SR 20 on the New River, forms 2,040-acre Bluestone Lake, providing recreational options such as boating, fishing and picnicking; phone (304) 466-2805 for information about Bluestone. *See Recreation Areas Chart.*

New River Gateway Convention & Visitors Bureau: 300 Second Ave., Hinton, WV 25951. **Phone:** (304) 466-5420 or (304) 466-5332.

Self-guiding tours: Brochures outlining a walking tour of Hinton's historic district, with more than 200 buildings of historic and architectural interest, are available at the convention and visitors bureau.

HUNTINGTON (C-1) pop. 49,138, elev. 565'
• Hotels p. 344 • Restaurants p. 344

Huntington lies in a semicircle between low hills and the Ohio River. Eleven miles of floodwalls protect the city. Founded in 1871 by Collis P. Huntington, who was then president of the Chesapeake & Ohio Railroad, the city has become a busy industrial center and trans-shipping point. Among the products manufactured in the area are chemicals, clothing, glass and steel.

The city's Big Sandy Superstore Arena, One Civic Center Plaza, draws convention business to Huntington and plays host to entertainment events; phone (304) 696-5990. Marshall University offers guided campus tours through its Recruitment and Welcome Center; phone (304) 696-3646 or (877) 464-3731. In partnership with Marshall University Department of Dietetics, Huntington's Kitchen offers lectures and cooking classes at 911 Third Ave.; phone (304) 522-0887. The community kitchen was started by British celebrity chef Jamie Oliver during the first season of "Jamie Oliver's Food Revolution."

The rose garden in Ritter Park, on McCoy Road between 8th and 12th streets, displays four species and 87 varieties of roses. Virginia Point Park, at the mouth of the Big Sandy River, has a boat-launching ramp and a camping area. The Ohio River also offers recreational opportunities. Public launching ramps and a marina provide boaters access to the river.

Camden Park, an amusement park just west of the city on US 60, offers more than 30 rides, including two wooden roller coasters and a 1907 carousel, as well as shows by nationally known recording artists; phone (304) 429-4321 or (866) 822-6336.

Cabell-Huntington Convention and Visitors Bureau: 210 11th St. #15, Huntington, WV 25701. **Phone:** (304) 525-7333 or (800) 635-6329.

Shopping: Huntington Mall, off I-64 exit 20B, counts JCPenney, Macy's and Sears among its stores. Heritage Station, a restored railway yard at 11th Street and Veterans Memorial Boulevard, offers shops and restaurants housed in old warehouses and boxcars and a farmers market in summer months. An array of antique stores and restaurants occupy downtown's Old Central City on West 14th Street.

HERITAGE FARM MUSEUM AND VILLAGE is off I-64 exit 8 (Fifth Street), 1 mi. w. on Johnstown

Road, then 1.7 mi. s. to 3300 Harvey Rd. Appalachian heritage is preserved in more than 12 restored buildings, including a sawmill, blacksmith shop, country store, one-room school and log church. A petting zoo, animal barn and nature walk are featured. Museum displays include farm machinery, steam tractors, covered wagons, early automobiles and home technology.

Note: Visitors are advised not to follow GPS directions to the farm from German Ridge Road, which is a narrow and winding country road not navigable by most vehicles. **Time:** Allow 1 hour minimum. **Hours:** Mon.-Sat. 10-3; last tour departs 1 hour before closing. Petting zoo open Sat. 10-3, May-Oct. Closed major holidays. **Cost:** Guided 1.5-hour tours $12; $10 (ages 65+); $8 (ages 3-12). Doll museum half-hour tour $8, by appointment (May 1-Dec. 1). Petting zoo/nature walk (with half-hour tour on scheduled days, May 1-Dec. 1) $5. Petting zoo only $5. **Phone:** (304) 522-1244. GT 🍴

DELTA HOTELS HUNTINGTON DOWNTOWN   304/523-8880

♦♦THREE DIAMOND SAVE Hotel. **Address:** 800 3rd Ave 25701

> **AAA Benefit:**
> Members save 5%
> or more!

FAIRFIELD INN & SUITES BY MARRIOTT   304/696-8777

♦♦THREE DIAMOND SAVE Hotel. **Address:** 536 Kinetic Dr 25701

> **AAA Benefit:**
> Members save 5%
> or more!

RAMADA LIMITED HUNTINGTON   304/523-4242

♦♦THREE DIAMOND Hotel. **Address:** 3094 16th Street Rd 25701

RED ROOF INN HUNTINGTON   304/733-3737

♦♦ APPROVED

Hotel

Address: 5190 US Rt 60 E 25705 **Location:** I-64 exit 15, just s. **Facility:** 125 units. 2 stories (no elevator), exterior corridors. **Amenities:** video games, safes. **Pool:** heated outdoor. **Guest Services:** valet laundry.

SAVE 🍴 🏊 📶 ✖ / SOME UNITS 🐾 📶 📺

SUPER 8   304/525-1410

♦♦ APPROVED Hotel. **Address:** 3090 16th Street Rd 25701

TOWNEPLACE SUITES BY MARRIOTT HUNTINGTON   304/525-4877

♦♦THREE DIAMOND SAVE Extended Stay Hotel. **Address:** 157 Kinetic Dr 25701

> **AAA Benefit:**
> Members save 5%
> or more!

WHERE TO EAT

HONEY BONES   681/204-5944

♦♦ APPROVED Chicken. Casual Dining. **Address:** 1533 Third Ave 25701

JEWEL CITY SEAFOOD   304/204-6658

♦♦ APPROVED American Seafood. Casual Dining. **Address:** 1317 4th Ave 25701

JIM'S RESTAURANT   304/696-9788

♦♦ APPROVED American. Casual Dining. **Address:** 920 5th Ave 25701

THE MARSHALL HALL OF FAME CAFE   304/697-9800

♦♦ APPROVED American. Casual Dining. **Address:** 857 3rd Ave 25701

HURRICANE pop. 6,284

HAMPTON INN WINFIELD/TEAYS VALLEY   304/760-7292

♦♦THREE DIAMOND SAVE Motel. **Address:** 511 SR 34 25526

> **AAA Benefit:**
> Members save up to
> 15%!

HOLIDAY INN EXPRESS   304/757-7177

♦♦THREE DIAMOND Hotel. **Address:** 4218 SR 34 25526

RED ROOF INN CHARLESTON WEST-HURRICANE, WV   304/757-6392

♦♦ APPROVED

Hotel

Address: 500 Putnam Village Dr 25526 **Location:** I-64 exit 39, just n on SR 34, then just e. **Facility:** 79 units. 2 stories (no elevator), exterior corridors. **Amenities:** safes. **Guest Services:** coin laundry.

SAVE 🍴 📶 ✖ / SOME UNITS 🐾 📶 📺 📺

WHERE TO EAT

FAT PATTY'S   304/757-5000

♦♦ APPROVED American. Casual Dining. **Address:** 5156 SR 34 25526

FIRESIDE GRILLE   304/757-4700

♦♦ APPROVED American. Casual Dining. **Address:** 439 WV SR 34 25526

INWOOD pop. 2,954

HAMPTON INN MARTINSBURG SOUTH-INWOOD   304/229-6677

♦♦THREE DIAMOND SAVE Hotel. **Address:** 4758 Gerrardstown Rd 25428

> **AAA Benefit:**
> Members save up to
> 15%!

WHERE TO EAT

VIVA MEXICO FAMILY RESTAURANT   304/229-1122

♦♦ APPROVED Mexican. Casual Dining. **Address:** 24 Annex Dr 25428

KEYSER (B-5) pop. 5,439, elev. 809'

The country around Keyser was a frequent battleground during the Civil War. A supply point for both armies, the community changed hands 14 times during the war. Nancy Hanks, mother of Abraham Lincoln, was born nearby on Doll Farm at Mikes Run.

Fort Ashby, on SR 46 near its intersection with SR 28, was built in 1755 and is the only remaining fort of the 69 that George Washington built to protect western Virginians. The fort is open by appointment; phone the visitors bureau at (304) 788-2513.

Mineral County Convention and Visitors Bureau: 40 1/2 Main St., Keyser, WV 26726. **Phone:** (304) 788-2513.

KEYSER INN   304/788-0913

APPROVED   **Address:** 51 Josie Dr 26726 **Location:** On US 220, 2.3 mi s. Next to Walmart. **Facility:** 44 units. 2 stories (no elevator), interior corridors. **Terms:** check-in 4 pm. **Guest Services:** coin laundry. **Featured Amenity:** continental breakfast.

Motel

SOME UNITS

SURESTAY PLUS HOTEL BY BEST WESTERN KEYSER
                304/597-1400

APPROVED   Hotel. **Address:** 70 N Tornado Way 26726

WHERE TO EAT

ROYAL RESTAURANT   304/788-9825

APPROVED   American. Casual Dining. **Address:** 88 N Main St 26726

LANSING (D-2) elev. 1,864'

Lansing serves as a base of operations for outfitters offering trips down the New River. The Canyon Rim Visitor Center, daily 9-5 except Jan. 1, Thanksgiving and Christmas, provides information about the New River Gorge National River; phone (304) 574-2115.

RECREATIONAL ACTIVITIES
White-water Rafting

• **Adventures on the Gorge** is .1 mi. n. of the New River Gorge Bridge exit off US 19, then .5 mi. w. on Ames Heights Rd.; bear left at the fork in the road. Other activities are offered. **Hours:** Trips depart daily, Apr.-Oct. **Phone:** (304) 574-0704 or (866) 343-0534.

LEWISBURG (D-3) pop. 3,830, elev. 2,300'
• Hotels p. 346 • Restaurants p. 346

Lewisburg's name was changed from Camp Union to honor Gen. Andrew Lewis, who organized the Virginia militia in 1774 for a campaign against the Shawnee. Lewis led his frontiersmen to victory at the Battle of Point Pleasant, said to be the first battle of the American Revolution. Andrew Lewis Park on N. Jefferson Street was the site where the militia assembled for the historic campaign.

The Civil War made yet another battleground out of Lewisburg. On May 23, 1862, the Confederate forces of Henry Heth clashed with the Union troops of George Crook, who later would win renown as the captor of Apache chief Geronimo. Although the Union force was victorious, Lewisburg remained a Confederate outpost for most of the war.

Some of Lewisburg's old buildings still bear scars of the battle, and a cross-shaped mass grave on McElhenny Road holds the remains of 95 unknown Confederate soldiers killed during the Battle of Lewisburg.

Carnegie Hall, 611 Church St., was a 1902 gift from Andrew Carnegie to the Lewisburg Female Institute, later known as Greenbrier College. The building now serves as an arts and education center; phone (304) 645-7917 for information about performances and exhibits.

Professional theatrical productions are staged by Greenbrier Valley Theatre. Musicals, dramas, comedies, children's plays, musical concerts, and literary and poetry readings are offered year-round; phone (304) 645-3838 or (866) 888-1411 for information.

The Greenbrier River Trail, a 78-mile pathway for hikers and bicyclers, runs along the Greenbrier River from Caldwell to Cass *(see place listing p. 336)*; the entrance to the trail at Caldwell is 3 miles east via US 60. The trail, originally part of the Chesapeake & Ohio rail system, provides access to the river for fishing, canoeing and cross-country skiing.

Greenbrier County Convention and Visitors Bureau: 905 Washington St. W., Lewisburg, WV 24901. **Phone:** (304) 645-1000 or (800) 833-2068.

Self-guiding tours: Booklets outlining tours of the Battle of Lewisburg and the 236-acre historic district, containing more than 60 18th- and 19th-century buildings of historic and architectural interest, such as North House Museum and Old Stone Church, are available at local lodgings and at the visitors center. Brochures containing information about self-guiding tours of the county's covered bridges, scenic overlooks and historic sites also are available at the visitors center.

LOST WORLD CAVERNS is 1.5 mi. n. via Court St. to 907 Lost World Dr. The caves were discovered in 1942 by speleologists from Virginia Polytechnic Institute. They contain a number of large rooms with stalactite, stalagmite and flowstone formations as well as impressive displays of pure calcite. Visitors descend about 100 feet below the entrance point and explore at their own pace by taking a self-guiding, half-mile loop trail through the caverns.

Some of the formations encountered include the Bridal Veil, a dazzling display of white calcite; the Snowy Chandelier, one of the largest stalactites in the United States at a whopping 30 tons; and the War Club, a 28-foot stalagmite. A subterranean stream and stalagmites jutting upward from the cave floor add to the mystique and beauty of this underground world. While the caverns' temperature is a constant 52 F, visitors can warm up in the facility's onsite museum, featuring an assortment of fossil and dinosaur replicas.

Note: Guided Wild Cave tours take four hours; full mobility is recommended. Warm clothing and comfortable shoes are recommended on all tours. **Time:** Allow 1 hour minimum. **Hours:** Daily 9-7, Memorial Day weekend-Labor Day; daily 9-5, day after Labor Day-day before Thanksgiving; daily 10-5, Mar. 1-day before Memorial Day weekend; daily 10-4, day after Thanksgiving-Jan. 1; Sat.-Sun. 10-4, rest of year. Last admission 45 minutes before closing. Closed Thanksgiving and Christmas. **Cost:** $12; $6 (ages 6-12). Wild Tour (ages 10+ only) $79; reservations required. **Phone:** (304) 645-6677 or (866) 228-3778. GT 🔄

NORTH HOUSE MUSEUM is .5 mi. w. on US 60 to 301 W. Washington St. The restored 1820 house displays antiques and artifacts dating from the early 1700s to the late 1800s, including Civil and Revolutionary war items and a Virginia Valley covered wagon. The library and its archives contain documents and family records from the same period.

Time: Allow 30 minutes minimum. **Hours:** Mon.-Sat. 10-4 or by appointment. **Cost:** Donations. **Phone:** (304) 645-3398.

FAIRFIELD INN & SUITES BY MARRIOTT LEWISBURG
304/645-7999

🔷 THREE DIAMOND
Hotel

Fairfield   **AAA Benefit:** Members save 5% or more!

Address: 273 Coleman Dr 24901 **Location:** I-64 exit 169, just s. **Facility:** 81 units. 4 stories, interior corridors. **Pool:** heated indoor. **Activities:** hot tub, exercise room. **Guest Services:** coin laundry. **Featured Amenity: full hot breakfast.**

HAMPTON INN BY HILTON LEWISBURG   304/645-7300

🔷 THREE DIAMOND
Hotel

Hampton   **AAA Benefit:** Members save up to 15%!

Address: 238 Coleman Dr 24901 **Location:** I-64 exit 169, just s. **Facility:** 60 units. 3 stories, interior corridors. **Pool:** heated indoor. **Activities:** hot tub, exercise room. **Guest Services:** valet laundry. **Featured Amenity: full hot breakfast.**

HISTORIC GENERAL LEWIS INN   304/645-2600
🔷 THREE DIAMOND Historic Country Inn. **Address:** 1236 Washington St E 24901

LEWISBURG HOLIDAY INN EXPRESS HOTEL & SUITES
304/645-5750
🔷 THREE DIAMOND Hotel. **Address:** 222 Hunter Ln 24901

QUALITY INN LEWISBURG CONFERENCE CENTER
304/645-7722

🔷 APPROVED
Hotel

Address: 540 N Jefferson St 24901 **Location:** I-64 exit 169, just s on US 219. Truck parking on premises. **Facility:** 162 units. 2 stories (no elevator), exterior corridors. **Pool:** outdoor. **Guest Services:** coin laundry. **Featured Amenity: breakfast buffet.**

SUPER 8   304/647-3188
🔷 APPROVED Motel. **Address:** 160 Village Dr 24901

WHERE TO EAT

CARLITO'S MEXICAN RESTAURANT   304/645-3891
🔷 APPROVED Mexican. Casual Dining. **Address:** 467 Greenbrier Valley Mall Dr 24901

FOOD & FRIENDS   304/645-4548
🔷 APPROVED American. Casual Dining. **Address:** 213 W Washington St 24901

THE JEFFERSON DINING ROOM   304/645-2600
🔷 THREE DIAMOND American. Fine Dining. **Address:** 301 E Washington St 24901

LIVERY TAVERN   304/645-9836
🔷 THREE DIAMOND American. Fine Dining. **Address:** 217 E Washington St 24901

MARTINSBURG (B-6) pop. 17,227, elev. 457'

Founded in the 18th century, Martinsburg developed into an important shipping center with the construction of the Baltimore & Ohio Railroad in the 1850s. During the late 19th century orchards were planted in surrounding areas, and today Martinsburg has become a distribution center for apples and peaches.

Martinsburg was torn apart by the Civil War because of Union and Confederate occupation, internal strife and the proximity of many battles. The town was the home of Belle Boyd, a beautiful 17-year-old Confederate spy who shot a Union soldier in her parents' home after he had made threats against her mother.

Martinsburg-Berkeley County Convention and Visitors Bureau: 126 E. Race St., Martinsburg, WV 25401. **Phone:** (304) 264-8801 or (800) 498-2386.

Shopping: Anchor shops at the Foxcroft Towne Center at Martinsburg, formerly Martinsburg Mall, between I-81 exits 12 and 13, are Hobby Lobby and Grand Home Furnishings.

COMFORT INN AIKENS CENTER   304/263-6200
🔷 THREE DIAMOND Hotel. **Address:** 1872 Edwin Miller Blvd 25404

FAIRFIELD INN & SUITES BY MARRIOTT MARTINSBURG
304/901-3003

♦♦♦ **THREE DIAMOND** [SAVE] Hotel. **Ad-**
dress: 451 Foxcroft Ave 25401

AAA Benefit:
Members save 5%
or more!

HAMPTON INN MARTINSBURG   304/267-2900

♦♦♦ **THREE DIAMOND** [SAVE] Hotel. **Ad-**
dress: 975 Foxcroft Ave 25404

AAA Benefit:
Members save up to
15%!

HILTON GARDEN INN MARTINSBURG   304/263-0101

♦♦♦ **THREE DIAMOND** [SAVE] Hotel. **Ad-**
dress: 65 Priority Dr 25403

AAA Benefit:
Members save up to
15%!

HOLIDAY INN MARTINSBURG   304/267-5500

♦♦♦ **THREE DIAMOND** Hotel. **Address:** 301 Foxcroft Ave 25401

WHERE TO EAT

BLUE WHITE GRILL   304/263-3607
♦ **APPROVED**   American. Casual Dining. **Address:** 101
N Queen St 25401

FIESTA TAPATIA BAR AND GRILL   304/260-0266
♦ **APPROVED**   Mexican. Casual Dining. **Address:** 201 S
Viking Way 25401

FINN THAI RESTAURANT & BAR   304/262-2200
♦ **APPROVED**   Thai. Casual Dining. **Address:** 748
Foxcroft Ave 25401

MINERAL WELLS pop. 1,950

COMFORT SUITES PARKERSBURG SOUTH   304/489-9600
♦♦♦ **THREE DIAMOND** Hotel. **Address:** 167 Elizabeth Pike 26150

HAMPTON INN BY HILTON PARKERSBURG/MINERAL WELLS
304/489-2900

♦♦♦ **THREE DIAMOND** [SAVE] Hotel. **Ad-**
dress: 64 Elizabeth Pike 26150

AAA Benefit:
Members save up to
15%!

HOLIDAY INN EXPRESS HOTEL & SUITES PARKERSBURG/
MINERAL WELLS   304/489-4111
♦♦♦ **THREE DIAMOND** Hotel. **Address:** 80 Old Nicholette Rd
26150

MICROTEL INN BY WYNDHAM   304/489-1234
♦ **APPROVED**   Hotel. **Address:** 94 Old Nicolette Rd
26150

WHERE TO EAT

NAPOLI'S   304/422-1111
♦ **APPROVED**   Italian. Casual Dining. **Address:** 102
Nicolette Rd 26150

MONONGAHELA NATIONAL FOREST
(C-3)

Elevations in the forest range from 900 ft. at
Petersburg to 4,861 ft. at Spruce Knob. Refer
to AAA maps for additional elevation
information.

Monongahela National Forest encompasses ten
West Virginia counties in the Allegheny Mountains.

Noted for its rugged terrain, highland bogs, blue-
berry thickets, vistas of exposed rocks, fast-moving
streams and thick cover of trees, the forest was established in 1920 after widespread cutting of eastern
forests. One of the 920,000-acre forest's best known
attractions is Spruce Knob, West Virginia's highest
peak at 3,861 feet *(see Spruce Knob-Seneca Rocks
National Recreation Area p. 354)*.

Seneca Rocks *(see Spruce Knob-Seneca Rocks
National Recreation Area p. 354)* and July-blooming
rhododendrons are among the region's highlights.

Access the four bogs of Cranberry Glades Botanical Area, which contains bog vegetation far south
of its normal range, from a half-mile-long boardwalk
at the Cranberry Mountain Nature Center (SRs 39
and 50), where you also can hike on a self-guiding
nature trail and see exhibits depicting forest ecology,
history and wildlife, including a live snake display.
The center is open mid-Apr. to mid-Oct.; phone (304)
653-4826 or (304) 846-2122 off-season.

Many good routes traverse the forest; some provide picturesque drives. The 43-mile Highland
Scenic Highway between Richwood and US 219 follows SR 39/55 for 21 miles, then SR 150 for 22
miles, offering spectacular views of the Allegheny
Highlands. US 250 offers some exceptional scenery.
Between Huttonsville and the Virginia line the
highway crosses 4,353-foot Top of Allegheny. A 60-
mile section of US 33 from Elkins east to Franklin
also offers splendid vistas.

Bears, deer, grouse, rabbits, squirrels and turkeys
can be hunted in season. The forest contains 129
miles of warm-water fishing and 576 miles of trout
streams. Gaudineer Scenic Area, off US 250 north
of Durbin, protects 140 acres of virgin red spruce.
The Dolly Sods Wilderness Area, 17,371 acres west
of Hopeville, offers wide views and upland bogs with
unusual plants. In the 20,698 acres of Otter Creek
Wilderness Area hiking trails thread through mountainous terrain. Fernow Experimental Forest, admin-
istered by the U.S. Forest Service, adjoins Otter
Creek; hunting is permitted in season.

Other wilderness areas within the forest are Cranberry, Laurel Fork North, Laurel Fork South, Spice
Run, Big Draft and Roaring Plains West. The forest
is traversed by some 500 miles of hiking trails and
an extensive backwoods road and trail system for
hiking, mountain biking and horseback riding. An excellent hiking guide to the forest is available for a fee
from the West Virginia Highlands Conservancy, P.O.
Box 306, Charleston, WV 25321.

For further information contact the Forest Supervisor, Monongahela National Forest, 200 Sycamore
St., Elkins, WV 26241; phone (304) 636-1800, voice
and TTY. *See Recreation Areas Chart.*

MORGANTOWN (B-4) pop. 29,660, elev. 869'
• Hotels p. 348 • Restaurants p. 348

Morgantown, on the east bank of the Monongahela River, is the seat of Monongalia County and the

home of West Virginia University (WVU). A highlight is Core Arboretum, the university's research facility and outdoor classroom that features trails and wildflowers, which is on Monongahela Boulevard, just south of the WVU Coliseum; phone (304) 293-0387. Near the Evansdale campus is the WVU Robert C. Byrd Health Sciences Center.

Coopers Rock State Forest, 13 miles east off I-68, offers 12,713 acres of forest, interesting rock formations, hiking trails, cross-country ski trails, camping and picnic areas, a 19th-century iron furnace and a spectacular view of the Cheat River Valley. Swimming and boating are popular activities at Cheat Lake, just east of town on I-68.

A 52-mile section of the West Virginia Rail Trail follows the Monongahela River through Morgantown. Ideal for walking, bicycling, jogging and inline skating, the trail is paved within city limits. Morgantown is at the western end of the scenic portion of I-68, which runs east to Hancock, Md.

Greater Morgantown Convention and Visitors Bureau: 341 Chaplin Rd., 1st Floor, Morgantown, WV 26501. **Phone:** (304) 292-5081 or (800) 458-7373.

Shopping: Morgantown Mall, at the junction of I-79 exit 152 and US 19, features JCPenney and Sears as well as more than 75 specialty shops. Seneca Center, in the old Seneca Glass Factory at 709 Beechurst Ave., contains specialty shops.

COURTYARD BY MARRIOTT MORGANTOWN   304/599-1080
🔷THREE DIAMOND SAVE Hotel. **Address:** 460 Courtyard St 26501

| | AAA Benefit: Members save 5% or more! |

EURO-SUITES HOTEL   304/598-1000
🔷THREE DIAMOND Hotel. **Address:** 501 Chestnut Ridge Rd 26505

FAIRFIELD INN & SUITES BY MARRIOTT   304/598-5006
🔷THREE DIAMOND   SAVE Contemporary Hotel. **Address:** 161 Lewis Dr 26501

| | AAA Benefit: Members save 5% or more! |

HOLIDAY INN EXPRESS   304/291-2600
🔷THREE DIAMOND Hotel. **Address:** 605 Venture Dr 26508

MICROTEL INN & SUITES BY WYNDHAM, MORGANTOWN
304/292-0055
🔷 APPROVED Hotel. **Address:** 15 Lawless Rd 26505

MORGANTOWN MARRIOTT AT WATERFRONT PLACE
304/296-1700
🔷THREE DIAMOND SAVE Hotel. **Address:** 2 Waterfront Pl 26501

| | AAA Benefit: Members save 5% or more! |

QUALITY INN-MORGANTOWN   304/296-9364
🔷 APPROVED Motel. **Address:** 225 Comfort Inn Dr 26508

RESIDENCE INN BY MARRIOTT MORGANTOWN
304/599-0237
 THREE DIAMOND
Extended Stay Hotel

Residence INN. **AAA Benefit:** Members save 5% or more!

Address: 1046 Willowdale Rd 26505 **Location:** I-79 exit 155, 2 mi s on US 19, then 0.9 mi e on SR 705. **Facility:** 104 units, some two bedrooms, efficiencies and kitchens. 4 stories, interior corridors. **Terms:** check-in 4 pm. **Pool:** heated indoor. **Activities:** exercise room. **Guest Services:** complimentary laundry.

SAVE 🔲 ♿ BIZ HS 📶 ✕
🔲 🔲 🔲 /SOME UNITS 🐾

SUPER 8 MORGANTOWN   304/296-4000
🔷 APPROVED Hotel. **Address:** 603 Venture Dr 26508

WHERE TO EAT

BLACK BEAR BURRITOS   304/777-4867
🔷 APPROVED Mexican. Casual Dining. **Address:** 3119 University Ave 26505

FLYING FISH AND CO.   304/225-3474
🔷 APPROVED Seafood. Casual Dining. **Address:** 5003 Mid-Atlantic Dr 26508

IRON HORSE TAVERN   304/451-1330
🔷 APPROVED American. Casual Dining. **Address:** 525 Granville St 26501

PEKING HOUSE   304/598-3333
🔷 APPROVED Chinese. Casual Dining. **Address:** 1125 Van Voorhis Rd 26505

PUGLIONI'S PASTA & PIZZA   304/599-7521
🔷 APPROVED Italian Pizza. Casual Dining. **Address:** 1137 Van Voorhis Rd 26505

STEFANO'S RESTAURANT   304/581-6930
🔷THREE DIAMOND Italian. Fine Dining. **Address:** 735A Chestnut Ridge Rd 26505

MOUNDSVILLE (B-3) pop. 9,318, elev. 647'

Moundsville, first known as Grave Creek, started as a cabin built in 1771 by Joseph, Samuel and James Tomlinson about 300 yards from the Grave Creek Burial Mound. In 1865 the town consolidated with Mound City and was named after the large prehistoric burial mound from the Adena Indian culture.

Marshall County Chamber of Commerce: 609 Jefferson Ave., Moundsville, WV 26041. **Phone:** (304) 845-2773.

WEST VIRGINIA PENITENTIARY is at 818 Jefferson Ave. This Gothic-style fortress was built by inmate labor in 1868 and was the state's first territorial prison. Guided 90-minute tours allow visitors to step inside a 5-foot-by-7-foot cell and see the electric chair, the gallows and North Hall, where the worst inmates were confined 23 hours a day. Handpainted murals, created by inmates, adorn the walls. Evening, night and paranormal tours also are available; phone ahead to confirm schedule and prices.

Hours: Tours depart on the hour daily 10:45-4, June-Aug.; Sun. and Tues.-Thurs. 10:45-4, Fri.-Sat. 10:45-3, Apr.-May and Sept.-Nov. Closed major holidays. **Cost:** $14; $11 (ages 55+); $8 (ages 6-16). **Phone:** (304) 845-6200.

SLEEP INN & SUITES   304/810-4000
THREE DIAMOND Hotel. **Address:** 8 Walmart Dr 26041

NEW RIVER GORGE NATIONAL RIVER
(E-3)

The New River Gorge National River encompasses 53 miles of the New River and its narrow gorge that wind through the Appalachian Mountains from Hinton to the New River Gorge Bridge (US 19) near Fayetteville. Contrary to its name, the New is believed to be one of the oldest rivers in North America; it was part of the ancient Teays River system, which originated more than 65 million years ago.

The river's human history began about 12,000 years ago when Native Americans lived and hunted in the area. The portion of the river within the park, however, was largely unsettled due to the dangerous and often impassable rapids and steep gorge walls. In 1873 the C&O Railroad was completed through the gorge and provided access to the exposed rich seams of coal in the mountains.

For the next 80 years the area was a booming industrial center, whose heart was the 18-odd communities in the lower canyon from Prince to Fayette Station. But as the mines were worked out, people began to leave the gorge's coal towns. Forest has since reclaimed most of the towns and mine sites.

General Information and Activities

The New is regarded as one of the best rivers in the state for small-mouth bass fishing. In addition, muskellunge, walleye, catfish and carp test the skill of anglers. Some of the river's tributaries are stocked with trout. The most popular portion of the New for fishing is the upper section from Hinton to McCreery.

The New River is said to rival the Colorado for its white-water rafting opportunities. The 30 miles of the lower portion from McCreery to the New River Gorge Bridge draw white-water rafting enthusiasts each year from early April to mid-October. Many outfitters with highly skilled guides provide both scenic and white-water trips through the gorge and are primarily located at the northern end of the river.

The sandstone cliffs along the New River, which range up to 120 feet tall, have become well-known among rock climbing enthusiasts. The peak climbing season runs from April through November.

Three visitor centers offer brochures, maps and historic background on the river and the surrounding area; park rangers provide information and orientation services. The Grandview's Center on SR 25 in the Thurmond railroad depot and SR 9 is noted for its overlooks, trails and spring display of rhododendrons. The Canyon Rim Visitor Center, (304)

574-2115, in Lansing and Sandstone Visitor Center, (304) 466-0417, in Sandstone are open year-round; all others are open seasonally.

Other popular recreational activities within the park include picnicking, camping, hiking, mountain biking, canoeing, kayaking and horseback riding. *See Recreation Areas Chart.*

ADDRESS inquiries to the Superintendent, New River Gorge National River, National Park Service, P.O. Box 246, 104 Main St., Glen Jean, WV 25846. Phone (304) 465-0508.

OAK HILL (D-2) pop. 7,730, elev. 2,014'

Though not the county seat, Oak Hill is Fayette County's largest city. The Coal Miner's Memorial Statue, at the visitor center on Oyler Avenue, stands as a reminder of the area's coal mining heritage; visitors are welcome to take a piece of coal as a souvenir.

At Oak Hill Public Library, 611 Main St., a bronze plaque notes legendary country singer Hank Williams "made his last stop on his last tour" in the community in 1953.

White-water rafting opportunities are numerous due to the city's proximity to the New River Gorge.

New River Gorge Convention and Visitors Bureau: 310 Oyler Ave., Oak Hill, WV 25901. **Phone:** (304) 465-5617 or (800) 927-0263.

RECREATIONAL ACTIVITIES
White-water Rafting
- **Ace Adventure Resort** is 11.2 mi. on US 19 to E. Main St. exit, following signs to New River Gorge Adventure Park. White-water rafting and other activities are offered. **Hours:** Trips depart daily, Apr.-Oct. **Phone:** (304) 465-0236 or (800) 787-3982.
- **River Expeditions** is 3.3 mi. n. on US 19, e. on Appalachian Dr., s. on SR 16, then just e. to 900 Broadway Ave. Other excursions also are available, including guided rafting trips, scenic float trips and zip line tours. **Hours:** White-water rafting trips on the New and Gauley rivers depart daily Apr.-Oct. **Phone:** (304) 574-2827 or (800) 463-9873.

HOLIDAY LODGE HOTEL AND CONFERENCE CENTER
                                                304/465-0571
THREE DIAMOND Hotel. **Address:** 340 Oyler Ave 25901

ORGAN CAVE (D-3) elev. 2,172'

ORGAN CAVE is .5 mi. e. on SR 63 to 242 Organ Cave Dr. Ninety-minute walking tours of the cave, discovered in 1704, feature fossils, stalactites, stalagmites and a Civil War refinery used by the Confederates to produce saltpeter. More than 200 passages have yet to be mapped. The cave, left as unaltered as possible, has more than 45 miles of passageways. Condensed walking tours and exploration expeditions also are available.

NOTE: Jackets are suggested year-round. GPS directions may not be accurate. **Time:** Allow 1 hour, 30 minutes minimum. **Hours:** Tours are given Mon.-Sat. 10-3:45, Apr.-Aug.; Mon.-Sat. at 11, 1 and 3, Sept.-Oct.; by appointment, rest of year. Closed Thanksgiving and Christmas. **Cost:** $16.50; $7.50 (ages 6-12). **Phone:** (304) 645-7600. 〔T〕 〔A〕

PARKERSBURG (B-2) pop. 31,492, elev. 151'

Parkersburg's strategic location at the confluence of the Little Kanawha and Ohio rivers aided its development as an industrial center. An early visitor was George Washington, who surveyed land above the city on the Ohio River. In 1810 the Virginia legislature passed an act to found the town, known as Neal's Station and Newport prior to being incorporated as Parkersburg. Improved transportation modes and routes to the area soon followed. West Virginia's first oil wells were drilled nearby in 1860, which made Parkersburg the supply and shipping point for the "black gold" fields.

The region also was blessed with natural gas fields, and gas soon became the major source of fuel for the growing number of industrial plants. More than 100 industries produce chemicals, glass, metals, plastics and other products.

A rails-to-trails conversion, the North Bend Rail Trail extends for 72 miles from its trailhead near Parkersburg to Wolf Summit near Clarksburg. The scenic trail runs through 10 tunnels constructed by the Baltimore and Ohio Railroad 1853-57 and crosses 36 bridges.

Greater Parkersburg Convention and Visitors Bureau: 350 Seventh St., Parkersburg, WV 26101. **Phone:** (304) 428-1130 or (800) 752-4982.

Self-guiding tours: Brochures outlining a walking tour of historic buildings are available at the convention and visitors bureau.

BLENNERHASSETT ISLAND HISTORICAL STATE PARK is in the Ohio River, reached by sternwheeler from Point Park on Second Street. Harman Blennerhassett, an Irish aristocrat, built his island mansion in 1798. He became involved with Aaron Burr in an alleged plot to establish an empire in the Southwest and was forced to flee the island with his family in 1806 when the conspiracy came to light. Both men were eventually acquitted of treason, but their lives were ruined.

Fire destroyed the abandoned mansion in 1811. The Palladian-style house has been reconstructed upon its original foundation, and guided tours of the interior are offered. Narrated horse-drawn wagon rides recount the island's history.

Time: Allow 3 hours minimum. **Hours:** Tues.-Fri. 10-4:30, Sat. 11-5:30, Sun. noon-5:30, early May-early June; Tues.-Fri. 11-4:30, Sat. 11-5:30, Sun. noon-5:30, early June-Labor Day; Thurs.-Sat. 11-4:30, Sun. noon-4:30, day after Labor Day-last Sun.

in Oct. Open all holidays that fall on Monday during the season. **Cost:** Sternwheeler fare $10; $8 (ages 3-12). Mansion tour $5; $3 (ages 3-12). Wagon rides $6.50; $5.50 (ages 3-12). Museum $4; $2 (ages 3-12). Combined ticket for Sternwheeler fare, Mansion tour, wagon ride and Blennerhasset Museum $25; $18 (ages 3-12). **Phone:** (304) 420-4800 or (800) 225-5982. 〔T〕 〔A〕

Blennerhassett Museum is downtown at 137 Juliana St. Three floors are dedicated to archeological and historical exhibits. A 13-minute video reveals the history of the Blennerhassett family and its island.

Time: Allow 30 minutes minimum. **Hours:** Tues.-Fri. 9-5, Sat. 10-6, Sun. 11-6, May 1-early June; Tues.-Fri. 10-5, Sat. 10-6, Sun. 11-6, early June-Labor Day; Tues.-Sat. 10-5, Sun. 11-5, day after Labor Day-last Sun. in Oct.; Tues.-Sat. 11-5, Sun. 1-5, rest of year. Closed Veterans Day, Thanksgiving and the day after Thanksgiving, Dec. 24-31. **Cost:** $4; $2 (ages 3-12). Combined ticket for museum, Sternwheeler fare, Mansion tour and wagon ride $25; $18 (ages 3-12). **Phone:** (304) 420-4800 or (800) 225-5982.

Sternwheeler departs for Blennerhassett Island Historical State Park from Point Park on Second Street. **Hours:** Trips depart on the hour Tues.-Fri. 10-3, Sat. 11-4, Sun. noon-4, early May-early June; Tues.-Fri. 11-3, Sat. 11-4, Sun. noon-4, early June-Labor Day; Thurs.-Sat. 11-3, Sun. noon-3, day after Labor Day-last Sun. in Oct. Open on all Monday holidays during the season. **Cost:** Fare $10; $8 (ages 3-12). Combined ticket for Sternwheeler fare, Mansion tour, wagon ride and Blennerhasset Museum $25; $18 (ages 3-12). Ticket office is located at Blennerhassett Museum *(see attraction listing)* **Phone:** (304) 420-4800 or (800) 225-5982.

OIL AND GAS MUSEUM, downtown at 119 Third St., commemorates the historical significance of those industries to West Virginia and southeastern Ohio through displays, exhibits and historic photographs. The museum also chronicles the city's history and culture and houses a Civil War room. **Time:** Allow 45 minutes minimum. **Hours:** Mon.-Fri. 11-5, Sat. 11-5, Sun. noon-5. **Cost:** $3; $2 (ages 0-6). **Phone:** (304) 485-5446.

WHERE TO EAT

JIMMIE COLOMBO'S ITALIAN RESTAURANT   304/428-5472
♦ **APPROVED**   Italian. Casual Dining. **Address:** 1236 7th
St 26101

J. P. HENRY'S   304/485-9390
♦ **APPROVED**   American. Casual Dining. **Address:** 5106
Emerson Ave 26101

PETERSBURG (C-5) pop. 2,467, elev. 937'

On the south branch of the Potomac River, Petersburg was settled in 1745. It was named after German colonist Jacob Peterson, who established the town's first store. During the Civil War the town served as a Union outpost along the contested border between the North and South. Nearby earthworks were constructed by troops from Illinois and Ohio in 1863.

Because it is near the entrance to Monongahela National Forest and Spruce Knob-Seneca Rocks National Recreation Area *(see place listings p. 347 and p. 354)*, Petersburg is considered a recreation center, and calls itself the "Home of the Golden Trout." Area outfitters provide information, equipment and guides for hunting, fishing and canoeing trips into the surrounding wilderness.

SMOKE HOLE CAVERNS is 8 mi. s.w. on SR 28/55. Knowledgeable guides lead visitors along an intricate system of walkways to observe the various wonders within the caverns, which include helictites, stalagmites and stalactites. Unusual formations include one of the world's longest ribbon stalactites and an underground lake and stream. Features pointed out along the tour include the Artesian Spring, Rainbow Falls, Flowstone Dome and the Crystal Cave Coral Pool, filled with trout.

The caverns were reportedly used by Native Americans to smoke meat and by enterprising settlers to make moonshine. A 19th-century still is displayed. A wildlife museum is on the grounds. The caverns maintain a constant temperature of 56 F. **Hours:** Guided tours daily every half-hour 10-4. Closed Easter, Thanksgiving and Christmas. **Cost:** $15; $13.50 (ages 65+ and military with ID); $10 (ages 5-12). **Phone:** (304) 257-4442 or (800) 828-8478.

HOMESTEAD INN MOTEL   304/257-1049
♦ **APPROVED**
Motel
Address: 1314 North Fork Hwy 26847 **Location:** On SR 55 and 28, 1.5 mi w. Located in a rural area. **Facility:** 12 units. 2 stories (no elevator), exterior corridors. **Activities:** health club.

WHERE TO EAT

SUE'S COUNTRY KITCHEN   304/257-9100
♦ **APPROVED**   American. Casual Dining. **Address:** 135
S Main St 26847

PHILIPPI (C-4) pop. 2,966, elev. 1,247'

The first land battle of the Civil War occurred at Philippi (FIL-uh-pee) on June 3, 1861. Col. B.F. Kelley and a detachment of Federal troops from George McClellan's army surprised and routed the newly recruited Confederates under the command of Col. George Alexander Porterfield.

Spanning the Tygart River is a covered bridge that was originally built in 1852 and was used by both Confederate and Union forces during the battles. The bridge burned in 1989 but has been completely restored and is the only covered bridge still in use as a federal highway. From Fairmont to the north, the scenic portion of US 250 passes through Philippi on its 73-mile journey to Huttonsville.

Barbour County Chamber of Commerce: 101 College Hill Dr., Box 2124, Philippi, WV 26416. **Phone:** (304) 457-1958.

ADALAND MANSION AND HISTORICAL BARN is at 324 Mansion Dr., 4 mi. n. on US 119 to SR 76, then 1 mi. n. to Adaland Rd. This 1870 brick mansion features Neo-Greek architecture, period wallpaper and antique furnishings. Details include woodwork of native hardwood, double porches, an outside walnut stairway, travelers' rooms and a metal roof with handmade brackets. A restored 1850 barn houses a display of early farm tools. The garden is in bloom April through October.

Time: Allow 1 hour minimum. **Hours:** Wed.-Thurs. and most Sat. 11-5, Sun. by appointment, May-Dec. Closed Thanksgiving and Christmas. **Cost:** Mansion $10; free (ages 0-11). **Phone:** (304) 457-1587 or (304) 457-2415. [GT]

MOUNTAINEER INN   304/457-5888
♦ **APPROVED**
Motel
Address: 14928 Barbour County Hwy 26416 **Location:** 2.5 mi s on US 250. **Facility:** 40 units. 2 stories (no elevator), interior corridors. **Guest Services:** coin laundry.

POINT PLEASANT (C-1) pop. 4,350, elev. 561'
• Restaurants p. 352

Point Pleasant is in a growing resort area near the confluence of the Kanawha and Ohio rivers. It is said that when George Washington surveyed this area in the 1740s, he referred to it as the Pleasant Point.

A reconstruction of Fort Randolph, the best known of the town's forts, is in Krodel Park and is open during special events. The 44-acre park also contains campsites and a playground, and allows fishing; phone (304) 675-6788, (304) 675-1068 or (304) 857-1490 for the campground.

The 11,772-acre Chief Cornstalk Public Hunting and Fishing Area, southeast of town, is accessible via a hard-surfaced road that branches west off SR 35 near Southside; phone (304) 675-0871.

Mason County Area Chamber of Commerce: 305 Main St., Point Pleasant, WV 25550. **Phone:** (304) 675-1050.

WEST VIRGINIA STATE FARM MUSEUM is 5 mi. n. on SR 62 to Fairgrounds Rd., following signs. This 50-acre museum features log cabins built in the early 1800s, a replica of an old Lutheran church, a one-room schoolhouse built around 1870, a print shop, a taxidermic collection, a doctor's office, a country store, farm equipment including a collection of tractors, a working blacksmith shop, an herb garden, railroad cars and a barn. **Time:** Allow 1 hour, 30 minutes minimum. **Hours:** Tues.-Sat. 9-5, Sun. 1-5, Apr. 1-Nov. 15. Closed major holidays. **Cost:** Donations. **Phone:** (304) 675-5737. 🅿

TUDOR'S BISCUIT WORLD　　　　304/675-6166
💎 **APPROVED** American. Casual Dining. **Address:** 2322 Jackson Ave 25550

PRINCETON (E-2) pop. 6,432, elev. 2,460'

Mercer County, at the southern tip of West Virginia, bears the name of General Hugh Mercer, a Revolutionary War hero who was mortally wounded in 1777 at the Battle of Princeton in New Jersey. The county seat, Princeton, honors the place where he died.

Princeton-Mercer County Chamber of Commerce: 1522 N. Walker St., Princeton, WV 24740. **Phone:** (304) 487-1502.

FAIRFIELD INN & SUITES BY MARRIOTT PRINCETON
　　　　　　　　　　　　304/913-5101
💎 **THREE DIAMOND** 💾 Hotel. **Address:** 107 Halls Ridge Rd 24739

| **AAA Benefit:** Members save 5% or more! |

HAMPTON INN　　　　　　304/431-2580
💎 **THREE DIAMOND** 💾 Hotel. **Address:** 277 Meadowfield Ln 24740

| **AAA Benefit:** Members save up to 15%! |

HOLIDAY INN EXPRESS PRINCETON　304/425-8156
💎 **THREE DIAMOND**
Hotel
Address: 805 Oakvale Rd 24740 **Location:** I-77 exit 9, just w. **Facility:** 70 units. 3 stories, interior corridors. **Pool:** heated indoor. **Activities:** hot tub, limited exercise equipment. **Guest Services:** valet and coin laundry. **Featured Amenity:** breakfast buffet.

💾 🛎 🚐 BIZ HS 📶 ✖
📷 🛏 📺 🖨 /SOME UNITS 🛋

QUALITY INN　　　　　　304/487-6101
💎 **APPROVED** Motel. **Address:** 136 Ambrose Ln 24740

SLEEP INN & SUITES　　　　304/431-2800
💎 **APPROVED** Hotel. **Address:** 1015 Oakvale Rd 24740

WHERE TO EAT

A TASTE OF MEMPHIS　　　　304/425-9667
💎 **APPROVED** Barbecue. Casual Dining. **Address:** 1249 Stafford Dr 24740

CAMPESTRE MEXICAN BAR & GRILL　304/487-0003
💎 **APPROVED** Mexican. Casual Dining. **Address:** 259 Greasy Ridge Rd 24739

RANSON pop. 4,440

HOLIDAY INN EXPRESS-CHARLES TOWN　304/725-1330
💎 **THREE DIAMOND** Hotel. **Address:** 681 Flowing Springs Rd 25438

RIVERTON (C-4) elev. 1,809'

SENECA CAVERNS is 3 mi. e. of US 33 via German Valley Rd. Visitors travel along a .75-mile passage on an hour-long guided tour through the caverns at a depth ranging from 25-165 feet below ground level. Lighted trails provide access to the caverns' unusual mineral formations including cave coral, rimstone, stalactites, stalagmites and travertine.

Other formations include Mirror Lake, a reflective underground pool, and the Grand Ballroom, featuring a natural balcony. The caverns served as a refuge for the Seneca Indians from cold winters and for ceremonial rituals during the 1400s and 1500s. Gemstone mining is available. Tours of undeveloped Stratosphere Cavern, reportedly the oldest cavern in the state, also are offered.

Warm clothing and comfortable walking shoes are recommended. **Time:** Allow 1 hour minimum. **Hours:** Guided tours depart Wed.-Mon. 10-4, Memorial Day-Labor Day; Wed.-Sun. 10-4, Apr. 1-day before Memorial Day and day after Labor Day-Oct. 31. **Cost:** Seneca Caverns tour $15; $13.50 (ages 65+ and military with ID); $10 (ages 3-12). Gemstone mining $5.95-$8.50 or $30-$70 for a full day. Stratosphere Cavern tour currently closed. Admission and schedule may vary; phone ahead. **Phone:** (304) 567-2691 or (800) 239-7647. GT 🍴 🅿

ROANOKE

STONEWALL RESORT　　　　304/269-7400
💎 **THREE DIAMOND** Resort Hotel. **Address:** 940 Resort Dr 26447

WHERE TO EAT

STILLWATERS RESTAURANT　　304/269-7400
💎 **THREE DIAMOND**
American
Casual Dining
$15-$39
AAA Inspector Notes: Authentic American cuisine is served here in a friendly and tranquil setting. Seasonal outdoor lakeside seating is an option. A buffet is available as well as diverse menu selections. **Features:** full bar. **Address:** 940 Resort Dr 26447 **Location:** I-79 exit 91, just e; in Stonewall Resort. B L D

SANDSTONE (D-3) elev. 1,362'

Sandstone is a rural community along the New River just south of I-64, characterized by its natural beauty and views of the river. Sandstone Falls State Park is south of town along SR-26. The falls stretch the full width of the river (about 1,500 feet) and it is the largest waterfall in the river. Visitors can enjoy hiking, fishing and mountain biking along the lush trails.

SHEPHERDSTOWN (B-6) pop. 1,734, elev. 402'

A quaint yet diverse college town on the banks of the Potomac River, Shepherdstown has much to offer visitors, including a thriving arts scene. The Contemporary American Theater Festival, held in July, presents works by well-known playwrights annually; phone (304) 876-3473 or (800) 999-2283. German Street is the town's cultural and social hub; Shepherd University's more than 4,200 students find time between classes to take a break at the street's cafés, boutiques and art studios. Catch a flick or live concert on weekends at the restored 1909 Shepherdstown Opera House, 131 W. German St; phone (304) 876-3704.

The town's history is well-represented in Federal, Greek Revival and Victorian homes and other buildings. On German Street are Shepherd University, built in 1871, and the Entler Hotel, built in 1786.

The site of one of the earliest settlements in West Virginia, Shepherdstown was established by English and German farmers who had crossed the river from Pennsylvania into this area before 1730. The legal grant to the land was purchased by Thomas Shepherd in 1732. Originally named Mecklenburg, the name was changed to Shepherdstown in 1798. While living in Shepherdstown in 1787, James Rumsey gave the first public exhibition of his steamboat. A monument on the banks of the Potomac commemorates this successful demonstration.

Shepherdstown Visitors Center: 201 S. Princess St., Shepherdstown, WV 25443-0329. **Phone:** (304) 876-2786.

BAVARIAN INN   304/876-2551

FOUR DIAMOND — Hotel — **Address:** 164 Shepherd Grade Rd 25443 **Location:** 0.3 mi n on SR 480; at south end of Potomac River Bridge. **Facility:** A gazebo and walkways add appeal to the gardens around these alpine-style chalets, all of which offer nice views of the Potomac River. Rooms have European elegance and luxury bedding. 60 units, some cottages. 2-3 stories, interior/exterior corridors. **Dining:** Bavarian Inn Dining Room, see separate listing. **Pool:** outdoor.

SAVE 🍴 🍸 ➔ BIZ 🛜 ✕ ▣ / SOME UNITS 🛏 📷

QUALITY INN SHEPHERDSTOWN   304/876-3160
APPROVED — Motel. **Address:** 70 Maddex Square Dr 25443

BAVARIAN INN DINING ROOM   304/876-2551

FOUR DIAMOND
Continental
Fine Dining
$18-$40

AAA Inspector Notes: German and American cuisines are served in a 1930s gray stone residence surrounded by well-manicured grounds. Wiener schnitzel is notably flavorful, and the well-presented torte is tasty and light. Service is courteous and prompt, servers are smartly attired and the dessert tray affords favorites like Black Forest and German chocolate cakes. **Features:** full bar. **Reservations:** suggested. **Address:** 164 Shepherd Grade Rd 25443 **Location:** 0.3 mi n on SR 480; at south end of Potomac River Bridge; in Bavarian Inn.

B L D

MARIA'S TAQUERIA   304/876-3333
APPROVED — Mexican. Casual Dining. **Address:** 108 E German St 25443

SNOWSHOE (C-4)

Recreation is at the heart of Snowshoe - with nearly 500,000 skiers taking to the mountains in the winter, and hikers and mountain bikers taking advantage of the Allegheny Mountain terrain in the warmer months.

RECREATIONAL ACTIVITIES
Skiing

- **Snowshoe Mountain Resort** is off US 219 at SR 66. Skiing and other activities are offered. **Hours:** Skiing daily, Thanksgiving-early Apr. **Phone:** (304) 572-1000, (304) 572-4636 for snow report or (877) 441-4386.

SOUTH CHARLESTON pop. 13,450

FAIRFIELD INN & SUITES CHARLESTON   304/744-4444
THREE DIAMOND SAVE Hotel. **Address:** 402 2nd Ave SW 25303

AAA Benefit:
Members save 5% or more!

HOLIDAY INN & SUITES CHARLESTON WEST   304/744-4641
THREE DIAMOND Hotel. **Address:** 400 2nd Ave SW 25303

HOLIDAY INN EXPRESS HOTEL & SUITES   304/746-4748
THREE DIAMOND Hotel. **Address:** 95 RHL Blvd 25309

MICROTEL INN & SUITES BY WYNDHAM CHARLESTON SOUTH   304/744-4900

APPROVED
Motel

Address: 600 2nd Ave 25303 **Location:** I-64 exit 56, just ne. Located in an industrial area. **Facility:** 84 units. 3 stories, interior corridors. **Activities:** exercise room. **Guest Services:** coin laundry. **Featured Amenity: continental breakfast.**

SAVE ➕ 🛜 / SOME UNITS 🛏 📷 ▣

SUZI' HAMBURGERS   304/744-3111
APPROVED — Breakfast Burgers. Casual Dining. **Address:** 239 MaCorkle Ave SW 25303

SPRUCE KNOB-SENECA ROCKS NATIONAL RECREATION AREA (C-5)

The Spruce Knob-Seneca Rocks National Recreation Area is composed of two sections within the Monongahela National Forest *(see place listing p. 347)*. The larger Seneca Rocks unit is especially noted for rugged terrain and white-water boating during high flows in spring and rock-climbing opportunities. Camping, fishing and hiking are popular during spring and summer. Hunting is permitted in season. Cross-country skiers prefer the higher elevations in the Spruce Knob unit, where trails are plentiful. For further information, phone (304) 567-2827 for Seneca Rocks Discovery Center or (304) 257-4488 for the Potomac Ranger District office. *See Recreation Areas Chart.*

SENECA ROCKS is off US 33 and SR 28 at the town of Seneca Rocks. Rising above the North Fork River, this 900-foot-tall mass of intricately eroded quartzite sandstone is one of the most impressive rock formations in the East and is considered to be an excellent rock-climbing area.

According to legend, Snow Bird, the beautiful daughter of Seneca chief Bald Eagle, held a contest to decide who should be her husband. The first warrior to scale the mighty cliff, which she had been able to climb since her early childhood, was eligible to marry her. **Phone:** (304) 567-2827 for Seneca Rock Discovery Center, or (304) 257-4488 for Potomac Ranger district office.

SMOKE HOLE CANYON lies along Smoke Hole Rd. in the Seneca Rocks unit; take SR 28/11 s. from jct. SR 28 at Cabins. The half-mile-deep gorge was formed by the south branch of the Potomac River as it ran between North Fork and Cave mountains. SR 2 leads northwest from US 220 north of Upper Tract, traverses a portion of the gorge and ends at the Big Bend Campground. Among Smoke Hole's notable formations is Eagle Rock, which towers upward from the river. **Phone:** (304) 257-4488 for the Potomac Ranger District office.

SPRUCE KNOB is w. of SR 28 via SR 33/4 about 2.5 mi. s. of Riverton. Spruce Knob is the highest point in West Virginia at 4,861 feet *(see Monongahela National Forest p. 347)*. Numerous overlooks provide scenic views on the road to the summit, which features an observation tower and an interpretive trail.

Nearby Spruce Knob Lake is stocked with trout and offers good fishing, especially during the spring and fall. **Note:** The road is twisting and steep and can be dangerous especially during hazardous driving conditions; caution is advised. The road should not be attempted by inexperienced drivers. **Phone:** (304) 636-1800.

STAR CITY pop. 1,825

BEST WESTERN MOUNTAINEER INN 304/599-5399

APPROVED

Hotel

Best Western.

AAA Benefit: Members save up to 15% and earn bonus points!

Address: 366 Boyers Ave 26505 **Location:** I-79 exit 155, 1.4 mi e on SR 7. **Facility:** 101 units. 3 stories, interior corridors. **Pool:** heated indoor. **Activities:** exercise room. **Featured Amenity:** full hot breakfast.

SUMMERSVILLE (D-3) pop. 3,572, elev. 1,926'

Nancy Hart, a Confederate spy, led an attack on Summersville in 1861. During the battle a Union force was captured, and the town was burned. Hart escaped to Confederate lines but returned after Gen. Robert E. Lee's surrender.

US 19, a 45-mile scenic highway linking I-79 at Sutton and the West Virginia Turnpike at Bradley, passes Summersville near Summersville Lake. The lake, West Virginia's largest with 60 miles of shoreline and more than 2,800 acres of water, offers swimming, fishing, boating, hiking, camping, scuba diving and picnicking opportunities *(see Recreation Areas Chart)*. Summersville serves as the county seat for Nicholas County.

The Gauley River National Recreation Area, between Summersville and Swiss, protects 25 miles of the Gauley River and 6 miles of its tributary, the Meadow River. The Gauley is known for its rapids, white-water rafting and fishing opportunities. The recreation area can be reached from Carnifex Ferry Battlefield State Park *(see attraction listing)* or Summersville Dam off SR 129 and from SR 39. Information is available at park headquarters, P.O. Box 246, Glen Jean, WV 25846; phone (304) 465-0508.

Summersville Area Chamber of Commerce: 19 Memorial Park Rd., Nicholas County Visitors Center, Summersville, WV 26651. **Phone:** (304) 872-1588.

WINERIES

• **Kirkwood Winery and Isaiah Morgan Distillery** is 2.7 mi. n.e. on SR 41, 1.1 mi. n. on US 19, then .5 mi. e. on CR 8 (Phillips Run Rd.), following signs. **Hours:** Tours and tastings Mon.-Sat. 9-5 (also Sun. 1-5, Apr.-Dec.). Closed Thanksgiving and Christmas. **Phone:** (304) 872-7332 or (888) 498-9463. GT

ECONO LODGE 304/872-6900

APPROVED Hotel. **Address:** 1203 S Broad St 26651

HAMPTON INN 304/872-7100

THREE DIAMOND
Hotel

 AAA Benefit: Members save up to 15%!

Address: 5400 Webster Rd 26651 **Location:** Just s on SR 41 from US 19. **Facility:** 74 units. 3 stories, interior corridors. **Pool:** outdoor. **Activities:** exercise room. **Guest Services:** coin laundry. **Featured Amenity:** full hot breakfast.

SAVE | CALL | BIZ

LA QUINTA INN & SUITES 304/872-0555
THREE DIAMOND Hotel. **Address:** 106 Merchants Walk 26651

QUALITY INN 304/872-6500
APPROVED
Motel

Address: 903 Industrial Dr N 26651 **Location:** US 19, 1.9 mi n of jct SR 39. **Facility:** 99 units. 2 stories (no elevator), interior corridors. **Pool:** heated outdoor. **Activities:** sauna, exercise room. **Guest Services:** coin laundry. **Featured Amenity:** continental breakfast.

SAVE | BIZ | SOME UNITS

SLEEP INN OF SUMMERSVILLE 304/872-4500
APPROVED
Motel

Address: 701 Professional Park Dr 26651 **Location:** US 19, 1.7 mi n of jct SR 39. Located at Northside Plaza. **Facility:** 94 units. 2 stories, interior corridors. *Bath:* shower only. **Pool:** heated outdoor. **Guest Services:** coin laundry. **Featured Amenity:** full hot breakfast.

SAVE | BIZ | SOME UNITS

SUPER 8-SUMMERSVILLE 304/872-4888
APPROVED Motel. **Address:** 306 Merchants Walk 26651

WHERE TO EAT

ALFREDO'S 304/872-3304
APPROVED Italian. Casual Dining. **Address:** 1210 Wal St 26651

TRIADELPHIA (A-3) pop. 811, elev. 741'

What was once a sleepy suburb east of Wheeling, W. VA., is now a destination for shoppers as they flock to The Highlands, a massive open-air shopping, dining and entertainment complex off of I-70. With more than one million square feet of retail space, there's something for everyone—pet lovers, shoe fiends, readers, electronics nuts, bargain hunters and fashionistas. A movie theater and spa add to the entertainment options. Triadelphia's actual city footprint looks like a wishbone, following the paths of Little Wheeling Creek to the north and Middle Creek to the south.

COMFORT INN & SUITES-WHEELING 304/547-0610
THREE DIAMOND Hotel. **Address:** 675 Fort Henry Rd 26059

HAMPTON INN & SUITES WHEELING-THE HIGHLANDS 304/547-4222

THREE DIAMOND
Hotel

 AAA Benefit: Members save up to 15%!

Address: 35 Bob Wise Dr 26059 **Location:** I-70 exit 10 (Cabela Dr), just w. **Facility:** 123 units. 4 stories, interior corridors. **Pool:** heated indoor. **Activities:** exercise room. **Guest Services:** valet and coin laundry. **Featured Amenity:** full hot breakfast.

SAVE | CALL | BIZ | SOME UNITS | HS

HAWTHORN SUITES BY WYNDHAM 304/218-2500
THREE DIAMOND Extended Stay Contemporary Hotel. **Address:** 20 Bob Wise Dr 26059

HOLIDAY INN EXPRESS & SUITES 304/907-4470
THREE DIAMOND Hotel. **Address:** 45 Wayfarer Dr 26059

MICROTEL INN & SUITES BY WYNDHAM 304/547-4550
APPROVED Hotel. **Address:** 85 Fort Henry Rd 26059

SUBURBAN EXTENDED STAY 304/547-1037
APPROVED Extended Stay Hotel. **Address:** 40 Robinson Dr 26059

WHERE TO EAT

EL PASO MEXICAN GRILL 304/547-0078
APPROVED Mexican. Casual Dining. **Address:** 410 Cabela Dr 26059

UNION (E-3) pop. 565, elev. 2,073'

The one-time hunting grounds of the Iroquois and other tribes also attracted pioneers from Virginia. James Alexander settled in what became Union in 1774 before serving in the Revolutionary War. When the area separated from Greenbrier in 1799, the town became the county seat of Monroe County. Though it was one of 50 that broke away from Virginia—an additional five counties formed later—residents were bitterly divided in their loyalties during the Civil War. A monument off US 219, memorializes local Confederates who died while another monument by the historic courthouse, 216 Main St., honors all veterans.

The area boasts farmland, timberland and mineral springs. Those same springs made it part of a popular resort region until the early 20th century. Historic structures still can be seen, especially on Main Street. North on US 219 is the Indian Creek Covered Bridge, part of a former Native American path called the Seneca Trail or the Warrior's Path. Nearby Moncove Lake State Park is a major recreation area *(see Recreation Areas Chart).*

Agriculture remains an economic force and a source of pride. Farmer's Day, an annual event in early June, celebrates agriculture with a parade, street dance and fireworks.

Monroe County Tourism: 261 Heath Center Dr. **Phone:** (304) 772-3003, ext. 15 or (866) 677-3003, ext. 15.

Self-guiding tours: Brochures outlining scenic drive trips, including the Rural Heritage Quilt Trail, which features decorated barns and businesses, and Civil War Trail, are available at the Monroe County Historical Society.

MONROE COUNTY HISTORICAL SOCIETY MUSEUM COMPLEX, at US 219/Main and Fairview sts., features historical buildings, Civil War-era exhibits and carriages in the National Historic District of Union. The 1810 Clark-Wiseman and Owen Neel II log cabins reveal pioneer life complete with period furnishings. Interior exhibits of the 1820 Hugh Caperton law office include Native American artifacts, historic tools and a uniform of J.W.M. Appleton, a recruiter for the 54th Massachusetts Infantry Regiment, the African-American troop portrayed in the 1989 Civil War film "Glory."

The Carriage House Museum showcases a John Stephenson Company omnibus, a sleigh and other 19th century horse-drawn vehicles. **Hours:** Tues.-Sat. 10-4, June-Oct.; by appointment rest of year. **Cost:** Donations. **Phone:** (304) 772-3946. GT

WEIRTON pop. 19,746

COMFORT INN-WEIRTON   304/723-0050
APPROVED   Hotel. **Address:** 167 AmeriHost Dr 26062

FAIRFIELD INN & SUITES BY MARRIOTT WEIRTON
304/723-0088
THREE DIAMOND SAVE Hotel. **Address:** 139 Amerihost Dr 26062

AAA Benefit: Members save 5% or more!

HOLIDAY INN   304/723-5522
THREE DIAMOND Hotel. **Address:** 350 Three Springs Dr 26062

WHERE TO EAT

CHICO FIESTA   304/723-3303
APPROVED   Mexican. Casual Dining. **Address:** 3110 Pennsylvania Ave 26062

DEE JAY'S BBQ RIBS & GRILLE   304/748-1150
APPROVED   Barbecue. Casual Dining. **Address:** 380 Three Springs Dr 26062

MARIO'S RESTAURANT & LOUNGE   304/748-1179
APPROVED   Italian. Casual Dining. **Address:** 3806 Main St 26062

WESTON (C-3) pop. 4,110, elev. 982'

Weston serves as a commercial center for an agricultural area and supports glass industries. Surveyed by Thomas "Stonewall" Jackson's grandfather, the town contains several rambling Victorian-era homes. The Trans-Allegheny Lunatic Asylum *(see attraction listing),* formerly called Weston State Hospital, is surrounded by vast landscaped grounds. The main building, begun in 1860 and completed in 1865, has 9 acres of floor space and is said to be the largest hand-cut stone building in the United States.

The Citizens Bank Building at 201 Main Ave. is noted among devotees of classic Art Deco architecture. Built 1928-30, this 54-foot tall Indiana limestone structure is believed to be the tallest single-story building in the United States; the wrought-iron work is by the noted artist Samuel Yellen. Inside, the woodwork is hand-carved American walnut, and the 45-foot suspended plaster ceiling has a relief of the Great Seal of West Virginia. Also of interest in nearby Horner is the Central West Virginia Genealogical and Historical Library and Museum, which is open to the public for research; phone (304) 269-7091.

Every Labor Day weekend, the city celebrates Jackson's Mill Jubilee, complete with Civil War re-enactments, heritage exhibits, music, fireworks and arts and crafts vendors.

Nearby Stonewall Resort State Park surrounds the state's second-largest lake. This park offers many recreational opportunities and facilities. For more information phone (304) 269-7400. *See Recreation Areas Chart.*

Lewis County Convention & Visitors Bureau/ Stonewallcountry: 499 US 33E, Suite 2, Weston, WV 26452. **Phone:** (304) 269-7328 or (800) 296-7329.

HAMPTON INN WESTON   304/997-8750
▼▼ THREE DIAMOND SAVE Hotel. **Ad-**
dress: 76 Hospitality Way 26452

AAA Benefit: Members save up to 15%!

HOLIDAY INN EXPRESS HOTEL & SUITES   304/269-3550
▼▼ THREE DIAMOND Hotel. **Address:** 215 Staunton Dr 26452

QUALITY INN   304/269-7000
▼▼ THREE DIAMOND **Address:** 2906 US Hwy 33 E 26452 **Lo-**
Hotel **cation:** I-79 exit 99, just e. **Facility:** 70 units. 2 stories (no elevator), exterior corridors. **Pool:** heated outdoor. **Activ-ities:** exercise room. **Featured Ame-nity: continental breakfast.**

WESTON SUPER 8   304/269-1086
◇ APPROVED **Address:** 100 Market Place Mall, Suite
Hotel 12 26452 **Location:** I-79 exit 99, just e. **Facility:** 61 units. 2 stories (no elevator), interior corridors. **Amenities:** safes. **Guest Services:** coin laundry. **Featured Amenity: continental breakfast.**

WHERE TO EAT

DON PATRON MEXICAN GRILL   304/269-0069
◇ APPROVED Mexican. Casual Dining. **Address:** 100 Market Place Mall 26452

STEER STEAKHOUSE   304/269-7666
◇ APPROVED Steak. Buffet Style. **Address:** 506 Market Place Mall 26452

WHEELING (A-3) pop. 28,486, elev. 645'
• Hotels p. 359 • Restaurants p. 359

Wheeling lies along the scenic portion of I-70, which continues into Pennsylvania to the east and Ohio to the west. The last battle of the American Revolution was fought in Wheeling Sept. 11-13, 1782, when Fort Henry was attacked by a force of 40 British soldiers and 260 Native Americans. The news of the peace had not yet reached this outpost. Ebenezer and Silas Zane, who founded the city in 1769, led the defending forces. Their sister, Betty, brought powder from the Zane cabin to the fort; her efforts saved the garrison. The site of the fort is marked by a memorial stone on Main Street.

When Virginia seceded from the Union, delegates from the western counties met at Wheeling and set up the "Restored Government of Virginia," with Wheeling as the capital. After West Virginia was formally admitted to the Union in 1863, Wheeling was the capital until 1870 and again 1875-85.

The 1,010-foot-long Wheeling Suspension Bridge, built in 1849, is one of the world's longest of its kind. Henry Clay, while visiting Wheeling a year after the bridge opened, described it as "a rainbow to behold."

Wheeling's history as a frontier port where the National Road met the Ohio River is evident in the Old Town section; some of the buildings are open to the public by tour.

From May through August the Wheeling Heritage Port Amphitheater hosts Wheeling's Waterfront Wednesdays where free concerts are featured.

In winter, the city is illuminated with one of the country's largest light shows, ▼ Festival of Lights, featuring a 6-mile driving tour through 300 acres.

Wheeling Visitors Center: 1401 Main St., Wheeling, WV 26003. **Phone:** (304) 233-7709 or (800) 828-3097.

Shopping: Eight miles west on I-70 in nearby St. Clairsville, Ohio, is Ohio Valley Mall, whose more than 150 stores include Macy's and Sears. North Main Street's North Wheeling Historic District (Old Town) has antique and specialty shops; from I-70 exit 1A go north on Main Street. Wheeling's Historic Centre Market, 2200 Market St., features antique and craft shops in and around the refurbished Centre Market House.

THE ECKHART HOUSE VICTORIAN HOME TOURS & TEAS is at 810 Main St. The 18-room 1892 Queen Anne town home maintains many original features, such as stained glass, fretwork, mantles, inlaid floors, pocket doors and original electric and gas light fixtures. Tours provide information about area history and the home's living and servants' quarters. Teas, including a sweet tea, an afternoon tea and a tea luncheon in the home's elegant dining room are presided over by a costumed hostess.

Time: Allow 1 hour minimum. **Hours:** Tours are given Sat. at 2, May-Dec. Tea Room open Sat. 10-5, mid-May to Dec. Closed major holidays. **Cost:** Tours $6. Afternoon tea $16. Sweet tea $12. Tea luncheon $20. Reservations are required 36 hours in advance for teas. **Phone:** (304) 232-5439.

OGLEBAY RESORT is off I-70 at US 40, then 3 mi. n. on SR 88 to 465 Lodge Dr. This 1,700-acre parklike resort offers gardens, nature trails, stables, a zoo, a spa, shops and museums. Activities include golf, tennis, swimming, trail rides, pedal-boating, fishing, skiing and snowboarding (see Recreation Areas Chart).

In November and December, one million holiday lights decorate the park for the ▼ Winter Festival of Lights.

Hours: Park open daily 9-dusk. **Cost:** All-day pass (excluding rental equipment and special programs) for zoo, museums, par 3 golf, miniature golf, tennis, fishing, pedal boats, train, trolley, and outdoor pool $18.95, Memorial Day weekend-Labor Day. Festival of Lights by donation, $9 per person for trolley rides. **Phone:** (304) 243-4000 or (800) 624-6988. 🔲 🍴 ✕ 🐾 ⛱

Bissonnette Gardens covers 16 acres between the museums at Oglebay Resort. Formal and herb gardens, an arboretum, landscape lighting and water displays are featured in this re-creation of gardens that existed at the turn of the 20th century. Spring arrives with tulips, summer offers displays of annuals, and mums are a fall highlight. **Hours:** Daily 9-dusk, mid-Apr. to late Oct. **Cost:** Free. **Phone:** (304) 243-4010 or (800) 624-6988. ⛱

Carriage House Glass Museum is on a hilltop at Oglebay Resort. The museum houses a large collection of glassware produced 1817-1939. Exhibits include flint glass, lead crystal, cut glass and a 21-gallon Sweeney punch bowl. Also featured are glass-blowing demonstrations and a video about the history of glassmaking in the valley.

Time: Allow 30 minutes minimum. **Hours:** Museum open daily 10-5. Last admission 1 hour before closing. **Cost:** $7; free (ages 0-12). Combination ticket with Mansion Museum $10. **Phone:** (304) 242-7272.

The Good Zoo at Oglebay, within Oglebay Resort, is named in memory of 7-year-old Philip Mayer Good, a young boy who loved nature and visiting Oglebay Park. The 30-acre zoo provides natural settings for 50 species, many of them rare and endangered, including African wild dogs, lemurs, otters and red pandas.

The Discovery Lab offers hands-on exhibits for children, while the Benedum Theater provides seasonal programs for all ages. A wetlands exhibit features animals and plants native to the region. An 1863 train tours the zoo along a 1.5-mile track and travels through the ostrich and zebra exhibits. An O-gauge model train is part of an indoor display.

Lorikeet Landing is an Australian walk-through aviary where cups of nectar can be hand-fed to the colorful birds that perch right on visitors' hands. Gray and red kangaroos and red-necked wallabies may be seen at the Outback Exhibit. A children's farm, a goat contact area, animal encounters and a gem mining sluice also are available.

Hours: Mon.-Fri. 10-4, Sat.-Sun. 10-6, in Aug.; Mon.-Fri. 10-4, Sat.-Sun. 10-5 (also 5-6 Labor Day weekend), in Sept. Lorikeet Landing and train ride Mon.-Fri. 10:30-4:30, Sat.-Sun. 10:30-5:30, June-Aug.; hours may vary rest of year (weather permitting). **Cost:** $9.95; $5.95 (ages 3-12). Train ride $2.95. **Phone:** (304) 243-4030 for zoo or (800) 624-6988.

Mansion Museum, within Oglebay Resort, contains historical material and is furnished with items reflecting Ohio Valley life in the early days. The mansion, the former summer home of Col. and Mrs. Earl W. Oglebay, is furnished to represent different eras

of Wheeling's past. Changing exhibits are presented. **Hours:** Daily 10-5. Last admission 1 hour before closing. **Cost:** $7; free (ages 0-12). Combination ticket with Carriage House Glass Museum $10. **Phone:** (304) 242-7272 or (800) 624-6988.

Schrader Environmental Education Center, within Oglebay Resort at 465 Lodge Dr., offers three nature trails that cover almost 5 miles, featuring overlooks, wildlife observation areas and waterfalls. More than 130 species of butterflies can be found in the flower gardens. **Hours:** Mon.-Sat. 10-5, Sun. noon-5. **Cost:** Free. **Phone:** (304) 242-6855 or (800) 624-6988.

Stifel Fine Arts Center is off I-70 exit 2B, .5 mi. n.e. on Washington Ave., then s. to 1330 National Rd. The center contains art exhibits by local, regional and national artists. Housed in an old mansion, the center is surrounded by lovely gardens. **Time:** Allow 1 hour minimum. **Hours:** Mon.-Fri. 9-5, Sat. 10-4. Closed major holidays. **Cost:** Free. **Phone:** (304) 242-7700.

WEST VIRGINIA INDEPENDENCE HALL MUSEUM is at 1528 Market St. This former Custom House is considered to be the Civil War birthplace of West Virginia. The state's separation from Virginia was the only change in the map of the United States resulting from the Civil War. From 1861 to 1863 the building housed the loyalist Union government of the Restored State of Virginia and the first constitutional convention for the state of West Virginia.

Restored rooms and a film interpret the building's history. A permanent exhibit of 3-D maps, artifacts and audiovisual displays depicts the rise to statehood and the war in West Virginia. The museum also features what is reputedly the largest exhibit of West Virginia Civil War battle flags and a Discovery Room for children. **Time:** Allow 30 minutes minimum. **Hours:** Tues.-Sat. 9-5. Closed major holidays. **Cost:** Free. **Phone:** (304) 238-1300 or (800) 225-5982.

WHEELING PARK is 4 mi. e. on US 40 at 1801 National Rd. The 406-acre park contains paddleboating facilities, a covered ice-skating rink, indoor and outdoor tennis courts, a miniature golf course, a nine-hole golf course, a playground with rubberized safety surface, and an Olympic-size swimming pool and waterslide *(see Recreation Areas Chart)*. **Hours:** Daily 9-7, late May-early Sept. Ice-skating rink open Nov.-Feb. **Cost:** Daily passes for pool $7.25; $6.25 (ages 4-12). Skating Rink $6.95; $5.95 (ages 3-12), with skate rental $4. Waterslide $1.95 per ride. Golf $13 for 9 holes (includes car). Miniature golf or pedal boat (15 minutes) $5.95. Tennis $4.95 per outdoor court, per half-hour; $39 per indoor court, per hour. Wristbands are available Memorial Day through Labor Day for $11.95 and include all-day admission for miniature golf, swimming pool, waterslide and pedal boating. **Phone:** (304) 243-4085, (304) 243-4185 or (800) 624-6988, ext. 4085. 🍴 ✕ ⛱

HAMPTON INN WHEELING   304/233-0440
THREE DIAMOND SAVE Hotel. **Address:** 795 National Rd 26003

AAA Benefit: Members save up to 15%!

OGLEBAY RESORT & CONFERENCE CENTER   304/243-4000
THREE DIAMOND Resort Hotel. **Address:** 465 Oglebay Dr 26003

SPRINGHILL SUITES BY MARRIOTT WHEELING
                                        304/232-8903
THREE DIAMOND SPRINGHILL SUITES MARRIOTT **Hotel**

AAA Benefit: Members save 5% or more!

Address: 908 National Rd 26003 **Location:** I-70 exit 2A, just e on US 40. **Facility:** 115 units. 5 stories, interior corridors. **Pool:** heated indoor. **Activities:** hot tub, exercise room. **Guest Services:** valet and coin laundry. (See ad this page.)
SAVE [symbols] CALL [symbols]
BIZ HS [symbols]

WHEELING ISLAND HOTEL-CASINO-RACETRACK
                                        304/232-5050
THREE DIAMOND Hotel. **Address:** 1 S Stone St 26003

WHERE TO EAT

ABBEY'S RESTAURANT   304/233-0729
APPROVED American. Casual Dining. **Address:** 145 Zane St 26003

COLEMAN'S FISH MARKET   304/232-8510
APPROVED Seafood. Casual Dining. **Address:** 2226 Market St 26003

FIGARETTI'S   304/243-5625
APPROVED Italian. Casual Dining. **Address:** 1035 Mt. DeChantal Rd 26003

GENERATIONS RESTAURANT & PUB   304/232-7917
APPROVED American. Casual Dining. **Address:** 338 National Rd 26003

LATER ALLIGATOR   304/233-1606
APPROVED American. Casual Dining. **Address:** 2145 Market St 26003

STRATFORD SPRINGS RESTAURANT   304/233-5100
APPROVED American. Casual Dining. **Address:** 100 Kensington Dr 26003

TJ'S SPORTS GARDEN RESTAURANT   304/232-9555
APPROVED American. Casual Dining. **Address:** 808 National Rd 26003

UNCLE PETE'S RESTAURANT   304/234-6701
APPROVED American. Casual Dining. **Address:** 753 Main St 26003

YE OLDE ALPHA   304/242-1090
APPROVED American. Casual Dining. **Address:** 50 Carmel Rd 26003

WHITE HALL

RED ROOF INN FAIRMONT   304/366-6800
APPROVED **Hotel**

Address: 42 Spencer Dr 26554 **Location:** I-79 exit 132, 0.3 mi s on US 250, just w, then just s. **Facility:** 108 units. 2 stories (no elevator), exterior corridors. **Amenities:** video games, safes.
SAVE [symbols] / SOME UNITS [symbols]

▼ See AAA listing this page ▼

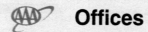

Offices

Main office listings are shown in **BOLD TYPE** and toll-free member service numbers appear in *ITALIC TYPE*.
All are closed Saturdays, Sundays and holidays unless otherwise indicated.
The addresses, phone numbers and hours for any AAA/CAA office are subject to change.
The type of service provided is designated below the name of the city where the office is located:

✛ Auto travel services, including books and maps, and on-demand TripTik ® routings.
● Auto travel services, including selected books and maps, and on-demand TripTik ® routings.
▣ Books/maps only, no marked maps or on-demand TripTik ® routings.
▲ Travel Agency Services, cruise, tour, air, car and rail reservations; domestic and international hotel reservations; passport photo services; international and domestic travel guides and maps; travel money products; and International Driving Permits. In addition, assistance with travel related insurance products including trip cancellation, travel accident, lost luggage, trip delay and assistance products.
✪ Insurance services provided. If only this icon appears, only insurance services are provided at that office.
◖ Car Care Plus Facility provides car care services.
▣ Electric vehicle charging station on premises.

AAA NATIONAL OFFICE: 1000 AAA DRIVE, HEATHROW, FLORIDA 32746-5063, (407) 444-7000

KENTUCKY

ALEXANDRIA—AAA CLUB ALLIANCE INC, 7005 ALEXANDRIA PIKE, 41001. WEEKDAYS (M-F) 7:30-7:30, TUE/THU 7:30-6:00, FRI 7:30-6:00, SAT 8:00-4:30. (859) 635-9777 ◖

BOWLING GREEN—AAA EAST CENTRAL, 1770 SCOTTSVILLE RD, 42104. WEEKDAYS (M-F) 9:00-5:30. (270) 781-7235 ✛▲✪

ELIZABETHTOWN—AAA EAST CENTRAL, 2914 RING RD, 42701. WEEKDAYS (M-F) 9:00-5:30. (270) 765-4109 ✛▲✪

FLORENCE—AAA CLUB ALLIANCE INC, 8711 US HWY 42, 41042. WEEKDAYS (M-F) 8:00-7:30, SAT 8:30-4:00. (859) 525-1690, *(800) 543-2345.* ✛▲✪◖

FT WRIGHT—AAA CLUB ALLIANCE INC, 476 ORPHANAGE RD, 41017. WEEKDAYS (M-F) 7:30-7:30, TUE/THU 7:30-6:00, FRI 7:30-6:00, SAT 8:00-4:30. (859) 341-6222 ▣◖

LEXINGTON—AAA CLUB ALLIANCE INC, 3008 ATKINSON AVE, 40509. WEEKDAYS (M-F) 9:00-6:00, SAT 9:00-2:00. (859) 233-1111, *(800) 568-5222.* ✛▲✪

LEXINGTON—AAA CLUB ALLIANCE INC, 3710 PALOMAR CENTRE DR, 40513. WEEKDAYS (M-F) 9:00-6:00, SAT 9:00-2:00. (859) 219-3333, *(800) 568-5222.* ✛▲✪

LOUISVILLE—AAA EAST CENTRAL, 1805 ROCKFORD LN, 40216. WEEKDAYS (M-F) 9:00-5:30. (502) 449-2529 ✛▲✪

LOUISVILLE—AAA EAST CENTRAL, 3614 FERN VALLEY RD, 40219. WEEKDAYS (M-F) 9:00-5:30, SAT 10:00-3:00. (502) 964-3787 ✛▲✪

LOUISVILLE—AAA EAST CENTRAL, 445 E MARKET ST STE #120, 40202. WEEKDAYS (M-F) 8:30-5:00. (502) 581-0665 ✛▲✪

LOUISVILLE—AAA EAST CENTRAL, 9421 VIKING CENTER DR, 40222. WEEKDAYS (M-F) 9:00-5:30, SAT 10:00-3:00. (502) 425-7885 ✛▲✪

NEWPORT—AAA CLUB ALLIANCE INC, 63 CAROTHERS RD, 41071. WEEKDAYS (M-F) 9:00-6:00, SAT 9:00-3:00. (859) 905-6280 ✛▲✪◖

OWENSBORO—AAA EAST CENTRAL, 1600 FREDERICA ST, 42301. WEEKDAYS (M-F) 9:00-5:30. (270) 683-8034 ✛▲✪

PADUCAH—AAA EAST CENTRAL, 2909 JAMES SANDERS BLVD, 42001. WEEKDAYS (M-F) 9:00-5:30. (270) 443-6478 ✛▲✪

WALTON—AAA CLUB ALLIANCE INC, 620 CHESTNUT DR, 41094. WEEKDAYS (M-F) 7:30-7:00, SAT 7:30-4:00. (859) 485-3430 ✛▲◖

OHIO

AKRON—AAA AKRON AUTO CLUB, 100 ROSA PARKS DR, 44311. WEEKDAYS (M-F) 9:00-5:00, SAT 9:00-12:00. (330) 762-0631 ✛▲✪

ALLIANCE—AAA EAST CENTRAL, 2322 S UNION AVE, 44601. WEEKDAYS (M-F) 9:00-5:00, SAT 9:00-12:00. (330) 823-9820 ✛▲✪

ASHLAND—AAA EAST CENTRAL, 1074 COMMERCE PKWY, 44805. WEEKDAYS (M-F) 8:00-5:00, MON 8:00-6:30, SAT 8:00-12:00. (419) 289-8133 ✛▲✪

ASHTABULA—AAA EAST CENTRAL, 2835 N RIDGE RD E, 44004. WEEKDAYS (M-F) 9:00-6:00, SAT 9:00-2:00. (440) 997-5586 ✛▲

ATHENS—AAA EAST CENTRAL, 130 E STATE ST, 45701. WEEKDAYS (M-F) 9:00-5:00, SAT 9:30-12:00. (740) 593-6677 ✛▲

AVON—AAA EAST CENTRAL, 35676 DETROIT RD, 44011. WEEKDAYS (M-F) 9:00-6:00, SAT 9:00-2:00. (440) 695-1795 ✛▲✪

BEAVERCREEK—AAA CLUB ALLIANCE INC, 3321 DAYTON-XENIA RD, 45432. WEEKDAYS (M-F) 7:30-7:00, SAT 7:30-4:00. (937) 427-5884, *(800) 624-2321.* ✛▲✪◖ ▣

BEAVERCREEK—AAA CLUB ALLIANCE INC, 3870 KEMP RD, 45431. WEEKDAYS (M-F) 7:30-6:00, SAT 8:00-4:30. (937) 426-8209 ◖

BELLEFONTAINE—AAA OHIO AUTO CLUB, 1790 S MAIN ST, 43311. WEEKDAYS (M-F) 9:00-5:00, SAT 9:00-12:00. (937) 599-5154 ✛▲✪

BOARDMAN—AAA EAST CENTRAL, 1275 BOARDMAN-CANFIELD RD, 44512. WEEKDAYS (M-F) 9:00-6:00, SAT 9:00-2:00. (330) 726-9083 ✛▲✪

BRUNSWICK—AAA OHIO AUTO CLUB, 3927 CENTER RD, 44212. WEEKDAYS (M-F) 9:00-5:00, SAT 9:00-12:00. (440) 808-8600, *(800) 323-5486 EXT 58202.* ✪

BUCYRUS—AAA OHIO AUTO CLUB, 314 S SANDUSKY AVE, 44820. WEEKDAYS (M-F) 9:00-5:30 (CLOSED 11:00AM-12:00PM). (419) 562-9969 ✛▲✪

CELINA—AAA OHIO AUTO CLUB, 1970 HAVEMANN RD, 45822. WEEKDAYS (M-F) 9:00-5:00, SAT 9:00-12:00. (419) 586-2460 ✛▲✪

CHILLICOTHE—AAA EAST CENTRAL, 141 W MAIN ST, 45601. WEEKDAYS (M-F) 9:00-5:00, SAT 9:30-12:00. (740) 702-3838 ✛▲✪

CINCINNATI—AAA CLUB ALLIANCE INC, 12000 CHASE PLAZA DR, 45240. MON 8:00-7:00, TUE/THU 8:00-6:00, WED 8:00-7:00, SAT 8:30-4:00. (513) 671-1886, *(800) 543-2345.* ✛▲✪

CINCINNATI—AAA CLUB ALLIANCE INC, 15 W CENTRAL PKWY, 45202. WEEKDAYS (M-F) 8:30-6:00. (513) 762-3301, *(800) 543-2345.* ✛ ▲ ✿

CINCINNATI—AAA CLUB ALLIANCE INC, 3663 STONE CREEK BL, 45251. WEEKDAYS (M-F) 7:30-7:30, TUE/THU 7:30-6:00, FRI 7:30-6:00, SAT 8:00-4:30. (513) 385-4010 ◖

CINCINNATI—AAA CLUB ALLIANCE INC, 3872 PAXTON RD, 45209. WEEKDAYS (M-F) 7:30-7:30, TUE/THU 7:30-6:00, FRI 7:30-6:00, SAT 8:00-4:30. (513) 631-1966 ◖

CINCINNATI—AAA CLUB ALLIANCE INC, 3998 RED BANK RD, 45227. WEEKDAYS (M-F) 9:00-6:00, SAT 9:00-3:00. (513) 247-8160, *(800) 543-2345.* ✛ ▲ ✿ ◖ ▭

CINCINNATI—AAA CLUB ALLIANCE INC, 471 OHIO PIKE, 45255. WEEKDAYS (M-F) 8:00-7:00. (513) 388-4222, *(800) 543-2345.* ✛ ▲ ✿ ◖

CINCINNATI—AAA CLUB ALLIANCE INC, 48 WEST COURT ST, 45202. WEEKDAYS (M-F) 7:30-6:00. (513) 412-7900 ◖

CINCINNATI—AAA CLUB ALLIANCE INC, 5362 RIDGE RD, 45213. WEEKDAYS (M-F) 7:30-7:00, SAT 7:30-4:00. (513) 458-2030 ◖

CINCINNATI—AAA CLUB ALLIANCE INC, 5977 HARRISON AVE, 45248. WEEKDAYS (M-F) 7:30-7:30, TUE/THU 7:30-6:00, FRI 7:30-6:00, SAT 8:00-4:30. (513) 598-2300 ◖

CINCINNATI—AAA CLUB ALLIANCE INC, 605 ANDERSON FERRY, 45238. WEEKDAYS (M-F) 7:30-6:00, SAT 8:00-4:30. (513) 922-2969 ◖

CINCINNATI—AAA CLUB ALLIANCE INC, 6558 GLENWAY AVE, 45211. WEEKDAYS (M-F) 9:00-6:00, SAT 9:00-3:00. (513) 598-2500, *(800) 543-2345.* ✛ ▲ ✿

CINCINNATI—AAA CLUB ALLIANCE INC, 8176 MONTGOMERY RD, 45236. WEEKDAYS (M-F) 9:00-6:00, SAT 9:00-3:00. (513) 984-3553, *(800) 543-2345.* ✛ ▲ ✿

CINCINNATI—AAA CLUB ALLIANCE INC, 9167 UNION CEMETARY RD, 45249. WEEKDAYS (M-F) 7:30-7:30, TUE/THU 7:30-6:00, FRI 7:30-6:00, SAT 8:00-4:30. (513) 677-5000 ◖

CINCINNATI—AAA CLUB ALLIANCE INC, 9401 KENWOOD RD, 45242. WEEKDAYS (M-F) 7:30-7:30, TUE/THU 7:30-6:00, FRI 7:30-6:00, SAT 8:00-4:30. (513) 793-0882 ◖

CINCINNATI—AAA CLUB ALLIANCE INC, 9718 COLERAIN AVE, 45251. WEEKDAYS (M-F) 9:00-6:00, SAT 9:00-3:00. (513) 385-0909, *(800) 543-2345.* ✛ ▲ ✿

COLUMBIANA—AAA EAST CENTRAL, 118 S MAIN ST, 44408. WEEKDAYS (M-F) 9:00-5:00, SAT 9:00-12:00. (330) 482-3836 ✛ ▲

COLUMBUS—AAA OHIO AUTO CLUB, 1075 W 3RD AVE, 43212. WEEKDAYS (M-F) 7:30-6:00, SAT 8:00-4:00. (614) 488-2197 ◖

COLUMBUS—AAA OHIO AUTO CLUB, 1335 BETHEL RD, 43220. WEEKDAYS (M-F) 7:30-6:00, SAT 8:30-4:00. (614) 451-2111 ◖ ▭

COLUMBUS—AAA OHIO AUTO CLUB, 2400 SOBECK RD, 43232. WEEKDAYS (M-F) 7:30-6:00. (614) 559-0000 ◖

COLUMBUS—AAA OHIO AUTO CLUB, 3646 E BROAD ST, 43213. WEEKDAYS (M-F) 7:30-6:00, SAT 8:00-4:00. (614) 237-6325 ◖ ▭

COLUMBUS—AAA OHIO AUTO CLUB, 5486 N HAMILTON RD, 43230. WEEKDAYS (M-F) 9:00-6:00 (CAR CARE PLUS: WEEKDAYS (M-F) 7:30-6), SAT 9:00-4:00 (CAR CARE PLUS: SAT 8-4). (614) 933-9600 ✛ ▲ ✿ ◖ ▭

COLUMBUS—AAA OHIO AUTO CLUB, 6600 PERIMETER LOOP RD, 43017. WEEKDAYS (M-F) 7:30-6:00, SAT 8:00-4:00. (614) 386-3200 ◖ ▭

COLUMBUS—AAA OHIO AUTO CLUB, 686 GRANDVIEW AVE, 43215. WEEKDAYS (M-F) 9:00-6:00, WEEKDAYS (M-F) 7:30-6:00, SAT 9:00-4:00, SAT 8:00-4:00. (614) 488-2197 ▰ ▲ ✿

COLUMBUS—AAA OHIO AUTO CLUB, 6971 E BROAD ST, 46017. WEEKDAYS (M-F) 7:30-6:00, SAT 8:00-4:00. (614) 759-7777 ◖

COLUMBUS—AAA OHIO AUTO CLUB, 8350 SANCUS BLVD, 43210. WEEKDAYS (M-F) 9:00-6:00, SAT 9:00-4:00. (614) 436-4005 ✛ ▲ ✿ ◖

DAYTON—AAA CLUB ALLIANCE INC, 14 W WHIPP RD, 45459. WEEKDAYS (M-F) 9:00-5:30, SAT 9:00-1:00. (937) 435-7447, *(800) 624-2321.* ✛ ▲ ✿

DAYTON—AAA CLUB ALLIANCE INC, 200 E THIRD ST, 45402. WEEKDAYS (M-F) 7:30-6:00, SAT 7:30-1:00. (937) 228-2144 ◖

DAYTON—AAA CLUB ALLIANCE INC, 6580 N MAIN ST, 45415. WEEKDAYS (M-F) 9:00-5:30, SAT 9:00-1:00. (937) 278-9195, *(800) 624-2321.* ✛ ▲ ✿

DEFIANCE—AAA CLUB ALLIANCE INC, 1007 N CLINTON ST #2, 43512. WEEKDAYS (M-F) 9:00-5:30. (419) 782-3876, *(800) 462-0045.* ✛ ▲ ✿

DELAWARE—AAA OHIO AUTO CLUB, 840 SUNBURY RD STE 502, 43015. WEEKDAYS (M-F) 9:00-5:00, MON 9:00-6:00, SAT 9:00-12:00. (740) 363-1928 ✛ ▲ ✿

EAST LIVERPOOL—AAA EAST CENTRAL, 516 BROADWAY ST, 43920. WEEKDAYS (M-F) 9:00-5:00, SAT 9:00-12:00. (330) 385-2020 ✛ ▲ ✿

FAIRFIELD—AAA CLUB ALLIANCE INC, 5031 DIXIE HIGHWAY, 45014. WEEKDAYS (M-F) 7:00-5:00, SAT 8:00-4:30. (513) 829-9989 ◖

FAIRLAWN—AAA AKRON AUTO CLUB, 2709 W MARKET ST, 44333. WEEKDAYS (M-F) 9:00-5:00, SAT 9:00-12:00. (330) 867-0694 ✛ ▲

FINDLAY—FINDLAY AUTOMOBILE CLUB, 1550 TIFFIN AVE, 45840. WEEKDAYS (M-F) 9:00-5:00, SAT 9:00-12:00 (NO INSURANCE ON WEEKENDS.). (419) 422-4961 ✛ ▲ ✿

FINNEYTOWN—AAA CLUB ALLIANCE INC, 6575 WINTON RD, 45224. WEEKDAYS (M-F) 7:30-6:00, SAT 8:00-4:30. (513) 542-7850 ◖

FRANKLIN—AAA CLUB ALLIANCE INC, 3439 PENDLETON CIR, 45005. WEEKDAYS (M-F) 7:30-6:00, SAT 8:00-4:30. (513) 424-8000 ◖

FREMONT—AAA OHIO AUTO CLUB, 2380 SEAN DR UNIT 4, 43420. WEEKDAYS (M-F) 9:00-5:00, SAT 9:00-12:00. (419) 332-2602 ✛ ▲

GALLIPOLIS—AAA EAST CENTRAL, 416 SECOND AVE, 45631. WEEKDAYS (M-F) 9:00-5:00, SAT 9:30-12:00. (740) 446-0699 ✛ ▲

GROVE CITY—AAA OHIO AUTO CLUB, 1730 STRINGTOWN RD, 43123. WEEKDAYS (M-F) 9:00-5:00, MON 9:00-7:00, SAT 9:00-12:00. (614) 277-1310 ✛ ▲ ✿

HARRISON—AAA CLUB ALLIANCE INC, 10764 HARRISON AVE, 45030. WEEKDAYS (M-F) 7:30-7:30, TUE/THU 7:30-6:00, FRI 7:30-6:00, SAT 8:00-4:30. (513) 367-2345 ◖

HILLIARD—AAA OHIO AUTO CLUB, 1513 HILLIARD ROME RD, 43228. WEEKDAYS (M-F) 9:00-5:00, MON 9:00-7:00, SAT 9:00-12:00. (614) 771-5777 ✛ ▲ ✿

HUBER HEIGHTS—AAA CLUB ALLIANCE INC, 8381 OLD TROY PIKE, 45424. WEEKDAYS (M-F) 8:00-5:30, SAT 8:30-4:00. (937) 281-3530 ✛ ▲ ✿

HUDSON—AAA AKRON AUTO CLUB, 178 W STREETSBORO RD, 44236. WEEKDAYS (M-F) 9:00-5:00, SAT 9:00-12:00. (330) 650-6727 ✛ ▲

INDEPENDENCE—AAA EAST CENTRAL, 5700 BRECKSVILLE RD, 44131. WEEKDAYS (M-F) 8:30-5:00, SAT 9:30-1:30. (216) 606-6300 ✛ ▲ ✿

IRONTON—AAA EAST CENTRAL, 624 S FOURTH ST, 45638. WEEKDAYS (M-F) 9:00-5:00, SAT 9:30-12:00. (740) 532-3242 ✛ ▲

JACKSON—AAA EAST CENTRAL, 126 E GAY ST, 45640. WEEKDAYS (M-F) 9:00-5:00, SAT 9:30-12:00. (740) 286-5077 ✚▲

LANCASTER—AAA OHIO AUTO CLUB, 714 N MEMORIAL DR, 43130. WEEKDAYS (M-F) 9:00-5:00, SAT 9:00-12:00. (740) 653-0912 ✚▲○

LEBANON—AAA CLUB ALLIANCE INC, 603 E MAIN ST, 45036. WEEKDAYS (M-F) 9:00-6:00, SAT 9:00-1:00. (513) 932-3300, *(800) 543-2345.* ✚▲○C

LIMA—AAA OHIO AUTO CLUB, 2115 ALLENTOWN RD, 45805. WEEKDAYS (M-F) 9:00-5:00, TUE 9:00-6:00, SAT 9:00-12:00. (419) 228-1022 ✚▲○

LYNDHURST—AAA EAST CENTRAL, 5356 MAYFIELD RD, 44124. WEEKDAYS (M-F) 9:00-6:00, SAT 9:00-2:00. (440) 473-0700 ✚▲○

MAINEVILLE—AAA CLUB ALLIANCE INC, 6269 RIVERSBEND DR, 45039. WEEKDAYS (M-F) 7:30-7:00, SAT 8:00-4:30, SUN 9:00-3:00. (513) 583-4674 C

MANSFIELD—AAA OHIO AUTO CLUB, 2114 PARK AVE W, 44906. WEEKDAYS (M-F) 9:00-5:00, MON 9:00-6:00, SAT 9:00-12:00. (419) 529-8500 ✚▲○

MARION—AAA OHIO AUTO CLUB, 1316 MT VERNON AVE, 43302. WEEKDAYS (M-F) 9:00-5:00, SAT 9:00-12:00. (740) 389-3517 ✚▲○

MASON—AAA CLUB ALLIANCE INC, 5123 BOWEN DR STE 100, 45040. WEEKDAYS (M-F) 9:00-6:00, SAT 9:00-3:00. (513) 683-5200, *(800) 543-2345.* ✚▲○

MASSILLON—AAA EAST CENTRAL, 1972 WALES RD NE, 44646. WEEKDAYS (M-F) 9:00-5:00, SAT 9:00-12:00. (330) 833-1084 ✚▲○

MEDINA—AAA OHIO AUTO CLUB, 150 NORTHLAND DR, 44256. WEEKDAYS (M-F) 9:00-5:00, THU 9:00-6:00, SAT 9:00-12:00. (330) 725-5669 ✚▲○

MENTOR—AAA EAST CENTRAL, 6980 HEISLEY RD, 44060. WEEKDAYS (M-F) 9:00-6:00, SAT 9:00-2:00. (440) 974-0990 ✚▲○

MILFORD—AAA CLUB ALLIANCE INC, 1246 STATE RT 28, 45150. WEEKDAYS (M-F) 7:30-7:00, SAT 8:00-4:30, SUN 9:00-3:00. (513) 831-0636 ■C

MOUNT VERNON—AAA OHIO AUTO CLUB, 1 PUBLIC SQ, 43050. WEEKDAYS (M-F) 9:00-5:00, MON 9:00-6:00, SAT 9:00-12:00. (740) 397-2091 ✚▲○

NEW PHILADELPHIA—AAA EAST CENTRAL, 1112 FOURTH ST NW, 44663. WEEKDAYS (M-F) 8:45-5:00, SAT 8:45-12:00. (330) 343-4481 ✚▲○

NEWARK—AAA OHIO AUTO CLUB, 1303 WEST MAIN ST, 43055. WEEKDAYS (M-F) 9:00-5:00, SAT 9:00-12:00. (740) 349-8529 ○

NEWARK—AAA OHIO AUTO CLUB, 135 DEO DR, 43055. WEEKDAYS (M-F) 9:00-5:00, MON 9:00-6:00, SAT 9:00-12:00. (740) 345-4017 ✚▲○

NILES—AAA EAST CENTRAL, 937 YOUNGSTOWN-WARREN RD, 44446. WEEKDAYS (M-F) 9:00-6:00, SAT 9:00-2:00. (330) 652-6466 ✚▲○

NORTH CANTON—AAA OHIO AUTO CLUB, 4895 PORTAGE ST NW, 44720. WEEKDAYS (M-F) 9:00-6:00, SAT 9:00-3:00. (330) 455-6761 ✚▲○

NORWALK—AAA EAST CENTRAL, 275 BENEDICT AVE, 44857. WEEKDAYS (M-F) 8:30-5:30. (419) 668-1622 ✚▲

OREGON—AAA CLUB ALLIANCE INC, 4041 NAVARRE AVE, 43616. WEEKDAYS (M-F) 7:30-6:00. C

PERRYSBURG—AAA CLUB ALLIANCE INC, 25740 NORTH DIXIE HWY, 43551. WEEKDAYS (M-F) 7:30-7:00, SAT 7:30-4:00. (419) 872-5000, *(800) 872-5620.* ✚▲○C

PORT CLINTON—AAA CLUB ALLIANCE INC, 2870-B E HARBOR RD, 43452. WEEKDAYS (M-F) 8:30-5:30. (419) 732-2161, *(800) 432-2161.* ✚▲○

PORTSMOUTH—AAA EAST CENTRAL, 1414 12TH ST, 45662. WEEKDAYS (M-F) 9:00-5:00, SAT 9:30-12:00. (740) 354-5614 ✚▲○

POWELL—AAA OHIO AUTO CLUB, 3897 W POWELL RD, 43065. WEEKDAYS (M-F) 9:00-5:00. (614) 761-3800, *(800) 323-5486 EXT 58002.* ○

POWELL—AAA OHIO AUTO CLUB, 8868 MORELAND ST, 43065. WEEKDAYS (M-F) 7:30-6:00, SAT 8:00-4:00. (740) 881-4400 C

RAVENNA—AAA EAST CENTRAL, 2641 ST RT 59, 44266. WEEKDAYS (M-F) 9:00-6:00, SAT 9:00-2:00. (330) 296-3406 ✚▲○

REYNOLDSBURG—AAA OHIO AUTO CLUB, 2036 BALT-REYNOLDSBURG RD, 43068. WEEKDAYS (M-F) 9:00-5:00, MON 9:00-7:00, SAT 9:00-12:00. (614) 864-2224 ✚▲○

SANDUSKY—AAA OHIO AUTO CLUB, 4201 MILAN RD UNIT A, 44870. WEEKDAYS (M-F) 9:00-5:00, SAT 9:00-12:00. (419) 625-5831 ✚▲○

SIDNEY—AAA SHELBY COUNTY, 920 WAPAKONETA AVE, 45365. WEEKDAYS (M-F) 9:00-5:00, SAT 9:00-12:00. (937) 492-3167 ✚▲

SOLON—AAA EAST CENTRAL, 34050 SOLON RD, 44139. WEEKDAYS (M-F) 9:00-6:00, SAT 9:00-2:00. (440) 248-9000 ✚▲○

SPRINGFIELD—AAA CLUB ALLIANCE INC, 755 BECHTLE AVE, 45504. WEEKDAYS (M-F) 8:30-5:00. (937) 323-8661, *(800) 303-9731.* ✚▲○

ST. CLAIRSVILLE—AAA OHIO AUTO CLUB, 51560 NATIONAL RD E, 43950. WEEKDAYS (M-F) 9:00-5:00, MON 9:00-6:00, SAT 9:00-12:00. (740) 695-4030 ✚▲○

STRONGSVILLE—AAA EAST CENTRAL, 17220 ROYALTON RD, 44136. WEEKDAYS (M-F) 9:00-6:00, SAT 9:00-2:00. (440) 783-3395 ✚▲○

TIFFIN—AAA OHIO AUTO CLUB, 191 E MARKET ST, 44883. WEEKDAYS (M-F) 9:00-5:00, SAT 9:00-12:00. (419) 447-0551 ✚▲○

TOLEDO—AAA CLUB ALLIANCE INC, 308 NEW TOWNE SQUARE DR, 43612. WEEKDAYS (M-F) 8:30-5:30, SAT 9:00-1:00. (419) 470-5665 ✚▲○C

TOLEDO—AAA CLUB ALLIANCE INC, 3200 MEIJER DR, 43617. WEEKDAYS (M-F) 8:30-5:30, SAT 8:30-1:00. (419) 843-1200 ■C

TOLEDO—AAA CLUB ALLIANCE INC, 5606 AIRPORT HWY, 43615. WEEKDAYS (M-F) 8:30-5:30, SAT 8:30-1:00. (419) 897-4455 ✚▲○C

TOLEDO—AAA CLUB ALLIANCE INC, 5750 JACKMAN RD, 43613. WEEKDAYS (M-F) 7:00-6:00, SAT 8:00-2:00. (419) 478-1309 C

TOLEDO—AAA CLUB ALLIANCE INC, 5916 W SYLVANIA AVE, 43623. WEEKDAYS (M-F) 7:00-6:00. (419) 882-4991 C

TROY—AAA CLUB ALLIANCE INC, 4 SOUTH STANFIELD RD, 45373. WEEKDAYS (M-F) 9:00-6:00, SAT 9:00-1:00. (937) 339-0112, *(800) 765-3753.* ✚▲

UPPER ARLINGTON—AAA OHIO AUTO CLUB, 3096 KINGSDALE CENTER, 43221. WEEKDAYS (M-F) 9:00-5:00, MON 9:00-7:00, SAT 9:00-12:00. (614) 457-2614 ✚▲○

WADSWORTH—AAA OHIO AUTO CLUB, 1090 WILLIAMS RESERVE BL, 44281. WEEKDAYS (M-F) 9:00-5:00, SAT 9:00-12:00. (330) 336-4900 ✚▲○

WASHINGTON COURT HOUSE—AAA EAST CENTRAL, 334 E COURT ST, 43160. WEEKDAYS (M-F) 9:00-5:00, SAT 9:30-12:00. (740) 335-3950 ✚▲

WEST CHESTER—AAA CLUB ALLIANCE INC, 4856 WUNNENBERG WAY, 45069. WEEKDAYS (M-F) 7:30-7:30, TUE/THU 7:30-6:00, FRI 7:30-6:00, SAT 8:00-4:00. (513) 870-6222 C

WEST CHESTER—AAA CLUB ALLIANCE INC, 7889 TYLERSVILLE RD, 45069. WEEKDAYS (M-F) 7:30-7:30, TUE/THU 7:30-6:00, FRI 7:30-6:00, SAT 8:00-5:00. (513) 755-0666 🦯

WEST CHESTER—AAA OHIO AUTO CLUB, 8210 HIGHLAND POINTE DR, 45069. WEEKDAYS (M-F) 9:00-6:00, MON 9:00-6:00, SAT 9:00-12:00. (513) 870-0951 ✛ ▲ ○

WESTERVILLE—AAA OHIO AUTO CLUB, 660 N STATE ST, 43082. WEEKDAYS (M-F) 9:00-5:00, MON 9:00-7:00, SAT 9:00-12:00. (614) 899-1222 ✛ ▲ ○

WESTLAKE—AAA EAST CENTRAL, 149 MARKET ST, 44145. WEEKDAYS (M-F) 9:00-6:00, SAT 9:00-2:00. (440) 788-3102 ✛ ▲ ○

WOOSTER—AAA OHIO AUTO CLUB, 3786 BURBANK RD STE 601, 44691. WEEKDAYS (M-F) 9:00-5:00, MON 9:00-6:00, SAT 9:00-12:00. (330) 345-5550 ✛ ▲ ○

WORTHINGTON—**AAA OHIO AUTO CLUB**, 90 E WILSON BRIDGE RD, 43085. WEEKDAYS (M-F) 9:00-5:00, MON 9:00-7:00, SAT 9:00-12:00. (614) 431-7901, *(800) 323-5486.* ✛ ▲ ○

ZANESVILLE—AAA OHIO AUTO CLUB, 3934 TARYN TRACE M5, 43701. WEEKDAYS (M-F) 9:00-5:00, MON 9:00-6:00, SAT 9:00-12:00. (740) 454-1234 ✛ ▲ ○

ZANESVILLE—AAA OHIO AUTO CLUB, 601 MARKET ST, 43701. WEEKDAYS (M-F) 9:00-5:00, SAT 9:00-12:00. (740) 452-2735 ○

WEST VIRGINIA

BECKLEY—AAA CLUB ALLIANCE INC, 1004 N EISENHOWER DR, 25801. WEEKDAYS (M-F) 9:00-5:30, SAT 9:00-3:00. (304) 255-4147, *(800) 244-2257.* ✛ ▲ ○

BRIDGEPORT—AAA EAST CENTRAL, 138 BARNETT RUN RD, 26330. WEEKDAYS (M-F) 9:00-5:30. (304) 842-2221 ✛ ▲ ○

CHARLESTON—AAA CLUB ALLIANCE INC, 1000 PARKWAY RD STE A, 25309. WEEKDAYS (M-F) 9:00-5:30, SAT 9:00-3:00. (304) 925-6681, *(800) 924-6681.* ✛ ▲ ○

HUNTINGTON—AAA EAST CENTRAL, 1126 SIXTH AVE, 25701. WEEKDAYS (M-F) 9:00-5:00. (304) 523-6423 ✛ ▲ ○

MARTINSBURG—AAA EAST CENTRAL, 284 RETAIL COMMONS PKWY, 25403. WEEKDAYS (M-F) 9:00-5:00, SAT 9:00-1:00. (304) 263-4619 ✛ ▲ ○

MORGANTOWN—AAA EAST CENTRAL, 482 SUNCREST TOWNE CTR DR, 26505. WEEKDAYS (M-F) 10:00-6:00, SAT 10:00-2:00. (304) 598-7470 ✛ ▲

VIENNA—AAA EAST CENTRAL, 1500 GRND CENTRAL AV #102, 26105. WEEKDAYS (M-F) 9:00-5:30. (304) 295-9715 ✛ ▲

WEIRTON—AAA EAST CENTRAL, 3126 WEST ST, 26062. WEEKDAYS (M-F) 9:00-5:00, SAT 9:00-12:00. (304) 748-1616 ✛ ▲

WHEELING—AAA EAST CENTRAL, 846 NATIONAL RD, 26003. WEEKDAYS (M-F) 8:30-5:30. (304) 233-1810 ✛ ▲ ○

Photo Credits

Page numbers are in bold type. Picture credit abbreviations are as follows:
- (i) numeric sequence from top to bottom, left to right - (AAA) AAA Travel library.

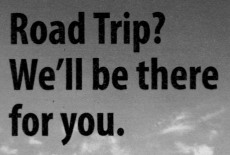

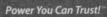